Victoria Crosses on the Western Front
27 January–27 July 1917

Victoria Crosses on the Western Front
27 January–27 July 1917

1917 to the Eve of Third Ypres

Paul Oldfield

Pen & Sword
MILITARY

First published in Great Britain in 2016 by
Pen & Sword Military
an imprint of
Pen & Sword Books Ltd
47 Church Street
Barnsley
South Yorkshire
S70 2AS

ISBN 978 1 47382 707 3

A CIP catalogue record for this book is available from the British Library

Typeset in Ehrhardt by
Mac Style Ltd, Bridlington, East Yorkshire
Printed and bound in the UK by CPI Group (UK) Ltd, Croydon,
CRO 4YY

Pen & Sword Books Ltd incorporates the imprints of Pen & Sword
Archaeology, Atlas, Aviation, Battleground, Discovery, Family History,
History, Maritime, Military, Naval, Politics, Railways, Select,
Social History, Transport, True Crime, and Claymore Press,
Frontline Books, Leo Cooper, Praetorian Press, Remember When, Seaforth
Publishing and Wharncliffe.

For a complete list of Pen & Sword titles please contact
PEN & SWORD BOOKS LIMITED
47 Church Street, Barnsley, South Yorkshire, S70 2AS, England
E-mail: enquiries@pen-and-sword.co.uk
Website: www.pen-and-sword.co.uk

Contents

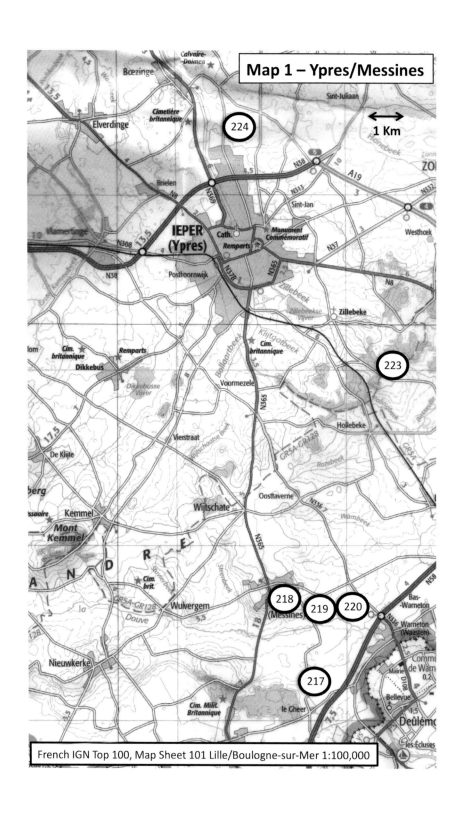

Map 1 – Ypres/Messines

1 Km

French IGN Top 100, Map Sheet 101 Lille/Boulogne-sur-Mer 1:100,000

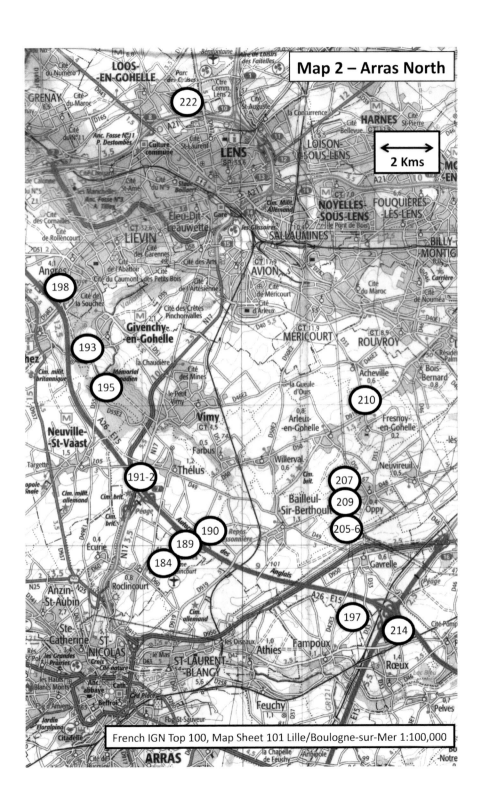

Map 2 – Arras North

2 Kms

French IGN Top 100, Map Sheet 101 Lille/Boulogne-sur-Mer 1:100,000

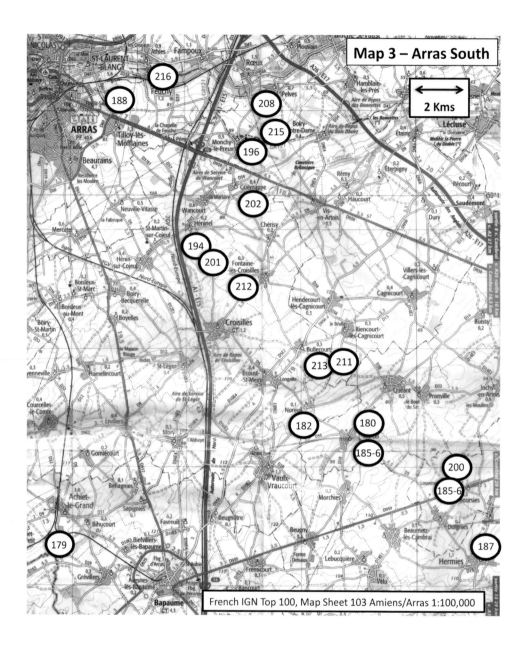

Map 3 – Arras South

2 Kms

French IGN Top 100, Map Sheet 103 Amiens/Arras 1:100,000

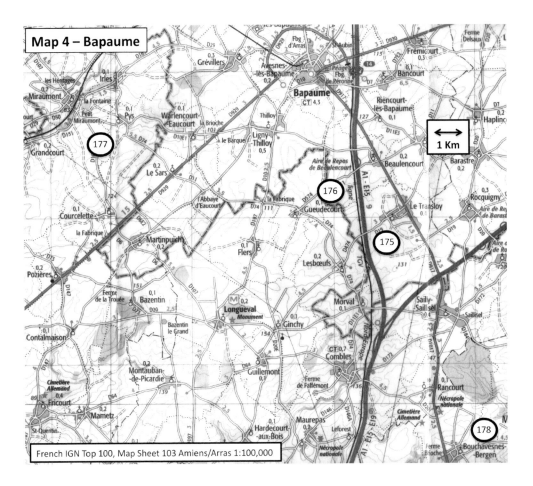

Map 4 – Bapaume

1 Km

French IGN Top 100, Map Sheet 103 Amiens/Arras 1:100,000

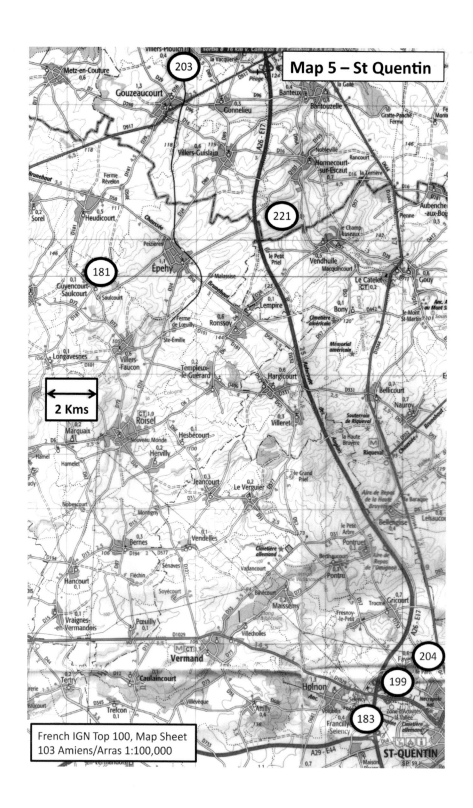

Map 5 – St Quentin

2 Kms

French IGN Top 100, Map Sheet
103 Amiens/Arras 1:100,000

Abbreviations

AAMC	Australian Army Medical Corps
ADC	Aide-de-Camp
ADS	Advanced Dressing Station
AIF	Australian Imperial Force
ARP	Air Raid Precautions
ASC	Army Service Corps
ATS	Auxiliary Territorial Service
Att'd	Attached
BA	Batchelor of Arts
BCh or ChB	Bachelor of Surgery
BEF	British Expeditionary Force
Brig-Gen	Brigadier General
BSM	Battery Sergeant Major
Bty	Battery (artillery unit of 4–8 guns)
Capt	Captain
CB	Companion of the Order of the Bath
CBE	Commander of the Order of the British Empire
CCF	Combined Cadet Force
CCS	Casualty Clearing Station
CE	Canadian Engineers
CEF	Canadian Expeditionary Force
CFA	Canadian Field Artillery
CGA	Canadian Garrison Artillery
Ch.B	Bachelor of Surgery
C-in-C	Commander-in-Chief
CM	Master of Surgery
CMG	Companion of the Order of St Michael & St George
CO	Commanding Officer
Col	Colonel
Cpl	Corporal
CQMS	Company Quartermaster Sergeant
CSgt	Colour Sergeant
CSM	Company Sergeant Major
CStJ	Commander of the Most Venerable Order of the Hospital of Saint John of Jerusalem

Cty	Cemetery
CVO	Commander of the Royal Victorian Order
CWGC	Commonwealth War Graves Commission
DAAG	Deputy Assistant Adjutant General
DCLI	Duke of Cornwall's Light Infantry
DCM	Distinguished Conduct Medal
DEMS	Defensively Equipped Merchant Ships
DL	Deputy Lieutenant
DLI	Durham Light Infantry
DPH	Doctor of Public Health
DSC	Distinguished Service Cross
DSO	Distinguished Service Order
Dvr	Driver
FM	Field Marshal
FRS	Fellow of the Royal Society
GC	George Cross
GCB	Knight Grand Cross of the Order of the Bath
GCMG	Knight Grand Cross of the Order of St Michael & St George
Gen	General
GOC	General Officer Commanding
GOC-in-C	General Officer Commanding in Chief
GSO1, 2 or 3	General Staff Officer Grade 1 (Lt Col), 2 (Maj) or 3 (Capt)
HE	His Excellency
HLI	Highland Light Infantry
HMAT	Her/His Majesty's Australian Transport/Troopship
HMCS	Her/His Majesty's Canadian Ship
HMHS	Her/His Majesty's Hospital Ship
HMS	Her/His Majesty's Ship
HMT	Her/His Majesty's Transport/Troopship/Hired Military Transport
HMNZT	Her/His Majesty's New Zealand Transport/Troopship
HRH	His/Her Royal Highness
HS	Hospital Ship
JP	Justice of the Peace
KBE	Knight Commander of the Most Excellent Order of the British
KCB	Knight Commander of the Order of the Bath
KCMG	Knight Commander of St Michael and St George
KCVO	Knight Commander of the Royal Victorian Order
KGStJ	Knight of Grace of the Most Venerable Order of the Hospital of Saint John of Jerusalem
KJStJ	Knight of Justice of the Most Venerable Order of the Hospital of Saint John of Jerusalem
Kms	Kilometres

KOSB	King's Own Scottish Borderers
KOYLI	King's Own Yorkshire Light Infantry
KRRC	King's Royal Rifle Corps
KSLI	King's Shropshire Light Infantry
LCpl	Lance Corporal
LDV	Local Defence Volunteers (predecessor of Home Guard)
LG	London Gazette
LM	Licentiate in Midwifery
LRCP&S	Licentiate, Royal College of Physicians & Surgeons
Lt	Lieutenant
Lt Col	Lieutenant Colonel
Lt Gen	Lieutenant General
Maj	Major
Maj Gen	Major General
MB	Bachelor of Medicine
MBE	Member of the Order of the British Empire
MC	Military Cross
MCh	Master of Surgery
MGC	Machine Gun Corps
MID	Mentioned in Despatches
MM	Military Medal
MO	Medical Officer
MP	Member of Parliament
MSM	Meritorious Service Medal
MSP	Member of the Scottish Parliament
MT	Motor Transport
MVO	Member of the Royal Victorian Order
NSW	New South Wales
NZEF	New Zealand Expeditionary Force
NZHS	New Zealand Hospital Ship
OBE	Officer of the Order of the British Empire
OC	Officer Commanding
OP	Observation Post
OStJ	Officer of the Most Venerable Order of the Hospital of Saint John of Jerusalem
OTC	Officers' Training Corps
PoW	Prisoner of War
PPCLI	Princess Patricia's Canadian Light Infantry
PPS	Parliamentary Private Secretary
Pte	Private
RA	Royal Artillery
RAF	Royal Air Force

RAFVR	Royal Air Force Volunteer Reserve
RAAF	Royal Auxiliary Air Force/ Royal Australian Air Force
RAC	Royal Armoured Corps
RAMC	Royal Army Medical Corps
RASC	Royal Army Service Corps
RCAF	Royal Canadian Air Force
RCHA	Royal Canadian Horse Artillery
RE	Royal Engineers
RFA	Royal Field Artillery
RFC	Royal Flying Corps
RGA	Royal Garrison Artillery
RHA	Royal Horse Artillery
RMA	Royal Marine Artillery
RMS	Royal Mail Ship/Steamer
RN	Royal Navy
RNR	Royal Naval Reserve
RSL	Returned and Services League
RSM	Regimental Sergeant Major
Sgt	Sergeant
SMLE	Short Magazine Lee Enfield
SNCO	Senior non-commissioned officers
Spr	Sapper
SS	Steam Ship
TA	Territorial Army
TD	Territorial Decoration
TF	Territorial Force
TMB	Trench Mortar Battery
Tr	Trench
TSS	Twin Screw Steamer
UN	United Nations
VAD	Voluntary Aid Detachment
VD	Volunteer Decoration
VC	Victoria Cross
VIP	Very Important Person
WAAF	Women's Auxiliary Air Force
WO1 or 2	Warrant Officer Class 1 or 2
YMCA	Young Men's Christian Association

Introduction

The fourth book in this series covers from the end of the 1916 Somme battles to just before the opening of the Third Battle of Ypres. This period includes the German withdrawal to the Hindenburg Line and the Battles of Arras and Messines Ridge, the curtain raiser to Third Ypres. Fifty VC recipients are included. As with previous books, it is written for the battlefield visitor as well as the armchair reader. Each account provides background information to explain the broad strategic and tactical situation, before focusing on the VC action in detail. Each is supported by a map to allow a visitor to stand on, or close to, the spot and at least one photograph of the site. Detailed biographies help to understand the man behind the Cross.

As far as possible chapters and sections within them follow the titles of battles, actions and affairs as decided by the post-war Battle Nomenclature Committee. VCs are numbered chronologically 175, 176, 177 etc from 27th January to 27th July 1917. As far as possible they are described in the same order, but when a number of actions were fought simultaneously, the VCs are covered out of sequence on a geographical basis in accordance with the official battle nomenclature.

Refer to the master maps to find the general area for each VC. If visiting the battlefields it is advisable to purchase maps from the respective French and Belgian 'Institut Géographique National'. The French IGN Top 100 and Belgian IGN Provinciekaart at 1:100,000 scale are ideal for motoring, but 1:50,000, 1:25,000 or 1:20,000 scale maps are necessary for more detailed work, e.g. French IGN Serie Bleue and Belgian IGN Topografische Kaart. They are obtainable from the respective IGN or through reputable map suppliers on-line.

Ranks are as used on the day. Grave references have been shortened, e.g. 'Plot II, Row A, Grave 10' will appear as 'II A 10'. There are some abbreviations, many in common usage, but if unsure refer to the list provided.

I endeavour to include memorials to each VC in their biographies. However, two groups have been omitted because they apply to them all and to include them in each biography would be unnecessarily repetitive. First, every VC is commemorated in the VC Diary and on memorial panels at the Union Jack Club, Sandell Street, Waterloo, London. Second, commemorative paving stones are being laid in every VC's birthplace in the British Isles on, or close to, the 100th anniversary of their VC action.

Thanks are due to too many people and organisations to mention here. They are acknowledged in 'Sources' and any omissions are my fault and not intentional. However, I would like to pay a particular tribute to Alasdair Macintyre, son of Western Front VC David Lowe Macintyre, who died in October 2015. Alasdair helped enormously with Scottish biographical research and nothing was ever too much trouble for him to tackle. He was a charming gentleman and will be missed by all members of the 'Victoria Cross Database Users Group' who also helped enormously – Doug and Richard Arman, Vic Tambling and Alan Jordan.

Paul Oldfield
Wiltshire
December 2015

Chapter One

Local Operations Winter 1917

27th January 1917

175 Sgt Edward Mott, 1st Border (87th Brigade, 29th Division), South of Le Transloy, France

The Somme offensive officially came to an end in November 1916, but the British maintained pressure on the Germans throughout the winter by a series of limited attacks, raids and bombardments. At the same time the British strengthened their defences and thinned out the line in order to train the maximum number of troops for forthcoming offensives in the spring. On 12th December 1916, Fourth Army extended its front southwards, taking over almost ten kilometres of the French line, and on 26th February 1917 the front was extended as far as the Amiens–Roye road near Le Quesnoy.

The first of the limited attacks by Fourth Army took place at 5.30 a.m. on 27th January. It involved two battalions of 87th Brigade (29th Division) on a frontage of 675m. The objective, known as Landwehr Trench to the Germans, was 360m north of the start line, astride the Le Transloy–Frégicourt road. Trench maps show the section attacked as Landsturm Trench, although it was continuous with Landwehr Trench. A formidable array of artillery was deployed in direct support and for counter-battery work. The attacking troops practised the attack repeatedly on similar ground out of the line and were thoroughly grounded in their tasks.

Preparations for the attack were complicated by the need to join the forward posts into a continuous line from which to launch the assault. This also delayed establishing forward dumps. There were no communications trenches in this area and the assault troops were limited to a single duckboard track from Ginchy Corner to the front line. This delayed their deployment into attack formation, but it was achieved on time.

At Zero hour, the barrage fell and 1st Royal Inniskilling Fusiliers on the right and 1st Border on the left moved forward rapidly. Each battalion had mopping-up parties attached from 2nd South Wales Borderers. Except for isolated pockets, the enemy was surprised and did not put up much of a fight. Indeed some of their machine guns were frozen. The morning was darker than usual and this resulted in a slight loss of direction, with the right converging on the centre. The following day this caused uncertainty about where the right flank of 1st Royal Inniskilling Fusiliers lay.

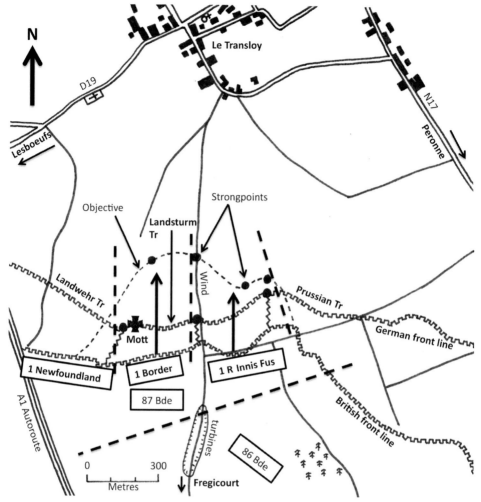

Leave Le Transloy on the D19 southwest towards Lesboeufs. Pass the church on the left and after 100m turn left on an unclassified road. After 300m turn right. Follow the track for a kilometre to the second wind turbine (SB02). Park off the track here and stand below the turbine looking north. You are halfway between 1st Border's start line behind you and Landsturm Trench about fifty metres to your front. Look half left about 275m at the top of a shallow re-entrant. This is where Edward Mott captured the machine gun post, which allowed the advance to continue.

From the second wind turbine looking northwards towards Le Transloy. Edward Mott's VC action was at the top of the re-entrant.

Cemetery

Shallow re-entrant

1st Border encountered heavy resistance on the left from a machine gun strongpoint and **Sergeant Edward Mott**'s company was pinned down. Despite being badly wounded in the eye, he dashed forward and after a fierce struggle succeeded in capturing the gunner and his gun. This cleared the way for the attack to continue and all objectives were taken by 2 p.m.

One strongpoint had to be evacuated later due to heavy retaliatory shellfire and three machine guns were knocked out during the day, but there was no counterattack. On the left flank, 1st Newfoundland saw an opportunity and dashed forward to seize seventy prisoners. Consolidation was made more difficult than normal due to the frozen ground and the men had to wrap sandbags around their feet to stop them slipping. During the night, two companies of 1/2nd Monmouthshire (Pioneers) dug two communications trenches to connect the old front line to the new positions. A third communications trench was dug by 1st King's Own Scottish Borderers, but it was not possible to relieve the attacking troops that night.

87th Brigade took 395 prisoners and three machine guns. It suffered about 200 casualties. 1st Border's share was 137 casualties and 204 prisoners before being relieved by 1st King's Own Scottish Borderers at 11 p.m. on 28th January.

4th–5th February 1917

176 Capt Henry Murray, 13th Battalion AIF (4th Australian Brigade, 4th Australian Division), Gueudecourt, France

In common with the rest of Fourth Army, I ANZAC Corps began to adopt a more offensive attitude from 10th January 1917 onwards. On 31st January, the Corps was allocated a number of small areas of the line to capture:

1. Cloudy Trench northeast of Gueudecourt.
2. The southern part of Finch Trench west of Le Transloy.
3. Butte de Warlencourt.
4. The Maze salient near Eaucourt-l'Abbaye.
5. Stormy Trench north of Cloudy Trench.

Le Transloy

6. Sunray Trench east of Cloudy Trench (added on 5th February).
7. Northern part of Finch Trench (added on 5th February).

The first of these attacks by I ANZAC Corps, and the second in the series of Fourth Army's limited attacks, took place on the evening of 1st February. It was launched against a 360m stretch of Stormy Trench, almost on the boundary between 4th and 5th Australian Divisions. It was on the neck of a shallow spur with a depression behind that could not be observed from the ANZAC lines. The first idea was for a silent dawn attack, but a belt of wire almost five metres thick in front of the objective required cutting beforehand by artillery or trench mortars. January was very cold and the ground hardened, enabling the trench mortars of X4A Battery to be positioned in what had been waterlogged emplacements.

Covered by an artillery shoot on 30th January, the trench mortars attempted to cut the wire, but many bombs bounced off the frozen ground and burst in the air. Another attempt was made on the 31st, but many rounds fell short. One

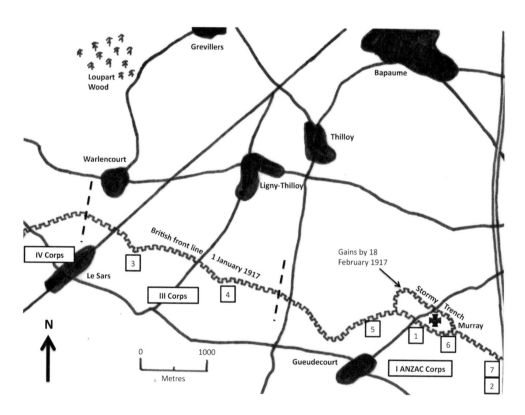

The position of Stormy Trench in relation to the other six planned attacks by Fourth Army in February 1916.

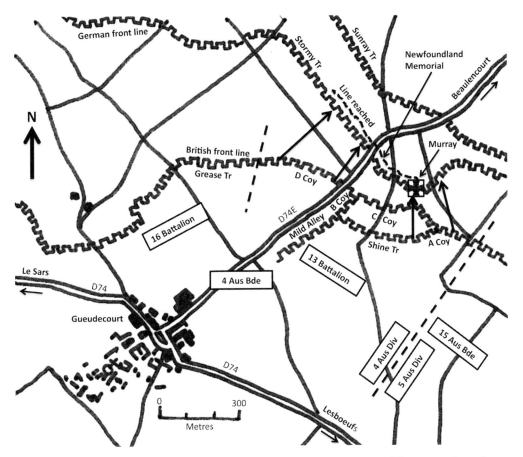

Leave Gueudecourt on the D74E northeast towards Beaulencourt. After a kilometre park at the Newfoundland Memorial on the right, which includes a small section of trench. Murray's VC action was 200m to the southeast of the memorial on top of the spur running away to the south.

exploded just outside one of the emplacements, killing or wounding the entire crew. Much of the wire remained uncut so the field artillery was turned on it during 1st February.

15th Battalion was ordered to make the attack at 7 p.m., following a bombardment of two minutes. There was a half moon until 2 a.m. However, the ANZAC front line was not continuous and some parts could not be approached in daylight. As a result, half a company had to lie up all day in a forward trench on the right. On the left, the company was able to assemble unseen at last light in Grease Trench.

At 7 p.m., a barrage crashed down on Cloudy Trench and other places as a diversion. The assault troops moved forward thirty metres under cover of the guns and, when they lifted, they attacked swiftly. The right was held up by uncut wire, but this had been anticipated and one of the platoons had joined the left attack. The troops on the left gained their objective and the left platoon bombed along Stormy Trench to the right and succeeded in taking most of it. Another company of 15th Battalion and forty men of 14th Battalion assisted in bringing up ammunition and

From the Newfoundland Memorial looking south. Part of the trench can be seen between the trees on the left. A line from the end of the trench through the fence corner post takes the eye to the top of the low spur upon which Henry Murray repelled numerous counterattacks and held on to the gains made. Gueudecourt is to the right of the picture.

food. The German counter-barrage made passage over no man's land very difficult, but immediate counterattacks were driven off.

Another counterattack at 1.55 a.m. was beaten off with the assistance of the artillery. However, at 4 a.m. next morning a strong German counterattack was launched. The Australian SOS signals were not seen by the artillery until they were repeated by Battalion HQ. The first shells came down at 4.50 a.m., but the barrage was not heavy enough to stop the attack. German shells destroyed both Stokes trench mortars supporting the forward troops, who by then had been driven out. 15th Battalion suffered 144 casualties, but came away with fifty prisoners and had inflicted more numerous casulaties on the enemy than it had suffered.

The decision was taken to repeat the attack at 10 p.m. on 4th February by 13th Battalion with C Company, 14th Battalion in support. This was to coincide with 5th Australian Division's attack on Finch and Orion Trenches on the extreme right of I ANZAC Corps. The scale was increased all round. The whole of 13th Battalion was involved, more artillery was allocated and 12,000 extra grenades were stockpiled in Grease Trench and Shine Trench. Another 8,000 grenades were held at Battalion HQ and there were also 1,000 rifle grenades. Individual bombers had at least twenty grenades and twenty bomb carriers per company behind them had another twenty-four each. Every infantryman stuffed more bombs into their greatcoat pockets. The leading companies also had 1,000 rifle grenades to outrange the German egg bombs.

Careful rehearsals were carried out and every company officer and NCO had time to carry out reconnaissance in no man's land. During assembly, boots were muffled on the frozed ground by tying sandbags around them. They were removed just before zero hour to avoid getting caught in the barbed wire. In the intense cold, the Lewis guns were kept from freezing by removing all thick grease and oil and smearing them with kerosene instead. Morale was high; some men due for leave stayed behind to take part and Lieutenant Kells, suffering from dysentery, rejoined **Captain Henry Murray's** A Company.

The 5th Australian Division attack on the right did not take place, as the Germans had already pulled back. However, there was plenty of activity elsewhere on the front to divert German attention. 1st Australian Division's artillery made a feint on The Maze and the British 2nd and 18th Divisions (II Corps) launched raids. At dusk, the assault troops assembled and the rum jar was passed around. On the right, one of Murray's platoons had to start from Shine Trench, 100m behind the rest. Due to the full moon, men had to trickle forwards in two and threes and some were not in position at 9.58 p.m. when the barrage fell.

The going across the hard snow-covered ground was easy and the platoon in Shine Trench hurried forward and soon caught up. The barrage was near perfect and in places the men were only a few metres behind it. A forward machine gun was overrun and another was silenced by the barrage. Within a few seconds, the left and centre had jumped into the enemy trench, just as the garrison came out of its dugouts. A barricade was thrown up on the left. The action was less intense there, but the German barrage was accurate. A counterattack at 10.50 p.m. was repulsed with the help of the artillery.

On the right, Murray's company found no gaps in the wire. Anticipating this, Murray led his men to the left, where the entanglement was known to be broken. They entered the point of the salient and found a maze of used and disused trenches just as the Germans hurled themselves into the attack from their dugouts. A vicious bombing exchange followed until the main trench had been blocked 100m short of where intended. Murray felt it was unwise to go further at that time.

Most of the Battalion's objective had been seized quickly and sixty-six prisoners were taken. However, the German retaliation was swift and by 10.09 p.m. their artillery was falling heavily. The counter-barrage was particularly heavy on the left, affecting bomb carriers, stretcher-bearers, prisoners going back and those holding the old front line. C Company, 14th Battalion, helped carry stores and ammunition as casualties amongst 13th Battalion's carriers mounted.

Twenty minutes after the attack, shadowy figures were seen approaching the right rear of Murray's position through no man's land. At first it was assumed they were from 58th Battalion (15th Australian Brigade), which was to dig a new trench to join up the flank. Simultaneously, Germans were seen moving southeast along their support trench. Murray got one of his Lewis guns to engage this target just as twenty grenades shattered the right barricade. Seven of the nine bombers there were killed or wounded and the rest were sent reeling back. Murray ordered Lieutenant Marper to fire the SOS signal at 10.47 p.m.

Within thirty seconds, the artillery of 4th and 5th Divisions crashed down, but the Germans pressed on. Several of Murray's men began to give ground, but he dashed forward, rallied them, shot three Germans and captured three more. His determined and timely action resulted in the position being held. Not content with just holding on, he led bombing parties and bayonet charges and also helped carry the wounded to safety. The Germans made five counterattacks here in rapid

From the southeast, the low spur upon which Henry Murray held off numerous counterattacks is to the left of the Newfoundland Memorial. The tree tops peeping over the skyline on the left are in Gueudecourt.

succession. Due to casualties, the bombers holding the right flank had to be replaced twice in this time. When the Germans finally pulled back, their barrage fell again heavily.

2435 Private (later Corporal) MD Robertson, one of the surviving bombers on the right, organised five riflemen to throw bombs back while he engaged the enemy more deeply with rifle grenades to cut off their support. He was wounded in the face, but continued until Murray gathered twenty bombers from the left. The Germans had occupied two trenches across that held by Murray's company, just out of Mills bomb range. 3136 Lance Corporal RB Withers on the right and a leaderless group on the left charged the enemy and drove them off.

A Company had two machine guns knocked out by the enemy shelling and these were replaced from reserves at Battalion HQ. There was a lull during which the CO, Lieutenant Colonel JMA Durrant DSO, arranged for a barrage on the depression behind Stormy Trench and also for one gun to fire in enfilade down the German front line just beyond Murray's right. Murray spent part of the night with Robertson reconnoitring the maze of old trenches. The company was too weak to occupy them, but they knew where to throw their grenades when the next attack came.

At 11.50 p.m., Murray telephoned Battalion HQ to report another counterattack. The CO checked Murray's precise position before bringing down the artillery again and this broke up the attack with heavy German casualties. The German shelling continued and eventually Battalion HQ was able to get an accurate bearing on a German 5.9″ battery, which was passed to the heavy artillery and dealt with.

Around 3 a.m., Murray spotted movement in Sunray Trench and fired the SOS signal at 3.07 a.m. This counterattack was broken up and on the far right some other Germans were driven off by rifle grenades. During the night a communications trench had been dug to connect with the old front line, but it was too shallow for daylight use. A German wireless message had been intercepted and another heavy counterattack was expected. At 7.45 a.m., the German bombers became active again, but no attack followed.

Having repulsed three major counterattacks, Murray's company was exhausted and its trenches were shattered. It was relieved, ahead of the rest of the Battalion at 7 p.m. on 5th February, by D Company, 16th Battalion. It came out with only forty-eight of the 140 who went into the attack the previous night. Murray's uniform was torn with bullet holes. Overall losses were heavier than in the attack on 1st February; 350 on this occassion, compared to about 250 Germans. 13th Battalion had 233 of these casulaties. Seventy-seven prisoners were taken. In addition to Murray, the CO also recommended Withers and Robertson for the VC, but they were both awarded the DCM (LG 26th March 1917).

The 12th Australian Brigade's hold over Stormy Trench was strengthen on 21st and 22nd February in two well executed bombing attacks. Fifty-five prisoners were taken.

16th/17th February 1917

> 177 LSgt Frederick Palmer, 22nd Royal Fusiliers (99th Brigade, 2nd Division), North of Courcelette, France

In early 1917, Fifth Army planned a series of attacks to improve its positions, the first of which was carried out on 17th February. The main attack south of the Ancre was to be carried out by 99th Brigade (2nd Division) and 53rd and 54th Brigades (18th Division). 6th Brigade (2nd Division) was to attack in support on the right against Desire Support and Guard Trenches, while 63rd Division on the left advanced north of the Ancre. Success would give the British command of the approaches to Pys and Miraumont and observation over the upper Ancre valley. The attack was named officially the Actions of Miraumont 17th–18th February 1917, but is also known as the Battle of Boom Ravine.

99th Brigade on the right had a frontage of 630m between the two Miraumont–Courcelette roads. Its objectives were Grandcourt Trench, then South Miraumont Trench beyond Hill 130 and finally the southern edge of Petit Miraumont. The assault battalions were 23rd Royal Fusiliers on the right and 1st King's Royal Rifle Corps on the left. D Company, 22nd Royal Fusiliers, was under command 23rd Royal Fusiliers to cover the right flank from the British front line to the first objective (Blue Line), a distance of 500m. Two companies of 22nd Royal Fusiliers were to

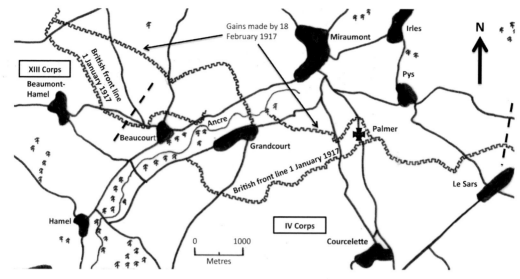

The gains made by Fifth Army astride the Ancre in February 1917.

pass through to take the third and final objective (Yellow Line), while B Company mopped up on the West Miraumont Road. 1st Royal Berkshire held the front line prior to the assault battalions forming up and was then in support. The attack was rehearsed meticulously behind the lines from 11th February onwards. Officers were to be dressed and equipped exactly as their men.

Frozen ground prevented the construction of assembly trenches but ironically, as the troops moved up into the forming-up positions, it thawed and turned into a quagmire. The night was very dark and when the move forward from Pozières began at 6 p.m., it was marked by signboards with luminous paint and tapes. Despite allowing ample time, the last troops were not in position until just after 5 a.m. The Germans may have learned of the attack from a deserter and from 4.30 a.m. bombarded the whole of the attack frontage, resulting in some losses.

The guns opened fire at 5.45 a.m. and the infantry set off in pitch darkness into a hail of small arms fire, particularly from the northeast. North of the Ancre, 63rd Division encountered little opposition and took all its objectives by 11 a.m. However, on the right, 6th Brigade's attack failed. Despite this, and the confusion caused by the unexpected mud and mist, the advance continued in the centre. On the left of 99th Brigade, 1st King's Royal Rifle Corps made good progress and gained the first objective. However, the reserve companies were pushed off the line of advance by 54th Brigade on the left and drifted as far right as the East Miraumont Road, from where they were driven back. Some soldiers gained the second objective, but were forced back to Grandcourt Trench. 23rd Royal Fusiliers had a very difficult time, but reached the first objective.

D Company, 22nd Royal Fusiliers, advanced as planned east of the East Miraumont Road. It had five Lewis guns and three machine guns with which to establish seven posts. The idea was to deploy the Lewis guns forward of and between the posts and

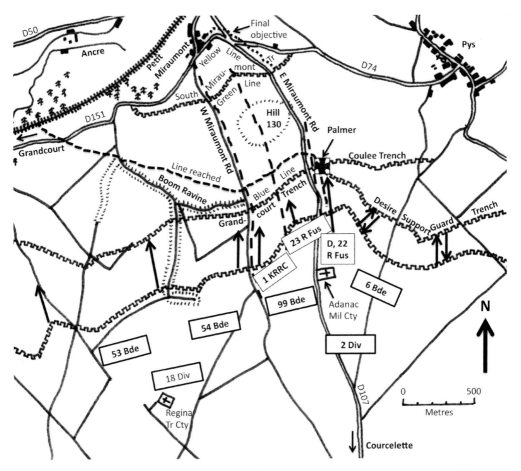

The point where Coulee Trench crossed the east Miraumont road is 675m north of Adanac Military Cemetery. However, there is nowhere safe to park on the roadside in that area, so leave your vehicle at Adanac and walk along the left side of the road to face the oncoming traffic. Coulee Trench crossed the road 200m after the sharp left hand bend. Frederick Palmer's VC action was to the east of the road at this point.

site the machine guns in the rear. As soon as the line was established, if prudent to do so, a proportion of the men were to be pulled back to form a support line. The advance was to be in seven parties, one per post, separated by about eighty metres. When the leading party reached the Blue Line, the whole company was to halt, turn right, face to the east and dig in.

The advance went well until it was halted by uncut wire. Fire from two machine guns on the right caused a considerable number of casualties, including the company commander, Major John Walsh, and second-in-command, Lieutenant GH Evans, who were both wounded, as were the other officers. Walsh died of his wounds on 19th February and is commemorated on a Special Memorial in Ovillers Military Cemetery.

Sergeant Frederick Palmer took command. Having arranged for Sergeant Arthur Mobley (awarded DCM for this action) and his section to engage the two

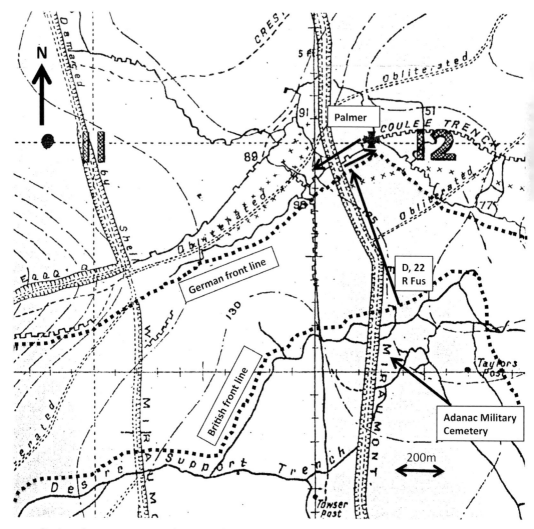

Section of contemporary trench map, updated just before the attack on 17th February 1917, showing in detail the area where Frederick Palmer defended Coulee Trench.

machine guns, Palmer took his men round the flank and managed to cut a gap through the wire. With just six men he then captured Coulee Trench, including the troublesome machine guns. They established a block and, having consolidated the position with men from several units, defended Coulee Trench for the next three hours against seven determined counterattacks. Palmer also rescued an injured runner, Skins Jennings, who had been shot in the buttock and was unable to walk.

When his small party ran out of bombs, Palmer went in search of a fresh supply. Just as he returned, at about 9 a.m., the Germans overran the post in their eighth attack. Although shaken from being blown off his feet by an exploding grenade, Palmer rallied his men and led them back to positions west of the East Miraumont

Looking across the East Miraumont road eastwards. D Company attacked from the right and seized Coulee Trench astride the road after Frederick Palmer's flank attack.

Road. There, with the support of 23rd Royal Fusiliers' Lewis guns, he held the enemy in Coulee Trench. His gallantry saved the situation on the right flank and averted a possible disaster. The other survivors in his party were awarded the DCM or MM.

Further west, A and B Companies found uncut wire and one platoon of C Company, west of the West Miraumont Road, was captured. They fell short of the final objective as a flanking move on the right forced them back to the first objective.

53rd and 54th Brigades managed to gain Boom Ravine in a day of confused and costly fighting, but could progress no further. Overall the attack was only a partial success and casualties were very heavy. The men were quickly exhausted by the fighting and the heavy going. Weapons became clogged with mud. Failure to secure beyond the first objective can also be attributed to the warning the Germans had, the inability of the artillery to adequately deal with Coulee Trench and the absence of a senior officer after the first objective to coordinate the next move and push up supports. An orderly retirement took place to the first objective, which was consolidated and held against heavy and repeated counterattacks.

By 6 a.m. on 19th February, 99th Brigade had been relieved by 6th Brigade. It had suffered 775 casualties and took over 200 prisoners. A few days later the enemy withdrew from this area to the Hindenburg Line, a few days earlier than originally intended.

8th March 1917

178 2Lt George Cates, 2nd Rifle Brigade (25th Brigade, 8th Division), East of Bouchavesnes, France

The German withdrawal to the Hindenburg Line (Siegfried Stellung) began on 24th February 1917. The British had the first inkling of the existence of the new defensive line in the middle of October 1916, but its full significance did not become apparent until the withdrawal operation was actually underway. A withdrawal is always a difficult and hazardous operation, but the German planning was meticulous and it went ahead by stages remarkably smoothly. The Allies were disadvantaged by following up over ground devastated by months of fighting and the German's scorched earth policy. A thaw also set in, making conditions even more intolerable. Moving artillery and ammunition forward was particularly difficult.

The withdrawal commenced on Fifth Army's front. Once the initial surprise had been overcome, commanders had to balance the obvious desire to pressurise the retreating enemy with caution, as the German rearguards were well armed, positioned and organised for their task. 2nd Australian Division was the first to learn this lesson in trying to enter Malt Trench near Warlencourt and finding it unexpectedly strongly held. Overall the troops lacked experience in mobile warfare and junior commanders were unused to taking the initiative. Lack of lateral communications between units resulted in delays and casualties.

In the Fourth Army area, a series of limited attacks had been planned before the start of the German withdrawal. In one such operation, at 5.15 a.m. on 4th March, 8th Division (XV Corps) attacked on a frontage of one kilometre, 800m northeast of Bouchavesnes. The aim was to secure the Bouchavesnes valley and the re-entrant leading towards Rancourt. Two brigades were employed, 24th Brigade on the left and 25th Brigade on the right. The latter attacked with only one battalion, 2nd Royal Berkshire, which was tasked to capture Pallas and Fritz Trenches and their respective support lines.

The attack, in falling snow, was successful and the gains were held, although the next day fierce German counterattacks caused some tense moments. On the night of 8th/9th March, 2nd Rifle Brigade relieved 1st Royal Irish Rifles in the front line. One company each was allocated to Fritz and Pallas Trenches, while half a company

Looking north from the track where you can park to overlook the Bouchavesnes valley. Cates' VC action was in one of the two trenches annotated.

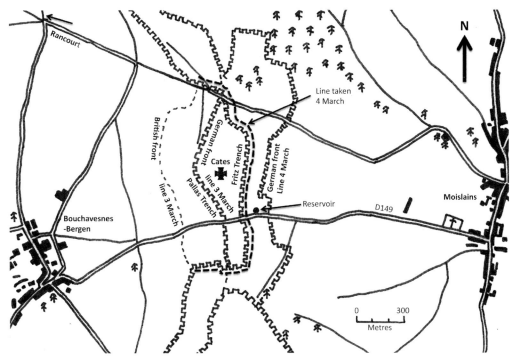

Midway between Moislains and Bouchavesnes-Bergen at the top of the hill on the north side of the D149 is a reservoir enclosed in a thick hedge. Continue 150m to the west where there is a convenient track on the south side of the road to park. Look north. The track is about midway between Pallas and Fritz Trenches. Cates' VC action was to your front in the low ground north of the road.

held the right flank between the old British front line and the captured trenches. The rest of this company was in support, and the fourth company was in reserve in the old front line.

Very little is known about the circumstances in which **Second Lieutenant George Cates** won the VC. The Battalion War Diary states that he was wounded

by shellfire and later died of wounds. However, this does not agree with the VC citation, which states that Cates was digging with his men to improve one of the captured trenches when his spade struck a buried bomb. The fuse immediately ignited and, in order to save those around him, Cates put his left foot on top of it. It exploded almost immediately wounding him mortally, but his men were spared serious injury. He died early the next morning.

Chapter Two

Advance to the Hindenburg Line

13th–17th March 1917

179 Pte Christopher Cox, 7th Bedfordshire (54th Brigade, 18th Division), Achiet-le-Grand, France

On 10th March, 53rd Brigade captured Irles. On the night of 12th/13th March, 54th Brigade relieved 53rd Brigade in the forward trenches in preparation for an attack on the Loupart Line. However, at about 3 a.m. on the 13th, an ANZAC patrol found Loupart Wood abandoned and by 6 a.m. it was clear that the enemy was withdrawing from the Bapaume–Achiet-le-Petit area. The attack was no longer necessary, but the Brigade remained in assault formation to follow the withdrawing Germans. 12th Middlesex was on the right, 6th Northamptonshire in the centre and 7th Bedfordshire on the left, with 11th Royal Fusiliers to form a left defensive flank. 7th Buffs (55th Brigade) was in close support for dugout clearance and carrying parties.

The overnight brigade relief was not completed until 6 a.m. on the 13th. There was also some delay in following up the Germans, as the troops had not previously seen the ground in front of them. However, by 10 a.m. the Brigade had occupied the Loupart Line between its junction with 6th Brigade (2nd Division) at the western end of Loupart Wood and the Miraumont–Achiet-le-Grand railway. 11th Royal Fusiliers formed a defensive left flank facing northwest on the forward slope of a spur running parallel to the railway north and northeast of Irles.

The three forward battalions pushed patrols northeast of the Loupart Line as far as the Grévillers–Achiet-le-Petit road. There was little opposition, but Achiet-le-Petit and the Bihucourt Line remained in enemy hands and patrols approaching them came under heavy fire. Between 5 p.m. and 8 p.m., 7th Bedfordshire pushed the Germans off the high ground around the 130m contour (128m on modern maps) and consolidated a line facing generally north with the left flank swung back to join with 11th Royal Fusiliers in the Loupart Line. During this operation **Private Christopher Cox**, a B Company stretcher-bearer, carried wounded men back from the Loupart Line through heavy shell and machine gun fire to the dressing station.

Before dawn on 14th March, 6th Northamptonshire was withdrawn into 54th Brigade reserve in the Loupart Line. At 1 a.m., C Company, 7th Bedfordshire

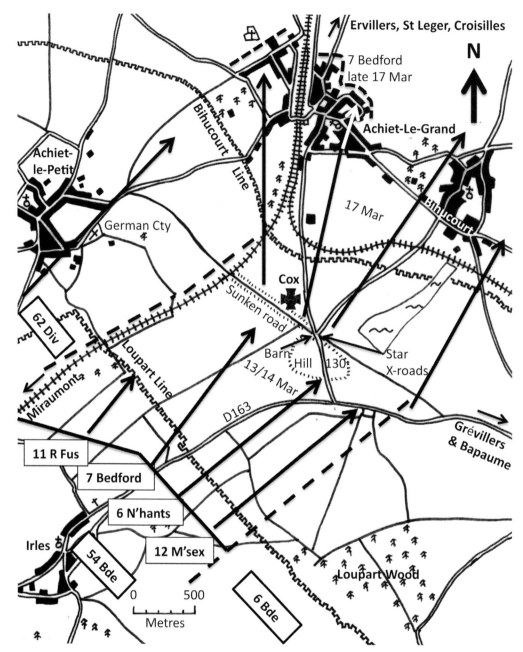

Leave Irles to the northeast on the D163 towards Grévillers, passing a cemetery on the left. After two kilometres pass three prominent trees on the roadside and turn left at the third tree. After 600m there is a barn on the left at Star Crossroads. A memorial to Christopher Cox is on the barn wall. Just north of the barn is the start of the sunken road captured by 7th Bedfordshire on 14th May. Cox's VC was awarded for his bravery in a number of places, but none more so that in the open ground northeast of the sunken road on 17th May.

occupied the sunken road between the Star Crossroads south of Achiet-le-Grand and the Miraumont–Achiet-le-Grand railway. D Company joined C Company in this new line, which connected with other troops on the right, while A and B Companies remained in close support. At 9 a.m., the Germans were seen massing in the Bihucourt Line around the railway junction south of Achiet-le-Grand. The concentrated fire of the artillery broke up the counterattack before it could develop.

The rest of the day was characterised by shelling and intense machine gun fire, under which B Company's stretcher-bearers assisted A Company to recover the wounded from the previous day in front of the Loupart Line. Cox carried two men 200m to safety whilst under machine gun fire all the way. In the evening, D Company took over the whole front line, allowing C Company to fall back into support.

Most of the action was on the left flank, where 62nd Division faced Achiet-le-Petit, but early on the morning of the 15th a 12th Middlesex patrol penetrated into Bihucourt and saw the German transport pulling back to the east. 12th Middlesex and 7th Bedfordshire advanced against the Bihucourt Line, but came under heavy machine gun fire from the two villages and were halted.

In this move, 7th Bedfordshire was led by C Company, supported by A Company. The first wave was hit by heavy fire from Achiet-le-Petit and Bihucourt Trench. The troops took cover in shell holes and dug in 200m down the hill. A Company did not advance, but held the line of the sunken road. After dark, C Company withdrew through A Company and went into reserve with D Company, while B Company supported A Company.

Despite the danger during the day, Cox worked across the bullet swept ground on Hill 130 looking for the wounded. He personally rescued four men, carrying them back on his shoulders. He was seen carrying a wounded man near the Star Crossroads, where artillery and machine gun fire was particularly heavy. The wounded man was hit again by machine gun fire and the impact knocked Cox to his knees, but he simply got up and carried on. A corporal he was carrying was also wounded a second time, such was the closeness of the enemy fire against individual targets. Having helped clear his own Battalion's wounded, Cox then assisted 12th Middlesex, continuing this fine work throughout the next few days. He also rescued some wounded machine gunners and returned for their ammunition to give to another team.

The 16th was uneventful except for a large fire observed in Achiet-le-Grand. At 6 p.m., B Company took over the front line. During the night reports from I ANZAC Corps indicated its patrols had entered Bapaume. Early on the 17th patrols found the Bihucourt Line abandoned. 12th Middlesex moved on Bihucourt, 7th Bedfordshire on Achiet-le-Grand and 62nd Division on Achiet-le-Petit.

C Company led 7th Bedfordshire's advance at 8 a.m. with D Company in support, while B Company made a secure left flank along the railway. The operation was carried out with great skill and energy. Some machine gun and heavy artillery fire was encountered entering Achiet-le-Grand, but by 10 a.m. the Bihucourt Line

From the embankment to the north of Star Crossroads looking north in the direction of 7th Bedfordshire's advance on 17th March. Christopher Cox was particularly active in this area over a number of days, rescuing the wounded under very heavy close fire.

had been occupied. At 3 p.m., the Battalion was occupying positions on the north and east sides of Achiet-le-Grand together with a strong flank along the railway to the west. During this advance, Cox again carried back several wounded cases from exposed forward positions through a bombardment. He also used bandages to mark gaps through the barbed wire for others to use.

Two troops of A Squadron, Yorkshire Dragoons, were pushed forward. Overnight patrols of 7th Bedfordshire and 12th Middlesex discovered the Germans had pulled back again and both battalions were ordered to push forward strong patrols up to 700m beyond the villages. On the 18th, an advanced guard was formed of A Squadron, Yorkshire Dragoons, 6th Northamptonshire, sections of artillery, engineers and 54th Brigade Machine Gun Company with 11th Royal Fusiliers in support. It moved forward to occupy Ervillers, while 7th Bedfordshire remained in Achiet-le-Grand and 12th Middlesex in Bihucourt. There was no opposition.

The advanced guard pressed on next day and took St Léger. On 20th March, 6th Northamptonshire was prevented from taking Croisilles by strong opposition. 7th Bedfordshire moved up to Ervillers and two companies moved to St Léger to support 6th Northamptonshire. 54th Brigade was relieved by 20th Brigade (7th Division) later in the day.

26th March 1917

180 Capt Percy Cherry, 26th Battalion AIF (7th Australian Brigade, 2nd Australian Division), Lagnicourt, France

By 20th March, the German retreat was slowing as it neared the Hindenburg Line and a series of outpost villages (Beaumetz, Lagnicourt, Noreuil, Longatte, Écoust and Croisilles) were held in front of it. On I ANZAC Corps' right, Beaumetz was abandoned before dawn on 21st March, but the Germans attempted to retake it in the early hours of 23rd March. 15th Australian Brigade's pickets were pushed back

and the village was entered from the north and southeast until the reserves cleared it again. Another German attempt early on 24th March failed completely.

V Corps was less advanced in its preparations than I ANZAC Corps and faced more formidable wire obstacles in front of Écoust and Croisilles than the Australians in front of Lagnicourt and Noreuil. Fifth Army therefore authorised the two corps to operate independently. I ANZAC Corps prepared to breach the outpost line on 26th March around Lagnicourt. Five siege and heavy batteries were established northeast of Bapaume.

The days before the attack were spent in patrolling and a post was seized at the junction of two sunken roads halfway down the valley towards Lagnicourt. Each night patrols set out from it to ensure the Germans had not withdrawn. The information gained by these patrols was added to air reconnaissance to build up an accurate picture of the enemy defences. There was very close cooperation with the RFC. The day before the attack, **Captain Percy Cherry**, 26th Battalion, became convinced that there was a trench round the southeast corner of the village. He requested further investigation. Lieutenant Cleaver, 3 Squadron RFC, and another officer worked out with Cherry what was required, returned to their airfield at Beugnettre and within two hours dropped a map to HQ 26th Battalion, marked with the German trench.

The plan involved elements of two Australian divisions, 2nd on the left and 5th on the right. 20th Brigade (7th Division, V Corps) would also be involved on the left flank against Écoust and Longatte, but was delayed due to the thick wire. On the right of Lagnicourt, 58th Battalion (15th Australian Brigade, 5th Australian Division) was to advance to the Lagnicourt–Beaumetz road and establish a line of posts 900m to the Doignies road to join with 2nd Australian Division.

7th Australian Brigade, under Brigadier General Wisdom, was the advanced guard of 2nd Australian Division. In addition to the Brigade it consisted of B Squadron 13th Light Horse, half of 6th Field Company, 4th and 5th Australian Field Artillery Brigades, two batteries of 60 Pdrs, a battery of 6″ Howitzers, half a company of 1st Anzac Cyclist Battalion and a bearer sub-division of 5th Field Ambulance.

The plan was for 26th Battalion on the right to send a company round each flank of the village (A Company right and B Company left), while C Company swept

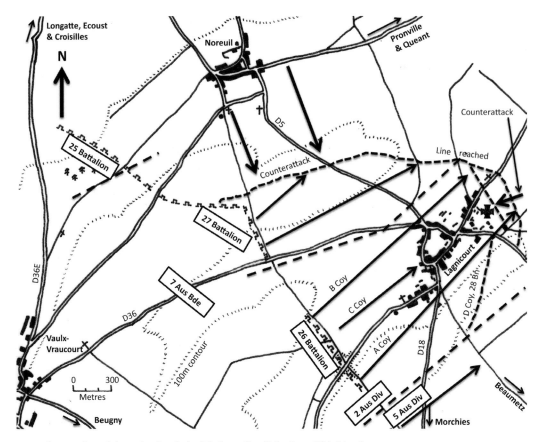

An overview of the action fought by 7th Australian Brigade on 26th March.

through the centre and D Company followed to mop up. A line of posts was to be established 700m beyond. A company of 28th Battalion was to clear the ground ahead of the assembly position and destroy an advanced machine gun post. It, and another company, was then to be the reserve. On the left, 27th Battalion was to advance with two companies along the spur between Lagnicourt and Noreuil, seize the road between the villages and establish a line of outposts beyond. On the extreme left a third company of 27th Battalion was to extend along the ridge to form a flank facing Noreuil. 25th Battalion was originally intended to attack Noreuil, but in the revised plan was to advance its right flank to connect with 27th Battalion's line and also keep in contact with 20th Brigade on the left.

26th and 27th Battalions assembled in the Noreuil–Morchies road, 1,200m from Lagnicourt. The barrage opened at 5.15 a.m. on the village outskirts for twenty minutes while the howitzers and heavy batteries shelled the crossroads in the village and the area beyond. When the infantry reached the barrage line, it began moving forward fifty metres every two minutes. This pace was intended to get the infantry to the edge of the village at daybreak.

The night before the attack was pitch dark and it drizzled throughout, making moving into position difficult. At Zero hour, B Company on the left of 26th Battalion

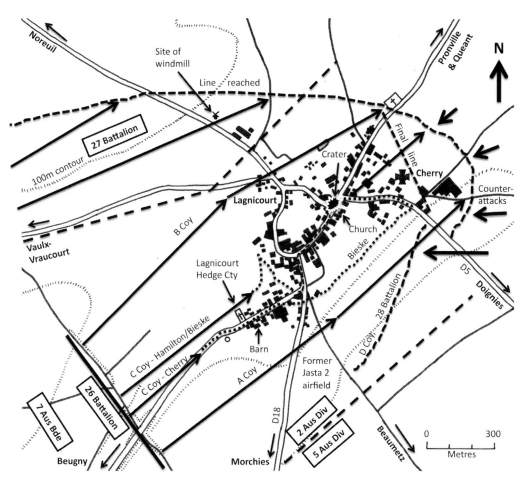

Percy Cherry's VC action is spread over a number of locations in and around Lagnicourt. Enter the village from the south on the D18 and just after turn left to Lagnicourt Hedge Cemetery and park there. Cherry's half of C Company advanced into the village towards you along the lane to the southwest. About fifty metres to the southeast of the Cemetery and slightly set back from the road on the south side is a large barn, which could be the one Cherry attacked. Turn round and drive back to the junction with the D18 and turn left. Follow the road round to the right for 350m to the church and park there. 100m on is the road junction where the crater was in 1917. Drive to the crater junction and turn right on the D5. After 300m turn left and park after 100m. Continue to walk along the track to the northeast, keeping a large metal barn on your right until you are under the power lines. To the north is the open area where the counterattacks were resisted and the final line was established.

had not arrived, so two platoons of the mopping up company (D) were diverted to cover the vacant flank. As soon as the barrage fell, the OC of B Company, Captain Cooper, was able to navigate by the flashes and arrived on time on the left edge of the village. The right of 26th Battalion was not in touch with 15th Australian Brigade. The OC of A Company, Lieutenant Lloyd, quickly strung out part of his second wave to help cover the gap and positioned some posts temporarily to cover the open flank.

As A Company passed the south of the village it was dazzled by a searchlight and halted until a Lewis gunner, firing from the hip, shot out the light. The advance continued and the Company closed round the east of the village. B Company on the left, with half the reserve company (D), made its way round the western side, losing some men to snipers in the village. Lagnicourt was cut off but was still held by about 250 men. As small groups of Germans escaped they were captured or shot down by the flanking companies.

In the centre, C Company under Captain Cherry encountered a barbed wire fence, but it did not stop the advance into Lagnicourt, where stiff resistance was met. Cherry split his company into two divisions. He led the right along the Beugny road into the southwest corner, while the left under Lieutenant Hamilton attacked the western outskirts. The plan was to meet in the open space in the centre of the village.

Hamilton's division came under heavy machine gun fire from the hedges fifty metres in front of the village. Many men were hit, including Hamilton. Lieutenant Bieske took command and led the men forward. They were fired on again and only Bieske and five men reached the trench behind the nearest hedge. The Germans fled, but fire continued to be received from the hedges to the left. Bieske's party made their way to this flank and bombed the machine gun without further loss.

Meanwhile Cherry had moved up the road into the village. He was fired upon from the windows and doors of the first building, a large courtyard farm. The attack was checked for a few minutes, until Cherry's bombers rushed both gates. Private Nutt fired his Lewis gun from the hip and hosed the inside of the barn with bullets. With the farm cleared, Cherry moved on the main street of the village and was shot

This is the road along which Percy Cherry led his half of C Company into Lagnicourt. The party under Lieutenant Hamilton, and later Lieutenant Bieske, was about 100m to the left of it. The Cross of Lagnicourt Hedge Cemetery is slightly left of and below the church tower.

The position of this barn matches the description of where Percy Cherry first came under fire as he moved along this road from right to left into the village. There is an Australian War Memorial photograph (P031 37.007) reputedly of the barn, but it has a large sign painted on it indicating the direction to Vaulx-Vraucourt and Noreuil, neither of which are on the road along which Percy Cherry's company advanced.

at from a stable. He headed straight into the yard and the defenders surrendered. The Lewis gunners fired with their weapons slung and the casings became so hot that they could only be aimed by holding the slings. In the central space of the village a large crater had been blown at the crossroads. It was defended resolutely from the rim and from loop-holed houses on the approaches. Lieutenant Corner was killed a

The cratered crossroads.

few metres from the crater and Cherry was checked. He sent for the trench mortars to be brought up, but became impatient waiting for them and decided to attack. Covered by the Lewis guns and rifle grenadiers, the bombers went round each flank and the strongpoint was cleared, the whole garrison being killed.

Cherry found Bieske lying at the bottom of the crater with a broken leg. Bieske had been unable to find Cherry and reached the eastern outskirts of the village to join up with A Company. He ran into a large German officer, whom he captured. Other Germans began to bolt and in the excitement of following them Bieske was attacked by his prisoner. The German was much heavier, but flabby and Bieske knocked him to the ground, where he was shot by another member of the party. In the dim light, figures were seen ahead and Bieske went forward to check who they were. At a corner of the road he found himself facing the rear of the Germans in the crater opposing Cherry. Bieske rushed them with his revolver and leapt over their heads just as they discharged their rifles at him. As he landed, he shattered his ankle and rolled to the bottom of the crater. The Germans were not expecting an attack in their rear and some left the crater to investigate. As they returned they were overwhelmed by Cherry's men and many were bayoneted. While Bieske was being carried to the rear on a door the carrying party was hit by a shell and three men lost their legs.

At 6.30 a.m. the troops on the flanks digging in beyond the village gave a cheer as Cherry's company emerged to join them. They had another stiff fight to clear dugouts by the roadside, but forced their way through. Cherry was due to fall back into reserve, but believed the Germans were preparing to counterattack and remained to strengthen the right, which was still not in touch with 15th Australian Brigade. Despite fighting through the village, it took D Company and a platoon of 28th Battalion until noon to mop up; and even then a few snipers evaded capture.

On the left, 27th Battalion killed a few Germans and forced back the rest from the sunken road between Lagnicourt and Noreuil. A line of posts was established along the ridge, including at Lagnicourt windmill, and part of the Lagnicourt–Noreuil road to the left was taken. Another post was established 200m further down the road, overlooking Noreuil. On the right, touch was gained with 26th Battalion, but on the left 25th Battalion was stopped by machine guns in Noreuil.

About 7.30 a.m., the Germans in Noreuil appeared to the left of the troops in the Lagnicourt–Noreuil road. Covered by snipers, the Germans were digging a line just over the crest from 27th Battalion, only fifty metres away in places. It was feared they might make a rush at any moment and many Australian rifles were still choked with mud. A number of men were hit and four Lewis gun teams on the ridge were reported destroyed. CO 27th Battalion called on 12th Battery, which had been keeping down the snipers in Noreuil, to turn its fire on the Germans on the crest.

27th Battalion was also under fire from a machine gun on the far left. A counterattack developed against the left from the Lagnicourt–Noreuil road, but when the officer leading it was shot it petered out. Covered by 12th Battery, the

Battalion crept forward over the crest to fire towards Noreuil and the Germans gradually withdrew.

The first counterattack did not affect 26th Battalion, but the Germans shelled Lagnicourt heavily until 10.30 a.m. About 1,000 Germans were seen deploying in small groups near the foremost entanglements of the Hindenburg Line near Pronville. The message to alert the artillery took forty minutes to arrive, by which time the Germans had gone. Soon after a message arrived from Cherry reporting that the enemy was counterattacking and requesting artillery support. The second company of 28th Battalion was sent forward and later the third and fourth companies. At 11.30 a.m. and 12.25 p.m., Brigadier General Wisdom (7th Australian Brigade) appealed to Brigadier General Elliott (15th Australian Brigade) to attack the enemy on the right, but this was delayed. Before the companies of 28th Battalion arrived, a crisis developed.

Lloyd's and Cherry's companies of 26th Battalion were deployed in posts about 300m beyond the northern and eastern outskirts of Lagnicourt. Most of the posts were dug into the banks of sunken roads overlooking open fields sprinkled with manure heaps. The men in some posts had levelled the heaps that were interrupting their field of fire, but when the Germans advanced the remaining heaps assisted their progress. On the ridge to the left of Lagnicourt, two machine guns opened fire on the Germans at 700m and stopped the counterattack in that area. However, on the right of Lagnicourt the flank post 350m down the Doignies road had to withdraw closer to the village under fire from a sniper. Working from one manure heap to another, the Germans came on steadily and began firing from front and flank into the northern posts. The Lewis guns were frequently clogged with mud and the riflemen struggled to keep their ammunition clean.

Cherry noticed that the Germans were firing yellow flares to show their positions to their artillery. He found some of these flares and fired them to cause the German

The area northeast of Lagnicourt between the Pronville and Doignies roads, where the German counterattacks were absorbed and where the final line was established.

artillery to lengthen its range and shell the further part of the village. With jammed Lewis guns on the left, the Germans were able to penetrate between the posts. Two other posts were outflanked and fell back closer to the village. Lieutenant Humphrys, commanding a fourth post, asked if he should withdraw, but was ordered by Lloyd to hold his position at all costs. The post held until Humphrys was killed (Villers-Bretonneux Memorial), the Lewis gun jammed and ammunition ran out. With the Germans on all sides, the survivors surrendered.

Meanwhile, the southern flank of the Germans had crossed the Doignies road, which 15th Australian Brigade was to have held, and worked round the right of the Lagnicourt posts. The first reinforcements from 28th Battalion arrived and four posts were established among the manure heaps southeast of the village. The Germans continued to advance and brought up a machine gun. The four new posts were all but annihilated and the flank was forced back to the edge of the village.

The Australians north and east of Lagnicourt had their backs against the village and the Germans were almost in some of the posts. The situation was desperate, but Cherry decided to hold on and soon after the encircling enemy appeared to lose heart. On the left, although within a stone's throw of success, they began to fall back under increasingly heavy fire from the Australians. The German machine gunners on the right took shelter in dead ground and were captured there. The rest of the German line in contact with the Australian posts withdrew under fire from the artillery. Later in the day a long line of Germans was seen digging in 900m from the Australian posts.

The Germans would not have penetrated so far had 15th Australian Brigade been in position. 60th Battalion was ordered to prepare for the attack and the officers reconnoitred the ground and made arrangements to cooperate with 26th Battalion. When the operation was postponed, 58th Battalion replaced the 60th, but it was only seventy-five minutes before the assault commenced that CO 26th Battalion was made aware. No mutual arrangements had been made and the two attacking companies of the 58th set off independently of the 26th. The right was resisted strongly by enemy posts on the road and failed to reach it. The left was hit by machine guns in a crater between the left of 58th Battalion and the right of 26th Battalion. The left flank post was established with some difficulty about 550m from the flank of 26th Battalion and under fire from a machine gun from the left rear. When the morning mist cleared, the German counterattack swept from Pronville across the front and the post withdrew.

Elliott placed 58th Battalion under Wisdom's command and sent 59th Battalion to counterattack; the German attack was driven off. That afternoon 58th Battalion seized the Doignies road and captured the troublesome German machine gun on the left.

The action at Lagnicourt cost 7th Australian Brigade 287 casualties, of which 179 were in 26th Battalion. German dead were estimated at 250–400. 26th Battalion believed it killed 200, took seventy prisoners and seized two machine guns and two trench mortars. The Germans did not renew their attempts to capture the village, but shelled it and the surrounding roads heavily. Around 4 p.m., a shell burst in a sunken road east of the village, killing Cherry and several other officers. The relief of 7th Australian Brigade began on the evening of 26th March, but it took until the 28th to complete.

27th March 1917

181 Lt Frederick Harvey, Lord Strathcona's Horse CEF (Canadian Cavalry Brigade, 5th Cavalry
     Division), Guyencourt, France

By 20th March, Fourth Army's line had advanced four to five kilometres east of the Somme. Next day the west bank of the canal south of Péronne was reached and the cavalry fought some small actions as it probed ahead. 23rd March was quiet, mainly due to the troops being exhausted. On the 24th, the corps cavalry regiments were relieved by 5th Cavalry Division, which had been put at Fourth Army's disposal. The Canadian Cavalry Brigade took over the front of XIV and XV Corps on the left of Fourth Army, while the Amballa Cavalry Brigade took over the front of III and IV Corps on the right. 5th Cavalry Division's orders were to locate advanced enemy outposts, prevent them advancing, give instant warning of any withdrawals and follow them closely.

As the Germans retreated, they adopted a 'scorched earth' policy. All useful war material was removed, villages were evacuated and razed, livestock was carried away and wells were filled or polluted. To delay the Allied advance, trees were felled across roads, large craters were blown at crossroads and liberal use was made of ingenious booby traps. Rearguards covered the German withdrawal with great skill and by 19th March twenty-nine divisions had pulled back with minimal interference.

The troops following up the German withdrawal found movement increasingly difficult. Each corps had to employ at least one of its divisions, in addition to normal labour units, as working parties to restore communications. All supplies had to be carried by horse because the roads were blocked, cratered or impassible in the thaw. Extended supply lines also put great strain on logistical support.

On 22nd March the Canadian Cavalry Brigade began moving forward from Saleux to Cerisy and by the end of the following day was around Péronne. On the 24th, the advance was led by Royal Canadian Dragoons on the right and Fort Garry Horse on the left. They took over a line of posts from XIV and XV Corps Cavalry Regiments, extending from Tincourt northwards to Bertincourt, a distance of about eighteen kilometres. Patrols were pushed forward.

On the 25th, the Amballa Cavalry Brigade took over the southern part of the outpost line from Royal Canadian Dragoons, which pushed patrols round Longavesnes and Liéramont, but could not occupy them. Later Fort Garry Horse

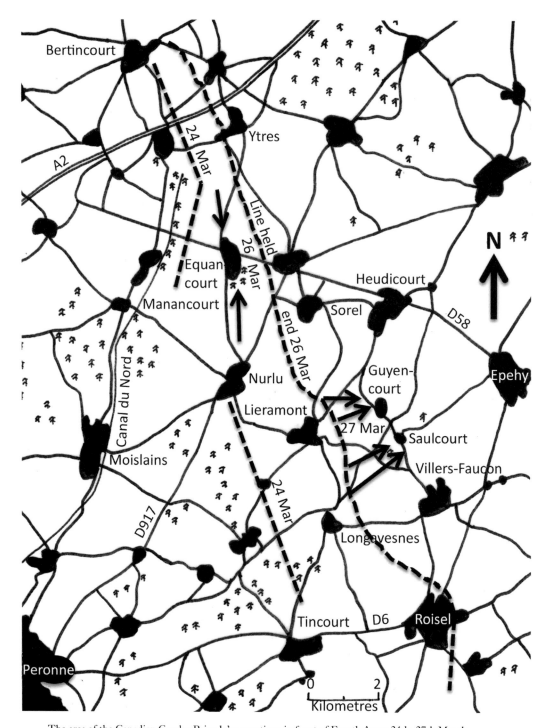

The area of the Canadian Cavalry Brigade's operations in front of Fourth Army 24th–27th March.

pushed the Germans out of two woods south of Ytres and took the railway station. On 26th March, a company of 1/4th Oxfordshire & Buckinghamshire Light Infantry (III Corps), with two squadrons of 18th Bengal Lancers (Amballa Cavalry Brigade) and two armoured cars, captured Roisel.

In another operation that day, the Canadian Cavalry Brigade was tasked to capture Équancourt and the wood to the south. Lord Strathcona's Horse and Fort Garry Horse were detailed to lead with a battery of RCHA in support. Reconnaissance was pushed forward up to three kilometres and by 5.30 p.m. the units involved were in position. Fort Garry Horse made slow progress, advancing with one squadron from the north. It was not until 12.30 a.m. next morning that a bombing party made contact with the infantry, who were by then holding Équancourt.

Meanwhile Lord Strathcona's Horse had surprised the Germans with a mounted attack by A and C Squadrons from the south, while B Squadron attacked frontally from Manancourt. The village and wood were seized by 6.15 p.m. The village came under heavy shrapnel and high explosive artillery fire, but casualties were relatively light; five men wounded, three horses killed and another six had to be destroyed. Outposts were set up, but the Germans made no attempt to counterattack. By 2.30 a.m. on 27th March, 2nd Lincolnshire had taken over the village and Lord Strathcona's Horse had pulled back to camp at Moislains.

The task for the cavalry on 27th March was to seize a line from the high ground south of Villers-Faucon and the village, the high ground west of Grebaussart and the Wood, Saulcourt village and Wood and Guyencourt. XV Corps Cavalry Regiment and N Battery RHA were attached. The Amballa Brigade was on the right, with its left boundary a line from Longavesnes to Villers-Faucon, both inclusive.

While the Amballa Cavalry Brigade captured Villers-Faucon, the Canadian Cavalry Brigade's advance was focussed against Saulcourt and Guyencourt. Both brigades operated with great dash, using armoured cars in the direct approach to draw the enemy machine gun fire, while the cavalry went round the flanks.

Brigadier General Jack Seely, commanding the Canadian Cavalry Brigade, personally reconnoitred the ground. The centre was open but the flanks were undulating, offering some cover for the approach. His intention was to turn the flanks of the objective (Saulcourt Wood–Saulcourt–Guyencourt), from north and south. The Royal Canadian Dragoons was the advanced guard, with the rest of the Brigade following ready to deploy.

By 4.30 p.m., Lord Strathcona's Horse had moved to a rendevous west of Lieramont, which had been taken by the infantry during the night. The horse artillery opened fire on Guyencourt and Saulcourt until 5.15 p.m., when it lifted beyond. The advance of the cavalry squadrons was to have commenced at 4.30 p.m., but a blinding snow storm delayed the start of the march until 5.15 p.m.

The leading squadron of Fort Garry Horse galloped to the last piece of cover and positioned two machine guns on Hill 140, which enabled progess to be made on the right and along the whole front. A second squadron pushed round the hill and

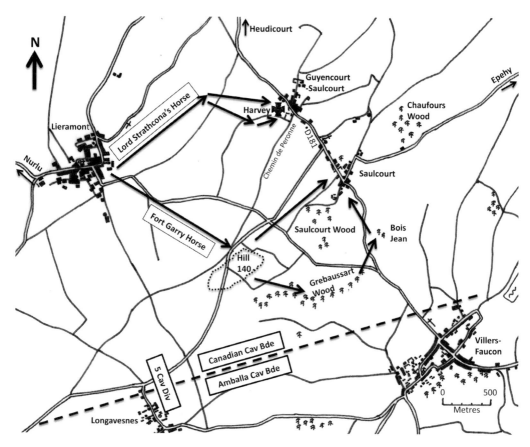

The movements of Fort Garry Horse and Lord Strathcona's Horse on 27th March. Harvey. Approach Guyencourt-Saulcourt on the D181 from the south. Just in the village take the left turning on Chemin de Peronne towards a large barn on the right side of the road. Park just beyond the barn and walk down the track to the southwest for 100m. Look north and about 100m into the field is where Harvey stormed the German trench.

got into Grebaussart Wood and Jean Copse, south of Saulcourt, while the reserve squadron moved up in close support on Hill 140. Progress was then rapid from the south and west and contact was maintained with the Amballa Cavalry Brigade, which entered Villers-Faucon on the right at 5.20 p.m.

On the left, Lord Strathcona's Horse led with C and A Squadrons and B Squadron, less one troop, in reserve. XV Corps Cavalry Regiment, less one squadron, was protecting the left flank northeast of Nurlu from the direction of Sorel and Heudicourt. It had one squadron on the Sorel le Grand spur and came under machine gun fire from the direction of Heudicourt, which held up the advance of the left flank of the whole attack. As a result, the leading squadron of Lord Strathcona's Horse had little space to manoeuvre and had to attack Guyencourt from the right front.

The German artillery engaged Lord Strathcona's Horse as it approached Guyencourt. As the leading troops topped the last rise, hostile machine gun fire

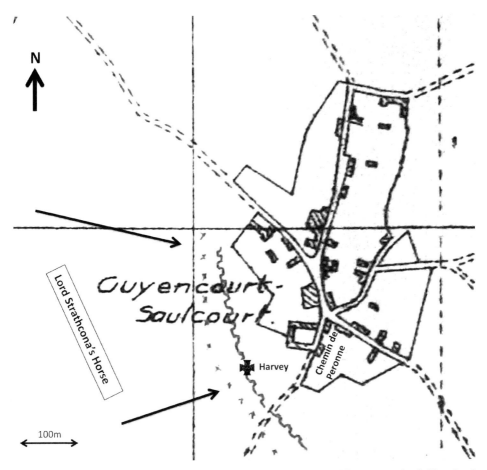

N

Lord Strathcona's Horse

Guyencourt-Saulcourt.

Harvey

Chemin de Peronne

100m

Contemporary map showing the location of the trench and wire in front of Guyencourt that held up Lord Strathcona's Horse until Frederick Harvey captured the machine gun post. The VC is shown in the most likely location for Harvey's action, as accounts are not specific enough to be more accurate.

was added to the artillery. One man and seven horses were killed and five men were wounded at this point. The supporting squadron was able to swing a little wider and came up on the left of the leading squadron. In the last bound before reaching the edge of the village the squadrons advanced at the gallop in open order, covered by machine guns on a ridge west of Guyencourt and two batteries of horse artillery.

Once in the shelter of the valley, the squadrons dismounted and with bayonets fixed, the attack went in on foot. **Lieutenant Frederick Harvey** commanded the leading troop (2nd Troop, C Squadron) of Lord Strathcona's Horse. A party of the enemy ran forward to a wired trench in front of the village and opened rapid rifle and machine gun fire at very close range. Casualties were suffered, but Harvey dashed ahead of his men, jumped the wire entanglement, shot a machine gunner and captured the gun. This broke the enemy resistance in front of the village and they were driven out of the trenches. Three prisoners and a machine gun were taken.

The view from the point where the trench attacked by Frederick Harvey crossed the Chemin de Péronne.

By 5.40 p.m. both leading regiments had gained footings on both flanks and in places in front. Ten minutes later the enemy was pulling back, blowing up an ammunition dump at Saulcourt as they departed. By 6 p.m. the objective had fallen and both regiments deployed their reserve squadrons. The enemy fell back towards Épehy, suffering considerable casualties from machine guns, despite the covering fire of their own. The Germans were too strong in Épehy to follow up, but a troop and two machine guns were pushed forward to Chaufours Wood, 500m northeast of Saulcourt. The gains were consolidated and put into a state of defence.

The infantry began moving forward, but Lord Strathcona's Horse could not withdraw immediately because the left flank was still open. About 11.30 p.m., 23rd and 24th Brigades began taking over the gains and the cavalry remained until 12.30 a.m. next day. The Canadian Cavalry Brigade withdrew to camp at Moislains at 6 a.m., except for a few elements, which remained to protect the infantry until dawn. Communications had improved sufficiently to allow another general move forward, but it took until 5th April to drive in the German outposts in front of the Hindenburg Line completely.

2nd April 1917

182 Pte Joergen Jensen, 50th Battalion AIF, (13th Australian Brigade, 4th Australian Division) Noreuil, France

In late March, General Gough directed I ANZAC Corps to capture the Hindenburg Line outpost villages of Doignies, Louveral and Noreuil, while V Corps was to take Longatte, Écoust St Mein and Croisilles. I ANZAC Corps had seized Lagnicourt on 26th March and this proved valuable when the next move was made against Noreuil on 2nd April. After Lagnicourt, 4th Australian Division relieved 2nd Australian Division on the left of I ANZAC Corps.

On the right of 4th Australian Division, the attack on Doignies and Louveral was carried out by 14th Australian Brigade. Only the field artillery and two extra batteries were available, so a surprise pre-dawn attack offered the best chance of success. In the dark there was some confusion and instead of from the rear the attack on Doignies came in from the north. Although the village was taken quickly, many

Leave Lagnicourt on the D5 northwest towards Noreuil. After 1,100m pull over carefully on the crest of the hill to overlook the scene of Joergen Jensen's gallantry just before the right hand corner on the road below. The dashed arrows on the map indicate the route taken by the German garrison retreating from Noreuil, followed by Seager's platoons.

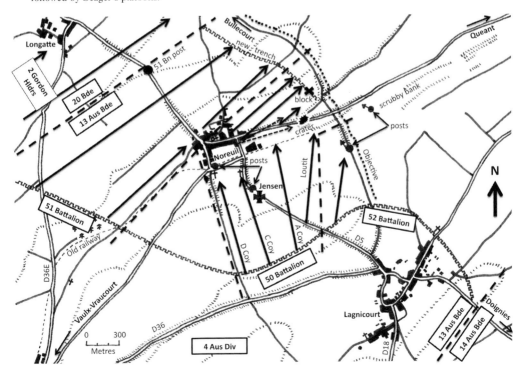

of the garrison escaped. At Louveral the fighting was fierce, but the objective was secured and counterattacks against both villages were broken up. 14th Australian Brigade had 400 casualties.

On the left, the attack on Noreuil was made by 13th Australian Brigade (Brigadier General TW Glasgow). German posts in front of Noreuil had been located by patrols. For two nights the village was shelled and its approaches were kept under intermittent artillery and machine gun fire to wear down the defenders. 1st April was showery, but the night was frosty and clear. The plan was for 51st Battalion on the left to advance northeastwards to meet 50th Battalion on the right advancing through Noreuil from the south. 52nd Battalion was to push forward its left to conform to the right of 50th Battalion.

After midnight a half moon helped with the move into the attack positions. About 2.30 a.m., the two assault battalions took up their positions, which had been marked with white tapes. At 5.15 a.m. they advanced as the rather thin barrage fell.

51st Battalion was to advance along the spur between Noreuil and Longatte, with its left in touch with 2nd Gordon Highlanders (20th Brigade), which was to seize Longatte. 2nd Gordon Highlanders had mistakenly assembled to the rear rather than alongside 51st Battalion, but there was no time to rectify the error before Zero hour. 51st Battalion was met with machine gun fire from left, right and the sunken Noreuil–Longatte road directly ahead. About eighty men were hit and the remainder took cover in front of the road. Lieutenant Earl crawled forward with a few men on the right, entered the road and crept along its bank; Earl shot the crew of the nearest machine gun. On the left Longatte had not yet been taken by 2nd Gordon Highlanders, so a post was formed on the road where it dipped towards that village, covering the ground to the northwest. The rest of the line advanced along the open spur. The right met some of 50th Battalion and worked through the northern outskirts of Noreuil, where opposition was slight.

51st Battalion was soon beyond the village and continued towards the Bullecourt road 630m further on. About 225m short of it, the troops were surprised to find a new trench, which had not been reported by patrols or aircraft. Some troops went on and entered the road, but two German machine guns were firing from the right rear and the officers decided to hold the new trench. The flanks appeared to be safe, as men of 50th Battalion were in the same trench on the right and part of 2nd Gordon Highlanders was on the left. However, it was clear that Noreuil and Longatte had not yet been mopped-up and the troops of both flanking battalions appeared to be out of touch with the main body of their units.

50th Battalion on the right had an excellent start position on the ridge overlooking Noreuil from the south. However, there were several advanced posts in the sunken roads leading into the village, which had to be taken before the village could be reached. Two posts behind barricades were to be bombarded by Stokes mortars and a third on the left was to be attacked by a platoon of bombers. On the right, A Company headed to the east of the village. On reaching a railway cutting in the valley, it was to wheel right and wait for the rest of the Battalion before continuing the advance eastward to the Bullecourt road. The centre (C) and left (D) companies were to cross the railway and road, fight through the village and emerge from the eastern end to join A Company and also wheel right to reach the Bullecourt road. C and D Companies were followed by sixty moppers-up to clear the dugouts and houses.

As 50th Battalion advanced down the hill towards Noreuil, the barrage was too thin to suppress the garrison. The first German posts behind barricades in the sunken roads were quickly overcome by Stokes mortars and bombers. However, at the German cemetery just south of the western corner of the village, a platoon with a machine gun, well protected by a barricade, steep bank and wire, was able to enfilade the advance; there were many casualties. Further right, the advance was also checked by a platoon behind a second barricade on the Noreuil–Lagnicourt road. As a result, a gap opened between the right and centre companies. The Stokes mortars had not reduced the post and A Company had to leave these Germans in its rear.

Sergeant Wilson, commanding the last wave of C Company in the centre, detached his bombers to assist with the situation on the right. One of them, **Private Joergen Jensen**, arranged for a mate to cover him by sniping the machine gunners. With five comrades he attacked the barricade behind which were about forty-five Germans and a machine gun. One of the party shot the machine gunner then Jensen rushed the post on his own and threw in a bomb. He had another in his other hand and retrieved a third from his pocket. Removing the pin with his teeth, he threatened the enemy with both bombs held high. He told them that they were surrounded and should surrender, which they did. One prisoner pointed out the location of another enemy party and was sent to tell it to surrender, which it also did. The latter party was fired on in ignorance by another party of Australians. Despite the danger, Jensen stood on the barricade, waved his helmet and stopped the firing before sending the prisoners back.

The centre and left companies then swept on into the village with the Lewis gunners firing from the hip to keep the enemy down. The Germans at the cemetery were left to the special bombing party and most were killed or captured. A Company, on the right under Captain Todd, was temporarily held up by wire, but pressed on and took thirty prisoners. It made the change of direction as planned and, with its right on the bottom of the valley, moved forward towards the objective on the sunken Bullecourt road.

About halfway, A Company was seen by a German post further south where the road crossed the spur near Lagnicourt. This post should have been seized by 52nd Battalion, but it had not been able to advance that far. At the same time, another post lower down and further back under a scrub-covered bank sighted A Company and opened fire. Todd's company suffered heavy losses and stopped short of the objective except at the bottom of the valley, where a small party succeeded in reaching it. The

The post seized by Joergen Jensen and his comrades was astride this road in the area of the trees just before the corner. Noreuil is on the right and Lagnicourt behind the camera.

Company was isolated and under heavy fire that it could not suppress, particularly from the right. All the officers were casualties. The survivors split into small parties to seek shelter in craters, the sunken road and the southern end of the trench that was soon after occupied further up the slope by 51st Battalion.

D and C Companies, under Captains Armitage and Churchill Smith, emerged from the village, wheeled right and advanced across the open. They did not at first notice A Company. On reaching the trench beside 51st Battalion, they became aware of a fusillade to their right rear and then saw Todd's men being closely attacked. In the shallow trench they were also enfiladed by the same machine guns and could do little to help. A contact aeroplane came over and they lit their flares. The observer reported the line lying along the shallow trench and at the crossways in the valley, where Todd's Lewis gun was holding on the objective.

It was almost over for A Company. Germans from the Bullecourt road were trying to force their way into a sunken road occupied by some of Todd's men. The moppers-up in Noreuil were too weak to deal with the village, allowing most of the garrison to escape along the bottom of the valley. They saw A Company part lying in the open with their backs to them or lining the bank of the road along which they were withdrawing. They opened fire. Todd ordered a couple of Lewis guns to fire to the rear, but the Germans were screened by Australian prisoners in front of them. Within a short time each element of A Company was surrounded and captured.

The Germans then lined the sunken road along the valley at right angles to the other companies and began to attack the southern end of the shallow trench. They were covered by enfilade fire from machine guns on the spur near Lagnicourt. 52nd Battalion eventually arrived higher up the crest and dug-in, but the German machine guns were sheltered from that Battalion's fire and the situation remained serious.

At 7.00 a.m., D and C Companies reported the gap in the line on the right where A Company should have been. Captain Armitage sent Sergeant Wilson to the critical point on his right with orders to take charge and hold it. The enemy bombing up the trench were beaten back three times, but the Lewis gunners were shot down by the enfilading machine guns. At 8.45 a.m., Armitage reported the position on the right was precarious, but although casualties were increasing, the forward troops were holding. A few minutes later, he was shot through the head. Wilson built a barricade in the trench and several Lewis crews arrived to assist. When the Germans attacked again, Wilson's party had fallen back thirty metres from the barricade. They allowed the enemy to reach it before throwing a shower of bombs and the Lewis gunners swept the top of the barricade. The attack was halted and for some time the enemy effort ceased.

Lieutenant Colonel Salisbury, CO 50th Battalion, had received no word from A Company, but did receive the message sent by D and C Companies at 7 a.m. Salisbury knew that Noreuil had not been cleared properly and sent two platoons of B Company in reserve under Captain Seager to move through it. After they left, he received a message that A Company was in difficulties. Salisbury sent the last platoon of his reserve under Lieutenant Esson Rule to assist, but he found no trace of A Company; Rule was mortally wounded (Noreuil Australian Cemetery – A 24).

Salisbury then sent Major Loutit, who quickly grasped the situation. In the valley where A Company's line should have been, he saw Germans with their backs half-turned lining the road and firing into the flank of the Australians in the shallow trench. The situation was critical so Loutit decided not to wait for Seager's two platoons, which were still working through the village. The Germans were so intent on their task that Loutit was able to lead Rule's platoon into a branch of the road about 100m behind them. Unobserved he lined the platoon on the bank, told each man to pick his target and then gave the word to fire. The line of Germans slid down the bank out of sight.

Loutit's party was seen by the German post on the scrubby bank further down the valley and its machine gun opened fire. To avoid heavy losses, Loutit withdrew 225m to a large mine crater at the point where the road branched. Seager's platoons emerged from the village and charged the objective road, but they were stopped by very heavy machine gun fire from further down the valley. A second attempt also failed. Loutit decided to hold the crater and suppressed the enemy in the road with fire, which kept the machine gun high on the slope quiet. Loutit informed Salisbury that the gap in the line, although not filled, was commanded by fire and could be held as it was.

Shortly before dusk 51st Battalion observed Germans massing to its front to counterattack; they were broken up by the artillery. At dusk, B Company, 50th Battalion, pushed two posts out to connect Seager's position with 52nd Battalion on the right. Seager intended to rush the Bullecourt road at dawn, but while patrolling at 2.30 a.m. he found it abandoned and at once occupied it. During the night, B Company, 49th Battalion took over the front line from C and D Companies, 50th Battalion.

On the left, the attack on the other villages met with similar difficulties, but ultimately succeeded. As a result the left of Fifth Army's front had successfully removed the last significant obstacles in front of the Hindenburg Line and all divisions began pushing their posts closer to the main defences.

13th Australian Infantry Brigade suffered 776 casualties, eighty-three of whom were taken prisoner. The Brigade captured about 130 Germans, seven machine guns, four trench mortars and a number of bomb throwers. 50th Battalion's share of the losses was 351, including ninety-five killed. The Battalion took seventy to eighty prisoners, two machine guns, two trench mortars and four bomb throwers.

3rd–4th April 1917

183 Maj Frederick Lumsden, Royal Marine Artillery attached Headquarters 32nd Division, Francilly, France

In early April 1917 the Germans held a series of outpost villages in front of Fourth Army while they completed the main Hindenburg Line defences. HQ Fourth Army resolved to reduce these outposts in a series of small operations, designed to force the enemy back to their main positions before they were fully prepared. One of these operations was launched by V Corps on 1st April.

The plan was for 61st and 32nd Divisions to envelop Holnon Wood by passing north and south of it respectively. 32nd Division's part in the attack began with 97th Brigade capturing Savy at dawn. 96th Brigade then took Bois de Savy, suffering heavy casualties as it crossed 4,500m of open ground. The final objective, on the St Quentin railway line, was secured by 8.30 p.m. At 5 a.m. next morning, 14th Brigade continued the advance with its left on the Holnon–Savy road. Within forty-five minutes, 1st Dorsetshire on the left had taken Holnon, while 2nd Manchester on the right captured Francilly-Selency and Selency. Two companies of 15th Highland Light Infantry advanced to take the ridge at Point 138 on the extreme right, which 96th Brigade had previously been unable to secure. Shortly afterwards the envelopment was completed when 2nd King's Own Yorkshire Light Infantry (97th Brigade) made contact with 61st Division north of Holnon Wood, by which

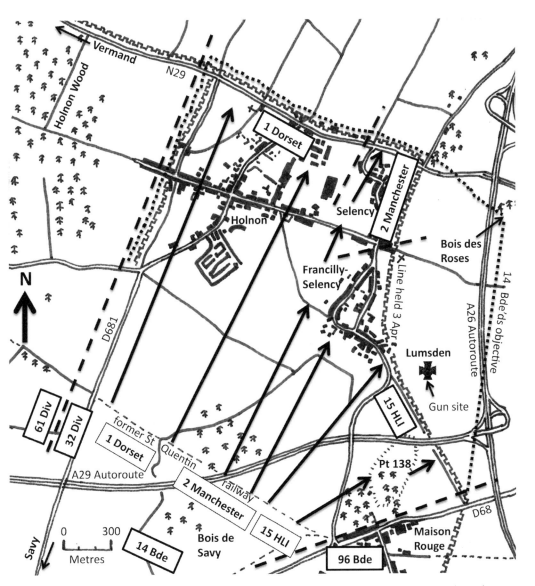

Drive through Francilly-Selency from north to south passing the church on the right. As you leave the village the road swings to the right and there is a disused track in front going straight on. Park along it. The British front line ran parallel with this track on the eastern side. Look east towards St Quentin. The guns seized by Frederick Lumsden and his team were in the field 200m to your front. Point 138 (128 on modern maps) was later the site of the famous stand of 16th Manchester on 21st March 1918, for which Lieutenant Colonel Wilfrith Elstob was awarded a posthumous VC.

time the Germans had withdrawn most of their guns and troops. The Germans retaliated with heavy artillery fire on 14th Brigade's line for the rest of the day from 6.30 a.m., but consolidation proceeded as planned.

Not all the German guns escaped. A battery of 77mm field guns was captured by C Company, 2nd Manchester, but there is conflicting evidence as to precisely where this took place. Accounts refer to locations east, southeast and even 1,125m

From the disused track south of Francilly-Selency looking east over the British front line on 3rd April 1917.

northeast of Francilly-Selency. However, HQ 14th Brigade's war diary gives a precise map reference (S15b62) and this has been taken as the true location. The battery was captured in a simultaneous frontal and flanking attack, during which there was hand-to-hand fighting with the gunners.

Meanwhile, A Company lost direction, advanced to within 1,350m of St Quentin and had to remain there until dusk. Bois des Roses was still held by the Germans and this necessitated the right flank being turned back towards Francilly-Selency. Despite these setbacks, the attack was a success and 2nd Manchester sustained relatively light casualties of twelve killed and fifty-eight wounded. Seventeen prisoners were taken. Attempts by Lieutenant GR Thomas, Adjutant of 2nd Manchester, and men from A/161st Brigade RFA to drag the guns back with ropes proved impossible, due to the broken ground and the enemy shelling from only 800m away. The guns remained 300m in front of the British lines and the Germans kept them under constant observation with the intention of recovering them at the earliest opportunity. They also protected them with a box barrage on Francilly-Selency, making any recovery attempt extremely hazardous.

Major Frederick Lumsden was sent by HQ 32nd Division to see what could be done. At 8.30 p.m. on the evening of 3rd April, Lumsden and Lieutenant CW Ward (161st Brigade RFA) led thirty men of 15th Highland Light Infantry and four horse teams from 161st Brigade in a second attempt to recover the guns. Covering fire was provided by a company and a half of 15th Highland Light Infantry. Approaching from a different direction to the previous evening, they galloped through the barrage, losing one of the teams. Having got the three remaining teams into cover, Lumsden led the infantry forward through a hail of small arms and artillery fire. They reached the guns and dragged them out of their pits one by one to where the teams, led by Lieutenant RC Trappes-Lomax MC, could come forward, hitch them up and drive away.

With the first three guns secured, Lumsden waited at the gun position for the teams to return, all the time under constant close range rifle fire. Another gun was hitched up and driven away, but the Germans chose this moment to attempt a rescue and their infantry closed in. The fifth gun was stuck and was abandoned during the German attack, but it was eventually manhandled out and driven away.

About a hundred Germans then broke through the infantry screen, reached the last gun and blew up the breechblock. Despite this, Lumsden resolved to recover it and collected another party from 15th Highland Light Infantry. They drove the enemy back long enough for the damaged gun to be dragged away.

5th April 1917

> 184 Sgt William Gosling, 3rd Wessex Brigade Royal Field Artillery attached V/51 Heavy Trench Mortar Battery (51st (Highland) Division), Near Arras, France

Sergeant William Gosling was a member of 3rd Wessex Brigade RFA, a Territorial Force unit that departed Britain on 9th October 1914 with 43rd (Wessex) Division and spent the rest of the war in India. From 1916 many men were transferred to reinforce other theatres, in particular the Western Front. However, it seems unlikely that Gosling went to India and returned to Britain in time to deploy to France on 6th May 1915. It seems more likely that 3rd Wessex Brigade RFA was up to establishment by the time he returned from Canada and he was retained in Britain. His arrival date in France coincides with the deployment of 51st Division. However, V/51 Heavy Trench Mortar Battery did not form until 18th October 1916 and there are no records revealing which unit he served with until then.

In April 1917 Gosling was serving with V/51 Heavy Trench Mortar Battery at Roclincourt and was involved in the preparatory bombardment for the forthcoming Arras offensive. 51st Division had twenty-eight medium trench mortars for the offensive. They were divided into six batteries to cut wire and bombard trenches in six lanes (A to F) in conjunction with the field artillery. The nine heavy trench mortars (9.45″) were split into three groups of three mortars, each covering two of the six lanes.

On 5th April Gosling was commanding a heavy trench mortar dug in ten metres forward of a British trench and 270m from the enemy positions. However, the trench mortar trace in the Brigade war diary suggests that the closest heavy mortar to the enemy lines was more like 670m away. The mortar had fired four rounds without a problem, but the fifth bomb only flew ten metres due to a faulty

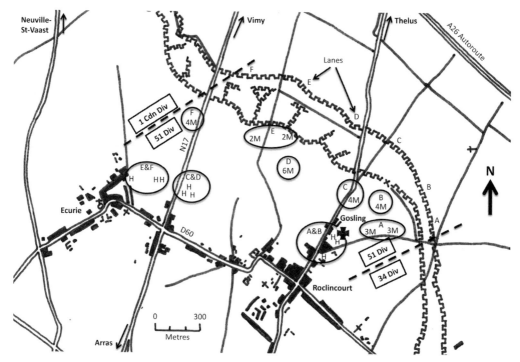

Enter Roclincourt from the southeast on the D60. At the crossroads in the centre turn right. After 250m take the right fork signed for two CWGC cemeteries and stop after 150m. The most likely heavy mortar location for Gosling's VC action was in the wood yard on the left side of the road. There were two heavy mortars here, with the third in this group being on the other side of the road about 100m closer to the centre of the village. This map is based upon the Divisional trench mortar trace. Each ellipse shows the position, number and type of mortar deployed there and the lane/lanes they were to engage; M = medium, H = heavy and A to F indicate the lane.

propellant cartridge. The fuse had been ignited and landing so close to the mortar position the bomb would destroy it and the crew when it exploded. Gosling sprang out of the position and, in full view of the enemy, dragged the nose of the bomb out of the ground, unscrewed the fuse and hurled it away just before it exploded. This incredibly brave action undoubtedly saved many lives and ensured the mortar remained in action.

In 1964 an unsubstantiated eyewitness account appeared in the Daily Sketch. It confirmed that the crew of six had fired four bombs that night, but the fifth landed only ten yards away, fortunately with a faulty fuse. They could not fire from that position again for fear of detonating the bomb. As they were about to dismantle the mortar and pull back, Gosling came up with an ammunition party. Gosling believed the crew sergeant should go out and defuse the dud, but he was reluctant to do anything. They agreed to toss for it. Gosling lost and went over the top to defuse the bomb. The eyewitness was recalling events from forty-seven years previously, so a few discrepancies with other accounts are to be expected. However, there are three major differences that bring the account into question. First, he says Gosling was

The wood yard, which had two 9.45" Heavy Trench Mortars sited within it in April 1917. It seems the most likely location for William Gosling's VC action, but by no means certain. The enemy lines were almost 700m away and out of view to the right.

bringing up ammunition, whereas official accounts are clear that he was the mortar commander. Second, he says the incident was at night. If so, how could Gosling be in full view of the enemy? Third, there would have been no time for the discussion overheard by the eyewitness before the burning fuse detonated the mortar bomb.

7th–14th April 1917

185 Capt James Newland, 12th Battalion, AIF (3rd Australian Brigade, 1st Australian Division), Boursies & Lagnicourt, France

186 Sgt John Whittle, 12th Battalion, AIF (3rd Australian Brigade, 1st Australian Division) Boursies & Lagnicourt, France

187 Pte Thomas Kenny, 2nd Battalion, AIF (1st Australian Brigade, 1st Australian Division) Hermies, France

200 Lt Charles Pope, 11th Battalion, AIF, (3rd Australian Brigade, 1st Australian Division), Boursies, France

By 7th April, most of the outposts that it was necessary to capture before the start of the Arras offensive had fallen. However, on the right of Fifth Army, Hermies, Demicourt and Boursies held out. 1st Australian Division was given the task of capturing the remaining villages. It had taken over an extended front from 5th Australian Division to allow 4th Australian Division on the left to concentrate on

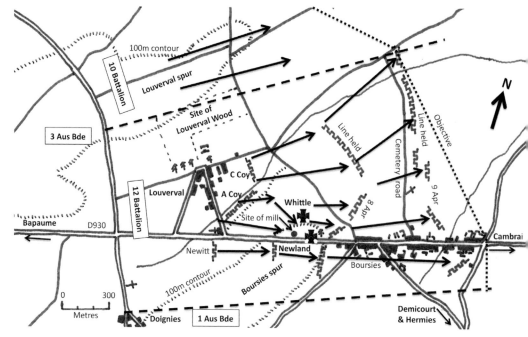

Approach Boursies from the west on the D930. 700m before the village stop at the Louverval Memorial on the left. The tree covered bank behind which Newland's A Company formed up for the attack runs away to the northeast. Look along the D930 towards Boursies. The clump of trees on the left of the road is about 150m beyond where the mill stood, of which today there is no trace. Continue towards Boursies. It is possible to pull over momentarily on the right side of the road at the crest of the Boursies spur, but ensure you are completely off the road as it can be both busy and fast. The mill was on the other side of the road, just short of the crest.

its diversionary role for the Arras offensive. As a result, 1st Australian Division's front included the whole of the Lagnicourt sector previously held by 4th Australian Division. 3rd Australian Brigade was north of the Bapaume–Cambrai road and 1st Australian Brigade to the south.

The attack on the three villages was to coincide with the opening of the Arras offensive. It was to be a phased operation, commencing with a night attack from Louverval to capture the high ground north of the Bapaume–Cambrai road

From behind A Company's forming up position looking in the direction of the attack towards Boursies.

overlooking Boursies. The following night, Boursies would be taken from the north and then two columns would strike against Hermies, which would be surrounded before being cleared. When Boursies and Hermies fell, the Germans were expected to abandon Demicourt and a battalion of 1st Australian Brigade was stood by to occupy it.

At 3 a.m. on 8th April, 3rd Australian Brigade advanced against the high ground north of Boursies. Two companies of 12th Battalion advanced immediately north of the Bapaume–Cambrai road, and two companies of 10th Battalion, which had relieved part of 12th Battalion, advanced north of Louverval Wood. This was the first occasion in which the new platoon attack tactics were used, employing Lewis gunners, rifle grenadiers, bombers and riflemen as an integrated force.

10th Battalion faced an advance on Louverval spur varying from 800m to 1,200m in places. There was no barrage. The left and right companies, each about a hundred strong, had frontages of 1,450m. Each company had been divided into fourteen posts, each of three or four riflemen and two or three bombers under an NCO. Despite the silent approach, they were soon spotted. Flares went up from the German posts and fire was opened. The advance of the right company continued until all the officers had been hit. The position reached was 200–360m beyond the corner of Louverval Wood and about 800m in advance of the old front. The forward companies were reinforced by the support and reserve companies, which also filled a gap between the two. 10th Battalion suffered eighty-five casualties in this action.

Immediately southeast of Louverval Wood, 12th Battalion advanced on a narrower front of about 400m. C Company on the left, pushing down the valley between the Louverval and Boursies spurs, came under the same fire that stopped 10th Battalion and came to rest after 450m on roughly the same line and in touch with its right.

A Company on the right, under **Captain James Newland**, assembled under a bank in the valley just north of the Cambrai road with all four platoons in line. Slightly south of the road on the Boursies spur was a detached platoon of B Company under Lieutenant Newitt. It was to advance within sight of the enemy and lie quietly. When fire was opened, it was to make as much noise as possible to divert the enemy's attention.

Louverval Memorial

Cambrai - Bapaume road

Louverval

Covered by this noise, Newland's company climbed the Boursies spur, wheeled to the right and swept on to the mill north of the Bapaume–Cambrai road. At the same time, Newland led the bombers up the main road to attack the mill. A Company covered half the distance to the objective before the enemy spotted it and the main posts in front of the village opened fire. A number of men were hit and a few were killed, but with a shout the line charged. Under heavy fire, Newland led a bombing attack against a strongpoint and secured the outskirts of the village. By the time the enemy trenches were reached most of the Germans had escaped, taking their machine guns with them. Posts were formed by 12th Battalion at the mill, near the entrance to the village and in a trench northeast of it. The left was bent back along a sunken road to the valley with C Company on the left.

The small salient gained by 10th and 12th Battalions north of Boursies created a gap in the defences of the village. The defenders rushed back to their supports in the next sunken road (cemetery road), which ran northwards halfway through the village. The full objectives had not been gained and local counterattacks began at once against the mill by parties creeping up the main road. These were largely checked. An exception was a post near the roadside, which held off the enemy with a Lewis gun until about 8.00 a.m. when a shower of bombs was thrown by the Germans. The post was driven back to a ruined factory, where it held.

Throughout the day a few German field guns and some machine guns kept the area under fire. At 2 p.m., under cover of a blizzard, the Germans tried to rush the

The opposite view from the previous picture, looking towards Louverval in the right distance from the D930. The mill was in the field just to the right of the camera position. The line of bushes across the middle of the picture is A Company's start position.

Alongside the D930 looking east into Boursies with the site of the mill on the left. This area saw much of the fighting during the German counterattacks.

mill, but were driven off. At 10 p.m. the post at the mill was heavily bombarded and the Germans attacked along the road and from the northeast. Most of the advanced posts were driven back, where they were reorganised by **Sergeant John Whittle**, commanding the left platoon. South of the road, Lieutenant Newitt's platoon swept the Germans with fire. Private Butler's Lewis gun accounted for ten men and when they fell back, Newitt pushed on with a platoon of D Company in support and occupied a trench south of the mill. Newland, assisted by Whittle, stemmed the retirement. He was at every threatened point instilling confidence, leading, arranging for ammunition and directing reinforcements to weak spots. When he was reinforced by a platoon from D Company under Lieutenant Harrison, Newland charged and regained the lost ground.

At 4 a.m. on 9th April, elements of B, C and D Companies, with two platoons of B Company, 11th Battalion, attacked the cemetery road. On the left, C Company and the 11th Battalion platoons attacked from the sunken road in three waves, but came under heavy machine gun fire from the left and were halted. The 11th Battalion platoons joined up with B Company on the right. Meanwhile two platoons of B Company and one of D Company attacked another trench, which was taken with little loss and two machine guns were captured, one being turned on its retreating former owners. At 12 p.m. a move was made round the south of Boursies and through it to establish posts on the far side. Two hours later the Germans were seen to be withdrawing.

That evening, Newland's A Company was so worn out that it had to be withdrawn. During 10th April the rest of 12th Battalion handed over to 1st Australian Brigade and 11th Battalion. The action cost 12th Battalion 256 casualties, including sixty-two killed and ten missing.

The main attack on Hermies by 1st Australian Brigade (Brigadier General WB Lesslie), went ahead as planned at 4.15 a.m. on 9th April. There was no artillery preparation, but heavy guns were turned on Demicourt, the beetroot factory to the

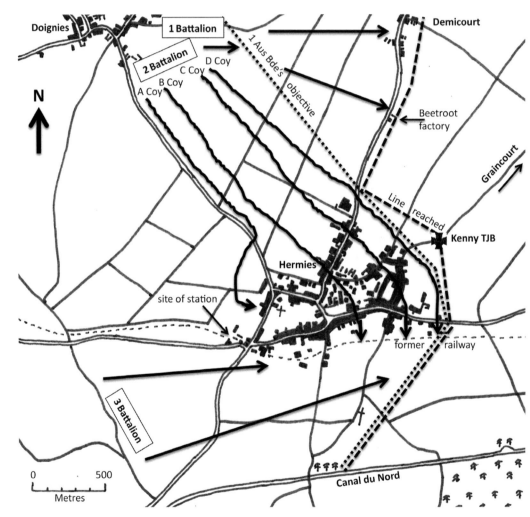

From the centre of Hermies head east on the D5 towards Havrincourt. After 350m turn left onto Rue Neuve and follow the lane round to the right for 600m. At that point there are a few trees and the lane becomes sunken. Park in one of the field entrances, ensuring agricultural traffic has access if required, and climb to the top of the bank. This sunken section of the lane is the part described as a sandpit and is where Kenny silenced the machine gun post and captured the position to complete the line of posts around the village.

south of it and other targets. The approach to the village was from the northwest, behind the enemy's frontal defences and wire. Shortly after dark the previous evening, 1st Battalion on the left advanced some posts 550–675m east of Doignies to create space for the assembly for the attack and also to cover the left flank. During the attack it was to maintain contact with 2nd Battalion's left. 2nd Battalion in the centre was to advance astride the Doignies–Hermies road through Hermies to the railway and then establish a line of posts north and east of the village. 3rd Battalion was to advance on the right to establish a line of posts south of the railway, while 4th Battalion remained in reserve.

In front of 2nd Battalion the German wire bent back as far as the Doignies–Hermies road, so A Company on the right was to assemble ahead of the rest along the east side of the road until the wire was passed, when it would cross to the west. Three companies would then attack in line, A Company on the right, B Company in the centre and C Company on the left, through the village to the line of the railway. The line was not to be crossed, as two companies of 3rd Battalion were to advance from the southwest to reach the railway from the opposite direction. D Company, advancing behind C Company, was echeloned to the left rear. It was to move east of Hermies and form a line of posts to cut off the garrison. Once the objective on the railway had been secured and contact established with 3rd Battalion, each of the three assault companies was to assist D Company by taking over part of the eastern flank.

At 3.30 a.m., while the troops were lying out waiting for zero hour, a flare from a German post in front of the two right companies set fire to a heap of straw. The Australians were spotted and the German post opened fire. Several men were hit and one company commander decided to advance immediately. The next company also set off. The Germans on the right withdrew, but in front of B Company a post on a scrubby 200m long bank opened fire. The Company lost heavily, including all its officers, but advanced by rushes under its NCOs until close enough to see German heads and then charged. The Germans ran and B Company followed over the bank into the dip beyond, where it lined up for the attack. It was short of the start line, but this was noticed by C Company's commander on the left, who ensured that the line moved forward again.

Both companies were ready to attack as the sky lightened. A distant cheer was heard on the right and the two companies rushed forward through the hedges and ruins. The Germans in the outskirts offered little opposition. Many others were found asleep in the cellars and were captured. The advance swept through the village, reorganised in a dip beyond and went on to form a series of posts, enclosing Hermies from the east.

A Company on the right advanced just inside the frontal defences. As it approached the end of the bent back wire, fire was opened. Some recently arrived young soldiers thought the battle was over and raised the cheer that was heard all over the battlefield. The advance continued and passed over the trench from which the fire had come and was assumed to be empty. The Company turned half-right, crossed the road and moved around to take the main defences of Hermies from the rear.

The western outskirts were reached when shouts, flares and rockets indicated A Company had been detected. A machine gun caught it at the foot of the hill, but it succeeded in advancing some way up the slope before having to seek cover. The defenders on the extreme right, cut off by the attack, faced rearwards and fired into the Australian flank. It seemed the Company would be shot to pieces and the commander, Lieutenant Millar, resolved to rush the position as soon as there was enough light to see the opposition, but suddenly the German fire ceased. Millar's company advanced over the crest. The sudden collapse of the Germans was caused by fire on their rear from B Company. It had escaped the fire on the flanks and pushed on, passing an outpost, which was cleared by the rear platoon, and entered the village. Half the company remained on the outskirts until daybreak. The CSM was tasked to bomb the Germans along the railway as C Company on the left advanced into Hermies.

The encircling left company (D) was already in position. As one platoon approached the crest traversed by the sunken Hermies–Graincourt road northeast of the village, it was fired on from a sandpit bordering the road. At first they thought they had lost their way, but the bombing section NCOs recognised three trees from an aerial photograph as their objective. On their own initiative the eight bombers crossed the road to a small cemetery on the flank of the Germans. Taking cover behind some manure heaps, they opened fire to cover the advance of other bombers. Private Brayshaw crawled towards the trees and shot a German sharpshooter, but was wounded, as was one of the NCOs. A corporal asked **Private Bede Kenny**, an exceptionally powerful bomber, to throw a grenade to the trees, but it fell halfway. Kenny then got two mates to cover him and rushed over the intervening hundred metres to the trees under very heavy close-range fire. He killed a German in front of the post who attempted to block him and then threw three bombs into the sandpit.

The former sandpit east of Hermies, which is on the extreme left of picture. Bede Kenny's attack came in from across the fields on the right.

Sandpit

Hermies

D Coy

C Coy

2nd Battalion's start line

2nd Battalion's left flank from its start position. The small clump of trees is on the site of the sandpit where Bede Kenny overcame the last German post and complete the encirclement of the village.

The last bomb silenced the post and Kenny entered it alone, took the survivors prisoner and occupied it. The line of posts was then completed around the east of Hermies, sealing it off completely.

The three companies in the village drove a few Germans who still resisted towards the posts and by 6 a.m. Hermies had fallen. Except for a few of the garrison who escaped through the gap left for a time at the sandpit, the rest were killed or captured. Over 200 prisoners were taken at a cost of 253 casualties in the battalions engaged. 2nd Battalion had 186 casualties, but it took 173 prisoners and counted ninety-one dead Germans.

The collapse of the defence was assisted by the advance of two companies of 3rd Battalion against the southwest corner. The plan was to approach frontally and hold the enemy while 2nd Battalion attacked from the left flank and rear. 3rd Battalion assembled nearer to the town than 2nd Battalion and began its advance at 3.45 a.m. in two widely extended waves. It was fired upon immediately, but continued until the left was within 200m of the railway station, where it was held. The right continued to edge forward and a machine gun was captured, while the extreme right flank seized a German bridgehead on the canal. With the right secured by about 5.30 a.m., the resistance on the left collapsed shortly afterwards. Another machine gun was captured and 3rd Battalion joined 2nd Battalion on the railway line. The troops on the railway then moved towards their final positions in the fields to the east. An erroneous report that Demicourt had also fallen led to heavy losses to machine guns in the follow up by 1st Battalion, but by noon it too had been taken.

15th April 1917

To assist Third Army at Arras, Fifth Army planned an operation at Bullecourt on the right flank of the main offensive. Third Army's axis was towards Cambrai and Bullecourt was only a few miles from the main Arras–Cambrai road. If a breach was made, 4th Cavalry Division was to pass through to join with the Cavalry Corps advancing from Arras. What happened in this attack on 11th April and in subsequent operations is covered in the section on the Battle of Bullecourt at the end of Chapter Three.

On the night of 13th April, 2nd Australian Division relieved 4th Australian Division. Next day, on the right of I ANZAC Corps, 1st Australian Division pushed forward its outposts to within 900m of the Hindenburg Line. During the night of 14th/15th April several of these posts heard movement in front. At midnight an advanced post of 4th Battalion just south of the main Bapaume–Cambrai road a few hundred metres east of Boursies reported Germans in front. Just before 4 a.m. a short bombardment fell about the old outpost line at Hermies and Boursies, and

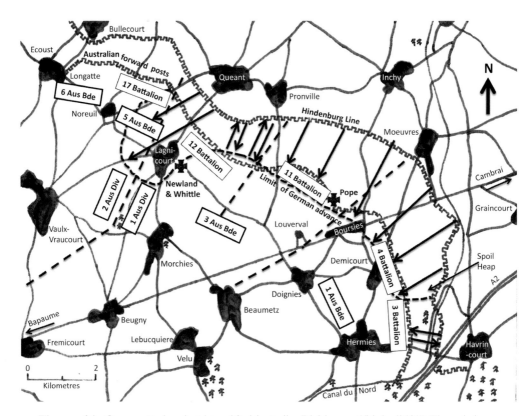

The area of the German attack against 1st and 2nd Australian Divisions on 15th April 1917. The main losses were at the junction of the two divisions around Lagnicourt, but most were regained later.

on the villages immediately in rear from Beaumetz to Vaulx-Vraucourt. A sentry in the post nearest to the Spoil Heap spotted a party of Germans coming up the hill and a warning was telephoned to company and battalion headquarters in Hermies.

Minutes earlier, nine kilometres to the northwest, Sergeant Gaskill of 17th Battalion, commanding the extreme right post of 2nd Australian Division, walked the fifty metres to the left post of 1st Australian Division held by 12th Battalion. He asked the corporal if he could hear movement and the two men walked to the top of a rise, but could hear nothing. Gaskill thought he must have been mistaken, but the Germans were unusually silent and there were almost no flares. Soon afterwards the sentry in another post reported a party coming in from the right. A patrol was expected and the men were warned not to fire, but as the party passed between two posts it was clear that they were wearing German helmets. Warnings were passed and a Lewis gun opened fire, but the Germans continued. Other posts joined in from 12th Battalion on the right and the 17th Battalion post on the left. By then three other posts of 17th Battalion were falling back.

Shortly afterwards the whole front of 1st Australian Division, except for the two right companies, was under attack. On the left, where the Germans overran the posts silently, warning messages did not get back. Elsewhere, except at one point in the centre, the posts opened rapid fire and were able to stop the first advance. Some incursions were cleared up, but the SOS barrage in front of the posts was not heavy due to a shortage of guns and ammunition. By dawn the posts had almost exhausted their ammunition, but supplies were brought up by runners and the attack ceased.

On the right of 2nd Australian Division, the ground in front of 1st Australian Brigade was covered with German dead. 3rd Battalion had lost only a dozen men and nowhere was its line penetrated. To the north, 4th Battalion, in front of Demicourt and Boursies, also beat off the first attack, but the struggle that followed was tougher because the enemy could take advantage of a number of depressions. 4th Battalion had 3,500m of front and each of its three forward companies held a line of three to six posts. Each company had two platoons behind in support in sunken roads or strongpoints. The Germans made repeated attempts to reach the posts by rushes, but were beaten off, except in the depressions where they made headway quickly.

In the southernmost depression the Germans attempted to get behind 4th Battalion's flank, but a counterattack stopped them 900m east of Demicourt. Two posts to the north held their ground, but north of them was another valley that the Germans used to get forward. During the fourth attempt they overcame the posts and tried to push up the valley to the rear of Demicourt, but fire from a support platoon stopped them. A platoon of the reserve company strengthened the supports and a company of 1st Battalion from Doignies was sent forward as a reserve.

On the next height to the north was the main Bapaume–Cambrai road through Boursies. To the northeast a deep valley led to Moeuvres, behind the Hindenburg Line, which the Germans used to force past 4th Battalion's left flank. Gradually fire from the posts slackened as they ran short of ammunition. Despite losses, the resistance gave time for three platoons of the reserve company to prolong the flank along the northern edge of Boursies. Three companies of 1st Battalion arrived to strengthen 4th Battalion and the line was stabilised.

After daybreak in this area German stretcher-bearers came out under Red Cross flags to collect their wounded. This was permitted until Germans behind the stretcher bearers were seen digging in and a machine gun was seen on a stretcher. The Australians waved the Germans away then opened fire. The Germans responded, but the stretcher-bearers managed to complete their task without interference.

Drive east through Boursies on the D930 towards Cambrai. Almost at the end of the village take the left turn and follow it for 1,300m to a right turn. Park here. Look southwest along the valley. Pope's post was about 400m away, on the north side of the valley.

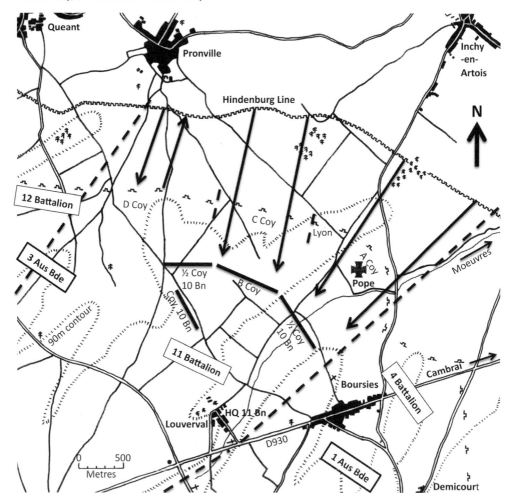

On the left of 1st Australian Division was 3rd Australian Brigade. 11th Battalion was on the right, with two companies of 10th Battalion in support; and 12th Battalion was on the left, with two companies of 9th Battalion in support. 11th Battalion had D Company on the left, C Company in the centre and A Company on the right, with B Company in reserve. Each company held its sector with posts well forward on the wide spur and one platoon in close support. One company of 10th Battalion was behind in a sunken road and the other was split, with half in support of A Company on the right and half supporting C Company in the centre.

At 4 a.m. an intense barrage opened on the forward posts, working back towards Louverval and beyond over a period of fifteen minutes. Hurried warnings were sent back before the posts were engaged by the advancing enemy. Two posts of D Company on the left under Captain O'Neill were behind some old German entanglements and the sentry on the far side of the wire alerted them to movement ahead. One German reached an Australian trench, but the rest were driven by fire to the edge of the slope, where several snipers established themselves close to the wire. The Germans made no progress here, although the left flank was open for a while when 12th Battalion was forced back. Eventually the attackers pulled back 180m and dug in. That evening the right post of D Company was overrun and a half company in reserve was sent up to consolidate an adjusted line.

The posts of A Company on the right under Captain Hemingway, although not protected by wire, checked the enemy by well-controlled fire, but they broke through in C Company's area in the centre. **Lieutenant Charles Pope**, commanding a post in the valley, kept his men quiet when the Germans went to ground and fired only when they rushed. Lieutenants Lyon and Beattie did much the same higher up the slope.

A large body of Germans creeping up the valley bottom in the dark had passed between Pope and the next post without either being aware. The Germans came out several hundred metres in Pope's rear. Most were beaten back by machine guns and the supports under Captain Hemingway, but some reached a short section of an old trench 630m behind Lyon's post on the left of A Company, close to the supports. Neither Pope nor Lyon could see this in the dark, but from shouts on all sides,

Looking south over the valley below Boursies along which the Germans infiltrated behind Pope's post.

Pope concluded that the enemy had got around him. He held on and sent a runner, Corporal AGC Gledhill, for ammunition. After about a hundred metres, Gledhill almost ran into the back of a line of Germans along the valley, but he managed to escape their attention. He then ran into two Germans, who left him alone, before stumbling on a German lying down who put up his hands. Gledhill swore at him and continued to A Company HQ. Hemingway sent Pope an NCO and fifteen men with ammunition.

With day breaking, this party found its way barred by fifty Germans on its right front and another fifty to its left, so returned to Hemingway. The other posts were in the same situation as Pope. A messenger sent by Lyon for ammunition reached a sunken road and was taken prisoner, having been hit on the head by a rifle butt. Lieutenant Simmons, commanding a post of C Company in the centre, was shot through the head from the rear. Sergeant Plunkett, in charge of another post, was also killed. In desperation Pope charged with the men of his post and they were overpowered and killed, but accounted for eighty enemy. Pope's last order before he was shot dead was to hold. Lyon ordered his men to fight to their last round and then destroy their Lewis guns. These posts were just out of sight from the supports, but their bomb and rifle grenade bursts could be seen. Firing was heard until hours after daybreak, but suddenly there was silence and it was clear that these positions had been captured. However, their resistance had enabled A Company to form a line further back connecting the supports; and a gap on the left was covered by two Vickers machine guns.

The support line of 11th Battalion and its immediate reserves repelled the attack without difficulty. One and a half supporting companies of 10th Battalion were brought up shortly after daybreak and continued the line held by B Company. Two platoons were used by Hemingway to dislodge the enemy in the old trench to his front, covered by a Lewis gun from the flank. Some Germans surrendered, but most ran back to the rim of the hill formerly held by the Australian posts and held on there and in the gullies. Later a company of 2nd Battalion filled a gap between the right of B Company and the left of A Company to complete the consolidation.

12th Battalion was not attacked on its right. That part of the Battalion knew nothing of events until daybreak, when it sighted the enemy to its left rear and its posts fell back on their supports. It was against D Company on the left and the right company of 17th Battalion (2nd Australian Division) that the blow fell. At their junction, about 1,600m north of Lagnicourt, the outposts discovered the Germans streaming through them in the dark. The extreme right of 17th Battalion was forced back, exposing the left flank of 12th Battalion's D Company. At the same time D, A and C Companies were attacked from the front. D Company was soon under attack from the front, left and rear. As it was about to be surrounded, the OC ordered the men to break out. The other companies tried to fall back in good order upon their supports, but the Germans were too strong. The flank posts of the two battalions

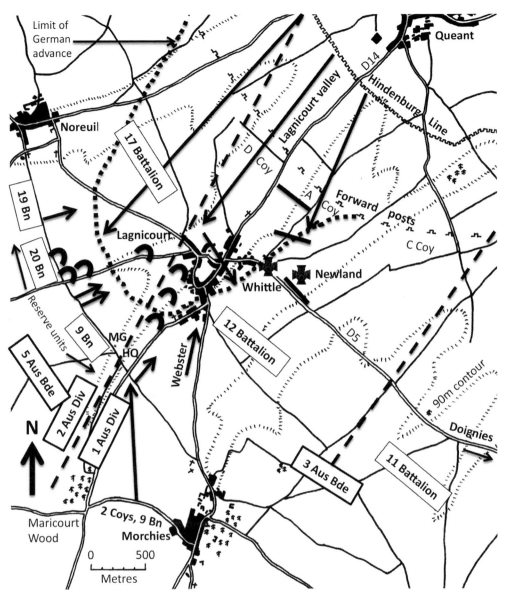

Leave Lagnicourt northeast on the D14 towards Quéant. Pass the cemetery on the left and after 800m turn right onto a track and park. Look back towards Lagnicourt. Newland's forward posts were 200m in front of and parallel with the track. He pulled his men back in stages up the hill in a generally southerly direction to the left of the large rust coloured barn and power lines on the skyline. Retrace your steps back into Lagnicourt and turn left on the D5. After 300m turn left again and park. Return to the D5 and walk along the sunken section of the road to the southeast for 350m. This was the centre of the last position held by A Company before it went forward again. At one time Newland's men were defending both banks of the road in opposite directions. Walk back to your car. Just as you enter Lagnicourt is where John Whittle captured the German machine gun before it could be brought into action against A Company's left flank. On the map battery positions are marked by semi-circles, the three successive A Company positions by solid black lines and the black dotted line is the limit of German penetration.

From A Company's original position looking back along its line of retirement to the road beyond the large barn left of centre. Lagnicourt village is on the right.

joined forces in falling back and stumbled on the back of a line of Germans lying down firing at some Australian supports. A close quarter fight to the death followed in which few of either party escaped.

The posts of 12th Battalion fell back 1,200m, losing heavily. Gun batteries behind were left unprotected and it was decided to withdraw the breechblocks and dial sights and retire. The guns of four batteries were abandoned and shortly afterwards another three in some disorder. Only a few men got through in the dark into a sunken road south of Noreuil, where they found 19th Battalion (5th Australian Brigade).

The right company of 17th Battalion became separated from 1st Australian Division, but its posts fell back in better order than the left of 12th Battalion, onto the supports in the sunken Lagnicourt–Noreuil road. An exception was one post on the right that was surrounded. Machine guns were positioned to defend the right flank, but the enemy continued to attack the road frontally and worked up the spur on the other side of the valley to establish a machine gun enfilading the road. The left was also threatened so a withdrawal to another trench was ordered. The supporting troops of 2nd Australian Division were much closer and more densely deployed than in the widely extended 1st Australian Division, so the trench was already partly occupied by a reserve company of 17th Battalion. The left of the company withdrew, but the right was under heavy fire and many were killed and wounded. The enemy penetrated along the bottom of the valley and set up a machine gun in front of Noreuil. About thirty Australians remaining in the road were charged from the right and captured. The enemy lined the road and placed two machine guns there, but their advance was halted. Thus on the northern side of the breach the Germans had bent back but had not broken through 17th Battalion.

On the southern side, around Lagnicourt, the situation was more serious. The enemy had broken through D Company, 12th Battalion, north of the village but

failed to break A Company in the centre under **Captain James Newland**, who the previous week had rallied 12th Battalion during its difficult attack on Boursies. Newland's posts held off the Germans for fifteen minutes and when they outflanked them he fell back to a position in the open halfway to the supports, where they had an excellent field of fire but no protection. After another stand, Newland, who was everywhere in the defence, ordered them to fall back on the sunken Lagnicourt–Doignies road southeast of the village.

Newland's company fired from the bank until shortly after 5 a.m., when day began to break. HQ 12th Battalion was at the crossroads 675m southwest of the village. It became aware that the enemy was advancing towards 1st Australian Field Artillery Brigade halfway up the Lagnicourt valley, and was also coming out of Lagnicourt along the Morchies road. CO 12th Battalion, Lieutenant Colonel Elliott, reported to the brigade commander that the right of 2nd Australian Division had fallen back, but he was forming a defensive flank and was confident that he could hold on. He sent his intelligence officer, Lieutenant Webster, with a hurriedly gathered platoon to gain contact with Newland, while batmen and other HQ details lined the bank of the road and opened fire on the enemy coming up the valley.

Webster mistook Elliott's intention, tried to enter Lagnicourt and was met by heavy fire. Webster was shot and captured, while his men were driven back. Despite the failure, Webster's action probably checked any penetration towards Morchies. Meanwhile Elliott transferred an anti-aircraft machine gun to the road bank from where it fired on Germans on the edge of Lagnicourt clustered around some abandoned howitzers. They fled for cover and the machine gun was turned on other Germans near the guns of 1st Australian Field Artillery Brigade and stopped their advance.

By 5.30 a.m. the Germans in the Lagnicourt valley were 2,400m behind the original Australian line when the first support arrived. This was the nearest company of 9th Battalion, which had been alerted about 5.20 a.m. by a stray man of

The reverse view from the previous picture. This is the section of the D5 Lagnicourt–Doignies road to which James Newland skillfully withdrew A Company and held off further German attacks. At one time they were defending both banks in opposite directions.

12th Battalion reporting that the Germans had broken through. The company lined up with bayonets fixed along the bank of the Morchies–Maricourt Wood road and went forward to HQ 12th Battalion. It arrived at 6.20 a.m. and Elliott positioned it along the bank of the road. Fire was opened and the Germans were stopped only a few hundred metres away.

An attempt by the Germans to come eastwards out of Lagnicourt behind Newland's line and between him and Elliott had also been foiled. Shortly after

This is where the German machine gun was being set up on A Company's left flank. Had it not been for John Whittle's quick and determined reaction it would have wiped out the resistance in the sunken road and may have led to the loss of the whole Lagnicourt position.

5 a.m. Newland's men in the Doignies road were fired upon from their left and rear by Germans coming along the roads from that side of Lagnicourt. Newland turned some of his men about to line the rear bank of the road while others remained covering the front, and the enemy was driven back.

A German machine gun crew attempted to set up its gun directly on Newland's flank in the same road. **Sergeant John Whittle** instantly grasped the seriousness of this move and he ran out alone. He bombed and killed the crew before they could open fire and brought back the gun.

12th Battalion stopped the enemy south and west of Lagnicourt. Looking behind, they saw troops approaching over the open and doubling along the roads towards them. These were the two reserve companies of 9th Battalion sent up to reinforce Elliott and two companies of 20th Battalion that had been sent by the neighbouring 5th Australian Brigade (2nd Australian Division). Eventually the Germans were forced back towards Quéant and were subjected to very effective artillery and small arms fire all the way. A number were also cut off and taken prisoner. The line was re-established about 11 a.m., by when A Company, 12th Battalion, was down to thirty men. The Battalion suffered 125 casualties.

14th April 1917

199 Sgt John Ormsby, 2nd King's Own Yorkshire Light Infantry (97th Brigade, 32nd Division),
     Fayet, France

When the Battle of Arras opened on 9th April 1917, Fourth Army to the south was still closing up to the Hindenburg Line. The French were about to launch their own offensive and requested a British attack on the village of Fayet to protect their left flank. General Rawlinson feared the fire of the St Quentin defences into his

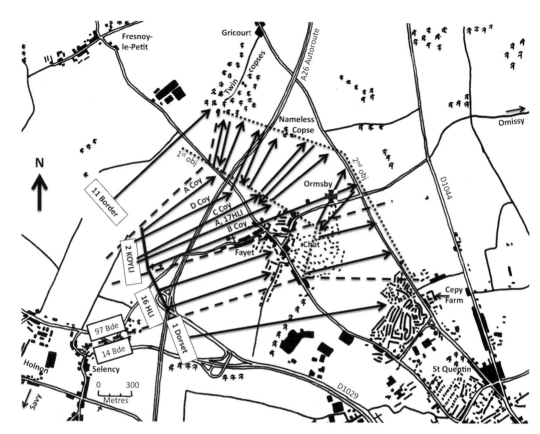

Approach Fayet from the east by driving south along the D1044 St Quentin – Bellenglise road and turning right onto the C4 heading southwest signed for Fayet. After 700m go straight on at the roundabout. After 300m pull over on the left hand side where there is a large parking area and some recycling bins. Look north across the road. The isolated clump of trees is Nameless Copse. B Company's attack in the afternoon led by John Ormsby, came out of the village behind you and across the fields to your front half right to the Gricourt road.

own flank and agreed to support the French with artillery, but would attack only if conditions allowed.

1st Dorsetshire (14th Brigade, 32nd Division) was ordered to maintain contact with the French, who attacked at 5 a.m. on 13th April. The French were successful on their right, but the left was pushed back and Rawlinson ordered 32nd Division to take Fayet next day to assist them. 97th Brigade was tasked with taking the village and to press on to the St Quentin–Gricourt road, while on the right 1st Dorsetshire was to take Cepy Farm to protect the flank. 97th Brigade was led by 2nd King's Own Yorkshire Light Infantry on the left supported by two companies of 17th Highland Light Infantry and 16th Highland Light Infantry on the right.

At 9 p.m. on 13th April, 2nd King's Own Yorkshire Light Infantry began moving forward. At 12.30 a.m., it halted for an hour between Savy and Holnon to have a hot meal. By 4.15 a.m., it was formed up ready on the taped start line. A Company on the left was to advance using a trench as its axis, while B Company on the right attacked astride the Fayet–Selency road. They were followed by D and C Companies on the left and right respectively. The attack commenced on time at 4.30 a.m., preceded by a creeping barrage moving forward at fifty metres per minute. At the same time, the artillery of 61st Division bombarded Gricourt to the north to protect the left flank.

A Company advanced to the left of the village and cleared up to the Fayet–Fresnoy-le-Petit road by 5.10 a.m., followed by D Company. Forty prisoners were taken and a few dugouts were bombed along the road. The advance continued at 5.20 a.m., but opposition stiffened and the company commander, Captain George Hendley Staveley, was killed (Serre Road Cemetery No.2 – Holnon Communal Cemetery Memorial 6) as he led his men out of the sunken road. 2nd Lieutenant Dibblee took over and despite the difficulties, the advance continued to just short of the copses on the left where it was held up by machine guns and wire. D Company came up and positioned itself to the right of A Company.

On the right, B Company, followed by C Company, took the village, where many occupied dugouts had to be cleared. **Sergeant John Ormsby**, who was acting as CSM, displayed total indifference to the heavy fire and set a fine example to the men. He also cleared out many snipers lurking in the area after the attack. Having cleared the village, the advance swept on behind the barrage to the final objective at 5.30 a.m., but in doing so lost contact with A Company on the left.

The Germans launched a counterattack at 6.40 a.m. B Company's commander, Captain John William Woods MC, was killed (Chapelle British Cemetery, Holnon – III B 9) and the Company's left flank was turned. A few men were lost, including twelve taken prisoner, and the Company was forced to fall back to the eastern edge of the chateau grounds with its left on the Fayet–Omissy road. A new line was dug facing east and the Germans were held off by two Lewis guns.

C Company moved up on the left of B Company, intending to fill the gap between A and B Companies. It reached the second objective at 6 a.m. where it was in touch with D Company on its left, but there was a gap of about 700m on the right before B Company in the chateau grounds. C Company dug in 180m west of the road on a ridge. It was also hit by the 6.40 a.m. counterattack, but forced the enemy back with its Lewis guns. The Germans took up an enfilade position in Nameless Copse and engaged C Company's line with machine guns. The position was untenable and at 8.30 a.m., C and D Companies were forced to fall back a short distance. C Company took up positions around a crater on the sunken Fayet–Fresnoy road. A Company also fell back to continue the new line on the left of D Company.

At 9 a.m., the Battalion's position ran just east of the Fayet–Fresnoy-le-Petit road facing northeast with A Company on the left, D Company in the centre and C Company on the right. A Company, 17th Highland Light Infantry filled the gap on the right, in touch with C Company on its left and B Company on its right in the chateau grounds. Another company of 17th Highland Light Infantry was ordered to swing round to hold the northern outskirts of Fayet.

From the parking area on the Fayet–Omissy road looking north into the area attacked by 2nd King's Own Yorkshire Light Infantry on 14th April. John Ormsby led the B Company attack on the right.

At 1 p.m. 11th Border captured the twin copses on the left from where hostile fire was delaying the advance. 2nd King's Own Yorkshire Light Infantry was then able to press on to the final objective. Leaving B Company to clear the chateau grounds, the Battalion resumed its advance at 1.50 p.m., supported by A Company, 17th Highland Light Infantry. The objective lost in the morning (essentially a line through Nameless Copse facing north) was regained at 2.15 p.m.

Having cleared the chateau grounds, B Company attacked at 2.30 p.m. to conform to the rest of the Battalion. It was led by its only officer, Second Lieutenant Pickering, who was wounded almost immediately (awarded MC). Sergeant Ormsby assumed command and led the Company over 360m of fire swept ground to rejoin the Battalion along the Gricourt–Cepy Farm road by 3.15 p.m. The Battalion dug in, in expectation of another counterattack. Ormsby distinguished himself again by organising his Company's line with skill and holding it with great determination.

At 9.30 p.m. another advance took place to bring 2nd King's Own Yorkshire Light Infantry into line with 11th Border on the left and 16th Highland Light Infantry on the right. Next evening the Battalion was relieved and marched back to billets in Beauvois-en-Vermandois having lost thirty-eight men killed, seventy-five wounded and fourteen missing.

On the right of 97th Brigade, 16th Highland Light Infantry had a difficult time reaching the start position as it was constantly held up behind 2nd King's Own Yorkshire Light Infantry. The right rear company was still getting into position when the attack commenced. However, the fight through Fayet was conducted quickly, with light casualties. At 10.30 a.m. 1st Dorsetshire (14th Brigade) attacked on the right and seized Cepy Farm. 16th Highland Light Infantry no longer had to worry about that flank and it advanced to the second objective without difficulty. At 7 p.m. the Battalion extended its front to include Cepy Farm, where it relieved 1st Dorsetshire.

24th April 1917

203 Cpl Edward Foster, 13th Battalion The East Surrey Regiment (120th Brigade, 40th Division), Villers-Plouich, France

On 15th April 1917, XV Corps commenced a series of minor operations to close up to the Hindenburg Line. Three divisions were involved; from the left these were 20th, 40th and 8th. The latter took Villers Guislain on the 15th and Gonnelieu on the 21st. The same day, 40th Division advanced its positions in preparation for an attack on Villers-Plouich and Beaucamps and 20th Division probed forward into Trescault.

40th Division attacked at 4.15 a.m. on 24th April. The right flank was covered by 8th Division on Cemetery Ridge. On the right, 119th Brigade attacked the spur north of Gonnelieu. The left achieved its objective with a handful of wounded, but the right encountered significant belts of wire and had a more difficult time getting forward. However, all objectives were achieved by 9.40 a.m.

On the left of 40th Division, 120th Brigade headed for Villers-Plouich and Beaucamps. The right assault battalion, 13th East Surrey, was ordered to take Villers-Plouich, while 14th Argyll & Sutherland Highlanders on the left was to seize Beaucamps. 13th East Surrey formed up in a newly dug trench running northwest from Fifteen Ravine. B and A Companies formed the first wave, supported by D and C Companies on the right and left respectively. 13th East Surrey was supported by 14th Highland Light Infantry, with a particular view to driving home the assault on the Ravine on the final objective.

When the attack commenced, 14th Argyll & Sutherland Highlanders got through Beaucamps with some difficulty, but soon afterwards all three leading company commanders became casualties. The Battalion pulled back to 200m south of the village. Patrols in the afternoon got into the village but could not hold on there.

13th East Surrey secured the first trench within seven minutes, but the leading companies came under heavy fire as they approached the village. At 5.30 a.m. the Battalion reached the edge of the village and split into three parties. The left

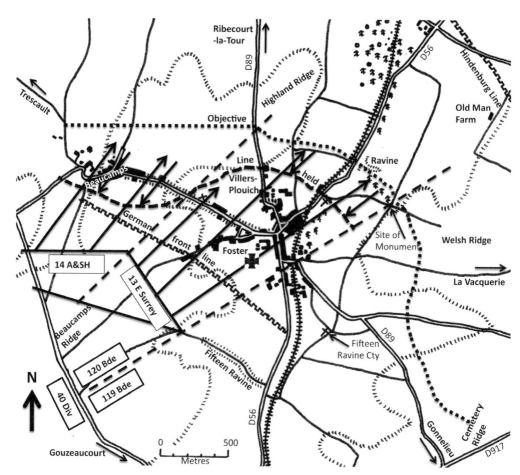

Enter Villers-Plouich from the north on the D56. Pass the church on the right and 100m after turn right, signed for Beaucamps. After 150m take the left fork and follow the track for about 900m until it bends left and opens out onto a plateau. There is hard standing on the left for parking on 13th East Surrey's start line. Look eastwards. Fifteen Ravine is in the low ground to your right and the right party of 13th East Surrey advanced across your front towards the village. Edward Foster's VC action was in the low ground between where you are standing and the church.

Villers-Plouich from 13th East Surrey's start line to the west of the village. The right party swept across the open ground from right to left. Edward Foster's VC action was in front of the village.

stormed a strongpoint on the Villers-Plouich – Beaucamps road and took over a hundred prisoners, but could proceed no further due to 14th Argyll & Sutherland Highlanders on the left being forced out of Beaucamps. The centre party went through the west of the village and took up positions on Highland Ridge.

The right party, under Captain Edward Crocker, was tasked to reach the Ravine 630m northeast of the village, but was held up by two machine guns in a trench in front of the village protected by a thick belt of barbed wire. It seemed the attack would fail until **Corporal Edward Foster,** commanding two Lewis guns, assisted by Lance Corporal Reed, volunteered to silence the guns. Armed with a Lewis gun each and some grenades, they rushed across the open ground and got to the wire before the Germans realised what was happening. Under heavy rifle and machine gun fire, they forced their way through the wire and entered the trench.

Reed's Lewis gun jammed and before he could clear it the Germans were upon them. Foster dashed to the rescue and threw a few Mills bombs to deter the enemy, while Reed cleared the stoppage. The Germans pulled back along the trench, leaving a few dead behind. With both Lewis guns back in action, Foster followed the retreating Germans closely. At the first machine gun post he opened fire from a few metres away and wiped out the entire crew and its protection party. A few minutes later, Foster and his companion reached the second machine gun post, killed all the enemy gunners and captured the machine guns. The way was clear for the company to advance again and sweep through the village.

There is some uncertainty over precisely where this action took place. Secondary sources tend to locate it at the objective in the Ravine. However, the VC citation does not support this, …*the advance was held up <u>in a portion of a village</u> by two enemy machine guns, which were <u>entrenched</u> and strongly covered by <u>wire entanglements</u>… Foster… succeeded in <u>entering the trench</u> and engaged the enemy guns….* The citation clearly places the action in a trench covered by wire entanglements in a village, no mention of a ravine. It is known that the Germans had trenches forward of the village and these would have been protected by wire. Wire entanglements around the Ravine, although not impossible, seem less likely. The citation also states that Foster's action *enabled the advance to continue*, but the Ravine was the objective, so no further advance was required once it was taken. The citation is supported by a

La Vacquerie

Right party

Fifteen Ravine

Military Intelligence 7b (1) document, which talks of the company being held up in front of the village and that after the trench had been cleared by Foster and Reed it was able to sweep through the village to its objective on the further side. The evidence therefore points to the VC action being in the German positions on the southwestern edge of Villers-Plouich.

A counter-bombardment at 6.40 a.m. resulted in the commanders of the centre and right parties being killed (Captain Crocker is buried in Fifteen Ravine British Cemetery, Villers-Plouich (II D 9) with eleven other East Surreys from 24th April 1917). Due to a misunderstanding, the forward platoon of the right party pulled back and the right and centre parties fell back to the eastern edge of the village. Second Lieutenant Carmichael DSO of 14th Highland Light Infantry immediately appreciated the situation and made a rapid advance to retake the Monument position, along with twenty prisoners. At 7 a.m. the line was advanced by 270m, where it held and two strongpoints were constructed.

At 8 a.m. Captain LB Mills, commanding 13th East Surrey, was wounded and command passed to Captain HP Naunton. A German bombardment commenced at 8.30 a.m. and lasted until 12 p.m., causing heavy casualties, but the line held. In this action 13th East Surrey suffered 199 casualties, but took over 300 prisoners. In addition to Foster's VC, the Battalion received nine other gallantry awards, including a DCM for Lance Corporal Reed. Next day patrols pushed forward and in the early hours of 26th April re-took Beaucamps in conjunction with 20th Division. 120th Brigade was relieved by 121st Brigade.

28th April 1917

204 CSM Edward Brooks, 2/4th Battalion, The Oxfordshire and Buckinghamshire Light Infantry (184th Brigade, 61st Division), Fayet, France

While the Battle of Arras raged on in Third Army's area, Fourth Army continued to maintain pressure on the right flank with a number of small actions designed to chip away at the Hindenburg Line outposts. One action was a raid by D Company (three platoons) and half of C Company, 2/4th Oxfordshire and Buckinghamshire Light Infantry, at Fayet on 28th April.

The Battalion went into the front line on 26th April after spending six days in support. The raiding party was to pass through a gap in the enemy trench opposite Fayet, which was thought to be unoccupied, as were several copses in the area. The attack was to be in normal formation with wire cutters and moppers-up on the left flank. The moppers-up, wearing white armbands to distinguish them, were to ensure no surviving Germans could fire into the backs of the men as they advanced along the enemy trench. Before the final objective was reached the wire cutters

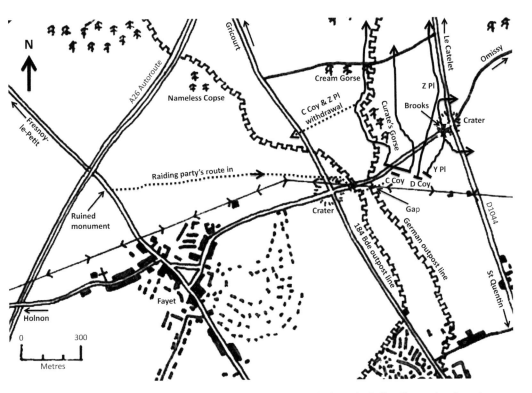

N

Gricourt

Le Catelet

Omissy

Cream Gorse

A26 Autoroute

Nameless Copse

Z Pl

C Coy & Z Pl
withdrawal

Curate's Gorse

Brooks

Crater

Fresnoy-
le-Petit

Raiding party's route in

Y Pl

C Coy

D Coy

D1044

Ruined
monument

Crater

Gap

German outpost line

184 Bde outpost line

St Quentin

Fayet

Holnon

0   300

Metres

Approach Fayet from the east by driving south along the D1044 St Quentin–Bellenglise road and turning right onto the C4, heading southwest signed for Fayet. The crater at this junction was where CSM Edward Brooks' VC action took place. Continue 450m to where the road bends to the right and park in the track entrance on the left. Look towards Fayet. The gap in the wire through which the raiders passed was about 50m to the left of the road. Look back along the road you have just driven to the junction with the D1044. C Company approached the crater from the low ground to the right of the road. North of the road, Curate's and Cream Gorses are where they were in 1917.

would turn left, cross the enemy trench, make a gap in the wire and hold it for the withdrawal of the main party.

Y Platoon of C Company was to seize and hold a crater and 100m of the St Quentin–Le Catelet road on either side, and prepare to cover the withdrawal of the rest of the raiders. Z Platoon, also C Company, was to follow Y Platoon as far as the crater, then wheel left and advance northwest astride the road ahead of the main attack party to protect its right flank and to cut off any enemy attempting to escape to the east. Both Y and Z Platoons were to have a patrol east of the road. The withdrawal was to be through the gap cut by the wire cutters, with D Company passing through first, followed by the moppers-up, Z Platoon and finally the wire cutters. They were to pull back to the road near the monument. Y Platoon was to fall back from the crater along the road to the southwest and then rejoin the rest of the raiding party.

The raiders moved from Holnon to reach the monument on the sunken lane leading to Fayet from Fresnoy-le-Petit. Here they found the lane full of troops organising a relief and support for the raid. C Company continued to the Gricourt–Fayet road to avoid enemy shelling and reached a large crater close to the gap in the German defences.

Fire support consisted of a creeping barrage by the artillery and six machine guns of 184th Machine Gun Company. The latter had two guns firing to the east of the St Quentin–Le Catelet road throughout. Four other machine guns neutralised targets to the north of the attack area from Zero onwards.

At 3 a.m., Captain GK Rose MC led C Company over the open ground east of Fayet, passed through the gap in the enemy wire and lay down to await the bombardment. They made it with seconds to spare. At 4.20 a.m., covered by the artillery, C Company set off in pitch darkness. Y Platoon rushed the crater on the St Quentin–Le Catelet road, where it initially surprised the enemy, but resistance soon stiffened. **CSM Edward Brooks** of D Company was advancing in the second wave when he saw the first wave checked by close range machine gun fire. Dashing past the first wave and completely disregarding the danger, he reached the position, where he shot the gunner with his revolver and bayoneted another man. The rest of the crew fled and Brooks turned the machine gun on them as they escaped to the northeast. His quick action undoubtedly saved many casualties.

Another machine gun, 500m east of the crater, was put out of action by 184th Brigade Machine Gun Company. Z Platoon advanced 100m north along the road and bombed three dug outs. Another machine gun was engaged by a Lewis gun and was eventually put out of action by a rifle grenade section. A prisoner was taken and sent back with one of the captured machine guns. The platoon Lewis gun was put to good effect enfilading the road down which the Germans were beginning to return. However, the enemy on the St Quentin–Le Catelet road kept the crater under constant fire. This fire intensified and was added to from the trench northeast of Curate's Gorse (also know as Squaw Copse).

The raiders assembled in this sunken lane below the monument before setting off for their assault positions.

The attack positions and directions of assault. Edward Brooks was with Y Platoon on the right.

Meanwhile the main party of C Company had rushed on under fire from the front and also from the right along the St Quentin–Le Catelet road, but reached the southeast corner of Curate's Gorse. There it encountered the enemy in a trench running northwest. The Germans here appeared to be confused as they were sending up flares and firing to the west rather than at the raiders coming from the southeast. A small trench at the southeast corner of Curate's Gorse was deep and wired but unoccupied. The left platoon bombing squad worked along it into the copse. They cleared three dugouts and accounted for several Germans in the trench. Two machine guns were also taken and members of both teams were killed while the rest ran off. About twenty Germans fled along the trench towards Cream Gorse (also known as Indian Copse).

The advance continued to the northern end of Curate's Gorse where it came under fire from the right front and the right. The Lewis guns of both leading platoons and the reserve platoon were used to suppress this fire, but it took some time to win the fire-fight and allow the advance to continue. It passed over a cross-trench and past the eastern end of Cream Gorse. The bombers of the left platoon went on some distance along the trench, but resistance from the St Quentin–Le Catelet road 200m north of the crater hampered the advance of the right platoon over the open; but it managed to force its way through some thin wire and bombed its way up to Cream Gorse.

As ammunition and grenades ran low the Germans counterattacked into the flank and rear of the raiders, while heavy fire was poured into the front. At 5 a.m., Rose ordered the withdrawal through the gap in the wire, covered by two Lewis guns. C Company extricated itself as it began to grow light, although some men were forced to hide in shell holes until nightfall. The last to leave was the covering party in the crater, which got away at 5.30 a.m. straight down the road towards Fayet. The platoon came under heavy fire from Curate's Gorse, but 184th Machine Gun Company dealt with the machine gun there. Only one man was lost in the withdrawal.

The raiders retired to Holnon Wood and rested in a railway cutting before withdrawing to Attilly. One prisoner (3rd Jäger Regiment) and two machine guns

Reverse view of the previous picture showing how exposed C Company would have been to flanking fire had the two D Company platoons not been employed along the St Quentin–Bellenglise road.

were recovered (including the one captured by Brooks). More prisoners would have been taken, but in the chilling words of the war diary, *…the situation did not allow of this and they had to be dealt with in the usual manner*. In the immediate aftermath reports indicate the raiders lost eleven to seventeen killed (including both leading platoon commanders in C Company), forty-three wounded and between three and nine missing. The CWGC records twenty-two fatalities in the Battalion that day, all but one commemorated on the Thiepval Memorial, indicating their bodies were left behind enemy lines and subsequently lost. The only one with a known grave is 203779 Private VR Evans, who is buried in Nesle Communal Cemetery (A 18), some thirty kilometres from the scene of the raid. No.21 Casualty Clearing Station was at Nesle April-June 1917, so it seems likely that he died of wounds there.

Chapter Three

The Arras Offensive

First Battle of the Scarpe 9th April 1917

188 Sgt Harry Cator, 7th East Surrey (37th Brigade, 12th Division), near Arras, France

189 LCpl Thomas Bryan, 25th Northumberland Fusiliers (103rd Brigade, 34th Division), near Arras, France

190 Pte Ernest Sykes, 27th Northumberland Fusiliers (103rd Brigade, 34th Division), near Arras, France

194 Pte Horace Waller, 10th King's Own Yorkshire Light Infantry (64th Brigade, 21st Division), south of Heninel, France

196 LCpl Harold Mugford, 8th Squadron Machine Gun Corps (8th Cavalry Brigade, 3rd Cavalry Division) Monchy-le-Preux, France

197 Lt Donald Mackintosh, 3rd attached 2nd Seaforth Highlanders (10th Brigade, 4th Division), north of Fampoux, France

On 15th November 1916 the French and British commanders-in-chief met at Chantilly as the Battle of the Somme was drawing to a close. Losses on the Somme and at Verdun during 1916 had been enormous, but as the year ended the allied armies were still growing numerically. In early 1917 they had the advantage of nearly one and half million men more than the Germans. Increased war production had also resulted in masses more guns and shells arriving at the front. The question for early 1917 was where to exert this numerical advantage? The Chantilly conference established the Western Front as the main theatre of war, but where to strike along it?

In Britain, David Lloyd George had replaced Herbert Asquith as PM, beginning a stormy relationship with British commander-in-chief, Douglas Haig. In France, Joffre was replaced as commander-in-chief by General Robert Nivelle, who had risen to prominence by retaking in a few hours what the Germans had required eight months to achieve at Verdun. On 21st December Nivelle outlined his ideas to Haig for a series of enormous, coordinated and surprise attacks in Artois and Champagne to end the war. Nivelle's plans relied on the artillery destroying all defences and the infantry simply mopping up; it was essentially back to the tactics of July 1916. Haig wanted to attack in Flanders, but Nivelle persuaded him it would be better to wait until his own offensives came to fruition, forcing the Germans to denude Flanders for other areas. Haig was aware that by agreeing to that he would limit the time available to reduce the Messines Ridge, a vital prerequisite for a Flanders offensive. The French also wanted the British to take over another thirty-two kilometres of front. This would have reduced the British contribution to the proposed offensive in Artois to a supporting role, rather than being part of the main event.

It was not until a conference at Calais on 26th–27th February 1917, that agreement was reached on the respective roles of the French and British and the command arrangements. However, the German withdrawal to the Hindenburg Line resulted in existing plans for offensive operations having to be abandoned and new ones substituted.

Preparations commenced three months before the offensive opened and were complicated by the German withdrawal. The winter was severe, with temperatures well below zero for long periods. The frozen ground was so hard that construction work was not possible. Then when it thawed the ground conditions made the movement of vast quantities of men, animals, stores and ammunition extremely arduous. Over 650 kilometres of roads were repaired and maintained. Masses of guns were moved into position. Thousands of metres of old and new trenches were constructed and/or maintained. Tramways were laid, gun emplacements and OPs for artillery and mortar observers were constructed and water storage established. Communications cables were dug-in and masses of Nissen huts were constructed to accommodate the troops, particularly in areas devastated by the Germans during the retreat. The army was now almost totally composed of wartime soldiers. The vast majority of pre-war regulars and territorials had been used up. Experience was at a premium.

The Battle of Arras essentially developed out of the need to draw German reserves away from the French Nivelle offensive on the Aisne. The outline plan was for Third Army to attack eastwards astride the River Scarpe, while First Army captured Vimy Ridge to the north. Fifth Army to the south was to attack northwards two days later around Bullecourt. If there were a breakthrough Haig would throw in his reserves. If not he intended keeping them for a new offensive in Flanders. The initial attack would be made by fourteen divisions, the same as on 1st July 1916 on the Somme. However, the artillery support available by April 1917 was in a completely different league in terms of quantity and how it was used. The creeping barrage was standard and was followed as closely as possible by the infantry. In addition, defective shells were much more uncommon than a year previously due to improvements in manufacturing quality.

The Arras battlefield is relatively open and uncluttered. South of the Scarpe the main feature is the high ground around Monchy-le-Preux, which offers the occupier observation over the whole Douai plain. To the north Vimy Ridge dominates everything. Just behind the British lines, Arras provided excellent cover for the assembling troops and was connected to the forward lines by an extensive tunnel network.

A staggering amount of artillery was amassed for the attack. First Army employed 1,106 guns along just six kilometres of front; a gun for every six metres. Third Army

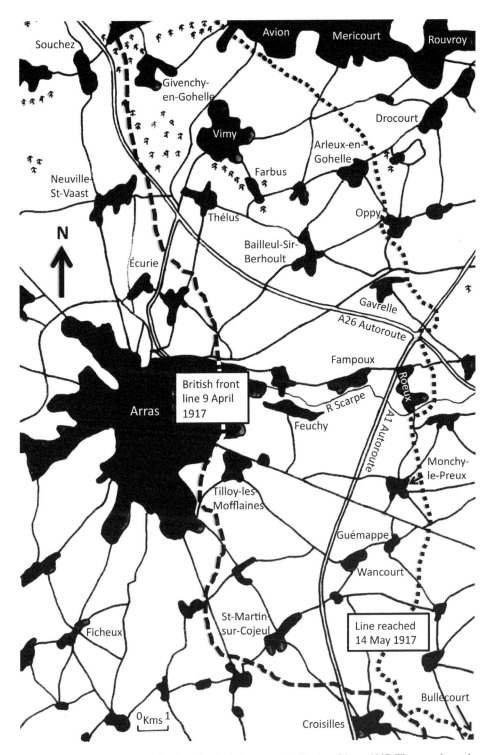

The area covered by the various battles collectively known as the Battles of Arras 1917. The map shows the British front line on 9th April and where the lines came to rest on 14th May 1917. Most of the place names mentioned in the various accounts are shown.

had 1,779 guns and Fifth Army another 519. They were provided with enormous stockpiles of shells. However, in the skies above the battlefields the situation was less positive. The RFC at this time was technically and tactically inferior to the German air forces. As they waited for new models of aircraft to arrive, the pilots did their best to support ground operations, but at enormous cost.

In the last few days before the offensive gas was employed extensively to debilitate the enemy by forcing him to wear masks for extended periods. The advantage in gas warfare lay with the Allies, with the prevailing westerly winds on their backs blowing towards the German lines. The preparatory bombardment lasted for five days and in places laid waste to the German defences to a depth of almost a kilometre. Efforts by the defenders to repair damage at night were dashed when they were shattered again next day. When practice barrages for the attack were fired there was little German reaction. Numerous raids were launched and patrols were mounted into no man's land to obtain identification and to check on the damage caused by the bombardment.

The attack was set for 8th April, but the French requested a delay of a few days. Haig would only agree to twenty-fours hours, until 5.30 a.m. on the 9th, Easter Monday. The main French attack was set for 15th April. In the First Battle of the Scarpe, Third Army attacked with three corps each of four divisions. From south to north these were VII, VI and XVII Corps. In the first phase, XVII and VI Corps were to take the Black Line; VII Corps was already on it. In the second phase, all three corps were to capture the Blue and Brown Lines within eight hours of zero, which was a very ambitious undertaking. The final objective was the Green Line, entailing an advance of just over seven kilometres in all.

VII Corps' four divisions attacked in echelon. The plan was for the two northern divisions (14th and 56th) to break into the enemy lines at Neuville Vitasse and Telegraph Hill, while the two southern divisions (30th and 21st) were to close up to the Hindenburg Line. In 21st Division, on the extreme right, three battalions of 64th Brigade advanced at 3.54 p.m. towards the Hindenburg Line, 900m away. In places there were no gaps in the wire, but it was well cut elsewhere and a number of lodgements were made. A and C Companies, 10th King's Own Yorkshire Light Infantry, reinforced 1st East Yorkshire and 15th Durham Light Infantry as they held 900m of the Hindenburg Line. 30th Division took St Martin in the afternoon, but made no impression on the Hindenburg Line beyond it. As a result the Germans were able to concentrate all their efforts on the small lodgements made by 21st Division, but despite considerable pressure they were unable to evict them. By the end of the day 21st Division had taken about two-thirds of the front line trench of the Hindenburg Line. 14th Division took Telegraph Hill and pressed on with 56th Division. They breached the Hindenburg Line, took Neuville Vitasse and the forward troops were about 700m short of the Wancourt–Feuchy (Brown) Line.

VI Corps attacked with three divisions in line. From the south these were 3rd, 12th and 15th Divisions. The objective was the Wancourt–Feuchy Line, 3,400m

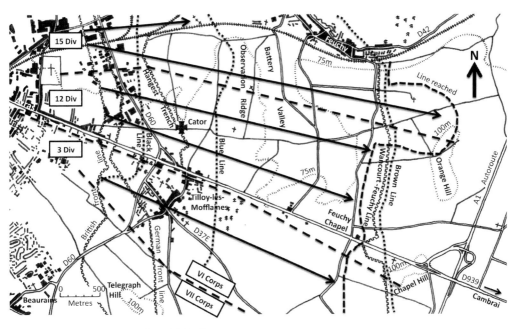

The area of VI Corps' attack on 9th April.

from the start line. At that point, 37th Division would pass through to take the Green Line beyond Monchy and Guémappe. On the right, 3rd Division encountered only isolated resistance in the early stages of the attack, but by evening heavy fire had halted the advance about 700–1100m short of the Wancourt–Feuchy Line.

In 12th Division, 37th Brigade on the right and 36th Brigade on the left were to advance to the Blue Line, where 35th Brigade would continue to the Brown Line. This area was dominated by Observation Ridge, which ran parallel with the Blue Line. However, such was the extent of the dugouts and tunnels, that 7th East Surrey in the front line had no casualties in the six days before the attack. Each brigade attacked with two battalions in line. In 37th Brigade, north of the Arras–Cambrai road, 6th Queen's was on the right and 7th East Surrey on the left. The enemy barrage in this area did not commence until three minutes after zero and the whole of 7th East Surrey passed over no man's land before it fell. Although the assault battalions drifted slightly to the right, the Black Line fell at 6.23 a.m. However, resistance stiffened as the reserve battalions (6th Buffs and 6th Royal West Kent) passed through at 7.30 a.m. on their way to the Blue Line, from where there was heavy machine gun fire.

At that time **Sergeant Harry Cator** of 7th East Surrey (coincidentally 37th Brigade was commanded by an unrelated Brigadier General ABE Cator) was consolidating a portion of captured trench with his platoon when they came under machine gun fire from Hangest Trench between the Black and Blue Lines. Many casualties were caused and 6th Royal West Kent's advance was also held up. Cator realised that the machine guns must be dealt with quickly. Taking a man with him, he dashed towards the enemy positions. His accomplice was killed after covering

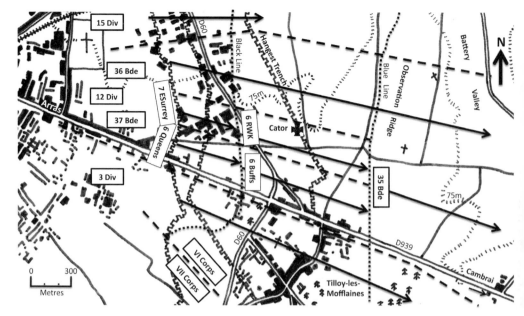

Leave Arras on the D939 southeastwards towards Cambrai. After 2.3 kilometres go straight on at the roundabout with the D60. 400m on turn left, signed for Bunyans Cemetery. Follow this track for 550m along Observation Ridge to a crossroads and park. Look slightly north of west towards Arras. 500m along that line is a hedgerow. Cator's VC action was at the right end of it in line with a prominent church tower in Arras. One wonders how long it will be before the industrial estate swallows up Cator's VC site.

fifty metres, but Cator reached the northern end of the hostile trench, picking up a discarded Lewis gun and some magazines on the way. From the trench Cator saw a bombing party commanded by Sergeant Jarrott pinned down by a German machine gun. Setting up the Lewis gun, Cator killed the entire crew, including the officer in charge, and brought back his papers. Covered by Cator the bombers then cleared the trench, taking a hundred prisoners and five machine guns. Cator also dealt with some snipers annoying those consolidating the Black Line.

By this time 35th Brigade was advancing and the sight of this fresh body of troops was too much for the weak German garrison. They abandoned the Blue Line to the

From Observation Ridge overlooking Hangest Trench and into Arras beyond. The initial attack by 7th East Surrey was towards the camera to the Black Line, which straddled the D60 road below. Harry Cator knocked out the machine gun post about where the hedge ends on the right.

From the Black Line in 7th East Surrey's area looking east onto Observation Ridge. Hangest Trench ran along the hedge at the bottom of the Ridge. Harry Cator's VC action was about where the hedge ends on the left.

forward brigades. Resistance on Observation Ridge was overcome and 35th Brigade rushed on into Battery Valley where thirty-one guns were taken, some being quickly put into use against their former owners. Although the advance had been reasonably successful, it was well behind the artillery programme and the Wancourt–Feuchy Line proved too tough to crack without it.

15th Division on the Corps left followed a very similar plan to 12th Division. Thirty-six guns were captured in Battery Valley, Feuchy was taken and by 5.30 p.m. the Brown Line had been secured along the whole divisional front. In the evening a lodgement was made on Orange Hill, just under five kilometres from the start point.

XVII Corps' frontage extended from the Scarpe northwards to the lower slopes of Vimy Ridge. Its three assault divisions, from south to north were 9th, 34th and 51st Divisions. They were to secure the Brown Line, which in this area encompassed parts of the Oppy–Méricourt and Point du Jour Lines. 4th Division was then to

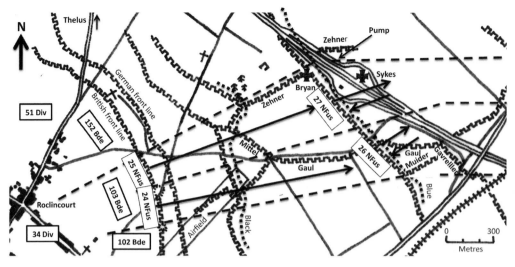

Access to where Sykes won his VC is difficult. One option is to drive northwest along the A26 Autoroute and pull in at the services (Aire de repos de la Cressonnière). Otherwise the closest point is on a track to the northeast. Leave Bailleul-Sir-Berthoult southwestwards on the D919. Go under the railway and 750m on turn right onto a farm track. Follow it for 800m until opposite the service area, which is some 450m away to the southwest. The location where Bryan won his VC is as problematical to reach as that for Sykes. There is a direct approach from the northwest towards Le Bon Lieu Farm, but that road is private! You could drive along the A26 Autoroute southeastwards and come off at the service area (Aire de repos des Trois Crêtes) and look over the fence on the southwest side. Otherwise the closest point you can reach is near Roclincourt Valley Cemetery, but you need to allow some time as it involves a long walk. Enter Roclincourt from the southeast on the D60. At the crossroads in the centre turn right. After 250m take the right fork signed for two CWGC cemeteries and follow it for 800m to a cross-tracks, where you can park. Take the track heading just east of north and follow it for 625m to Roclincourt Valley Cemetery, but keep going beyond for another 125m to the junction with the private road. Look east, with the autoroute on your left and Le Bon Lieu Farm in the trees to your front. Bryan's VC action was to the left of the Farm on the edge of the autoroute service area.

pass through to take the Green Line, consisting of 2,250m of the Oppy–Méricourt Line and the village of Fampoux.

After a hard fight 9th Division secured its objectives, taking 2,100 prisoners. During the afternoon 12th Brigade (4th Division) passed through and took Fampoux, but further progress towards the Green Line was halted by machine guns on the railway embankment to the southeast. By the end of the day the line in this area had been advanced 5,400–6,100m, the longest single day's advance since trench warfare began.

34th Division attacked with its three brigades in line. The leading battalions of 101st Brigade, on the right, and 102nd Brigade, in the centre, reached their objectives on the Black and Blue Lines, supported by a very effective machine gun barrage.

On the left of 34th Division, 103rd Brigade attacked with 24th and 25th Northumberland Fusiliers on the right and left respectively, supported by 26th Northumberland Fusiliers, with 27th Northumberland Fusiliers behind in

Divisional reserve. About 2.30 a.m. patrols ascertained that the Germans were holding their trenches in strength and were fully alert. The assault battalions were complete in their assembly trenches by 3.45 a.m. The plan was for the leading battalions to take the Black and Blue Lines before 26th Northumberland Fusiliers passed through them to the Brown Line. All three battalions advanced promptly at Zero hour in order to avoid the enemy counter-barrage. In the event the German barrage was fairly weak and there were very few casualties from it.

News was slow in reaching Brigade HQ, but the main portion of the Black Line was taken, and a message from 25th Northumberland Fusiliers, timed 9.07 a.m., confirmed this. At that time there was no news about the Blue Line. On the left, 51st Division was slower in getting forward and at 9.35 a.m. a message reached HQ 103rd Brigade that it was held up in front of the Blue Line, but half an hour later 51st Division realised it was in fact still in the Black Line. 27th Northumberland Fusiliers was sent forward by HQ 34th Division to investigate and take appropriate action. Meanwhile 26th Northumberland Fusiliers closed up and reported the Black Line was being consolidated, while elements of 24th and 25th Northumberland Fusiliers had pressed on towards the Blue Line.

Setting off from the Black Line, 25th Northumberland Fusiliers had A Company on the right and B Company on the left. They ran into heavy machine gun fire from the left at the Pump, or Zehner Weg, where 51st Division had not been as quick to get forward and was somewhat scattered. B Company was hit very badly.

Looking along the axis of advance of 25th and 27th Northumberland Fusiliers on 9th April into the German rear areas from the German front line. The cross track where you can park in the foreground. Roclincourt Valley Cemetery is signed off to the left. In the left distance is a prominent clump of trees surrounding Le Bon Lieu Farm. The low line of trees in the centre distance is the autoroute service area. Thomas Bryan's VC action was on the edge of the service area in line with the right of the trees around the farm.

From the junction with the private road near Roclincourt Valley Cemetery looking east. The track running past Roclincourt Valley Cemetery lead to the parking area at the cross-tracks.

Reinforcements were sent up Gaul and Zehner Wegs from the Black Line by 25th Northumberland Fusiliers to deal with the machine guns, which were stopping the advance from reaching the Blue Line. This was coordinated with similar efforts by 51st Division on the left. A Company obtained some cover from the fire from Pump (or Zehner Weg), as it advanced mainly to the south of the ridge. In the supporting C and D Companies all the officers became casualties very soon after the start of the advance.

There was much confusion along Mittel Weg, which was compounded when 51st Division strayed south across the line of advance and 26th Northumberland Fusiliers closed up too quickly from the rear. However, the mess was sorted out and they pressed on down Zehner and Gaul Wegs to deal with the machine guns. A Company, supported by C Company, managed to get eighty men into the Blue Line and worked along the trench towards B Company's objective on the left.

Although wounded, **Lance Corporal Thomas Bryan** went with Captain JF Huntley along Zehner Weg to see what could be done about a machine gun that was causing heavy casualties. Huntley was shot dead by a sniper (Roclincourt Valley Cemetery – II A 18) as he looked over the parapet with his field glasses, but Bryan continued. He surprised three Germans, who surrendered, two of whom gave him their watches. Having sent them to the rear guarded by some other men, Bryan

The autoroute service area (Aire de repos de la Cressonnière) from the northeast, where Ernest Sykes' VC action took place. The autoroute is behind the hedge on the left.

Arras

Roclincourt Valley Cemetery

pressed on and joined forces with CSM Foster, with whom he captured a German officer. A few minutes later he took another prisoner, but continued his search for the machine gun post. He was spotted as he closed in and was shot through the right arm. At this he opened rapid fire at the post and it fell silent. Working his way behind it, he rushed the crew, bayoneted two of them and disabled the gun. The continued advance of the whole Brigade to the Blue Line depended upon this gallant action.

A portion of the Blue Line around its junction with Gaul Weg and southwards was taken. However, the rest of 24th and 25th Northumberland Fusiliers, supported now by 26th Northumberland Fusiliers and the leading elements of 27th Northumberland Fusiliers, in the Black Line could not get forward to support and expand the gains in the Blue Line. A great deal of time had already been lost and there was no immediate prospect of pressing on to seize the Brown Line.

At 12.25 p.m. 26th and 27th Northumberland Fusiliers were ordered to pass through the leading battalions and take over the lead to the Brown Line. However, it was not until 1.30 p.m. that the two battalions had moved up to the Blue Line and 2 p.m. before the move towards the Brown Line commenced. They were hit by heavy machine gun fire from the left about Zehner Weg, the junction of Gavreller Weg and Gaul Weg and higher up the hill on Gaul Weg itself. There were considerable losses and on the left 152nd Brigade (51st Division) had still not caught up.

As **Private Ernest Sykes** advanced with 27th Northumberland Fusiliers (not on 19th April as is often stated), his company was halted by the intense fire after covering only 300m. Despite the danger, Sykes went out and recovered four wounded. On his fifth journey it appeared inevitable he would be killed, but he managed to reach a number of the wounded too badly injured to be moved. Sykes remained with them and bandaged their wounds, all the while exhibiting utter contempt for the danger around him.

It was not until 4 p.m. that 152nd Brigade on the left reported it had captured the Blue Line. Due to the delays, 103rd Brigade could not get far beyond the Blue Line that day. It consolidated its position, while machine guns in Zehner Weg were mopped up and posts were pushed forward along Muiden Weg and Gaul Weg. Contact with 102nd Brigade was established on the right in Gavreller Weg and with 152nd Brigade (51st Division) on the left. While 26th and 27th Northumberland Fusiliers held the forward positions, 24th and 25th Northumberland Fusiliers consolidated in the Black Line.

51st Division cooperated with the Canadians, whose objectives did not coincide with those of XVII Corps. In addition, resistance was stiffer in front of 51st Division. The Black Line was taken, but resistance stiffened beyond it and the troops swung to the right. The advance petered out in some confusion short of the Point du Jour (Brown) Line.

10th April 1917

On 10th April XVII Corps continued to press its attacks towards the Green Line. 34th Division established itself quickly on the objective and 51st Division made some progress, but was still short of the Green Line at the end of the day. VI Corps' plan was to take the remainder of the Wancourt–Feuchy Line, following which 12th Division was to capture Chapel Hill and 37th Division (Corps reserve) was to capture Monchy-le-Preux. When Monchy had fallen, 3rd and 15th Divisions were to advance on either flank of 37th Division to consolidate the Green Line.

During the night 15th Division's bombers fought southwards, capturing 550m of the Wancourt–Feuchy Line, which was of great assistance to 12th Division. Elements of 35th and 36th Brigades attacked from the left flank through 15th Division's area, while three other battalions assaulted from the front. The attack was a complete success and Chapel Hill was taken soon afterwards. 3rd Division's attack was also a complete success and 37th Division took up the advance. Further gains were made, but Monchy and Guémappe were not taken. The troops were at least 1,600m from the final objective on the Green Line.

Just before midday, 2nd and 3rd Cavalry Divisions were put on stand by to exploit success in the Monchy area. 8th Cavalry Brigade (3rd Cavalry Division) had moved earlier due to erroneous reports that 37th Division had already entered Monchy, but it was still 450m short of the western edge. At 2.30 p.m., 6th and 8th Cavalry Brigades moved to the south and north respectively of Monchy, but came under heavy fire and had to retire. 8th Cavalry Brigade was covered by a convenient snowstorm and bivouaced just west of the Feuchy–Feuchy Chapel road.

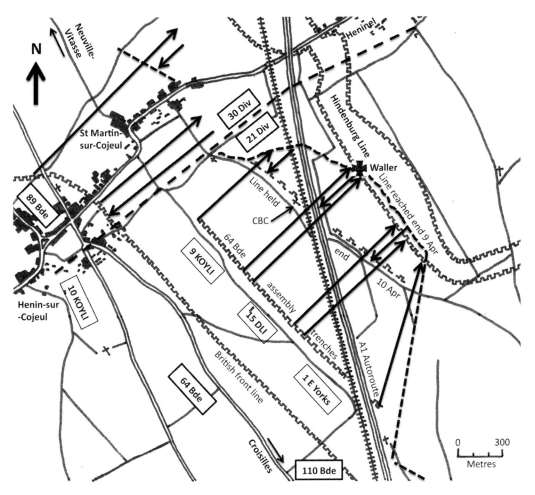

The site of Horace Waller's VC action is remote and access has been affected by the construction of the A1 Autoroute and TGV railway line. More recently tracks in the area that used to lead almost to the VC site have been realigned to service wind turbines. The closest position that can be reached by car is from Héninel village. Approach it on the D33 heading northeast from St Martin-sur-Cojeul. In the centre of Héninel turn right at the Mairie, signed for six CWGC cemeteries. Pass the church on the right after 100m and follow the road round the sweeping right bend, signed for Héninel-Croisilles Road Cemetery. The main road swings left at a house on the left corner, but go straight on here for 450m and turn left up the hill. Continue for 575m and stop at a concrete pillbox on the left. There are several more in the fields to the east. Look across the fields to the right of the road slightly south of west. About 300m on this line is where Horace Waller defended the bombing post block. The original attack came from the far side of the autoroute and railway line. Cojeul British Cemetery, where Horace Waller is buried, is just west of the TGV railway line, marked as 'CBC'.

In VII Corps on 9th April, 14th and 56th Divisions on the left made progress against the Wancourt–Feuchy Line, but 30th and 21st Divisions made only limited gains on the right in the Hindenburg Line. On the left of 21st Division, 64th Brigade set off on time at 3.54 p.m. and advanced up the slight slope towards the German positions 900m away. Much of the ground was open, but there were some dips and folds to cover the advance. The German barrage was largely ineffectual

From the pillbox looking northwest. 64th Brigade attacked towards the camera from the other side of the autoroute/TGV railway. There are very few local features in this wide-open agricultural landscape.

and covering fire was provided by the Brigade's machine guns. Some gaps in the enemy wire were exploited quickly, but elsewhere Stokes mortars had to be used to blast a way through. 1st East Yorkshire on the right and 15th Durham Light Infantry in the centre got into the front line of the Hindenburg Line. However, beyond it the wire was uncut in front of the second line and they could make no further progress.

On the left, 9th King's Own Yorkshire Light Infantry met heavier machine gun fire and found fewer gaps. Eventually the men had to shelter in shell holes amongst

This pillbox, on the Hindenburg support line, makes a convenient place to stop to consider 64th Brigade's attack and overlook the site of Horace Waller's gallantry.

the lines of barbed wire. 15th Durham Light Infantry bombed northwards along the front trench of the Hindenburg Line to assist 9th King's Own Yorkshire Light Infantry, but after 270m was forced back when the bombs ran out. The Germans then launched strong bombing attacks again both flanks of 64th Brigade's gains, making some initial progress on the left against 15th Durham Light Infantry, but they were then held. At 7.10 p.m., 10th King's Own Yorkshire Light Infantry was sent up from reserve to support the gains and to dig a support line along the line of the road in front of the Hindenburg Line. 9th King's Own Yorkshire Light Infantry was eventually withdrawn as it was very exposed and 89th Brigade on the left in 30th Division had not been able to advance on its right.

During the night of 9th/10th April, B and D Companies, 10th King's Own Yorkshire Light Infantry, assisted by engineers and pioneers, dug the support line just behind the sunken road occupied by 9th King's Own Yorkshire Light Infantry. A and C Companies remained in the front line with 15th Durham Light Infantry and 1st East Yorkshire while the new trench was being dug. These companies later took over the line when 9th King's Own Yorkshire Light Infantry pulled back. By 3.30 p.m. the new trench was ready and occupied by B and D Companies as well as Battalion HQ. A communications trench had also been dug to link the front line.

64th Brigade's memorial in Cojeul British Cemetery, close to Horace Waller's grave. The inscription reads, "To the honoured memory of the officers and men of the 64th Infantry Brigade who fell on April 9th 1917 in capturing the part of the Hindenburg Line close to this place".

C Company, 10th King's Own Yorkshire Light Infantry, relieved the left flank posts of 15th Durham Light Infantry and a bombing post block was established at the point where the British line met the German held part of the trench. From 8 a.m. the enemy launched repeated bombing attacks to regain the lost trench and pressure was maintained against the block all day. It was held by a party of bombers, including **Private Horace Waller**. The position was held with the utmost determination against repeated attacks and all the men became casualties, including five killed. Over 300 bombs were thrown in this action. Waller was the last man standing. He continued throwing bombs on his own for an hour until the enemy had been repulsed. In the evening the Germans returned to the attack and everyone in the party was hit again including Waller, but he continued to fight for half an hour, until he was mortally wounded.

A little after 7 p.m. the Germans launched the heaviest attack of the day, preceded by a trench mortar barrage. On the right, 1st East Yorkshire was driven into the open and the rest of 64th Brigade had to conform by pulling back 200m to the support line dug the previous night. 64th Brigade was relieved by 2 a.m. on 11th April.

11th April 1917

VI Corps' main effort on 11th April was against Monchy. 111th Brigade (37th Division) captured the village after a hard fight, assisted by four tanks (all were knocked out), while 15th Division cleared the area to the north up to the Scarpe.

The general area of 3rd Cavalry Division's operations on 11th April.

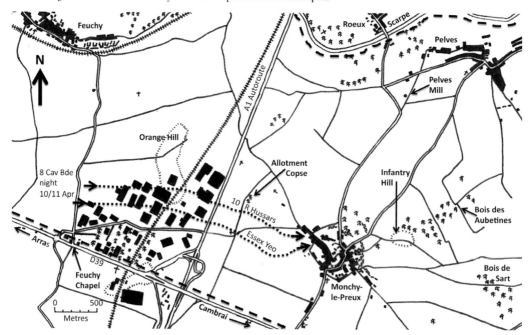

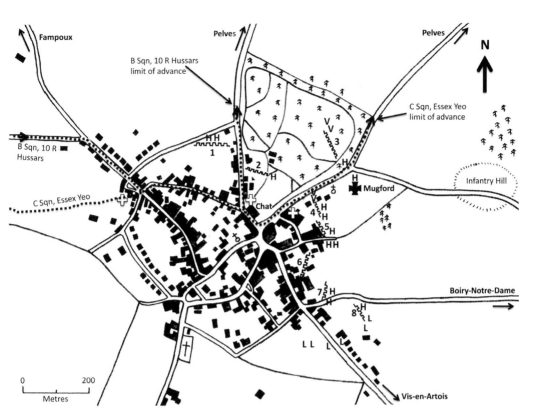

Leave the centre of Monchy-le-Preux on the easternmost of the two roads to Pelves, the D33E. Pass a chapel on the right and park at the track junction on the right after 50m. Mugford's machine gun position was probably on this corner, a few metres into the field, where the ground is slightly higher.

Detailed overview of the positions in Monchy. Machine gun posts are marked with a letter; H = Hotchkiss, V = Vickers, L = Lewis. Harold Mugford's position is not known for certain, but given the descriptions the best choice seems to be the one shown. Cavalry unit positions are shown thus; 1 = A Sqn 10th Royal Hussars, 2 = A Sqn, Essex Yeomanry, 3 = Sqn 10th Royal Hussars, 4 = Sqn 10th Royal Hussars, 5 & 6 = B Sqn, Essex Yeomanry, 7 & 8 = C Sqn, Essex Yeomanry. Big white crosses mark the dressing stations.

With the fall of Monchy the cavalry had its chance. At 8.30 a.m. 3rd Cavalry Division, operating between the Scarpe on the left and the Arras–Cambrai road on the right, began moving forward elements of 6th (right) and 8th (left) Cavalry Brigades.

8th Cavalry Brigade was to seize the high ground, villages and woods on the eastern spurs facing the Scarpe from Bois des Aubepines to Pelves Mill, about 3,600m east and northeast of Monchy. If this was achieved, a further advance was to be made to the final objective, from Bois de Sart to the eastern end of Pelves. C Squadron, Essex Yeomanry, was the advanced guard on the right and B Squadron, 10th Royal Hussars on the left, each with a section of the Brigade Machine Gun Squadron attached. The weather throughout the subsequent operations was very trying, with sleet and snow driven by high winds.

As they moved north of the village crossing Orange Hill they were hit by heavy machine gun fire from across the Scarpe, particularly from Roeux. This fire had been encountered during an attempt to get forward the previous day. If it occurred again the contingency plan was to move through the comparative shelter of Monchy village. Accordingly they swerved past Allotment Copse into the northwest of Monchy, but as the two squadrons emerged from the eastern and northern sides of the village on the two Pelves roads they were met by heavy artillery and machine gun fire and driven back. As the rest of these regiments closed up in the village, the Germans bombarded it, causing many casualties to man and beast. The troopers dismounted and occupied a defensive line in the southeast, east and north of the village. They also made two strongpoints in the chateau grounds and at the northeast exit from the village.

A Squadron, 10th Royal Hussars, held the secondary road to Pelves on the north face of Monchy. A Squadron, Essex Yeomanry, was on the east side of the road close by the chateau gardens and a squadron of 10th Royal Hussars held the sunken road to Pelves in the northeast corner. Another squadron of 10th Royal Hussars, plus B and C Squadrons, Essex Yeomanry, faced east and southeast, covering the roads to Boiry-Notre-Dame and Vis-en-Artois. Machine guns were placed in the strongpoints, while abandoned infantry Lewis guns were deployed on the east and southeast fronts. By 11 a.m. the village was in a state of 'semi' defence, according to the 8th Cavalry Brigade's war diary, but it was not until 6 p.m. that the defences were described as 'passable'.

The CO of 10th Royal Hussars, Lieutenant Colonel Philip Hardwick DSO, was wounded about 10 a.m. and the CO Essex Yeomanry, Lieutenant Colonel Francis Henry Douglas Charles Whitmore DSO, assumed command of both regiments. By the end of the battle Whitmore was shell shocked, but remained at duty. The brigade commander, Brigadier General Charles Bulkeley Johnson, and the Brigade Major went forward to conduct a reconnaissance and assess the situation. The Brigadier General was killed (Gouy-en-Artois Communal Cemetery Extension – A 30) and Lieutenant Colonel Lord Tweedmouth DSO assumed command.

Monchy from the west looking along the axis of 8th Cavalry Brigade's advance into the village. The road used by B Squadron, 10th Royal Hussars is on the left of picture with a car travelling along it. The track used by C Squadron, Essex Yeomanry runs parallel with the road, but on the right of picture.

Work to improve and strengthen the defences went on all day and into the night. The remnants of elements of five infantry battalions in Monchy, mainly from 111th Brigade, were collected in the west of the village and put to work collecting tools, bringing in the wounded and helping to dig the defences.

In the Brigade Machine Gun Squadron, No.3 Section lost its ammunition packs to shellfire and No.6 Section lost a gun after dismounting. The remaining gun of No.6 Section and those in No.4 Section were in position all day and engaged some long range targets. At 11 a.m. the Royal Horse Guards and Nos 1 and 2 Sections were ordered forward to support the two regiments in Monchy. The leading squadron of the Royal Horse Guards was badly mauled by shellfire before it reached Monchy and retired to reform at Feuchy Chapel crossroads. No.2 Section lost its ammunition pack animals.

By 9.30 a.m. half the garrison in Monchy had become casualties. At 2 p.m. a squadron of Royal Horse Guards and No.1 Section got into the village and set up in the line held by the Essex Yeomanry. By 2.50 p.m. four infantry machine guns had also been sent to reinforce the defences. At 5 p.m. squadrons of Royal Horse Guards and No.1 Section northwest of Feuchy Chapel moved back 1,600m owing to shellfire and halted north of the Arras–Cambrai road.

The Germans massed for counterattacks on a number of occasions during the afternoon and early evening, but they were driven off. This was partly due to the effective fire brought down by **Lance Corporal Harold Mugford**'s machine gun. Although under very heavy shell and machine gun fire, Mugford moved into an exposed position, from where he could deal with the enemy threat. His No.2 was killed almost immediately and Mugford was severely wounded. He was ordered to move the gun to a new position and then go to the dressing station to have his wound attended to. Mugford moved the gun, but refused to go to the rear and continued to engage the enemy, causing them great loss. A shell broke both his legs, but he continued firing and refused to leave his position, telling his comrades to leave him alone and to take cover. When the danger had passed he was carried to a dressing station, where he was wounded again, this time in the arm.

The most likely position for Harold Mugford's machine gun post is to the northeast of the village just off the eastern Pelves road.

Monchy had been secured, but this was the only major success of the day. At dusk the enemy was digging in 300m from the northeast outskirts of the village and on Infantry Hill. The ad hoc garrison held on until relieved by 12th Division on 12th April. However, on the north side of Monchy it was not possible to relieve Captains Palmes and Canning with fifty men of 10th Royal Hussars and Nos 1 and 4 Sections of the Machine Gun Squadron until the next night. By then the Machine Gun Squadron had lost forty men (including nine killed and two missing) and ninety-seven horses. CWGC records show eleven fatalities in the Brigade Machine Gun Squadron on 11th April 1917. Two are buried side by side in Tilloy British Cemetery at Tilloy-les-Mofflaines and the other nine appear on the Arras Memorial.

In XVII Corps, 4th Division was ordered to secure the line Plouvain–Greenland Hill–Hyderabad Redoubt. The attack was made by all three brigades in line and zero hour was set for 12 p.m. While 11th Brigade guarded the left flank, 12th Brigade on

Reverse of the previous view showing the exposed position Mugford was in.

the right secured the area around Roeux and took the Green Line. Further advance was halted by heavy fire from Mount Pleasant Wood.

In the centre, 10th Brigade was led by 1st Royal Irish Fusiliers on the right and 2nd Seaforth Highlanders on the left. The two battalions moved forward through Fampoux until reaching a crossroads, where they turned left into the sunken Fampoux–Gavrelle road and followed it northwards into their start positions. A German aircraft flew low over the road and must have seen the two assault battalions forming up. It flew off immediately over the German lines and five minutes later shells began to fall around the road.

The start line was not ideal. Elements of 12th Brigade were in front and there had been insufficient time to conduct a proper reconnaissance and move forward earlier. There was also no time to set up proper communications between brigade and battalion headquarters. Visual signalling was to be relied upon but before it could be used the first objective had to be taken. Until then all messages had to be passed by runner. As soon as the leading battalions of 10th Brigade advanced,

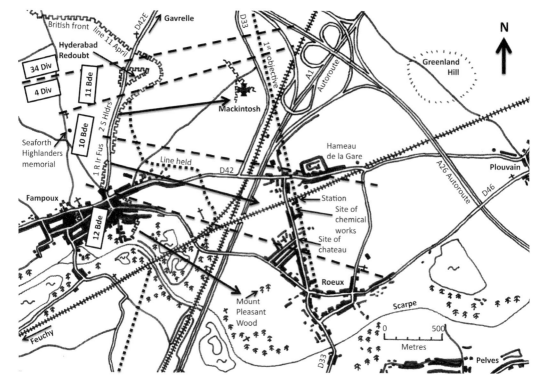

A view of the whole of 10th Brigade's area can be obtained from the Seaforth Highlanders Memorial north of Fampoux. However, it is 1,500m from where Donald Mackintosh won his VC. From the Memorial return southwards into Fampoux and at the crossroads turn left on the D42. After 1,150m turn left on the D33 for Gavrelle. For 600m this road runs parallel with the TGV railway line on the right and then bends left. 200m after the bend there is a track on the left. Turn in here and park. 200m to the southwest of this junction is where Donald Mackintosh seized the unknown trench. Look along the track to the southwest. Just to the right of the track, almost on the skyline, is the Seaforth Highlanders Memorial. The exposed nature of 2nd Seaforth Highlanders' line of advance is all too evident.

The open ground over which 10th Brigade had to advance, with the 2nd Seaforth Highlanders Memorial in the foreground and Fampoux on the right.

they were to be replaced in the sunken road by the support battalions (Household Battalion and 1st Royal Warwickshire). Once the second objective had fallen to the leading battalions, the support battalions were to pass through to the final objective.

1st Royal Irish Fusiliers advanced into a hail of machine gun fire. One platoon of the right company managed to get within 200m of the objective at the station, but was in danger of being surrounded and cut off, so it had to fall back. Some men joined 12th Brigade on the railway embankment and that was the extent of the advance that day.

2nd Seaforth Highlanders set off in snow with three companies leading (C right, A centre and B left), but the attack soon broke down due to heavy fire from the chateau, chemical works, station and railway embankment. There was also a lack of artillery support, as the guns could not be brought forward due to the soft ground. However, a number of small isolated parties pressed on.

One party was led by **Lieutenant Donald Mackintosh** in A Company. Despite the heavy fire, he pressed home his attack. He was almost crippled by a bullet in the right leg, but by a superhuman effort regained his feet and hobbled towards the enemy. His men hesitated and he shouted, *Never mind, Seaforths, keep it up.* He reached an unknown German trench on the Roeux–Gavrelle road about 150m west of the first objective, where two privates assisted him into the trench. The majority of his company joined him and captured the enemy trench. Elements of another company that had lost all its officers were forced back into Mackintosh's position. He gathered together these men and those of his own company and repulsed a counterattack, during which he was wounded again and rendered unconscious. He came round a few minutes later but could not stand. His men dragged him to a position of relative safety and propped him against a dugout, from where he continued to direct operations.

Mackintosh realised that if the line was to be held he must seize the part of the trench still held by the enemy. With only fifteen unwounded men he struggled in agony to clamber out of the trench towards the objective. With a supreme effort, he rushed the position with his party. As the enemy were being forced back, he was hit again, but tried to struggle to his feet and refused all help until he knew the position had been cleared. He died soon afterwards.

The support battalions moved forward on time, ten minutes after Zero, and met the same heavy machine gun fire. They were halted halfway to the first objective and were unable to influence the outcome. At 2 p.m., HQ 4th Division ordered another attack on the first objective. 32nd Brigade RFA was tasked to re-bombard the first objective from 3 p.m. onwards and the two assault battalions were ordered to attack again at 3.30 p.m. Runners failed to get through until 4 p.m. and the 10th Brigade commander (Brigadier General Charles Gosling CMG was killed by shellfire on 12th April 1917 and is buried in Hervin Farm British Cemetery, St Laurent-Blangy – C 6) decided, in view of the disorganised situation and heavy casualties, that a renewed attack was not possible. He ordered 1st Royal Warwickshire up on the right

Almost a reverse view of the previous picture from the track west of the D33.

of 1st Royal Irish Fusiliers and the three forward battalions dug in where they were. 10th Brigade suffered 1,085 casualties, including 390 in 2nd Seaforth Highlanders. In the five leading assault companies of 2nd Seaforth Highlanders (three) and 1st Royal Irish Fusiliers (two), not one officer returned unwounded.

To the north, 34th Division made some progress on its right when the enemy withdrew from the Green Line. The Germans also abandoned the Brown Line in 51st Division's area, which was occupied during the evening. That night 51st Division was relieved and its 2,100m frontage passed to First Army.

Battle of Vimy Ridge
9th April 1917

191 Pte William Milne, 16th Battalion CEF (3rd Canadian Brigade, 1st Canadian Division), Thélus, France

192 LSgt Ellis Sifton, 18th Battalion CEF (4th Canadian Brigade, 2nd Canadian Division), Neuville St Vaast, France

193 Capt Thaine MacDowell, 38th Battalion CEF (12th Canadian Brigade, 4th Canadian Division), Vimy Ridge, France

195 Pte John Pattison, 50th Battalion CEF (10th Canadian Brigade, 4th Canadian Division), Vimy Ridge, France

198 Cpl John Cunningham, 2nd Leinster (73rd Brigade, 24th Division), Bois-en-Hache, France

The part played by Third Army in the opening days of the Battle of Arras (First Battle of the Scarpe) was described in the previous section. To the north of Third Army was First Army, commanded by General Sir Henry Horne, facing the daunting task of capturing Vimy Ridge. The Germans had held the position as a front line since May 1915 and had made it an immensely strong defensive position with deep trenches, concrete machine gun positions and thick belts of wire. Existing caves in the chalk were extended and numerous tunnels connected strongpoints, allowing troops to shelter and emerge to resist an attack almost unscathed by a preparatory bombardment.

Fampoux

2nd Seaforth Highlanders

The eastern edge of the Ridge drops away sharply, but is much more gentle to the west. The French had failed to retake it in 1915, but had pushed back the Germans to narrow the defensive belt running along the eleven kilometres of its length. So although the defences were strong, they lacked the depth encountered by Third Army to the south. The British took over the sector in the spring of 1916. It was clear that the key to capturing the Ridge was the overwhelming use of heavy artillery. However, although Vimy Ridge is chalk, which drains well, it is overlaid by clay mixed with decomposed chalk and sand. When wet it produces a very slippery mud that holds water and does not drain easily. Firing over 1,135,000 shells (double the concentration achieved on the Somme on 1st July 1916) onto the Ridge churned up the mud and made the movement of heavy equipment across it extremely difficult.

The order issued to First Army on 2nd January 1917 was to secure observation over the Douai plain and assist Third Army on its right. Planning commenced for two linked operations. The main southern operation, to be launched simultaneously with the Third Army attack astride the Scarpe, was entrusted to the four divisions of the Canadian Corps (Lieutenant General Sir Julian Byng) supported by the British 5th Division. It was to seize the crest of the Ridge, essential if Third Army's left flank was to be protected as it advanced to the south.

The northern operation was to be launched later against The Pimple (Hill 120) and Bois en Hache at the northern end of the Ridge. This was the responsibility of I Corps (Lieutenant General (later Sir) Arthur Holland) assisted by the left of 4th Canadian Division. The rest of First Army was to fire an artillery diversion beginning six days before the offensive.

Confirmatory orders for the First Army attack were issued on 12th March. Adjustments were made to the line and formations were rotated to allow all four Canadian divisions to move into position in numerical order from the south. The Canadian lines ran from north to south and the advance was to be due east. However, the German lines ran southeast to northwest. As a result, the right of the Canadian Corps had 3,600m to cover to reach its final objective, but on the left the distance was only 650m. Each division was to attack with two brigades and one in reserve. The British 5th Division was allocated to the Canadian Corps. Its 13th Brigade was attached to 2nd Canadian Division for the final stage of the initial advance, while 15th and 95th Brigades formed the Canadian Corps reserve. With the addition of

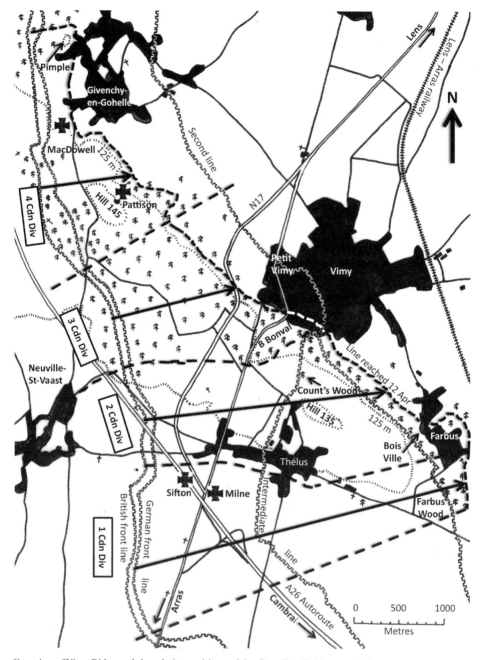

Overview of Vimy Ridge and the relative positions of the Canadian divisions and VCs.

5th Division and other British units (artillery, engineers and labour), the Canadian Corps swelled to 170,000 all ranks, of which 97,000 were Canadian.

The first phase of the operation was to take the German first system of three trench lines in thirty-five minutes (Black Line), which involved an average advance of 675m. On the left, this would bring 4th Canadian Division onto Hill 145, overlooking the Douai plain. The advance would resume after forty minutes with twenty minutes being allowed to gain the Red Line. In this phase 4th Canadian Division was to seize the German reserve trenches on the eastern slopes of Hill 145, while 3rd Canadian Division pushed forward to the edge of the Ridge. 3rd and 4th Canadian Division would then be on their final objectives.

1st and 2nd Canadian Divisions would still have two more objectives, which were allocated to their reserve brigades. The advance from the Red Line would follow after a pause of two and a half hours. 2nd Canadian Division's area widened as it advanced and the British 13th Brigade was to deploy on its left to the final objective, which was to be covered in two bounds. By Zero plus five hours and twenty minutes, 1st and 2nd Canadian Division would have taken Thélus, Hill 135, Bois de Bonval and Count's Wood (Blue Line). They would pause there for ninety-six minutes before the final advance. By Zero plus seven hours and forty-eight minutes, the final objective on the German second position was to be reached in Farbus Wood, Bois de la Ville and the south of Bois du Bonval (Brown Line). Patrols would then push forward to the Lens–Arras railway, while the gains were consolidated against counterattack.

No attempt was made to hide the preparations; it would have been futile to do so. However, the date and time of the assault were kept secret. 3rd and 4th Canadian Divisions had six months to get to know the area and even 1st and 2nd Canadian Division had four weeks to familiarise themselves. Replica enemy positions were constructed behind the lines for every detail of the assault to be rehearsed. A large plasticine model was constructed at HQ First Army to be studied by officers and NCOs and air photographs were also distributed copiously.

First Army artillery was reinforced by numerous siege and heavy batteries. The Canadian Corps had two heavy artillery groups, which were reinforced by nine more British heavy groups. Two bombardment groups were allocated to each assault division. There was a heavy gun for every twenty metres of front and a field piece for every ten metres. On the right the field gun positions were almost 6,000m from the final objective and were unable to cover the final advance at their extreme range. Nine 18 Pounder and two 4.5″ Howitzer batteries were dug in at night 450–1,350m behind the front line. To maintain secrecy, registration of these guns was conducted under the cover of fire from batteries further back.

In addition to the usual artillery support, there was much closer liaison between the heavy artillery groups and the divisions. Counter-battery fire was given a very high priority. A sophisticated system was devised to link rapidly and accurately the aircraft and balloons observers, sound ranging units, flash spotters and ground observers with the counter-battery guns. Rather than attempt to destroy all trenches, fire was directed against junctions, dugouts, strongpoints, concrete emplacements and tunnel entrances. Behind the lines road junctions, dumps and other targets were hit out to 4,500m. The wire in front of the first trench line was bombarded comprehensively, but thereafter lanes were cut instead. The new No.106 fuse was used extensively to burst high explosive shells amongst the wire on first contact. Smoke shells were held in readiness to mask off observation posts that appeared to be intact when the attack was launched. The artillery bombardment commenced on 20th March, but with only half the batteries. The full weight of the bombardment commenced on 2nd April; a period described by the defenders as 'the week of suffering'.

Heavy and medium trench mortars joined in on the front trenches and wire. At night 280 machine guns (another seventy-eight were in reserve) harassed communications trenches, open approaches, dumps and gaps in the wire to prevent them being repaired. As the weather permitted, air photography allowed damage assessment to be carried out and to locate enemy batteries. It was later discovered that eighty-six percent of the active German batteries had been located accurately. The weight of fire was stupefying, but it could not hope to destroy the deep tunnels and dugouts. In addition, the distance to be advanced meant that the tunnel entrances could not all be seized in the first rush. As a result large numbers of enemy troops could survive and be ready to emerge at the last moment to fight off the attackers, as had happened on the Somme the previous year. In order to gain the maximum distance before resistance stiffened, surprise would be achieved by dispensing with a final bombardment.

Behind the lines a huge amount of engineering work was required to provide accommodation, water, ration and ammunition dumps and medical units. Bridges were prepared to allow artillery to cross enemy trenches and miles of roads were built or repaired. Much of the work was in full view of the German forward positions and so was undertaken at night. There was very little interference from the Germans. Four tunnelling companies gained the upper hand over the Germans underground. Twelve subways were extended right up to the front line and became the main routes by which to conduct trench reliefs and evacuate casualties. This involved digging 9,600m of tunnels eight metres below ground. The subways had electric lighting and also carried communications cables and water pipes. Brigade and battalion HQs were set up in the tunnels. Mines were pushed forward under some enemy positions to be blown at Zero hour. Two thousand gas projectors were installed, but on the day the wind was too strong and they were not used. Thirty-four kilometres of new cable routes outside the tunnels were dug to a depth of two metres. By April 1917 there were 2,400 kilometres of communications circuit.

Eight tanks were allocated to 2nd Canadian Division, but no reliance was placed upon them in the planning due to the state of the ground. Despite the Germans having superiority in the air at this time, the RFC managed to photograph the whole attack area. The weather in the preparatory period varied between snow, sleet, freeze, thaw and torrential rain, making work difficult and necessitating constant route maintenance.

Raids ascertained that the 15,000 Canadians in the initial assault would face five German regiments totalling about 5,000 men. There were another 3,000 in reserve about two hours march away. However, the Canadians had 12,000 in reserve and they were much closer to the front. Two German reserve divisions were at least four hours away. It seemed likely that 1st and 2nd Canadian Divisions, with the longest advance, would encounter these formations. The batteries supporting them had their allocation of shells increased to break up counterattacks.

After dark on 8th April the assault troops commenced the five kilometres approach march to their start positions. It was a dark and cloudy night, but the mud was partly frozen and the routes had been well signed and marked with luminous posts. Many men arrived at the front through the subways. Patrols reported the German wire was well cut. Parties cut lanes in the British wire and the assault troops made their way through them to lay up in ditches and craters in no man's land less that 100m from the German forward posts. Fifty-two battalions were deployed, with only a few local alarms being raised. Waiting ninety minutes for Zero was a cold and wet experience, with snow and sleet falling heavily.

At 5.30 a.m. on 9th April (Easter Monday) 983 guns and mortars opened fire and two mines were exploded under the German lines on the left. After three minutes the barrage began creeping forward ninety metres every three minutes. Four hundred metres ahead of the creeping barrage, 150 machine guns created a bullet-swept zone. All known German batteries and dumps were hit at the same time with high explosive and gas shell. A smoke screen was laid in front of Thélus and Hill 135.

As soon as the creeping barrage fell, the infantry set off. It was supposed to be first light, but thick cloud meant it was dark longer than expected. The wind came from behind the Canadians and drove the sleet and snow into the faces of the enemy.

Drive through Thélus eastwards on the D49. At the major crossroads with the D917 turn left. After just over 200m there is hard standing on the right on which to pull over. Cross the road to the west side and look in that direction. Thélus is on the left. The attack came from behind you over the road. Zwolfer Graben ran parallel with the road and about 125m to the east of it. This is where William Milne's main VC action took place.

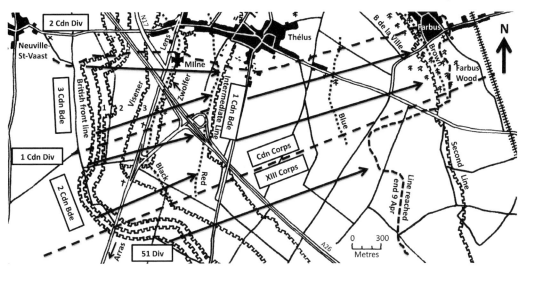

The German artillery response was ineffective and there were very few casualties initially.

On the right, 1st Canadian Division (Major General Arthur Currie) had a frontage of 1,800m. 2nd Canadian Brigade on the right rushed the first trench before the sentries could alert the men in the deep dugouts. The entrances were guarded to await the moppers-up while the advance continued with the creeping barrage. 3rd Canadian Brigade on the left had a few more casualties until three machine guns were knocked out. Both brigades pressed on to the second trench, where there were a few more casualties, but the trench fell easily. In the third trench both the 14th and 16th Battalions of 3rd Canadian Brigade met strong resistance. Four machine guns were overcome by 14th Battalion.

16th Battalion, on the left of 3rd Canadian Brigade, had moved into the front line via Bentata Tunnel and suffered very few casualties. However, the Battalion HQ had gone forward overland to avoid congestion in the tunnel system and was hit by a shell. Most were killed or wounded and only the CO, Lieutenant Colonel CW Peck, was able to continue to the Battle HQ. The advance was led by 3 and 4 Companies, right and left respectively, followed by 1 and 2 Companies in support. Each company had its own piper. The Battalion faced the Claudot and Vissec groups of mine craters; up to six metres deep with slippery sides and often holding two metres of muddy water at the bottom.

16th Battalion advanced on the first German positions in the face of heavy machine gun fire. Groups dashed forward and to the flanks to deal with machine gun posts with grenades and bayonet. **Private William Milne** captured one machine gun in the first trench. The cost was high, particularly in officers and NCOs, but the advance moved on. Machine guns were encountered frequently in front and to the flanks. Strong resistance was encountered in Visener Kreuz Weg, just short of the Arras–Lens road. It had escaped much of the artillery bombardment and the garrison fought hard for it, but was overcome.

The next objective beyond the Arras–Lens road, which could not be distinguished in the mud and debris, was Zwolfer Graben. 3 Company was able to proceed without difficulty, but on the left 4 Company was held up as soon as it left Visener Kreuz Weg. A machine gun opened up from half left and there were many casualties. Groups of soldiers crept towards it, but were unable to silence it. While a fresh assault party

The view westwards from the N17 with the line of Zwolfer Graben marked. William Milne's VC action was at the left end of the trench.

was being organised for another attempt, grenades were heard exploding around the machine gun position. Milne had crawled forward on hands and knees to within bombing distance of the machine gun position and put the entire crew out of action before capturing the gun. This gallant action prevented many casualties. Milne jumped up out of a shell hole and signalled his comrades to advance again. Later, between the Black and Red Lines, he cleared another machine gun position that was holding up the advance. He was killed shortly afterwards, one of about 350 casualties amongst the 647 who went into action in the Battalion that day.

The right flank was delayed and suffered casualties before overcoming resistance on the track to Roclincourt but, despite setbacks, by 6.05 a.m. 1st Canadian Division was on its first objective on the Black Line. Although the German machine gunners had fought well, most of the garrison appeared to be dazed and happy to surrender. The position was consolidated and the advance by the support companies of the leading battalions continued after forty minutes. The next stage of the advance was across a 650m wide saucer shaped depression south of Thélus. On the far side lay the next objective, a single trench Intermediate Line (Zwischen-Stellung), beyond which the ground rose to the crest of the Ridge. The defenders had excellent observation, but the driving snow hid the advance and they were overcome quickly. Shortly after 7 a.m. the second objective (Red Line) was secured, except on the right.

After the Intermediate Line south of Thélus, 1st Canadian Division's frontage narrowed to 900m. At 7.30 a.m., 1st Canadian Brigade in reserve advanced from the assembly trenches to its forming up area, having lost a few men to spasmodic shelling. There was almost no opposition and soon after the troops were looking over country unspoiled by the barrage.

Two belts of wire protected the German concrete casemates in Farbus Wood and Bois de la Ville and the second line positions, which were aligned northwest – southeast, whereas the previous advance had been easterly. The final advance therefore included a half left wheel beginning on the right to bring the forward edge of troops into line. The rearward batteries were now out of range and the secreted advanced batteries took over the barrage. By 1 p.m. the leading companies were closed up to the barrage, but 1st Canadian Brigade found insufficient gaps had been cut in the wire by the artillery and more had to be cut by hand. The two leading battalions followed the barrage through both belts of wire. The German gun positions were overrun and most of the crews were found sheltering from the

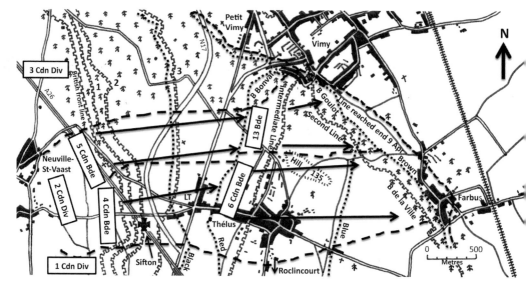

The area around the second German trench, where Ellis Sifton captured the machine gun and allowed C Company to continue its advance, has been comprehensively altered by the construction of the A26 Autoroute and the upgraded N17. As a result it bears no resemblance to the landscape of 1917. However, it is possible to get very close to the site. Drive through Thélus eastwards on the D49. At the major crossroads with the D917 go straight over, signed for Neuville-St-Vaast. Cross over the N17 bridge and immediately after it and before going over the A26 bridge, stop in the turning on the left. It allows service access to the autoroute and a gas installation so please do not block it. Look to the east. C Company advanced over the autoroute and N17 towards Thélus. Ellis Sifton's VC action was in front of you in the area of the gas installation. LT = Les Tilleuls.

barrage. 51st Division on the right was delayed and a defensive flank was formed back to the Intermediate Line.

2nd Canadian Division had a frontage of 1,300m. 4th Canadian Brigade on the right and 5th Canadian Brigade on the left each attacked with two battalions, a third was in support and the fourth acted as carrying parties. 18th Battalion was on the right of 4th Canadian Brigade and, despite heavy enemy artillery fire during the move

From the D49 just west of the N17 bridge. As close as can be ascertained, Ellis Sifton captured the machine gun post in the area of the gas installation on the far side of the bridge.

to the start positions, had no casualties. The last company was in position by 3.45 a.m. The first trench was taken with very little opposition and the German artillery fell behind the assault troops in no man's land before becoming haphazard. The support line fell without difficulty and soon after the Battalion was on the Black Line.

However, there were isolated areas of resistance and C Company in the centre was held up and suffered heavy losses from two machine guns in the second trench. **Sergeant Ellis Sifton** spotted one of the hidden emplacements, leapt into the trench, overthrew the gun and bayoneted the crew single-handed. A party of Germans then moved against him down the trench and he held them off with his bayonet and rifle used as a club until his comrades arrived to relieve him. He was killed later by one of the Germans he had wounded, one of 166 casualties suffered by 18th Battalion that day.

The left of 4th Canadian Brigade (19th Battalion) and the whole of 5th Canadian Brigade managed to avoid heavy fire and overran the enemy trenches with most of the defenders still in their dugouts. As the advance continued to the second trench, more opposition was encountered and there were numerous acts of gallantry to overcome these machine guns. However, by 6.05 a.m. 2nd Canadian Division was on the first objective.

The support battalions of each brigade led the advance to the next objective. In 4th Canadian Brigade, 21st Battalion overcame two machine guns in Les Tilleuls and captured a number of prisoners and a field gun in the ruins. Half an hour later a large cave (Felsenkeller) was discovered and 106 Germans surrendered, including two battalion headquarters. 5th Canadian Brigade swept ahead to its objective and, with the moppers-up, took 390 prisoners and four machine guns.

2nd Canadian Division reached the Red Line, halfway to the final objective, but was still 450m short of the Intermediate Line. 6th Canadian Brigade and the British 13th Brigade were to carry out the attack on Hill 135 and Thélus in one movement, passing through 4th and 5th Canadian Brigades respectively. The creeping barrage resumed at 9.35 a.m., closely followed by the leading five battalions of the two brigades. They advanced rapidly and rushed the Intermediate Line between

Thélus and Bois de Bonval. The wire was well cut and the trench had been all but obliterated. Success was signalled at 9.55 a.m. and soon after the advance was resumed by both brigades. Tanks were to have assisted in the next phase, but due to ground conditions none crossed no man's land. Two battalions of 6th Canadian Brigade advanced either side of the Thélus main street and at the same time 13th Brigade advanced round the north side of Hill 135. Machine guns were brought up while the artillery covered the consolidation along the Roclincourt–Thélus track for ninety minutes.

6th Canadian Brigade's final advance encountered only limited resistance from a machine gun and a gun battery. The advance surged on and 250 prisoners were taken after securing the eastern edge of Bois de la Ville. 13th Brigade completed the capture of Bois du Goulot and a gun battery that opened fire from only 200m was rushed and captured. The whole of the final objective (Brown Line) was taken.

3rd Canadian Division had two of the longest subways emerging in its sector (Goodman and Grange). It attacked with 8th Canadian Brigade on the right and 7th Canadian Brigade on the left. The front line fell before the defenders could react. Some were half-dressed as they emerged from Schwaben Tunnel and over 150 prisoners were taken. The third trench was so damaged by shellfire that many did not recognise it and went beyond. The rear companies passed though on time and reached the final objective, Bois de la Folie. Here 7th Canadian Brigade suffered the majority of its casualties in clearing trenches and dugouts. Counterattacks were repulsed and by 7.30 a.m. the western edge of the wood had fallen. In places consolidation utilised former German trenches, but elsewhere it meant digging a new line. Casualties mounted from snipers and there was no contact with 4th Canadian Division at Hill 145, so a defensive flank was established. However, the value of having brigade Vickers machine guns well forward in the advance was demonstrated when two set up on the Vimy–Lens road ahead of the advancing infantry and inflicted a hundred casualties on the enemy.

4th Canadian Division had the task of securing Hill 145, the highest point on the Ridge and where the Canadian National Vimy Memorial now stands. The Hill afforded excellent observation in all directions, but as the Germans lacked depth in their positions in this area they had made them particularly strong to compensate. Hill 145 was double ringed by trenches and there were deep shelters, particularly on the rear slope (Hangstellung). Achieving surprise here was more important than anywhere else. Zouave Valley lay just behind the assembly trenches and was a regular target for German artillery. Six subways of 300–1350m in length were constructed to avoid this fire and assembly trenches were dug 140m from the German lines. They could not be closer due to the uncertain nature of the mining beneath.

Pivoting on its left at Kennedy Crater, 4th Canadian Division attacked with 11th Canadian Brigade on the right and 12th Canadian Brigade on the left, with 10th Canadian Brigade in reserve. The first objective was to be consolidated as the main line of resistance and the support battalions would pass through for another 235m

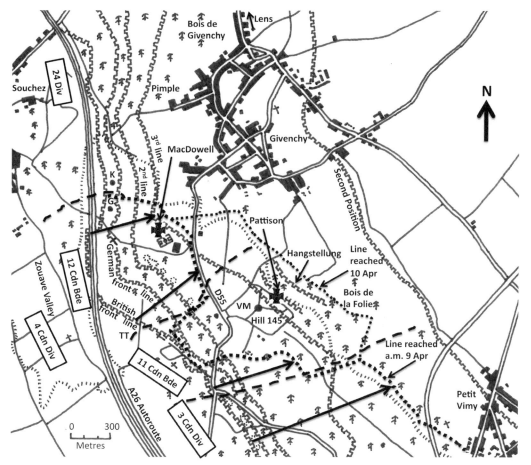

Leave the Canadian National Vimy Memorial car park and turn right on the D55. After 525m there is riding school on the left with plenty of space to park. It is also the entrance to the local sports pitch. On the south side of the riding school is a track forbidden to motor vehicles. Walk along it for 500m to Givenchy-en-Gohelle Canadian Cemetery. On the way note the heavily cratered landscape in the wood on the left of the track. This is the area of Craters 1–7. At the Cemetery look a little north of east into the fields. About 140m along that line is where Cyrus Trench joined Baby Trench and where MacDowall's VC action took place. K = Kennedy, G = Gunner, TT = Tottenham tunnel and VM = Canadian National Vimy Memorial.

to the Hangstellung on the reverse slope of the Ridge, which would be held with Lewis gun posts for observation beyond.

The right of 11th Canadian Brigade reached its final objective with little trouble, but on the left it was a different story. A German strongpoint commanded the exit from Tottenham Tunnel from 360m away. Half the leading waves were casualties before the German front line was reached and wire prevented the strongpoint being rushed, giving the Germans time to man their second trench. The objective was reached at considerable cost, but on the left 54th Battalion was forced back and became entangled with 12th Canadian Brigade. By 7 a.m., when the barrage moved on, the left was still short of the summit and snipers drove back many of the most advanced troops.

12th Canadian Brigade was the left wing of the whole offensive and only required an advance of a few hundred metres to bring it to its objective. 38th Battalion was on the right, 72nd Battalion in the centre and 73rd Battalion on the left, with 78th and 46th (10th Canadian Brigade) Battalions in support. 78th Battalion was on the right flank, which required the longest advance. The left flank was screened by smoke to prevent interference from the Pimple at the extreme northern end of the Ridge.

The attack was to be preceded by firing two mines at Zero, one near Gunner Crater and the other close to Kennedy Crater. Specially designated parties were to seize the resultant craters. A company of 72nd Battalion was to seize the eastern lip of the new crater near Gunner Crater. Two companies of 73rd Battalion companies also provided two crater-rushing parties. One was to seize the western and northern lips of the new crater near Gunner Crater, while the other seized the new crater near Kennedy Crater. Upon consolidation each battalion, assisted by engineers, was also to dig a new communications trench to the rear.

72nd Battalion in the centre captured the first trench with little opposition, but lost the barrage and suffered many casualties before the second trench was taken by bombing along it from a flank. A footing was gained in the third trench but, as the smoke cleared from the Pimple, intense machine gun fire from it stopped further progress. 73rd Battalion on the left only had to take the first German trench. As the

The overgrown remains of Crater 6.

barrage opened, the two mines killed many in the German garrison. The survivors fled and the objective was taken within seven minutes. Contact was established with I Corps on the left.

38th Battalion on the right led with A Company on the right and D Company on the left, supported by C and B Companies respectively. The first wave was to deal with the first objective and the second wave the second objective. The last two waves were to capture the existing Craters 1–7 and establish strongpoints beyond them, each held by a platoon. The remainder were to fall back and help with the consolidation of the second objective, which was to be the main line of resistance in this area. The Battalion's left flank was also to extend 150m north to join the captured German front line with the British front line. The Battalion moved up using Erzatz communications trench and Blue Bull Tunnel, which also housed the Battalion HQ.

The Battalion seized the first trench with few casualties, but they increased as the advance resumed over particularly difficult ground. Some shell holes were so deep and full of water that wounded men drowned in them. German defenders appeared in unexpected places in the second trench from deep dugouts. A machine gun position was encountered near the junction of Cyrus and Baby Trenches. **Captain Thain MacDowell** with his two orderlies, 788589 Private James Thomas Kobus and 144589 Private Arthur James Hay, bombed up Baby Trench, killing some of the crewmen and capturing one of the guns.

A detailed map of the area around the junction of Cyrus and Baby Trenches.

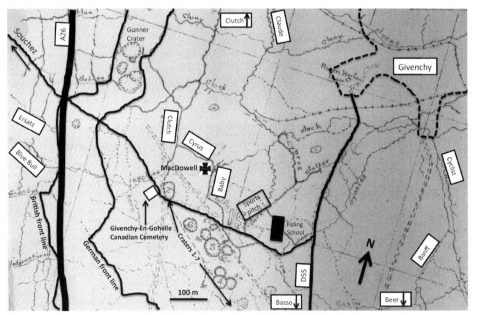

The surviving crewmen and the other gun disappeared into a large dugout at the junction of Cyrus and Baby. It was about twenty-three metres deep and had three entrances. MacDowell threw in a few grenades and then went down to find an enormous shelter capable of housing 250–300 men. He tricked the occupants into believing he had a large force behind him. There were seventy-seven Germans in the shelter, including two officers, and they had two machine guns. MacDowell filed them out six at a time to be passed from one runner to the next. However, nearby a Canadian sniper had set up and shot the first twelve, not knowing that they were already prisoners. MacDowell stopped the prisoners leaving the dugout and found the sniper to ensure he stopped firing. A few of the prisoners turned on MacDowell's party when they realised how small it was. They were dealt with immediately and drastically and the remainder caused no further trouble. The surviving prisoners were then sent back to the Canadian lines with a few parting shots to keep them moving. MacDowell's bold action allowed the Battalion to reach its second and final objective by 5.54 a.m. and ten minutes later a telephone signal station was set up on the south side of No.6 Crater.

MacDowell sent back a series of reports to ensure Battalion HQ was aware of the situation. At 8 a.m. he reported that he was on his objective but with very few men, no officers or NCOs and most weapons were clogged with mud. The men were cleaning them as best they could and he was bringing in isolated men, but he needed reinforcements as his only machine gun had lost its cocking piece. His position had a field of fire of 350m from west round to east through north and a couple of Brigade machine guns would make all the difference to holding on. They also needed tools, as none had got through in the advance. He finished by apologising for the state of his writing.

From the Givenchy-en-Gohelle Canadian Cemetery looking northeast towards the site of the trench junction seized and held by Thain MacDowell, with the assistance of Privates James Kobus and Arthur Hay. The morning the picture was taken was wet, misty, cold and miserable. The visibility was not unlike the conditions encountered by the Canadians early on 9th April 1917.

Junction o
Cyrus & B

Givenchy-En-Gohelle
Canadian Cemetery

Another report was sent at 10.30 a.m. He had fifteen men by then, but two were stretcher-bearers and two more were wounded. He had two Lewis guns but only four pans of ammunition and mud was still a problem in the weapons. The dugout he had captured had a tunnel heading towards the British lines but he had not explored it. He could see no sign of 78th Battalion in front and he was under fire from two machine guns and snipers. This fire was subsequently discovered to be coming from the junction of Claude and Clutch to the north. A German aircraft flew over and saw some of his men outside the dugout entrance and shortly afterwards the area was shelled. Reinforcements were required. As a result a reserve Lewis gun team was sent up. Private CJP Nunney (DCM for this action and VC in September 1918) was having a wound dressed and volunteered to take up another Lewis gun. He had thirty-two pans of ammunition, but needed a carrying party for them. A Brigade machine gun and crew were also sent forward to assist MacDowell. Three officers and some specialists out of the line at Chateau de la Haie were ordered forward to reinforce MacDowell as well.

By 2.45 p.m., MacDowell was able to report that he had explored the start of the tunnel but no further, as he feared it was wired for destruction. All visible wires had been cut and he requested tunnelling officers be sent to investigate further. He believed that the tunnel led towards No.7 Crater and would make a useful underground communications trench. One room in the dugout was packed with explosives, later estimated to weigh five tons. However, on the plus side they had discovered a plentiful supply of good cigars and Perrier water. Although they had been under fire from German heavy artillery from the southeast, there had been no casualties, although he admitted to being *half scared to death … by a big brute*. He reiterated the strength of his position and how it would almost certainly be a target for counterattack. There were large numbers of wounded in front. They had to resort to using German rifles as their own were too contaminated with mud to be cleaned properly. By then he had three Lewis guns and fifteen pans of ammunition.

Riding stables and sports pitch

Cratered area

Track to riding stables, 500m

An officer named Kelty had joined him, but he still had no NCOs. He finished with, *Tell Ken to come up for tea tomorrow if it is quiet….*

MacDowall remained at his post and continued to hold the position for a further five days under heavy fire until relieved. Kobus and Hay were awarded the DCM for their part in this action. Of the 744 (562 actually in the assault) all ranks of 38th Battalion who took part in the operation, 325 became casualties, out of a total of 1,344 casualties in 12th Canadian Brigade. The Battalion captured five tons of explosives, a heavy mortar, two light mortars, four machine guns and a host of other weaponry and equipment, as well as 150 prisoners.

78th Battalion was to pass through 38th Battalion but was affected by the delay to 11th Canadian Brigade on the right. It was subjected to enfilade fire from Hill 145, both flanks and also from Banff Trench. This, combined with the heavy ground, meant the creeping barrage was lost, but the Battalion pressed on and reached the second trench. However, by the time its support companies had reached the third trench at about 8.30 a.m., they were severely depleted and a counterattack from a dugout in the rear overwhelmed them in Cyclist Trench. The Germans continued towards their second trench, but it was well held with Lewis guns and they were forced into shell holes until retiring into Cyclist and Banff Trenches at 7.30 p.m.

Except for the section in front of 11th Canadian Brigade at Hill 145, all of the Canadian Corps' objectives had been captured. A brilliant victory had been gained by thorough planning, preparation, rehearsal, plentiful artillery and determined execution. Over 3,400 prisoners had entered the cages before midnight and many more were heading towards them.

As soon as the operation had been completed patrols, including two of cavalry, were pushed forward and the construction of the main line of defence commenced, using existing belts of German wire. Roads, tramways and pipelines were extended and a vast army of engineers and carriers appeared. The artillery started moving up but could not get beyond the old front line that night. Work commenced on a plank road to connect the Arras–Souchez and Arras–Lens roads.

During the rest of 9th April 3rd Canadian Division threw back a defensive left flank against Hill 145. Contact was eventually made with 4th Canadian Division, but as a precaution the defensive flank was continued all the way back to the original front line. 11th and 12th Canadian Brigades suffered casualties all day from machine guns and snipers on Hill 145. However, HQ 4th Canadian Division did not know exactly where its forward troops were and did not order a renewed bombardment. However, by 1 p.m., Stokes mortar and machine gun barrages had been organised. These allowed bombers to work along the front trench of Hill 145, which was secured with sixty prisoners and two machine guns being taken.

About midday two battalions of 10th Canadian Brigade at the disposal of 11th and 12th Canadian Brigades were used to reinforce the inner flanks of both brigades. 11th Canadian Brigade also received two companies of 85th Battalion to attack the nearside of the summit. At the last moment it was decided not to risk the bombardment that had been arranged, but it was too late for modified orders to get through. The two companies crossed the first trench held by Canadian bombers at 6.45 p.m. Despite the lack of fire support and the ground conditions, they reached the second trench, captured it and took or killed ninety-two Germans. Further advance to the final objective met little resistance. At the same time two companies of 46th Battalion, attached to 12th Canadian Brigade, advanced on the left and captured Craters 1–3 beyond the German second trench. The fire to which 3rd and 4th Canadian Divisions had been subjected throughout the day then ceased.

10th April 1917

During the night the clouds cleared and the near full moon gave light for reorganisation. Early on the morning of the 10th a machine gun drove off a German counterattack on Hill 145 at the same time as they made another abortive attempt to regain Hill 135. At 4.15 a.m. patrols discovered the third German trench was unoccupied and it was quickly taken by parties of 85th and 75th Battalions just before parties of the enemy tried to recover it from the Hangstellung.

11th Canadian Brigade was exhausted so 10th Canadian Brigade was ordered to carry out the advance to the final objectives. The task fell to 44th (right) and 50th (left) Battalions. 50th Battalion had moved forward to Music Hall support line late on 9th April from the Quarry with Battalion HQ in the Souchez Tunnel. Soon after midday it advanced across Zouave Valley and was in its assembly positions in Basso Trench at 2.45 p.m. 50th Battalion's assault was to be led by C Company on the right and A Company on the left, with D and B Companies in support respectively. A slow barrage fell at 3.04 p.m. on Banff Trench and at 3.15 p.m. it intensified. By

From whichever direction you approach, follow signs for the Canadian National Vimy Memorial and leave your vehicle in the large car park just off the D55 Neuville-St-Vaast – Givenchy-en-Gohelle road. Walk to the Memorial and look down the slope on the far side to the east. On 10th April this is where 44th and 50th Battalions swept over the top of Hill 145, on which the stunning Memorial now stands, and rushed the Hangstellung along the tree-line beyond the path. John Pattison destroyed the machine gun post between the Memorial and the Hangstellung to allow the advance to continue.

From the Canadian National Vimy Memorial looking east. The attack on 10th April came from behind the camera and swept down the slope to the Hangstellung in the tree-line. Although visibility was limited when the picture was taken, the domination of the Ridge over the Douai plain is all too apparent.

then 50th Battalion had worked forward to Beer Trench. Both battalions moved forward under cover of the artillery and four minutes later, when it lifted, they charged and entered the trench. On the right parties of 44th Battalion pressed on through the northern end of Bois de la Folie and made contact with 3rd Canadian Division on the right. Within thirty minutes the two battalions had cleared the dugouts of both trenches of the Hangstellung. 50th Battalion took 125 prisoners alone, together with two machine guns and a mortar. However, heavy casualties were suffered rushing down the hill and in the subsequent close fighting; 50th Battalion lost 229 men.

During the attack the advance was held up by a machine gun causing heavy casualties. **Private John Pattison**, with utter disregard for his own safety, sprang forward and jumped from shell hole to shell hole to get within thirty metres of the gun position. Despite the heavy fire he exposed himself to throw in some bombs, which killed or wounded some of the crew. He then rushed in and bayoneted the surviving five crewmen, allowing the advance to continue and saving the situation. Unusually his exploits are not mentioned in either the British or Canadian Official Histories.

The fall of the Hangstellung gave complete command of the rear slopes of the Ridge. 12th Canadian Brigade was able to move its right forward and complete the capture of its original objectives. 47th Battalion completed taking over the line from 44th and 50th Battalions by 1 a.m. on 11th April. The two relieved battalions moved back into Zouave Valley to prepare for the attack on the Pimple.

12th April 1917

The northern operation against the Pimple and Bois en Hache should have been delivered twenty-four hours after the southern operation. It had to be delayed by a day because the assault troops of 10th Canadian Brigade had been diverted to take Hill 145. The attack was launched at 5 a.m. on 12th April. On the right, 10th

Canadian Brigade was to secure the Pimple and the head of the Bois de Givenchy spur. On the left, 73rd Brigade (24th Division) faced Bois en Hache, the last German foothold on the Lorette Ridge.

44th and 50th Battalions and two companies of 46th Battalion of 10th Canadian Brigade moved north from Zouave Valley at 1.45 a.m. on 12th April. Because of the casualties suffered on 10th April, 50th Battalion was reorganised into two composite companies, No.1 and No.2, each with a strength of 150. They moved up the slope to the assembly trenches only a few hundred metres from the crest of the Ridge. During the night the artillery pounded the German rear areas and Livens projectors fired over forty gas drums into Givenchy. Capture of the first German trench was to be followed by a further advance of 350m.

44th Battalion on the right was to take the eastern end of the Pimple spur and its right was to gain contact with 73rd Battalion on the left of 12th Canadian Brigade. 50th Battalion on the left was to take the Bois de Givenchy spur, keeping in contact with 44th Battalion on the inner flank. 50th Battalion's assault was to be made by No.1 Company, while No.2 Company mopped up and started work on the main line of resistance in Carry and Carrion Trenches. It was reinforced by two companies of 46th Battalion on the left and was to throw back a line along the northern slope of the spur to connect with the original front line of I Corps in the Souchez Valley.

At 4 a.m. the two companies of 46th Battalion were detected, but the fire opened against them mainly went high. By 4.15 a.m. the units were in position and snow began falling at 4.30 a.m., driven by a strong westerly wind. At 4.50 a.m. two siege groups of heavy and medium artillery opened fire and ten minutes later the shrapnel barrage fell and the infantry set off across no man's land. The wind increased and helped push the attackers across the difficult ground while also blinding the defenders. The ground was so heavy that the infantry lost the barrage, but they got into the first trench. The second and third trenches hardly existed and the garrison was firing mainly from shell holes. With visibility down to ten metres at times, the Canadians cleared the position at close quarters.

By 6 a.m. 44th Battalion had fought its way into the quarry on the high ground of the Pimple and rushed the dugouts. One hundred Germans were cut down by

Lewis guns as they tried to escape downhill into Givenchy. Seventy-seven prisoners were taken. The only real setback was on the right, where a platoon of 73rd Battalion did not attack as expected to support 44th Battalion. A party of Germans managed to hold on between 44th Battalion and the flank of 12th Canadian Brigade and a bombing party of 73rd Battalion failed to shift this resistance point.

50th Battalion made good progress through the mud and shattered stumps of Bois de Givenchy. Only isolated resistance was encountered and the enemy was either bayoneted or captured. The final objective of 50th Battalion was reached at 5.45 a.m. The 46th Battalion companies also overcame the opposition quickly. The leading company lost direction and became involved in the main assault on the right, but the rear company reached the objective overlooking the Souchez stream on the northern slope of the spur and set up Lewis guns to secure the left flank. 50th

Drive through Angres on the D58E2 southwest towards Souchez. Just before going under the autoroute bridge turn right and drive to the top of the hill where there is a telecommunications mast with some hard standing to park on the right. Look back the way you came. The A26 Autoroute is on the right and Bois en Hache (Bois Soil on modern maps) is on the left. 2nd Leinster's front line ran through the field parallel with the track you drove up. The Pimple is on the high ground to the southeast (Bois de Givenchy) on the far side of the Souchez stream.

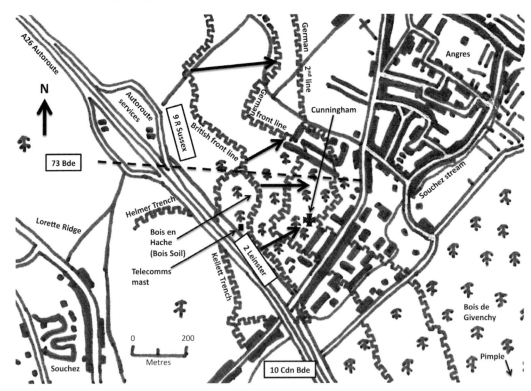

Battalion sent back fifteen prisoners, but only one reached the former British lines. Four machine guns and two minenwerfers were also taken. The German artillery shelled the captured positions heavily and snipers were very active on the left. As daylight broke the snowstorm abated and the sun came, out allowing the men of 10th Canadian Brigade to see the two most important features on the Ridge that they had captured over the previous three days – Hill 145 and the Pimple. The final objective was consolidated while the rear companies entrenched a main line of resistance some 300m behind.

50th Battalion went forward again at 5.30 p.m. to take up a new line along Crash, Clannish and Cancan Trenches. Four 77mm guns were captured. The German artillery remained active and counterattacks seemed to threaten but did not materialise. At 8.30 p.m., the Battalion was relieved and moved back to Vancouver Camp, having suffered 271 casualties in the two operations.

Bois en Hache covers the eastern end of the Lorette Ridge and was the last German foothold on that feature. The attack against it was simultaneous with that against the Pimple. 73rd Brigade attacked with two battalions on a frontage of 450m. 2nd Leinster was to take the south and centre of the wood, while 9th Royal Sussex took the north and the slopes beyond. Each battalion was reinforced with a section of 129th Field Company RE, a platoon of 12th Sherwood Foresters (Pioneers), two Stokes mortars of 73rd Light Trench Mortar Battery and a sub-section of 73rd Machine Gun Company. The engineers would also construct two communications trenches across no man's land, one behind each battalion.

The first German trench would be consolidated as a main line of resistance while the advance continued 200m to the final objective, the German second line trench on the reverse slope of the Ridge, which overlooked the Douai Plain. This would give the British the advantages previously enjoyed by the Germans in the opposite direction. The attack was rehearsed repeatedly beforehand. No assembly trenches were dug due to the appalling state of the ground. The attack would commence from the existing front line.

C Company, 2nd Leinsters was to take the front line trench and then A and B Companies were to pass through to take the second line. D Company was in reserve. A final rehearsal took place on the afternoon of the 11th, following which the Battalion left its billets at Fosse 10 near Petit Sains at 7.30 p.m. via Aix Noulette and the Arras Road for the trenches in the Souchez sector. Heavy snow fell until 11.45 p.m. On arrival in the trenches area the men were served rum and tea and given extra equipment such as grenades, tools, wire cutters etc. 2nd Leinster entered the front line along Helmer Trench, with the supports in Kellett Trench behind.

At 4 a.m. on 12th April the leading companies left the front line trench and deployed in front of the wire, while the rear companies lay down just beyond the parapet. At 4.31 a.m. 2nd Leinster was in position and the enemy did nothing to interfere. The barrage opened at 5 a.m. and the attackers suffered a few casualties from it as they set off in darkness. The enemy fire was inaccurate due to being

From the telecommunications mast looking south, with the autoroute on the right, the high ground of the Bois de Givenchy straight ahead and Bois en Hache on the left.

blinded by the snowstorm. Progress across no man's land was very slow due to the shell holes and mud up to a metre deep, but the German wire presented no obstacles and his artillery was weak. At 5.10 a.m. the barrage lifted and the front line, which was lightly held, was stormed. Most of the casualties were incurred on the right by fire from Bois de Givenchy across the Souchez Valley and from trenches behind Long Sap (not identified, but assumed to be within the German trenches in Bois en Hache). Casualties were particularly heavy in the right platoon detailed to form the defensive flank. The Lewis gunners were noted during this phase wielding their guns as clubs. Amongst them was **Corporal John Cunningham** in the right platoon. German survivors ran back to the second trench.

As daylight broke the advance continued down the slope towards the second line. The ground was in even worse condition here than in no man's land and the

Reverse view of the previous picture.

attackers again came under heavy enfilade fire from south of the stream. All the officers in the leading waves were hit and the survivors took cover where they could. Small parties pressed on and broke into the trench in two places, which was cleared after fierce hand-to-hand fighting. In places the trench had been obliterated.

Many in Cunningham's section were killed and wounded but, although wounded himself, he pressed on. Their objective was an embankment but after the intense bombardment of the previous week it was difficult to recognise and some men overran it. However, they gained the objective, Long Sap and the trench behind it, which was in good condition and strongly held. A stiff fight followed and there were casualties on both sides. The survivors under Lieutenant EJ Magner established a post. Cunningham set up his Lewis gun and accounted for at least twenty Germans. The weakened platoon was attacked by about forty Germans from the trenches in the valley below and from behind Long Sap. They held on for about forty-five minutes, inflicting many casualties on the Germans. Cunningham was wounded in four places but continued to hold the post almost single handed. The few survivors of the platoon made their way back to the embankment and eventually to the German front line. They were deployed on the right flank facing south to keep touch between the British front line and the captured German front line.

Cunningham held on in his post near Long Sap until attacked by another party of about twenty Germans. He fired off all his ammunition and then continued the fight with bombs, fully exposed to the enemy fire throughout the engagement. Inevitably he was wounded again, but picked himself up and continued to throw bombs until he had none left. He then made his way back to the front line where it was discovered he had a broken arm and numerous other wounds. His stand averted a disaster on the right flank, but it cost him his life as he died of his wounds on 16th April, one of 216 casualties in the Battalion.

9th Royal Sussex on the left had sixty casualties in the first few minutes of the attack and 106 in total. The left company reached the objective with relatively few problems, whereas the right company lost all its officers and only small parties reached the objective, where contact was made with 2nd Leinster. Survivors of both battalions grouped into small parties to hang on to their gains in the line of resistance with advanced posts thirty-five metres in front. 2nd Leinster brought up a machine gun and two Stokes mortars to help hold the right flank.

The interior of Bois en Hache is thickly overgrown in places and there are vestiges of trenches and shell holes everywhere. The low bank on the right on the southern edge of the wood may be the embankment referred to in contemporary accounts. John Cunningham's VC action was in this area.

Having withdrawn the forward troops from the German second line, consolidation proceeded along the original German front line, assisted by 129th Field Company RE and 12th Sherwood Foresters (Pioneers). Tactically the loss of the German second line was of little consequence as the front line overlooked the second line and beyond. Next day 2nd Leinster pushed over the Souchez on the right and gained contact with 10th Canadian Battalion.

Meanwhile on the 12th, it became clear that the Germans were withdrawing and vigorous patrols were ordered to follow up along the entire Canadian Corps front. This resulted in a considerable move forwards to include Willerval, Vimy, Petit Vimy and Givenchy. On the flanks, XIII Corps and I Corps reached Bailleul station and Angres. Prisoners confirmed that the Germans were pulling back to the Oppy–Mericourt Line and the Avion Switch, the original third position. The advance continued on the 13th and 14th with little opposition until it approached the new German front. The Oppy–Mericourt Line was far enough east to minimize the advantages of observation from Vimy Ridge. First Army was in no position to assault the new line until it had moved its artillery forward across the shattered Vimy battlefield. Until the roads were repaired and extended there could be no resumption of the offensive in this area. In the meantime the infantry established a new line as close as possible to the German lines. It would remain there almost to the end of the war.

The Battle of Vimy Ridge was a spectacular success for the Canadian Corps. It had advanced 4,100m and captured an impressive array of enemy manpower and equipment – over 4,000 prisoners in addition to many more killed, fifty-four guns, 104 mortars and 124 machine guns. However, the success came at a price. The Canadians alone suffered 10,602 casualties up to 14th April, of whom 3,598 were killed or died of wounds.

Second Battle of the Scarpe

23rd April 1917

201   Capt Arthur Henderson, 2nd Argyll & Sutherland Highlanders (98th Brigade, 33rd Division), Fontaine-lès-Croisilles, France
202   Capt David Hirsch, 4th Yorkshire (150th Brigade, 50th Division), near Wancourt, France

The momentum of the first two days of the Arras offensive could not be maintained, mainly for logistical reasons. Roads had to be laid across the destroyed battlefield before the heavy artillery could be moved forward into new positions. Rations, water, ammunition and medical units also had to be brought up. It was a similar situation encountered throughout the war; the momentum and successes of the first few days could not be maintained and the offensive bogged down. Exhausted units were rotated and fresh formations were brought into the line, but many had only been rested briefly and the weather conditions and lack of accommodation meant they were tired when they returned. The pause also allowed the Germans to rotate their units and bring reinforcements from other areas. There was no prospect of achieving surprise when the offensive was renewed. German batteries were more numerous than on 9th April and there was not enough time to locate them accurately for counter-battery fire.

The aims of the next phase of the offensive were to keep the initiative and to break through in support of the French on the Aisne. However, after 16th April it became clear that Nivelle's offensive was failing. The British were then under pressure to keep attacking at Arras to take pressure off the French. A small action was fought at Lagnicourt on 15th April when the Germans realised that 1st Australian Division was holding twelve kilometres of front. They occupied Lagnicourt, but the Australians counterattacked and restored the line.

Following days of poor visibility and freezing weather, Third Army went back onto the offensive at 4.45 a.m. on 23rd April. The attack was launched on fourteen kilometres of front from Croisilles to Gavrelle, astride the Scarpe. Elements of First Army also took part to the north at Gavrelle. The day dawned with thick mist, which was added to by the smoke of the barrage, but this cleared later, allowing good visibility. The German artillery was very effective and more damaging than their machine guns.

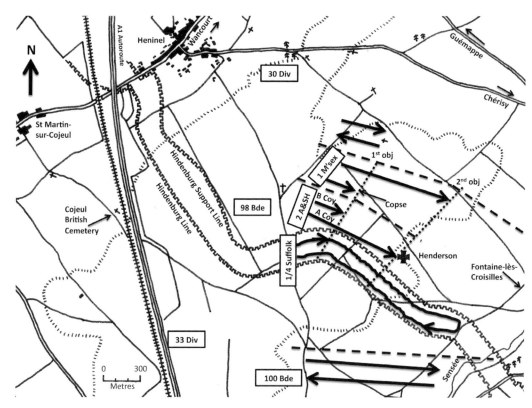

Enter Fontaine-lès-Croisilles along the D9 from the southwest from Croisilles. At the t-junction in the village turn left and after 100m go straight on but be aware that traffic from the right is on the priority route. Follow the road round to the left for 900m and take the right fork. Follow it for 500m and stop. Henderson held out with his company about 100m into the field on the left of the road. Continue up the hill to the northeast to the small copse that caused so much trouble. Look back towards Fontaine-lès-Croisilles to appreciate the strength of the Hindenburg position.

The small copse that held up the inner flanks of 2nd Argyll & Sutherland Highlanders and 1st Middlesex. Arthur Henderson led A Company over the skyline past the copse and down the slope to the left, where they held on despite being cut off by a counterattack in their rear.

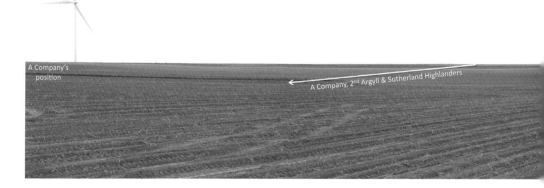

All three corps of Third Army took a full part in the attack. Of the nine divisions committed to battle on 23rd April, four had attacked on the 9th. Despite the break, the troops had not recovered fully and faced a much strengthened enemy. On the right, VII Corps attacked with 33rd, 30th and 50th Divisions. In addition to the general advance, 33rd Division attacked on the right to secure the Hindenburg Line on the east bank of the Sensée. The aim was to prevent flanking fire into the main attack. A previous attempt on 16th April was only party successful. 100th Brigade was to make the lodgement across the Sensée while 98th Brigade on the left fought its way south astride the Hindenburg Line to link up.

100th Brigade gained its objectives, but about 2 p.m. was thrown back to its start positions. 98th Brigade attacked with three battalions in line. While the right (1/4th Suffolk) bombed down the Hindenburg Line to link up with 100th Brigade, the centre (2nd Argyll & Sutherland Highlanders) and left (1st Middlesex) were to advance over the high ground to the north to assault their objectives frontally, 1,350m from the Sensée.

1/4th Suffolk, supported by two companies of 2nd Royal Welsh Fusiliers (19th Brigade) and a tank, swept along the Hindenburg Line, taking hundreds of prisoners, but was halted on the Chérisy–Croisilles road only 275m from the final objective. Platoons of 4th King's, in 98th Brigade reserve, were sent up with fresh supplies of bombs. A counterattack at 10.45 a.m. pushed the Battalion back to its start positions by 11.50 a.m. despite being reinforced by two companies each from 2nd Royal Welsh Fusiliers and 4th King's and a company of 5th Cameronians. Later another company of 5th Cameronians went up to support.

In the centre, 2nd Argyll & Sutherland Highlanders attacked with A Company on the right and B Company on the left. D Company was in support with C Company in reserve. Four minutes after Zero, A Company, led by **Captain Arthur Henderson**, and a platoon of B Company reached the first objective. The remainder of B Company was checked by a machine gun in an isolated copse and, although two

platoons of D Company were sent forward, no progress was made. At 6.20 a.m. A Company continued over the crest to the final objective overlooking Fontaine-lès-Croisilles, where it gained touch with 1st Middlesex on the left and 1/4th Suffolk on the right. Henderson was wounded in the left arm during the initial attack, but had pressed on to the objective and organised the consolidation. However, the inner flanks between 1st Middlesex and 2nd Argyll & Sutherland Highlanders were held up by the same machine gun as B Company.

At 7.45 a.m. two platoons of 4th King's were sent to A Company with ammunition and bombs. At 8.30 a.m. one and a half platoons of C Company were also sent with bombs and ammunition to A Company. A counterattack from the northeast at 10 a.m. succeeded in getting behind the forward companies. 1/4th Suffolk was forced back and lost the Hindenburg Support Line, exposing A Company's right flank. 30th Division on the far left had failed to reach its objectives, resulting in the small enclave being completely exposed on both flanks. At 11 a.m. the Germans succeeded in bombing along a trench leading from the Hindenburg Support Line to the sunken road east of the copse, thus cutting off all communications with the forward troops.

Undaunted by being cut off, Henderson resolved to hold on as long as possible. He led a bayonet charge against one counterattack and was constantly moving around encouraging the men. He was killed later, but not before he had ensured that the position could be held. The 1st Middlesex companies on the left were also surrounded, but fought with great determination and held the position, despite being attacked from three sides simultaneously. They were able to enfilade part of the Hindenburg Line and caused a great nuisance to the Germans.

At 6.24 p.m. a fresh attack was launched by 2nd Royal Welsh Fusiliers, supported by those elements of 1st Middlesex and 2nd Argyll & Sutherland Highlanders not committed to the morning attack. With little time for organisation, the attack failed

Reverse of the previous view looking towards the Sensée valley, with the Hindenburg Support Line on the far right.

and the survivors organised their trench for defence. At 7 p.m. reinforcements arrived.

Next day a German withdrawal in 33rd Division's area was followed up and 19th Brigade relieved 98th Brigade. When 2nd Argyll & Sutherland Highlanders was withdrawn from the line at 7.30 a.m. on the 24th, it had to abandon its cut off A Company. 2nd Royal Welsh Fusiliers sent out patrols and ascertained that A Company was still holding out with some of 1st Middlesex. It was impossible to attempt a withdrawal in daylight, but they managed to pull out at 11.30 p.m. In addition to Henderson's VC, A Company received fifteen other gallantry awards for this isolated action. 2nd Argyll & Sutherland Highlanders suffered 314 casualties out of the total of 926 for 98th Brigade.

In the centre of VII Corps, 30th Division's attack against the high ground overlooking Chérisy failed to reach all of its objectives. On the left, 50th Division attacked with two battalions of 150th Brigade leading, supported by two tanks. At Zero, 1/4th East Yorkshire on the right and 1/4th Yorkshire on the left advanced towards the first objective, supported by 1/5th Yorkshire and 1/5th Durham Light Infantry respectively. 1/4th Yorkshire's boundaries were the railway line on the right and the Cojeul River on the left. The creeping barrage was too slow, resulting in a number of casualties. The German counter-barrage also fell promptly. Officer casualties were particularly heavy and as a result information passed back to HQ 150th Brigade was patchy.

1/4th East Yorkshire met light resistance at first and pushed forward on the right, but was held up on the left by fire from Kestrel Copse. On the right of 1/4th Yorkshire, W Company made slow progress and sustained many casualties from rifle and machine gun fire. The survivors took cover in shell holes fifty metres short of the enemy front line and eventually won the fire fight with the assistance of a tank. They then swept over the enemy trench, taking many prisoners. Z Company on the left had to dig in 135m west of the objective, but in the centre X Company reached the enemy line with fewer casualties than the companies on the flanks. The advance

A Company's position ← A Company, 2nd Argyll & Sutherland Highlanders — Hindenburg Support Line — Copse

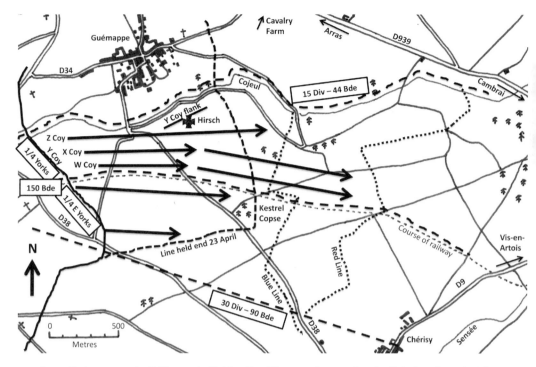

Leave Guémappe on the D38 towards Chérisy. One kilometre after crossing the Cojeul, park on the left at Kestrel Copse. A memorial to David Hirsch at the corner of the copse was missing when visited in October 2015. Although the memorial was placed there, the VC site is out of sight in dead ground some 700m away in the direction of Guémappe. A closer view can be gained from the side of the D38, from the right hand bend 150m after the Cojeul bridge. There is a flat area to park on the north side of the road. Walk round the corner and climb the bank for views along the Cojeul valley to where Philip Hirsch established a secure left flank overlooking the stream and Guémappe. Nowadays trees along the stream obscure most of the view to the north.

continued to the support line which was taken at 5.25 a.m., but the attackers were weakened by casualties and there was no sign of the units on the flanks – 1/4th East Yorkshire on the right and 44th Brigade on the left beyond the Cojeul River. The advance continued a little further and three field guns were taken before a line was dug 100–200m short of the Blue Line (1st objective). Most enemy fire had ceased,

From the Hirsch memorial at the corner of Kestrel Copse alongside the D38. 1/4th Yorkshire advanced across these fields from left to right.

From the D38 road bend just after crossing the Cojeul bridge.

except for a machine gun firing into the left flank from close to Cavalry Farm on the Arras–Cambrai road across the river.

During the early advance Y Company, led by **Captain David Hirsch**, was in support. He was wounded twice and by 6.05 a.m. was the only officer remaining in the Company. At 7.55 a.m. he sent a message saying it was impossible to check the advance of the troops as so many Germans were surrendering and the men were rushing forward to take them. As a result the left flank had become very exposed. When the advance ground to a halt in front of the Blue Line, he set about establishing a defensive flank on the left above and parallel with the River. He moved about the position tirelessly, encouraging the men and remained in full view of the enemy, despite the hail of machine gun bullets being directed at him. He also organised the resistance to a counterattack, again with complete disregard for his own safety. Almost inevitably he was killed and for a period his Company was commanded by Lieutenant Luckhurst, 150th Brigade Light Trench Mortar Battery.

The line was extended on the right by A Company, 1/5th Durham Light Infantry, but this flank remained in the air. The enemy was seen massing for further counterattacks in the Cojeul valley, in front of Vis-en-Artois and from the right rear. As a result it was decided to withdraw and the move back was conducted skilfully by the junior NCOs. By 8.10 a.m. the Battalion was back on its start line. By 11.30 a.m. the whole of 150th Brigade was back on its start line, having lacked support on either flank.

Another attack was launched at 6 p.m. by 1/5th Border on the right and 1/9th Durham Light Infantry on the left, both provided by 151st Brigade. They were supported by 150th Brigade's support battalions, 1/5th Yorkshire and 1/5th Durham Light Infantry respectively. Three minutes later the German barrage fell. The attack made progress, as did the brigade on the left and prisoners were soon streaming back, but the brigade on the right was held up on its left. The 151st/150th Brigade attack carried all the objectives except on the left. At 8.30 a.m. command of the sector passed from HQ 150th to HQ 151st Brigade. The Battalion HQs of 1/4th East Yorkshire and 1/4th Yorkshire were ordered to pull back and the remnants of these battalions came under 1/8th Durham Light Infantry. By the time 150th Brigade had been fully relieved, it had suffered 1,184 casualties. 1/4th Yorkshire had fifty-three killed, 185 wounded and 125 more were missing.

By the end of 24th April, VII Corps had reached the Blue Line, with 33rd and 30th Divisions advancing 1,350m and 50th Division up to 1,600m. Further north, VI, XVII and XIII (First Army) Corps had some success after very hard and difficult fighting, but overall the results were disappointing. Third Army suffered over 8,000 casualties.

Battle of Arleux

28th/29th April 1917

205 2Lt Reginald Haine, 1st Honourable Artillery Company (190th Brigade, 63rd Division), Gavrelle, France

206 2Lt Alfred Pollard, 1st Honourable Artillery Company (190th Brigade, 63rd Division), Gavrelle, France

207 Cpl James Welch, 1st Royal Berkshire (99th Brigade, 2nd Division), Oppy, France

The French Nivelle offensive on the Aisne was not going well at the end of April 1917. The British had subordinated their desire to attack at Ypres in order to support the French, and it was a blow to learn that their efforts at Arras had been largely wasted. However, as long as the French continued to attack, the British had to support them. The next phase at Arras was an attack by First and Third Armies on 28th April.

First Army's objectives were Arleux (Canadian Corps) and Oppy (XIII Corps), while to the south XVII Corps moved against Greenland Hill. It is XIII Corps' part in this attack that is of particular interest. On the right at Gavrelle, 63rd Division was to create a secure flank for 2nd Division on the left as it attacked Oppy. 63rd Division had previously attacked in this area on 23rd April. Although the left had been held up by uncut wire and the final objective was not reached, Gavrelle was seized. However, the failure of flanking formations to keep up had resulted in a dangerous salient.

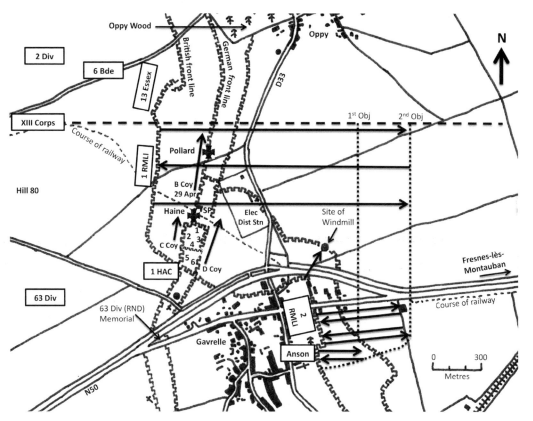

The whole area involved in 1st Honourable Artillery Company's action on 28th/29th April 1917 is now covered in a confusion of electricity distribution lines. Without wading through ploughed fields or standing crops it is difficult to get anywhere near the site of the strongpoint and there are no traces of the former railway line. There are two vantage points from which to gain a reasonable view of the scene of the action. Leave Gavrelle northwards on the D33 towards Oppy. Pass the electricity distribution station on the left and 150m beyond turn left on to a single-track road. Drive along it for 250m until in line with the western fence of the distribution station. This is where the German front line trench cleared by Pollard crossed the road. Look south-southwest towards an overgrown water tower on the D49. This is the line of the German trench and Haine's and Pollard's parties attacked towards your position. The strongpoint was 275m from where you stand, in line with the water tower. Look in the other direction towards Oppy Wood. Pollard advanced another 160m along this line. Continue to the end of the track and turn left on the D49 for 700m to the overgrown water tower. Just after it on the opposite side of the road is a turning where you can park. Walk round the perimeter of the water tower to the north side to gain the opposite view towards Oppy Wood. Due to the shape of the ground, there is less to see from this perspective. The small trenches mentioned are indicated on the map as follows – 1 = Foggy, 2 = Fabric, 3 = Flurry, 4 = Folly, 5 = Falcon and 6 = Flabby. There is a café and a restaurant at the crossroads in the centre of Gavrelle.

The 63rd Division attack, at 4.25 a.m. on 28th April, was made by two battalions of 188th Brigade, 1st and 2nd Royal Marine Light Infantry. They were to cover the right flank of 2nd Division's advance to the north and were supported by two battalions of 190th Brigade, 1st Honourable Artillery Company in support and 10th Royal Dublin Fusiliers as carriers.

On the left, patrols of 1st Royal Marine Light Infantry ominously found that the enemy wire was uncut. As it moved to take up its assault positions, the tapes could not found, so it aligned itself with 13th Essex (6th Brigade, 2nd Division) to the north. Falcon, Folly and Flabby trenches were temporarily abandoned to allow the artillery more freedom in cutting the enemy wire. These trenches were to be reoccupied immediately the barrage lifted at Zero by 1st Honourable Artillery Company. During this time trench mortars and rifle grenades were to be directed on Foggy Trench to prevent the enemy from taking advantage and gaining footholds in Fabric and Flurry. Casualties from shelling were suffered during the night.

When the attack started the Battalion came under enfilade fire from a strongpoint just north of the railway that had not been captured on the 23rd. The advance began to break down immediately and with very heavy losses. At 6.30 a.m. 1st Honourable Artillery Company was ordered to attack northwards along the German trenches to seize the strongpoint, link up with 1st Royal Marine Light Infantry and allow its advance to continue. Not making provision to attack the strongpoint earlier was a serious flaw in the plan, particularly as it had been partly responsible for the failure of the attack on 23rd April. To the north, 6th Brigade had taken the first two objectives, but there was no contact with 1st Royal Marine Light Infantry and a defensive flank was established facing south.

C Company, 1st Honourable Artillery Company, commanded by **Second Lieutenant Reginald Haine**, was tasked was to bomb northwards to seize the strongpoint north of the railway. Covered by a trench mortar bombardment, Haine advanced along the trench from the south and then dashed thirty metres over open ground to the strongpoint. At the same time, D Company attacked along the German support line. Just after 7 a.m. Flabby and Flurry Trenches were cleared, but there was no sign of 1st Royal Marine Light Infantry.

Haine led three attacks against the strongpoint, but it held out and he suffered heavy casualties. He decided to pause while a trench mortar was brought up. Meanwhile D Company bombed up the support line to a position north of the strongpoint, from where it could support C Company, and 6th Brigade attempted to

From the middle of no man's land looking towards the German lines, with Oppy on the left and Gavrelle on the right.

bomb southwards to link up. Without waiting for the mortar, Haine attacked again at 8.50 a.m. This time he took the strongpoint along with fifty prisoners and two machine guns. 188th Brigade's war diary states that the advance was then continued 460m northwards from the railway, presumably to the northern brigade boundary. Haine's force was pushed back by a counterattack at 10 a.m. and the strongpoint was lost. Haine fell back to the south of the railway line where he organised the defence and manned a block against no fewer than seven separate counterattacks that continued into the night.

It seems that the leading waves of 1st Royal Marine Light Infantry had managed to get through the largely intact wire and, despite suffering horrific casualties, some had reached the second objective. However, there they were met with a massive counterattack from the north from the direction of Oppy Wood. The right of 6th Brigade was overwhelmed, as were the few survivors of 1st Royal Marine Light Infantry. By the time Haine seized the strongpoint at around 9 a.m., it was too late for 1st Royal Marine Light Infantry. To all intents and purposes the Battalion had been wiped out as a fighting unit suffering more than 500 casualties. The survivors fell back to the start line, joined Haine's party or took shelter in shell holes.

By 10.20 a.m. the Germans were reported to be west of the British front line. The attack in this area had been turned into a desperate defensive battle. By 12.30 p.m. 1st Honourable Artillery Company had formed a defensive flank around Folly Trench. The Howe Battalion was moved to Hill 80 behind 1st Royal Marine Light Infantry's start positions to prevent a German break-in and 14th Worcestershire (Pioneers) was moved forward to plug gaps in the line. Gradually the front was stabilised. Occasionally flares were seen, fired by isolated parties of 1st Royal Marine Light Infantry, but these petered out as they were overcome.

2nd Royal Marine Light Infantry on the right advanced eastwards with C Company, Anson Battalion, on the right. The rest of the Anson Battalion was to follow later to form strongpoints. The wire was uncut except for one gap through which 2nd Royal Marine Light Infantry streamed. At 5 a.m., C Company, Anson Battalion, set off and was halted by fire from a strongpoint near the Gavrelle–Fresnes road, but this was overcome by 2nd Royal Marine Light Infantry. The Windmill and first objective were taken. The attack pressed on towards the final objective, but the Battalion was

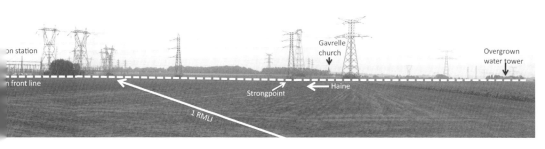

under heavy fire from both flanks. C Company, Anson Battalion, was still under heavy fire and the enemy to its front actually advanced 100m. Another Anson company was sent forward, but the situation remained uncertain and the Anson companies were not in contact with 2nd Royal Marine Light Infantry. However, the latter secured all its objectives by 7.25 a.m., albeit with heavy casualties and with no sign of 1st Royal Marine Light Infantry on the left. The Anson companies were still struggling to secure the right flank and were incurring many casualties. At 10 a.m. the CO withdraw them. This left 2nd Royal Marine Light Infantry in a deep salient without support on either flank. At 10.10 a.m. counterattacks commenced in increasing strength against the forward companies (A, C and D), while B Company had been unable to get through the gap in the wire and consolidated in the German front line. By 11.30 a.m. the three forward companies were isolated, but the Windmill was held and prisoners were sent back. Initially the German counterattacks were halted or forced back by the artillery, but gradually they gained the upper hand and many groups of Royal Marines were forced to surrender. The last German attack at 8.30 p.m. was beaten off with the help of the artillery and the line stabilised a little. 2nd Royal Marine Light Infantry suffered almost 600 casualties and at the end of the day only held the Windmill.

Without flank protection 2nd Division's attack stood little chance of success. It had to break through the Oppy Line, fight through the tangle of Oppy Wood and then take the village. The attack was carried out by 5th and 6th Brigades on the left and right respectively. The village was reached by elements of 6th Brigade, but by evening the Germans had pushed them back to their start line. 5th Brigade was successful on its left, where it benefited from the successful Canadian attack on Arleux, but it was forced back on the right. 99th Brigade began to take over from 6th Brigade on the right at 4.55 p.m.

Both divisions attacked again at 4 a.m. on the 29th. 63rd Division's attack was made under 188th Brigade, delivered by a composite battalion of 190th Brigade (7th Royal Fusiliers and 4th Bedfordshire) under Lieutenant Colonel John Collings-Wells (awarded the DSO for this action and the VC in March 1918). It reached its objectives, but was immediately pushed back by a counterattack.

The opposite view from the overgrown water tower is not as extensive due to the shape of the ground.

At the same time as the renewed general attack, Colonel Charles Fortscue Osmond, CO 1st Honourable Artillery Company, ordered Haine to attack the strongpoint again. Haine suggested that Pollard and B Company might take it on as they had been rested the previous day, but the CO said, *Bill, I dare not risk it.* So C Company had to attack again. A German with a bandage around his head started running away in front. Haine stopped his men opening fire and the German ran back to the strongpoint. This seemed to cause a panic as fifty Prussians surrendered. By 7.15 a.m. Haine and the remnants of C Company had recaptured the strongpoint taken and lost the previous day.

B Company, under **Lieutenant Alfred Pollard**, passed through and established itself in trenches in front of the strongpoint, allowing C Company a breathing space in which to consolidate the position. A little later a strong German bombing party was seen approaching from the north and the Germans opened a furious barrage all the way along the line south of Oppy Wood. Men from 188th Brigade began to fall back and Pollard helped the other officers to rally them, while B Company maintained its support positions behind. He deployed some of the rallied Royal Marines in shell holes either side of the trench and told them to fire at anything in order to help rebuild their will to resist. Satisfied that the line would hold, Pollard went to investigate, accompanied by two bombers, 4208 Private Reginald Hughesdon (also his runner) and 3850 Lance Corporal Victor Goodwin Scharlach, plus L/12179 Lance Corporal John McCarthy, 13th Royal Fusiliers.

Pollard established a simple system for clearing the trench. He would move from traverse to traverse and when his companions heard his pistol, they were to pitch two grenades fifteen metres forward into the next traverse. They covered 200m with no sign of the enemy, but coming round the next traverse Pollard encountered and shot a German. Two grenades went over and another German appeared. Pollard shot him too, causing the last two grenades to be thrown, but by then the enemy survivors had fled. To keep them from reorganising, Pollard dashed after them until he reached a portion of trench blown in by a shell. Here he posted McCarthy armed with seven fully loaded German and British rifles, while the rest of the party went off to find some German bombs.

Ten minutes later the Germans were back and grenades were soon flying in both directions. Pollard's party picked up those thrown by the Germans and tossed

Gavrelle

D49   N50

them back over the parapet before their longer fuses exploded. Pollard threw off his helmet and gas mask carrier in order to throw more easily. When the party had only six bombs remaining, the enemy once again pulled back. A few minutes later the second-in-command (Lieutenant Ernest Lambert Samuel) brought up the rest of B Company and a supply of bombs. Lewis guns were established fifty metres out on each flank. Rifle grenadiers (including Scharlach) were positioned to engage at fifty and one hundred metres while Pollard and Hughenden stood ready to throw more hand grenades. In the face of these dispositions, the next attack was beaten back easily. About 275m of trench was cleared to the north and contact made with Lieutenant Stanley Ferns Jeffcoat's party of 22nd Royal Fusiliers (99th Brigade, 2nd Division). Once the line had been secured, Pollard brought up the troops who had lost it, before pulling his men back. When the Battalion was relieved that night it was holding 1,800m of trench with only 120 men. In addition to Haine's and Pollard's VCs, Hughesdon was awarded the DCM (and MM for a previous event and was commissioned later) and Scharlach and McCarthy the MM. McCarthy was killed either later that day or the next and is commemorated on the Arras Memorial (he had been posted as a deserter in December 1914).

While in Gavrelle a visit can be made to the Royal Naval Division Memorial at the extreme western end of the village. Keep going west along the main street until the road almost runs out and there is a No Entry sign before the N50. The Memorial is on the right where there is space to park, although when backing out take great care of traffic coming off the N50 at speed into Gavrelle. When visited in October 2015 the memorial was run down and in need of some renovation.

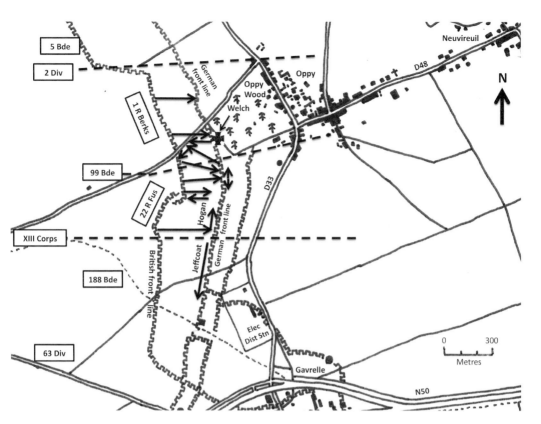

Drive through Oppy northwestwards on the D50. Pass the church on the right and continue 325m. Turn left and continue with Oppy Wood on the left for 750m until the road begins to bend right and there is hardstanding on the left on which to park. Look back towards Oppy Wood. The pylon directly in front, five metres south of the road, is just behind the British front line. The German front line ran from the left corner of the Wood at the roadside to the right up the slope towards the electricity distribution station at Gavrelle. From where you stand, James Welch's VC action was approximately fifty metres this side of the centre of the tree line. There is a path along the edge of the Wood and it is worth walking to the southern tip. Notice the Wood is as thick and impenetrable today as it was in 1917.

In 2nd Division, 5th Brigade and 99th Brigade, left and right respectively, attacked in conjunction with 63rd Division on the right. 99th Brigade's attack was led by 22nd Royal Fusiliers (strength 358) on the right and three companies of 1st Royal Berkshire (strength 240) on the left. A company of 23rd Royal Fusiliers was in support and the remainder of that Battalion was in reserve. Two parties, each of an officer and fifty men of 1st King's Royal Rifle Corps, acted as carriers for the leading battalions. The Brigade had forty-six machine guns of its own and 6th, 92nd and 94th Brigade Machine Gun Companies in support.

99th Brigade took over the line from 6th Brigade during the night and a strongpoint was established on the right in case 63rd Division's attack failed. Shortly before Zero some of the forward dumps of ammunition, bombs and water were destroyed by German shellfire and this affected the outcome later.

The wire in front of 22nd Royal Fusiliers was largely intact, particularly in front of its right company. It was held up, the barrage moved on and many men were lost to small arms fire. However, against the odds, the platoon on the right under Lieutenant Stanley Jeffcoat broke into the forward German trench and killed or captured the garrison before bombing north and south along the trench. The Germans to the south resisted strongly all the way, but after 360m Jeffcoat made contact with the right of 63rd Division. Meanwhile CSM Hogan had bombed northwards from Jeffcoat's (mortally wounded later – Roclincourt Military Cemetery II B 17 and Mentioned in Despatches) entry point and established a block there until forced back by repeated counterattacks when grenades ran out. The left company of 22nd Royal Fusiliers was shot down in front of the wire. However, the left platoon did get through the wire and bombed north and south along the trench. A block was established on the right and contact was made with 1st Royal Berkshire on the left. The 1st King's Royal Rifle Corps detachment dug in to form a defensive right flank, while a company of 23rd Royal Fusiliers garrisoned the old British front line on the right flank. Another company of 23rd Royal Fusiliers was sent up to support both leading battalions. It bombed north along the Oppy Line and recaptured it up to 200m south of Oppy Wood, forming a block there.

The wire in front of 1st Royal Berkshire was generally well cut except on the far right. The creeping barrage was effective, but it did not neutralise three machine guns in the west corner of Oppy Wood. Fortunately their fire was mainly high and did little damage. The German front line (Oppy Trench) was reached at 4.15 a.m. and found to be heavily damaged and so it offered little protection. While it was being consolidated, snipers entered the Wood and captured the three machine guns, which were put to good use. Both flanks were open except for a small party of 22nd Royal Fusiliers on the right. There was also a 200m gap before 5th Brigade on the left.

During the initial attack **Corporal James Welch** in B Company reached the enemy trench where a German attacked him with a dagger, cutting open Welch's

From the British front line on the Oppy–Bailleul-Sir-Berthoult road (no longer sunken) looking in the direction of 1st Royal Berkshire's attack on 29th April.

tunic. Welch shot the German with his revolver and took his dagger. He then set up his Lewis gun on a high point to support C Company on the left, which was held up by machine guns. He held off a counterattack and this allowed C Company to gain the German front line. By then his gun team of six had been reduced to himself and Private Walker. Then, armed with just his revolver, he chased four German snipers about 100m away, firing after them as he advanced. He eventually captured them, but by then his revolver was empty. Having brought them in under heavy shellfire, he handed over the prisoners and returned to his Lewis gun, which Walker had manned in his absence.

The Germans launched a second counterattack and entered the captured trench on the right. Welch was ordered to search for ammunition and spare parts to keep the Lewis guns in action. While engaged in this work under heavy fire, he was wounded for a second time, this time in the cheek. His Company was in danger so he took up a position where he was able to fire along the trench to the right. The German counterattack penetrated for about 100 metres, but was bombed back again. During the third German counterattack, Welch went to the left of Oppy Wood and took up position on some higher ground. He had to keep going out to collect ammunition and spare parts and Walker was wounded. Although alone, Welch kept the Lewis gun in action under very heavy short-range fire. He was hit by a piece of shell, but kept firing until exhausted through loss of blood. After five hours he had to hand over the Lewis gun to a comrade and left the firing line.

Between 5 a.m. and 9.30 a.m. five counterattacks were launched against the right of the Battalion. The enemy suffered devastating losses and the first four attacks were pushed back, but A and B Companies were very exposed, holding 450m of front and their strength had been reduced to about thirty-five men each. The supply of bombs ran out during the fifth counterattack and A and B Companies were forced to withdraw to the sunken road running southwest from the west corner of Oppy Wood. However, a German grenade dump was found and they were able to go forward again to regain the lost ground. A defensive flank was formed along the sunken lane. The combined strength of A and B Companies was then down to

Reverse of the previous view from the German front line.

thirty-five men. On the other side of the sunken lane, C and D Companies were also down to about the same number and were forced to move north along the trench, taking their wounded and the three captured machine guns with them. They joined hands with 5th Brigade and came under command of 17th Royal Fusiliers. A block was established and the three enemy machine guns were set up. The Germans shelled these positions for the rest of the day.

The rest of 1st Royal Berkshire in the sunken road then had its left flank in the air. With ammunition and grenades running low, it retired to the start point around 10 a.m. The Battalion was relieved at 11 p.m. by 13th East Yorkshire, bringing out seventy prisoners and the three machine guns. In view of the small numbers involved, casualties were heavy, a total of 158 (sixteen killed, ninety-three wounded and forty-nine missing). CWGC records fifty-three fatalities in 1st Royal Berkshire in the period 28th–30th April. Fighting throughout the area eventually died down. The German strength had been seriously underestimated and the few gains were not worth the losses involved. 99th Brigade had 414 casualties in this action, but on the other hand it had captured ninety-three prisoners and estimated it had killed over 500 other Germans.

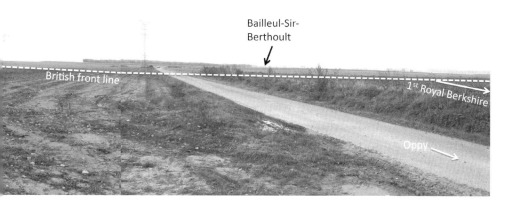

Third Battle of the Scarpe and Subsequent Capture of Roeux
3rd May 1917

208 Cpl George Jarratt, 8th Royal Fusiliers (36th Brigade, 12th Division), near Pelves, France
209 2Lt John Harrison, 11th East Yorkshire (92nd Brigade, 31st Division), Oppy, France
210 Lt Robert Combe, 27th Battalion CEF (6th Canadian Brigade, 2nd Canadian Division), Acheville, France

By early May 1917 it was clear that the French Nivelle offensive was going to fail. Haig wanted to switch British attention to Flanders; but he could not disengage from Arras immediately as the French were to make another attempt on 4th May. However, with little prospect of the French joining him on his right flank, he realised that Cambrai could no longer be reached. His priorities therefore changed to establishing a firm defensive line from which he could launch small surprise attacks to pin the Germans down before launching the Flanders offensive later in the year.

Meanwhile, to assist the French, he ordered a supporting attack be launched at 3.45 a.m. on 3rd May on a frontage of twenty-two kilometres by Fifth, Third and First Armies. The Fifth Army attack by I ANZAC Corps at Bullecourt, which lasted two weeks, is described later in the book. It was hoped that adding this second prong to the assault would force the Germans to retreat further eastwards. In the event, neither attack made a significant advance.

Some commanders wanted to attack in the dark, but others did not feel their troops were up to such a challenge and wanted Zero hour to be in daylight. A compromise was reached that pleased no one. Zero would be at 3.45 a.m., effectively a night attack in the early stages, as sunrise was not until 5.22 a.m. The timing of

Zero did not reach the assault troops until very late in their preparations. Assuming it would be a daylight assault, no arrangements to maintain direction had been made such as guiding markers, accurate compass bearings and intermediate objectives. To add to the difficulties, the moon was due to set behind the assaulting troops sixteen minutes before Zero, thus silhouetting them against the skyline and making them easier targets.

All three Corps of Third Army took part. VII Corps on the right attacked southeast in conjunction with Fifth Army's attack northwards. There was much confusion in the dark, compounded by the very heavy and accurate German artillery response. A returning tank resulted in an order to retire and by the time the mess was sorted out the barrage had been lost. Some gains were made as the Germans willingly sacrificed limited areas of ground, but all were subsequently lost because supports could not get up in time to counter heavy German counterattacks.

VI Corps in the centre attacked with three divisions; from the right, 56th, 3rd and 12th Divisions. All had been involved in the first stages of the Arras offensive. 56th Division made a few gains, some of which were held until the early hours of 4th May, but all were subsequently lost. 3rd Division had been in the line for ten days and had suffered 464 casualties just holding the line in the very active sector around Monchy. The Germans clearly knew the attack was coming as just prior to Zero their artillery fired gas and high explosives along the attack frontage. British batteries were deluged with gas, but continued the barrage wearing respirators. The infantry too had to assemble in their respirators. 9th Brigade on the left made some progress, but could not continue due to the failure of 8th Brigade on its right and 12th Division on its left. The German artillery fire was so intense that the reserve battalions of 9th Brigade suffered 350 casualties and never crossed the British front line.

On the left of VI Corps, 12th Division was to form a protective left flank for 3rd Division, but its final objective in Pelves was not to be attacked until Roeux, in the XVII Corps area to the north, had fallen. It was to reach a line running northwest from Keeling Copse (Brown Line) and await orders. Meanwhile Pelves was to be bombarded with 15″ Guns and 12″ Howitzers while 6″ Guns kept Boiry and Vis-en-Artois under fire all day. 3rd Special Company RE was attached to lay a smoke screen along the Scarpe on the left flank with its 4″ Stokes mortars. The attack was made by two battalions each of 37th Brigade and 36th Brigade on the right and left respectively. 37th Brigade's leading battalions were cut off by a counterattack behind them and few escaped. After dark another attack also failed.

36th Brigade's objectives were Rifle and Scabbard Trenches. It was led by 8th and 9th Royal Fusiliers, left and right respectively. C Company on the left and B Company on the right led 8th Royal Fusiliers' assault. Two platoons of D Company were detailed to mop up Scabbard Trench and another platoon was allocated for Pelves Lane and to form a strongpoint to protect the Battalion's left flank. A Company was in reserve.

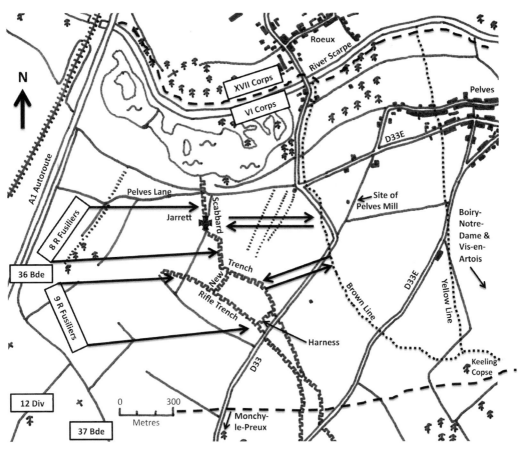

Leave Monchy-le-Preux on the D33, the westernmost of the two roads to Pelves. After just over a kilometre the road sweeps around a left bend. 300m later at the crossroads turn left into the start of a track. Park at this junction and walk west along the track for 500m until reaching another track running off to the left (south). Walk up the hill for 160m then turn round. This is the point where Scabbard Trench crossed the track from the left (west) side. When there are no crops the outline of the trench line can be seen as a lighter chalky band. It was somewhere along this trench that George Jarratt saved his comrades.

The first objective, the Brown Line, was taken by 10 a.m. despite heavy flanking fire from Roeux, where XVII Corps' attack had failed. This fire caused much damage to the second wave and the moppers-up. At the Brown Line the assault troops waited for orders to continue the advance and encountered strong enemy bombing parties counterattacking along the Scarpe. The Brigade was pushed out of Scabbard Trench and some men were surrounded, cut off and taken prisoner in the confusion. A bombing stop established at the junction of New and Scabbard Trenches held the enemy.

At 12.10 p.m. two companies of 7th Royal Sussex succeeded in gaining a lodgement in Scabbard Trench after a bombardment of ten minutes. Forty-five prisoners were taken, but no further advance was possible in daylight. During the consolidation of the German front line, the bombers threw grenades into each dugout to winkle

This is the point where Scabbard Trench crossed the track leading south from Pelves Lane.

out any enemy surviving below. **Corporal George Jarratt** of 8th Royal Fusiliers had been taken prisoner during the initial assault in the morning. He was in one of the dugouts with a number of the wounded when a grenade came through the entrance. Without hesitation he jumped on top of it with both feet to protect the others. The grenade blew off both of his legs, but his bravery saved everyone else. He died before he could be evacuated to an aid station. Jarratt's VC is unusual as it was awarded for actions resulting from an assault by British, not enemy, troops.

At 9.45 p.m. 9th Royal Fusiliers made another attempt and reached the Brown Line, but lack of support on the right and heavy fire forced it to fall back on Scabbard Trench, which at the end of the day was held from the Scarpe to Harness Lane. Despite this setback, 36th Brigade made the only gains in Third Army. 8th Royal Fusiliers was relieved late on 4th May having suffered 282 casualties. The CO, Lieutenant Colonel Neville Elliott-Cooper, was awarded the DSO for this action and went on to win the VC in November 1917.

North of the Scarpe, XVII Corps attacked with two divisions against the by then familiar objectives of Roeux, the chemical works and Greenland Hill. Following previous failures in this area, the artillery fired a lengthy and heavy preparatory bombardment. 4th Division's attack lapsed into confusion in the darkness. Some men reached the first objective and a few even got to the second, but few returned from either. On the left the railway embankment and cutting caused problems and, despite some successes, after dark any survivors made their way back to the start positions. 17th Division suffered similarly and in the confusion there were instances of friendly forces attacking each other. The action of XVII Corps was little short of a disaster.

First Army's attack was preceded by a low level attack by the RFC, shooting down four German observation balloons and damaging the remaining four. By May

1917 the RFC was beginning to overcome its disadvantages with new machines and new tactics, but it would be a long haul.

XIII Corps attacked with two divisions. 31st Division on the right was fresh after a period in reserve, but 2nd Division on the left was much reduced by recent operations. Accordingly, 31st Division took over half of 2nd Division's front in addition to that of the outgoing 63rd Division. As a result, 31st Division's frontage was 3,200m and 2nd Division's only 1,000m. The operation was also complicated by the Germans continuing to hold almost 700m of the Oppy Line west of Oppy Wood.

31st Division faced a difficult task, particularly on its left, where Oppy Wood was a tangled mass of fallen trees, making a considerable obstacle. The artillery in this area was firing at extreme range, so it was reinforced by nine field batteries from 2nd and 63rd Divisions, plus sixteen Vickers machine guns from 63rd Division and eight Hotchkiss guns from XIII Corps Cavalry. 93rd Brigade was on the right and 92nd Brigade on the left.

The three assault battalions of 93rd Brigade managed to reach the final objective in some places, but when 92nd Brigade on the left failed to keep up, strong counterattacks drove it back. Gavrelle Windmill was lost, but recaptured by 18th Durham Light Infantry.

92nd Brigade ran into severe problems. The attack was made by 10th, 11th and 12th East Yorkshire, each deploying three companies in line, with 13th East Yorkshire in reserve providing carrying parties. A combination of the German barrage prior to Zero, the darkness and the black mass of Oppy Wood in front, meant the lifting of the creeping barrage was not noticed immediately. 10th East Yorkshire on the right failed completely.

11th East Yorkshire's task in the centre was to clear the Wood and village plus Oppy Support Trench 350m beyond it. The Battalion crossed a low ridge 900m from the enemy as it moved into its assembly positions, and was silhouetted against

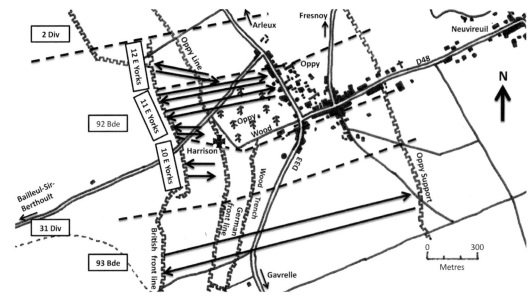

Drive through Oppy northwestwards on the D50. Pass the church on the right and continue 325m. Turn left and continue with Oppy Wood on the left for 750m until the road begins to bend right and there is hardstanding on the left on which to park. Look back towards Oppy Wood. The pylon directly in front, five metres south of the road, is just behind the British front line. The German front line ran from the left corner of the Wood at the roadside to the right up the slope towards the electricity distribution station at Gavrelle. John Harrison was killed 100m from the southern tip (right as you look at it), between the tip and the solid metal pylon. There is a path along the edge of the Wood and it is worth walking to the southern tip. Notice the Wood is as thick and impenetrable today as it was in 1917.

the setting moon. Although it must have been seen, the Germans took no action at that stage, but the assembly positions, in places only 100m from the western edge of Oppy Wood, were bombarded twice before Zero starting at 1.40 a.m.

When the attack got underway the leading companies (from the right B, C and D), kept fifty metres from the creeping barrage, advancing at a rate of 100m every four minutes. However, the darkness, smoke and dust made it impossible

From the Gavrelle–Oppy road looking north over the ground where 11th East Yorkshire attacked on 3rd May 1917.

to distinguish when the barrage had lifted off the enemy front line. Heavy small arms fire was received, but in spite of it B Company on the right surged forward. This attack was repulsed, but undeterred the Company attacked again and was again pushed back. **Second Lieutenant John Harrison** reformed 6 Platoon in no man's land and attacked for a third time, but they made no progress against three belts of wire and a machine gun at the southern tip of the Wood. Harrison ordered his men into shell holes, from where they were to keep the machine gun under rifle and grenade fire. He charged the gun on his own, armed only with a revolver and a Mills bomb. As he threw the grenade, he was hit and fell face down, but it found its mark and the machine gun was silenced. Despite Harrison's heroism, his platoon could still not get forward and spent the rest of the day sheltering in shell holes.

In the centre and left some parties reached the village, but were driven out by counterattacks at 6 a.m. or cut off there. Harrison's remains were never identified; he was one of 269 casualties in the Battalion that day. The survivors were relieved at 10 p.m. by 11th East Lancashire (94th Brigade). 31st Division suffered 1,900 casualties, but by the end of the day had no new ground to show for them. 92nd Brigade's share of the casualties was 810, including 74% of the officers involved in the attack.

On the left of XIII Corps, the exhausted and severely weakened 2nd Division could only muster a composite brigade of four composite battalions with a combined strength of about 1,800. A Battalion was from 5th Brigade, B Battalion from 6th Brigade and C and D Battalions from 99th Brigade. The assembly was delayed by enemy shelling and some companies were not in position at Zero. B Battalion on the right made some progress before being driven back by a counterattack. C Battalion on the left reached its final objective on its left to cover the Canadian Corps as it captured Fresnoy. Counterattacks threatened this tenuous gain and the composite brigade formed a block 350m south of the Division's left boundary, with posts in contact with the Canadians southeast of Fresnoy. It succeeded in holding the attacks, but the cost was high.

Oppy Wood

Oppy

Gavrelle

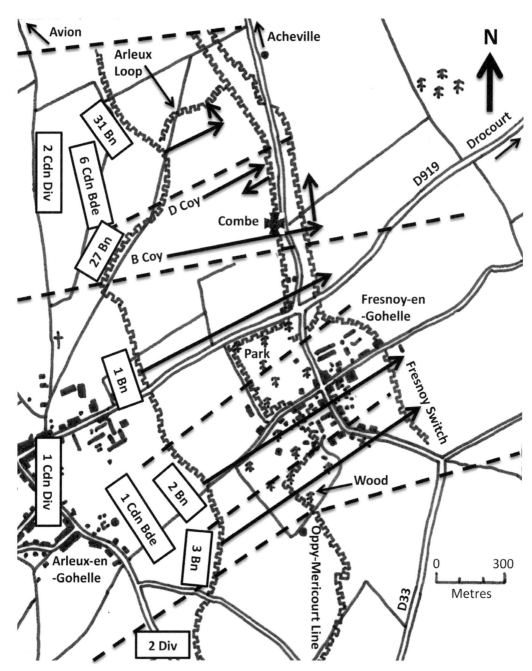

Drive through Fresnoy-en-Gohelle northwards on the D33 towards Acheville. Pass the church on the left and continue 400m to the crossroads with the D919. Go straight over and after 350m turn right onto a single track road. There is enough room to park hard up on one side or the other to allow other vehicles to pass. Face west. Robert Combe secured the German front line trench (Oppy-Mericourt Line) fifty metres on the other side of the road. There is a café back at the crossroads.

The Canadian Corps attacked with 1st and 2nd Canadian Divisions, each with one brigade forward, 1st and 6th Canadian Brigades respectively. The objective included Fresnoy village, Wood and Park. It was essentially a continuation of the successful attack on the Arleux Loop five days before. Although the Germans knew an attack was coming and periodically bombarded the assembly trenches, they did not expect a night assault and surprise was achieved. Despite this, within a minute of Zero, their artillery was laying fire across no man's land, causing losses to the rear waves.

On the right, 1st Brigade attacked with three battalions on a frontage of 1,300m. The gaps cut in the wire by the artillery were hard to find in the dark, but darkness made the German fire less effective. 3rd Battalion overran Fresnoy Wood and captured seventy-five prisoners in dugouts. Soon after 5 a.m. it captured the support trench (Fresnoy Switch) 400m beyond the Wood, but in so doing one company was reduced to just twenty-five men. 2nd Battalion made similar progress in overcoming initial resistance. Three machine guns in Fresnoy were outflanked and put out of action, allowing the advance by two companies to pass through the village where there was little opposition. The final objective 550m beyond, was reached about 4.30 a.m. and over 200 Germans surrendered. 1st Battalion attacked astride the Drocourt road on the northern boundary of Fresnoy Park. The left reached the final objective in the support trench by 4.50 a.m.

On the left, 6th Canadian Brigade on a frontage of 825m had the complicated task of also forming a strong left flank facing northeast. It was to capture the network of trenches at the junction of the old Arleux Loop with the Oppy–Méricourt Line 450m south of Acheville. The attack was led by 27th Battalion on the right and 31st Battalion on the left, with 28th Battalion in support and 29th Battalion in reserve. The wire had not been well cut and the barrage was ragged. The German artillery retaliated quickly and intensely when the attack started, including enfilade fire from batteries near Avion. As a result the creeping barrage was lost.

27th Battalion had 600m of open ground to cross to reach the German front line. D Company on the left gained it quickly, but the moppers–up got lost. With no one on either flank, the company commander ordered his men to about turn and attack back over their gains to clear the Germans in the front line from the rear as they emerged from their dugouts. Thirty prisoners were taken and the survivors were driven towards the Canadian lines. D Company then had to dig in short of its first objective.

B Company on the right was stopped in front of the front trench by the enemy barrage. A handful of men under **Lieutenant Robert Combe** managed to get to the objective. It was due to his magnificent courage that the position was carried, secured and held. Using enemy grenades when their supplies ran out, they captured 235m of trench to the left and took eighty to a hundred prisoners. Contact was also made with 1st Battalion (1st Canadian Brigade) on the right. Just as C Company in support managed to get round on the right, Combe was killed. A Company in

From just behind the German front line at the point where Robert Combe led B Company into it.

reserve reached the enemy wire, where it was planned to consolidate, but it was later filtered forward into the forward gains to reinforce B Company, which was down to six men plus the survivors of two sections of machine guns and a section of trench mortars. C Company cleared another 135m of trench, formed a block and helped consolidate the position. The German support trench was found to be unoccupied and a Lewis gun was set up there soon after sunrise, but 200m of the objective were not taken. The captured section was blocked at its northern end while arrangements were made to make contact with 31st Battalion on the left. A counterattack was broken up by the artillery and after dark 29th Battalion helped 27th Battalion to extend its hold on the support trench. The action cost 27th Battalion 267 casualties.

31st Battalion on the left faced a recently dug trench about halfway to the German front line. It was not occupied by night but the wire in front was intact. On reaching the wire the first waves were swept by enfilade fire from the trench junction to the north. The attack split, with some following the new trench northwards into the old

Reverse of the previous view, looking along the axis of 27th Battalion's advance.

Arleux Loop Trench where machine guns caused heavy losses and halted further movement. Others reached the German front line, but were isolated and unable to secure it. The new German trench was occupied and a block was established in the Arleux Loop Trench where the new trench joined it. Touch was gained with 27th Battalion on the right and a 360m long connecting trench was dug after dark.

About 10.30 a.m. the Germans were seen about 700m away preparing to counterattack. When they advanced the Canadians were ready. Small arms and artillery fire inflicted heavy losses, breaking up the attack, and only one small party got to within 200m of the Canadian positions. They tried again in the afternoon with the same result, but attempts by both battalions to bomb forward were held up. German artillery and machine gun fire remained a problem for the rest of the day. By 6.05 a.m. on 4th May, 27th and 31st Battalions had been relieved by 28th and 29th Battalions. A plan to complete the seizure of the original objectives was ruined when the German artillery knocked out much of the supporting field artillery. An attempt in the evening to bomb into the honeycomb of trenches was only partly successful. 29th Battalion gained the rest of 31st Battalion's objective, but on the right 28th Battalion was held and suffered heavy casualties. That night an assembly

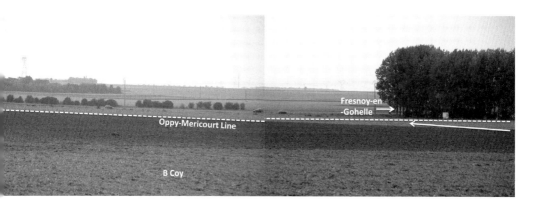

trench was dug preparatory to another attack on 5th May, but it was concluded that possession of the honeycomb would not improve observation and the attack was cancelled.

Fresnoy was another success for the Canadians, coming a month after seizing Vimy Ridge. However, the cost was high, with 1,474 casualties. Without this success and that of 36th Brigade south of the Scarpe, the Third Battle of the Scarpe would have been a complete failure. As it was, there was little to show for the sacrifices involved.

6th May 1917

212 Pte Michael Heaviside, 15th Durham Light Infantry (64th Brigade, 21st Division), near Fontaine-lès-Croisilles, France

During the offensive on 3rd May 1917 (Third Battle of the Scarpe), 21st Division had been on the right of both VII Corps and Third Army. In 64th Brigade, in the centre, 15th Durham Light Infantry attacked with one company leading in both the Hindenburg Line front and support trenches. They immediately ran into heavy enemy artillery fire, resulting in heavy casualties. On the left, the support trench company was held by machine guns and barbed wire blocks, despite fourteen attempts to get through. A tank allocated to this attack turned up an hour late and was then subjected to heavy trench mortar fire, which crippled the tank and forced the supporting infantry into cover. An attempt by nine men, including the company commander, to get over the enemy block in the trench resulted in seven men being knocked out by a shell. The attack on the front line resulted in all the officers being lost and was also halted. Two platoons of 10th King's Own Yorkshire Light Infantry went forward to reinforce this attack, but made little difference.

A little later an attack across the open by the left and support companies was stopped by a belt of uncut wire. In the afternoon the Battalion was relieved by 1st

From 15th Durham Light Infantry's front line. The two assault companies each used one of the Hindenburg Line trenches as its axis. Michael Heaviside's VC action was in the field in the foreground between the British and German front lines.

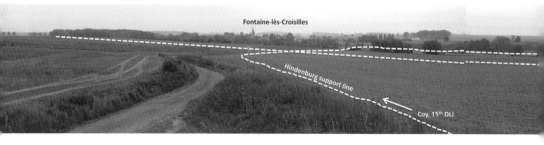

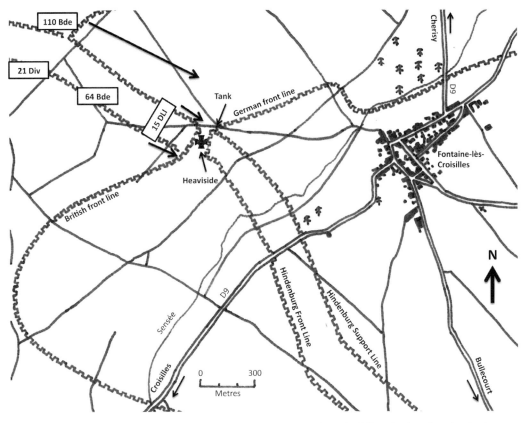

Enter Fontaine-lès-Croiselles along the D9 from the southwest from Croisilles. At the t-junction in the village turn left and after 100m go straight on, being aware of traffic on the priority route from the right. Follow the road round to the left for 1,100m almost to the crest of the hill, where there is some hard standing on the left on which to park just after a track junction. Look towards Fontaine-lès-Croisilles. At this point the Hindenburg support line hugged the road you have just driven along eastwards for 200m and then swung round to the south. The Hindenburg front line ran parallel with it about 250m to the south. Michael Heaviside's brave rescue occurred somewhere in the open ground before you.

East Yorkshire with nothing to show for its efforts except 124 casualties. It withdrew to the trenches in the Hindenburg Line that it had held on the morning of 2nd May. On the evening of 5th May, the Battalion went back into the trenches it had attacked on the 3rd to man the barricades. The enemy was only 100m away and snipers and machine guns were very active on both sides.

At 2 p.m. on 6th May a man was seen waving a water bottle from a shell hole about forty metres from the German lines. It was assumed that he was wounded, but it was impossible to send a stretcher party out in daylight. Despite the danger, one of the stretcher bearers, **Private Michael Heaviside**, volunteered to take food and water to the man. As he crawled over the parapet, Heaviside became the focus of attention for all the enemy snipers and machine gunners. By making intelligent use of the ground and the numerous shell holes he reached the man, who had lain in the shell hole for almost four days and three nights. He was almost demented with thirst and Heaviside's water almost certainly saved his life. After dark Heaviside returned to the British lines and guided a rescue party to recover the wounded man.

12th May 1917

214 Pte Tom Dresser, 7th Yorkshire (Green Howards) (50th Brigade, 17th Division), near Roeux, France

When the French acknowledged their inability to continue the Nivelle offensive, the roles of the two nation's armies were reversed, with the British increasingly taking the lead. Operations continued around Arras while reserves were moved north in preparation for the attack on Messines Ridge. The change in emphasis made the task of Third and First Armies at Arras even more difficult as they tried to maintain pressure on the Germans with exhausted troops and a diminishing amount of artillery.

Of necessity the Arras operations were limited. One small action began with a 4th Division attack on the evening of 11th May against the chemical factory, cemetery, chateau and station at Roeux. Previous attacks had failed due to being launched at dawn, as expected, with insufficient artillery preparation and too great a distance between objectives. On this occasion XVII Corps' artillery was in support, while the VI and XIII Corps artillery on either flank extended the barrage to help mask the objective from the enemy. The assault troops remained hidden in trenches throughout the day. Despite being weak from constant fighting (less than 2,500 bayonets were available for this attack), the troops followed the barrage closely at Zero (7.30 p.m.). It was the thickest they had ever known. The attack was a complete success.

At 6.30 a.m. next day the attack was continued by the left of 4th Division (11th Brigade) and 17th Division on the left. 4th Division was again completely successful, but suffered a total of 539 casualties over the two days. 17th Division attacked with 50th Brigade on the right north of the Arras–Douai railway and 52nd Brigade on the left, supported by nine field artillery brigades. Early in the day a German aircraft flew over 52nd Brigade and it seems likely that the troops were spotted, for when the attack began this area was bombarded heavily. Only a few gains were made and were retaken by the Germans within twenty minutes.

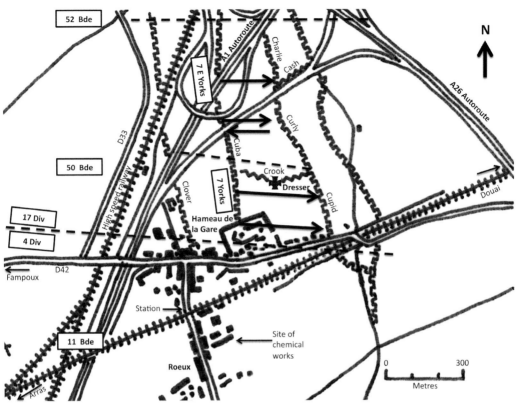

Pass through Roeux northwards on the D33. Cross the railway and take the next right after 200m on the D42. After 675m, just before the railway crossing, turn left onto a track running northwards. Park here and walk along the track for 300m. About 130m to the west of this point is where Tom Dresser delivered his message at the junction of Cupid, Curly and Crook Trenches.

50th Brigade attacked with 7th Yorkshire on the right and 7th East Yorkshire on the left, with 10th West Yorkshire in support. Two companies of 6th Dorset were in reserve, the other two companies being attached to 4th Division.

7th East Yorkshire's objective was Charlie Trench and part of Curly Trench. It got to Charlie on the left, but the centre and right were held by heavy fire from Curly and did not reach their objective. On the left flank, 52nd Brigade did not get forward, so the left of 7th East Yorkshire was isolated, with both flanks open and exposed. It was heavily bombed and had to withdraw to the original front line, but occupied part of Cash. Later the Battalion tried to rush the northern end of Curly to link up with 7th Yorkshire, but heavy small arms fire stopped it. An officer and twelve men did reach the junction of Curly and Charlie, where a bombing fight took place. None of the party returned.

7th Yorkshire's objective was Cupid Trench from the railway north to the junction with Crook Trench. B and C Companies, right and left respectively, attacked from new assembly trenches running from Crook Trench to the southern end of Cuba Trench. The support companies (A right and D left) started from Clover Trench. The Battalion took Cupid Trench by 7.30 a.m., although it suffered heavily from

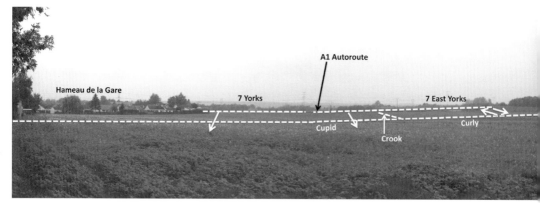

Looking northwest from the track just north of the D42 railway crossing. Tom Dresser's VC action was in the area of Crook Trench.

machine gun fire on the left. Mopping-up parties dealt with Crook and Crow Trenches where some of the garrison put up a stiff fight. The Battalion then tried to bomb north along Cupid Trench into Curly Trench to assist 7th East Yorkshire, which was held up. The fighting then centred on the junction of Cupid and Curly Trenches at the point where Crook Trench ran at right angles to the front line, but it remained no man's land all day. Eventually a bombing party established a block forty metres beyond the junction in Curly Trench on the left of the captured position. A bombing fight developed for possession of the block and it was apparent that the position could not be held indefinitely.

Captain Groom asked for a volunteer to go to Battalion Headquarters to bring up more bombs. **Private Tom Dresser** set off with the vitally important message. It was a bright sunny morning and he had the whole of no man's land to cross, but he managed to cover the open ground and gain the safety of a communications trench. The Germans did little to stop him, even though they had the whole area under observation from balloons. It is possible that they guessed his mission and were waiting for him to return with reinforcements before opening fire.

Dresser delivered his message and was given a reply stating that D Company was to hold onto its gains and reinforcements were on their way. Accompanied by two men laden with Mills bombs, he headed back along the communications trench until he heard the whine of approaching shells and threw himself into a shell hole away from the trench. When the shelling stopped he was surprised to discover that he was unhurt, but the trench had been completely obliterated. He had no option other than to make his way over the open, dodging from shell hole to shell hole. As he neared the British positions he could see the bombing contest in progress, resembling a schoolboy's snowball fight. Enemy bullets got closer as the Germans endeavoured to stop him. He heard an explosion much closer than the others and a terrific blow in his right shoulder flung him to the ground. His helmet was knocked

off, but he managed to reach the cover of a shell hole, where he took off his jacket and used his handkerchief to bandage the wound in his damaged arm. To ensure the message was not lost even if he was killed, Dresser tied it around his neck with his identity disc cord.

Once the wound was dressed he set off again towards the front line. Machine gunners and snipers turned their full attention onto him immediately he broke cover and he was forced to dive flat again. Undeterred he crawled on and as he neared the trench he was hit a glancing blow by a bullet in the jaw and knocked over again. His comrades feared the worst, but were astonished to see Dresser stagger to his feet and, half running and half crawling, continue towards them. He sent the two men with the Mills bombs ahead as they were needed urgently. Hardly noticing a flesh wound in the leg, with a final supreme effort he threw himself over the parapet. Too weak to speak he pointed to the message around his neck. Sergeant Major Elliott managed to give him a drink before he blacked out. Later Dresser joked he knew he had done well as sergeant majors seldom performed such acts of kindness for private soldiers. The reinforcements eventually arrived and the situation was saved.

Another attempt was made to take Curly Trench at 2.30 a.m. next day. The Germans kept the area illuminated with Very lights and the attackers were driven back by small arms fire. Bombing continued all day in the southern portion of Curly Trench. 7th Yorkshire gained ten metres of the trench at 3.30 p.m., but could get no further. The fire of 4.5″ Howitzers on Charlie and Curly day and night undoubtedly assisted 7th Yorkshire to hold on to Curly Trench despite constant attacks. The Battalion was relieved over the next two nights, having suffered 221 casualties.

Battle of Bullecourt

6th May 1917

211 Cpl George Howell, 1st Battalion AIF, (1st Australian Brigade, 1st Australian Division), Bullecourt, France

213 Lt Rupert Moon, 58th Battalion AIF (15th Australian Brigade, 5th Australian Division), Bullecourt, France

When the Arras offensive opened on 9th April, it was planned for Fifth Army to attack the Hindenburg Line at Bullecourt to assist Third Army in its general offensive to the north. However, delays in cutting the wire meant the attack could not be simultaneous with the opening of the main offensive. A surprise attack on 10th April was decided upon, using ten tanks ahead of the artillery barrage. This required a rapid reshaping of plans, with only 4th Australian Division (I ANZAC) attacking on a frontage of 1,350m. If the Hindenburg Line was breached, units were to swing west into Bullecourt and 62nd Division (V Corps) on the left would also advance. 4th Cavalry Division was poised to exploit the breach.

The infantry assembled on time, but the tanks were delayed by a snowstorm. The attack was cancelled and the Australian infantry retired unseen in a snow flurry. 62nd Division was not aware of the cancellation and sent forward strong patrols as planned, suffering 162 casualties.

The attack was rescheduled for the morning of 11th April, by when it was known that the wire was fairly well cut, so the infantry were to advance fifteen minutes after the tanks regardless of their progress. Only four tanks reached their start positions by Zero hour at 4.30 a.m. and the Germans heard them coming despite the noise of covering machine gun fire. Some tanks attacked outside the area of the assault and others developed problems, were knocked out or bogged down.

4th Australian Brigade on the right overtook the tanks in a hail of small arms fire. Countless flares lit up the sky, but the troops got through gaps in the wire to take the first trench. Although the wire in front of the second trench was undamaged, the infantry infiltrated through gaps left by the Germans and along communications trenches to secure the second trench.

12th Australian Brigade on the left was delayed waiting for the tanks. By the time it started the artillery had lifted off Bullecourt. Despite the difficulties, by 6.50 a.m. both brigades were on their objectives in most places in the Hindenburg Line, but were too weak to go on towards Riencourt and Bullecourt. It was difficult to support the forward troops in daylight and a gap between the brigades could not be filled. Confusion over the location of the tanks caused delays in putting down adequate protective artillery fire in front of the forward positions.

Reports that the tanks had succeeded triggered 62nd Division's advance against Bullecourt. Reports reaching HQ Fifth Army indicated all was going to plan and

4th Cavalry Division was ordered to push on towards Fontaine-lès-Croisilles and Chérisy. The cavalry advance soon petered out under heavy fire.

At 10 a.m. counterattacks began from all sides. As bombs ran out the infantry were forced back and it was impossible to resupply them in daylight over the bullet swept no man's land. By 12.25 p.m. the last were ejected and came back to their start positions. The Australians suffered 3,167 casualties, including 1,164 taken prisoner. Too much reliance had been put on the tanks and the failure to thoroughly bombard Bullecourt contributed to the disaster.

A renewed attack was planned, but the Australians naturally did not want to rely upon tanks. There was also a need for thorough artillery preparation and the Army commander, Gough, did not want to move until Third Army to the north had reached the Sensée. As a result, the renewed attack did not take place until early

The attack by 2nd Australian and 62nd Divisions on 3rd May 1917 set the conditions for subsequent operations during which Snowy Howell (6th May) and Rupert Moon (12th May) were awarded the VC.

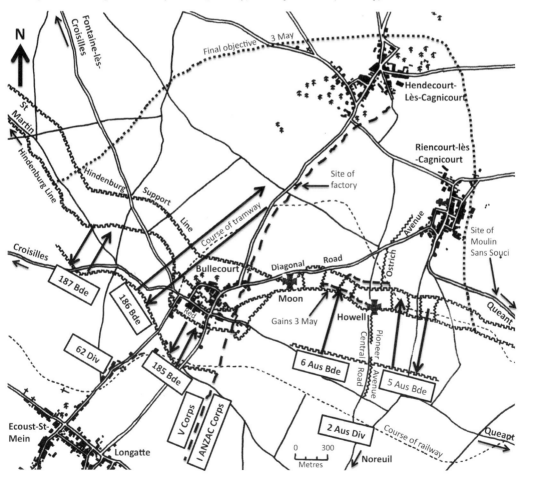

May by when there was no prospect of Fifth Army assisting Third Army in a great victorious sweep forward. Instead the Battle of Bullecourt, like the Third Battle of the Scarpe, was aimed mainly at holding the Germans in place.

The plan was for I ANZAC Corps to attack with 2nd Australian Division in about the same area as on 11th April. V Corps' front on the left was extended 450m eastwards in order that 62nd Division could attack Bullecourt simultaneously. V Corps had tanks in support; I ANZAC Corps did not!

There were three objectives; first the Hindenburg support trench; second the road from Fontaine to Quéant; and finally an egg shaped perimeter including Riencourt (I ANZAC Corps) and Hendecourt (V Corps). Holding this prominent salient could not be achieved unless the attack by VII Corps to the north (Third Battle of the Scarpe) was also successful and the two thrusts joined.

The heavy artillery was reinforced, giving forty-eight batteries between the two corps, in addition to a 15″ Gun and 12″ Howitzer battery under Fifth Army control. Each assault division was strongly reinforced with field batteries from other formations. Moving up the guns and ammunition necessitated road improvements and establishing dumps well forward. The artillery preparation commenced on 12th April and grew steadily in intensity.

The attack was set for 3rd May. 2nd Australian Division attacked with 5th Australian Brigade on the right and 6th Australian Brigade on the left, with 7th Australian Brigade in support. Initially the creeping barrage moved forward ninety metres every three minutes, but later slowed to five minutes. Ninety-six machine guns were also used for overhead and flanking barrage fire. The front to be attacked was deliberately narrow, with the intention of widening it by bombing outwards having made an initial lodgement. However, there was a 275m section between the two assault divisions that was not attacked or engaged by the artillery.

5th Australian Brigade's attack failed. Troops bunched up and in front of the German wire, which was well cut, they came under heavy machine gun fire from in front and from the right and left. They paused to await the barrage lifting two minutes later, but the German front line was fully manned despite being under heavy shellfire. As soon as the barrage lifted, German fire rose in intensity. Someone gave the order to retire and the troops fell back to the sunken Bullecourt–Quéant road. A few men got into the Hindenburg front line trench on the left and fired the success rocket. At 4.17 a.m. there was a report that the second trench had also been taken.

6th Australian Brigade found the wire well cut and reached the first Hindenburg trench, except on the left, where the left of 22nd Battalion was forced back by enfilade fire from Bullecourt. 24th Battalion on the right had the advantage of being in a depression alongside the sunken Central Road. It took the second trench at 4.18 a.m., as did the right of 22nd Battalion. At 4.57 a.m. 6th Australian Brigade reported that 5th Australian Brigade had been forced back, but HQ 5th Australian Brigade still believed its troops had been successful. 6th Australian Brigade sent forward a company of 26th Battalion to the sunken road to rally the troops there and lead them forward again. The advance commenced at 5.45 a.m. and 200 men of 5th Australian Brigade followed as a second wave. It was apparent from the intense fire from the Hindenburg Line that it was still strongly held by the Germans. Only a few got to the front line on the left, but under Captain Walter Gilchrist, of 6th Field Company, a party of 24th Battalion advanced along the deserted trench eastwards to east of Central Road. He bombed the enemy while also trying to induce men lying out in no man's land to join him. He was wearing a grey cardigan, without a hat throughout.

Meanwhile the rest of 6th Australian Brigade pressed on to the second objective on the Fontaine–Quéant road. On the right a party of 24th Battalion went on a little further to a tramway. A party of 23rd Battalion, detailed to take the third objective, came up on the right at the crossroads southwest of Riencourt, but the right flank was open where 5th Australian Brigade had failed. The Germans were standing up to fire across Central Road into the flank of 6th Australian Brigade. Captain PGR Parkes wheeled his men right and established a flank along the road.

On the left of 6th Australian Brigade the attack had failed and a fierce bombing fight was in progress in the Hindenburg trenches. It was impossible for the Brigade to continue the advance in the face of opposition on both open flanks. When it was clear that the attack had broken down on the right and in 62nd Division's area on the left, a protective barrage beyond the second objective was maintained. An attempt by 25th Battalion (7th Australian Brigade) to assist 62nd Division by attacking Bullecourt from the southeast met with heavy fire and was stopped.

In the Hindenburg trenches the bombing fight continued. Gilchrist's party made considerable progress, but he was killed (Villers-Bretonneux Memorial) and his party was driven back to Central Road. In the support trench a post was established 140m east of the road. On the left the bombers were stopped where the support trench crossed the Riencourt–Bullecourt road. A counterattack from Riencourt against the second objective was driven off, but the position was untenable and the defenders were hit by their own artillery dropping short along the tramway. They were forced back in small parties to the Hindenburg trenches.

28th Battalion (7th Australian Brigade) was attached to 5th Australian Brigade to secure its original objective in the Hindenburg Line. It moved up Central Road, which afforded some cover, and at 2 p.m. commenced bombing eastwards along the Hindenburg trenches. Three times the bombers reached the Riencourt–Noreuil road 450m east of Central Road and were forced back again, the last time at 8.40 p.m. Soon after, survivors from 5th Australian Brigade, who had been lying in no man's land in shell holes, were seen retiring across the open towards Central Road. In the gloom they appeared to be Germans advancing under cover of a bombardment attempting to get behind the forward Australian troops and cut them off. An erroneous report spread amongst 28th Battalion that 6th Australian Brigade behind them was falling back, so the order was given to withdraw. No such instruction had been given to 6th Australian Brigade and it held on, filling gaps left by the retirement.

62nd Division, in its first major action, attacked with all three brigades in line, with 22nd Brigade (7th Division) in reserve. It was supported by ten tanks of D Battalion. On the right, 185th Brigade headed for Bullecourt. 2/6th West Yorkshire on the right was blinded by smoke from the northeast and drifted left, where it became intermingled with 2/5th West Yorkshire. The first trench and the village were taken, with posts being established on the northern edge.

186th Brigade in the centre was to go through to the final objective beyond Hendecourt. The right reached the support line, but the left was held up by the wire. The rear waves closed up, causing confusion and no progress was made. They fell back to the railway, rallied and went forward again, but to no avail. Meanwhile the right had been reinforced by the support battalions and went on to the factory north of Bullecourt.

On the left, 187th Brigade was only to advance to the second objective and establish a protective left flank. Part of the right reached the support trench. The left crossed the front line, but attempts to get further forward were met with withering fire. It was forced back to the St Martin road, with some men going back as far as the railway. The barrage was brought back for a new attack at 9.30 a.m. but it also failed.

Efforts to reach the isolated parties in the German lines failed and by noon all had been bombed back except the party at the factory, although this was not known at the time. 62nd Division was incapable of renewing its attack, having suffered almost 3,000 casualties. However, Bullecourt had to be taken if the Australians were to hold onto their gains. It was reported that VII Corps had taken Chérisy, adding more urgency to press on. V Corps ordered 7th Division to take over 62nd Division's right brigade sector and attack Bullecourt again. 22nd Brigade was to make the attack, but could not be ready until 10.30 p.m. Two battalions were to attack from the railway and having reached the centre of the village, the support battalions were to pass through to take the remainder. One battalion reached the second objective and the other the first, but strong counterattacks drove them out, except for ten men of 2nd Honourable Artillery Company, who held on in Bullecourt for three days. Another attempt at 4 a.m. next morning was broken up by the supporting artillery.

On 4th May, 1st Australian Brigade (1st Australian Division) was put at the disposal of 2nd Australian Division. A communications trench had been dug overnight parallel with Central Road at some cost in lives to the pioneers and was named Pioneer Avenue. 3rd Battalion filed along it to the Hindenburg support line and 1st Battalion to the front line. Another counterattack had to be repulsed before the remnants of 6th Australian Brigade could be relieved and HQ 1st Australian Brigade took over. Meanwhile 2nd Battalion passed along Pioneer Avenue to the 5th Australian Brigade area, but had to remain in the communications trench as only the head of the column could engage the enemy.

At 1 p.m. 1st Battalion began bombing westwards along the Hindenburg front line and an hour later 3rd Battalion commenced along the support line. Both pushed ahead for 135m and made contact with each other via a lateral communications trench. 2nd Battalion's attack eastward, supported by 4th Battalion, was delayed for artillery registration. The advance began at 3.40 p.m. and met stubborn resistance, but reached a communications trench west of the Riencourt–Noreuil road at 4 p.m.

By 9 p.m. the German artillery fire had increased and counterattacks were launched from both flanks and frontally. The left attack made some ground in the support trench, but the others were driven back. During the night 11th and 12th Battalions (3rd Australian Brigade) took over east of Central Road and 2nd and 4th Battalions were relieved. After dark 22nd Brigade was ordered to send patrols into Bullecourt to make contact with isolated parties still thought to be there. They could not get past a belt of fresh wire put out by the Germans.

On 5th May attempts to push ahead east of Central Road came to nothing as the troops were hard pressed just to hang on. At times the shelling here was as bad, if not worse, than anything experienced at Pozières the previous year. The left flank of 1st Battalion was attacked three times from Bullecourt by German bombers between 10.30 a.m. and 4 p.m., but they were forced back on each occasion. At 10 p.m. the Germans tried to bomb down Ostrich Avenue and Central Road, but the SOS signal was put up by the right of 3rd Battalion and the protective barrage stopped the hostile movement.

Leave Riencourt-lès-Cagnicourt on the unclassified road to the southwest towards Bullecourt. 400m after the last houses park on the left at the track junction. Walk 150m towards Bullecourt and turn left onto a track and continue walking along it (Central Road) to the south for 500m to a clump of trees on top of the bank on the left of the track. This is where the Hindenburg front line crossed Central Road and where Snowy Howell forced the Germans back to the east.

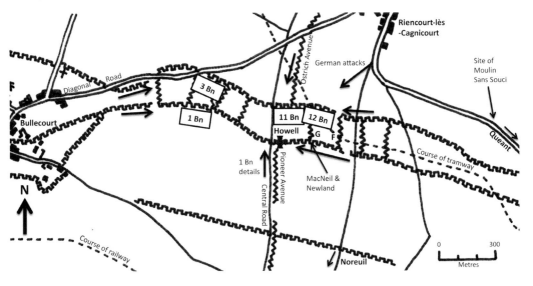

At 1 a.m. on 6th May the enemy artillery fell on the front line trenches on the right, Pioneer Avenue and the railway. Posts were shattered and many men were buried. German infantry was seen moving about and at 3.30 a.m. the SOS signal was fired to bring down the Australian protective fire. The German fire continued unabated, but a very welcomed reinforcement of a company of 10th Battalion arrived via Pioneer Avenue. At 5 a.m. the German guns lifted and their infantry advanced from the Moulin Sans Souci road and down Ostrich Avenue. At that moment the barrage to cover a cancelled Australian attack also came down and the Germans ran into it, ending the attack in this area. A new type of Germans bomb was reported, resembling a stick grenade but filled with an incendiary mixture.

However, other German troops attacked along the Hindenburg Line trenches. The support trench block was pushed back forty metres before stabilising, but the Germans made rapid progress against 11th Battalion along the front trench to Central Road and the survivors were forced back down Pioneer Avenue. Australians in the support trench turned their attention to the south and poured fire into the Germans advancing along the front line. Trench mortars were sited to stop such attacks. In the front line trench there was one 100m behind the block, two more were in cross-trench 'G' about 135m further back and another was held in reserve. As soon as the sounds of bombing were heard, they opened fire. The easternmost mortar fired on the trench and those in 'G' fired into no man's land further north.

Germans in the support trench bombed down cross-trench 'F' from the north. The flank bombing post turned to counter this move and was caught by the main German party advancing along the front line with two flamethrowers, which in the dark were particularly terrifying. The post fell back and the Germans followed up rapidly, positioning machine guns and bombers out to the flanks as they advanced. Some of the crew of the first mortar carried it back, while 931 Corporal Julian North (DCM for this action), 3rd Australian Light Trench Mortar Battery, and others threw mortar bombs as well as grenades at the Germans a few metres away. The reserve mortar was brought into action, firing into the trench, while the two in 'G' shortened their range. As the 'G' trench mortars were being pulled back by 778 Corporal Emanuel Victor Hockey (MM for this action and DCM August 1918), Lieutenant Alexander MacNeil (DSO for this action, recommended for

Looking northwards along Central Road to the Hindenburg front line. Snowy Howell's VC action was where the Hindenburg Line crossed Central Road at the prominent bushy topped tree.

Bullecourt

Hindenburg Front Line

VC), both of 3rd Australian Light Trench Mortar Battery, held the enemy back from the trench junction. He waited until the leading flamethrower came round the corner and watched the flame roar past him before throwing a grenade, killing the flamethrower carrier. MacNeil was joined by Captain James Newland (awarded the VC for his actions on 7th–15th April 1917) with a box of bombs. The two kept the enemy back while the mortars were taken back to Central Road and came back into action again. The small party with MacNeil and Newland was very exposed. Newland was hit in the arm and chest and eventually made his way back over the open to Central Road. MacNeil continued throwing grenades from a shell hole near to the trench. Although the second flamethrower was also destroyed, there was some panic in the trench garrison and they moved back sharply to Central Road.

1st Battalion to the west of Central Road had initially not been affected by this attack. About 6 a.m. **Corporal George Howell**, commanding the post nearest to Central Road sent a message to his acting CO, Captain Alexander Kenneth Mackenzie (MC for this action and DSO September 1918) (Major Philip Woodforde had been killed – Grévillers British Cemetery III D 6), that the battalion on the right was retiring. Mackenzie sent the signals officer, signallers, batmen and any other hands available to stop the German thrust and push it back. When they reached the entrance to the Hindenburg front line they were showered with German grenades. The 1st Battalion party lined the road bank and threw bombs back. Within the German party of about eighty, both officers and twenty-five men were killed. Machine guns in 'G' and Central Road 180m south of the Hindenburg Line kept the Germans' heads down.

At this point Howell dashed out from the post and ran alongside the front Hindenburg Line trench, throwing bombs into it and forcing back the enemy bombers. He was followed and supported by Lieutenant Thomas James Richards (MC for 4th May 1917) with a Lewis gun. Howell was wounded and fell into the trench, but his action gave time for the survivors of 11th and 12th Battalions to rally and, with a party of 1st Battalion, go back into the attack. With the flamethrowers out of action, the Australian bombers pushed the Germans back, covered by Lewis guns in shell holes out to the flanks. Troops in the support trench bombed down cross-trench 'F' to catch the retiring Germans in the flank. The fight went on for forty-five minutes and the block in the front line was established further east than when the counterattack started.

Riencourt-lès
-Cagnicourt

Central Road

The area where the 1st Battalion signallers and batmen lined the bank along Central Road to hold the German attack and where Snowy Howell started his counterattack.

The opposite view of the previous picture, with Bullecourt in the background.

That evening 10th Battalion took over on the right and the trench ends were firmly barricaded off, it being recognised that in the short term at least there was no prospect of continuing the advance. By the time 1st Battalion had been relieved it had suffered 317 casualties, including forty-nine killed and another twenty-nine missing (CWGC records seventy-four dead in the Battalion 5th–8th May 1917).

Despite this success, after four days and using four divisions, there was little to show for the efforts and sacrifice involved. There were only two options open, pull out or continue to batter away in the hope that Bullecourt could be taken; the former was unthinkable.

12th May 1917

On 7th May 7th Division attacked Bullecourt from the southeast. The southwest corner was to be kept under heavy artillery fire to deter machine gun fire until it could be cleared later. This area became known as the Red Patch. 2nd Australian Division had been scheduled to bomb along the Hindenburg Line the previous day up to 7th Division's objective, but it was not possible to start this operation until 11 p.m. It was therefore agreed to postpone the Australian attack and launch them simultaneously at 3.45 a.m. on 7th May.

20th Brigade, which had relieved 22nd Brigade, attacked with 2nd Gordon Highlanders. The Battalion dashed across no man's land and seized the first and second objectives together with 106 prisoners and three machine guns. Contact was made with 1st Australian Brigade in the Hindenburg Line at 5.15 a.m. It had bombed along the Line with great skill, covered by trench mortars and Lewis and machine guns. Heavy German artillery fire forced 2nd Gordon Highlanders to abandon a small portion of the second objective on the left.

On 8th May 8th Devonshire attacked Red Patch by bombing down the trench south of Bullecourt. Rain overnight had turned the trenches into sticky mud, but some progress was made before being driven back. 2nd Border relieved 2nd Gordon Highlanders and established a post at the northeast corner of Red Patch. Meanwhile 1st Australian Brigade had been relieved by 2nd Australian Brigade. 8th Battalion bombed down the Hindenburg support line for 135m towards Bullecourt as a diversion.

By this time most troops of 2nd and 1st Australian Division had been used and fresh ones were needed. 5th Australian Division was resting around Albert when it received unexpected orders to deploy two brigades. 14th Australian Brigade relieved 3rd Australian Brigade east of Central Road on the night of 8th May; and the following night 15th Australian Brigade took over from 2nd Australian Brigade west of Central Road. On 10th May 5th Australian Division assumed command of the sector. Meanwhile, on 9th May, 8th Devonshire renewed its attack and made some progress before being driven back. On the night of 10th May the exhausted 20th Brigade was relieved by 91st Brigade.

By 9th May orders had been issued for half the heavy artillery supporting I ANZAC Corps to begin moving north for the forthcoming Flanders offensive. The move was to begin on 15th May limiting the time left to create a defendable front at Bullecourt.

At 3.40 a.m. on 12th May 91st Brigade attacked with 2nd Queen's and 1st South Staffordshire with the intention of taking the whole of Bullecourt, while 15th Australian Brigade advanced westwards to join 91st Brigade at the crossroads northeast of the village. 2nd Queen's took the objective up to the church, but the left of 1st South Staffordshire on the left failed. The right reached the north and northwest outskirts of the village. On the left, 185th Brigade of 62nd Division reached the Crucifix but was bombed back again.

From the parking place for Snowy Howell's VC action continue towards Bullecourt another 900m and park at the Australian Memorial on the left. The pillbox captured by Moon's party was where the statue stands now.

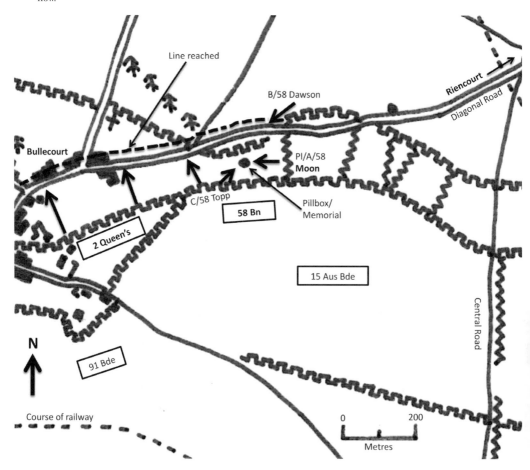

To avoid the British barrage, B Company, 58th Battalion, was to advance along the Hindenburg support trench fourteen minutes later than 91st Brigade. Its objective was a large dugout on Diagonal Road and it was reinforced by two platoons of A Company. It was to be preceded by a platoon of A Company taking a machine gun pillbox between the front and support lines. C Company was to advance from the front line trench to take a German strongpoint west of the crossroads. Two companies of 60th Battalion were to occupy the vacated trenches. The area to be attacked had been included in a massive artillery duel during the early hours and many casualties had been suffered. A company of 59th Battalion had to be brought forward to strengthen the troops holding the Hindenburg front line.

The attack along the support trench led by Lieutenant Forbes Campbell Dawson (MC for this action and DSO later) was held up, despite showers of rifle grenades and bombs being used. The attack on the pillbox by **Lieutenant Rupert Moon**'s platoon was also held up. Part of C Company directed against the objectives further west became involved in the fight for the pillbox. While C Company's commander, Lieutenant Samuel Topp, tried to redirect his men onto their real objective, he was shot through the head and killed (Villers-Bretonneux Memorial).

Moon had been hit in the face and temporarily dazed, but recovered. Seeing his men were wavering he called on them, *Come on boys don't let me down.* After ten minutes hard fighting, the garrison was driven out of the pillbox and fell back on the support trench. Moon was being supported by Lieutenant George Patrick Hooper and was followed by a carrying party of 58th and 60th Battalions. Moon continued

From the site of Snowy Howell's VC action looking towards the Australian Memorial, where the pillbox captured by Rupert Moon stood. Bullecourt is off picture to the left and Reincourt to the right.

The Australian Memorial from the Bullecourt–Reincourt road.

the attack over the open and caught the enemy resisting Dawson in their right flank. Dawson's party was still attacking the barricade and had been reinforced by four bombing squads of 60th Battalion plus some rifle grenadiers and Lewis guns. The combined onslaught was too much for the Germans. While Dawson reorganised the disparate groups, Moon with 806 Lance Corporal Charles Edward Free DCM led the bombers.

Moon put a Lewis gun in a shell hole on the left and after a few minutes of bombing, the Germans fell back towards Diagonal Road. Moon emerged alone into the cutting and emptied his rifle into them, but was forced back by hostile bombers. Free shot the leading German bomber and Moon then organised a shower of grenades into the cutting and led the men nearest to him into it. The closest

From the Hindenburg front line looking in the direction of the attack on 12th May 1917.

Germans were shot down, but the rest pulled back into the shelter of the dugout entrances in the sunken Riencourt–Bullecourt road. Moon's party opened fire, trapping the Germans inside and kept them there until Dawson's party appeared. The Australians numbered only about thirty. While Moon consolidated in the cutting, Dawson mopped up the dugout; 186 Germans surrendered (another 150 dead were counted after the action). Moon positioned a Lewis gun to fire along the road to the left as no contact had yet been made with friendly troops in that direction. As he peered over the edge of the cutting a sniper's bullet shattered his jaw and he bandaged it roughly to carry on with the consolidation, but the wound eventually put him out of action. Dawson was forced back a little by snipers and the crossroads was not secured until after dark. The cost to 58th Battalion was 149 casualties (CWGC records forty-nine dead for the Battalion 12th–13th May 1917).

C Company reached the road bank a little west of the crossroads, having advanced across the open from the Hindenburg front line trench and established contact with 2nd Queen's on the left. The whole village was held except for Red Patch. That night 15th Australian Brigade was relieved by 173rd Brigade (58th Division, attached to 7th Division), leaving I ANZAC Corps responsible only for the area east of Central Road held by 54th Battalion of 14th Australian Brigade.

On 13th May a complicated operation was attempted against Red Patch from southwest and northeast simultaneously. The artillery fell short on one battalion and no progress was made, nor later in the day when it was tried again. On 14th May 1st Royal Welsh Fusiliers (22nd Brigade under 91st Brigade) attacked Red Patch three times from the east. The third attempt succeeded partially, just as their bomb dump was blown up. That night there were three battalions in Bullecourt under the CO 1st Royal Welsh Fusiliers, two from 22nd Brigade and one from 91st Brigade.

Just before 4 a.m. on 15th May saw the last but largest German counterattack. An intense bombardment the previous night caused heavy casualties and destroyed much of the repaired trenches of the Hindenburg Line. Trench mortars joined in and levelled the trenches. British field batteries were hit by gas but put down the protective barrage. With so many signal rockets flying around it was impossible for observers to be sure what was required and by whom. The German frontal

attack on 54th Battalion on the right was smashed, but on the extreme right parties broke in and captured 135m of the Hindenburg support trench and part of the communications trench leading back to the front line until they were expelled.

Further west 173rd Brigade under Brigadier General Bernard Freyberg VC, in its first battle, beat off the attack and sent some reserve companies to help the Australians on the right to restore their line. In Bullecourt there was a protracted struggle. 91st Brigade held on to the village east of the Longatte road, but was ejected from the west side. Later another attack forced the line back from the road to the southeast corner of the village, but a counterattack restored the line along the road. 7th Division was exhausted after twelve days and 91st Brigade was relieved that night by 174th Brigade of 58th Division, which next morning assumed command of the sector west of Central Road. The Hindenburg support line was captured on the 16th as far west as the eastern road to Hendecourt.

At 2 a.m. on 17th May 174th Brigade attacked the Red Patch frontally from the railway after a hurricane bombardment of two minutes. The Red Patch was secured quickly, following which another company, facing west on the Longatte road, passed in front of the attacking battalion and cleared the rest of the village. The Germans were preparing the cellars for demolition prior to evacuation. Local engagements continued for a few days, but this was effectively the end of the Battle of Bullecourt. The cost was immense. I ANZAC Corps had 7,488 casualties (in addition to those suffered in the battle in April) and V Corps suffered another 6,800. This battle was one of the most deadly of all in trench warfare. Its conduct shook Australian confidence in British command, particularly after the errors of 11th and 12th April.

Chapter Four

Local Operations Summer 1917

19th May 1917

215 Sgt Albert White, 2nd South Wales Borderers (87th Brigade, 29th Division), Monchy, France

The Battle of Arras ended on 16th May and heavy artillery and reserve formations began moving north for the forthcoming offensive in Flanders. However, operations around Arras continued on a reduced scale in order to support the French and tie down German forces. In addition a massive reorganisation was undertaken to hand over part of the front up to the Omignon to the French and to adjust Army boundaries. First and Third Army therefore faced having to continue offensive operations with tired, under strength formations and reducing artillery and others assets. Small attacks with limited objectives were all that could be undertaken.

29th Division took over the front line from 3rd and 12th Divisions on the night of 14/15th May, with orders to capture Infantry Hill (Hill 100) and Bois des Aubepines on 19th May. 56th Division was to protect the right flank by securing a section of Tool Trench with five platoons of 1/8th Middlesex. The main attack was made by elements of three battalions of 87th Brigade (29th Division). On the right was 1st Royal Inniskilling Fusiliers, with 1st Border on the left. D Company, 2nd South Wales Borderers, was attached to 1st Border on the extreme left. During 18th May an assembly trench was dug and communications trenches were improved in preparation for the attack.

The enemy was fully alert and it is possible they knew the time of the attack. German SOS signals went up only five seconds after the advance commenced at 9 p.m. and their barrage began falling within forty seconds. The objective of D Company, 2nd South Wales Borderers, was a section of Devil's Trench astride, but mainly to the right of, Bit Lane. To cover the advance a rifle grenade section was positioned in an abandoned trench in no man's land. When Devil's Trench fell, bombers were to press northwards to establish a block and strongpoint. A Company was to follow as a carrying party and occupy Snaffle and Shrapnel Trenches with B Company when D Company went forward.

As soon as the assault began the troops were raked by machine gun fire from the left of Bit Lane. Casualties mounted quickly, but the attack was pressed home.

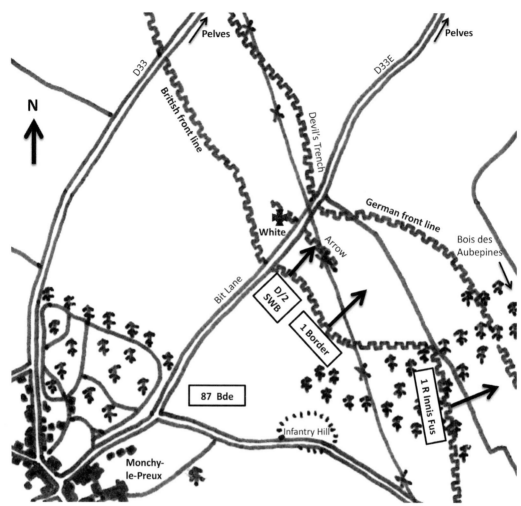

Leave Monchy-le-Preux on the easternmost of the two roads to Pelves, the D33E. After 750m pass under the power lines and park immediately on the right in the track entrance. Only do this if the ground is dry. There is a small area of hard standing a little further on where a vehicle may be left for a short while. Arrow Trench crossed the road a few metres southwest of the power lines. Albert White attacked the machine gun post in Arrow Trench just north of the road (Bit Lane).

From the German front line looking southwest towards Monchy-le-Preux. The attack was towards the camera. Albert White assaulted the machine gun position in Arrow Trench right of the D33 Monchy–Pelves road.

There were heavy losses in D Company as it reached the waterlogged Arrow Trench on the right. **Sergeant Albert White** realised the attack would fail unless the machine guns were silenced. He charged the nearest gun, followed by Corporal Newell. White reached the German infantrymen covering the gun team, shot three of them and bayoneted a fourth. He then charged the gun, but before reaching it was riddled by bullets. His self sacrifice diverted attention from his comrades, but it was not sufficient to allow them to gain the objective. The survivors sheltered in shell holes until darkness fell. Of the 116 men in D Company who went into action only sixty-one returned, of whom half were wounded.

The attack was also a complete failure everywhere else. 1st Royal Inniskilling Fusiliers made a lodgement in the enemy front line, but these men were cut off and few escaped.

4th June 1917

216 2Lt Thomas Maufe, 124th Siege Battery, Royal Garrison Artillery, Feuchy, France

Little is known about the circumstances under which **Second Lieutenant Thomas Maufe** was awarded the VC. The Arras offensive was over and only routine line holding operations were taking place in the area. On 4th June the Battery war diary records firing a few rounds at Hausa and Delbar Woods without observation. The Battery came under intermittent shelling throughout the afternoon. From 5.15 p.m. until 7 p.m. the shelling intensified and the telephone line between the forward and rear positions was cut. Unaided and on his own initiative, Maufe repaired the cable under fire, thereby enabling the Battery to open fire on the enemy.

Although no damage was caused to the guns or ammunition, a dump of 4.5″ Howitzer gas and high explosive shells across the street was hit and blown up. Disregarded the very grave risk, particularly from the gas shells, which he knew were in the dump, Maufe saved what might have been a disaster by extinguishing the resultant fire. All the gas shells were lost but he saved most of the high explosive.

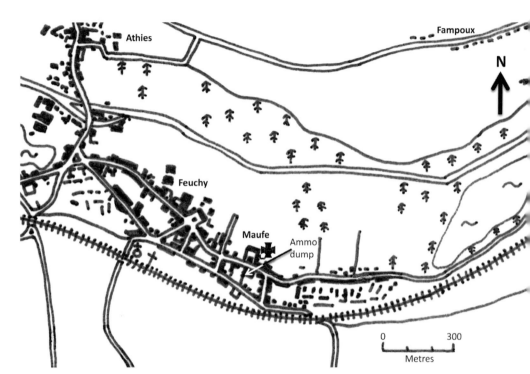

Enter Feuchy on the D37 heading east. Pass the church and Feuchy British Cemetery on the right and continue 250m, then turn left and after fifty metres turn right. Continue on this road for 150m and park. 124th Siege Battery was on the left of the road and the burning 4.5" Howitzer ammunition dump was opposite on the right.

Looking northwest through Feuchy. 124th Siege Battery was in the field on the right behind the bus stop. The burning 4.5" Howitzer dump was on the left of the road beyond the junction on the left.

24th–25th June 1917

221 2Lt John Dunville, 1st (Royal) Dragoons (6th Cavalry Brigade, 3rd Cavalry Division), Épehy, France

1st (Royal) Dragoons spent May and June 1917 dismounted in the trenches in the Épehy and Vendhuille area. The British line was about 725 yards from the enemy and consisted of a series of connected redoubts with a line of posts to the front. On

Approach Ossu from the north along the unclassified road running south from Honnecourt-sur-Escaut, parallel with and west of the St Quentin Canal. 650m after passing the village sign there is a chapel on the left. Continue another 125m and turn sharp right up a sunken track, passing house No.28 on your left. In good weather this is drivable with care in a normal car. In the wet it is advisable to park at the bottom and walk. After 350m the track bends slightly to the right. Just after some bushes, climb the bank on the left. About 100m into the field is where Dunville's VC action took place. Look half right. The raiders left No.1 Post at the top of the slope about 140m west of the track to take up their assault positions.

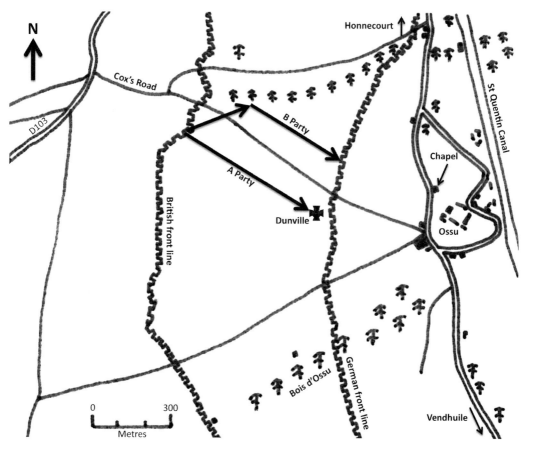

24th June the Regiment was relieved except for a raiding party of five officers and ninety-six other ranks.

The raiders were divided into two parties. On the right A Party was commanded by Lieutenant Ronald Henry White Henderson, assisted by **Second Lieutenant John Dunville**, the Regimental Scout Officer. On the left B Party was commanded by Lieutenant Robert Barnard Helme, assisted by Second Lieutenant Vincent Clinton Rice, North Somerset Yeomanry Scout Officer. Overall direction of the raid was under Lieutenant Colonel Frederick William Wormald DSO, CO Royal Dragoons. Although the Royal Dragoons provided the majority of the raiding party, detachments from other units were also involved:

- North Somerset Yeomanry – six scouts in B Party commanded by Second Lieutenant Rice.
- 3rd Dragoon Guards – six scouts and a Hotchkiss detachment.
- 6th Machine Gun Squadron – six guns and Lieutenant John Burgon Bickersteth to command the covering group for A Party.
- Six sappers with Bangalore torpedoes.

In the week before the raid, Dunville spent nearly every night in no man's land, acquainting himself with the ground. At 12.50 a.m. on 25th June the raiders left the northern end of No.1 Post and advanced 400m into no man's land. A Party on the right was to operate south of the Ossus (now Ossu) Wood road and B Party to the north. Progress was slowed by head high thistles, which made direction keeping by compass difficult. On reaching the start point they lay down to await the barrage, which opened at 1.10 a.m.

South of the road Dunville was followed by three sappers and six scouts, the latter laying tapes for the assault party to follow. As they neared the main enemy wire they encountered a narrower belt of low wire, which Dunville and the sappers cut by hand. They then ran forward to the main belt of wire, followed closely by the assault parties. A Bangalore torpedo was needed to breach the main wire, but the assault groups had come too far forward for safety and the sappers sent them back a little. By then the Germans, who seemed to be largely unaffected by the barrage, were firing into no man's land and throwing grenades. It was assessed afterwards that the Germans were fully aware that the raid was coming.

In crossing no man's land a joint of the Bangalore torpedo tube came apart and needed to be repaired before it could be used. Dunville lay between the sapper corporal and the enemy to shield him from fire. While the corporal dealt with the torpedo, Dunville urged him to keep cool and gave him the confidence to finish the repair and position the torpedo. The little party withdrew a short distance and the torpedo was fired at 1.23 a.m. The assault group went forward covered by Bickersteth's Hotchkiss on the right. As they reached the gap in the wire Dunville's left arm was shattered by a grenade. At another time he received a serious chest wound, probably caused by a bullet as he shielded the sapper corporal. The enemy fire increased and almost immediately the assault party encountered another belt of wire. Henderson ordered another Bangalore torpedo be brought forward and they were covered by the Hotchkiss while they waited. Before the second torpedo could be used the recall rocket went up. The retirement was carried out in an orderly fashion and the wounded were brought back. The Brigade war diary says that this party did eventually reach the enemy trench and killed a few Germans before withdrawing, but this is not supported by other sources.

The left party got through the first belt of wire and was about to blow a gap in the second belt when white posts were found marking a German track through the entanglement. A listening post connected to the front line by a sap was entered by the scouts. Three Germans were killed there and a machine gun was blown up. Second Lieutenant Rice had an arm broken by a bullet, but managed to kill two Germans and remained with his men until the action was over (MC for this action). The party got into the German trench and moved north along it. Corporal Jull bayoneted some Germans and Sergeant Howell bombed a dugout. They remained for a few minutes, accounting for several more defenders and taking one prisoner. The Germans then bombarded their own trench to the north with trench mortars, probably killing several of their own men. The prisoner died before reaching the British lines, but the raiders returned with sufficient material to identify the German unit as 2nd Battalion, 124th Infantry Regiment.

Despite his wounds, Dunville walked back to the British lines. While being attended to by his squadron commander, Captain Edward William 'Billy' Tremayne

From the middle of no man's land looking over the German lines towards Ossu. John Dunville's VC action was to the right of Cox's Road and in front of the German trench.

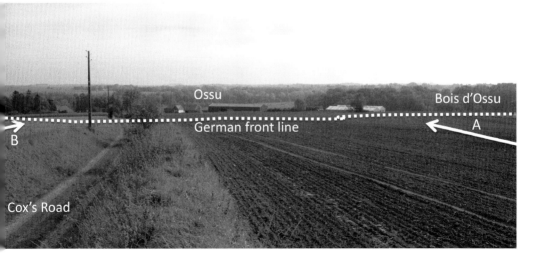

Miles, he was quite cheerful and even apologised to the CO for not being able to get into the enemy trenches. He was taken to Villers-Faucon by ambulance, where his left arm was amputated by a surgeon named Lockwood, called in from a casualty clearing station at Tincourt. A second operation was performed to counteract blood poisoning, but Dunville died at 3.00 a.m. on 26th June without regaining consciousness.

There were five other fatalities amongst the raiders, plus nine wounded and two missing (later discovered to have been killed). Amongst the dead was B Party's commander, Lieutenant Robert Barnard Helme, who is also buried in Villers-Faucon Communal Cemetery (A 23). The other men killed were 4450 Sergeant WT Hicks and 13038 Lance Corporal Frederick Boast, both of 3rd Dragoon Guards; and 8865 Lance Corporal Alexander Nisbet, 8809 Private James Allan Barr Leitch, 911 Private Richard Grizzell and 7698 Private John Miles all of 1st (Royal) Dragoons. Nisbet, Leitch, Boast and Hicks are buried in Villers-Faucon Communal Cemetery (C 24–C 27). Grizzell and Miles were the two missing and are commemorated on the Thiepval Memorial.

Chapter Five

Battle of Messines and Prelude to Third Ypres

7th June 1917

217 Pte John Carroll, 33rd Battalion AIF (9th Australian Brigade, 3rd Australian Division), St Yves, Belgium

218 LCpl Samuel Frickleton, 3rd New Zealand Rifle Brigade NZEF (3rd New Zealand (Rifle Brigade) Brigade, New Zealand Division), Messines, Belgium

219 Capt Robert Grieve, 37th Battalion AIF (10th Australian Brigade, 3rd Australian Division), Messines, Belgium

At the Chantilly Conference on 15th November 1916 the Allies agreed to coordinate simultaneous offensives during 1917. The intention was to put the Central Powers under such pressure that a breakthrough would be created somewhere. The Franco–British commanders decided to coordinate their spring offensives on the Arras and Aisne fronts before the British effort shifted to Flanders. This met the primary British War Committee aim for 1917 of seizing the Belgian ports. However, the failure of the Nivelle offensives in April and May and the resultant French mutinies forced the Allies to review their plans. The British had to take the lead, while the French mainly went onto the defensive to rebuild their morale and await the arrival of the Americans. The possibility of Russia seeking a separate peace with the Central Powers also loomed. In this situation there was no prospect of ending the war in 1917 and so a process of wearing down the enemy was to be pursued. The British hoped at least to clear the Belgian coast and deny the Germans the use of two U-boat bases there.

No major offensive operations had taken place in Flanders since spring 1915. However, the British had wanted to clear the Belgian coast since December 1914, but pressure to undertake operations elsewhere had prevented any action being taken until the middle of 1917. Before the Arras offensive ended the BEF began transferring reserves north into Flanders. A prerequisite for a successful offensive around Ypres was control of the strongly defended Messines–Wytschaete Ridge, to deny the Germans observation over the Salient from the south.

Second Army's preparations, under General Sir Herbert Plumer, took a year. Plumer planned a broad advance over the Ridge on a front of sixteen kilometres with objectives limited to penetrations of 1,600–3,200m. From the south, II ANZAC, IX and X Corps were to make the attack, each deploying three divisions

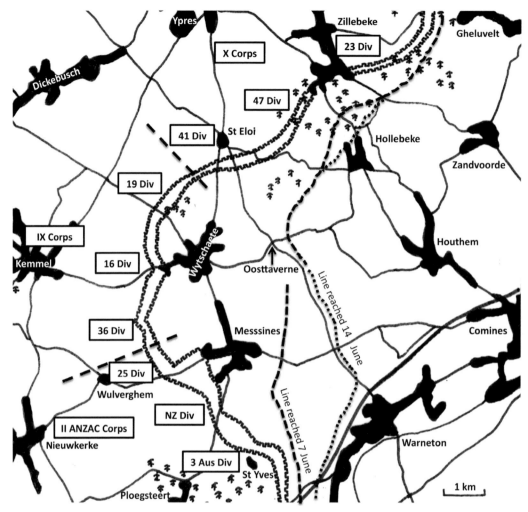

The Battle of Messines 7th–14th June 1917. The formations making the initial assault are shown. The position held late on 7th June is shown by a dashed line and the extra gains made by 14th June by a dotted line.

in line and retaining a fourth in reserve. XIV Corps was in GHQ Reserve sixteen kilometres behind. As the German line on the Ridge bulged out to the west, the right and left corps had only 725–1,100m to cover to reach their objectives, but IX Corps in the centre faced an advance of 1,800m. To compensate for this imbalance, IX Corps' frontage narrowed as the advance progressed from 4,600m at the start to just 1,800m at the final objective.

Preparations and rehearsals were meticulous. The assault troops trained on replica ground and commanders down to platoon level were briefed on a minutely detailed model near Scherpenberg. Many of the divisions also produced their own clay models. Raids were conducted to assess the strength of enemy positions and to harass and wear them down. Working parties constructed six lines of assembly trenches, some in no man's land within 150m of the German front line. Engineering preparations were enormous in scale:

- 280 kilometres of broad and narrow gauge railway were laid.
- 300,000 tons of stores were in-loaded.
- Water piping was laid to deliver each corps 200,000 gallons per day.
- 31,450 labourers were involved in building/improving roads, establishing depots, working quarries, laying cables, building shelters and stocking dumps etc.

The artillery was organised into two groups per assault division, one per forward brigade. Each group was split into two sub-groups, one per battalion frontage, each of six field batteries. The bombardment by 2,266 guns (including 756 medium and heavy) opened on 21st May, with pillboxes receiving individual attention. The fortress villages of Wytschaete and Messines were systematically destroyed. Over 3,500,000 shells were fired up to 6th June. Two dress rehearsals of the creeping barrage were carried out on 3rd and 5th June to force the Germans into unmasking their batteries. As a result over 200 German battery positions were recorded for counter-battery fire on the day of the attack.

The RFC had 300 aircraft to achieve air superiority over the battle area and allow almost unrestricted reconnaissance and observation of the defences. Targets out of range of the artillery were bombed by the RFC, including airfields, railway stations, villages and camps. Seventy-two new Mk IV tanks were also available.

Twenty-five mines, with galleries up to 650m long, were driven under the German front line, twenty to forty metres below the surface, where they were less likely to be detected. They were dug through the upper layers of sandy loam, semi liquid sand and clay slurry, into the blue London clay beneath. Clay kicking, a technique used to construct the London Underground tunnels, was employed to dig the galleries. At the peak of the mining effort there were 4,000 miners supported by 4,000 pioneers and infantrymen. Most of the mines were ready by August 1916. An incessant silent battle went on underground, as the mines had to be maintained and sometimes fought for.

Zero hour was set for 3.10 a.m. on 7th June. The previous day Plumer told his staff, *Gentlemen, we may not make history tomorrow, but we shall certainly change the geography.* They did both.

The assault troops moved into position overnight, some making it just in time, and were briefed on the mines at the last possible moment. From 2 a.m. onwards aircraft flew low over the German positions to cover the noise of the tanks moving forward. Half an hour before dawn all was quiet and nightingales were heard singing. Within nineteen seconds of Zero, nineteen huge mines, totalling 470 tons of explosives, exploded along the German front line from Hill 60 in the north to near Ploegsteert Wood in the south. The pre-dawn silence was shattered. Germans in Lille, twenty-four kilometres away, rushed into the streets panic stricken by the earthquake effect.

The detonations were heard in London. A British witness observed, *Suddenly … great leaping streams of orange flame shot upwards, each a huge volcano in itself … followed by terrific explosions and dense masses of smoke and dust, which stood like great pillars towering into the sky, all illuminated by the fires below.*

Six mines were not used; Peckham II, La Petit Douve Farm and three of the four at Le Pelerin/Birdcage are still there. The fourth Le Pelerin/Birdcage mine exploded in July 1955 during a thunderstorm, leaving a crater seventy-five metres across and eighteen metres deep.

Huge numbers of Germans were killed and wounded, others were too stunned to resist or fled in panic. The artillery opened fire simultaneously, including firing seventy tons of gas shells onto enemy gun positions. Three belts of artillery fire, in total 650m deep, moved ahead of the infantry, while the medium and heavy guns fired standing barrages on defences and approaches further back. Counter-battery fire accounted for a quarter of the German field guns and half of the heavies. The British gun flashes were so close together that the western horizon seemed to be ablaze. Within seconds 80,000 men were advancing up the slopes of Messines Ridge. Visibility was limited to about fifty metres due to the hour and the dust and smoke from the mine explosions and artillery fire. Some units lost direction, but the German artillery did not respond for five to ten minutes after Zero, by which time the assault battalions were well clear of their assembly trenches.

Resistance was negligible at first and the first objective was gained in thirty-five minutes. The advance was so swift that the tanks could not keep up. Any resistance was quickly cleared up by a combination of rifle grenades, Lewis guns, bombers and trench mortars. This method of countering pillboxes, found to be so successful on Vimy Ridge, would become very familiar for the rest of the year in the Flanders offensive. The support battalions in each brigade then passed through to continue the advance to the next objective some 450–750m away. The barrage dealt with local counterattacks, but as the advance approached the forward posts of the German second position resistance began to stiffen.

II ANZAC Corps was to attack northeast to capture the southern shoulder of the Ridge, including Messines. It was to consolidate the southern flank of the attack from St Yves across the slopes of the Ridge to meet the Oosttaverne Line east of Messines and then along it to the Corps northern boundary. 3rd Australian Division on the right, the New Zealand Division in the centre and 25th Division on the left were to advance to the first Corps objective on the Black Line, 450m east of Messines, having passed through subsidiary objectives on the Blue, Brown and Yellow Lines. Patrols were to be pushed out another 275m to the Black Dotted Line, which was to be the start line for the assault on the final Corps objective (Green Line) by 4th Australian Division passing through the New Zealand and 25th Divisions. The Black Dotted Line would then form the support line to the new front. 57th Division was in reserve. The Corps was allocated twenty tanks, the routes being carefully planned and bridges readied for crossing the Douve. One

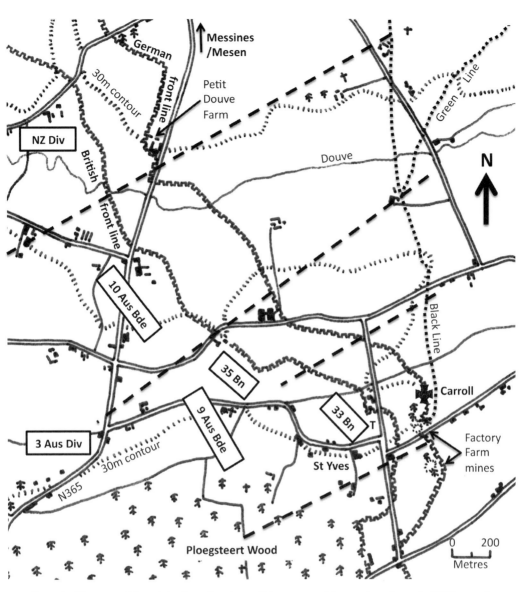

From the Ploegsteert Memorial, where there is a café/restaurant, drive northwards on the N365 towards Mesen (Messines). The road goes round a right hand bend and climbs a hill. At the top turn right, signed for Bruce Bairnsfather's cottage and the site of the 1914 Christmas truce. Pass Prowse Point Military Cemetery on the right and continue to the t-junction. Turn left and after 150m stop at the telecommunications tower (marked with a T on the map) at the highest point on the left. Cross the road and climb the bank on the right side for a view over 33rd Battalion's area of attack.

hundred and forty-four machine guns were allocated for a barrage 450m in front of the advancing infantry.

3rd Australian Division on the right had a frontage of 1,800m. It had a difficult three miles approach march through Ploegsteert Wood, which was deluged with German gas shells as the assault troops moved through it. There were 500 casualties. However, the men persevered in their respirators and, despite some loss of direction, they reached the assembly positions in good order. The assault was delivered by 9th and 10th Australian Brigades on the right and left respectively, assisted by the four Trench 122 and Trench 127 mines. Some troops had only just arrived in the assembly trenches at Zero and went straight into the attack. The mine craters caused some confusion as the troops tried to keep direction. In some places waves joined together, but the tasks were well known and the men were able to sort themselves out and reform as they advanced to their objectives.

9th Australian Brigade identified the troops to take each objective with coloured patches – front line black, support line white and Black Line pink. The initial assault was by 33rd Battalion on the right and 35th Battalion on the left. 34th Battalion was to pass through the latter later and 36th Battalion was in reserve. Each battalion attacked with three companies and smoke was laid by Stokes mortars to mask off the right flank.

33rd Battalion advanced with D Company on the right, C Company in the centre and B Company on the left. It was to seize the Black Line and consolidate it as the new support line. It was also to capture the northern of the two Factory Farm/Trench 122 mine craters on the extreme right. A platoon of A Company was under D Company for this task. At Zero the Battalion encountered some resistance in front, in addition to enfilade fire from the open right flank. D Company only reached the start line as the mines exploded and there was no time to reorganise, so it went over in one wave. The wire was well cut and there was little opposition in the German front line. Most of the surviving enemy were still in their dugouts. **Private John Carroll** rushed the enemy trench and bayoneted four men. He noticed a comrade in difficulties and went to his assistance, killing another German. He then discovered a machine gun team of four men in a shell hole and attacked them alone. He killed three of the crew and captured the gun. Following a shell explosion, he rescued two comrades who had been buried.

The advance continued to the support line, where the Germans resisted more strongly. A machine gun opened up and three men were hit, but the gun was taken

From the road bank at the telecommunications tower looking east. 33rd Battalion's front line was just in front of the road and the German front line ran parallel with it through the copse just right of centre, within which is the northernmost of the Factory Farm mine craters. Ploegsteert Wood is just visible on the extreme right. John Carroll's VC action was to the left of the copse.

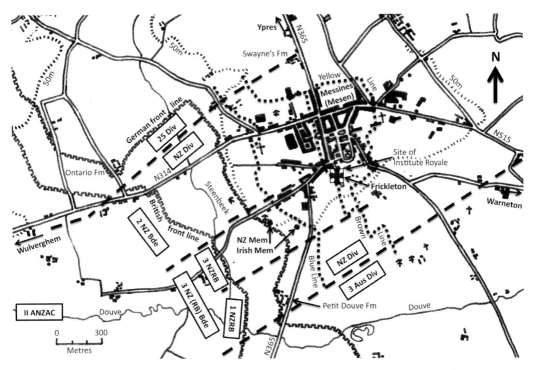

Map labels:
Ypres · Swayne's Fm · N365 · 50m · German front line · 25 Div · NZ Div · Yellow Line · Messines (Mesen) · N515 · 50m · Site of Institute Royale · Ontario Fm · N314 · British front line · 2 NZ Bde · Steenbeek · Frickleton · Warneton · Wulverghem · 3 NZRB · 3 NZ (RB) Bde · NZ Mem · Irish Mem · 1 NZRB · Blue Line · Brown Line · NZ Div · 3 Aus Div · Petit Douve Fm · Douve · II ANZAC · Douve · 0 · 300 · Metres · N365 · N

From the site of Robert Grieve's VC action drive west along Waastenstraat to the t-junction after 800m with Rijselstraat. There is space to park for a short period around the junction. Look west into the outskirts of Messines, where Samuel Frickleton stormed the machine gun positions.

by a team of five men led by Private James Spence DCM. During the final advance to the Black Line, where the flank rested on the northern Factory Farm mine-crater, another machine gun opened fire from a concrete shelter ninety metres up a communications trench, Ultimo Avenue. It was kept under sniper fire until 4 a.m., when a Stokes mortar of 9th Light Trench Mortar Battery drove the gun crew back into shelter with twelve rounds. By 5 a.m. the Battalion was reporting all its objectives had been taken and were being consolidated.

The New Zealand Division in the centre had a frontage of 1,400m. It had twelve of the twenty tanks allocated to II ANZAC Corps. In addition to the usual support of the corps artillery, the Division had nineteen 18 Pounder batteries and six 4.5" Howitzer batteries. In addition, fifty-six of the one hundred and forty-four machine guns in the Corps were allocated to the Division. The attack was made by 3rd New

Zealand (Rifle Brigade) Brigade on the right and 2nd New Zealand Brigade on the left. 3rd New Zealand (Rifle Brigade) Brigade's advance was led by 1st New Zealand Rifle Brigade on the right and 3rd New Zealand Rifle Brigade on the left, the latter reinforced by two platoons of 2nd New Zealand Rifle Brigade.

The New Zealand Division had avoided the gas that affected 3rd Australian Division in the approach march and reached its assembly trenches without problems. On the left flank there was a bulge in the line at Ontario Farm, from where the Germans could enfilade the New Zealand advance. An early advance was considered in this area, but it would have compromised the rest of the attack. So the left flank was protected by an enfilade barrage and smoke screen in addition to the Ontario Farm mine.

The leading battalions crossed the dry Steenbeek and, despite the La Petite Douve Farm mine being abandoned (the only one of twenty-five lost to countermining – 50,000 lbs of explosives remain twenty-five metres under Petit Douve Farm), they took the front trench system (Blue Line) within sixteen minutes. The leading companies halted in the support trench and the support companies in each battalion passed through and moved up the slope towards Messines and the Brown Line. The going was difficult in the dark, negotiating craters up to five metres deep, but by advancing on compass bearings they reached their objectives.

In 3rd New Zealand (Rifle Brigade) Brigade, 1st New Zealand Rifle Brigade on the right captured seventy prisoners and four machine guns. 3rd New Zealand Rifle Brigade on the left reached the Brown Line almost without opposition, then two machine guns at the edge of Messines opened fire. The commander of C Company on the left was killed and others fell rapidly as the advance was checked. **Lance Corporal Samuel Frickleton** was slightly wounded, but called on his section and led it through the barrage. He rushed and bombed one machine gun before dashing in with the bayonet and finishing the survivors. He then went on to tackle the other machine gun twenty metres away. He killed the three-man crew and then

Looking west from southeast of Messines. 3rd New Zealand Rifle Brigade attacked towards the camera. The top of the Irish Memorial shows above the houses on the left.

accounted for six others in the same post in a dugout. The advance then swept on to take the trench. Frickleton's action saved many casualties, but he was later severely wounded. 3rd New Zealand Rifle Brigade took almost one hundred prisoners and three machine guns up to the Brown Line. It lost forty-two men killed, 201 wounded and had forty-nine missing. Only nine officers remained.

On the left of 2nd New Zealand Brigade, machine guns at Swayne's Farm, 350m north of the village, held up the advance until a tank crashed through it and forced thirty Germans to surrender. 4th New Zealand Rifle Brigade (3rd New Zealand (Rifle Brigade) Brigade) and 2nd Canterbury (2nd New Zealand Brigade) passed through the leading battalions and continued through the wire and outer trench system into the village. By then the creeping barrage had slowed to ninety metres every eleven minutes. Messines village was a fortress ringed by two lines of trenches and barbed wire. Inside the trench ring were five strongpoints based on concrete pillboxes and the existing cellars had also been strengthened.

The village was divided equally between the two battalions and each area was allocated to a platoon or company. Every man had a map showing what to expect and where the strongpoints were located. Snipers fired from the remains of houses or threw bombs from behind walls. Numerous machine guns were rushed, outflanked or silenced by rifle grenades. The German commandant and staff were captured in a massive dugout under an orphanage (Institute Royale). In all, twenty-three machine guns were taken in Messines. By 4 a.m., except on the left, where a flank was formed to await the arrival of 25th Division, the New Zealand Division had taken the second system of trenches on the Yellow Line.

25th Division on the left had its assembly trenches 550–725m back on higher ground as a result of the salient in the German line at Ontario Farm. Its front was narrower than the other two divisions in II ANZAC Corps to compensate for the greater distance to be covered. The mine at Ontario Farm assisted the attack of both brigades (74th and 7th), and they soon came up level with the New Zealand Division on the Messines–Wytschaete road on top of the Ridge. The only real opposition was at Hell Farm, 650m northwest of Messines, where a sharp fight resulted in fifty Germans surrendering and eight machine guns being taken.

In the centre, IX Corps advanced due east astride the Spanbroekmolen saddle to capture the central sector of the Ridge, including Wytschaete. 36th Division on the right and 16th Division in the centre were assisted by a number of mines, which killed or stunned the defenders. Resistance in the shambles that remained was overcome quickly, although there were some casualties due to the late firing of some mines. Except for L'Hospice at the northern end of Wytschaete Wood, which held out until 6.48 a.m., the rest of the objective was gained just after 5 a.m. 19th Division on the left had a similar experience; the enemy ran or surrendered and there was little fight in them.

X Corps on the left flank attacked southeast to gain the northern part of the Ridge as far north as Hill 60. The defences in this area were particularly strong to maintain observation over the British rear areas east of Ypres. 41st Division on the right met little resistance. In Damm Strasse and its numerous dugouts there were some sharp fights, but the advance moved on irresistibly. 47th Division in the centre and 23rd Division on the left were assisted by the Caterpillar and Hill 60 mines and a smoke screen along the Comines Canal covered the initial advance.

Soon after 5 a.m. the second intermediate objective, which included the first trench of the German Second Line had been taken along the entire attack front. The next objective, 365–460m away across the flat top of the Ridge, included the rear trench of the Second Line. A pause of two hours was allowed to bring forward fresh battalions, during which strongpoints were established and pack animals moved forward ammunition, water and rations. At 7 a.m. the standing barrage intensified and began creeping forward again.

On the right flank of II ANZAC Corps, 3rd Australian Division had taken the German front and support lines. The support battalions in 9th and 10th Australian Brigades passed through to continue the advance to the second objective (Black Line). North of the Douve, 10th Australian Brigade was held up by a machine gun on top of a concrete post north of Grey's Farm. It was overcome and eventually so was opposition near Bethleem Farm. 9th Australian Brigade, south of the Douve, was led by 34th Battalion, while 33rd Battalion held the right flank. 34th Battalion met stiff resistance from a number of machine gun positions until they were taken. Both brigades reached the Black Line and began digging in on their objective. By 5.15 a.m. the Division had completed its main part in the attack.

In the New Zealand Division in the centre of II ANZAC Corps, 1st Wellington and 1st Auckland in 1st New Zealand Brigade passed through 3rd New Zealand (Rifle Brigade) and 2nd New Zealand Brigades and advanced rapidly left and right of Messines. An artillery HQ at Blauwen Molen, 450m east of the village, was overrun. On the left Fanny's Farm was secured after a tank knocked in the walls and a hundred Germans surrendered.

In 25th Division on the left, 75th Brigade passed through the leading brigades. The only real resistance was at Lumm Farm but, with the assistance of 36th Division to the north, it was rushed and the garrison was either killed or captured.

In the centre, IX Corps' advance continued. 36th Division on the right captured a German battalion headquarters in a house near the Messines road. 16th Division, in the centre, faced Wytschaete village, the northern buttress of the whole German position on Messines Ridge. Although visibly ruined, it was a fortress, with all round defence based upon machine gun positions in reinforced cellars. A tank led two battalions through and around the village and by 8 a.m. the objective beyond the St Eloi–Messines road had been taken. On the left, 19th Division had little trouble in reaching its objectives. At 8.40 a.m., a company from each leading battalion advanced behind the barrage to the observation line a few hundred metres down the eastern slope of the Ridge. They were supported by eight tanks and patrols of the Corps cavalry. RFC aircraft strafed any Germans they saw in front. The observation line, from Bethleem Farm south of Messines through Despagne Farm and along the eastern side of Oosttaverne Wood, was reached with few casualties. It was to be the start line for the afternoon's assault and was accordingly marked with tape and flags.

X Corps on the left, generally had a more difficult time. 41st Division on the right crossed 450m to the objective on the back of the Ridge, meeting only occasional resistance. However, 47th Division in the centre had some bitter fighting. Its objective included the 365m long Spoil Bank on the north side of the Comines Canal. The attack was checked by machine guns on the south bank and in Battle Wood and at 9 a.m. the assault troops withdrew for a re-bombardment of the objective. Meanwhile, south of the canal, White Chateau was captured. On the left 23rd Division had heavy losses clearing Battle Wood.

By 9 a.m. the line along the entire length of the Ridge had been established from the Douve to the east of Mount Sorrel. Artillery observers could see into the German rear areas for the first time since October 1914, but not to the base of the Ridge, due to the convex slope. Casualties had been a fraction of those predicted, but as a result the top of the Ridge became congested and led to unnecessary losses. German reserve divisions were expected to arrive at this time and batteries of XIV Corps in reserve, that had not revealed their positions, were ready for them. However, it was not until 11 a.m. that enemy troops could be seen marching towards the front about four kilometres away.

At 1.45 p.m. German troops crossed the Oosttaverne Line in ten waves on a frontage of 900m from east of Messines to Lumm Farm. The New Zealand Division was not affected by the German artillery barrage and had a clear field of fire. To the north, 25th Division met the attack with the frontal and enfilade fire of twelve machine guns. At 2.10 p.m. the British protective barrage intensified as a counterattack appeared imminent. The combined fire of artillery and machine guns stopped the attack before it reached the observation line. However, in view of the counterattack the corps commanders did not believe a further immediate advance to the Oosttaverne Line was practicable. Five hours was allowed in the plan for each corps to bring forward its reserve division and some artillery before this advance commenced, but two more hours were added, so the attack was to commence at 3.10 p.m. Forty batteries were moved forward and one hundred and forty-six machine guns were to fire an overhead barrage. Twenty-four tanks were available.

In II ANZAC Corps, two brigades of 4th Australian Division took up the lead on the left of 3rd Australian Division, each with two battalions. On the right 12th Australian Brigade passed through a heavy barrage while crossing the shoulder of the Ridge, but had few casualties. Only then was it told that the advance had been delayed for two hours. The troops had to wait in the open and exposed to enemy artillery and machine gun fire. Despite this, many men were so tired that they slept through it all. On the left 13th Australian Brigade did receive the message to delay the start and held back until 1.40 p.m. before commencing the move to the start line.

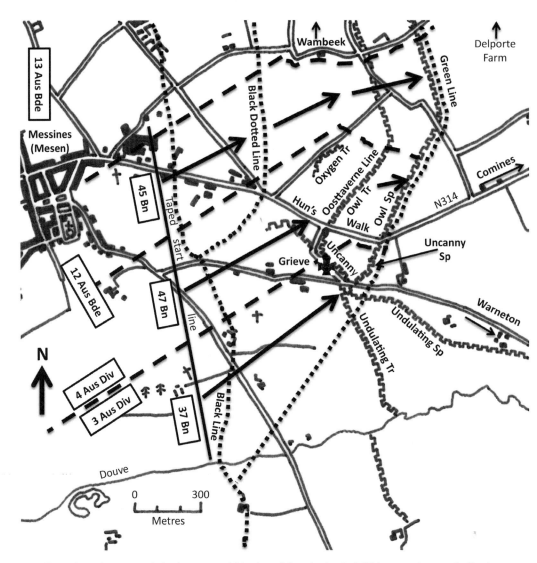

From the main crossroads in the centre of Messines (Mesen) take the N314 eastwards towards Comines (Komen). After 1,350m turn right just before a house on the corner onto Vier Koningenstraat. This lane bends to the left after 100m. Continue to the t-junction after another 200m and turn right. Drive on for 200m and park outside some houses on the left. Walk back to the junction 200m behind. This was where Uncanny Support, Undulating Support and Undulating Trench met. The pillbox stormed by Robert Grieve was in Uncanny Trench, which ran parallel with and about thirty metres east of the road, running northwest from this junction.

While waiting for the barrage to creep forward again, the survivors of the German counterattack were seen taking up positions in front of and along the Oosttaverne Line and reinforcements were seen arriving south of the Messines–Warneton road. The Australians realised that they faced some hard fighting. However, **Captain Robert Grieve** in 37th Battalion described this waiting period as being more like a picnic than a battle. At 3.10 p.m. the creeping barrage began moving forward again and the advance resumed towards the Green Line.

12th Australian Brigade had 37th Battalion attached from 3rd Australian Division on the right. The Brigade's objective was 900m of the rear trench of the Oosttaverne Line. The leading companies were to take the front trench when the barrage lifted at 3.30 p.m. and the support companies were to pass through to seize the support trench when the barrage lifted at 3.45 p.m. Moving closely behind three tanks, 47th and 45th Battalions, right and left respectively, were swept by machine guns from hedges, trenches and pillboxes and suffered heavily. Most resistance was centred on pillboxes in the Oosttaverne Line 275m ahead. With the support of the tanks, Oxygen Trench was overrun and 120 prisoners were taken. North of the Messines–Warneton road, 45th Battalion was held up by machine guns and field guns in concrete emplacements near Delporte Farm. South of the road, 37th and 47th Battalions reached the pillboxes screened by the dust of the barrage and many savage fights took place as each strongpoint was outflanked and overcome. Many surrendered as soon as they realised their defences had been outflanked, but some fought on and others were shot down or ran into the barrage as they tried to flee.

37th Battalion advanced with C Company on the left and D Company on the right, with A Company and D Company of 40th Battalion following in support respectively. B Company was in reserve. A Company, under Captain Grieve, on the left was to capture Uncanny Support in the Green Line from Hun's Walk to the junction of Undulating Support and Undulating Trench. During consolidation it was to establish a strongpoint behind its front line, which was to include a trench mortar and a machine gun. To ensure various parties could be recognised easily, coloured shoulder straps were worn – scouts green, runners red, signallers blue, carriers yellow, moppers-up white etc.

During the advance many previously unknown machine gun positions were encountered and sections of the enemy trenches were found to be largely undamaged by the barrage. As a consequence casualties were heavy. A Company was passing through a gap in the German wire while the barrage was still on the German front line, when a machine gun opened fire. Half the company was hit, including all the officers except Grieve, and they were held up 175m south of the road. Grieve avoided further casualties by getting his men into the cover of shell holes. He saw the fire was coming from a loopholed concrete pillbox in Uncanny Trench and went off to find the Vickers and Stokes crews who were advancing with his company. Both crews had already been hit either by artillery or machine gun fire. The Machine Gun Officer, Lieutenant AJ Fraser (MC for this action), repaired the Vickers with wire cut from the entanglement, but as he mounted the gun to fire he and the gun were hit.

Grieve set off alone and approached the machine gun position from a flank, knowing that the arc of fire was limited by the loophole. As he closed in on the pillbox he threw bombs towards it. Each one caused the gunners to cease firing momentarily, allowing him to move from shell hole to shell hole under the cover of the dust from the explosions and get closer on each occasion. Having passed out of the arc of fire he got into the deserted trench, which was still under the British

From the junction of Uncanny Trench with Undulating Support and Undulating Trench. 37th Battalion attacked towards the camera position. Uncanny Trench, where Robert Grieve captured the pillbox, ran parallel with Vier Koningenstraat.

barrage. He posted two bombs through the loophole and inside the pillbox found the whole crew either dead or wounded. Grieve signalled the company to move ahead again and it occupied the trench. Germans fleeing down a communications trench were shot down by Lance Corporal William Babington's Lewis gun (killed next day – Ypres (Menin Gate) Memorial). Grieve was still standing on the roof of the pillbox signalling to his men when he was wounded by a sniper. Meanwhile the right had rushed the trench and taken eighty prisoners as soon as the barrage lifted. A Company began consolidating thirty metres short of Uncanny Support. By the time the Battalion was relieved on 9th June, it had suffered 402 casualties, including sixty-seven killed.

On the left, 13th Australian Brigade was held up 450m short of the Oosttaverne Line as was the left of 12th Australian Brigade, and suffered heavy losses. The left of the Brigade was unsupported at that time by 33rd Brigade and inclined left, trying to make touch. This took the advance across the Wambeek spur instead of straight down it and a gap opened in the centre of the Brigade. However, the move filled the gap on the flank until 33rd Brigade arrived and ensured the Brigade did not have Germans in its left rear. The Oosttaverne Line was reached, but 900m north of where it should have been. About 4.30 p.m. units of the delayed 33rd Brigade began to arrive and seized Joye and Van Hove Farms.

IX Corps' frontage had narrowed during the advance, so only 33rd Brigade of 11th Division in reserve was required. Messages to move forward were delayed and the Brigade did not reach the start line until 3.50 p.m., forty minutes after the attack was due to start. When the error was realised, two battalions of 57th Brigade (in reserve to 19th Division) were sent forward to seize 550m of the Oosttaverne Line from Van Hove Farm to the road junction south of Bug Wood. This reduced the section to be taken by 33rd Brigade to 1,100m. Commanders in 57th Brigade had no time to familiarise themselves with the task other than to move in a certain direction

and keep up with the barrage. Fortunately German opposition and artillery fire were light and the two battalions occupied the Oosttaverne Line within twenty minutes.

In X Corps, 17th and 73rd Brigades of 24th Division reached Damm Strasse before 1 p.m. without incident and moved onto the start line soon afterwards. They gained their objectives easily, taking 289 prisoners and six guns. One brigade suffered only six casualties. 73rd Brigade ran its left flank back to join with 47th Division, which was still held up at Spoil Bank, north of the canal.

In the southern area an SOS barrage was called for at 5.30 p.m. to check a counterattack astride the Warneton road. A contact aircraft flew over, but the advanced and isolated elements of 47th and 37th Battalions were reluctant to fire their flares to identify themselves, fearing they would reveal their positions to the enemy. Contact was made by signal lamp as the enemy counterattack approached. It was met with a hail of small arms fire and the attack melted away on the left but continued on the right. The British barrage then fell behind the forward troops. At first it was thought to be German fire, but it was soon realised that it was the protective barrage. It moved forward and hit the forward elements of 12th Australian Brigade, which was 230m ahead of where it should have halted, but this was not known further up the chain of command. The attack was halted but the artillery fire continued to cause friendly casualties. A junior officer ordered a retirement back through the barrage. This move was continued to left and right despite more senior officers trying to stop it. There were many casualties. Some companies fell back through the observation line to the first objective before they could be reorganised. New Zealanders on the first objective believed the retirement heralded a counterattack and asked for the barrage to be shortened to in front of the observation line. This fire hit those Australians on the proper objective, including 37th Battalion on the right, forcing those units to also pull back through the barrage with considerable losses. 37th Battalion fell back from the open area north of the Douve, but part of it held on to the first Oosttaverne trench south of Hun's Walk. By dusk the whole of the southern part of the Oosttaverne Line had been given up or remained uncaptured.

The arrival of German reinforcements in front of IX Corps looked like a counterattack and at 8.30 p.m. the SOS barrage came down causing friendly casualties. Many men fell back, including the garrison of Van Hove Farm. Rumours spread that the forward brigades had been pushed back and the protective barrage was shortened to in front of the observation line. This made it intolerable for those still in front of it. The situation was not restored until 10 p.m., when the artillery ceased and IX Corps' sector of the Oosttaverne Line was reoccupied.

Despite these unnecessary setbacks, the British could move freely in daylight on the western slopes of the Ridge for the first time since October 1914. The southern end of the Ypres Salient had been wiped out. Only the Spoil Bank, at the bend of the Comines Canal in X Corps area, and a 900m section of the Oosttaverne Line at the junction of II ANZAC and IX Corps had not been taken or had been lost. At 10.45 p.m., 3rd and 4th Australian Divisions were ordered to reoccupy all the lost ground, but HQ II ANZAC Corps was unaware that the Blauwepoortbeek sector had never been taken nor that part of 13th Australian Brigade was out of place in IX Corps area.

The attack was to be made by 44th Battalion in 3rd Australian Division and 48th Battalion in 4th Australian Division. At Zero, 44th Battalion was on the start line, but there was no sign of 48th Battalion on their left. It advanced alone at 3 a.m. next morning and stopped short of the Oosttaverne Line in a partially dug trench in front of the German wire. Under fire from its own artillery the Battalion pulled back a little, with both flanks refused. 48th Battalion was delayed due to orders arriving too late. Eventually a thin line was organised and advanced 135m to an unknown trench, which made an ideal start line. More of the Battalion arrived and a patrol successively found Oxygen Trench and the front and support Oosttaverne Line trenches unoccupied. Platoons dashed forward to occupy them. Despite missing the start time, 48th Battalion still gained all its objectives.

The situation north of the Warneton road was not appreciated by HQ II ANZAC Corps for many hours. It was not until 4 a.m. when GOC 4th Australian Division and two brigade commanders went forward to Messines that it was learned that part of 13th Australian Brigade (52nd Battalion) was holding most of 33rd Brigade's front, but only 200m of its own. It was decided that 33rd Brigade would take over its proper front from 52nd Battalion that evening. 52nd Battalion was then to move round to support the advance of 49th Battalion into the Blauwepoortbeek gap to take the only remaining section of the objective from the previous day. While 33rd Brigade was being relieved, the Germans opened fire with their artillery. This appeared to 25th Division to herald a German attack and the withdrawal of 52nd Battalion looked like a counterattack. The SOS signals were fired and the area was again deluged with shells. This caused the Germans to believe that they were going to be attacked and added their SOS barrage. There were heavy casualties and the attack on the Blauwepoortbeek had to be postponed.

The confusion resulted from having two separate defence organisations; one under the reserve divisions along the Oosttaverne Line and another under the original attack divisions on the Ridge, each with its own supporting artillery. The situation was not unravelled until 9th June, when a front defence system on the forward slope was supported by a main line of resistance on the Ridge top, both under the unified command of the forward divisions.

At 10 p.m. on 10th June 13th Australian Brigade attacked down the Blauwepoortbeek, while bombers moved north from the captured section of the Oosttaverne Line. Preparatory fire by the heavies was erratic, probably due to excessive barrel wear and there were some friendly casualties. The attack was only partly successful. Further south 3rd Australian Division advanced at 11 p.m. and strengthened advanced posts established the previous night south of the Douve in order to cover the whole right flank of the operation. During the 11th the Germans fell back from the part of the Oostataverne Line still held by them to the Warneton Line. Patrols followed up and secured the last part of the original final objective except for the Spoil Bank.

14th June 1917

220 Pte William Ratcliffe, 2nd South Lancashire (75th Brigade, 25th Division), Messines, Belgium

The days following the successful storming of Messines Ridge on 7th June 1917 were spent in consolidation, during which the Oosttaverne Line was taken. Here it was discovered that observation over the German lines was not as extensive as expected and a short general advance on the whole front was ordered for 14th June. II ANZAC Corps' part in this was to push forward its left and centre about 900m to include Gapaard Spur and Ferme de la Croix, while its right advanced from Ploegsteert Wood eastward towards the Lys. However, the Germans pulled back on the night of 10th/11th June, evacuating many of the positions to be attacked.

25th Division was under command of II ANZAC Corps at this time. 75th Brigade was in reserve until it took over the front line from 4th Australian Brigade on 12th June. The Brigade was given the task of capturing the line from Ferme de la Croix through Gapaard to Deconinck Farm and establishing a chain of strongpoints. 2nd South Lancashire was the right assault battalion and 8th Border the left, each advancing with three companies forward and one in support.

The approaches to the front line in this area were under observation by the Germans and there were few communications trenches. The attack was set for the evening and it was not desirable to have the assault troops crammed into the forward trenches all day. During the previous night improvements were made to communications to allow the move into the start positions to be conducted in daylight. However, the communications trenches in 2nd South Lancashire's area were still incomplete and men had to be moved forward in small parties over

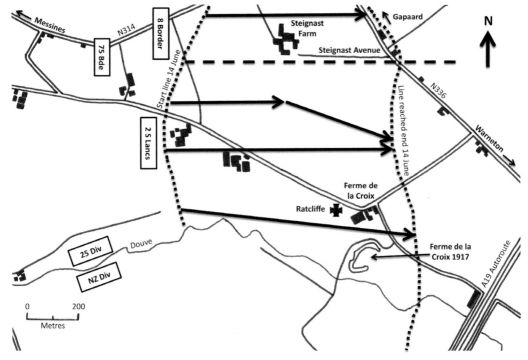

From the main crossroads in the centre of Messines (Mesen) take the N314 eastwards towards Comines (Komen). After 1,350m turn right just before a house on the corner onto Vier Koningenstraat. Continue to the t-junction after 300m (Robert Grieve's VC action) and turn left. Drive on for 1,200m and park just before Ferme de la Croix on a left bend. The original farm was behind the current buildings.

carefully reconnoitred routes. It took four and a half hours and was completed at 6.30 p.m. with only three casualties.

2nd South Lancashire's three assault companies formed up in the open while under fire from pockets of enemy located in shell holes. The attack, commencing at 7.30 p.m., was to be preceded by a standard creeping barrage. This happened perfectly in front of 8th Border, but in front of 2nd South Lancashire the guns immediately jumped back to the final standing barrage line beyond Ferme de la

William Ratcliffe's VC action was in front of the modern Ferme de la Croix.

Croix. Knowing it was vital to keep up with the artillery, the troops doubled forward and the speed of their advance surprised the enemy, who were mostly overcome with little effort. The German barrage came down five minutes after Zero and fell to the rear of the advancing troops.

Although the German artillery made little impact on the advance, machine gun posts were a different matter. Several were located near Ferme de la Croix, the objective of D Company under Second Lieutenant Henry Ernest Howse (MID for this action). He and his men managed to outflank the enemy and drive them out with rifle grenades, but one party retired into the ruins of the Ferme, where it continued to resist stoutly.

It was here that one of the stretcher-bearers, **Private William Ratcliffe**, distinguished himself. As he followed his platoon near the first objective, he noticed a machine gun firing into the flank and rear of his comrades. Dropping his stretcher, he seized a rifle and went straight at the machine gun post, bayoneting the officer and the crew of five. He picked up the gun and ammunition, hurried after his Company and brought it into action. When the objective had fallen, he went back to his stretcher and spent the rest of the day bringing in the wounded under a heavy barrage. It is understood he recovered a pistol from the German officer and sold it for seventy-five francs.

A and B Companies on the left reached their objectives without great difficulty and within a short time a new line was being consolidated. By 9.20 p.m. confirmation reached Brigade HQ that 8th Border had taken all its objectives and the same was received from 2nd South Lancashire at 10 p.m. Contact was made with flanking brigades to the south at Ferme de la Croix and to the north.

However, 2nd South Lancashire's left company had lost direction after Steignast Farm and drifted right, leaving a gap of 450m. 8th Border pushed out additional posts south of Steignast Avenue and 2nd South Lancashire covered the gap with a machine gun and two Lewis guns. The gap was also patrolled by both battalions. 2nd South Lancashire remained in the line until the night of 17th/18th June. In addition to Ratcliffe's VC, the Battalion received thirty-three other gallantry awards for this action.

The Battle of Messines came to a close. Casualties in the first stages were light, but had mounted thereafter mainly due to crowding on the ridge. Second Army suffered 24,562 casualties up to 12th June. The Germans admitted to 23,000 casualties to 10th June, but their figures do not include lightly wounded, whereas British figures do. Amongst the Germans losses were 7,354 prisoners, forty-eight guns, 218 machine guns and sixty mortars.

28th June 1917

222 2Lt Frank Wearne, 11th Essex (18th Brigade, 6th Division), east of Loos, France

In the interval between the capture of Messines Ridge and the start of the Flanders campaign, Haig ordered a series of feint attacks by First Army along twenty-two kilometres of front between Gavrelle and Hulluch. In one operation on 28th June 1917 all three Corps were ordered to improve their positions. The Canadian and I Corps attacked south and north of the Souchez River respectively, with the aim of taking the German salient between Avion and Lens.

The bombardment opened at 7 p.m. along the whole Army front, to give the impression that a full scale offensive was about to take place. Some artillery on its way north for the forthcoming Flanders offensive was diverted to take part. The infantry attack at 7.10 p.m. was accompanied by a violent thunderstorm and torrents of rain. On I Corps' right north of the Souchez, 46th Division captured most of Avion, Eleu dit Leauwette and the eastern slopes of Reservoir Hill.

On 46th Division's left a diversionary raid was launched by 18th Brigade (6th Division), with 2nd Durham Light Infantry on the right and 11th Essex on the left each providing a company. 11th Essex was commanded by Lieutenant Colonel Frederick Gordon Spring. In the preceding three days various artillery shoots had been fired in rehearsal for the raid and to give the impression that attack was impending at 8 p.m. To enhance this impression to an aerial observer, early on the morning of 28th June over 1,000 dummies were deployed in the front and support lines held by 2nd Durham Light Infantry. Wire cutting was conducted by the artillery and also by patrols with Bangalore torpedoes.

C Company 11th Essex, commanded by Captain Sydney Edwin Silver MC, and twenty men of A Company, were allocated for the raid, divided into four parties as follows:

- A Party – thirty men in three sections commanded by Lieutenant Magnus Rainier Robertson.
- B Party – thirty men in two sections commanded by **Second Lieutenant Frank Wearne**.
- C Party – an NCO and six men.

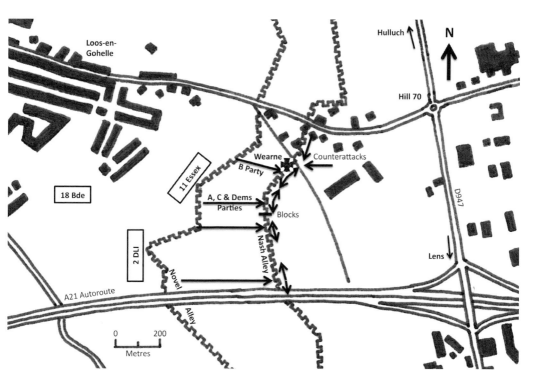

From the square in the centre of Loos, where there are a couple of cafés, drive northeast on the D165 towards Hulluch. After 150m turn right on Rue Kleber, signed 'Halle de Tennis'. Continue 200m and turn left, signed 'Stade Eric Sikorsa'. Take the right fork after 100m, signed 'Ecole O Leroy' and continue 850m. Turn right on Chemin de la Voie Perdue and park on the hard standing on the right. Walk along the road southeast towards a large industrial building on the left. After 250m turn to face west and fifty metres into the field is where B Party entered the German trench. Frank Wearne held the left flank from that point to the road you are standing on. Further south in the field are the remains of a concrete pillbox. This is where Nash Alley turned from running northwards to northeastwards and where A Party entered the German trench.

• Demolition party of twenty-one sappers from 3rd Australian Tunnelling Company. The plan was for A Party to enter the enemy lines, establish itself and then to collect prisoners and demolish dugouts. The left section was to bomb northwards towards B Party while a block was established in a communications trench leading to the rear. B Party was to make its entry either side of a sap and turn left and right to protect its flanks. C Party was to cross a trench block held by the right section of A Party and rush a German block. It was to be followed by the demolition party to destroy mine shafts and dugouts. All parties were to withdraw exactly one hour after zero.

There was insufficient artillery available for the raid, but the 18 Pounders were assisted by trench mortars and machine guns targeting communications trenches to the rear. Smoke and burning oil canisters were also projected by Royal Engineer special companies. As a result, the barrage worked well and at 7.10 p.m. A and B Parties left the British lines and entered the enemy trenches as planned. The wire proved to be no obstacle. The inside sections of A and B Parties met up, but no contact

From behind the German front overlooking the area of the raid on 28th June.

was made with 2nd Durham Light Infantry on the right. A Party encountered little opposition initially, but suffered heavy casualties later in a counterattack. C Party took the block without opposition. When the enemy in a nearby dugout refused to surrender the sappers threw in a charge to destroy it. Wearne led B Party forward despite the opposition and gained his objectives. The left section encountered continuous counterattacks from the left along the trench and from the German support line over the open. Of the fifteen men involved in the fighting there, only one escaped unwounded.

The enemy bombarded their own front line and an aircraft flew overhead dropping red flares. Wearne knew the importance of holding the left flank. At a critical moment he jumped onto the parapet and, followed by the left section, ran along the top of the trench firing and throwing grenades into the enemy. This daring and unexpected action threw them back in disorder. Wearne was severely wounded in the leg, but refused to leave his men and continued to organise the defence. Just before the order to withdraw was given, he was wounded again in the back of the neck. While he was being assisted back he was hit a third time and killed.

After an hour in the enemy lines the withdrawal was conducted under heavy enemy pressure. Of the 104 men engaged in the raid, forty-eight became casualties, including twelve killed and six missing believed killed (CWGC records eighteen dead in 11th Essex on 28th June 1917, including ten commemorated on the Loos Memorial). Enemy casualties were also heavy with two dugouts and three mine shafts being destroyed. One prisoner of the 153rd Regiment was brought back.

In addition to Wearne's VC, Lieutenant Colonel Spring was awarded the DSO, Captain Silver a Bar to his MC and Lieutenant Robertson the MC. Silver was killed on 20th November 1917 and is buried in Fifteen Ravine British Cemetery, Villers-Plouich (IV II 20). Lieutenant Robertson was killed on 22nd August 1918 and is buried in Méaulte Military Cemetery (G 15).

7th July 1917

223 2Lt Frederick Youens, 13th Durham Light Infantry (68th Brigade, 23rd Division), near Hill 60, Ypres, Belgium

Since taking part in the Messines offensive, 13th Durham Light Infantry had been out of the line, but returned to the trenches near Klein Zillebeke late on 5th July to relieve 8th King's Own Yorkshire Light Infantry. At 12.15 a.m. on 7th July, **2nd Lieutenant Frederick Youens** led out a three man patrol from the Battalion's right flank with the intention of gaining touch with the neighbouring unit, 1/17th London (141st Brigade, 47th Division). Shortly afterwards a party of forty Germans was seen carrying materiel into a strongpoint. The enemy covering party tried to surround Youens' patrol and take them prisoner, but they fought back. Although Youens and one of his men were wounded they all regained the British lines.

From 1.45 a.m. to 3 a.m. a heavy bombardment fell on 13th Durham Light Infantry's front and support line trenches. At 2.30 a.m. about fifty Germans raided

13th Durham Light Infantry's front line ran across this field in July 1917. Frederick Youens helped repel the German raid just the other side of this road (Werviksestraat).

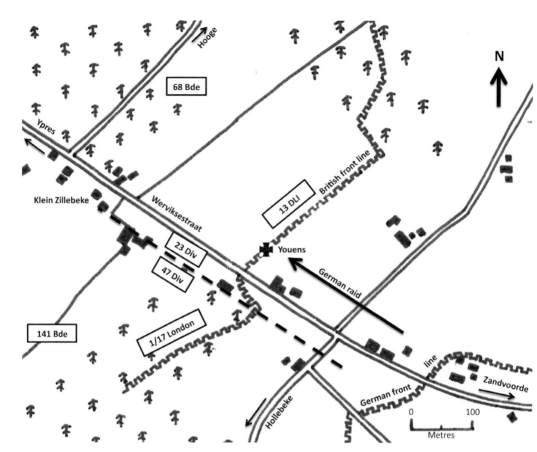

Leave Zillebeke in a southeasterly direction towards Zwarteleen. Go through the village and pass the turning to Hill 60 on the right. Continue 900m from that junction and park outside a house on the right of Werviksestraat. Look across the road to the field on the left/north side. This is where the British front line crossed the road and where Frederick Youens defended it against the German raid.

the right company's position. The shelling scattered a Lewis gun team and it seemed inevitable that the enemy would break in.

Youens was in a nearby dugout having his wounds attended to, but dashed out without shirt or jacket and took control. He quickly got the Lewis gun into action. A bomb landed in the gun position, which Youens caught and threw out again. Another bomb was thrown and Youens grabbed it, but before he could throw it back, it exploded, injuring him seriously and some of his men. Despite this, the raid was foiled, mainly due to Youens' resolute leadership and quick thinking. He died two days later. The Battalion lost another three killed and twelve wounded in this short action.

27th July 1917

After taking part in the attack on Messines Ridge, 11th Division moved north in preparation for the forthcoming Flanders offensive. On 15th/16th July, 33rd Brigade took over the entire frontage of XVIII Corps from 118th and 154th Brigades and came under command of 51st Division. Initially the front was held by three battalions. On 24th July, 7th South Staffordshire took over 33rd Brigade's left sub-sector. The tour in the forward trenches was scheduled for two days, but the delay in the start of the offensive resulted in an extension until 29th July.

On 25th July patrols at the northern end of the Fifth Army front reported that they had walked into the German front line without opposition. On the 26th there was a reorganisation of the forward positions, resulting in the XVIII Corps front being held by just two battalions; 7th South Staffordshire remained on the left with 6th Lincolnshire on the right. Early on the afternoon of the 27th RFC reports indicated that the enemy had abandoned his front line. The Guards Division on the extreme left flank took advantage of this and crossed the Yser Canal near Boesinghe to occupy 2,750m of the former enemy front line.

In XVIII Corps' area, 7th South Staffordshire received orders at 2.40 p.m. to prepare fighting patrols to push forward in conjunction with 6th Lincolnshire on the right, as it was suspected the enemy had withdrawn to the Black Line (Canopus Trench–Kitcheners' Wood–Hurst Park–Canister Trench–Cane Trench). All 6th Lincolnshire's patrols met with strong resistance and were forced back. 7th South Staffordshire's objective was the Blue Line (Kultur Farm–Muller Cot–Hindenburg Farm – Contour 23), with an advanced post at Racecourse Farm. At 4.10 p.m. orders were received to advance at 5 p.m.; there was to be no artillery support. The aim was to gain touch with the enemy, but patrols that were heavily engaged were to retire rather than fight pitched battles. By the time the company commanders had been briefed and returned to their companies it was almost time to advance.

7th South Staffordshire sent out five patrols each, consisting of an officer and twenty-five men with a Lewis gun, preceded by three scouts. The departure times were staggered from 5.30 to 6.10 p.m. and their objectives were:

• First patrol, on the extreme right – contact 6th Lincolnshire at Kultur Farm and send a small party to Racecourse Farm.
• Second patrol – reach No Man's Cottage and Muller Cottage after establishing contact with the patrols on its right and left.

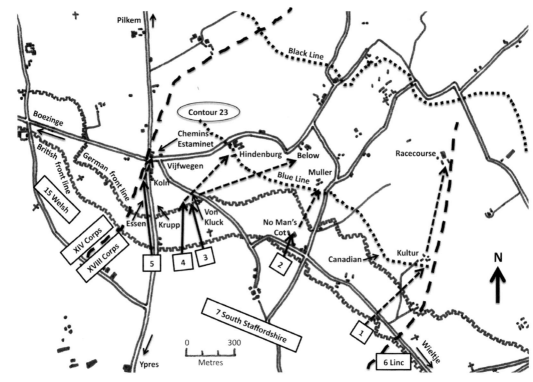

At the crossroads in Pilkem drive south along Pilkemseweg for 1,400m and at the crossroads at Vijfwegen turn left into Moortelweg and park. The buildings to the south on the east side of the road to Ypres are on the site of Koln Farm. The fifth patrol approached these buildings from the south and this is where Thomas Barratt covered his comrades while they withdrew. The patrols are marked by numbered boxes. Solid arrows show their progress and dashed arrows the intended objectives that were not reached.

- Third patrol – advance through Von Kluck Cottage to Below Farm.
- Fourth patrol – advance through Von Kluck Cottage to Hindenburg Farm.
- Fifth patrol, on the extreme left – pass through Krupp and Essen Farms to gain contact with 15th Welsh at Chemins Estaminet (Vijfwegen).

Koln Farm on the Pilkem–Ypres road, scene of Thomas Barratt's VC action on 27th July 1917.

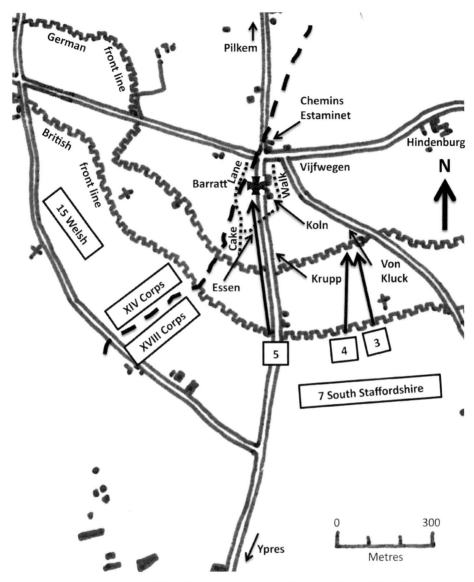

Details of the patrol action around Koln Farm. Beware when walking alongside the Pilkem–Ypres road as it can be both busy and fast.

All patrols gained the enemy front line, except on the extreme right, which was pinned down by machine gun fire from Canadian Farm until nightfall. The second and third patrols gained their initial objectives, but then encountered stiff opposition and flanking counterattacks. A prisoner confirmed that the ruse had been designed to entice the British into a trap. These two patrols withdrew successfully to the British front line.

The two patrols on the left provided by D Company reached the enemy front line, but encountered heavy opposition further on. The left patrol had the most difficult task of the two. It never made contact with 15th Welsh and its left flank was dangerously exposed throughout. On the way forward to Essen Farm several snipers were stalked and killed, mostly by one of the scouts, **Private Thomas Barratt**. This was the only opposition until they approached some strongly held houses at Koln Farm, between Cake Lane and Cake Walk. Here the patrol had to extricate itself from a very dangerous situation. While the Lewis gun and grenadiers tried to silence the enemy posts, the two rifle sections worked their way back. The whole of the Lewis gun section became casualties and meanwhile a strong enemy party worked its way around the right flank.

The opposition intensified and both patrols realised they had to withdraw as quickly as possible or be cut off and annihilated. The withdrawal on the extreme left was only possible due to Barratt, who voluntarily covered his platoon until the last possible moment. He shot at least six of the enemy during the withdrawal although under heavy small arms fire throughout. Barratt made his way back unaided, which was a considerable feat in itself. During the withdrawal on the left, five men were killed and eight wounded. Had it not been for Barratt's effective covering fire the casualties would have been much higher. Just after reaching the British lines he was killed by a shell, one of thirty-two fatalities suffered by the Battalion that day, eighteen of whom remain missing and are commemorated on the Ypres (Menin Gate) Memorial.

Biographies

17114 PRIVATE THOMAS BARRATT
7th Battalion, The South Staffordshire Regiment

Thomas Barratt was born on 5th May 1895 at 9 Foundry Street, Darkhouse, Coseley, Dudley, Staffordshire. He was known as Tom. His father, James Barratt (1862–1914), a coal miner, married Sarah Ann Bailey (c.1865–98) on 21st July 1884 at Coseley parish church; her maiden name appears as Bayliss on the marriage certificate. James was the illegitimate son of Thomas Jones, a collier. The family was living at 11 Foundry Street, Coseley in 1891 and at 38 Webb Street, Coseley in 1901. Sarah died on 11th January 1898 at 23 Foundry Street due to complications with childbirth. By then James was in poor health, suffering a form of paralysis, and was forced to go into the Dudley Workhouse (later Burton Road Hospital). Tom had four siblings:

- Clara Ellen Barratt (1886–1962) married Samuel Smout (1878–1969) in 1904. They lived at 12 Ebenezer Street, Roseville, Coseley and had ten children – Cyril Smout 1905, Isaac Smout 1906, Nancy Smout 1907, Samuel Smout 1910, Clara Smout 1915, Doris Smout 1917, Albert Smout 1918, John Smout 1920, Leslie Smout 1924 and Phyllis Smout 1925. John served in the Scots Guards (2702024) and was killed in action on 11th August 1944. He is buried in St Charles de Percy War Cemetery, France (V E 2).
- James Barratt (1888–1950), born at Warrington, Lancashire, married Miriam Butler (1890–1962) in 1910. They were living at Albert Street, Prince's End, Coseley in 1917. They had eight children – Albert J Barratt 1916, Thomas Barratt 1918, Isaac Barratt 1921, Irene Barratt 1924, James Barratt 1926, Dorothy Barratt 1928, Ethel M Barratt 1931 and Ronald Barratt 1933.
- Elizabeth Maud V Barratt (1890–92) was born at Warrington, Lancashire. Her birth and death were both registered as Barrett.
- Bert 'Bertie' Barratt (born 1892).

Little is known about his paternal grandparents. His maternal grandfather, William Caddick (1843–1901), was a foundry labourer and later a watchman at an iron works. He is believed to have married Mary Ann Bailey (born 1848), a fruit seller in Tipton, in 1873. Her surname has also been seen as Bayley. The family was living at 22 Foundry Street, Coseley in 1881 and at 27 Foundry Street by 1891. In addition to Sarah they had eight other children:

The Dudley Poor Law Union was created in 1836 and in 1859 the Burton Road Workhouse was completed. It later became Burton Road Hospital, which closed in 1993 and was demolished a year later. Most of the site has been redeveloped for private housing.

- Mary Jane Caddick (born 1868).
- Benjamin Caddick Bayley (1870–72).
- Noah Caddick (1872–1947) was a puddler in an iron works in 1891 and may have served in the police in India.
- Thomas Caddick (born 1876).
- Edith Caddick (1881–1957) married James Holden (1880–1949) in 1904. They had nine children – Alice Maud Holden 1905, John Thomas Holden 1907, Leonard Holden 1909, Frederick Holden 1911, James D Holden 1914, Bert Holden 1915, Norman Holden 1917, Edith M Holden 1920 and Jeffrey Holden 1922. John 'Jack' Thomas Holden (1907–2004) represented England in international cross-country 1929–39, winning in 1933, 1934, 1935 and 1939. He was the Amateur Athletic Association's six miles track winner three times before the war, during which he served in the RAF as a PT instructor. He was four times Amateur Athletic Association marathon champion 1947–50 and represented Great Britain in the marathon at the 1948 London Olympics, but having gained the lead he had to retire after seventeen miles with severe blistering. At the Empire Games in Auckland in February 1950, he won the marathon, running the last nine miles barefoot because his waterlogged plimsolls fell apart. Six months later he won the European marathon title by thirty-two seconds.

Jack Holden the international distance runner, was Tom Barratt's cousin.

- Hannah Caddick (1883–1955) married John McNicholas (McNicholls on the marriage certificate) in 1905 at Holywell, Flintshire. They had twelve children – John McNicholas 1905, Winifride McNicholas 1906, Thomas McNicholas 1908, Timothy McNicholas 1909, Mary McNicholas 1911, William McNicholas 1913, James McNicholas 1914, Patrick McNicholas 1915, George D McNicholas 1920, Catherine McNicholas 1922, Ann P McNicholas 1924 and Michael McNicholas 1927.

- Maud Victoria Caddick (born 1887).
- Bertie Caddick (born 1889).

Following William Caddick's death, Mary Ann married Samuel Haynes (1866–1928) in 1904. Samuel, a coal miner, had previously married Dinah Evans (died 1900) in 1885 and had six children – Samuel, William, Isaac, Selina, Edith and Joseph. Samuel and Mary lived at 35 Darkhouse Lane, Coseley.

Following the death of his mother in 1898, Tom was under the care of the Poor Law Guardians at Dudley Workhouse. He frequently ran away and on one occasion arrived at the home of his brother James at Albert Street, Coseley. James was at work and his wife Miriam did not want him in the house, so gave him some bread and cheese and told him to go back to the workhouse. Tom then went to his grandmother, Mary Ann Haynes, who, with her husband Samuel, agreed to adopt him in 1907. Tom was educated at Darkhouse Baptist Chapel School, Coseley where he was considered an unruly child although he regularly attended Bible classes at Darkhouse Baptist Chapel. Following school, he was employed at Cannon Foundry and later at Thompson Brothers, boilermakers of Lower Bradley, Bilston.

Darkhouse Baptist Chapel.

Tom enlisted on 14th January 1915 and landed at Suvla, Gallipoli on 11th September. He later served in Egypt before going to France. **Awarded the VC for his actions near Boesinghe, north of Ypres, Belgium on 27th July 1917, LG 6th September 1917.** He was killed shortly after the VC action and is buried in Essex Farm Cemetery, Boesinghe, Belgium (1 Z 8). As Tom never married, the VC was presented to his brother, James, by the King at Buckingham Palace on 20th October 1917. Tom is commemorated in a number of places:

THOMPSON BROS.
BRADLEY BOILER WORKS, **BILSTON.**
Postal and Telegraphic Address, THOMPSON BROS., BILSTON.   Telephone No. 780.
ESTABLISHED 1810.
MAKERS OF GALVANIZING BATHS OF ALL DESCRIPTIONS.
Patentees and Sole Makers of the Dished and Recessed Annealing
COVERS AND DISHES.

WELDED IRON OR STEEL PANS AND TANKS FOR CHEMICAL WORKS, Which are more suitable than Rivetted or Cast for Heat and Expansion, and require less fuel.	COLLIERY FURNISHERS. SKIPS, BOWKS, PIT COAL TUBS, PIT TANKS, WROUGHT IRON SLEEPERS, AIR PIPES OR VENTILATING TUBES FOR COLLIERIES.

PARTICULARS AND PRICES ON APPLICATION.

ALSO MAKERS OF STEAM BOILERS, GIRDERS, IRON BOATS, &c., AND ALL KINDS OF WELDED WORK.

A Thompson Brothers advertisement.

- Barratt Court, Batmans Hill Road, Princes End, Coseley dedicated in April 1962. A new plaque was unveiled in May 2012 by the Mayor of Sandwell, Councillor Joyce Underhill, and Barratt's nephew, Ronald Barratt, after the original disappeared during renovations in 2011.
- Named on the war memorial at Christ Church, Church Road, Coseley.

Suvla Bay from Anzac on the Gallipoli peninsula.
Tom Barratt landed there on 11th September 1915.

Tom Barratt's grave in Essex Farm Cemetery. The advanced dressing station located there is believed to where John McCrae composed 'In Flanders Fields' May 1915.

- Memorial inside Christ Church, Coseley unveiled by Colonel FW Law and dedicated by the Lord Bishop of Stafford on 17th March 1918.
- Memorial at Darkhouse Baptist Chapel, unveiled by Brigadier General TE Hickman on 9th December 1917. It was transferred to the Garrison Church, Whittington Barracks, Lichfield when the old chapel building was demolished.
- Named on a Thompson Brother's war memorial in the firm's canteen. When the building closed in 1987 the memorial went to the Staffordshire Regiment Museum.
- Named on a memorial plaque to all South Staffordshire Regiment VCs at the Garrison Church, Whittington Barracks.

In addition to the VC he was awarded the 1914–15 Star, British War Medal 1914–20 and Victory Medal 1914–19. The VC group was acquired by the Staffordshire Regiment on 12th March 1987 with a grant from the Museums and Galleries Commission and other funds. The VC is held by the Staffordshire Regiment Museum, Whittington Barracks, Lichfield, Staffordshire.

The war memorial at Christ Church, Coseley where Tom Barratt is commemorated.

201154 COMPANY SERGEANT MAJOR EDWARD BROOKS
2/4th Battalion, The Oxfordshire and Buckinghamshire Light Infantry

Edward Brooks was born at Oakley, Buckinghamshire on 11th April 1883. His father, Thomas Brooks (1854–1922), was a general labourer in 1881, a woodman and allotment holder in 1901 and a farm labourer by 1911. His mother was Selina née Siviter (1857–1922), a nailer in 1871. Thomas and Selina married on 13th September 1875 at St Thomas, Dudley, Worcestershire. The family was living at Titford Lane, Cakemore, Worcestershire in 1881 and by 1891 they were at the Common, Oakley, Buckinghamshire. Edward had eleven siblings:

St Thomas, Dudley, Worcestershire where Edward's parents married in 1875.

- Ellen Jane Brooks (1876–1940), married Matthew George Henry Piper (1869–1931) c.1899. He was a waiter who had previously married Ada Bird in 1895. Ellen and Matthew had a daughter, Doris May Piper in 1900.
- Rhoda Brooks (1877–1962) married William George Wright (1878–1937), a tailor, in 1906. He was the brother of Edwin Ernest Wright, who married Rhoda's sister Selina. Rhoda and William were living at 13 Walton Well Road, St Giles, Oxfordshire in 1911. They had a son, William Brooks Wright, in 1907.
- John Thomas Brooks (1879–1920) was an allotment holder and woodman in 1901. He married Edith Lovell (born 1878) in 1905. By 1911 he was the manager of a firewood provision business, living with his family at Worminghall Road, Oakley, Buckinghamshire. John and Edith had three children by 1911 – Edith Gladys SS Brooks 1906, John Thomas Brooks 1908 and either Alice Daisy Brooks 1907 or Annie Mabel Brooks 1909.
- James Brooks (born c.1882).
- Albert Martin Brooks (born and died 1884).
- Charles Brooks (born 1888) was a farm labourer.
- Selina Brooks (1889–1940) married Edwin Ernest Wright (born 1886) in 1911.
- Henry 'Harry' Brooks (born 1891) was a farm labourer.
- Lizzie Brooks (born 1893).

- Mary Brooks (born 1896) was a general servant in 1911, living with her brother Edward and his family.
- Owen Brooks (1899–1980) married Lily/Lillie G Harris (c.1902–78) in 1923. They had six children – Barbara J Brooks 1924, Kathleen J Brooks 1925, Audrey Brooks 1928, Stanley Brooks born and died 1931, Major A Brooks 1932, and Arnett M Brooks 1937.

Edward was educated at Oakley village school. He left home aged thirteen to work at the Huntley and Palmer biscuit factory in Reading. When it was discovered that he was underage, he was employed without wages, but received a suitable weekly tip. Later he worked for Messrs Knowles & Sons, a building firm in Oxford that still exists. Edward enlisted into 3rd Grenadier Guards (10080) on 9th January 1902. He was a member of a guard of honour during one of Kaiser Wilhelm II's visits to Britain. Having served three years in England, Edward transferred to the Reserve on 8th January 1905, until discharged on 8th January 1914. He returned to work for Messrs Knowles & Sons.

Edward Brooks married Elsie May née Danbury (1885–1958) on 12th March 1910 at Bicester, Buckinghamshire; his name was recorded as Edward George Brooks. Elsie was a domestic servant in 1901 at 81 Iffley Road, Cowley, Oxfordshire. They lived initially in New Headington, Oxford and were at 15 High Street in 1911, at Southill Cottages on New High Street in 1912 and on South (later Gardiner) Street in 1914, before moving to 16 Windsor Street in 1915. They later moved to 42 Morrell Avenue, Oxford. Edward and Elsie had five children:

Edward worked at the Huntley and Palmer biscuit factory in Reading. The company was founded in 1822 and at its height employed over 5,000 people. By 1900 it was the world's largest biscuit manufacturer. Production ceased in Reading in 1976 and there is little of the factory remaining.

New High Street in New Headington. Southill Cottages, where Edward and his family lived in 1912, are the four houses beyond the shop on the left.

- Doris Rhoda Brooks, born on 31st August 1910, married Sydney Church (born 1904) in 1931 and they had five children – Dennis S Church 1932, Jean E Church 1934, Roy H Church 1936, Myra E Church 1944 and Alan E Church 1946.
- Harold Gilbert Brooks (18th August 1912–1957), married Dorothy E Surman (1918–97) in 1937 and they had four children – Sheila M Brooks (later Wilson-Brooks) 1938, Carol A Brooks 1944, Keith E Brooks 1946 and Kim KH Brooks 1958. Dorothy married Matthew N Wilson in 1972.
- Stephen James Brooks, born on 21st May 1914, married Renee L Green in 1937 and they had four children – Rita D Brooks 1937, David H Brooks 1939, Joan Brooks 1940 and Diane M Brooks 1948.
- Nora Ida Brooks, born on 18th December 1918, married Arthur W Pearce in 1941 and they had a son, Terence S Pearce in 1947.
- Barbara Brooks (3rd June 1924–1991), married Harry Jordan in 1942 and they had two daughters – Susan B Jordan 1945 and Ruth L Jordan 1952.

Sergeant Edward Brooks, standing left, with a group of officers and NCOs of the Battalion before going to France.

Edward enlisted in 2/4th Oxfordshire and Buckinghamshire Light Infantry on 19th October 1914 (3516 later 201154) and was promoted lance corporal the same day. Promoted sergeant 13th May 1915 (substantive 24th May 1916). Edward was a first class shot and had won many prizes. As a result, he was employed initially as a rifle and drill instructor and also taught members of the Headington Miniature Rifle Club to shoot. Edward went to France on 24th May 1916 and was appointed company sergeant major on 29th July. He returned home for ten days leave in November 1916.

Awarded the VC for his actions at Fayet, near St Quentin, France on 28th April 1917, LG 27th June 1917. The VC was presented by the King outside Buckingham Palace on 21st July 1917. He returned to Oxford, where he was received by the Mayor and Corporation at the Great Western Railway station before being driven to Headington, where he was presented with a framed illuminated address and monies donated from the neighbourhood.

Edward returned to the front, but was admitted to hospital on 15th December 1917 with rheumatism. He was evacuated to England on 20th December and was treated at 3rd Southern General Hospital, Oxford until 22nd January 1918, in the part of the Hospital based in University College's Durham Buildings. He was posted to 4th Reserve Battalion on 15th January 1919 and was discharged on 15th May 1919 with twenty percent disability for myalgia. He worked at the Morris Motor Works at Cowley from December 1919 for twenty-five years in the Sub-Assembly Department. Later he was a works fireman and finally worked in the stores when he

Edward Brooks meets the Prince of Wales during a royal visit to the Cowley factory.

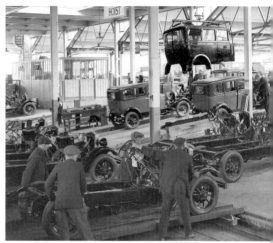

A production line at the Morris Motor Works at Cowley. The firm began as WRM Motors Ltd in 1912 when bicycle manufacturer William Morris commenced car manufacturing. The Cowley factory opened in 1913 on the site of the former Oxford Military College. By 1924 it was Britain's largest car manufacturer. None of the Morris buildings remain, having been demolished after the sale of the site by British Aerospace in 1992. It is now Oxford Business Park. The adjacent former Pressed Steel site remains and is operated by BMW to assemble the Mini.

turned sixty. Edward was presented to the Prince of Wales during a royal visit to the factory.

On 6th May 1935, he attended the dedication of the 61st (South Midland) Division Memorial at Holy Trinity Church, Stratford. The Memorial was unveiled by Sir Ivor Maxse, commander of XVIII Corps, to which 61st Division had belonged in March 1918. Edward raised the divisional flag at the ceremony.

Edward Brooks died at his home at 42 Morrell Avenue, Oxford on 26th June 1944 and is buried in Rose Hill Cemetery, Oxford (G2 119). He is also commemorated at:

- Edward Brooks Barracks, Cholswell Road, Abingdon, Oxfordshire opened by the Duchess of Gloucester on 18th July 2009. Three of his grandchildren attended the ceremony.
- Brooks Taylor Court, Albion Place, St Ebbes, Oxford named after Edward Brooks and a member of the Women's Army Corps.

In addition to the VC, he was awarded the British War Medal 1914–20, Victory Medal 1914–19 and George VI Coronation Medal 1937. His VC is held by the Royal Green Jackets (Rifles) Museum, Winchester.

Holy Trinity Church, Stratford-upon-Avon, where Edward attended the dedication of the 61st (South Midland) Division Memorial on 6th May 1935. The church is better known as the burial place of William Shakespeare and Anne Hathaway.

22040 LANCE CORPORAL THOMAS BRYAN
25th Battalion (2nd Tyneside Irish), The Northumberland Fusiliers

Thomas Bryan was born at Bott Lane, Lye, near Stourbridge, Worcestershire on 31st January 1882. His father, also Thomas Bryan (1858–1935), was a coal hewer. His mother was Sarah née Hoskins (1855–1904). Their marriage was registered in the 2nd quarter of 1881 at Stourbridge. The family was living at 8 Hunt Street, Whitwood Mere, Castleford, Yorkshire in 1891. In 1911, Thomas senior was living there with boarders Sarah Ann Waller and her son Sydney. He later moved to 29 Hunt Street.

His paternal grandfather, John Bryan (c.1829–1909), was born at Stourbridge, Worcestershire. He was a scythe smith in 1861, a brickyard labourer by 1891 and a retired carter in 1901. He married Ann Maria née Clews (c.1831–1907) in 1858 at Stourbridge. She was a nail maker in 1871. The family lived at Belbroughton, Worcestershire and by 1871 had moved to Spring Street, Green Lane, Lye, Worcestershire. In addition to Thomas they had five other children, the first four being registered as Brian at birth – Mary Bryan 1859, Marian Bryan 1861, John Bryan 1863, Albert Bryan 1864 and Susannah Bryan 1870.

His maternal grandfather, John Hoskins (c.1820–83), an agricultural labourer, was born at Lulsley, Worcestershire. He married Louisa née Poyner (c.1817–71) at Ombersley, near Droitwich, Worcestershire in 1843. The family was living at Park Street, Stourbridge, Worcestershire in 1851 and Lye Farm, Lye, Worcestershire in 1871. In addition to Sarah they had six other children – Ellen Hoskins 1844, Ann Hoskins 1846, Mary Hoskins 1849, Louisa Hoskins 1853, Elizabeth Hoskins born and died 1858 and John Hoskins 1859.

Thomas was educated at the Potteries Council School and also attended the United Methodist Church Sunday School, both in Whitwood Mere, Castleford. He was employed as a miner around Castleford and just before the war was working for Henry Briggs & Co at Whitwood Colliery. He played rugby league and was a member of the Castleford Northern Rugby Football Union team during the 1906/07 season.

On 26th December 1903, Thomas Bryan married Sarah née Smart (1884–1954) at Whitwood Mere Parish Church, Castleford. They were living at 29 Hunt Street, Whitwood Mere in

The High Street in Lye.

Whitwood Colliery.

Whitwood Mere Parish Church, Castleford
(J Burrow).

1911 and later at 11 Fairfield Villas, Norton, Castleford. Thomas and Sarah had five children:

- Thomas Alfred Bryan (1904–74) married Mary Fox (born 1904) in 1923. They had three children – Frank Bryan 1924, Mabel Bryan 1925 and George W Bryan 1928.
- Fanny Bryan (1906–07).
- Albert Bryan (born 1908) married Constance Laura Mangan (1896–1985) in 1935. They had two sons – Thomas D Bryan 1936 and Albert M Bryan 1940.
- Sarah Bryan (1911–88) married George William Weston (1906–71) in 1936. They had a son, Alex, in 1944.
- Evelyn Bryan (1913–90) married Alexander Ingram in 1940. They had a daughter, Evelyn A Ingram, in 1942.

Thomas enlisted in the Northumberland Fusiliers on 11th April 1915 and went to France on 22nd December with 25th Battalion. He fractured his ankle and was evacuated to England in April 1916, but returned to France on 4th October. Promoted lance corporal 26th March 1917. **Awarded the VC for his actions near Arras, France on 9th April 1917, LG 8th June 1917.** He was evacuated

A group of patients at Alnwick Military Convalescent Hospital with the Commandant, Colonel Broome Giles and the Scottish singer and comedian Harry Lauder (later Sir Harry) on 9th August 1916. His only son, John, was killed on 28th December that year serving with 8th Argyll & Sutherland Highlanders. As a result Harry wrote the song 'The End of the Road', one of the most famous of the First World War.

St James' Football Ground in Newcastle-upon-Tyne during a Cup match in 1913.

Newcastle's Empire Theatre.

Thomas Bryan receives his VC from the King at St James' Football Ground in front of a crowd of 40,000.

to England and treated at Alnwick Military Convalescent Hospital, Northumberland. The VC was presented by the King at St James' Football Ground, Newcastle-upon-Tyne on 17th June 1917, in front of a crowd of 40,000. On 27th July, he and Private Ernest Sykes VC received a civic reception at the Empire Theatre, Newcastle. The Lord Mayor presented them with war loans, a clock and a wallet of Treasury notes.

On 29th July 1918, while being treated at Norwich War Hospital, he rescued a three-year old girl, Phyllis Richardson, from drowning in the river at Thorpe,

The Annexe of Norwich War Hospital.

The river at Thorpe, Norwich where Thomas rescued Phyllis Richardson from drowning.

Thomas and Sarah later in life.

Askern Colliery.

Norwich and resuscitated her. Thomas was discharged on 16th September 1918 having been wounded three times.

Post-war he went back to mining at Castleford. From 1926 he was employed at Norton Colliery near Doncaster and from 1934 at Askern Colliery, Doncaster. He gave up mining in 1935 due to ill health caused by war wounds and the effects of gas poisoning and opened a greengrocer's shop at Bentley with Arksey, Doncaster.

Thomas Bryan died at 44 Askern Road, Bentley, near Doncaster, Yorkshire on 13th October 1945 and is buried in Arksey Cemetery, Doncaster (J 237). He is also commemorated in three places in Castleford:

• Bryan Close.
• Memorial plaque in the foyer of the Civic Centre.
• Named on the memorial at the Library in Carlton Street.

In addition to the VC, he was awarded the 1914–15 Star, British War Medal 1914–20, Victory Medal 1914–19 and George VI Coronation Medal 1937. The medals were sold for £9,800 to an anonymous buyer at a Christie's auction on 25th July 1989. On 28th June 2000 they were sold at a Dix Noonan Webb auction to Lord Ashcroft for £60,000. The medals are held in the Lord Ashcroft Gallery in the Imperial War Museum.

Thomas Bryan's CWGC style headstone in Arksey Cemetery (Memorials to Valour).

1804 PRIVATE JOHN CARROLL
33rd Australian Infantry Battalion AIF

John Carroll, known as Jack, was born on 16th August 1891 at Brisbane, Queensland, Australia. His father, also John Carroll (c.1863–1919), was born in Tipperary, Ireland. He married Catherine 'Kate' née Wallace on 23rd December 1888, also born in Tipperary, Ireland. They emigrated to Brisbane, Queensland, Australia before 1891, moved to Donnybrook, Western Australia in 1893 and then to Yarloop. In 1905 they settled at Kurrawang, where he and his son John were labourers with the Goldfields Firewood Supply Company. On 3rd December 1919 he was a guard directing the shunting of seven trucks to the sawmill siding at Kurrawang. His son-in-law, James Sexton, was the driver. John fell between the truck, where both legs were severed and he also suffered head injuries; death was instantaneous. Kate was living at Yarloop, Western Australia around 1931 and at 184 Shaftesbury Avenue, Bedford Park, Western Australia around 1968. John junior had six siblings:

- Michael George Carroll (1889–1945) is reputed to have been wounded at Gallipoli and on three other occasions in France serving in the AIF. He started a relationship in 1920 with Elizabeth Charlotte Ann Fitzgerald, wife of Maurice Fitzgerald, hotelkeeper at Kurrawang, Western Australia. Maurice and Elizabeth were divorced in 1922. They had four children. Michael subsequently married Elizabeth and she became a nurse. They lived at 55 Hanbury Street, Kalgoorlie and had two children – Dorothy Carroll and Sheila Carroll.
- Martin Thomas Carroll (1896–1933) enlisted on 24th February 1916 (244) at Kalgoorlie. He gave his occupation as locomotive guard and his mother was his next of kin. He was described as 5′ 9″ tall, weighing 164 lbs, with ruddy complexion, grey eyes, brown hair and his religious denomination was Roman Catholic. He was posted to 52nd Depot Company on 3rd March, 22nd Depot on 4th April and 44th Battalion on 29th April. Martin embarked on HMAT A29 *Suevic* at Fremantle on 6th June and disembarked at Plymouth on 21st July. While aboard he was admitted to the ship's hospital with venereal disease 13th–29th June. He was serving in 7th Training Battalion at Rollestone Camp, Salisbury Plain on 7th November. He went to France on 19th November on SS *Outward* from Folkestone and joined 28th Battalion on 4th December from 2nd Australian Division Base Depot, Étaples. On 16th January 1917 he transferred to 1st ANZAC Light Railway Operating Company (later 3rd Light Railway Operating Company). Absent without leave on 9th June and forfeited one day's pay. He was granted

leave to England 29th November–14th December. Admitted to 3rd Australian Casualty Clearing Station on 9th May 1918 with scabies. He was discharged on 7th July and sent on leave 8th–29th July, but failed to return on time and was absent without leave until 6th August in London. He was awarded fourteen days Field Punishment No.2 and forfeited twenty-three days' pay. He rejoined his unit on 17th August. On 25th March 1919, he was confined to barracks for five days and £5 was stopped from his pay for damage to a magneto. He departed France on 2nd April for Codford, Wiltshire and departed England on 11th May aboard HMAT A30 *Borda*, disembarking in Australia on 23rd June. Martin was discharged at Perth on 25th August 1919. He married Gwendoline Preddy in 1924 and worked as a railway guard for the Goldfields Firewood Supply Company. He played cricket for Merryman's Cricket Club and was returning home after playing at the Foundry Ground, Kalgoorlie on 26th March 1933 when his car overturned and he was killed instantly. Two passengers, George Stinchcomb and Robert George Jones, survived.

- Mary Anne Carroll (born 1898) married James Sexton, a train driver.
- Thomas Carroll (born 1901).
- Kathleen 'Kate' Carroll (1905–75) married Sydney James Smith (born 1904), a blacksmith, in 1929. They had three children including – Phyllis Smith and Terrance Martin Smith.
- May Carroll married as Barfoot.

It is not known where John was educated. He worked alongside his father at the Goldfields Firewood Supply Company as a labourer before working as a miner at the Kalgoorlie gold mines and at nearby Kurrawang. He was a good athlete and was a prominent member of the local Australian rules football club.

John Carroll enlisted in the AIF at Kalgoorlie, Western Australia on 27th April 1916, understating his age by one year. He was described as 5′ 8″ tall, with ruddy complexion, blue eyes, had a scar on his right cheek and upper lip and his religious denomination was Roman Catholic. He was posted to 44th Battalion (2nd Reinforcements) (1804) at Blackboy Hill, Northam, Western Australia. He embarked

The Kalgoorlie gold mines.

Kalgoorlie town centre.

Troops at Blackboy Hill Camp, Northam, Western Australia queuing for inoculations (Australian War Memorial).

SS *Miltiades* (6,793 tons) was built in 1903 at Glasgow for G Thompson & Co Ltd of London (Aberdeen Line) for the London to Australia service. Her maiden voyage from London to Sydney via Cape Town and Melbourne commenced on 3rd November 1903. She was rebuilt in 1912, during which a second funnel was added and her weight increased to 7817 tons. On 1st November 1914 she assembled with the first convoy at King George's Sound, Albany, Western Australia to transport the First Detachment of the Australian and New Zealand Imperial Expeditionary Forces. In 1915 she was requisitioned as a troopship and returned to commercial service in June 1920. She was purchased by the Royal Mail Steam Packet Company and renamed *Orcana* and was transferred to the Pacific Steam Navigation Company in 1922 on the South America service. She was scrapped in Holland in 1924.

for England from Fremantle aboard HMAT A28 *Miltiades* on 9th August. While at sea on 29th August he was absent from roll call and was awarded seven days detention and forfeited nine days pay. Having disembarked at Plymouth, Devon, he joined 11th Training Battalion on Salisbury Plain on 1st October followed by 3rd Division Amalgamated Training Battalion. He joined 44th Battalion at Larkhill Camp, Salisbury Plain on 11th November and transferred to 33rd Battalion on 14th November. John embarked at Southampton for France on 21st November 1916. He was in hospital 27th January–13th February 1917 and was charged with being absent without leave for failing to appear on parade at Regina Barracks on 3rd May and for losing his small box respirator. He was awarded two days Field Punishment and ordered to pay for a replacement respirator costing £0/12/6.

Awarded the VC for his actions at St Yves, Belgium 7th–12th June 1917, LG 2nd August 1917. John was wounded in the chest near Messines on 9th July and was evacuated to 14th General Hospital, Boulogne on 10th July and from there to No.1 Convalescent Unit. He forfeited a day's pay for being in a café against orders on 18th July. He rejoined his unit on 19th August and was promoted lance corporal on 19th September. He received a gunshot wound to the right buttock near Passchendaele on 12th October and was evacuated to England on HMHS *St Andrew* on 20th October, where he was treated at 2nd Birmingham War Hospital, Northfield from 21st October. He was transferred to 3rd Australian Auxiliary Hospital at Dartford, Kent on 28th November and later to the Depot at Sutton Veny, Wiltshire. On 27th January 1918 he was assaulted while returning from Warminster, resulting in a fractured left fibula, and was admitted to the Military Hospital at Sutton Veny next day. He was discharged to No.1 Command Depot on 6th March.

The VC was presented by the King at Buckingham Palace on 23rd March 1918. Reports that he deliberately missed three previous investitures and then repeatedly called out the Buckingham Palace Guard, a mythical right due to all VCs, are without foundation. John suffered from dermatitis and was admitted to 1st Australian Dermatological Hospital, Bulford, Wiltshire on 8th May. He was charged again with absence without leave from Sandhill Camp at Longbridge Deverill on 3rd June, but was admonished and forfeited three day's pay.

John was held at the Overseas Training Brigade, Longbridge Deverill until he embarked from Folkestone, Kent for the Australian Infantry Base Depot at Le Havre on 19th June and rejoined 33rd Battalion on 27th June. On 27th July he was ordered to report to AIF Headquarters in London. He disembarked at Folkestone on 1st August and was held at No.2 Command Depot, Weymouth, Dorset on 22nd August. Two days later he embarked on HMAT D21 *Medic* on 24th August with fellow VCs John James Dwyer, Reginald Inwood, Joergen Jensen, Thomas Kenny, Leonard Keysor, Stanley McDougall, Walter Peeler, William Ruthven and John Whittle. They were being returned home to assist in recruiting for the all-volunteer AIF. John was discharged in Perth, Western Australia on 1st January 1919.

TSS *St Andrew* (2,528 tons) was built by John Brown in 1908 for the Fishguard & Rosslare Railways and Harbours Board. During the First World War she was used as a hospital ship. In 1932 she was renamed *Fishguard* to free her name for a replacement TSS *St Andrew* and was scrapped in 1933. The second *St Andrew* also served as a hospital ship in the Second World War.

John worked as a guard on the Kurrawang line in Western Australia, then worked as a railway truck examiner at Hoffman's Mill, Yarloop, Western Australia. On 1st November 1927 he slipped while boarding a train during shunting operations. His right foot was crushed and it had to be amputated at St John of God Hospital, Perth. He continued to work as a labourer for many years

2nd Birmingham War Hospital, Northfield.

The Australian Infantry Base Depot at Le Havre.

St Mary's Catholic Cathedral, Perth, Western Australia where John Carroll married Mary Brown on 23rd April 1923.

afterwards. John Carroll married Mary Brown (c.1892–1971) on 23rd April 1923 at the St Mary's Cathedral (Cathedral of the Immaculate Conception), Perth, Western Australia. They settled at 184 Shaftesbury Avenue, Bedford Park, Perth after 1956. There were no children.

On 17th March 1920 he was one of fourteen VCs mounted on white horses as a Guard of Honour for Catholic Archbishop of Melbourne Daniel Mannix as he led 10,000 ex-servicemen and women in the St Patrick's Day march. John was at the Anzac Commemoration Service on 25th April 1927 at the Exhibition Building, Melbourne, Victoria in the presence of The Duke of York (future King George VI). In the march past the twenty-six VCs conceded pride of place to blinded soldiers who insisted on marching. On 11th November 1929 he attended a lunch hosted by Colonel Sir William Campion KCMG DSO TD, Governor of Western Australia, at Government House, Perth to honour those VCs who could not attend the VC Reunion in London. He attended the Sydney Anzac Day Reunion on 25th April 1938 and the VC Centenary Celebrations at Hyde Park, London on 26th June 1956, travelling with other Australian VCs on SS *Orcades*.

John Carroll died at the Repatriation General Hospital, Hollywood, Perth, Western Australia on 4th October 1971. He is buried in Karrakatta Cemetery, Perth (one of nine VCs buried there) (Roman Catholic Section KA, Plot 658). He is also commemorated in a number of other places:

A memento of the St Patrick's Day celebrations in Melbourne on 17th March 1920.

- Carroll Street, Canberra, Australian Capital Territory.
- John Carroll Ward, Sylvia Perry MBE Wing, Hollywood Private Hospital, Perth (formerly the Repatriation General Hospital) opened on 24th July 2002 by Danna Vale MP, Minister for Veterans' Affairs.
- Victoria Cross Memorial on the corner of Howse and Derrick Streets, Campbell, Canberra, dedicated on 24th July 2000, commemorating ninety-six Australians who have been awarded the VC.
- Victoria Cross Memorial, Queen Victoria Building, George Street, Sydney, New South Wales.
- Memorial plaque at the State War Memorial, King's Park, Perth, dedicated on 26th January 1996.
- Named on one of eleven plaques honouring 175 men from overseas awarded the VC for the Great War. The plaques were unveiled by the Senior Minister of State at the Foreign & Commonwealth Office and Minister for Faith and Communities, Baroness Warsi, at a reception at Lancaster House, London on 26th June 2014 attended by The Duke of Kent and relatives of the VC recipients. The Australian plaque is at the Australian War Memorial.
- The Secretary of State for Communities and Local Government, Eric Pickles MP announced that Victoria Cross recipients from the Great War would have commemorative paving stones laid in their birthplace as a lasting legacy of local heroes within communities. The stones would be laid on or close to the 100th anniversary of their VC actions. For the 145 VCs born in Australia, Belgium, Canada, China, Denmark, Egypt, France, Germany, India, Iraq, Japan, Nepal, Netherlands, New Zealand, Pakistan, South Africa, Sri Lanka, Ukraine and United States of America, individual commemorative stones were unveiled at the National Memorial Arboretum, Alrewas, Staffordshire by Prime Minister David Cameron MP and Sergeant Johnson Beharry VC on 5th March 2015.

In addition to the VC he was awarded the British War Medal 1914–20, Victory Medal 1914–19, George VI Coronation Medal 1937 and Elizabeth II Coronation Medal 1953. After his death his medals were bequeathed to the Kalgoorlie Returned Services League Club. The VC was too valuable to display and was held in a safe in Kalgoorlie. In October 1989 the medals were presented to the Australian War Memorial. The family objected, claiming they were not consulted, but the presentation went ahead. His medals are now held in the Hall of Valour, Australian War Memorial, Anzac Parade, Canberra, Australian Capital Territory.

SECOND LIEUTENANT GEORGE EDWARD CATES
2nd Battalion, The Rifle Brigade (The Prince Consort's Own)

George Cates was born at 86 Hartfield Road, Wimbledon, Surrey on 9th May 1892. His father, also George Cates (1852–1935), was born at Dunmow, Essex. He was variously employed as a warehouseman, wholesaler of Manchester ware, handkerchief agent and a commercial traveler. He married Alice Ann née Livermore (1854–1942), who was born at Kelvedon Hatch, Essex, on 13th July 1879 registered at Hastings, Sussex. The family lived at various addresses:

1881 – 10 Winslade Road, Lambeth, London.
1891 – 86 Hartfield Place, Wimbledon, Surrey.
1901 – 11 Springfield Road, North Wimbledon.
1911 – Sonning Common, Reading, Berkshire.
1915 – 221 Kingston Road, Wimbledon.
1918 – 39 Compton Road, Wimbledon.

George had nine siblings:

- Francis George Cates (1881–1937) was a dry goods warehouseman in 1901 and a salesman in 1911. He married Emily Maude Blundell (born 1878) in 1905. They were living at 10A Albany Terrace, Queen's Road, Wimbledon in 1907 and 69 Stuart Road, Wimbledon Park, Surrey in 1911. They had two children – Wilfrid George Henry Cates 1907 and Gladys EA Cates 1912.
- Ethel Catherine Mary Cates (1883–1950) never married.

Kingston Road, Wimbledon where the Cates family lived in 1915.

- Charles Bertram Cates (1884–1964) was an apprentice mechanical engineer in 1901 and a traveller in 1911. He married Frances Margaret Anne Towers (1886–1980), a short hand typist, in 1912 and they were living at 39 Compton Road, Wimbledon in 1917. Charles enlisted in the Motor Transport Section of the RFC on 23rd October 1917, transferred to the RAF on 1st April 1918 and the RAF Reserve on 21st February 1919. They had a son, Geoffrey Charles Cates (1918–2003), who was ordained priest. He married Mary Lee Buckton (1924–2002) in 1946. Geoffrey's appointments included Chaplain at Butlin's Holiday Camp, Clacton-on-Sea, Essex 1949–52; Bishop of Accra's Chaplain to the Chamber of Mines, West Africa 1952–53; Vicar at Kumasi, Ashanti, Ghana 1954–61; Dean of St George's Chapel, Georgetown, Demerara-Mahaica, Guyana 1961–71; Rector of Sacred Trinity, Salford, Lancashire 1971–82; Honorary Canon, Manchester Cathedral 1981–82; Social Responsibility Adviser of St Edmundsbury & Ipswich Diocese 1982–88; and Honorary Canon, St Edmundsbury Cathedral, Ipswich 1985–88.

- Alice Mabel Cates (born 1886) was a governess at Widmerpool Rectory, Nottingham in 1911. She married the Reverend Sydney Walter Drewer (1886–1971) in 1919. He was Rector of Poughill Parish Church, Cornwall. They had two children – Robert W Drewer 1920 and David W Drewer 1929.

- William Frederick Cates (1888–1917) enlisted in the Canadian Army Medical Corps (962) on 31st March 1915, giving his employment as clerk of supplies and costkeeper. He was described as 5' 6½" tall, with dark complexion, blue eyes, dark brown hair and his religious denomination was Church of England. He was lost at sea when HMHS *Llandovery Castle* was torpedoed and sunk 120 miles off Ireland on 27th June 1918. He is commemorated on the Halifax Memorial, Nova Scotia, Canada and left £206/19/10 to his sister Ethel and brother Harry.

- Harry Arthur Cates (1890–1953). He was educated at Wimbledon and sat the Cambridge Senior Examination in 1905 followed by the London matriculation. He went to Canada in 1908 to study medicine at the University of Toronto and qualified as a physician. He served in the war as a Canadian Army Medical Corps captain in Salonika, possibly with No.4 (University of Toronto) General Hospital, which was there from November 1915 until the summer of 1917. On enlistment he was described as 5' 3½" tall, with fair complexion, blue grey eyes, fair hair and his religious denomination was Church of England. Harry married Muriel Constance Hearn (1892–1973) in 1918 and they lived at 1557 Bloor Street West, Toronto. They had two sons – Geoffrey Cates (died 1988) and George Cates (1919–65). Harry became Professor of Anatomy and Director of Physical and Health Education at the University of Toronto.

HMHS *Llandovery Castle*, built in 1914 for the Union-Castle Line, was one of five Canadian hospital ships. She was torpedoed off southern Ireland on 27th June 1918 and there were only twenty-four survivors; 234 doctors, nurses and patients died. It was Canada's worst naval disaster and an infamous atrocity. In 1921, the Captain of U-*86*, Lieutenant Helmut Patzig, and two of his officers were committed for trial. Patzig left Germany and although both other officers were sentenced to four years in prison, at the Court of Appeal both were acquitted on the grounds that the captain was responsible.

• Geoffrey Cates (1893–1918) was a clerk in 1911, boarding at 135 South Park Road, Wimbledon. He enlisted in 18th Royal Fusiliers (1345) at the Institute of Mechanical Engineers, Westminster on 15th September 1914 and was a bank clerk at the time. He was described as 5′ 7″ tall with fair complexion, blue eyes, fair hair and his religious denomination was Church of England. On 25th October 1915 he was taken into hospital for the removal of his appendix and was discharged on

Geoffrey Cates' name on the Arras Memorial.

13th November. He was posted to 28th Battalion on 14th November and back to 18th Battalion in France on 9th February 1916. Geoffrey applied for a commission on 10th March, returned to England on 25th March and joined No.1 Officer Cadet Battalion next day. He was commissioned in 10th Durham Light Infantry on 4th August 1916 and was killed in action at Morchies, France on 21st March 1918 while attached to 2nd Durham Light Infantry. He is commemorated on the Arras Memorial, France and left £351/3/4 to his brother Charles.

John Henry Stephen Dimmer VC (1883–1918) was a fellow pupil at Rutlish School.

• Dorothy Maud Cates (1894–95).
• Marjorie Eliza Cates (1901–77) never married.

His uncle, Isaac Charles Livermore (1856–1931) was a captain in the Merchant Navy, retiring before 1896, by when he was a farmer. He married his cousin, Fanny Ann Livermore (1862–1944), a hospital nurse, in 1896. They were living at Little Laver and Abbess Roding, Ongar, Essex in 1911 and had three children – Isaac Owen Livermore 1897, John Eustace Livermore 1900 and Edward Charles Livermore 1904.

George was educated at Rutlish School, Merton, Surrey and Mr Sutherland's King's College Private School in Worple Road Wimbledon (closed in 1912). Rutlish Science School was previously attended by John Henry Stephen Dimmer, who was awarded the VC in 1914, and later by John Major, British Prime Minister 1990–97. George was employed as a clerk with the Royal Insurance Company. In his free time, he was Assistant Scoutmaster with 2nd Wimbledon Scout Troop and was also a member of the YMCA.

Sir John Major KG CH was Prime Minister of the United Kingdom 1990–97 having served under Margaret Thatcher as Chancellor of the Exchequer and Foreign Secretary. (*Getty*)

2/28th London (Artists Rifles) in camp at Richmond Park in 1915.

Rutlish School.

George enlisted as a signaller in 28th London Regiment (Artists' Rifles) on 8th December 1914 (3035 later 760384). He transferred to 2nd (Reserve) Battalion on 26th December, 2/28th Battalion on 17th April 1915, 3/28th Battalion on 26th June and to 1/28th Battalion on 30th June. He went to France on 11th August and joined his unit in the field on 16th August. George was commissioned in 2nd Rifle Brigade on 26th February 1917.

Awarded the VC for his actions east of Bouchavesnes, France on 8th March 1917, LG 11th May 1917. He died of wounds received during his VC action at 137th Field Ambulance, Bouchavesnes on 9th March 1917 and is buried in Hem Farm Military Cemetery, Hem-Monacu (I G 15). His commissioned service was so short that there is no entry for him in the Army List. He left £475/17/6 in his will, which was administered by his sister Ethel. George is commemorated in a number of other places:

Putney Vale War Memorial, Wimbledon Common.

George Cates' grave in Hem Farm Military Cemetery, Hem-Monacu.

ROLL OF FAME

V.C. CPL. A. G. DRAKE	1915
V.C. MAJ. W. la T. CONGREVE	1916
V.C. 2/LT. G. E. CATES	1917
BRIG. GEN. R. C. MACLACHLAN	1917
GEN. SIR J. S. COWANS	1921
COL. W. W. C. VERNER	1922
F. M. SIR H. H. WILSON BT.	1922
V.C. GEN. SIR W. N. CONGREVE	1927
MAJ. GEN. SIR C. R. H. NICHOLL	1928
MAJ. GEN. SIR F. H. HOWARD	1930
MAJ. GEN. SIR L. V. SWAINE	1931
GEN. THE RT. HON. SIR N. G. LYTTELTON	1931
V.C. RFN. A. E. DURRANT	1933
GEN. SIR CAMERON DEANE SHUTE	1936
LT. COL. LORD AILWYN	1936
MAJ. GEN. SIR RONALD B. LANE	1937
MAJ. GEN. SIR VICTOR A. COUPER	1938
LT. GEN. SIR H. F. M. WILSON	1941
SGT. LATER LT. C. V. CALLISTAN	1944
V.C. C.S.M. LATER LT. COL. H. DANIELS	1953
GEN. SIR REGINALD STEPHENS	1955
GEN. SIR J. T. BURNETT-STUART	1958
LT. GEN. SIR RALPH EASTWOOD	1959
V.C. L/SGT. LATER CAPT. J. E. WOODALL	1962
F. M. LORD WILSON OF LIBYA & STOWLANGTOFT	1964
V.C. CPL. W. BEESLEY	1966
V.C. SGT. W. GREGG	1969

ROLL OF FAME

MAJ. GEN. V. W. STREET	1970
GEN. SIR MONTAGU STOPFORD	1971
MAJ. GEN. J. M. L. RENTON	1972
V.C. LT. COL. V. B. TURNER	1972
LT. GEN. SIR RICHARD FYFFE	1972
V.C. SGT. W. F. BURMAN	1974
MAJ. GEN. SIR VICTOR PALEY	1976
F.M. SIR FRANCIS FESTING	1976
MAJ. GEN. D. L. DARLING	1978
MAJ. GEN. THE VISCOUNT BRIDGEMAN	1982
MAJ. GEN. J. T. W. REEVE	1983
GEN. SIR JAMES GLOVER	2000
LT. GEN. SIR PETER HUDSON	2000
V.C. L/SGT. D. W. BELCHER	1915
V.C. SGT. A. J. KNIGHT	1917
LT. GEN. SIR JAMES WILSON	2004

Part of the Rifle Brigade Memorial in Winchester Cathedral. George Cates' name is third down from the top of the left panel (Paul Goodwin).

• A plaque in St Mary's Church, Wimbledon, Surrey.
• The Rifle Brigade Memorial, Winchester Cathedral, Hampshire.
• Putney Vale War Memorial, Wimbledon Common.

George never married and the VC was presented to his father by the King in Hyde Park on 2nd June 1917. In addition to the VC, he was awarded the 1914–15 Star, British War Medal 1914–20 and Victory Medal 1914–19. The VC was lost in a fire in 1951 and a replacement was provided. It is held by the Royal Green Jackets (Rifles) Museum, Peninsula Barracks, Winchester.

G8/5190 SERGEANT HARRY CATOR
7th Battalion, The East Surrey Regiment

Harry Cator was born at Drayton, Norwich, Norfolk on 24th January 1894. The family name is sometimes seen as Cater. His father was Robert Cator (1864–1939), a railway platelayer of Caston, Norfolk. His mother, Laura née Shinn (1867–1933), a general servant, married Robert on 2nd April 1893 at St Nicholas, Great Yarmouth, Norfolk. The family was living at Fakenham Road, Drayton in 1901 and High Road, Drayton in 1911. Harry had a brother, Arthur Cator, born in 1898.

Harry's paternal grandfather was Henry Cator (c.1836–1907), an agricultural labourer living at Northacre, Caston, Norfolk. He married Emily née Whiterod (1839–1931) in 1858. In addition to Robert, they had eleven other children:

• George Henry Cator (1859–1928) was a farm labourer. He married Harriet Louisa Gooch (1860–1933) in 1879. They were living at The Views, Stow Bedon, Norfolk in 1891, Traice Road, Fundenhall in 1901 and Shrubb Farm, Larling and Roudham in 1911. They had six children including – Edith Louisa L Cator 1880, Charles Daniel Cator 1882, Delilah May Cator 1886, Kate Ellen M Cator 1895 and Dorothy Victoria Cator 1897.
• Rosa 'Rose' Cator 1860.
• Louisa Cator 1861.

Drayton, near Norwich.

St Nicholas, Great Yarmouth where Harry and his parents were married.

- Walter Cator (born 1862) married Martha Ann Brunton (1859–1934) in 1881 and they were living at Sharpe Street, Catfield, Norfolk in 1911. They had ten children including – Edward James Cator 1884, Robert Henry Cator 1885, William Frederick Cator 1889, John Ernest Cator 1891, Wilfred Walter Cator 1894, Stanley Percy Cator 1897 and Arthur Cator 1900.
- Henry Cator 1866
- William Herbert Cator (born 1868), a stationary engineman, married Louisa Dawson (born c.1871) in 1895. In 1911 the family was living at 98 George Street, Great Yarmouth. They had ten children including – Daisy Cator 1893, Violet Cator 1899, William Cator 1900 and Herbert Cator 1908.
- Emma Cator (1869–1944) had a son, Alfred Henry Cator in 1890 at Croydon, Surrey. She married Frederick Thurley (1864–1937), a bricklayer, in 1891. They were living at 11 Lancaster Road, Enfield, Middlesex in 1891. They had five children including – Eliza May Thurley 1892, Fred Thurley 1893, Emma Thurley 1895 and Ernest William Thurley 1898.
- Ellen Cator 1872.
- Herbert Cator (1873–1959), (registered as Carter), married Alice Barnard (1874–1939) in 1899. Herbert was a butcher's labourer in 1901 and a watchman at a shipyard in 1911. The family lived at 29 St Margaret's Road and later at Laundry Lane, both in Lowestoft, Suffolk. They had three children – Herbert Charles Cator 1899, Louisa Alice Cator 1902 and Henry James Cator 1908.
- Amelia Cator (1875–1952) married George William Sussams (1870–1855), a farm labourer, in 1894 (registered as Sussame). They had three children – Mary Sussams 1895, Frederick William Sussams 1897 and Florence Emma Sussams 1903.
- Arthur Cator (1878–1918) married Ellen Edith Bambridge (born 1876) in 1900. They had a son, Albert Thomas Cator in 1901. Ellen married William Eagling in 1919.

His maternal grandfather, Isaac Shinn (born c.1834), was a shepherd. He married Lucy née Aves (c.1835–68) in 1857. They were living at Long Lane, Feltwell, Norfolk in 1861. By 1881 Isaac had moved to 1 California, Snetterton, Norfolk, where he was living with his children and Maria Shinn, a widow, who was his housekeeper. In addition to Laura, Lucy and Isaac had five other children:

- Thomas Burton Shinn (1858–1921) married Annie Norton (1851–1932) in 1875. He was a railway porter and later a pulleyman and fruiterer. The family was living at Sculcoates, Kingston-upon-Hull, Yorkshire in 1881 and at 26 Brigham Terrace, Hull by 1901. They had seven children – Lucy Elizabeth Shinn 1876, George Thomas Shinn 1878, Selina Mary Shinn 1880, Laura Annie Shinn 1882, Frederick Burton Shinn born and died 1884, John Willie Shinn 1884 and Gertrude Maria Shinn 1886.

- Mary Ann Shinn born in 1860.
- Lucy Shinn (1861–1945), a nursemaid, married James Pinner (1859–1913), a farm labourer, in 1883. They were living at Larling and Roudham, Thetford in 1911. They had six children – William Isaac Pinner 1885, John Pinner 1888, Rose Mabel Pinner 1890, Alfred Pinner 1893, Laura Pinner 1897 and George James Pinner 1899.
- Maria Shinn (1864–1941), in addition to being Harry's aunt was also his mother-in-law. She was living with her uncle, James Amos, and his wife Susan in 1871 at Bridgham, Norfolk. By 1881 she was a servant at 8 Columbia Terrace, Great Yarmouth. Maria married William John Morriss (1862–1942), a carpenter, in 1885. They were living at 37 St Paul's Terrace, Great Yarmouth in 1891. Harry was living with them at 27 Salisbury Road, Great Yarmouth in 1911. Maria and William had five children – William George S Morriss born and died 1888, Maria Laura Morriss 1889, George Isaac Morriss 1890, John Stowards Morriss born and died 1891 and Rose Alice Morriss 1895, who married Harry.
- John William Shinn (1865–1930) was a shepherd's page in 1881. He moved to Hull, where he was employed as a dock labourer. He married Alice Roberts (c.1866–1886) in 1885. John was boarding with his brother Thomas in 1901.

Harry was educated at Drayton School, Norwich and was also a boy scout. He was employed by the Midland and Great Northern Joint Railway as a porter at Thursford Station near Fakenham, Norfolk and at Beach Station, Great Yarmouth. Later he worked for Chateau and Company in Great Yarmouth. Harry married his cousin, Rose Alice née Morriss (1895–1969) on 2nd September 1914 at the parish church of St Nicholas, Great

Beach Station, Great Yarmouth, where Harry worked as a porter.

Yarmouth. He was living at 5 Beaconsfield Road, Great Yarmouth at the time. They lived at 'Otago', 36 Allens Lane, Sprowston St Faith and Aylsham, Norwich. Rose and Harry had a son, Harry WR Cator, in 1922. He married Nancie DJ Herbert (born 1923) in 1943 and they lived at Mytchett, Aldershot, Hampshire. Harry and Nancie had three children – Robert P Cator 1944, Richard HL Cator 1946 and Rosanne D Cator 1950.

Harry enlisted on 3rd September 1914, the day after his marriage, promising his wife that he would do his best to win the VC. He went to France on 23rd June 1915 and was promoted sergeant in July. **Awarded the MM for rescuing thirty-six wounded men from the German barbed wire at Ovillers on the Somme on 3rd July 1916, while the Battalion was clearing the dead from the failed 37th Brigade attack, LG 23rd August 1916.**

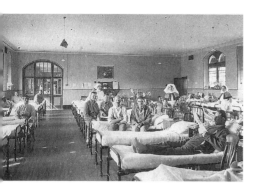

Beaufort War Hospital was the Bristol Lunatic Asylum prior to the First World War. It eventually had 500 beds, including thirty for mental cases and a ward of ten beds for German prisoners. The first wounded arrived on 24th May 1915 and the hospital closed in February 1919, having treated 29,433 patients. Post-war it became Glenside Hospital and in 1996 was sold when Avon and Gloucestershire College of Health and Bath and Swindon College of Health Studies, joined the University of the West of England's Faculty of Health and Community Studies.

Harry Cator being congratulated by fellow patients (Eastern Daily Press).

Awarded the VC for his actions at Hangest Trench, near Arras, France on 9th April 1917, LG 8th June 1917. Both his jaws were broken by shell fragments on 12th April and he was evacuated to Beaufort War Hospital in Bristol, where he underwent several operations. Some fragments were still embedded in his shoulder when he died in 1966. Harry was offered a commission, but he declined. The VC was presented by the King outside Buckingham Palace on 21st July 1917. **Also awarded the French Croix de Guerre for his part in the Arras battles, LG 14th July 1917.** He was discharged in January 1919 and in March he was given a civic reception in Drayton.

Harry was a member of the VC Guard at the interment of the Unknown Warrior on 11th November 1920. He set up a shoe repair business and worked for the Post Office in Norwich from February 1929. He may also have worked for the RAF on clerical duties and later was a clerical officer with the National Assistance Board, which was established in 1948.

Norwich Post Office, where Harry worked from February 1929.

On 12th April 1927, Harry became a Freemason, being Initiated into the Wanderers Lodge (No.1604) in London. He was Passed to the Second Degree on 11th October and was Raised on 8th November. On 6th May 1929 he became a Joining Member of the Naval and Military Lodge (No.3678), meeting at Saint Giles' Street, Norwich, and served as Worshipful Master in 1944. He was appointed Provincial Grand Sword Bearer for the Province of Norfolk in 1949. Harry was also a prominent member of the British Legion and acted as standard-bearer for the Drayton branch, as well as being active in the Old Comrades' Association.

He was commissioned on the General List of the Army Emergency Reserve on 3rd October 1942. Promoted war substantive lieutenant and temporary captain to be the Quartermaster of 6th Norfolk Battalion Home Guard on 3rd January 1943. Later he was the Quartermaster of Denton Transit Camp at Newhaven and then Commandant of a PoW camp near Cranwich, Norfolk. He treated his prisoners very fairly and spent holidays with some of them in Germany after the war. Harry was released from embodied service and relinquished his Emergency Commission when he transferred to the Territorial Army Royal Artillery as a lieutenant on 19th December 1947. Promoted captain 28th April 1948 and continued to serve in 284th (1st East Anglian) Heavy Anti-Aircraft Regiment, Royal Artillery TA until he retired on 12th January 1951 (244007).

Harry Cator died at the Norfolk and Norwich Hospital on 7th April 1966 and is buried in the churchyard of St Mary's & St Margaret's Church, Sprowston, Norfolk. He left the net sum of £2,895/13/- in his will. He is also commemorated by Cator Road, off School Road, Drayton, Norwich built in 1947–48.

Denton Transit Camp at Newhaven, where Harry was the Quartermaster.

In addition to the VC and MM, he was awarded the 1914–15 Star, British War Medal 1914–20, Victory Medal 1914–19, Defence Medal, War Medal 1939–45, George VI Coronation Medal 1937, Elizabeth II Coronation Medal 1953 and the French Croix de Guerre. The medals were sold by Spink's at the Cavendish Hotel, Jermyn Street, London on 6th June 1985 for £10,500. They were sold again by Spink's in 1996 for £28,500 and were purchased by Michael Ashcroft. The medals are held in the Lord Ashcroft Gallery in the Imperial War Museum.

A post-war picture of Harry, on the right in the middle, with some of his former German prisoners.

CAPTAIN PERCY HERBERT CHERRY
26th Australian Infantry Battalion AIF

Percy Cherry was born on 4th June 1895 at Murradoc, Drysdale, Victoria, Australia. His father, John 'Jack' Gawley Cherry (1863–1940) was born at Benalla, Victoria. He was a horse breaker and roughrider as a teenager for the Victoria Police, and competed in buckjumping contests against Bob Simpson and Tommy Lawless, noted roughriders of the time. On 26th June 1880, the notorious Kelly gang killed a police informer and headed for Glenrowan, where Jack Cherry was a witness to what happened thereafter. Next day the gang gathered the whole population of Glenrowan, sixty-two people, in Mrs Jones' hotel. The police arrived and a fire fight followed, during which Superintendent Hare was shot in the wrist. Among those caught in the crossfire was fifty-eight year-old Martin Cherry, an unmarried platelayer born in Limerick, Ireland, whose relationship to Jack Cherry is unknown. Martin was found with a groin wound behind the main building and was administered the last rites by Father M Gibney; he died within half an hour. The son of Mrs Ann Jones, the owner of the hotel, was also killed. Overnight Ned Kelly escaped from the hotel and attacked the growing police force from the rear at dawn. He was overwhelmed, having been shot several times in the limbs and groin, but his armour saved him from any fatal wounds. The other three members of the

The remains of the burned out Glenrowan Hotel after the police action against the Kelly gang on 27–28th June 1880. Percy Cherry's father, Jack, witnessed the event.

Ned Kelly in chains in Melbourne Gaol 1880.

gang were still in the hotel. Joe Byrne was shot dead and the remaining hostages escaped. The police then set the hotel on fire and the two others, Dan Kelly and Steve Hart, probably committed suicide before the flames reached them. Ned Kelly was tried on 19th October and was hanged at Melbourne Gaol on 11th November.

Jack went on to manage large horse and cattle stations for twelve years at Cape Otway and Merrydock, Drysdale, Victoria and then ran a cattle station in South Africa for eighteen months, helping to stamp out Rinderpest. Returning to Victoria c.1902, he ran the Rose of Australia Hotel in Melbourne for eighteen months then moved to Gippsland for a few months. Jack relocated to Tasmania and took over an apple orchard at 'Cherry Vale', Cradoc, Huon. He was also a Codlin moth inspector for five years. Percy's mother, Elizabeth née Russell (c.1861–1927), was born in Victoria. Jack and Elizabeth married at Guildford, near Campbell's Creek, Castlemaine, Victoria in 1883. Percy had four siblings:

- John Andrew Cherry (1900–66), an orchardist on the family property, married Georgina Edna Lee (1901–67). He was an office keeper in 1949 and was living with his family at 21 Harrington Street, Hobart. They had two children – Eardley Harold 'Pat' Cherry 1925 and Frederick James Cherry.
- George William Cherry (1903–83) was also an orchardist on the family property.
- Florence May Emmaline Cherry (1893–1984) married Cyril George Edmund Batchelor (born c.1890). He enlisted in 12th Australian Infantry Battalion AIF (125) on 17th August 1914 and served abroad as a corporal, but returned to Australia on 15th August 1915. They had six children – Dorothy June Batchelor 1919, Cyril Edward Batchelor 1921, Percy Strickland Archibald Batchelor 1922, Olive Dawn Batchelor 1923, Gloria Faith Batchelor 1925 and Herbert Walter Batchelor 1931. Percy served in the Royal Australian Navy during the Second World War.
- Elizabeth 'Lizzie' Cherry (born 1905) married Harry Mark Large (1908–73) and had at least one child, Bronwyn Large.

Percy's paternal grandfather, George Gawley Cherry (1825-85) was born at Aughnamullen, Co Monaghan, Ireland. He married Caroline née Milligan (1821-88) who was also born in Ireland. George became a road contractor and famer at Benalla, Victoria. In addition to Jack they had a number of other children including - George Gawley Cherry 1847, Joseph Cherry 1849, Margaret Jane Cherry 1853, George James Cherry 1855 and Caroline Cherry 1861.

Percy was educated at Cradoc State School, Huon, Tasmania until 1908 and received private tuition thereafter. He rowed with the Franklin Rowing Club, played cornet in the Franklin Brass Band and sang in the Church of England school choir. He worked for his father in the apple orchard and became an expert picker. He won one picking competition by packing thirty-five cases in one hour. Percy joined the Army Cadet Force in 1908 and was an excellent shot. He won the President's Trophy and Gold Medal in 1911 at Franklin Rifle Range. At the time he was the youngest member of the unit. He was later appointed lieutenant with 93rd Infantry Regiment (Militia).

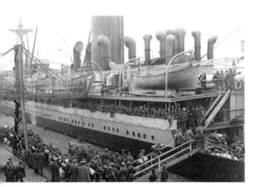

Troops boarding HMAT A60 *Aeneas*. SS *Aeneas* (10,049 tons) was built in Belfast in 1910 for the Ocean Steam Ship Co (Blue Funnel Line) on the South Africa–Australia service. She was requisitioned by the Australian Government during the First World War and her first voyage as a troopship was on 29th June 1915, departing Brisbane with 25th Battalion and 1st Reinforcements of 26th Battalion. In May 1918 she ran aground on Rathlin Island off Ireland. She returned to the Australian service on 29th May 1920 and in 1925 transferred to the Far East route. On 2nd July 1940, as part of convoy OA 1776 from London to Glasgow, she was sunk in an air attack off Start Point, Devon with the loss of nineteen lives.

HMHS *Oxfordshire* arriving in Sydney in September 1945. SS *Oxfordshire* was built by Harland & Wolff for the Bibby Line in 1912. On 2nd August 1914, she was the first ship requisitioned for war service and was converted at Tilbury into Naval Hospital Ship No.1 with 562 beds. In April 1915, she was the base hospital ship at Mudros and in 1916 was used in the Persian Gulf and off German East Africa. In 1918 she was a shuttle hospital ship between Britain and France. By the time she was decommissioned on 24th March 1919, she had made 235 voyages, covered 172,000 miles without a breakdown and carried 50,000 wounded, the highest number of any hospital ship in the war. On 3rd September 1939, she was requisitioned again and converted at the Royal Albert Dock, London into Hospital Ship No.6 (500 beds). She was the base hospital ship at Freetown, Sierra Leone until September 1942 when she deployed to the Mediterranean. In 1944 she went to the Adriatic, where on 29th October she was damaged by a near miss between Ancona and Bari. That November she went to the Far East and was loaned to the US 7th Fleet during the taking of Okinawa. Following the defeat of Japan, she was used to repatriate wounded from Hong Kong and in May 1946 brought home the sick from the Near and Far East. She also repatriated Indian troops from Basra to Bombay as well as making four Atlantic crossings with refugees. In 1948 she arrived home with troops from Palestine and on 19th July was decommissioned at Southampton after carrying 22,321 casualties, once again the highest of any hospital ship. In April 1949 she made her first voyage for the International Refugee Organisation to Australia with emigrants and in 1950–51 was used as a troopship between Trieste and Port Said. On 13th April 1951, she sailed from Liverpool as the *Safina-el-Arab*, having been sold to the Pan-Islamic Steamship Co of Karachi and was used on the Karachi–Jeddah route to ferry pilgrims between June and October. She was broken up at Karachi in 1958.

On 5th March 1915, Percy enlisted in the Australian Imperial Force at Franklin and was immediately appointed quartermaster sergeant. He qualified for a commission, but was considered too young at the time. He was described as 5′ 8″ tall, weighing 133 lbs, with fair complexion, grey eyes and brown hair. He was posted to 26th Battalion and embarked for the Middle East with D Company at Brisbane aboard HMAT A60 *Aeneas* on 29th June. The Battalion disembarked at Alexandria, Egypt and moved to Camp Heliopolis.

The Battalion embarked at Alexandria for Lemnos on 4th September. Percy was appointed company sergeant major on 13th September 1915 and took part in operations at Gallipoli. He was wounded in the head by shrapnel on 1st December and treated at 7th Field Ambulance and 13th Casualty Clearing Station before being transferred to Mudros on 2nd December. From there he was evacuated on HMHS *Oxfordshire* to Alexandria on 3rd December and treated at No.2 Australian General Hospital.

No.2 British Red Cross Hospital at Rouen.

Percy was commissioned on 8th December 1915. He transferred to Helouan Convalescent Depot, Cairo on 20th January 1916 and returned to duty at Tel el Kebir on 26th January. Having attended a machine gun course in February and March, he was posted to 7th Machine Gun Company at Moascar Garrison, Egypt on 3rd March. He embarked at Alexandria on 14th March and disembarked at Marseilles, France on 21st March. While he was at the front, his mother sent him posies of flowers, which he would kiss and return to her for preservation in the family album.

During the fighting near Pozières on the Somme on 5th August, Percy and a German officer spent some time sniping at each other until they both fired simultaneously and both were wounded. Percy was hit in the neck, but the German was mortally wounded. Percy crawled to him and the German gave him a bundle of letters, asking in English if he would post them to his family; Percy agreed. The German said, *And so it ends* and died. Percy was treated at No.2 British Red Cross Hospital, Rouen, on 6th August, before being evacuated to 3rd London General Hospital at Wandsworth, London on 12th August.

He was promoted lieutenant on 25th August and appointed adjutant at Wareham, Dorset on 16th September. He returned to France on 8th November, where he was appointed temporary captain

In August 1914, the Royal Victoria Patriotic School in Wandsworth became the 3rd London General Hospital, one of four Territorial General Hospitals in London. It was built in 1859 as the Royal Victoria Patriotic Asylum, an orphanage for the daughters of soldiers, sailors and marines who had fought in the Crimean War. In 1914, a temporary railway station was built to enable wounded to be brought easily from the south coast. Hutted wards were added in the grounds, bringing capacity to 2,000 beds by May 1917. The Hospital closed in August 1920, having treated 62,708 patients. The building now contains twenty-nine apartments, several studios and workshops, a drama school and a restaurant.

No.2 Australia General Hospital in Egypt with the first of casualties from Gallipoli.

Percy Cherry's original grave at Lagnicourt. His remains were subsequently moved to Quéant Road Cemetery, Buissy, near Arras (Australian War Memorial).

Percy Cherry's grave in Quéant Road Cemetery.

and OC C Company, 26th Battalion on 1st December and assumed temporary command of A Company on 9th December. Promoted captain on 14th February 1917.

Awarded the MC for his actions on 2nd March 1917 in an attack on Malt Trench at Warlencourt. He was wounded, but refused to leave his post and managed to find a gap in the wire to charge two enemy gun positions. He captured both and turned one of the guns on the enemy. He continued fighting and managed to clear the enemy from their positions, LG 26th April 1917.

Awarded the VC for his actions at Lagnicourt, France on 26th March 1917, LG 11th May 1917. He was recommended by Brigadier General Evan Wisdom, Commander

Sir Francis Newdegate, Governor of Tasmania presented Percy's VC to his father on 6th October 1917.

The imposing Australian War Memorial, Anzac Parade, Canberra where Percy Cherry's VC is held.

Hobart City Hall where the VC presentation to place (Mike Krebs).

7th Australian Infantry Brigade, on 3rd April 1917 and it was supported by Major General NM Smyth VC, GOC 2nd Australian Division. Percy was killed in action near Lagnicourt, France on 27th March 1917 and is buried in Quéant Road Cemetery, Buissy, near Arras, France (VIII C 10). Percy never married and the VC was presented to his father by Sir Francis Newdegate KCMG, Governor of Tasmania, at Hobart City Hall on 6th October 1917.

In addition to the VC and MC, he was awarded the 1914–15 Star, British War Medal 1914–20 and Victory Medal 1914–19. His VC is held at the Australian War Memorial, Anzac Parade, Canberra, Australian Capital Territory, Australia. Percy is commemorated in a number of places:

• Victoria Cross Memorial, Campbell, Canberra dedicated on 24th July 2000.
• Victoria Cross Memorial, Hobart Cenotaph, Tasmania dedicated on 11th May 2003.
• Victoria Cross Memorial, Queen Victoria Building, George Street, Sydney, New South Wales.
• Carved wooden statue and plaque at Channel Highway, Cradoc Park, Cradoc, Tasmania.
• Memorial plaque at Huonville Primary School, 74 Wilmot Road, Huonville, Tasmania.
• Named on one of eleven plaques honouring 175 men from overseas awarded the VC for the Great War. The plaques were unveiled by the Senior Minister of State at the Foreign & Commonwealth Office and Minister for Faith and Communities, Baroness Warsi, at a reception at Lancaster House, London on 26th June 2014 attended by The Duke of Kent and relatives of the VC recipients. The Australian plaque is at the Australian War Memorial.
• The Secretary of State for Communities and Local Government, Eric Pickles MP announced that Victoria Cross recipients from the Great War would have commemorative paving stones laid in their birthplace as a lasting legacy of local heroes within communities. The stones would be laid on or close to the 100th anniversary of their VC actions. For the 145 VCs born in Australia, Belgium, Canada, China, Denmark, Egypt, France, Germany, India, Iraq, Japan, Nepal, Netherlands, New Zealand, Pakistan, Sri Lanka, South Africa, Ukraine and

United States of America, individual commemorative stones were unveiled at the National Memorial Arboretum, Alrewas, Staffordshire by Prime Minister David Cameron MP and Sergeant Johnson Beharry VC on 5th March 2015.

LIEUTENANT ROBERT GRIERSON COMBE
27th Battalion (City of Winnipeg), Canadian Expeditionary Force

Robert Combe was born on 5th August 1880 at St Machar, Aberdeen, Aberdeenshire, Scotland. His father, James Combe (1845–1901), was born at Kirkbean, Kircudbrightshire. He was a butler at Elm Hall, Penny Lane, Wavertree, Lancashire in 1871, a hotel waiter in 1881 and keeper of the Central Hotel, Holburn, Old Machar, Aberdeen in 1901. James married Elizabeth 'Betsey' née Jardine (1835–1909) on 21st September 1869 at St John's, Liverpool, Lancashire. She was born at Caerlaverock, Dumfriesshire. In 1881 the family was living at 18 Holburn Road, Old Machar, Aberdeen. By 1891  they were at 2 Millburn Street, Aberdeen and moved to 24 Ferryhill Place, Aberdeen the following year. Robert had five siblings:

- James Combe (1864–89) was registered as Combs at birth. He was a confectioner's apprentice in 1881 and drowned accidentally in Surrey Docks, London on 1st February 1890.
- Elizabeth Combe (born 1870) was a teacher in 1891.
- Mabel Combe (born 1872) was also a teacher in 1891.
- Jessie Catherine Combe (born 1875) was a bookkeeper in 1901. She married Ernest Eustace Benham (born 1874), an electrical engineer, in 1903 at Ferryhill Parish Church, Aberdeen.
- George Alexander Combe (born 1877) was a student of arts in 1901.

His paternal grandfather, Alexander Combe (1810–88), born at Haugh of Urr, Dalbeattie, Dumfriesshire, was an agricultural labourer. He married Elizabeth née Grierson (1814–89) in 1831. She was born at Durisdeer, Dumfriesshire. By 1871 they were living at 39 & 41 Queensberry Street, Dumfries with their son Robert. In

St Machar, Aberdeen.

addition to James they had five other children – Janet Combe c.1835, Margaret Combe c.1838, William Combe 1840, John Combe 1841 and Robert Combe 1855.

His maternal grandfather, George Jardine (born c.1806), was a ship's carpenter. He married Margaret née Boyd (born c.1811) and they were living at Kelton, Dumfriesshire in 1841. In addition to Betsey they had four other children – James Jardine c.1828, John Jardine c.1831, Margaret Jardine c.1838 and Mary Jardine 1841.

Melville Railway Station, Saskatchewan.

Ferryhill School, Aberdeen.

SS *Pretorian* (6,508 tons) was launched in 1900 for the Allan Line for the north Atlantic routes. In 1917 she was taken over by the Canadian Pacific Line and was scrapped in 1926. She is seen here in Prince's Dock, Glasgow.

Aberdeen Grammar School dates from c.1257. In 1863 it moved to its current location on Skene Street. Originally fee paying, it became successively a council grammar school, a comprehensive and co-educational from 1973. In 1986 it was devastated by a fire and rebuilt over a number of years. Famous alumni include Lord Byron, former Foreign Secretary Robin Cook (1946–2005), actor Andrew Cruikshank and mathematician Hector Munro Macdonald.

Robert was educated at Ferryhill School, Aberdeen and Aberdeen Grammar School 1894–97. He was an apprentice pharmacist with William E Hay of Aberdeen and London. He served for about a year in 1st Volunteer Battalion, Royal Fusiliers in London. In April 1906 he emigrated to Canada, sailing on SS *Pretorian* from Liverpool, and settled at Moosomin, Saskatchewan, where he found employment in a drugstore.

Moosomin, Saskatchewan.

He opened his own drugstore at Melville, Saskatchewan in 1908 and a second later in Dubuc. He was prominent in the life of the community:

- President of the Melville Board of Trade.
- Served for a year in 16th Light Horse.
- Director of Melville Hockey Club and a founder member of Melville Millionaires Hockey Club.
- Member of Union Church, Melville.
- Member of the Order of Knights of Pythias, a fraternal and secret society founded in Washington DC in 1864. It now has 2,000 lodges worldwide.

On 18th August 1909, Robert Combe married Jean Traquair Donald (c.1886 – 12th April 1963) at Melville. She was a teacher who worked at Coverdale, New Brunswick and Moosomin, Saskatchewan. They had no children. Jean's father, John Gordon Donald (1843–1919) was born at Cairnie by Huntly, Ruthven, Aberdeenshire. He emigrated to Canada and married Agnes née Barbour (born 1853 in New York, USA) in 1881 in Ontario,

Melville Millionaires Hockey Club won the Allan Cup in 1915.

Canada. Her parents came from Scotland. The family moved to Moosomin, Saskatchewan in 1889, where John became postmaster in 1897.

Robert enlisted on 1st April 1915 and was commissioned as a lieutenant in 53rd Battalion at Prince Albert, Saskatchewan. He was described as 5′ 10″ tall, weighing 160 lbs, with black hair, brown eyes, fresh complexion and his religious denomination was Presbyterian. He was also stationed at Camp Sewell, Western Manitoba. He sailed to Britain in September 1915 and joined 30th Reserve Battalion. He also appears to have

Prince Albert, Saskatchewan.

Camp Sewell, a military training area in Manitoba was used from 1909 to 1934. It was renamed Camp Hughes in 1915 after Major General Sir Sam Hughes, Canadian Minister of Militia and Defence.

been in 32nd Battalion for a short period. He completed 5th Officers' Course 3rd January–18th March 1916 and sailed for France on 27th March, joining 27th Battalion in the field on 29th March. On 1st–7th May he attended a Stokes Gun Course.

On 31st May, Robert was evacuated to 5th Canadian Field Ambulance with lumbago and moved to a casualty clearing station next day. He returned to the Battalion on 5th June, but was admitted to No.10 Casualty Clearing Station on 13th June with the same complaint and

No.10 Casualty Clearing Station was at Abeele, near Poperinghe, Belgium at the time Robert Combe was admitted.

No.14 General Hospital at Wimereux the following day. He was discharged to duty Class B on 24th June, but recovery was slow and he was admitted to No.2 General Hospital at Le Havre on 26th June. He was evacuated to England on HS *Panama* and admitted to Miss Pollock's Hospital, 50 Weymouth Street, London on 29th June; posted to the General List the same day.

A Medical Board at 86 Strand, London on 18th July decided he needed a month for recovery and recuperation. He was treated at Bath Officers' Hospital, 26 Marlborough Buildings, Bath until 6th August then went on leave to Aboyne, Aberdeenshire. A Medical Board at 86 Strand on 18th August allowed a further three weeks for recovery and on 8th September he was found fit for Home Service. As a result he was attached to 11th Reserve Battalion at Shorncliffe on 11th September and was taken on strength on 6th November. On 13th November he transferred to

Miss Pollack's Hospital for Officers at
50 Weymouth Street, London was one
of two hospitals for colonial officers
established by Sir Robert Hudson
Borwick (1845–1936). The other was run
by Miss Bertha Lancaster at 29 Wimpole
Street. Miss Pollack's Hospital had
twelve beds and was affiliated to Queen
Alexandra's Hospital, Millbank (Lost
Hospitals of London).

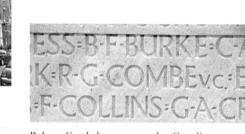

Robert Combe's name on the Canadian
National Vimy Memorial.

This part of Shorncliffe Camp was known as 'Tin Town'.

The Canadian National Vimy Memorial
stands on the highest point of Vimy
Ridge, Hill 145.

the permanent cadre of 11th Reserve Battalion.
He was attached to 31 Rifle Party at the School
of Musketry, Hythe, Kent 28th November –
23rd December.

A Medical Board on 19th March 1917 found
him fit for General Service. He was struck
off strength to 27th Battalion and sailed for
France on 20th April, arriving at the Canadian
Base Depot on 22nd April and rejoined the
Battalion on 25th April. **Awarded the VC for his actions near Acheville on 3rd
May 1917, 27th June 1917.** He was killed during his VC action on 3rd May 1917
and is commemorated on the Canadian National Vimy Memorial, France. Robert is
commemorated in a number of other places:

- Honours Board, Aberdeen Grammar School.
- The family headstone at Allen Vale Cemetery, Aberdeen.
- Aberdeen War Memorial.
- Combe Lake, North Saskatchewan.
- Combe Branch, Royal Canadian Legion, Melville.
- Portrait in the Peace Tower, Ottawa, Ontario.
- Portrait in Melville Museum, Saskatchewan.
- Canadian Book of Remembrance.
- Two 49 Cent postage stamps in honour of the ninety-four Canadian VCs were issued by Canada Post on 21st October 2004 on the 150th Anniversary of the first Canadian VC's action, Alexander Roberts Dunn.

Aberdeen War Memorial and Cowdray Hall are part of Aberdeen Art Gallery. The memorial was unveiled on 29th September 1925 by King George V when he opened Cowdray Hall.

- Victoria Cross obelisk to all Canadian VCs at Military Heritage Park, Barrie, Ontario dedicated by The Princess Royal on 22nd October 2013.
- Named on one of eleven plaques honouring 175 men from overseas awarded the VC for the Great War. The plaques were unveiled by the Senior Minister of State at the Foreign & Commonwealth Office and Minister for Faith and Communities, Baroness Warsi, at a reception at Lancaster House, London on 26th June 2014 attended by The Duke of Kent and relatives of the VC recipients. The Canadian plaque was unveiled outside the British High Commission in Elgin Street, Ottawa on 10th November 2014 by The Princess Royal in the presence of British High Commissioner Howard Drake, Canadian Minister of Veterans Affairs Julian Fantino and Canadian Chief of the Defence Staff General Thomas J Lawson.

The Legislative Building in Regina, Saskatchewan where the Prince of Wales presented Robert Combe's VC to his widow in October 1919, during his two months' visit to Canada.

Aboyne Castle was used as an auxiliary hospital during the First World War. The building dates back to 1233 and has been in the Huntly family since the 15th Century.

In 1915 Bangour Village Hospital was taken over by the War Office and was known as Edinburgh War Hospital. The first wounded arrived in June. By 1918 the hospital had a capacity of 3,000 patients. It reopened as a psychiatric hospital in 1922, but in 1939 once again became Edinburgh War Hospital. Bangour General Hospital closed in 2004.

Jean followed her husband to Britain and trained with the British Red Cross for a year before being posted to Aboyne Castle Hospital, Aberdeenshire, where she was appointed Quartermaster. She lived at 252 Great Western Road, Aberdeen. She was posted to Edinburgh War Hospital, Midlothian working with the Voluntary Aid Detachment. She also lived at 1 Hazel Grove, Yelverton, Devon for a time. Jean was invited to investitures at Buckingham Palace on two occasions, but declined both through ill health. The VC was eventually presented to her by the Prince of Wales at the Legislative Building, Regina, Saskatchewan, Canada on 4th October 1919.

Jean returned to Canada following her husband's death and trained as a physiotherapist at Hart House, Toronto, Ontario. When qualified she was employed at Tuxedo Military Hospital, Winnipeg, Manitoba. She was demobilised at the end of the war and joined the staff of Dr Galloway's Clinic in Winnipeg. She moved to 155 Linden Avenue, Victoria, British Columbia in 1925. In 1942 she was appointed Supervisor of the Blue Triangle Leave Center for Servicewomen at Balmoral, Victoria until it closed in 1946. She attended the Victoria Cross Centenary celebrations in London in 1956 and was living at Brentwood Bay, Vancouver Island, British Columbia at the time. Jean returned to Victoria in February 1963, fell ill shortly afterwards and died in hospital at Victoria on 12th April 1963. Former members of 27th (City of Winnipeg) Battalion acted as pallbearers at her funeral.

In addition to the VC he was awarded the British War Medal 1914–20 and Victory Medal 1914–19. His next-of-kin is eligible to receive the Canadian Memorial Cross. His medals are held by Provincial Archives, 3303 Hillsdale Street, Regina, Saskatchewan, Canada.

13908 PRIVATE CHRISTOPHER AUGUSTUS COX
7th Battalion, The Bedfordshire Regiment

Christopher Cox was born at Kings Langley, Hertfordshire on 25th December 1889. His father, William Cox (1850–90), a labourer, married Elizabeth 'Betsy' Carter (1848–82) in 1869. They were living at Canal Bridge, Kings Langley in 1871 and at Waterside, Kings Langley in 1881. Christopher's mother was Susannah late Frazer née Chilvers (1843–1916). She married Dial Frazer (1843–79), a groom, in 1866 at Wisbech St Peter, Cambridgeshire. In 1871 they were living at 25 Great South Street, Wisbech. William Cox married Susannah Frazer on 1st June 1882 at Kings Langley. She was a shirt needle woman in 1891, when the family was living at Waterside, Kings Langley. By 1901 Susannah had moved to Church Lane, Kings Langley. Christopher had ten siblings from his parents' three marriages:

- Herbert William Cox (born 1871).
- Alice Cornelia Cox (born 1873).
- Eliza Cox (born c.1875).
- Elizabeth Charlotte Cox (born 1880).
- Edith Cox (twin with Florence) (1883–84).
- Florence Cox (twin with Edith) (born and died 1883).
- Henry 'Harry' Norman Cox (1884–1970) was a pulping machine boy in a paper mill in 1901. He served in the Royal Navy (307357), enlisting on 12th September 1904 for twelve years initially, serving much of the time as a Stoker 1st Class. He

The Flour Mill at Kings Langley.

Church Lane, Kings Langley, where Christopher's mother was living in 1901.

was described as 5′ 6″ tall with light brown hair, blue eyes and fair complexion. He served on numerous ships and shore establishments, including HMS *Nelson, Firequeen, Victory, Exmouth, Royal Arthur, Crescent, Edgar, Hindustan, Dreadnought, Latina, President, Daedalus, Pembroke, Bee, Vernon, Thunderer, Cardiff, Greenwich, Dido, Ready* and *Rosalind* until transferring to the Reserve on 17th September 1936. He then worked as a porter for the General Post Office. He married Edith Smith in 1917 and reportedly had a daughter, Thora.

• Ellen 'Nell' Susannah Cox (born 1886) was a paper stainer in 1901. She married Alfred James Hopkins in 1916.
• James Percy Cox (1888–1916) was an agricultural labourer in 1901 and a chaff cutter in 1911. He emigrated and settled at Port Augusta, South Australia. He enlisted in 48th Battalion, Australian Imperial Force (2789) on 9th July 1915 and served in Egypt and France. He died of wounds on 3rd October 1916 and is buried in Lijssenthoek Military Cemetery, Poperinge, Belgium (X B 22).
• Rose Cox (born and died 1888).

Christopher's uncle, James Cox (born 1841), enlisted in the 96th Regiment (108) at Westminster on 6th October 1857 and served in South Africa for two years and eight months and the East Indies for eight years and six months. He was awarded Good Conduct Pay on 25th April 1862, 5th October 1865, 2nd June 1870 and 8th October 1875 and received the Long Service & Good Conduct Medal on 8th October 1875. He was discharged at Aldershot on 14th June 1877 as unfit for further service due to chronic ophthalmia caused by the climate and exposure during his service. His character was assessed as Good, with two entries in the Regimental Defaulters Book. On discharge he was described as 5′ 7½″ tall, with fresh complexion, grey eyes and light brown hair. His intended place of residence was Langley Lodge Farm, Langley, Hertfordshire. James married Sarah Ann Morton (born 1847) in 1878 and they had four children – Thomas James Cox 1879, Ethel Mary Cox 1881, Reuben William Cox 1883 and Harry Cox 1886.

At least three of Christopher's maternal uncles moved to the United States:

• Robert Chilvers (1828–96) died in Chicago, Illinois.
• John Thomas Chilvers (1829–82) died in Illinois.
• William B Chilvers (1831–1916) married Jane Johnson (1824–1908) in 1852. She was born in England. William and Jane had eight children – Mary Jane Chilvers 1852, Ellen Maria Chilvers 1855, William Henry Chilvers 1857, Emma Chilvers 1860, Sarah Ann Chilvers 1863, Abraham L Chilvers 1866, David Chilvers 1868 and Agnes Clara Chilvers 1870. William and Jane died at Brookfield, Cook County, Illinois.

Christopher was educated at Kings Langley Church of England School. He was employed as a farm hand at Balls Pond Farm and injured the tips of his fingers in a turnip mincing machine. He was a coal carman in 1911. Christopher married Maud May née Swan (17th January 1890–16th July 1976) on 5th October 1912 at Queen's Road Wesleyan Chapel, Watford. She was a nursery maid for the Stirling family in Watford in 1911. They lived at Blackwall Lane and later at 81 Coniston Road, Kings Langley. Christopher and Maud had nine children:

Queen's Road Wesleyan Chapel, Watford where Christopher Cox married Maud Swan in 1912.

- Christopher William Cox (1913–96) served in the Royal Army Medical Corps during the Second World War with his brother Reg during the siege of Malta and later in Italy. He married Elizabeth Kirtley in 1944 and had a son, David C Cox in 1949.
- Reginald James Cox (1915–71) served in the Royal Army Medical Corps during the Second World War with his brother Chris and was also at the siege of Malta and in Italy. He became a tobacconist and later a civil servant. He married Margery Alice Lilian Sweatman (born 1930) in 1951 and they had three children – Stephen J Cox 1952, Hilary A Cox 1955 and Alison M Cox 1957.
- Violet Beatrice Maud Cox (1918–2010).
- Joyce Rose Cox (born 1920) married Alfred H Cox in 1943.
- Elizabeth May Cox (born 1922) married Malcolm WC Chapman in 1945.
- Norman Victor Cox (1924–2010) served in the Royal Scots Fusiliers during the Second World War and landed on Gold Beach in Normandy on 6th June 1944, attached to 6th Border. He was wounded in the leg in November 1944 and was later awarded the French Legion d'Honneur, Chevalier Class, for his part in the D-Day landings. Norman married Rosemary R Brown (1929–2007) in 1951. They had two children – Lorna GN Cox 1955 and Victoria L Cox 1957.
- Dennis Abyss/Abbiss Cox (born 1927).
- Ian Herbert Cox (1928–2011) served in the army during the Second World War and was in Berlin shortly after its capture by the Russians. He married Maria Fruhauf in 1949 and they lived at Abbott's View, Watford. Ian featured in a documentary about VE Day in June 2010. He was highly regarded locally and Kings Langley Parish Council allocated a bench on the corner of Abbots View and Abbots Rise in his memory. Ian and Maria had two children – Anita M Cox 1954 and Marina E Cox 1958.
- Stella Iris Cox (1930–2012) married Leslie A 'Mick' Lewis (1924–2014) in 1959. Mick flew Lancasters during the Second World War and was shot down over France.

One of Maud's sisters, Mary Eliza Swan (1875–1960) married James Pearson (1867–1930) in 1896. James served in the East Kent Regiment until 14th May 1905. They had eight children and emigrated to Australia on 8th October 1912, where they ran a boarding house at St Kilda, Melbourne, Victoria.

One of Maud's brothers, Lewis Christian Victor Swan (1887–1966), was an errand boy when he enlisted in the Royal Navy (227768) on 23rd August 1903. He was described as 5′ 2½″ tall, with brown hair, dark grey eyes and fresh complexion. He served aboard HMS *Lion*, *Impregnable*, *Boscawen III*, *Ganges*, *Victory*, *Amethyst* and *Excellent*. When he became eighteen on 25th December 1905, he signed on for twelve years, but was discharged by purchase on 12th August 1907. He married Mabel Clara Auger (born 1884) in 1907 and they had four children. Lewis was a journeyman baker in 1911, living with his family at 34 Acme Road, Watford.

Christopher enlisted on 7th September 1914 and went to France on 26th July 1915. He was wounded in the thigh on 1st July 1916 on the Somme and spent two months in hospital. **Awarded the VC for his actions at Achiet-le-Grand, France on 13th–17th March 1917, LG 11th May 1917.** A number of officers and senior NCOs submitted reports recommending Christopher for recognition for his actions, including Second Lieutenants RJ Clarke (A Company), FE Dealler and SR Chapman (B Company), Sergeants F Bayford (5 Platoon), FS Nicholson (8 Platoon), BW Eakins and Corporal WV Simmonds (6 Platoon). A formal recommendation was submitted on 29th March 1917 by Lieutenant Colonel GP Mills, CO 7th Bedfordshire, and it was supported by Lieutenant Colonel CC Carr, commanding 54th Infantry Brigade and Major General RP Lee, GOC 18th Division.

The VC was presented by the King outside Buckingham Palace on 21st July 1917. On 28th July, Lord Clarendon presented him with a £50 War Loan and a gold watch at Church House, Kings Langley on behalf of the inhabitants. At some time Christopher rescued a relative of Major General Lee, GOC 18th Division.

Christopher Cox receives a hero's welcome on his return to Kings Langley.

Queen Mary Military Hospital, Whalley, Blackburn.

Christopher and Maud in their garden.

The nutritional value of barley malt was discovered in 1865 by Dr George Wander, a Swiss chemist, who manufactured malt extract and sold it as a food drink, 'Ovomaltine'. In 1909 his son, Albert, established the British company, A Wander Ltd, and changed the name to 'Ovaltine' for the British market. In 1913 a factory was built at Kings Langley with a workforce of thirteen, but the business expanded rapidly to cope with demand and by 1950, there were 1,400 employees. A radio programme aimed at children, *The League of Ovaltineys*, was broadcast by Radio Luxembourg 1935–39 and from 1952. At the height of its popularity the programme had five million listeners. The Kings Langley factory continued until 2002 and has since been converted to housing.

Christopher later sustained serious wounds to his left foot during an attack and was evacuated to England for treatment at Queen Mary Military Hospital, Whalley, Blackburn, Lancashire. He was demobilised on 24th February 1919.

He worked for a builder until October 1922, when he was employed as a maintenance worker by A Wander Ltd at the Ovaltine factory. During the Second World War, he served in the Home Guard as a corporal in the Kings Langley unit. The Griffin public house was bombed and the publican, Ted Carter, was missing. Christopher assisted others in searching the ruins and Carter's body was found in the rubble.

Christopher was forced to give up work in 1956 after a fall at the factory resulted in serious head and other injuries. He spent the next few years in and out of

Hill End Hospital, St Albans.

King's Langley Church where there is a memorial to
Christopher Cox.

The memorial at the Star Crossroads
outside Achiet-le-Grand dedicated in
March 2007 by Christopher's son, Ian.

hospital and died at Hill End Hospital, St
Albans, Hertfordshire on 28th April 1959. He
is buried in Kings Langley Cemetery and is
commemorated in a number of other places:

• Memorial unveiled by his son, Ian, at the Star
  Crossroads outside Achiet-le-Grand on 17th March 2007, the 90th anniversary
  of the VC action.
• Kings Langley and Achiet-le-Grand were twinned on 8th November 2009 in
  honour of Christopher's VC action.
• Memorial in Kings Langley Church.

In addition to the VC, he was awarded the 1914–15 Star, British War Medal 1914–
20, Victory Medal 1914–19, George VI Coronation Medal 1937 and Elizabeth II
Coronation Medal 1953. The VC is owned privately, but is on loan to the Imperial
War Museum, Lambeth Road, Kennington, London where it is displayed in the
Lord Ashcroft Gallery.

8916 CORPORAL JOHN CUNNINGHAM
2nd Battalion, The Prince of Wales's Leinster Regiment (Royal Canadians)

John Cunningham was born at Hall Street, Thurles, Co Tipperary, Ireland on
22nd October 1890. His father, Joseph Cunningham (c.1868–1907), was a general
labourer. He married Johanna née Smith (c.1866–1941), a general domestic servant,
on 11th November 1889. In 1901 the family was living at 55 Stradavoher Street,
Thurles. By 1911 Johanna was a charwoman. John had four siblings:

- Patrick 'Packie' Cunningham (c.1895–1915) served initially in the Royal Irish Regiment (10381). He was an acting corporal in 1st Leinster (10181) when he was severely wounded and evacuated home. He died on 4th June 1915 and is buried in Thurles (St Mary) Church of Ireland Churchyard.
- Hanora 'Nora' Cunningham (1893–1966) married Francis Michael Morrissey (1889–1973) in 1919. They moved to Middlesbrough, Yorkshire and had eight children including – Joan Anne Morrissey 1923, Norah Morrissey 1927, John Morrissey 1931 and Francis Michael Morrissey 1934.
- Mary Ann Cunningham (1897–1969) married William Arthur Littler (1894–1969) in 1915 at Edmonton, Middlesex.
- Joseph Cunningham (1904–71) married Alice Bennett (1910–51) in 1931 and they later moved to Plymouth, Devon. They had ten children including – Elizabeth Mary Cunningham 1934, Frederick Cunningham 1944, twins Pamela and Patricia Cunningham (both born and died 1947), Maureen Cunningham 1948 and Peter M Cunningham 1949.

The main street in Thurles.

John was educated at the Christian Brothers School, Thurles and was then employed as a farm labourer. Having enlisted, he went to France on 19th December 1914. **Awarded the VC for his actions at Bois-en-Hache, France on 12th April 1917, LG 8th June 1917.** He was seriously wounded during his VC action and died of wounds near Barlin, France on 16th April 1917 and is buried in Barlin Communal Cemetery, near Noeux-les-Mines, France (I A 39). He is also commemorated on a memorial stone at Stradavoher, Thurles, Co Tipperary on the site of his former home.

As he was unmarried, the VC was presented to his mother by the King outside Buckingham Palace on 21st July 1917. In addition to the VC he was awarded the 1914–15 Star, British War Medal 1914–20 and Victory Medal 1914–19. The VC was withdrawn from sale at Sotheby's on 21st March 1979. His medals were acquired on loan by the Imperial War Museum in August 2006 and are displayed in the Lord Ashcroft Gallery.

John Cunningham's grave in Barlin Communal Cemetery, near Noeux-les-Mines.

242697 PRIVATE TOM DRESSER
7th Battalion Alexandra, Princess of Wales's Own (Yorkshire Regiment)

Tom Dresser was born at Laund (also seen as Lawnd) House Farm, Huby, near Sutton-on-the-Forest, Easingwold, Yorkshire on 9th April 1891. His father, Thomas James Dresser (1862–1921), married Clara née Ward (1867–1947) in 1887 at Easingwold, Yorkshire. They were living with her parents at Laund House Farm, Huby in 1891. By 1901 he was a groom on a stud farm living with his family at No.2 The Cottages, Little Langton, Yorkshire. By 1911 he was a tobacconist and newsagent, living with his family at 65 Marton Road, Middlesbrough, Yorkshire. However, there must have been moves between Census returns as the other children were born in Pontefract and Kingsclere, Hampshire. Clara was living at 159 High Street, Redcar, Yorkshire at the time of her death. Tom had two siblings:

- Annie Dresser (1887–1975) was working as an assistant in her father's shop in 1911. She married George Joynson (1888–1940) in 1919 and they had a daughter, Annie Joynson in 1920.
- Joe Dresser (1896–1916) was born at Kingsclere, Hampshire. He was working as an assistant in his father's shop in 1911 and was a well-known swimmer involved in cross-Channel racing. He enlisted in the Northumberland Fusiliers (12078) on 28th September 1914 at Newcastle. He was described as 5′ 7¾″ tall, weighing 126 lbs, with fresh complexion, blue eyes, dark brown hair and his religious denomination was Church of England. He transferred to 8th East Yorkshire next day and served with the Divisional Cyclist Company 19th–22nd February 1915 on probation. He was admitted to Rivet Hospital, Aylesbury 16th–30th March with enuresis. Joe served in France with 8th East Yorkshire 9th 30th September and was evacuated to Britain was a gunshot wound to the left thigh. It is not known where he was treated initially, but he was admitted to Lichfield Military Hospital 5th–14th December. He returned to the Depot on 15th January 1916 and was posted to 3rd Battalion on 18th May. On 7th July he was posted to 11th Battalion and went to France next day. On 23rd September he transferred to 9th York & Lancaster (34479) and was killed in action on 2nd October 1916. His body was never recovered and he is commemorated on the Thiepval Memorial.

Tom's paternal grandfather, Joseph Dresser (1826–78), married Tabitha née Batty (c.1828–96) in 1848. He was a farmer of 104 acres in 1851, employing three men and living at Clifton House, Whenby, North Yorkshire. By 1871 he was a pork butcher and the family was living at 14 New Bridge Street, St John Micklegate, York. After his death, Tabitha continued the business and was employing three men in 1881. She was living at Huby, Yorkshire in 1891. In addition to Thomas they had two daughters – Elizabeth Ann Dresser 1861 and Mary Annie Dresser 1864.

His maternal grandfather, Thomas Ward (c.1821–1902), was a farmer of 208 acres at Lawnd House, Huby, Yorkshire,

Joe Dresser's name on the Thiepval Memorial.

employing four men. He took over the farm from his mother, the family having farmed there since 1820. He married Tabitha née Morfoot (1835–1902) in 1861 at Alne, Yorkshire. In addition to Clara they had seven other children – Eliza Ward 1862, Isaac Ward 1869, William George Ward 1871, John Thomas Ward 1872, George Ward 1874, Ann Dora Ward 1875 and William Morfoot Ward 1878.

Tom was educated at St John's and Hugh Bell Schools in Middlesbrough. He was employed at Dorman, Long's Dock Street Foundries, Middlesbrough before assisting his father as a newsagent. He was a member of the Cleveland Sketching Club and supplied artwork for the local Sports Gazette.

Tom enlisted at Richmond, Yorkshire on 28th February 1916 (28425) and carried out basic training at Rugeley Camp, Cannock Chase, Staffordshire probably with 11th Reserve Battalion. He went to France on 2nd September 1916 and joined his battalion on 21st September. He served with 1/5th and 6th Battalions and was wounded in the foot on 10th November, evacuated to England on the 19th and was treated in Birkenhead 21st November–19th December, probably in one of the four section hospitals that were part of 1st Western General Hospital based

Hugh Bell School in Middlesbrough opened in 1892 and was named after a long serving mayor, Hugh Bell (1844–1931). The school was demolished to make way for Teesside Magistrates' Court.

Dorman Long works in Middlesbrough.

at Fazakerley, Liverpool on the other side of the Mersey. In common with all Territorial soldiers he received a new number (242697) on 1st March 1917. He returned to France on 4th March 1917, joined 37th Infantry Base Depot on 20th March and 7th Battalion next day.

Awarded the VC for his actions near Roeux, France on 12th May 1917, LG 27th June 1917. He was wounded during the VC action, evacuated to England on 19th May and was treated at Roseneath Auxiliary Hospital, Wrexham and at Ripon, Yorkshire until 23rd November. Tom had no idea that he had been recommended for the VC until a nurse brought him the Daily Mail on 30th June. The VC was presented by the King outside Buckingham Palace on 21st July 1917. He was presented with a gold watch and 100 guineas by the people of Middlesbrough after being invested. He was also presented with a silver watch and chain by the Hull Soldier's Club.

Rugeley and Brocton Camps on Cannock Chase had a collective capacity of 40,000 troops. They were self-contained towns with their own churches, post offices, bakeries and a theatre. Early in the war the camps were used by newly raised service battalions to train before going abroad. Later, reserve battalions moved there to train individual soldiers and they eventually formed into training reserve battalions and brigades.

On 6th April 1918 he was appointed unpaid lance corporal on transfer to the Machine Gun Corps (138867). He transferred from 3rd (Reserve) Battalion MGC at Grantham on 21st June to Clipstone and remained there until 25th September. He reverted to private on returning to France on 26th September and reported to the MGC Base Depot at Camiers on 27th September. Tom joined 74th Battalion MGC on 3rd October. He returned to England on 30th March

Tom Dresser receives his VC from the King outside Buckingham Palace on 21st July 1917.

1919 and was discharged on 27th April with 20% disability.

In 1925 Tom took over his father's newsagent business at 65 Marton Road, Middlesbrough. While running the shop, he kept his VC in a tobacco tin behind the counter and willingly produced it when asked.

Tom Dresser married Teresa Josephine née Landers (1904–65) in the 2nd quarter of 1925 and they lived over the shop. They had four sons:

- Joseph Dresser (1926–91).
- Peter Dresser, a twin with Tom (1931–78).
- Thomas 'Tom' Dresser, a twin with Peter, (born 1931) married Rita P Gray (born 1933) in 1953 and they had three sons – Paul Dresser 1955, Brian Dresser 1958 and John T Dresser 1961.
- Brian James Dresser (1938–93) married Hannah Adamson (born 1937) in 1958 and they had two sons – Mark A Dresser 1958 and David Dresser 1960.

Teresa's father, Michael Landers (1859–1912), a labourer, married Bridget née McDonald (1863–1944) in 1885. In 1891 they were living at 26 Feversham Street, Middlesbrough and by 1901 had moved to 17 Graham Street, Middlesbrough. In addition to Teresa they had twelve other children, including – Thomas Landers 1888, John Landers 1891, Catherine 'Kate' Landers 1894, Leo Landers 1896, Edward Landers 1898, Margaret Landers 1899, Bridget and Ellen Landers 1902 and Michael V Landers 1905.

Tom Dresser, in the centre, at the ceremony in 1972 when the Green Howards received the Freedom of Teesside.

Teresa and Tom Dresser's gravestone in Thorntree Cemetery, Middlesbrough.

The Victoria Cross Holders Memorial in the Town Hall, Middlesbrough.

Tom served in G Company, 8th North Riding (Middlesbrough) Battalion Home Guard in the Second World War and was awarded a certificate of merit by GOC-in-C Home Forces in 1943. He was given the Freedom of Middlesbrough on 13th May 1944, the same day as Edward Cooper VC. Tom ran the shop until June 1979, when the council required the property for a redevelopment project. He received compensation and moved to 63 Erroll Street, Middlesbrough. Tom died there on 9th April 1982 and is buried in Thorntree Cemetery, Middlesbrough (Ref 26183, RC Section, Grave 1901) with his wife. Due to fears that the gravestone might be desecrated at the height of the IRA campaign, his name was not added until 2015. He is also commemorated on the Victoria Cross Holders Memorial, Town Hall, Middlesbrough with Stanley Hollis and James Alexander Smith.

In addition to the VC he was awarded the 1914–15 Star, British War Medal 1914–20, Victory Medal 1914–19, George VI Coronation Medal 1937, Elizabeth II Coronation Medal 1953 and Elizabeth II Jubilee Medal 1977. The VC is owned by the family but since May 1983 has been on loan to the Green Howards Museum, Richmond, Yorkshire.

SECOND LIEUTENANT JOHN SPENCER DUNVILLE
1st (Royal) Dragoons

John Dunville was born at 46 Portland Place, Marylebone, London on 7th May 1896. His father, John Dunville Dunville CBE DL (1866–1929) of Redburn, Holywood, Co Down, Ireland, was educated at Cambridge, where he was Master of Staghounds 1886–87. John senior was Political Private Secretary to 8th Duke of Devonshire 1890–1908 and became Chairman of Dunville & Co Whiskey Distillers on the death of his father in 1910. John married Violet Ann Blanche née Lambart (1861–1940) of Beauparc, Co Meath, Ireland on 7th January 1892. They were both passionate hot air balloonists and competed frequently in international competitions. He twice crossed the English Channel, the first time accompanied by Violet in November 1908. Flying balloon 'La Mascotte', he won the Northcliffe Challenge Cup in September 1907, flying 300 kilometres from London to Wales. In December 1908 he won the Cup again, flying from Chelsea Gas Works to Crailsheim near Stuttgart in Germany, accompanied by CF Pollock and Philip Gardner, in thirteen hours. That year he also competed in the Gordon-Bennett Cup. Twenty-one balloons left Berlin and he was temporarily judged the winner, after being airborne for almost thirty-seven hours. However, the winners were a Swiss team (Theodor Schaek and Emil Messner), who flew 1,190 kilometres in seventy-three hours before falling into

46 Portland Place, Marylebone, the Dunville family home in London (Stephen Richards).

John Dunville's parents, Violet on the left and John in the centre with Bobby Dunville on the right at the start of the Gordon-Bennett Cup at Solbosch, Brussels in September 1923 (Gordon Thompson).

the sea and were picked up by a trawler. Violet won the Hedges Butler Challenge Cup three years running in 1912, 1913 and 1914. The Cup was awarded for the longest distance flight by any type of flying machine, starting from London. As she won it three times in succession, the Cup became hers. John was Master of the Meath Hounds 1911–15 and served for many years in the Meath Militia (5th Leinster). He was commissioned as a temporary flight lieutenant in the Royal Naval Air Service on 30th March 1915 and was promoted to flight commander on 1st January 1916. He was appointed squadron commander of No.1 Balloon Training Wing, Roehampton, London on 30th June 1917. He transferred to the Royal Air Force on 1st April 1918 as a major/temporary lieutenant colonel Kite Balloon Officer. John was involved in the formation of the RAF Reserve Squadron in Belfast and was the first commander of RAF Aldergrove in 1918. He was awarded the CBE for his services during the war (LG 3rd June 1919) and transferred to the RAF Reserve on 17th August 1926 as an honorary wing commander. During the

Redburn House, Holywood, Co Down, the Dunville family home in Northern Ireland, was built for Robert Grimshaw Dunville in 1865. It had seventy rooms and was set in 170 acres of land, with views over Belfast Lough and the Antrim hills. A stables block for sixty-four horses and a walled courtyard were added in 1879. John's mother, Violet, was the last Dunville to live there. When she died in 1940 the House was commandeered to accommodate members of the Women's Auxiliary Air Force. After the war it became derelict and was later demolished. The land has since been redeveloped into a cemetery, school, housing estate and Redburn Country Park.

Beauparc, Co Meath, Ireland, home of the Lambart family.

John's father was Political Private Secretary to Spencer Compton Cavendish, 8th Duke of Devonshire (1833–1908), who had the distinction of leading three political parties; the Liberals in the House of Commons 1875–80, succeeding William Gladstone, the Liberal Unionists 1886–1903 and the Unionists in the House of Lords 1902–03. He held numerous posts in government, including Postmaster-General, Chief Secretary for Ireland, Secretary of State for India 1880–82 and Secretary of State for War 1882–85. In 1884 he helped persuade Gladstone to send a relief mission to Khartoum to support General Gordon. In 1891 he succeeded as the Duke of Devonshire. Three times he refused to become Prime Minister.

Sinn Fein troubles he was also a Commandant of the Special Constabulary Force in Belfast. He travelled to New Zealand in 1927 with a party of British anglers, spending several weeks fishing off North Island. Every year he and his wife laid a wreath in memory of their son John at the war memorial in Holywood, Co Down, Northern Ireland. The family had three residences:

46 Portland Place, St Marylebone, London.
Redburn House, Belfast, Ireland.
Sion House, near Navan, Co Meath, Ireland.

After John died in 1929, Violet presented the Northcliffe Cup to the Officers' Mess at RAF Aldergrove. When Violet died at Redburn House, Belfast on 7th March 1940, she left £196,569/5/9 in her estate. She bequeathed £500 to Holywood Parish Church to found a John Spencer Dunville VC Trust. The income from the investment was to be used to make gifts on Armistice Day to ex-servicemen, their dependants or the poor of the parish. As part of the bequest, the Rector and Churchwardens were to place a wreath on Armistice Day in the form of a Victoria Cross on the war memorial in memory of her son. Redburn House was commandeered to accommodate members of the Women's Auxiliary Air Force after Violet's death and after the war it became derelict and was later demolished. The land has been redeveloped into a cemetery, school, housing estate and Redburn Country Park. John junior had three siblings:

- Robert Lambart Dunville (1893–19), also known as Bobby, was commissioned in 1st Life Guards on probation in September 1913 but retired due to ill health. He was commissioned in the Buckinghamshire Yeomanry (Royal Buckinghamshire Hussars) on 6th October 1914; he was 6′ 1¾″ on joining. A medical board at the Military Hospital, Cottonera, Malta on 19th April 1915 recommended he be sent home to be operated on for appendicitis. He was admitted to 3rd Southern General Hospital, Oxford for the operation on 20th May. A medical board at Tidworth found him fit for General Service on 11th September. He transferred as a lieutenant to 5th (Reserve) Battalion Grenadier Guards on 24th November 1915. He was later a captain in 3rd Battalion, but does not appear to have seen any active service. On 24th April 1916 during the Easter Rising he was travelling from Belfast to Kingstown (now Dun Laoghaire) with his chauffeur to catch the ferry to England to rejoin his unit. They were captured by Sinn Feiners at Castlebellingham, Co Louth. With four policemen they were stood against some railings. A man got out of a car and fired a rifle at Robert, the bullet passing through his chest from left to right. Robert was left for dead, but survived, although he never fully recovered. Constable McGee was hit four times and died a few hours later. Robert was granted leave until 23rd April 1917 to recover. A medical board at Belfast on 13th June 1916 found him unfit for any service. He received a wound gratuity of £125 in March 1920, but was not eligible

Dunville & Co was founded in Belfast to blend whiskey and import tea by John Dumvill, who changed his surname to Dunville in 1825. Dunville's VR, its most popular whiskey, began production in 1837. In the 1860s tea was given up to allow expansion of the whiskey business. John built the Royal Irish Distilleries, seen here, in 1869. American Prohibition lost the company a large market and its repeal did not result in recovered sales. The last chairman, Robert Lambart, died in 1931 and the company was run by its Directors until 1936, when it went into liquidation. In 2013, the Echlinville Distillery revived the brand.

The Northcliffe Cup was presented by Lord Northcliffe to the Aero Club in 1906, to be awarded annually to the Briton who made the longest flight during the preceding year. John Dunville Dunville won the cup in consecutive years and was allowed to keep it. After he died, Violet presented the Cup to the Officers' Mess at RAF Aldergrove, where he had been station commander in 1918.

for a wound pension. He was demobilised on 20th January 1920 and relinquished his commission on 1st April. He was Master of the County Down Staghounds Hunt 1926–27 and succeeded as Chairman of Dunville & Co following the death of his father in 1929. Robert collected wild animals from all over the world and kept them in a private zoo in the grounds of Redburn House. On 9th April 1918 he married Winifred Phyllis Combe (1891–1961) at the Guards' Chapel, London. Unusually, the guard of honour, a detachment of Grenadier Guards, formed an archway with Lewis guns as they left the Chapel. Winfred's uncle, Boyce Combe, married Mabel Katherine Tombs on 17th December 1898, daughter of Henry Tombs VC. Robert and Winifred had a daughter, Maureen Eileen Anne Dunville, on 18th September 1919. She married Wing Commander Herbert Montague 'Monty' Robertson DFC RAF (1918–61) in 1941 at Moose Jaw, Saskatchewan, Canada. Monty was a prisoner of war at Stalagluft I, Barth, Pomerania, Germany and postwar became a diplomat. From the time Winifred fell pregnant with Maureen, Robert neglected her and spent most of his time away from home. In May 1920 she obtained a decree of restitution of conjugal rights. In September 1920 Robert appeared at Marylebone Police Court charged with being drunk in charge of a motorcar and assaulting Police Sergeant Collins. Dr Thomas J Crean VC DSO, called for the defence, said that Dunville had developed nervous symptoms as a result of the incident with Sinn Fein in 1916. Robert denied he was drunk, but admitted to drinking whisky, port and Chartreuse. Despite strong evidence against him he was acquitted. In January 1921, Winifred was granted a divorce on the grounds of Robert's desertion and adultery. Robert had been living in a flat at Albert Mansions, Northumberland Street with Evelyn Redfern née Buckley from March 1919 to June 1920. Robert and Evelyn had a child, Patricia Iona Violet Dunville (1920–61). Winifred married Hon Francis Nathaniel Curzon (1865–1941) in April 1922. Amongst the wedding guests was Oswald Mosley MP, founder of the British Union of Fascists in 1932. Robert married Kathleen Kirkpatrick Shaw (née Morice) (1895–1977) on 18th June 1927. She was born in Transvaal, South Africa and was previously married to Cyril Hay Shaw by whom she had two children. They travelled to South Africa in 1930 and intended going on to Australia to see his brother, William, but he became ill and died of heart failure at Carltonion, Johannesburg on 10th January 1931. The animals in his private zoo were given to the Belfast Zoological Gardens, which opened to the public in 1934. His combined estate in Ireland and Britain was valued at £381,307. Kathleen's third marriage in 1932 was to Desmond Meyler

Robert Lambart Dunville with one of the animals from his private zoo.

Shean (1906–88), who was commissioned in the Royal Ulster Rifles in 1926 and rose to brigadier. Following their divorce she married a fourth time, Henry JF Hunter (born c.1895), in 1949.

- William Gustavus Dunville (1900–56) served in the Grenadier Guards. He went to Canada, sailing in April 1921 on SS *Aquitania* from Southampton to New York. However, he was back in Britain by March 1922 when he married Ruth Glover (born c.1901) at Trinity Church, Marylebone. They may have had three daughters. The marriage ended in divorce in 1927. He was commissioned in the Green Howards TA and was promoted captain 24th August 1939 and temporary major 24th October 1941. He last appears in the Army List in April 1943. William married Ivy Evelyn Coombs (1906–67) and they moved to Nundle, New South Wales, Australia to run a sheep station. They had two daughters – Shirley June Dunville 1933 and Avis Zoe Pamela Dunville 1935. The family later went to Canada, where he was a salesman.

Thomas Crean VC was a defence witness at Robert Dunville's trial in September 1920.

- Una Dunville (1903–58) was born with Down's Syndrome and she was placed in Normansfield Hospital, Teddington, Middlesex in 1907. The hospital was founded in 1868 by Dr John Haydon Langdon Down (1828–1896), who first recognised Down's Syndrome as a condition. The hospital closed in 1997. Una is the subject of a chapter in 'Tales of Normansfield' by Andy Merriman.

John's paternal grandfather, Robert Grimshaw Dunville (1838–1910), was appointed Chairman of Dunville & Co in 1874. He was a founder member of the Reform Club and member of the Liberal

Robert Lambart Dunville was distantly related to Henry Tombs VC.

Party until William Gladstone advocated Home Rule for Ireland, when be became a Liberal Unionist. Under his chairmanship, the annual output of whisky from the Distillery increased from one and a half million gallons in 1887 to two and a half million gallons in 1890. He gifted Dunville Park to Belfast in 1891, its first public park. Robert was Deputy Lieutenant Co Down and High Sherriff of Co Meath. He married Jeanne née Chaine (1842–1914) and their only child was John Dunville Dunville.

His maternal grandfather, Gustavus William Lambart (1814–86), was State Steward to the Lord Lieutenant of Ireland, Deputy Lieutenant Co Meath and

Una Dunville on her mother's knee, with brother Robert.

Normansfield Hospital, Teddington, Middlesex 1868–1997.

Secretary of the Order of St Patrick. He lived at Beau Parc, Navan, Co Meath. Gustavus married Lady Frances Caroline Maria née Conyngham (1827–98) in 1847, daughter of General Sir Francis Nathaniel Conyngham, 2nd Marquess Conyngham (1797–1876) and Lady Jane Paget (1798–1876). In addition to Violet they had eleven other children:

- Gustavus Francis William Lambart (1848–1926), 1st Baronet Beau Parc, married Kathleen Barbara Sophia Moore-Brabazon (born 1882) in 1911. They had a son, Oliver (later Sir Oliver) Francis Lambart (1913–86).
- Amy Gwendoline/len Lambart (1852–1927), Maid of Honour to Queen Victoria 1877–84, married Captain (later Lieutenant Colonel) Sir Henry Charles Legge (1852–1924) Coldstream Guards in 1884. He was the son of William Walter Legge, 5th Earl of Dartmouth (1823–91), who served in the Coldstream Guards

John's paternal grandfather, Robert Grimshaw Dunville.

Dunville Park was gifted to Belfast by Robert Grimshaw Dunville in 1891. The Royal Victoria Hospital is in the background.

as a major, and Lady Augusta Finch (1822–1900). Henry was Groom-in-Waiting 1889–93 and Equerry-in-Waiting to Queen Victoria 1893–1901, Edward VII 1901–10 and George V 1910–15, Registrar and Secretary of the Order of Merit 1907, Extra Equerry 1915 and Paymaster to the Royal Household 1915–20; GCVO 1920. Amy and Henry had two children:

○ Victoria Alexandrina Stella Legge (1885–1965) married Major Richard Gerard Wellesley Williams-Bulkeley (1887–1918) in 1909 and they had three children – Victoria Sylvia J Williams-Bulkeley 1910, Richard HD Williams-Bulkeley 1911 and David Williams-Bulkeley 1915. He served in the Welsh Guards and was awarded the MC for gallantry at Loos. He was wounded in December 1915, died on 28th March 1918 and is buried in East Finchley Cemetery (D 3A 18). Victoria married Captain Roland Frank Holdway Norman, Leicestershire Regiment (later wing commander RAF) in 1921. They had a son, Robert Chares Francis Norman (1923–42) who served as an Ordinary Seaman (P/JX 323216) and died at sea aboard MGB 335 on 11th September 1942 (Great Yarmouth (Caister) Cemetery, Norfolk – A 68). Victoria and Norman divorced in 1944 and she resumed her first husband's name by deed poll in 1946.

○ Nigel Walter Henry Legge-Bourke (1889–1914) was Page of Honour to Edward VII 1902-06 and was promoted lieutenant in the Coldstream Guards on 6th June 1910. He changed his surname to Legge-Bourke by Royal Licence on 26th April 1911 in accordance with the will of Hon Henry Lorton Bourke. Nigel married Victoria Alexandria Wyn-Carington (1892–1966) at the Royal Military Chapel, Wellington Barracks, Westminster, London on 3rd June 1913. The witnesses were Alexandra, widowed Queen of Edward VII, and Prime Minister HH Asquith. They lived at The Manor Cottage, Clewer Green, Windsor and had a son, Edward Alexander Henry Legge-Bourke, in May 1914. Nigel was killed at Reutel on 30th October 1914 serving with 2nd Coldstream Guards (Ypres (Menin Gate) Memorial, Belgium). Kitchener expressed his sympathy in the notification telegram to Lady Legge-Bourke. His son, Edward, was Page of Honour to George V 1924–30. During the Second World War he served as a major in the Royal Horse Guards (Blues), was wounded and became ADC to the British Ambassador in Cairo 1941–42. Post-war he was Conservative MP for the Isle of Ely 1945–73 and DL Cambridgeshire 1955; KBE 1960. His son, William Nigel Henry Legge-Bourke, was the father of Alexandra 'Tiggy' Shân Legge-Bourke MVO, nanny to Princes William and Harry and a personal assistant to Prince Charles 1993–99. Victoria married Major Hon Edric Alfred Cecil Weld-Forester in April 1916 and lived at 53 Princes Gate, London. They had three children – Mary Cecilia Georgina Weld-Forester 1917, Charles Robert Cecil Weld-Forester 1919 and Elizabeth Rosalind Weld-Forester 1923.

• Cecil Jane Lambart (1854–1900).

• Constance Una Elizabeth Lambart (1856–1925) married Hon Henry Lorton Bourke (1840–1911), son of Robert Bourke, 5th Earl of Mayo (1797–1867) and Annette Charlotte Jocelyn (1799–1867).

- Georgina Rose Lambart (1859–1907) married John McDonald in 1882. She was living at 12 Cavendish Place, Cavendish Square, London at the time of her death, leaving £19,831/5/9.
- Julian Hamilton Lambart (born and died 1863).
- Lilian Fannie Ermengarde Lambart (1864–1927).
- Cyril Henry Edward Lambart (1866–1955). He emigrated to Australia and married Ethel Caroline Annie (1871–1960). They had two children – Charles Albert George Julian Lambart 1901 and Lillian Edith Sylvia Lambart 1907.
- George James Richard Lambart (1867–1908).
- Bertha Madeline Collins Lambart (1869–1949).
- Adeline Octavia Lambart (1872–1958) married John Pascoe Grenfell (1869–1948), brother of Francis Octavius Grenfell VC. John was commissioned in the Buckinghamshire (Royal Bucks Hussars) Yeomanry and served in South Africa in 1900 and during the Great War as a lieutenant colonel, MID (LG 12th January 1918). They had five children – Harold Francis Pascoe Grenfell 1906, Cecil John Grenfell 1908, Victor Cyril Grenfell 1909, Cynthia Maud Grenfell 1912 and Hersey Constance Grenfell 1913. Harold, Cecil and Victor all served as commanders in the Royal Navy during the Second World. Harold was awarded the DSC and Victor was awarded the DSO and was also MID.

John was educated at Ludgrove School at Cockfosters and Eton College until the summer of 1914 (OTC from May 1912). At Eton he was a member of Mr William's House and later Mr Robeson's House. He passed matriculation for Trinity College, Cambridge. He applied for a commission at Cambridge on 31st August 1914. He was 6′ tall and weighed 131 lbs. He was commissioned in 5th Reserve Cavalry Regiment

Ludgrove School was founded in 1892 in north London and in 1937 moved to Wokingham. Famous alumni include Princes William and Harry, Alex Douglas-Home, Prime Minister 1963–64 and Bear Grylls, the mountaineer and survival expert. The original building seen here is now private flats (Philafrenzy).

Eton College was founded in 1440 by Henry VI. John Dunville is one of thirty-seven Etonian VCs, the largest number of any school. The College has educated numerous members of the Royal Family, including Princes William and Harry, and nineteen British prime ministers.

The Dunville family grave in Holywood Priory Church Graveyard, Northern Ireland.

John Dunville's grave in Villers-Faucon Communal Cemetery. Hardy Falconer Parsons VC is also buried there.

on 16th September 1914. An application to transfer to the Royal Flying Corps on 7th April 1915 was accepted and he passed the medical at York on 19th April, but his course was cancelled and he transferred to 6th (Inniskilling) Dragoons and went to France on 6th June 1915. During the Battle of Loos on 26th/27th September, he led a party detailed to cover the withdrawal of a howitzer battery that had been temporarily abandoned. His application for a permanent commission on 7th December was supported by Brigadier General DGM Campbell, commanding 6th Cavalry Brigade; John had been his ADC for a short period. John transferred to 1st (King's) Dragoon Guards on 4th January 1916 and was attached to 6th Dragoon Guards (Carabiniers).

The Eton College For Valour Memorial to its thirty-seven VCs.

He was admitted to hospital on 19th April with trench fever and embarked on the HMHS *St Denis* at Boulogne on 9th May, arriving at Southampton next day. A medical board at Osborne, Isle of Wight on 14th May found him unfit for General Service for six weeks and he was sent on leave until 24th June, extended to 17th July and then to 7th August. Subsequent medical boards on 26th May, 26th June, 17th July, 7th August and 6th September found him unfit for various periods. He transferred to 1st Royal Dragoons on 8th July with seniority from 4th January 1916 and he joined 5th Cavalry Reserve Regiment in York on 8th August. A medical board at York on 2nd October found him fit for General Service and he returned to France on 22nd December to serve with 1st (Royal) Dragoons.

Awarded the VC for his actions near Épehy, France on 24th/25th June 1917, LG 2nd August 1917. As he never married, the VC was presented to his father by the King at Buckingham Palace on 29th August 1917. John died of wounds resulting from his VC action at 5th Cavalry Field Ambulance at 3.20 a.m. on 26th June 1917 and is buried in Villers-Faucon Communal Cemetery (A 2 1). He is commemorated in a number of other places:

- John Spencer Dunville VC Trust.
- His grandfather's gravestone in Holywood Graveyard, Northern Ireland.
- Named on a plaque at Holywood Church of Ireland (St Philip and St James) commemorating all parishioners who died during the Great War and also on an individual memorial.
- Eton College Cloisters For Valour Memorial, unveiled by the Queen on 27th May 2015.

In addition to the VC he was awarded the 1914–15 Star, British War Medal 1914–20 and Victory Medal 1914–19. His VC is held by the Household Cavalry Museum, Combermere Barracks, St Leonard's Road, Windsor.

13290 CORPORAL EDWARD FOSTER
13th Battalion (Kensington), The East Surrey Regiment

Edward Foster was born at 14 Tooting Grove, Wandsworth on 4th February 1886. His father, Charles Foster (c.1848–99), was a brewer in 1875 and a labourer by 1891. His mother was Mary Ann née Biggs (born 1852). Charles and Mary were married on 25th December 1875 at St Barnabus, Kensington. In 1891 the family was living at 15 Tooting Grove, Wandsworth. By 1901, Mary was living at 27 Tooting Grove, Tooting Graveney, Wandsworth. In 1911, a woman matching Mary Ann's description for birth, year of marriage and number of children was living with George James Lucock (born 1878) and Elizabeth Jane Lucock (formerly Howe née Lilley) (born 1877) and family at 139 Blackfriars Road, Southwark. She was recorded as an aunt, but the relationship between them has not been verified. Edward had three siblings:

- Amelia Foster (1881–1901), a domestic servant, was a patient at Greenwich Union Infirmary, Vanbrugh Hill at the time of the 1901 Census.
- Charles Foster (born 1883) was a carman in 1901. The death of a Charles Foster of the correct age was registered in the 4th quarter of 1918 at Wandsworth, London.
- George Foster (born 1891).

Edward was educated at Tooting Graveney School, Wandsworth and was employed as a dustman with a contractor, FW Surridge, and later with Wandsworth Borough Council. He married Alice Jane née Donovan (22nd October 1883–11th October 1972) on 8th May 1910 at Croydon, Surrey. They lived at 48 Fountain Road, Tooting Broadway and later moved to 92 Fountain Road, Tooting Broadway. Their only child was Dennis Edwin Foster, whose birth cannot be traced but is thought to have been in May 1923. Dennis served in the Royal Navy as a petty officer for four years during the Second World War as a diesel engineer on minesweepers.

The Médaille Militaire, the third highest award of the French Republic, given to other ranks for meritorious service or bravery in action. It was established in 1852 by Emperor Napoleon III.

He married Lucy M MacNamara (born 1922) in 1941 at Wandsworth and was living at Quadring, Spalding, Lincolnshire when he died in 2002. Dennis and Lucy had five children – Veronica M Foster 1942, Dennis A Foster 1944, Carol A Foster 1945, Christine E Foster 1947 and Stella D Foster 1956.

Alice's father, John Donovan (1845–92) was a labourer when he enlisted in the 58th Regiment (551) at Westminster on 22nd July 1859, giving his age as eighteen. He was promoted corporal on 6th January 1862, sergeant 1st January 1865 and colour sergeant on 20th May 1866. He qualified for Good Conduct Pay on five occasions and was awarded the Long Service and Good Conduct Medal on 22nd July 1880. During his service he was in India for nine years and seven months. He was discharged on 6th July 1880 as a sergeant instructor in musketry, with his conduct and character assessed as Very

Edward Foster in 1936 (DE Foster).

Good. His intended address was 9 Lemon Terrace, Stepney Green, London. In 1877 he had married Ann Davis (born c.1849) at Portsea. In addition to Alice they had three other children – Ann Elizabeth Donovan 1879, Sarah Donovan 1880 and John Daniel Donovan 1890. He was a staff sergeant in 1881 at the Royal London Militia Barracks, City Road, St Luke, London. By 1891 he was a commercial traveller and the family was living at 5 De Maria Terrace, Mile End Old Town, London.

Edward enlisted on 27th July 1915. He was known as Tiny, being 6′ 2″ tall and weighing twenty stones. He went to France with the Battalion on 3rd June 1916. **Awarded the VC for his actions at Villers Plouich, France on 24th April 1917, LG 27th June 1917.** The VC was presented by the King outside Buckingham Palace on 21st July 1917. **Awarded the French Medaille Militaire, LG 14th July 1917.** Edward was discharged on 24th October 1918.

Post war, Edward worked as a dustman inspector for Wandsworth Borough Council covering Wandsworth, Putney and Roehampton. He was a member of the VC Guard at the interment of the Unknown Warrior on 11th November 1920. He died at St James' Hospital, Balham, London on 22nd January 1946 and is buried in Streatham Cemetery, Tooting (Section F15, Grave 357). A new headstone was dedicated on 7th June 1997. He is also commemorated by Foster's Way, a path alongside the River Wandle in King George's Park, Wandsworth; and on a plaque at Villers-Plouich, France.

On 29th September 1920, Wandsworth Borough Council decided to assist Villers-Plouich and funds were sent to help rebuild the school and water supply. A marble plaque was erected in the village by the grateful villagers, and each Armistice Day they honour their own and the dead of 13th East Surrey.

In addition to the VC he was awarded the British War Medal 1914–20, Victory Medal 1914–19, George VI Coronation Medal 1937 and French Médaille Militaire. The VC was purchased in 1981 by Bob Richardson of Brisbane, Queensland, Australia. He sold it at Sotheby's on 30th June 1988 for £12,100 to Lord Ashcroft. It is held in the Lord Ashcroft Gallery in the Imperial War Museum.

6/2133 LANCE CORPORAL SAMUEL FRICKLETON
3rd Battalion, New Zealand Rifle Brigade

Samuel Frickleton was born on 2nd April 1891 at Old Lodge, Slamannan, Stirlingshire, Scotland. The surname also appears as Freckleton.

His father, also Samuel Frickleton (c.1851–1913), a coal miner, was born at Airdrie, Lanarkshire. He married Elizabeth née Logan (1857–1941) in 1877 at Holytown, Lanarkshire. In 1901 they were living at 24 Moubray Row, Bannockburn, Stirlingshire. The marriage failed and Elizabeth emigrated to

New Zealand in 1904 with five of her sons and a daughter and settled at Clifford Street, Blackball, Greymouth, West Coast, South Island. She travelled to Canada aboard SS *Aoramoi* from Sydney, New South Wales with her son James, arriving on 27th April 1928 at Victoria, British Columbia. She died on 12th April 1941 at Greymouth, Grey, New Zealand and is buried with her daughter Mary and her granddaughter Elizabeth Logan Symons. By 1911 Samuel senior had moved to 21 Roxburgh Row

Slamannan High Street.

Lane, Plean, Stirlingshire with his son John, daughter-in-law Jeanie (wife of his son Henry) and their children Katie and Lizzie. Samuel junior had nine siblings, all born in Scotland. All of the brothers served in the war and three were wounded:

- Jane Frickleton (c.1878–1950), a domestic servant, married Alexander McLuckie Small (1874–1940), a coal miner, in 1898 at Reddingmuirhead, Polmont, Stirlingshire. They had a son, William Small, in 1903.
- Marion Logan Stewart Frickleton (c.1880–1950) married James Cramb (1873–1957), a coal miner, in 1900 at Cowie, Bannockburn, Stirlingshire. They had three children, all born at Cowie – Elizabeth Marion Logan Cramb 1901, James Cramb 1902 and Samuel Freckleton Cramb 1904. The family moved to Nanaimo, British Columbia.
- John Frickleton (1882–1970), a coal miner hewer, was adopted and changed his name to John Logan Frickleton. He married Elizabeth (born c.1883) and emigrated to Canada before moving to Shoal Creek, Bond, Illinois, USA. They had twelve children including – John Frickleton c.1905, Lizzie Frickleton c.1906, Samuel C Frickleton c.1909, Janie Frickleton c.1911, Bertha Frickleton c.1913, Isabelle Frickleton c.1916, Dorothy Frickleton c.1917, James Frickleton c.1918, Mary Frickleton c.1919, June L Frickleton c.1925 and Ingrid H Frickleton c.1927. All were born in Illinois except John, who was born in Canada

William Frickleton's grave in Flatiron Copse Cemetery at Mametz.

- Henry Frickleton (1884–1971) was a coal miner drawer in 1901. He married Mary Jane 'Jeanie' Marrs (born c.1884), a domestic servant, in 1906 at Reddingmuir, Polmont, Stirlingshire. They had five children including – Catherine 'Katie' Boulter Marrs Millar Frickleton 1909 and Elizabeth 'Lizzie' Frickleton c.1911. They emigrated to Canada and were living at Five Acres, Nanaimo, British Columbia in 1921 and had moved to Grisham, Montgomery, Illinois, USA by 1930.

- Mary Frickleton (c.1887–1943). She married as Buchanan and had at least a daughter, Elizabeth Logan Symons (sic) (c.1910–16).
- William Twaddle Frickleton (1889–1916) served as a private (6/2135) in 1st Canterbury NZEF and was killed in action on 28th September 1916. He is buried at Flatiron Copse Cemetery, Mametz, France (I G 41).
- James Frickleton (born c.1893).
- Thomas McCreary Frickleton (1895–1959). He married Minnie Josephine Jeffries in 1925.
- Alexander Small Frickleton (born 1897).

In addition to their own children, Samuel and Elizabeth Frickleton adopted John Logan after 1891. It is believed he was John Logan born on 7th July 1881 at Holytown, near Bellshill to John Logan (born c.1848) and Margaret Prentice (born c.1845). They were living at Smith's Land, Main Street, Holytown in 1891, but could not be found in the 1901 Census of Scotland. By 1911 the adopted John was a coal miner hewer, living with his adoptive father as John Frickleton.

Samuel's paternal grandfather, Henry Frickleton (c.1827–84), was born at Keady, Co Armagh, Ireland. He married Jane née Stewart (1828–56) in 1846. In addition to Samuel senior they had three other children – William Stewart Frickleton c.1848, John Frickleton c.1853 and Henry Frickleton 1855. Henry senior married Margaret McCreary (1839–1914) in 1859 at Slamannan, Stirlingshire. They had ten children – James Frickleton 1859, Henry Frickleton 1861, Thomas Frickleton 1863, Hugh Frickleton 1866, Andrew Frickleton 1868, Robert Frickleton 1870, Eliza Frickleton 1871, Joshua Frickleton 1874, David Frickleton c.1880 and Joseph Frickleton c.1882. Henry, Thomas and Andrew emigrated to the United States.

His maternal grandfather, John Logan (born c1806), was a coal miner. He married Elizabeth Logan (born c.1821). In addition to Elizabeth they had eight other children – Margaret Logan c.1836, Richard Logan c.1838, Marion Logan c.1844, James Logan c.1847, John Logan c.1851, Agnes Logan c.1853, John Logan c.1855 and Ann Logan c.1860. The family was living at Woodhall Square, Old Monkland, Lanarkshire in 1861. John senior married secondly, Margaret (born c.1819) and they were living at 4 Pine Street, Hutchesontown, Lanarkshire in 1881.

Samuel was probably educated at Slamannan. He worked as a coal miner at Blackball, Greymouth, West Coast, South Island, New Zealand. On 12th February 1915 he enlisted in the New Zealand Expeditionary Force. He was described as 5′ 10″ tall, weighing 158 lbs, with brown eyes and dark hair. His accent remained broad Scottish. He was promoted corporal and embarked for Egypt in the Canterbury Infantry Battalion with the 5th Reinforcements on 13th June, arriving on one of three ships between 24th July and 6th August. Having contracted tuberculosis, he was returned to New Zealand for treatment and discharged medically unfit on 11th November.

Samuel re-enlisted on 13th April 1916 and embarked for Britain with the 15th Reinforcements on 26th July (HMNZT *Waitemata*) or 29th July (HMNZT *Ulimaroa*). *Waitemata* arrived on 3rd October and *Ulimaroa* on 28th September at Devonport. He arrived in France in November and was posted to 3rd Battalion New Zealand Rifle Brigade on 7th December. Promoted lance corporal February 1917 and was detached to the Grenade School 3rd–12th May 1917.

Awarded the VC for his actions at Messines, Belgium on 7th June 1917, LG 2nd August 1917. He was evacuated to Britain to recover from his wounds and rejoined his unit in July. Appointed acting sergeant 11th August. The VC was presented by the King at Ibrox Park, Glasgow on 18th September 1917. Evacuated through illness in October. Samuel commenced training at one of the officer cadet battalions at Cambridge and was commissioned on 26th March 1918. However, he became seriously ill in May, suffering from pulmonary tuberculosis and gas poisoning, and was returned to New Zealand from Avonmouth as medically unfit, arriving on 12th June. He was given a civic reception and was presented with a sum of money on 15th June at Wellington Town Hall.

Samuel Frickleton receives his VC from the King at Ibrox Park, Glasgow on 18th September 1917 (Auckland Daily News).

Samuel ceased service with the NZEF on 20th December 1918, but was appointed a temporary staff officer and Assistant Provost Marshal, Wellington Military District 21st December 1918–30th June 1919. He transferred to Canterbury Military District on 1st July and to the New Zealand Staff Corps as a lieutenant in October. He retired on medical grounds on 1st April 1927.

Samuel Frickleton married Valeska Gembitsky (10th August 1894–9th May 1984) on 12th January 1922. They lived at Glen Flats, Rara Street, Naenae. They had a son, Logan Samuel Frickleton (1928–84) at Lower Hutt, near Wellington. Logan married and had a daughter, Leigh.

Samuel went into business in Wellington in 1927, later turning to farming in Wakanae and finally became a house manager. He resumed service in the Territorial Force in 1934 and was promoted captain. He commanded the Guard of Honour for the visit of the Duke of Gloucester to New Zealand in December 1935. Samuel attended the coronation of King George VI in 1937 as a member of the New Zealand contingent before retiring. He was recalled as an Inspector New Zealand Forces in 1939, serving until 1948. He attended the VC Centenary Celebrations at Hyde Park, London on 26th June 1956. Samuel was a Freemason and was a member of Lodge Kawatiri (now Kawatiri – Wesport No. 152), Scinde No.5 of Napier and Lodge Taia No. 229 of Kilbirnie. He was also an active member of the Returned Services Association of New Zealand.

Victoria Cross Corner, Dunedin Returned
Services Association Memorial Hall.

Samuel Frickleton's memorial plaque outside
Messines church unveiled on the 90th anniversary
of his VC action on 7th June 2007.

Samuel died following a long illness in
Hutt Hospital, Naenae, Lower Hutt City,
near Wellington on 6th August 1971. He
is buried in Plot 1188, Taita Servicemen's
Cemetery, Naenae. He is commemorated
in a number of other places:

- Frickleton Barracks, Linton Military
  Camp, near Palmerston North, New
  Zealand, named on 30th June 2010.
- Narcissus 'Frickleton V.C.' is a large-
  cupped daffodil with white petals and
  rich-yellow cup.
- Frickleton Street, Taradale, Napier,
  New Zealand.
- A sundial in the centre of the War
  Memorial Wall, Caroline Bay, Timaru
  bears the names of eleven New Zealand
  VCs, including Samuel Frickleton.
- Named on a plaque listing 22 New
  Zealand VC winners dedicated by the Reverend Keith Elliott VC on 29 January

The New Zealand Post 60c Samuel Frickleton
stamp issued on 14th April 2011.

1956 and unveiled by Governor General Sir Willoughby Norris. The plaque is
on Victoria Cross Corner outside the Dunedin Returned Services Association
Memorial Hall opened on 24 May 1921.

- Plaque outside Messines church unveiled on 7th June 2007 by Annette King, New Zealand Minister of State Services, Police, Transport and Food Safety during a ceremony marking the 90th anniversary of the Battle of Messines. The ceremony was attended by two of Samuel Frickleton's grandchildren – Mrs Julia Tatam of Hawke's Bay and Mr Mark Frickleton of Stokes Valley, Wellington. New Zealand Defence Force staff based in London and Ministry of Foreign Affairs staff from Brussels also attended.
- Memorial cairn at Slamannan, Stirlingshire unveiled on 3rd April 2010 following a memorial service attended by relatives, a representative of the New Zealand Army, the Lord Lieutenant of Stirling and Falkirk and several MPs and MSPs.
- An issue of twenty-two 60c stamps by New Zealand Post entitled 'Victoria Cross – the New Zealand Story' honouring New Zealand's twenty-two Victoria Cross holders was issued on 14th April 2011.
- Named on one of eleven plaques honouring 175 men from overseas awarded the VC for the Great War. The plaques were unveiled by the Senior Minister of State at the Foreign & Commonwealth Office and Minister for Faith and Communities, Baroness Warsi, at a reception at Lancaster House, London on 26th June 2014 attended by The Duke of Kent and relatives of the VC recipients. The New Zealand plaque was unveiled on 7th May 2015 to be mounted on a wall between Parliament and the Cenotaph. The ceremony was attended by Defence Minister Gerry Brownlee, Defence Force Chief Lieutenant General Tim Keating and Corporal Willie Apiata, New Zealand's only living VC.
- Victoria Cross Memorial next to the cenotaph in Queens Gardens, Dunedin, New Zealand.

In addition to the VC he was awarded the 1914–15 Star, British War Medal 1914–20, Victory Medal 1914–19, George VI Coronation Medal 1937, Elizabeth II Coronation Medal 1953 and the New Zealand Long and Efficient Service Medal. His widow presented the medals to the Queen Elizabeth II Army Memorial Museum (now the National Army Museum) in November 1977, where they are held. On 2nd December 2007, ninety-six medals were stolen from the Museum by James Joseph Kapa and Ronald van Wakeren, including nine VCs (Andrew, Elliott, Frickleton, Grant, Hinton, Hulme, Judson, Laurent and Upham) and two GCs. A $300,000 reward was offered by medal collector Lord Michael Ashcroft and Nelson businessman Tom Sturgess and the collection was recovered on 16th February 2008. The medals returned to the Museum in October 2008. Kapa was jailed for six years and van Wakeren for eleven years for this and other crimes. Consequent upgrades to security at the Museum cost NZ$1.4 million.

645112 SERGEANT WILLIAM GOSLING
3rd Wessex Brigade Royal Field Artillery attached V/51 Heavy Trench Mortar Battery Royal Field Artillery

William Gosling was born at Wanborough, near Swindon, Wiltshire on 15th August 1892. His father, Albert Gosling (1850–1906) was born in Gloucestershire and farmed at Somerset Farm, Lower Wanborough, Wiltshire. He married Elizabeth Ellen née Duck (1861–1922) in 1888 at Bath, Somerset. She ran the farm after Albert's death and was living at Swindon Road, Wroughton in 1911. William had three siblings:

(Sue Knight)

- Albert Tudor Gosling (born 1888) was an agricultural labourer in 1911 working for his mother. He married Winifred Dorothy Cundell (born 1890) in 1917. They had a daughter, Mary E Gosling, in 1918 who married George Sidney E Shearing in 1939 and had three children.
- Francis John Gosling (1890–1959) was an agricultural labourer in 1911 working for his mother. He married Cicely Mary Hancock (born 1886) in 1918 and they had three children.
- Annie Louisa Gosling (1895–1917) married Thomas James Greenman (1890–1918) in 1916. He was assisting his father as a butcher and farmer in 1911. Louisa died giving birth to a daughter, Violet L Greenman, who also died. Thomas

3rd Wessex Brigade RFA band prior to the First World War.

married Kate Alma Hitchcock in 1918, but died later the same year.

William's paternal grandfather, John Gosling (1799–1890), was the uncle of his maternal grandmother, Ann Duck née Adams, daughter of John Gosling's sister Elizabeth Adams née Gosling (1808–1907).

William was educated at Wanborough Village School. He was employed as a wheat farmer, probably helping his mother, and served in 3rd Wessex Brigade RFA (TF) 1908–09 (118). He went to Canada, departing from Liverpool, Lancashire on SS *Tunisian* on 19th October 1911, bound for Montreal. He lived for a while with his uncle Walter Sydney Duck in Winnipeg. Walter (1859–1921) married Elizabeth Priscilla Martin (born 1859) in 1881 at Newport, Monmouthshire and

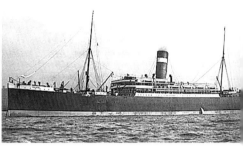

SS *Tunisian* was launched in 1900 for the Allan Line on the North Atlantic route from Liverpool to Halifax, Portland, Québec and Montréal. Early in the First World War she was used for prisoner of war accommodation off Ryde, Isle of Wight before becoming a troopship. In 1917 she was taken over by Canadian Pacific and in 1922, following reconfiguration, she was renamed *Marburn*. Until 1927 she operated between Liverpool, Glasgow, Hamburg, Antwerp and London and was broken up in 1928.

was a gardener at Maidstone Cemetery in 1901. He and his family emigrated to Canada only a month before William, departing Southampton, Hampshire on the *Ausonia* on 19th September 1911 bound for Quebec. William worked at various times on grain silos, as a fireman on the Canadian Pacific Railway and as a lumberjack.

When war broke out, William returned to Britain and re-enlisted in 3rd Wessex Brigade RFA (TF). He went to France on 6th May 1915. **Awarded the VC for his actions at Roclincourt near Arras, France on 5th April 1917, LG 14th June 1917.** The VC was presented by the King outside Buckingham Palace on 21st July

Wroughton High Street.

Main Street, Winnipeg around the time William Gosling was there.

1917. In August 1917, he was presented with a cheque for £130/5/6 and a silver salver by the Mayor of Swindon at the Town Hall. He was also presented with an illuminated address later in the year. William was later appointed battery sergeant major and was discharged in 1919.

Post war he was a tractor driver in Essex, where he met his wife, until he took tenancy of Summerhouse Farm, Wharf Road, Wroughton, Wiltshire in 1920 and worked it for the rest of his life. He was Vice President of the Wroughton British Legion until 1933 and was a parish councilor for the last few years of his life. He also ran a shop in Wroughton between the wars, *W Gosling VC Dairyman & Confectioner*.

William Gosling married Martha Beverley née Crow (3rd May 1888–9th April 1974) on 20th September 1919 at Billericay, Essex. So he was a Gosling, his mother was a Duck and he married a Crow. William and Martha had two children:

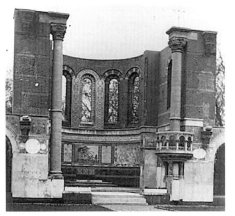

St George's Chapel, the Woolwich Garrison Church before it was destroyed by a V1 in the Second World War. The Royal Artillery VC Memorial is on the curved wall behind the altar.

A post-Second World War picture of the remains of St George's Chapel.

William Gosling's grave in St John and St Helen's Churchyard Cemetery Extension, Wroughton (Wroughton One Place Study).

St John and St Helen's Church, Wroughton.

- Alan Desmond Gosling (born 1923) married Peggy J Saunders in 1946 and had three children – Susan P Gosling 1947, William PJ Gosling 1948 and Patricia E Gosling 1951.
- Marion Gosling (born 1924).

King George VI Coronation Medal 1937.

During the Second World War, William was a captain in 9th Wiltshire (Cricklade) Battalion Home Guard from 1st February 1941 and was promoted major 17th January 1943. As a member of the Home Guard he would have qualified for the Defence Medal after three years service, but it does not form part of his medal group and he may not have had sufficient service. He was a Freemason (Gooch Lodge No.1295).

William died at Summerhouse Farm, Wroughton, Wiltshire on 12th February 1945 and is buried in St John and St Helen's Churchyard Cemetery Extension, Wroughton. He is commemorated on the Royal Artillery VC Memorial in the ruins of St George's Chapel, the former Garrison Church at Woolwich, which was reduced to a roofless shell by a V1 in 1944.

In addition to the VC, he was also awarded the 1914–15 Star, British War Medal 1914–20, Victory Medal 1914–19 and King George VI Coronation Medal 1937. His medals are held privately.

CAPTAIN ROBERT CUTHBERT GRIEVE
37th Australian Infantry Battalion AIF

Robert Grieve was born on 19th June 1889 at Brighton, Melbourne, Victoria, Australia. His father, John Grieve (1858–99), was a clerk before forming the firm Connibere, Grieve and Connibere, soft goods merchants, in 1889. He married Annie Deas née Brown (1861–1930) at Fitzroy, Victoria in 1885. The family lived at Erne Lodge, 254 Bay Street, Brighton. Later Annie lived at 301 Flinders Lane, Melbourne before moving to 13 Beaver Street, East Malvern, Victoria. Robert had two brothers:

- Frank Edward Grieve (1898–1936).
- John Whyte Grieve (1892–1948) was commissioned as a captain in the Australian Army Medical Corps on 17th February 1917. He attested in the AIF on 30th March and was described as 5′ 11″ tall, weighing 172 lbs, with fair complexion, blue eyes, fair hair and his religious denomination was Presbyterian. He embarked

Flinders Lane, Melbourne.

on HMAT A9 *Shropshire* on 11th May and disembarked at Plymouth on 19th July. John joined AAMC Training Depot, Parkhouse Camp, Tidworth, Hampshire on 20th July and went to France on 23rd August, where he joined 3rd Australian General Hospital on 25th August. He was detached to the Chinese General Hospital 20th September–24th October and transferred to 1st Australian Division on 2nd December and to 3rd Australian Field Ambulance next day. He was detached to 12th Australian Field Artillery Brigade 21st December 1917–9th January 1918, the Australian Corps Medical Officers School 30th January–6 February and 11th Battalion 21st February–2nd March. John sprained his back falling from a gun carriage on 20th April, but appears to have recovered quickly as he was detached to 9th Battalion on 29th April. He was mentioned in Sir Douglas Haig's Despatch of 16th March 1919 (LG 11th July 1919). Granted medical leave in Britain 3rd April–3rd July and embarked at Devonport on 18th July for return to Australia on HMAT *Takada*, disembarking on 7th September. His appointment with the AIF was terminated on 7th October 1919. He was appointed a captain in the Reserve of Officers, 3rd Military District on 1st January 1920 and transferred to AAMC Reserve on 1st July 1925. Appointed honorary major on 8th December 1937. John went into private practice at 12 Collins Street, Melbourne, but later changed to 318 Flinders Street. He was living at 15 Beaver Street, East Malvern, Melbourne in 1923.

Robert's paternal grandfather, also Robert Grieve (1829–1907), was born at Water of Leith, Edinburgh, Midlothian, Scotland. He was a grocer in Edinburgh in 1851 before emigrating to Australia for the gold rush, sailing from Leith aboard the *Yarra* (possibly the *Yarra Yarra*) on 30th September 1852, arriving at Melbourne, Victoria on 1st March 1853 with his half brother John (1831–1905). He settled in Eaglehawk, Victoria where he was manager of the canvas tent store of Messrs Dunn and Bayne. He subsequently purchased the store and in 1860 purchased part of Allotment 10 from William Gruby, the original landowner and publican of the Camp Hotel, on which he erected a general store. He became a borough councillor with the first Eaglehawk Council and was postmaster there in June 1858. Robert married Janet née Whyte (1830–85) in Melbourne on 2nd January 1857. She worked as a post ringer for Donald Mackay in Sandhurst, Victoria but was recorded as a confectioner in 1857. In addition to John they had seven other children, most of whom died very young, all but one born at Eaglehawk – Agnes Whyte Grieve 1859, Robert Grieve 1860, Annie Cuthbert Grieve 1861, stillborn infant 1863, Jessie Whyte Grieve 1865, Margaret Ann Grieve 1868 (born at Bridge of Allan, Scotland) and Jessie Grieve 1870. About 1868 the family returned to Scotland and he rented his grocery business to his half-brother Thomas, who had also emigrated to Australia in the 1850s. Grieve Street in

Eaglehawk High Street in the early 1900s.

Eaglehawk is named after the brothers. The family returned to Melbourne, Victoria c.1870. Robert married Cecilia Wilson Stewart (1855–1935) in 1890 at Melbourne. She was a daughter of the VC's maternal grandmother's first marriage. Robert and Cecilia had seven children – Effie Stewart Grieve 1891, Cecilia Stewart Grieve and Robert Cuthbert Grieve 1893, Jessie Grieve 1895, James Stewart Grieve 1896, George Grieve 1898 and Alexia Lyell Grieve 1899.

His maternal grandfather, Edward Henry Brown (1832–79), emigrated to Victoria where he was a wholesale grocer. His maternal grandmother was Euphemia late Stewart, née Lyell (1833–96). She emigrated from Fife, Scotland to Victoria, Australia with her parents in 1849. She married John Motherwell Stewart (1831–57), an ironmonger, in 1854 and they had two children – Cecilia Wilson Stewart 1855 and John Motherwell Stewart 1857. Euphemia and Edward married in 1861 and lived at Erne Lodge, 254 Bay Street, Brighton, Victoria. In addition to Annie they had six other children – James Brown 1864, Euphemia Lyell Brown 1866, Margaret Brown 1869, Mary Jane Brown 1871, Alexia Brown 1874 and Edward Henry Brown 1878.

Robert was educated at Caulfield Grammar School, Melbourne and Wesley College, Melbourne. He was a keen footballer and cricketer, playing football for the

Caulfield Grammar School, an independent day and boarding school, was founded in 1881. In 1961 it amalgamated with Malvern Memorial Grammar School and became coeducational in 1981. It now has over 3,000 pupils over three campuses.

Wesley College, Melbourne, established in 1866, is independent, coeducational and Christian. It is the largest school in Australia, with 3,100 students.

Collegians, one of Melbourne's amateur clubs. On one occasion he could not play because of a dinner engagement, but went to watch the first half. His team was four men short so he took off his jacket, rolled up his trousers, donned his football boots and joined in. The team ended up winning, even though still three short.

He worked as an interstate commercial traveller in soft goods and gave his occupation as warehouseman when he enlisted in the AIF on 16th June 1915. He had spent the previous eight months with the Victorian Rangers at Brighton. He was described as 5′ 10″ tall, weighing 182 lbs, with fresh complexion, blue eyes, light brown hair and his religious denomination was Presbyterian. He was posted to the Depot on 25th June and to Q Company, 5th Depot Battalion, Broadmeadows, Victoria 23rd October 1915–21st January 1916. Robert was commissioned from the Officers' Training School, Broadmeadows on 17th January 1916. He was posted to 4th Depot Battalion on 22nd January and promoted lieutenant on 1st May 1916. He departed Melbourne on 30th May 1916 on HMAT *Persic*, disembarking at Plymouth, Devon on 25th July. He was assigned to A Company, 37th Battalion from 16th June. The unit moved to Larkhill Camp on Salisbury Plain for training. He was seconded to 10th Light Mortar Battery at No.5 Camp, Larkhill on 5th August and went to France on 22nd November from Southampton. He was posted to 10th Light Mortar Battery on 15th January 1917 and rejoined 37th Battalion on 15th February, when he was appointed acting captain to command A Company. Promoted captain 19th April.

Awarded the VC for his actions at Messines, Belgium on 7th June 1917, LG 2nd August 1917. Exceptionally, as there were no officers left in the company, the recommendation came from other ranks' eyewitness reports. Robert received a gunshot wound to the right shoulder resulting in a fractured scapula during his VC action. He was admitted to 9th Australian Field Ambulance and 2nd Australian Casualty Clearing Station on 8th June and 8th General Hospital, Rouen on 10th

SS *Persic* was built by Harland and Wolff in 1899 for the White Star Line, one of five Jubilee Class ships for the Liverpool–Cape Town–Sydney route. She was requisitioned as a troopship during the war and on 7th September 1918 was torpedoed by a U-boat near the Isles of Scilly. She was badly damaged, but limped to port. She was scrapped in 1927.

Larkhill Camp sprang from almost nothing in August 1914 to a small town able to accommodate thirty-four battalions under training. The first Army airfield was established there in 1910 and the first Military Aeroplane Trials were held there in 1912. After the First World War it became mainly an artillery centre. This photograph looks west along the central road of the camp, the Packway.

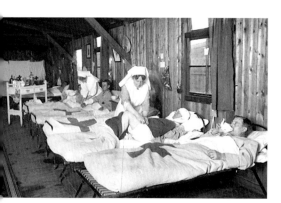

2nd Australian Casualty Clearing Station opened on 29th July 1916 at Trois Arbres, Steenwerck. Its workload increased from May 1917 onwards and additional staff was provided by No.2 Australian General Hospital. Robert Grieve was a patient 8th–9th June. In July it was bombed, resulting in four sisters being awarded the MM. At other times it came under shellfire and bombproof shelters were constructed for the nurses to sleep in. May Isabel Bowman was posted to 2nd Australian Casualty Clearing Station on 27th January 1918. Her future husband was admitted on 11th January and remained until 26th February. On 11th March 1918 shelling forced the CCS to close and the remaining patients were evacuated. The nursing staff, including May, left for No.10 Stationary Hospital (Australian War Memorial).

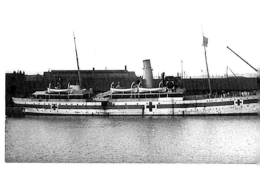

SS *Aberdonian* (1,648 tons) was built in 1909 at Glasgow for the Aberdeen Steam Navigation Co. She was requisitioned as a hospital ship 16th October 1915–16th June 1919 and as a depot ship at Fort William and Dartmouth 1940–45. She was sold in 1946 to Shahin Steamship Co Ltd and was renamed *Taishan Peak*. She was renamed *Parviz* in 1948. Following typhoon damage at Hong Kong in 1948, she was broken up at Bombay in 1950.

June. He embarked for England from Rouen on SS *Aberdonian* on 12th June and was admitted to 3rd London General Hospital, Wandsworth next day and transferred to 5th Australian Auxiliary Hospital, Welwyn on 18th July. While in hospital he received a letter, *Sir, NCO's* [sic] *and men of your Company, and especially those who had the honour of being led into action at the Battle of Messines, wish to take this the earliest opportunity to congratulate you upon the very high honour it has pleased His Majesty the King to confer upon you at this time, and also the honour of bringing our Battalion the first VC.* ... Robert was discharged from hospital on 24th September to Perham Down. The VC was presented by the King at Buckingham Palace on 20th October 1917.

Robert returned to Le Havre, France from Southampton on 24th October and joined II ANZAC Reinforcement Camp on 26th October, 3rd Australian Division Base Depot on 27th October and returned

5th Australian Auxiliary Hospital opened on 16th June 1915 at Digswell House, Welwyn and closed on 31st January 1919.

to 37th Battalion on 29th October. He was granted leave to Abbeville 22nd–26th November. On 11th January 1918, he was admitted to 9th Australian Field Ambulance and 2nd Australian Casualty Clearing Station suffering from acute trench Nephritis (inflammation of a kidney) and double pneumonia. While there he was nursed by his future wife. He was moved to 5th British Red Cross Hospital at Wimereux on 26th February and evacuated to England aboard HS *Cambria* on 10th March and admitted to 3rd London General Hospital, Wandsworth. The complaint was classified as severe

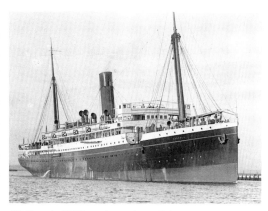

SS *Karoola* (7391 tons) was Australia's largest liner when she was built in 1907 for the McIlwraith, McEacharn's Line Pty Ltd, Melbourne. In the First World War she was used as a troop transport until converted into a hospital ship and served until June 1919.

and he was scheduled for return to Australia and sent on leave on 18th March. He left Britain aboard *Dunluce Castle* on 8th April and re-embarked at Suez, Egypt on HMAT *Karoola* on 27th April, arriving in Australia on 25th May. His appointment was terminated on 28th June 1918 and he was posted to the Reserve of Officers as honorary captain with seniority from 19th April 1917 and captain on 1st October 1920.

Robert founded the soft-goods firm of Grieve, Gardener and Co at 301 Flinders Lane, Melbourne in 1919 and remained its managing director until his death in 1957. On 7th August 1918 he married May 'Mabel' Isabel Bowman (1880–1929) at Scots Church, Sydney, New South Wales and they lived at 15b Mont Albert Road, Canterbury, Victoria. There were no children.

May was a nurse at Marrickville Cottage Hospital, Sydney and was also head nurse for four months at Parkes District Hospital and matron at Tumut Hospital

Scots Church, Sydney where Robert and May married in August 1918.

Robert and May on their wedding day (Richmond Guardian, Victoria).

for seven months. She enlisted in Sydney as a staff nurse in the Australian Army Nursing Service on 26th April 1915. She was described as 5′ 3″ tall, weighing 132 lbs, with dark complexion, brown eyes, brown hair and her religious denomination was Church of England. She departed Melbourne on 17th June and Fremantle, Western Australia aboard HMAT A62 *Wandilla* on 25th June. *Wandilla* arrived at Suez on 17th July, Port Said on 19th July and Alexandria, Egypt on 21st July. She served in 1st Australian General Hospital in Egypt and was detailed for duty with 4th Auxiliary Hospital, Abbassia on 16th February 1916. She was admitted to 1st Australian General Hospital, Heliopolis with influenza 27th February–1st March. She embarked with 1st Australian General Hospital at Alexandria on 29th March and disembarked at Marseilles on 6th April. The Hospital opened for patients at Rouen racecourse on 19th April. May joined No.26 Ambulance Train on 9th May and was admitted to 24th General Hospital, Étaples with bronchitis on 3rd August. She was transferred to the Nurses Home at Le Touquet next day and rejoined her unit at Rouen on 12th September. May was on leave in Britain 7th–23rd February 1917 and was promoted sister on 1st September. She was on leave in England again 19th September–5th October. On 27th January 1918 she was posted to 2nd Australian Casualty Clearing Station and while serving there met her future husband and helped nurse him. May was posted to 10th Stationary Hospital on 11th March and went on leave to Britain on 18th March, being retained there pending discharge due to marriage. She was detached to 1st Australian Auxiliary

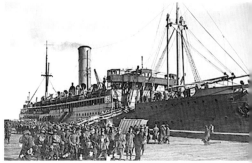

SS *Wandilla* (7,785 tons) was built in 1912 for the Adelaide Steamship Co on the Fremantle–Sydney route. In 1915 she was requisitioned as a troop transport and was converted to a hospital ship in 1916. She was hit by a torpedo from a U-boat in February 1918, but it failed to explode. In 1921 she was sold to the Bermuda & West Indies Steamship Co and renamed *Fort St George*. She collided with RMS *Olympic* in 1924 in New York. In 1935 she was sold to Lloyd Triestino and renamed *Cesarea* and *Arno* in 1938. In the Second World War, she was used by the Italian Navy as a hospital ship. She was sunk by British aircraft near Tobruk on 10th September 1942. On the face of it this was a war crime, but the British claimed an intercepted German radio message on 31st August proved the ship was carrying supplies to Benghazi, thus making it a legitimate target. The sinking was not investigated after the war. (Josiah E Barnes)

The staff of No.1 Auxiliary Hospital, 1st Australian General Hospital at Heliopolis, Egypt in 1915. May Isabel Bowman is on the far right of the third row from the front.

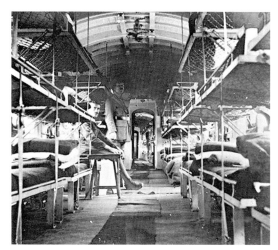

The interior of a hospital train, such as the one May worked on from May 1916.

Hospital, Harefield on 2nd April. On 21st April she embarked on HMAT A29 *Suevic* for transport duty to Australia, arriving on 7th June. On 17th June she applied for discharge in order to serve at home and was released on 26th June 1918. May died during a visit to London on 9th August 1929.

May's father, Arthur Charles MacQuarie Bowman (1844–1913), married Clarissa née Tuckerman (1844–80) in 1868 at Windsor, New South Wales and they had seven children – Florence Alice Bowman 1869, Charles Huffington Bowman 1870, Percival Stephen Bowman 1871, Ethel Marian Bowman 1874, Edward Horace Bowman 1875, Kathleen Constance Bowman 1877 and May Isabel Bowman 1880. Percival Stephen Bowman (1871–1956), manager of the Commercial Bank, Condobolin, New South Wales in 1915, married Clara Elizabeth Bell in 1895. They had four children, including:

• Geoffrey Charles Bowman (1895–1974) was a bank clerk at the time of his enlistment in 20th Battalion, 2nd Reinforcements (1663) at Liverpool, New South Wales on 20th May 1915. He was described as 5′ 8¾″ tall, weighing 143 lbs, with dark complexion, brown eyes, black hair and his religious denomination was Church of England. He returned to duty fit on 9th October and was attached to 20th Battalion, 6th Reinforcements. Admitted to 1st Auxiliary Hospital, Cairo with influenza 15th February–22nd March 1916. Taken on strength 5th Training Battalion at Tel el Kebir on 19th April and transferred to 56th Battalion next day. He embarked on HMAT *Huntsend* at Alexandria on 16th June and disembarked at Marseilles on 29th June. Promoted lance corporal 21st August and was granted leave in Britain 13th–30th December. He was commissioned in 56th Battalion on 29th January 1917 and attended a course at the Lewis Gun School 9th–18th March. He received a gunshot wound, which fractured his left leg on 3rd April and was admitted to 15th Australian Field Ambulance. Transferred to 3rd Australian Casualty Clearing Station on 5th April and 8th General Hospital on 10th April where his leg was amputated above the knee. He embarked for Britain from Le Havre on HMAHS *Warilda* and was admitted to 4th London General Hospital on 17th April. Promoted lieutenant 28th May. He was admitted to Dover House, Roehampton on 6th November. A medical board decided he should be returned to Australia and he was sent on leave 13th–20th December 1917, extended to

28th January 1918. His engagement with the AIF terminated and he embarked on HMAT A14 *Euripides* for Australia on 30th January and disembarked on 22nd March. He was discharged on 21st September 1918 and was awarded Silver War Badge A71566. Geoffrey married Constance Ruby A Riedel (died 1972) at Sydney in 1920.

* Arthur Percy Bowman (1897–1918) was a bank clerk with two years service in 42nd Infantry, Citizen Forces when he enlisted at Parkes, New South Wales on 7th August 1917 (7016). He was described as 5' 7¼" tall, weighing 147 lbs, with dark complexion, brown eyes, brown hair and his religious denomination was Church of England. He joined at Show Ground Camp, Sydney on 14th August. Appointed acting lance corporal 17th August in B Company, 1st Infantry Depot Battalion. Granted leave 10th–14th September. He was allocated to 17th Battalion, 21st Reinforcements on 28th September and embarked at Sydney on HMAT A14 *Euripides* on 31st October as a private and disembarked at Devonport on 26th December. He joined 5th Training Battalion at Fovant, Wiltshire next day. Appointed acting lance corporal 28th December 1917–31st March 1918. He landed at Le Havre, France from Dover on 1st April 1918 and was taken on strength of 17th Battalion on 16th April. Arthur was killed in action at Mont St Quentin on 31st August 1918 and is commemorated on the Villers-Bretonneux Memorial, France.

Clarissa died in 1880 at Maitland, New South Wales following complications with the birth of May. Arthur married Anne Henrietta Boydell (born 1850) in 1882 and they had a daughter, Edith Mary Broughton Bowman, in 1883.

Robert was at the Anzac Commemoration Service on 25th April 1927 at the Exhibition Building, Melbourne, Victoria in the presence of the Duke of York (future King George VI). In the march past the twenty-six VCs conceded pride of place to blinded soldiers who insisted on marching.

Robert was appointed to the Unattached List on 1st April 1939 on the strength of the Deputy Assistant Director of Ordnance Services at Army Headquarters as honorary captain. He served with A Company, 4th Victorian Battalion of the Volunteer Defence Corps from June 1940. He was mobilised on 21st March 1942 for part time duty. At that time his address was Commercial Travellers Club, Flinders Street, Melbourne and his brother John was his next of kin. Promoted captain 12th June 1942 (V350783). He was discharged on 18th September 1944. His appointment terminated on the disbandment of 4th Battalion and he resumed as an officer on the Retired List on 31st October 1945. During a visit to Heidelberg Hospital, Melbourne in February 1954 the Queen spotted Robert in the crowd and went over for a chat. Robert Grieve collapsed from cardiac failure and died in his office in Melbourne on 4th October 1957. He is buried in the Presbyterian Section, Springvale Cemetery, Melbourne (Compartment C, Section 15, Grave 28). He is commemorated in a number of other places:

The Commercial Travellers Club, Flinders Street, Melbourne, where Robert lived after his wife died, is the second building on the left, behind the laden cart.

Robert Grieve's gravestone in Springvale Cemetery, Melbourne.

- Grieve Scholarship, Wesley College, Melbourne, Victoria was sponsored by him shortly before his death.
- Grieve Avenue, Wodonga, Victoria on White Box Rise estate built on land formerly part of Bandiana Army Camp.
- Grieve Street, Macleod, Victoria, Australia.
- Victoria Cross Memorial, Campbell, Canberra dedicated on 24th July 2000.
- Victoria Cross Memorial, Queen Victoria Building, George Street, Sydney, New South Wales.
- Named on one of eleven plaques honouring 175 men from overseas awarded the VC for the Great War. The plaques were unveiled by the Senior Minister of State at the Foreign & Commonwealth Office and Minister for Faith and Communities, Baroness Warsi, at a reception at Lancaster House, London on 26th June 2014 attended by The Duke of Kent and relatives of the VC recipients. The Australian plaque is at the Australian War Memorial.
- The Secretary of State for Communities and Local Government, Eric Pickles MP announced that Victoria Cross recipients from the Great War would have commemorative paving stones laid in their birthplace as a lasting legacy of local heroes within communities. The stones would be laid on or close to the 100th anniversary of their VC actions. For the 145 VCs born in Australia, Belgium, Canada, China, Denmark, Egypt, France, Germany, India, Iraq, Japan, Nepal, Netherlands, New Zealand, Pakistan, South Africa, Sri Lanka, Ukraine and United States of America, individual commemorative stones were unveiled at the National Memorial Arboretum, Alrewas, Staffordshire by Prime Minister David Cameron MP and Sergeant Johnson Beharry VC on 5th March 2015.

In addition to the VC he was awarded the British War Medal 1914–20, Victory Medal 1914–19, George VI Coronation Medal 1937 and Elizabeth II Coronation Medal 1953. He bequeathed his VC to Wesley College, Melbourne, where it was held from 1959. In 2003 it was presented on permanent loan to the Shrine of Remembrance, St Kilda Road, Melbourne, Victoria where it is held.

The Shrine of Remembrance on St Kilda Road, Melbourne was built as a memorial to the men and women of Victoria who served in the First World War, but was later dedicated to all Australians who have served in war. The foundation stone was laid on 11th November 1927, and the Shrine was dedicated on 11th November 1934, when this picture was taken. It is estimated 300,000 people attended.

'The Mates of Messines', a small group of those associated with Robert Grieve during the Battle of Messines on 7th June 1917, met on the anniversary of the battle each year. At each meeting, every member signed a book and a record was made of any happenings during the previous year. In the back of the book Robert Grieve wrote, *Time will eventually take its toll of the members of this gathering. It has been resolved that as and when through these circumstances, it becomes impossible for the remaining members to carry on, that they then shall pass this 'Book of Remembrance' to the National War Memorial, Canberra, when in judgement, this stage has been reached.* In the front of the book is an inscription, *To commemorate 'Messines', June 7th, 1917 and Armistice Day, November 11, 1918. Lest we Forget.* The first meeting was at Trois Abrés in 1925. Each year the numbers dwindled and the last gathering, held at the Naval and Military Club, Melbourne, was attended by only five members. The book was signed off in 1975 and was presented to the Director of the Australian War Memorial by the Chief of Operations, Major General John Whitelaw.

SECOND LIEUTENANT REGINALD LEONARD HAINE
1/1st Battalion, The Honourable Artillery Company Infantry

Reginald Haine, known as Bill, was born at Earlsfield, Wandsworth, London on 10th July 1896. His father, Harry James Haine (birth registered as Hain in Blandford, Dorset) (1864–1933), was a pupil teacher in 1881. He married Louisa Margaret née Smith (1859–1957) at Crewkerne, Somerset in 1891. She was an assistant schoolteacher in 1881 and a schoolmistress in 1891. By 1896 Harry was a Metropolitan Police officer and the family was living at 10 Wilna Road, Wandsworth, London. He was a detective sergeant by 1901 and the family had moved to 9 Sheendale Road, Richmond, Surrey by 1911. By 1920 Harry was working at Scotland Yard. The family later moved to 'Clipsham', Ringley Avenue, Horley, Surrey. Bill had an older brother, Harry Willis Haine (1892–1915).

Bill's paternal grandfather, William Haine (1840–1920) was born at Stourpaine, Dorset. He was a blacksmith in 1864, a carrier and grocer by 1881 and by 1891 he was a grocer and Hackney Carriage proprietor. He married Mary née Best (c.1831–1890) at Milton Abbas, Dorset in February 1862. The family lived at North Street and later at Foyle's Cottages, Stourpaine. In addition to Harry they had two daughters – Mary Elizabeth Haine (1866–1951) and Ellen Haine (1872–1953). After Mary died, William married Amelia Emily Fisher (1854–1920) in October 1892 at Medway, Kent. They were living at Foyle's Cottage, Stourpaine in 1911.

Bill's maternal grandfather, Walter Smith (c.1825–99), was born at Marshalsea, Dorset. He was a letter carrier in 1861, a postman and tailor in 1871, a tailor in 1881 and a letter carrier in 1891. He married Mary Ann née Willis (1827–1900) at Chard, Somerset in 1850. They lived at various times at 76 North Street, West Street and East Street, Crewkerne. In addition to Louisa they had eight other children – Ellen Jane Smith 1851, Henry A Smith 1852, Emma Caroline Smith (1854–1925), George Frederick Smith 1855, Robert Willis Smith 1857, Mary Ann Smith 1862, Charles Smith 1864 and William Smith 1866. Emma married Alfred George Flaxman (1852–1926), a blacksmith, in 1884. They had three children, including Walter James Flaxman (1888–1917), who was an assistant schoolmaster at Andover Grammar School. Walter applied for a commission on 17th July 1915. He

Earlsfield in the early 20th Century.

Scotland Yard at the time Bill's father worked there as a detective sergeant.

had suffered from diphtheria when aged fourteen and was short sighted, but was otherwise passed fit for service at 1st Eastern General Hospital on 16th July. He was commissioned in the Army Service Corps on 6th September 1915 and served initially with K Supply Company at Aldershot from 25th September. He was later posted to No.1 Lines of Communication Supply Company ASC and embarked on 24th October 1916 for Mesopotamia. On 27th May 1917 he was drowned accidentally and his body was not recovered. He is commemorated on the Basra Memorial, Iraq.

It is not known where Bill went to school, but he was a patrol leader with Petersham Boy Scout Troop. He was articled to a firm of accountants when he enlisted in the Honourable Artillery Company on 28th August 1914 (1496), eleven months underage. The Battalion was inspected by the King and moved into camp at Aveley near Purfleet, Essex expecting to have six months training. However, this was cut short and on 18th September it went to France. Bill was home on leave 9th–12th December. He was wounded on 16th June 1915 and rejoined the Battalion on 21st October. Promotion followed rapidly – lance corporal 5th December 1915, lance sergeant 19th February 1916 and sergeant 12th March. He was at the Corps School 9th–19th August. Bill was promoted company sergeant major on 15th November and was commissioned in the Battalion on 7th December. He attended a bombing course 19th–28th December and was on a Fifth Army course 28th February–12th March 1917. **He was Mentioned in Sir Douglas Haig's Despatch of 9th April 1917, LG 18th May 1917.**

Bill was appointed to the temporary command of C Company on 13th April. **Awarded the VC for his actions at Gavrelle, France on 28th/29th April 1917, LG 8th June 1917.** Lieutenant General Sir William Congreve VC, the commander of XIII Corps personally went to congratulate him and Alfred Pollard on their magnificent performances when the Battalion came out of the line on 1st May. Bill spent the period 7th–23rd May at a rest camp. The VC was presented by the King outside Buckingham Palace on 21st July 1917. Bill was the first Richmond man to be awarded the VC and the Mayor presented him with an illuminated address. The Council wanted to set up a subscription on his behalf, but he refused as he saw no connection between money and his action. He and Alf Pollard, who were firm friends, were invited to a celebratory lunch at Armoury House, headquarters of the Honourable Artillery Company, following their investiture. Alf had rarely had to speak in public before and when asked to do so,

Armoury House, headquarters of the Honourable Artillery Company.

General Sir Walter Norris
Congreve VC KCB MVO
was known as 'Squibs' or,
affectionately, to his soldiers
as 'Old Concrete'. He was
awarded the VC for his actions
in the Second Boer War in
1899. His son, Major Billy
Congreve, was awarded the VC
posthumously in 1916.

stood up and said, *Thank you very much everybody* and
sat down. The audience were not impressed and asked
Bill Haine to elaborate. He stood up and said, *I think
Alf's said all there is to say* and promptly sat down too.

He attended a Second Army Musketry Course 4th–
22nd December. Promoted lieutenant 7th June 1918.
Seconded on probation to the Indian Army on 6th
November as a lieutenant retaining his seniority. He
served with 1/35th Sikhs. Transferred to the Indian
Army on 11th January 1919 with seniority as second
lieutenant from 7th June 1917. Promoted lieutenant
Indian Army 11th January 1919 with seniority from 7th
September 1918. **Awarded the MC for his actions at
Dakka, Afghanistan on 17th May 1919; on many
occasions during the fighting near the summit of
the hill he did everything in his power to collect
the men for an attack on the enemy trenches in the
face of very heavy fire. When it was decided to take
up a position further down the hill he collected all
the men he could gather and before descending
assisted in getting all the wounded away, LG 29th
November 1919.** Captain Ernest Frank Bugler was also
awarded the MC for this action. Bill's MC was presented by the King at Buckingham
Palace on 10th March 1920.

Bill acted as Adjutant of 1/35th Sikhs as an acting captain 6th–17th May 1919.
He relinquished his appointment in the Indian Army on 12th January 1920, but
remained in the Honourable Artillery Company. He became a chartered accountant
in London with Messrs Andrew Low, Son & Co and was later a director of Jennings
Hotels Ltd.

Bill Haine married Dora Beatrice
née Holder (7th November 1898–3rd
October 1997) on 21st November 1923
at St Mark's Church, Woodcote, Purley,
Surrey. They lived at Cherry Cottage,
Woodcote Village, Purley and at Dawslea
Cottage, Hollist Lane, Easebourne,
Midhurst, West Sussex. Dora and Bill
had a daughter, Janet E Haine in 1924.
She married Stanley JC Stephens in
1954 and they had three daughters
– Sally C Stephens 1955, Amanda J

The Dakka area of Afghanistan.

Stephens 1956 and Rebecca L Stephens 1961.

Dora's father, Edward Holder (1865–1941) was a French drapery agent and was running his own business, E Holder & Co, from 75 Little Britain, London. He married Alice Beatrice née Beviss (1873–1925) in 1895. The family was living at Stanfield, Dowsell Avenue, Prittlewell, Essex in 1901 and by 1911 had moved to Beckhythe, Rose Walk, Purley and later lived at Cherry Orchard, Woodcote Valley, Purley. In addition to Dora they had three other children:

Purley, Surrey where Bill and Dora lived after they married in 1923.

- Edward Phillips Holder (1895–1978) joined the Honourable Artillery Company (1028) and was promoted through the ranks to sergeant. He went to France on 29th December 1914 and was commissioned in the Honourable Artillery Company on 7th December 1916. He continued to serve until 4th October 1923. In 1925 he married Olive Ainsley (1896–1980), sister of Mary Ainsley, first wife of Alfred Pollard VC MC DCM, with whom Bill Haine won the VC. Edward enlisted in the Royal Artillery TA (125069) and was promoted lance bombardier before being commissioned in the Royal Army Service Corps on 27th March 1940.
- Frank Douglas Holder (1897–1978) trained at the Royal Military College, Sandhurst and was commissioned in The Buffs (East Kent Regiment) on 26th January 1916. He carried out flying training at Farnborough, Hampshire and Mousehold, Norfolk and transferred to the Royal Flying Corps on 15th July 1916. He served in France from 21st July with 22 Squadron and received a gunshot wound to the left ankle during aerial combat over Le Transloy near Bapaume on 7 September. The aircraft petrol supply was also damaged and the aircraft fell the last thirty feet, resulting in bruises and abrasions. He embarked at Le Havre on 11th September on HMHS *Salta*, arriving at Southampton next day. A medical board at Osborne, Isle of Wight on 19th September found him unfit for service for one month and sent him on leave until 20th October. A medical board at Croydon War Hospital on 23rd October found him unfit for General Service for one month, but fit for Home Service and he was posted to 28 Squadron on 5th November. A medical board at Adastral House, London on 21st December found him fit for General Service and he was posted to Orfordness, Suffolk on 1st January 1917, where he was part of the Armament Experimental Station working on the first use of oxygen apparatus and electrically heated clothing for use in the air, in addition to testing machine guns, sights, ammunition, photography and pyrotechnics. Awarded the MC for shooting down Zeppelin L48 on 17th June 1917 with 506 Sergeant Sidney Ashby, who was awarded the MM, LG 7th August 1917. Also involved in the destruction of L48 was Lieutenant P Watkins and Captain

RHMS Saundby, who had previously served under Major Lanoe Hawker VC and in the Second World War, as Air Marshal Sir Robert Saundby, was Deputy to Air Marshal Sir Arthur Harris at HQ Bomber Command. Appointed temporary lieutenant on 26th July and temporary captain on 13th October. He was employed under the Air Ministry 1st April 1918–26th January 1920 and was re-seconded to the RAF on 30th October 1919, holding Regular Army and Temporary RAF commissions simultaneously. He transferred to the Reserve (East Kent Regiment) in February 1920. His commission in 5th Defence Force Battalion, The Buffs on 15th April 1921 was cancelled later as he already held a commission in the Regular Army Reserve of Officers. He served in the emergency 15th–21st April 1921, when he was living at 33 Queen's Road, Chelmsford. He resigned his commission, retaining the rank of lieutenant, on 23rd May 1924. Frank married Cynthia Olive Hart (1896–1956) in 1919 and they had four children – John Douglas Holder 1920, Anne B Holder 1923, Robert Woollard Holder 1925 and Susan I Holder 1936. Frank was commissioned as acting pilot officer in the Training Branch, Royal Air Force on 31st March 1941 (63006). Promoted flying officer on probation (Emergency) in the Administrative and Special Duties Branch on 3rd August 1942 and later squadron leader. His other appointments included – JP 1941, member of Chelmsford Council, Deputy Mayor 1950, DL Essex, HM Lieutenant Essex 1962 and Chairman No.276 (Chelmsford) Squadron Committee ATC. He was awarded the OBE, LG 10th June 1967. In 1957 he married Dorothy Ellen Sincock née Creasy (1901–76), widow of Leslie John Sincock (1905–55).

The wreckage of Zeppelin L48, shot down on 17th June 1917 just outside Theberton in Suffolk. L48 was a new type of lightweight Zeppelin able to climb higher to try to avoid night fighters. Her maiden flight was on 22nd May and she was lost on her first operational sortie when she was tasked to attack London. L48 bombed Harwich and Martlesham instead and was heading home but due to a frozen compass, went north instead of east. She was picked up by searchlights and four aircraft engaged her, of which three were credited with assisting in her destruction. In addition to Frank Holder's and Sergeant Sidney Ashby's FE2b, there was a DH2 flown by Captain Robert Saundby (awarded MC) and a BE12 piloted by Lieutenant P Watkins who was credited with the final kill. Frank Holder survived a crash at Eastbridge a few weeks later, but Ashby died in a crash at Martlesham on 16th March 1918 (Ipswich Old Cemetery). Of the nineteen Zeppelin crew, only three survived and one of those died of burns on 11th November 1918.

• Nancy Muriel Holder (1903–98).

Bill was promoted captain in the Honourable Artillery Company on 2nd January 1928 and he transferred to the TA Reserve of Officers on 15th June 1929. During

St Mary's Easebourne near Midhurst where Bill's funeral took place.

the Second World War he served in the Home Guard and was lieutenant colonel and CO of 58th Surrey (Purley) Battalion from 1st February 1941. Bill was a founder member of the Victoria Cross and George Cross Association in 1956 and joined the Committee. He was also Chairman of the Baltic Exchange Branch of the British Legion, meeting in Merchants Hall, London.

Bill Haine died at St Thomas's Hospital, Lambeth, London on 12th June 1982. His funeral was held at the Parish Church of St Mary Easebourne near Midhurst and he was cremated at Chichester Crematorium, Sussex where his ashes were scattered (Garden of Remembrance Section J-60). There is a memorial plaque at the crematorium. His estate was valued at £101,296. Bill is also commemorated in a number of other places:

Robert Henry Magnus Spencer Saundby (1896–1971) joined the Royal Warwickshire Regiment and was commissioned in 1915. He went to France, but in January 1916 joined the RFC, qualified as a pilot and served under Major Lanoe Hawker VC. In Iraq in the 1920s he served with Squadron Leader Arthur Harris developing bombing techniques. He served with Harris again at Worthy Down developing night bombing techniques. By 1937 Saundby was Deputy Director of Operations and in 1940 become Senior Air Staff Officer (SASO), HQ Bomber Command under Air Marshal Richard Peirse and later Bomber Harris with whom he appears in this picture; Saundby is on the left.

- Plaque on the wall of St Mary's Church, Easebourne, West Sussex and a memorial altar rail.
- One of twenty VC and GC holders born, lived, studied, worked or died in Wandsworth named on a memorial outside Wandsworth Town Hall.

In addition to the VC and MC he was awarded the 1914 Star with 'Mons' clasp, British War Medal 1914–20, Victory Medal 1914–19 with Mentioned-in-Despatches Oakleaf, India General Service 1908–35 with 'Afghanistan NWF 1919' clasp, Defence Medal, George VI Coronation Medal 1937, Elizabeth II Coronation Medal 1953 and Elizabeth II Jubilee Medal 1977. The VC is owned privately and is on loan to the Imperial War Museum, where it is displayed in the Lord Ashcroft Gallery.

SECOND LIEUTENANT JOHN HARRISON
11th Battalion, The East Yorkshire Regiment

John Harrison was born at Drypool, Sculcoates, Kingston-upon-Hull, Yorkshire on 12th November 1890. He was known as Jack to distinguish him from his father, also John Harrison (born 1860), who was born at Middlesbrough, Yorkshire. John senior worked for Earle's Shipbuilding in Hull as a boilermaker-plater. He married Charlotte née Carr (1862–1944), a domestic servant, in 1883. The family was living at 20 Williamson Street, Southcoates in 1891, 19 Brazil Street, Sculcoates in 1901, 107 New Bridge Road, Hull by 1911 and Ainslie House, Sculcoates in 1914. John junior had six siblings:

- Stanley Harrison (1901–18).
- Beatrice Harrison (1884–1972) was a pupil teacher in 1901. She married Fred Myers in 1914.
- Lilian Harrison (born 1886) was an assistant in a tobacconist's shop in 1901.
- Charlotte Ethel Harrison (born 1888) was a teacher in 1911.
- Elsie Harrison (born 1895) was an apprentice dressmaker in 1911.
- Elma Harrison (1899–1997) married Bramwell Butler (1896–1941) in 1924 and they had two sons – Stanley M Butler 1925 and Keith H Butler 1932. Bramwell was killed on the night of 31st March/1st April 1941 during an air raid on Hull. He was a firewatcher and was in the Ferensway air raid shelter when it received a direct hit. He was one of fifty-two killed and seventy-two seriously injured that night. One of Stanley M Butler's sons, Guy, attended the unveiling of John Harrison's memorial outside Hull's new Kingston Communications ground in 2003.

New Bridge Road, Hull.

Southcoates Lane, Hull.

John's paternal grandfather, William Ainsley Harrison (c.1839–89), was a blacksmith in 1871. He married Anne Elizabeth née Grange (c.1832–1909) in 1860 at Stockton, Co Durham. In 1871 the family was living at Southcoates, Hull and by 1881 at 9 Richards Terrace, Garbutt Street, Southcoates. In addition to John they had six other children – Elizabeth Harrison 1866, Thomas Harrison 1867, William Ainsley Harrison 1869, Edward Harrison 1872, George Harrison 1876 and Robert Harrison 1878.

John's maternal grandfather, Thomas Carr (c.1831–92), was a railway engine driver in 1871 and a blacksmith in 1881. He married Mary née Jackson (c.1828–1908) in 1850 at York. In 1871 the family was living at Myton, Yorkshire, in 1881 at 1 Prince of Wales Terrace, Myton and in 1891 at 2 Chapel Terrace, Campbell Street, Myton. In addition to Charlotte they had two other children – George Carr 1857 and William Carr 1864.

John Harrison was educated at:

- Craven Street Higher Grade School, Hull 1901–09. It became Malet Lambert High School when it moved to a new site in 1932 and a grammar school twelve years later.
- Hull Secondary School 1909–10.
- York Diocesan Teacher Training College (St John's College), Lord Mayor's Walk, York September 1910–July 1912.

John was well known as a sportsman in the north of England, being one of the finest Rugby League wing three-quarters in the Northern League. Initially he played for St John's College as captain and then for York Northern Union Rugby Football Club in the 1911–12 season before moving to Hull Northern Union Club, making his debut against York on 5th September 1912. He went on to make 116 appearances, scoring 106 tries and two goals. His record of six tries, in a match against Wakefield, stood until 1968. He scored one of the two tries in the Northern Rugby Union Challenge Cup Final (now the Rugby League Challenge Cup) to beat Wakefield Trinity 6–0 at Halifax on 26th April 1914. In the 1914–15 season he set an unbroken record of fifty-two tries in a single season. Before war broke out he was selected for the 1914 tour to Australia, which was cancelled. He is reputed to be the only professional Rugby League VC, but Thomas Steele VC played three matches as a professional for Broughton Rangers and Thomas Bryan VC played for Castleford in the 1906/07 season. John was one of twelve Hull players killed in the war.

John was a student teacher at Estcourt Street Senior School, Hull until September 1912 when he became an assistant master at Lime Street Senior Boys/Council School, Hull in the dockland area close to the river.

On 1st September 1914, John Harrison married Lilian née Ellis (1889–1977) at Sculcoates. They lived at 75 Wharncliffe Street, Hull and had one son, John 'Jackie' Harrison, born on 29th June 1915. He served as a temporary captain in 1st Duke

The Hull Northern Union Rugby Football Club winning team in the Northern Rugby Union Challenge Cup Final on 26th April 1914. John Harrison is on the far right of the middle row.

Estcourt Street School, where John Harrison was a student teacher, was established in 1902 with a capacity of 1,000 pupils. It was destroyed in the bombing in 1941.

of Wellington's (66137) and was killed in action on 1st June 1940 commanding C Company in the defence of the Dunkirk perimeter on the canal between Furnes and Bergues. He is buried in Dunkirk Town Cemetery (2 13 14).

Lilian's father, George Evans Ellis (1862–1935), born at Newhaven, Sussex, was a shipwright at Kellythorpe Crossing, Driffield, Yorkshire. He married Sarah née Hendey (1865–1946), who was born at Scarborough, Yorkshire, in 1888 at Sculcoates. The family was living at 8 Brentwood Avenue, Sculcoates in 1901 and 21 Dryden Street, Sculcoates in 1911. In addition to Lilian they had three other children –

George Ellis 1892, Gladys Ellis 1893 and Doris Ellis 1905. George junior served in 8th East Yorkshire (30982) and died of wounds on 30th April 1917. He is buried in Duisans British Cemetery, Étrun – II Q 12.

John enlisted in the Inns of Court OTC on 4th November 1915 (7203) and trained at No.14 Officer Cadet Battalion, Berkhamsted, Hertfordshire from March 1916. He was commissioned in the East Yorkshire Regiment on 5th August 1916 and was posted to 14th (Reserve) Battalion at Seaton Delaval near Newcastle-upon-Tyne. He went to France on 19th September, where he joined 6 Platoon, B Company, 11th East Yorkshire. **Awarded the MC for his actions on 25th February 1917 when**

John 'Jackie' Harrison's grave in Dunkirk Town Cemetery.

during the enemy retirement near Hébuterne he led one of two platoon strength patrols towards the enemy lines as part of an advance guard. He reached his objective, Slug Street, one mile into enemy territory and took a prisoner.

John Harrison's name on the Arras Memorial.

The advance was led with great courage and skill under very difficult conditions, LG 17th April 1917.

Awarded the VC for his actions at Oppy, France on 3rd May 1917, LG 14th June 1917. He was killed during his VC action and is commemorated on the Arras Memorial. He left £149/18/10 to his wife. The VC was presented to his widow by the King at Buckingham Palace on 2nd March 1918. John Harrison is commemorated in a number of other places:

• Jack Harrison VC Memorial Trophy presented by the Army Rugby League to the Combined Services Rugby League in 2000, to be contested annually by the Army and the Royal Navy in the Inter-Services Rugby League Championship.

The bronze memorial plaque unveiled at Lime Street School in 1920 is now in Hull's Guildhall (Memorials to Valour).

- Jack Harrison VC Memorial Trophy established in 2003 and awarded annually by the Jack Harrison Memorial Trust to the young handicapped person in Hull showing the most fortitude in overcoming disadvantage.
- Jack Harrison Memorial Trophy established by Hull Football Club Foundation and competed for annually by special schools in East Yorkshire. The trophy is presented to the winning school and all players receive a Jack Harrison Medal.
- Jack Harrison Court, Hull consists of fifty-seven flats for the elderly and was named in the 1980s.
- A bronze memorial plaque was unveiled at Lime Street School on 3rd May 1920. The school was bombed in the Second World War, but the plaque was rescued and taken to the Guildhall for safekeeping. It was rediscovered on the roof in 1978 and was displayed in the Rugby League Centenary Exhibition in 1995. It is now in the Guildhall's main ground floor corridor.
- Memorial plaque at Malet Lambert School, James Reckitt Avenue, Hull.
- Named on the East Yorkshire Regiment War Memorial, Beverley Minster, East Yorkshire.
- Named on St Mary's Church war memorial, Lowgate, Hull.
- Named on the Victoria Cross Memorial, Paragon Square, Hull.
- Named on the St John's College war memorial in the Chapel dedicated in 1921. There is also a portrait of John Harrison and his citation at the Sport Hall, Lord Mayor's Walk Campus, York St John University.

John Harrison's memorial at Malet Lambert School, Hull.

St Mary's Church, Lowgate, Hull where John is commemorated on the war memorial.

• Hull Rugby Club unveiled a memorial to Harrison at the Boulevard ground on 23rd November 1979. The Boulevard closed in 2003 after 107 years. On 11th November 2003 a memorial to Harrison was dedicated outside the club's new Kingston Communications ground by his great nephew, Guy Butler, and the Rugby Football League Executive Chairman, Richard Lewis. It was unveiled formally at the Great Britain v Australia Rugby League test match a few days later on 15th November 2003.

The John Harrison memorial dedicated on 11th November 2003 outside Hull Rugby Club's Kingston Communications ground.

In addition to the VC and MC he was awarded the British War Medal 1914–20 and Victory Medal 1914–19. When Lilian died, she bequeathed the medals to the East Yorkshire Regiment Museum in Beverley and they are now held by the Prince of Wales's Own Regiment of Yorkshire Museum, Tower Street, York. After the war Oppy was adopted by Hull. Lilian was living at Berne Villa, The Roundway, Anlaby Park Road, Hull in 1922. In 1923 her plight as a war widow was recognised by the local community and a fund was set up to pay for her son's education.

LIEUTENANT FREDERICK MAURICE WATSON HARVEY
Lord Strathcona's Horse (Royal Canadians), Canadian Expeditionary Force

Frederick Harvey was born on 1st September 1888 at Athboy, Co Meath, Ireland. His father was the Reverend Alfred Thomas Harvey (c.1843–98), who was Vicar at Kentstown Rectory, Navan, Co Meath and later at The Rectory, Athboy. He was also Succentor of St Patrick's Cathedral, Dublin. When he died he left £317/0/7 to his widow. Frederick's mother, Ida Suzette née Wegelin (c.1852–c.1943), born at Diessenhofen, Schaffhausen, Switzerland, was a governess and tutor. Alfred and Ida married on 3rd August 1875 at Killiney, Rathdown,

Ireland. She was living at 204 Marlborough Road, Pembroke West, Dublin in 1901, at 7 Wellington Road, Pembroke West in 1911 and 5 Leeson Park, Dublin in 1913. Frederick had six siblings:

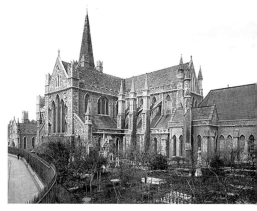

St Patrick's Cathedral, Dublin.

- Ida Mabel Harvey (1876–1953) was a teacher in 1901 and a secretary and organist in 1911. She married Frank Oswell (1863–1936) in 1913 in Dublin. Frank's father was William Cotton Oswell (1818–93), a renowned big game hunter and explorer who discovered Lake Ngami and was with Livingstone when the latter was attacked by a lion. Ida's brother, Thomas, officiated at the wedding with the Reverend Harrison Oswell, Frank's brother. They had two children, one of whom was William Brian Oswell (1919–91).
- Thomas Arnold Harvey (1878–1966), a clergyman, married Isabel Kathleen Burrows (born 1887) in 1911 and they had a son, Philip Harvey (1920–43). He was Rector of St Philip's and St James's, Booterstown, Co Dublin before being elected Dean of St Patrick's Cathedral, Dublin on 22nd June 1933.
- Charles Dacre Harvey (born 1879) was a bank clerk in 1901 and in 1914 was working for the Bank of Ireland. He enlisted in 7th Royal Dublin Fusiliers (14147) on 14th September 1914 and was described as 5' 9½" tall, with fresh complexion, hazel eyes, brown hair and his religious denomination was Church of England. He was promoted lance sergeant on 27th October and was commissioned on 24th December. The Battalion embarked on 10th July 1915 and

Frederick's sister's father-in-law, William Cotton Oswell, secured a position with the East India Company, after leaving Rugby School in 1837, and spent ten years learning languages and studying surgery and medicine. In South Africa he explored the Kalahari Desert and located Lake Ngami. He took part in expeditions to the Zambesi with David Livingstone. In the Crimean War he carried out medical duties and later traveled in North and South America.

he was wounded by shrapnel in the right shoulder when landing at Suvla Bay, Gallipoli on 7th August. Promoted lieutenant on 10th August and rejoined the Battalion on 25th November. He received a gun shot wound to the chest on 3rd October during the brief advance into Serbia from Salonica and rejoined the unit on 18th October. Charles was appointed acting adjutant 9th–20th May 1916 and adjutant on 15th July. He was mentioned in Lieutenant General GF Milne CB DSO's despatch of 8th October (LG 6th December 1916). He left his unit for a staff duties course in Egypt, embarking at Salonica on HMT *Kingstonian* on 1st January 1917 and arriving at Alexandria on 5th January. He embarked for Salonica on HMT *Chagres* from Port Said on 22nd February, arriving on 26th February. He was admitted to 27th Casualty Clearing Station 4th–11th March, commanded B Company 24th March–12th April and resumed as adjutant next day. Charles embarked for leave in Britain on 1st May, returned to Salonica on 8th June, rejoined his unit on 1st July and resumed as adjutant next day. He was attached to HQ 10th Division on 2nd August and his appointment as temporary captain was backdated to 1st July 1916. Having rejoined his unit on 18th August 1917, he embarked at Salonica on 2nd September, disembarked at Alexandria on 6th September and was appointed Staff Captain, HQ 29th Infantry Brigade on 10th September, assuming the duties on 16th September. He was appointed Acting Deputy Adjutant & Quartermaster General, HQ 10th Division on 15th October and joined the Desert Mounted Corps on 6th November. Charles was awarded the Order of the Nile 4th Class (LG 9th November 1918) and joined HQ 29th Brigade on 14th January 1919. He moved to HQ 10th Division on 3rd February and resumed duties as Acting Deputy Adjutant & Quartermaster General on 15th February. In March 1919 he was detached to work for the Military Governor of Haifa and on 1st October joined HQ Occupied Enemy Territory Administration (South) in Jerusalem as Paymaster and Senior Assistant Treasurer, Government of Palestine. He relinquished his appointment as Deputy Assistant Administrator on 26th August 1920 and was demobilised at Kantara the same day, but continued to be employed by the Government of Palestine.

• George Alfred Duncan Harvey (1882–1957) was a doctor (LRCP&S (Ireland) & LM 1904, DPH London 1920). He played rugby for Wanderers Football Club in Dublin and went on to play for Ireland in 1903 against England and Scotland, in 1904 against Wales and in 1905 against England and Scotland. He was commissioned as a lieutenant in the Royal Army Medical Corps on 30th July 1904 and served in the Straits Settlements 1905–07. Promoted captain 30th January 1908 and posted to Egypt 1908–10. He was a Specialist in Physical Training in 1912 and was seconded to the Egyptian Army 4th June–14th November 1914. Promoted major 1st July 1915 and appointed Deputy Assistant Director General, Army Medical Services 24th September 1915–28th February 1918. Went to France 20th March 1918. Appointed acting lieutenant colonel while CO of a field ambulance in France 11th July–8th December 1918 and 15th January–3rd February 1919 while Assistant Director of Medical Services HQ Army, France. Awarded the CMG 4th June 1917 and Mentioned in Despatches 27th July 1917. George married Gwendel Rothera (1893–1979) in 1916 and they had at least one child, Lesley C Harvey in 1917. He was appointed Deputy Assistant Director

General, War Office 5th February 1919–31st March 1921 and was posted to Gibraltar as Assistant Director of Medical Services 1921–25. He returned to the War Office as Assistant Director of Hygiene 20th March 1926–10th February 1930 and was promoted lieutenant colonel on 22nd October 1927. He was CO British Medical Hospital, Meerut 1930–33. Appointed brevet colonel 1st January 1931 and promoted colonel 13th February 1933 with seniority backdated to 1st January 1931. He remained in India as Assistant Director of Medical Services, HQ Waziristan District 13th February 1933–23rd March 1935 until returning to Britain as Assistant Director Medical Services, HQ London District June– October 1935. Promoted major general 6th October 1935 and went back to India as Deputy Director of Medical Services, HQ Western Command 10th November 1935–31st October 1938. Appointed King's Honorary Physician 1st March 1937. Awarded CB (LG 9th June 1938) and retired on 28th March 1939. On 20th February 1940, he was recalled as a colonel and served with the BEF in France as Assistant Director of Medical Services, HQ 4 Base Sub-Area from 22nd February. He was a prisoner of war in Germany from 1940 until repatriated in 1943. He then served with HQ Supreme Allied Command until reverting to retired pay as a major general on 12th May 1944.

• Frank Newenham Harvey (born c.1887) was a doctor, specialising in midwifery and was practising at 10 Marine Parade, Napier, New Zealand in 1913. He married Beatrice Dudgeon and they had a son, Newenham Deane Maurice Harvey (1919–96). Newenham was born at Napier, New Zealand, educated at Otago University (MB ChB 1942) and was commissioned in the New Zealand Medical Corps (412910) on 31st December 1943. He sailed for Britain aboard SS *Ruahine* as a captain on 6th September 1944 arriving at Liverpool on 29th October. He married Mary Patricia Roseby (1925–2003) in 1951 at Wortley, Yorkshire and they had four children. They moved to Roskill, Auckland, New Zealand in 1954 and later to Adelaide, South Australia.

• Dora Kathleen Harvey (born c.1891).

Frederick's paternal grandfather, George Newenham Harvey (c.1804–64), was Vice-Consul for the Kingdom of Sweden and Norway at Queenstown and Cork, Ireland at the time of his death. He married Sarah née Watson (1803–75) in 1834 at Monanimy Church, Co Cork. In addition to Alfred they had two other sons – George Newenham Harvey (c.1836–90) and William Watson Harvey born c.1844. Frederick's maternal grandfather, Rudolf J Wegelin of Diessenhofen, Canton Thurgau, Switzerland was deceased at the time of his daughter Ida's marriage in 1875.

Frederick was educated at Portora Royal School, Enniskillen, Ireland and Ellesmere College, Shropshire January 1899–April 1902, where he was in the School Cadets. John Henry Cound Brunt VC MC was a pupil at Ellesmere from 1934. Frederick was a keen sportsman and one of three VCs to play for Wanderers

Portora Royal School, Enniskillen, Co Fermanagh was founded by Royal Charter in 1608 by James I. It was attended at various times by James Gamble, founder of Proctor & Gamble, Samuel Beckett, Nobel prizewinner for literature and Oscar Wilde, the playwright.

Oscar Wilde.

Rugby Football Club, Dublin; the others were Thomas Joseph Crean and Robert Johnston. Frederick also played for Ireland against Wales in 1907 and France in 1911 as fullback. He emigrated to Canada in 1908 and worked as a surveyor in Northern Alberta and High River, before settling in Fort Macleod c.1911. He returned to Ireland by the time of the 1911 Census, when he was living with his mother. By 1914 he was a rancher at Medicine Hat, Alberta.

Frederick married Winifred Lillian Patterson (1890–1989) in 1914 and they had a son, Denis Frederick Harvey. Denis served as a lieutenant with the Royal Winnipeg Rifles and died on 16th February 1945 (Groesbeek Canadian War Cemetery, Netherlands – XI F 4). Winfred's parents, Robert Patterson (1856–1938) and Sarah Lucinda née Sayers (1861–1925), were born in Tipperary, Ireland and emigrated to Alberta, Canada, where they settled at Fort Macleod and Robert joined the North-West Mounted Police. He later became a superintendent in the Royal Canadian Mounted Police. Robert took up ranching in 1880 near Champion, moving to Bassano in 1886. In 1906 he returned to Fort Macleod and was elected as an Independent Member of the Legislative Assembly in 1911, sitting until 1917. In addition to Winifred they had five other children – Ethel Susan Patterson 1885, Arthur Courtney Patterson 1887, Robert Edward Patterson 1888, George W Patterson 1891 and Katherine M Patterson 1900.

Frederick served with 23rd Alberta Rangers at Fort Macleod, part of the

Ellesmere College was founded in 1879 and was originally called St Oswald's School. Other former pupils include the England rugby captain, Bill Beaumont, and John Brunt VC MC.

John Brunt was awarded the VC for his actions in Italy in December 1944 whilst serving with the Sherwood Foresters.

Fort Macleod grew up around the North-West Mounted Police barracks built there in 1874 and the town became an important railway centre. It was all but destroyed in a fire in 1906 and the local economy was devastated in the 1920s. In 1956 there was a famous UFO sighting over the town. The singer-songwriter Joni Mitchell was born there in 1943.

RMS *Olympic* (45,324 tons) was the lead transatlantic liner of the White Star line. Her sister ships, *Titanic* and *Britannic*, had short and tragic careers. *Titanic* sank after striking an iceberg in April 1912 with the loss of 1,514 lives. *Britannic* struck a mine and sank in the Mediterranean in November 1916 with the loss of thirty lives. *Olympic*'s first voyage from Belfast to Liverpool coincided with the launch of *Titanic* on 31st May 1911. On her maiden voyage on 14th June 1911 from Southampton to New York, *Britannic* was captained by Edward Smith, master of the *Titanic* on her maiden voyage the following year. The picture is from 2nd March 1912 as *Olympic*, on the left, is being manouvered into dry dock in Belfast for repairs to a propeller. On the right, *Titanic* is being fitted out ahead of her maiden voyage. On 27th October 1914, off the north coast of Ireland *Olympic* went to assist the battleship HMS *Audacious*, which had struck a mine. *Olympic* took off 250 of *Audacious*' crew, but on the way to Lough Swilly the towing cable parted and *Audacious* sank later. In May 1915, *Olympic* was requisitioned as a troop transport. On 12th May 1918, en route to France with US troops, she sighted U-*103* surfaced 500m ahead and opened fire. U-*103* crash-dived, but *Olympic*'s port propeller sliced through the pressure hull. U-103 surfaced and was scuttled and abandoned by her crew. *Olympic* reached Southampton via Cherbourg with some damage, but her hull was not breached. USS *Davis* picked up thirty-one survivors from U-*103*. *Olympic*'s master, Captain Hayes, was awarded the DSO. During the war, *Olympic* carried 200,000 troops and travelled 184,000 miles. In 1920 she returned to passenger service, carrying many celebrities, such as Charlie Chaplin, Mary Pickford and the Prince of Wales. The Depression and competition from new larger and faster liners had their effect and she left New York for the last time on 5th April 1935. She was broken up in 1936–37, having completed 257 Atlantic crossings, transporting 430,000 commercial passengers and travelled 1,800,000 miles (Robert John Welch).

South Alberta Light Horse, which raised three regiments of Canadian Mounted Rifles for service in the First World War: 3rd, 12th and 13th. Frederick enlisted on 8th February 1915 at Fort Macleod (13285) and served in 13th Canadian Mounted Rifles, which was raised on 15th March 1915. He was described as 6' tall with dark complexion, brown eyes, brown hair and his religious denomination was Church of England. He was promoted corporal on 15th February and acting sergeant on 24th February. Frederick was commissioned as a lieutenant on 20th March 1916 and was serving at Medicine Hat, Alberta in May. He sailed to England aboard RMS *Olympic* on 19th June, arriving on 5th July. His wife also went to England and worked in an ammunition factory.

He transferred to the Royal Canadian Regiment and Princess Patricia's Canadian Light Infantry on 19th July, following the disbandment of 13th Canadian Mounted Rifles. On 22nd July, he was attached to Lord Strathcona's Horse Reserve Regiment at Shorncliffe and proceeded to France on 22nd November to the Canadian Base Depot and joined Lord Strathcona's Horse in the field on 27th November.

Awarded the VC for his actions at Guyencourt, France on 27th March 1917, LG 8th June 1917. He was originally recommended for the MC, but it was upgraded to a DSO at Corps HQ and to a VC at HQ BEF. Frederick had a generous allocation of leave – 11th–23rd May, 12th–26th July (during which the VC was presented by the King in the Forecourt at Buckingham Palace on 21st July) and 31st December 1917–5th February 1918. He was detached to the Regimental Trench Party 20th February–6th March 1918.

Awarded the MC for his actions at Moreuil on 30th March 1918, LG 22nd June 1918. In an attack his fearless leading overcame the resistance of the enemy, although the latter were in superior numbers. He engaged many of them single-handed and, although wounded and suffering from loss of blood, continued to fight his way forward until he effected a junction with another mounted party, thus contributing in a great degree to the success of the attack. The action was fought by the Canadian Cavalry Brigade, commanded by Brigadier General JEB Seely, and resulted in the award of a posthumous VC to Lieutenant Gordon Flowerdew, who commanded the leading squadron of Lord Strathcona's Horse in the attack. Frederick received gunshot wounds to the right arm and left thigh and was evacuated to No.8 General Hospital at Rouen on 31st March and to Britain on SS *Caesarea* on 2nd April. He was admitted to Prince of Wales' Hospital for Officers, Marylebone, London on 3rd April until sent on leave 4th–24th May. The MC was presented by the King at Buckingham Palace on 10th July 1918. He was on the strength of the Canadian Reserve Cavalry Regiment from 27th May until proceeding to Canadian General Base Depot, France on 15th October and rejoined his unit on 19th October. **Awarded the French Croix de Guerre, LG 10th October 1918.**

Frederick was in England again 17th–23rd November and was granted fourteen days leave on 11th February 1919, extended to 4th March, and rejoined his unit

Brigadier General John Edward Bernard Seely CB CMG DSO TD PC JP DL (1868–1947) was a Conservative MP 1900–04 and a Liberal MP 1904–22 and 1923–24. He was Secretary of State for War until forced to resign over the Curragh Incident. Educated at Harrow, where he knew Stanley Baldwin and Winston Churchill, the latter becoming a lifelong friend. He was called to the Bar and served in the Hampshire Yeomanry. During the Boer War he was awarded the DSO serving with the Imperial Yeomanry. After the First World War, he and Churchill were the only members of the Cabinet to have seen active service. In 1933, Seely was raised to the peerage as Baron Mottistone. He married twice and his first son, Second Lieutenant Frank Reginald Seely was killed serving with 1st Hampshire on 13th April 1917 (Haute-Avesnes British Cemetery – C 14). In 1934, Seely wrote *My Horse Warrior* about his charger, who went through the entire war with him. Warrior died in 1941 aged thirty-three and in 2014 was awarded the Dickin Medal for bravery.

SS *Caesarea* (1,504 tons) was built for the London & Southwestern Railway Company in 1910 for the Southampton–Channel Islands service and was requisitioned for service throughout the First World War. In 1923, she struck a rock and sank just outside St Helier, Jersey. Following salvage and repairs, she was acquired by the Isle of Man Steam Packet Company and renamed *Manx Maid*. On 27th August 1939, she was requisitioned by the Admiralty as an armoured boarding vessel and was undergoing repairs at the time of the Dunkirk evacuation. She made two crossings later as the retreat moved westwards. On the first, she tried to get into St Malo, but the Germans had already occupied the port. In the second, to Brest, she rescued 3,000 troops. In October 1941, she became a Special Duties vessel and was renamed HMS *Bruce*. From March 1942 until March 1945 she was a Fleet Air Arm target vessel. After the war she returned to the Isle of Man until she was broken up in November 1950.

The Royal Military College, Kingston, Ontario was established in 1876 and continues to train and educate officers for the Canadian armed forces.

Lieutenant Gordon Flowerdew VC.

on 6th March. He returned to England on 17th April and was struck off strength of Lord Strathcona's House on 20th May. Next day he embarked at Liverpool and disembarked at Halifax, Nova Scotia on 28th May. On 4th June he was attached for temporary duty with Military District No.10.

Frederick was admitted to Manitoba Military Hospital, Winnipeg on 4th December 1919 with Ptomaine poisoning after eating spoiled oysters. He was granted Christmas leave on 22nd December and recovery leave 24th January–19th February 1920. On 1st April 1920 he was struck off strength of the Canadian Expeditionary Force to an appointment in the Permanent Force. Frederick was appointed Instructor of Physical Education at the Royal Military College, Kingston, Ontario 1923–27. He attended the VC Dinner at the Royal

The Great Central Hotel on Marylebone Road became the Prince of Wales Hospital for Officers in 1916. By 1917 it had 750 beds and in July 1919 the last patients were removed. The hotel was used as a convalescent hospital in the Second World War and later became the headquarters of the British Railways Board, known to railway staff as the Kremlin. It is now a hotel again.

Gallery of the House of Lords, London on 9th November 1929. In addition to his military duties, he excelled at equestrian sports and was a frequent entrant in horse shows. He also served as a judge of Hunter and Jumper divisions. However, his equestrian pursuits led to a number of injuries:

- 19th August 1929 – his horse threw up its head while he was umpiring an exercise at Sarcee Barracks, Calgary. One filling was knocked out and two crowned teeth were bent back at right angles.
- 27th July 1933 – playing for the regimental polo team during the Provincial Tournament at Sarcee Barracks, he collided with another player. His horse was thrown to the ground and he displaced a cartilage in his knee.
- 4th August 1934 – severe muscular strain to the right thigh when his horse refused a jump at Sarcee Barracks.

Currie Barracks, Calgary in the early 1940s.

Promoted lieutenant colonel and assumed command of Lord Strathcona's Horse (Royal Canadians) at Currie Barracks, Calgary on 15th December 1938. He went to England for a six-months course for senior officers at Sheerness, Kent. Promoted brigadier and appointed District Officer Commanding 13th Military District at Alberta, Canada on 10th July 1940. He went back to Britain in 1944 for a two-and-a-half months tour of the Canadian Army, during which he observed many improvements to training techniques, which he implemented on return to Canada. Frederick retired in December 1945 and was Honorary Colonel of Lord Strathcona's Horse 1st September 1958–3rd June 1966. After retirement he travelled to Australia, New Zealand, Ireland and Britain to attend various horse shows and races. He attended the VC Centenary Celebrations at Hyde Park, London on 26th June 1956.

Frederick Harvey died at Colonel Belcher Hospital, Trinity Lodge, Glenmore Trail, Calgary, on 24th August 1980. The funeral was held at St Stephen's Anglican Church, Calgary on 25th August 1980 followed by buried at Union Cemetery, Fort Macleod, Alberta. He is commemorated in a number of other places:

- Mount Harvey (2438m/8000'), in Willmore Park, Alberta, named after him in 1949.
- Sarcee Barracks, Calgary, Alberta was renamed Harvey Barracks in 1981. It closed after Lord Strathcona's Horse (Royal Canadians) moved to Edmonton, Alberta in 1996, where Harvey Building was named after him.
- Victoria Cross obelisk to all Canadian VCs at Military Heritage Park, Barrie, Ontario dedicated by The Princess Royal on 22nd October 2013.
- Named on one of eleven plaques honouring 175 men from overseas awarded the VC for the Great War. The plaques were unveiled by the Senior Minister of State at the Foreign & Commonwealth Office and Minister for Faith and Communities, Baroness Warsi, at a reception at Lancaster House, London on 26th June 2014 attended by

The Duke of Kent and relatives of the VC recipients. The Canadian plaque was unveiled outside the British High Commission in Elgin Street, Ottawa on 10th November 2014 by The Princess Royal in the presence of British High Commissioner Howard Drake, Canadian Minister of Veterans Affairs Julian Fantino and Canadian Chief of the Defence Staff General Thomas J Lawson.

- Two 49 Cent postage stamps in honour of the ninety-four Canadian VCs were issued by Canada Post on 21st October 2004 on the 150th Anniversary of the first Canadian VC's action, Alexander Roberts Dunn.

The VC plaque donated to Canada by the United Kingdom in June 2014.

In addition to the VC and MC, he was awarded the British War Medal 1914–20, Victory Medal 1914–19, Defence Medal, War Medal 1939–45, Canadian Volunteer Service Medal 1939–45 with Maple Leaf clasp, George V Jubilee Medal 1935, George VI Coronation Medal 1937, Elizabeth II Coronation Medal 1953, Elizabeth II Jubilee Medal 1977, Canadian Centennial Medal 1967, Canadian Forces Decoration with two Bars and French Croix de Guerre with Bronze Palm. His VC is held by Lord Strathcona's Horse (Royal Canadians) Museum, Calgary, Alberta. It is unique, being the only VC displayed so that both sides can be seen. His next-of-kin is eligible to receive the Canadian Memorial Cross.

Lord Strathcona's Horse modified its dress to honour its three VC winners. Two scarlet hose flashes are worn for Lieutenants Harvey and Flowerdew and a myrtle green flash for Sergeant Richardson.

The Canadian Volunteer Service Medal was awarded to members of the armed forces who served voluntarily on active service from 3rd September 1939 to 1st March 1947 and completed eighteen months service. In 2001, it was extended to individuals who were not members of the forces, including merchant mariners, Auxiliary Services, Corps of Canadian (Civilian) Fire Fighters who served in UK during the Blitz, Overseas Welfare Workers, Ferry Command pilots and others. In 2003, it was extended to members of the Royal Canadian Mounted Police who served voluntarily during the war. A bar with a maple leaf denotes sixty days service outside Canada. There are three other bars:

- Dieppe Bar for the Dieppe Raid on 19th August 1942.
- Hong Kong Bar for the Battle of Hong Kong 8th 25th December 1941.
- Bomber Command Bar for service in Bomber Command.

4/9720 PRIVATE MICHAEL WILSON HEAVISIDE
15th Battalion, The Durham Light Infantry

Michael Heaviside was born at Station Lane, St Giles, Durham on 28th October 1880. His father, John Wilson Heaviside (1853–1921), was a grocer in 1881, an under keeker (supervisor of hewers) at a colliery in 1901, a coal miner in 1905 and a keeker at a pit in 1911. He married Ann 'Annie' née Fawell (1859–97), a dressmaker, in 1886. The family was living at 4 Station Lane, St Giles, Durham in 1881, 18 Charles Street, Kimblesworth, Co Durham in 1891 and Gas House Cottages, Witton Gilbert, Co Durham in 1901. John was lodging with Eliza Hubber (his daughter Ethel's mother-in-law) and her family at Plawsworth Road, Sacriston, Co Durham in 1911. He was living at 27 William Street, Kimblesworth at the time of his death, registered in the 2nd quarter of 1921 at Durham, with his age being recorded as sixty-one. Michael had three siblings:

- Thomas Remmer Heaviside (1886–1943) was a coal miner. He married Emily Lofthouse (1891–1924) in 1918 and they had a son, Reginald Heaviside in 1920.
- Ethel Heaviside (1882–1946) was a grocer in 1901. She married James Henry Hubber (1878–1944) in 1902. They were living at 233 Fourth Cross Street, Sacriston, Co Durham in 1911. Ethel and James had seven children – John William Gregson Hubber 1903, Ada Lavinia Hubber 1905, Henry Ezra Hubber 1907, Oliver Hubber 1909, Herbert Hubber 1911, Leslie Hubber 1913 and Kenneth Hubber 1926.

The station at Witton Gilbert about the time Michael Heaviside lived there.

- Ann 'Annie' Heaviside (1883–1983) married James Powney (1883–1945), a coal miner, in 1904. They were living at 27 William Street, Kimblesworth, Co Durham in 1911 and had four children – John Powney 1904, Ella Powney 1906, Olive Powney 1910 and Henry Powney 1912.

Michael's paternal grandfather, Thomas Heaviside (c.1829–86), was an artist and photographer. He married Ann 'Annie' née Wilson (c.1831–88) in 1853. They were living at Paradise Lane, Durham St Nicholas in 1861 and at Queen Street, North

Bailey, Co Durham in 1871. In addition to John they had seven other children – Michael Heaviside 1855, Thomas William Heaviside 1857, Mary Annie Heaviside 1859, Frederick Heaviside 1861, James Heaviside 1863, Charles Edward Heaviside 1864 and Ada Lavinia Heaviside 1874. When Thomas died he left £5,939/19/7 to his widow and daughter Mary.

His maternal grandfather, John Fawell (c.1835–72), was a railway porter and by 1871 he was a painter. He married Elizabeth née Atkinson (1839–94) in 1857. The family lived at Bassington Street, Monkwearmouth, Sunderland before moving to Brockley Whins Villa, Boldon, Co Durham. In addition to Annie they had four other children – Mary Fawell c.1863, Stephen Fawell 1864, Margaret Jane Fawell 1866 and John Fawell 1869. By 1891 Elizabeth was a dressmaker living at Turks Head Yard, Gateshead, Co Durham.

Michael was educated at Kimblesworth Colliery School, Co Durham and was employed as a miner at Burnhope Colliery. He enlisted in the Royal Army Medical Corps (11796) and served in South Africa as a stretcher-bearer in the Second Boer War. He also served with No.11 General Hospital at Kimberley and is understood to have returned to Britain after contracting enteric fever. He was awarded the Queen's and King's South Africa Medals. However, a roll of RAMC personnel entitled to the King's South Africa Medal shows that Michael's was not awarded due to being discharged on 5th October 1903 for misconduct. He returned to mining and in 1913 moved to Oswald pit.

Michael Heaviside married Elizabeth née Draper (23rd May 1887–1967) on 30th December 1905 at the Register Office, Lanchester. At the time he was living at West Wood Row, Burnhope and she at 5 Cross Row, Burnhope. They were living at 3 Mavins Buildings, Anderson Square, Sacriston, Co Durham in 1911 and at Front Street, Craghead in 1917.

Elizabeth's father, Matthew Robson Draper (1848–1927) was a coal miner in 1891 and a mason by 1901. He married Isabella née Roddam (1853–1924) in 1869. The family was living at Waggon Hill, Penshaw, Co Durham in 1891, at 5 Cross Row, Lanchester, Co Durham in 1901 and they were boarding with their son-in-law, John Peveller, in 1911. In addition to Elizabeth they had ten other children – Robert Roddam Draper 1870, William Cook Draper 1873, Richard Draper 1874, Joseph Cook Draper 1878, Mary Ann Cook Roddam Draper 1880, Margaret Cook Draper 1882, Isabella Draper 1884, Ellen Roddam Draper 1885, Jane Roddam Draper 1888 and Matthew Robson Draper 1891. Robert Roddam Draper served in the

Front Street, Craghead where the family was living in 1917.

Northumberland Fusiliers during the war (24600). Jane Roddam Draper married Edward Henry Perry who served in 1/6th Northumberland Fusiliers (3508) and was killed on 26th April 1915 (Ypres (Menin Gate) Memorial). Matthew Robson Draper was a colliery banks man above ground in 1911 and enlisted in the Royal Army Medical Corps on 3rd November 1915 (81198). He went to France on 11th July 1916 and was posted to 58th Field Ambulance on 18th July. He was attached to the Royal Garrison Artillery and was awarded the MM, LG 26th May 1917. Having been admitted to 1st Northern General Hospital, Newcastle upon Tyne with suspected scarlet fever 30th November–21st December, he rejoined his unit on 23rd December. He transferred to the Base Depot at Étaples on 7th November 1918 and was discharged to the Class Z Army Reserve at Ripon, Yorkshire on 24th December 1918.

Michael and Elizabeth had fifteen children:

- Richard Draper Heaviside (1906–34) married Georgina Jackson (1908–2005) in 1928 and they had a daughter, Doreen Heaviside in 1929. Georgina had another daughter, Marlene Heaviside, in 1939. She married Wilfred E Ridge in 1944.
- John Wilson Heaviside (1907–75) married Elsie Robinson (1909–76) in 1927. They had two daughters – Sylvia Heaviside 1927 and Margaret E Heaviside 1930 – and were living at 27 Standerton Terrace, Craghead, Co Durham in 1939.
- Annie Heaviside (1909–90) married Walter Gordon (1907–61) in 1930 and they had a daughter, Edna Gordon, in 1931.
- William Draper Heaviside (1911–33).
- Norman Heaviside (1912–90) married Elsie Johnson (1918–99) in 1935. He served in the Army as a company sergeant major.
- Michael Wilson Heaviside (1914–88) married Rhoda Hilland (1915–2001) in 1936 and they had a son, Kenneth Heaviside, in 1938.
- Matthew Draper Heaviside (1915–83) married Annie Johnson (1916–87) in 1937.
- Victor Draper Heaviside (1917–44) served in 1/7th Royal Warwickshire (5114836) and was promoted corporal. He died on 9th August 1944 and is buried in Brouay War Cemetery, Calvados, France (I C 5).
- Thomas Heaviside (1918–19).
- Sarah Heaviside (1919–22).
- James Henry Heaviside (1922–87) married Mary E Ross in 1946 and they had two daughters – Christine Heaviside 1947 and Joan Heaviside 1948.
- Elizabeth Selina Heaviside (1924–87) married Slater Jobson Gourley (1923–95) in 1944 and they had four children – Eileen Gourley 1945, Lancelot J Gourley 1950, Michael Gourley 1953 and Gordon Gourley 1960.
- Margaret Heaviside (born and died 1926).
- Joseph W Heaviside (1929–97) married Joan M Thorne in 1951 and they had two sons – David M Heaviside 1964 and Keith W Heaviside 1965.
- Thomas Heaviside (1930–31).

Shield Row Station, renamed West Stanley in 1934, where Michael Heaviside was greeted by a large cheering crowd on 12th July 1917.

Michael Heaviside being welcomed home on 12th July 1917.

Michael enlisted on 7th September 1914 in 10th Durham Light Infantry and went to France on 10th June 1915. He transferred to 15th Battalion soon after. **Awarded the VC for his actions near Croisilles-les-Fontaine, France on 6th May 1917, LG 8th June 1917.** On 12th July he returned home by train arriving at Shield Row Station to be met by his father, three of his children, local dignitaries and a cheering crowd. He was taken by car to Stanley town hall, escorted by the South Moor Colliery Band, D Company, 1st Battalion Durham

St Thomas's Church, Craghead, where Michael Heaviside is buried, is now a private house.

County Volunteers and Church Lads' Brigade cadets from Beamish. After speeches the column continued through crowded streets to South Moor and Craghead football ground for more speeches and the presentation of a gold watch and chain and war bonds. The VC was presented by the King in the forecourt of Buckingham Palace on 21st July 1917. Michael was discharged on 8th June 1919. He became friends with Ernest Sykes VC.

Michael returned to mining at Craghead. The effects of gas poisoning, coal dust and heavy smoking resulted in his death at his home at 14 Bloemfontein Terrace, Craghead on 26th April 1939. He was buried in an unmarked grave in St Thomas's Churchyard, Craghead as the family could not afford a headstone at the time. Elizabeth Heaviside married John Cooper in 1939. Burial records for St Thomas's Churchyard were subsequently lost in a fire, but the grave was re-located by matching burial numbers to known graves and using a process of elimination for the remainder. A headstone, paid for by the family, the DLI Association and the Light Infantry, was dedicated on 1st November 1999. St Thomas's Church was later converted to a private residence, but pedestrian access is still permitted to the churchyard. Michael is commemorated in a number of other places:

Michael Heaviside's headstone in the former St Thomas's churchyard dedicated on 1st November 1999 (Durham Cow).

- Heaviside Wood, Shafto Terrace, Craghead. A memorial plaque was unveiled on 10th August 2001.
- Heaviside House, Durham Johnston Comprehensive School, Crossgate Moor, Durham. The school's other three houses are also named after Durham Light Infantry VCs – Annand, Kenny and Wakenshaw.
- Heaviside Place, Durham, Co Durham.
- Sacriston Working Men's Club roll of honour records the names of 255 men who served including sixteen who were killed. Michael Heaviside is recorded as Heavisides. In addition to his VC, the other men earned four DCMs, eight MMs and two MSMs.
- A commemorative stone honouring the eleven Durham Light Infantry soldiers awarded the VC was unveiled in the grounds of the Durham Light Infantry Museum on 8th September 2001 by Brigadier Robin MacGregor-Oakford MC. The stone was funded by the Durham Light Infantry veterans' group, 'The Faithful Inkerman Dinner Club'. The ceremony was attended by the Regiment's sole surviving VC holder, Captain Richard Annand.

In addition to the VC he was awarded the Queen's South Africa Medal 1899–1902 with three clasps (Cape Colony, Orange Free State and Transvaal), King's South Africa Medal 1901–02 with two clasps (South Africa 1901 and South Africa 1902), 1914–15 Star, British War Medal 1914–20, Victory Medal 1914–19 and George VI Coronation Medal 1937. His Victory Medal ribbon carries a Mentioned-in-Despatches Oakleaf, but no trace of it has been found in the London Gazette. On 12th July 1957 his son, CSM Norman Heaviside, presented the medals to the Durham Light Infantry, watched by Michael's widow and over thirty other members of the family. The medals are held at the Durham Light Infantry Museum, Aykley Heads, Framwell Gate, Durham.

CAPTAIN ARTHUR HENDERSON
4th attached 2nd Battalion, Princess Louise's (Argyll & Sutherland Highlanders)

Arthur Henderson was born at 18 Greenhill Road, Paisley, Renfrewshire, Scotland on 6th May 1893. His father, George Henderson (1853–1921), was a building contractor and magistrate, often referred to as Mr Baillie Henderson. He married Elizabeth née Purdie (1858–97) on 29th December 1882 at Lessuddon, St Boswells, Roxburghshire. She was working as a domestic maid at 16 Carlton Terrace, South Leith, Edinburgh, Midlothian in 1881. The family was living at 93 Grove Street, Glasgow, Lanarkshire in 1885 and at 21 Oakshaw Street, Paisley, Renfrewshire in 1901. George married Elizabeth Wilkins (1870–1943), a medical nurse, on 8th March 1906 at the Windsor Hotel, Glasgow. They were living at Egnal, 9 Riccartsbar Avenue, Paisley in 1911. George was awarded the OBE for his work as Chairman of the Paisley War Savings Committee, LG 30th March 1920. Arthur had six siblings:

- John George Henderson (1883–1917) was educated at Ferguslie School and the John Neilson Institution in Paisley. He worked in the building trade with his father as an apprentice mason before emigrating in 1911 to Lytton, British Columbia, Canada. He was employed in the Civil Engineering Department of the Canadian Northern Pacific Railway. George enlisted as a private in 172nd Battalion (Rocky Mountain Rangers) (687891) at Lytton on 24th February 1916 and carried out basic training at Vernon, British Columbia. He went to France on 17th January 1917 with 2nd Canadian Mounted Rifles and was listed as missing in action on 9th April 1917 near La Folie Farm during the attack on Vimy Ridge. His body was never recovered and he is commemorated on the Canadian National Vimy Memorial, France as George Henderson.
- Alexander Purdie Henderson (1888–96).
- William Purdie Henderson (1889–91).
- Agnes Imery Henderson (1885–c.1978) married Robert Martin Graham (1882–1927), a furniture merchant, in 1913. They lived at 10 Stewarton Street, Wishaw, Lanarkshire.
- Elizabeth Purdie Henderson (1895–1920) was a clerk. She contracted tuberculosis and died at Grampian Sanatorium, Kingussie, Inverness-shire on 20th September 1920.
- Ellen Miller Henderson (1908–47).

Arthur's paternal grandfather, John Henderson (c.1795–1869), was a fisherman and farmer. He married Margaret Grant and they had three children – John Henderson 1823, Ann Henderson 1827 and Alexander Henderson 1831. He married Arthur's grandmother, Helen née Miller (1820–65) in 1840. In addition to George they had eight other children – Margaret Grant Henderson 1841, Louisina 'Susan' Miller Henderson (1843–1914), Elizabeth Henderson c.1845, Hugh Sutherland Henderson 1846, Georgina Henderson 1848, Janet 'Jessie' Henderson c.1852, John Henderson 1856 and Helen Henderson 1858. Louisina married Sinclair Forbes (1845–1927) in 1871. He was a sergeant in the 93rd Highlanders in 1871. He was commissioned on 27th August 1884 and retired from the Argyll & Sutherland Highlanders on 27th February 1895. He was a captain in the Army Service Corps in 1901 and was appointed honorary captain on 18th October 1902. They were living at North Camp, Farnborough, Hampshire in 1891 and at 6 Union Road, Inverness in 1901.

Arthur's maternal grandfather, Alexander Purdie (c.1813–1904), was gamekeeper to Lord Polwarth in 1853. He married Agnes née Imery (c.1825–93) in 1852. By 1881 Alexander was a salmon fisherman, living with his family at Grosvenor Place, St Boswells, Roxburghshire. In addition to Elizabeth they had five other children – Margaret Purdie 1853, William Purdie 1857, Mary Agnes Purdie 1860, Wilhelmina Purdie 1863 and Alexander Purdie 1866.

Arthur was educated at John Neilson Institution, Paisley. He was a fine cricketer, playing for Ferguslie Cricket Club. After school he was employed as an accountant and stockbroker by Messrs R Easton & Co of Glasgow. He enlisted in 1/6th Argyll & Sutherland Highlanders on 2nd September 1914 (3448) and served in 1 Platoon, A Company with William Davidson Bissett, who was awarded the VC in 1918. Arthur was described as 5′ 7″ tall, weighing 158 lbs, with dark complexion, brown eyes and his religious denomination was Presbyterian. He was commissioned into 3/6th Argyll & Sutherland Highlanders on 5th April 1915, served with 4th Battalion and was attached to 2nd Battalion in France from 1st October. Appointed acting captain 19th August 1916.

Awarded the MC for his actions during the Battle of the Somme leading his company in an attack with great courage and determination, advancing our line and consolidating the position won with great skill, LG 10th January 1917. This action was probably on 27th–28th August

The John Neilson Institution was set up in 1852, initially for boys who had lived in Paisley for three years and whose parents were either poor or dead. By 1968 it had outgrown its premises and moved to Millarston as the John Neilson High School. The old building, known locally as the porridge bowl, was converted into flats.

1916. At 10 p.m. on the 27th, Arthur led A Company in an attack on Pommiers Redoubt, but was driven off. Next day he tried again and, despite a counterattack, he took the objective and held it. In November, Arthur and his brother George arrived in Paisley on leave within an hour of each other, having not met since 1911.

Awarded the VC for his actions at Fontaine-lès-Croisilles, France on 23rd April 1917, LG 5th July 1917. As he never married, the VC and MC were presented to his father by the King outside Buckingham Palace on 21st July 1917. Arthur was killed during his VC action on 24th April 1917 and is buried in Cojeul British Cemetery, St Martin-sur-Cojeul, France (B 61). He is also commemorated in a number of other places:

William Davidson Bissett VC, who served in 1/6th Argyll & Sutherland Highlanders with Arthur.

• Named with his brother George on a memorial at John Neilson Institution, Paisley unveiled on 30th November 1932 by the Earl of Home. The memorial consists of a bronze plaque and a book of remembrance recording the names of 700 former pupils and staff who served in the First World War, of whom about a hundred died.
• Named with his brother George on the roll of honour at Oakshaw West United Free Church, Paisley. In 1972, Oakshaw West Church united with South Parish Church to form St Luke's Church of Scotland.
• Memorial in the clubhouse at Ferguslie Cricket Club, MeikIeriggs, Corsebar Road, Paisley.
• Memorial in the tearoom of drapers Robert Cochran & Sons (later House of Fraser). The tearoom was once run by two female relatives who owned his medals and sold them to a member of the Scottish Military Collectors Society c.1966.
• Memorial to the five VCs from Paisley at Hawkhead Cemetery, Paisley, Renfrewshire unveiled on 26th June 2007 by two local children and Second World War sailor, Joe McGhee. About 800 people,

Arthur Henderson's grave in Cojeul British Cemetery, St Martin-sur-Cojeul. The grave of Horace Waller VC is in the row behind.

including family members, attended the ceremony during which nine wreaths were laid and each family released a dove. The other VCs are Samuel Evans, John Hannah, Hugh McIver and James McKechnie.

The memorial to Paisley's five VCs at Hawkhead Cemetery.

The roll of honour of Oakshaw West United Free Church, Paisley includes Arthur and his brother George.

In addition to the VC and MC, he was awarded the 1914–15 Star, British War Medal 1914–20 and Victory Medal 1914–19. His medals were sold at a Christie's auction on 4th July 1978 for £8,200, a world record at the time. On 27th November 1990 they were sold again by Christie's for £14,000 to Michael Ashcroft and are displayed in the Lord Ashcroft Gallery of the Imperial War Museum. The Michael Ashcroft Trust held an exhibition of eighteen VC groups, including Arthur Henderson's, at the Rugby Football Union Museum, Twickenham, London 16th–20th September 2008. The exhibition coincided with a rugby match on behalf of the charity 'Help for Heroes' between England Old 'Uns' and The Rest of the World Old 'Uns' on 20th September.

CAPTAIN DAVID PHILIP HIRSCH
1/4th Battalion, Alexandra, Princess of Wales's Own (Yorkshire Regiment)

Philip or 'Pip' Hirsch as he was known within his family was born at Leeds, Yorkshire on 28th December 1896. His father, Harry Hirsch (1871–1951), was born at Dundee, Forfarshire, Scotland and entered the firm of Messrs Julius Cohen & Josephy, wool merchants, in 1887. Harry married Edith née Brindley (1869–1946), who was distantly related to James Brindley, the canal builder, in 1895 at Leeds. The family lived at various addresses in and around Leeds – 4 Woodhouse Cliff, Park Side at Harehills, Weetwood Grove and High Leas at Adel. Harry eventually gained a principal interest in Messrs Julius Cohen & Josephy with a relative, Ernest Hermann Josephy. The firm's head office was at 8 Broad Street, Bradford and it had a woollen mill at Almonte, Ontario, Canada in addition to warehouses in

Toronto, at Boston, Massachusetts and in Berlin. The mill was destroyed by fire in September 1923. On 31st December 1933 the firm became Hirsch & Son, following Josephy's retirement. Harry was also in another business partnership with Ernest Josephy, known as Top Makers of Manor Row, Bradford, along with Frank Hirsch and Harold Kenningham. It was dissolved by effluxion of time from 15th June 1932. Its head office was at 6 Broad Street, Bradford. Harry was a member of the Board of Governors of Leeds Maternity Hospital and the Mill Hill Unitarian Church, Leeds. He founded the firm of Hirsch, Son & Rhodes, wool and yarn export merchants, in 1935 (dissolved 2008) and both he and his son Frank were well-known Yorkshire Shorthorn cattle breeders. Harry worked as a volunteer for the Ministry of Food during the Second World War. Late on 1st June 1946 Harry and Edith's car hit an abandoned lorry near Catchem Corner on the Otley–Pateley Bridge road. Edith suffered a fractured skull and died

Philip's mother, Edith née Brindley, was distantly related to James Brindley (1716–72) the engineer and canal builder. Amongst his work was the Bridgewater Canal opened in 1761, which includes the Barton Aqueduct, the Trent & Mersey Canal, the Staffordshire & Worcestershire Canal, the Coventry Canal, the Oxford Canal and others totalling 587 kms of waterways.

shortly afterwards in hospital. The lorry was stolen from haulage contractor Jack Robinson in Leeds and was abandoned in the middle of the road without lights. A verdict of death by misadventure was recorded at the inquest by the York District Coroner on 18th June. Harry left £142,883/6/- in his will. Philip had two siblings:

• Frank Brindley Hirsch (1898–1995) applied for a commission in 2/4th Yorkshire on 6th March 1916, but was rejected due to his age. He enlisted in 4th (Reserve) Cameron Highlanders at Ripon, Yorkshire on 11th May (4711) and applied again for a commission on 1st August. He went to France on 2nd August and transferred to 6th Battalion on 8th September (S/40438). Frank was recommended for a commission in 4th Yorkshire on 15th September, but received a gunshot wound to the right thigh that day. He was eventually evacuated to England on 20th November and treated at 2nd Northern General Hospital, Leeds, usually known as Beckett Park Hospital. He was discharged on 31st May 1917 no longer physically fit for war service and awarded the Silver War Badge (No.197658). A medical board at Cambridge on 12th December 1917 found the gunshot wound had shortened his right leg by 1¼″ and there was chronic flexion of the right knee joint. As a result he was graded to Category BII (garrison duty). Despite his physical condition he was sent to an officer cadet school and was commissioned in 1/5th Durham Light Infantry on 8th September 1918. He went to France in October to join 13th Durham Light Infantry. While he was on leave in England 7th–14th

February 1919 he asked for a medical board. Millbank Hospital in London issued a certificate that he was unfit to return and the medical board was convened at 2nd Northern General Hospital, Leeds on 24th February. It recommended he be permitted to resign his commission. As a result he was posted to the held strength of 3rd Durham Light Infantry at South Shields on 27th February and was sent home until he relinquished his commission on 23rd March on account of ill-health caused by wounds. Frank was examined by the Yorkshire Region Medical Board in Leeds on 6th January 1920 and his invalidity was assessed to be 30% and permanent. Frank

Mill Hill Unitarian Church, Leeds. Although there has been a Unitarian chapel in Leeds City Square since 1674, this building dates from 1848. Joseph Priestley (1733–1804) was the minister 1767–73. He is usually credited with the discovery of oxygen and a number of other gases including carbon monoxide. He also discovered the carbon cycle, invented the rubber pencil eraser and artificially carbonated water, which was taken up commercially by Johann Jacob Schweppe.

married Amy Helen Woodrow Megson (1899–1988) in 1921 at Cambridge. Her father, Edmund Victor Megson, was a Professor of Music. Frank became a partner in his father's firm, Hirsch & Son, and lived at Low Hall, Dacre, Yorkshire. He was commissioned in the Green Howards (144988) on a Regular Army Emergency Commission on 30th August 1940 and was promoted war substantive captain on 26th December 1942. He was released to the Unemployed List as an honorary major in late 1945, having served in Italy. Frank was a prominent local figure, providing a playing field, serving as a councilor and founding the Young Farmers' Club. Amy provided a home for a Canadian Battle of Britain pilot whose face was severely burned in 1941. Frank and Amy had three children:

- Dorothy B Hirsch (born 1922) married Geoffrey D Kilpin in 1947 and they had at least one child, Philip Kilpin.
- David Phillip Hirsch (1926–45) served as an officer cadet in the Green Howards (14494982) in India, where he died on 10th June 1945 and is buried at Kirkee War Cemetery, India (8 A 9).
- Pamela A Hirsch (born 1929) married Lionel B Holliday in 1955 and they had five children – Venetia A Holliday 1957, Giles PL Holliday 1959, twins Lionel CB and Thomas B Holliday 1962 and Phillip Brook Holliday 1966.
• Margery B Hirsch (1900–62) emigrated to Massachusetts, USA, where she married Frederick William Appleyard. They were living at 56 Yale Street, Winchester in

2nd Northern General Hospital, Leeds, usually known as Beckett Park Hospital, was based in a teacher training college built in 1913. It treated 57,200 soldiers between 1914 and 1918 and was used as a hospital again in the Second World War. It is now part of Leeds Beckett University.

July 1924. She returned to Britain and was living at Ghyll Bank, Gill Bank Road, Middleton, Ilkley, Yorkshire. She died on 23rd June 1962 leaving £72,843/1/8 to her husband and her brother Frank.

Philip's paternal grandfather, Hermann Anselm Hirsch (1820–87), was born at Teterow, Mecklenburg, Germany and was Jewish. He was a linen merchant moving frequently between Germany and Britain from 1839 to 1846. He married Elizabeth 'Betsy/Betty' née High (c.1837–1912) in 1863. She was born at Kinghorn, Fife, Scotland. The family was living at Daisy Bank Road, Moss Side, Lancashire in 1871 and at 3 Roundhay Terrace, Leeds, Yorkshire in 1881, by when he was a teacher of languages. Elizabeth was living with her children at 3 Tanfield Place, Leeds, Yorkshire in 1891. In addition to Harry they had seven other children all born at Dundee, Scotland – Albert Hirsch 1864, Bernard William Hirsch 1865, William Paul Hirsch 1868, Elizabeth Mary Hirsch 1869, David Hirsch 1872, Charles Otto Hirsch 1874 and Hermann Hirsch 1876.

Philip's maternal grandfather, Richard Prince Brindley (1842–1925) was a footman

Frank Hirsch's home at Low Hall, Dacre, Yorkshire.

56 Yale Street, Winchester, Massachusetts was built in 1923. Margery Hirsch lived there, having married Frederick William Appleyard.

in 1861 at the home of Benjamin Rigby Murray, cotton spinner. He married Fanny née Laverack (1843–1909) in 1868. Richard was the publican of the White Swan, Call Lane, Leeds in 1871 and founded RP Brindley & Co Ltd, wine and spirit merchants of Claypit Lane, Leeds c.1875. The family was living at Victoria Road, Headingley, Yorkshire in 1881 and at 7 St John's Terrace, Leeds in 1891. By 1911 Richard was a corn merchant living at 33 Maldon Road, Wallington, Croydon, Surrey. He was President of the Yorkshire Bottler's Association and was a member of the North-West Ward on the City Council. He was also a Freemason. At the time of his death he was living at 21 White Rock, Hastings, Sussex. In addition to Edith they had four other children – Alice Brindley 1874, Bessie Brindley 1879, Kate Brindley 1883 and Richard Brindley 1884. He served as a gunner in D Battery, 311th Brigade RFA (781208) and was killed in action on 3rd June 1917. He is buried in St Quentin Cabaret Military Cemetery (II J 2).

Philip was educated at Willaston School, London Road, Nantwich, Cheshire from 1908, where he was the head boy in his final year. He was a talented athlete, holding the record for the mile and as a cricketer he took more wickets for the school than any previous bowler. He won an open exhibition in modern history for Worcester College Oxford, but left in December 1914 and joined Leeds University OTC.

Philip was commissioned into 11th West Yorkshire on 7th April 1915 and later served in 13th (Reserve) Battalion. He transferred to 1/4th Yorkshire on 22nd September 1915 and attended a machine gun course before going to France in April 1916. He was wounded in September at Eaucourt l'Abbaye while commanding the Battalion's machine gun section. Promoted temporary lieutenant 23rd September and acting captain on assuming command of Y Company on 16th November. Promoted temporary captain March 1917.

Mentioned in Sir Douglas Haig's Despatch dated 9th April 1917, LG 22nd May 1917. Awarded the VC for his actions near Wancourt, France on 23rd April 1917, LG 14th June 1917. He was killed during his VC action and is commemorated on the Arras Memorial. As he never married, the VC was presented to his parents by the King outside Buckingham Palace on 21st July 1917. Although he was killed in April 1917, he continued to appear in the Army List under the West Yorkshire Regiment and in June 1918 his VC was included. Philip Hirsch is commemorated in a number of other places:

• Hirsch Close, Nantwich, Cheshire.
• Captain David Hirsch VC swimming pool at Willaston School, London Road, Nantwich, Cheshire was endowed, and a dedication plaque was unveiled, by his parents in 1924. The School closed in 1937 and became St Joseph's RC College until 1987, when it became Elim Bible College. It was renamed Regents Theological College in 1996 and in 2009 became a hostel for Reaseheath College.
• Plaque outside Leeds City Art Gallery, Leeds, Yorkshire.

- A seat presented to the Wood and Garnett Almshouse Charity by Nantwich Town Council outside the almshouse in Wall Lane.
- Plaque at Victoria Gardens, Leeds Garden of Rest, The Headrow, Leeds commemorating all Leeds VCs.
- Named on the Mill Hill Chapel war memorial with his nephew, David P Hirsch.
- A bedroom at the Florence Nightingale Men's Memorial Home, Great Hucklow, Derbyshire

Philip Hirsch's name on the Arras Memorial.

was opened in his honour by his father on 17th May 1931. It later became a holiday and conference centre.
- A memorial cross was placed near where he was killed, but over the years it deteriorated. On 23rd April 2012, ninety-five years after he died, a new cross, similar in design to the original, was placed at Kestrel Copse by his niece, Mrs P Holliday and his great-nephew, Jarvis Browning. It was replaced by a granite memorial on 18th October 2015, which will not be dedicated formally until April 1917.

In addition to the VC he was awarded the British War Medal 1914–20 and Victory Medal 1914–19 with Mentioned-in-Despatches Oakleaf. The medals passed to his brother, Frank, on the death of their father in

The granite memorial to Philip Hirsch erected on 18th October 2015 at the corner of Kestrel Copse alongside the D38. It replaced a replica of the original iron memorial placed there by some of the men who were with him during the VC action. It is outside 1/4th Yorkshire's area, but the corner of Kestrel Copse was probably chosen because it is accessible and overlooks the general area of the VC action about 700m away. The inset top right shows the detail of the new memorial and top left the original iron memorial (Tony Goddard).

Philip and his nephew, David P Hirsch, are both named on the Mill Hill Chapel war memorial.

1951. Frank owned them until his death, when they passed to his grandson, Philip D Kilpin of Elgin, South Africa. He presented them on loan to the Green Howards Museum, Trinity Church Square, Richmond, Yorkshire in September 1995.

2445 CORPORAL GEORGE JULIAN HOWELL
1st Australian Infantry Battalion AIF

George Howell, known as 'Snowy' because of his blue eyes and blond hair, was born on 19th (also seen as 21st and 23rd) November 1893 at Enfield, New South Wales, Australia. His father, Francis 'Frank' John Howell (1857–1923), was born in Brighton, Sussex, England. He was a carpenter and emigrated to New South Wales with his parents in 1874. Frank enlisted in the AIF on 16th July 1915 'for Home Duty only' and was discharged on 30th December as 'unlikely to become an efficient soldier'. He re-enlisted in 54th Infantry Battalion (2666) on 16th June 1916 as Frank Howell, giving his age as forty-three, and sailed for Britain on HMAT *Ceramic* from Sydney on 7th October. He joined his unit in France, sailing from Folkestone, Kent on *Princess Victoria* on 21st December. His true age was eventually discovered and he was evacuated to England on 18th July 1917 and to Australia on 27th August, where he was discharged on 22nd November. Frank married Martha née Sweeny (1858–1926) in 1881 in Sydney and they lived at 53 Burnett Street, Redfern. Martha was living in Boyle Street, Enfield in 1916 and at Valo, Boyle Street, Enfield when she died in 1926. Snowy had seven siblings:

- Frederick Francis Howell (1882–1965) was a carpenter. He enlisted in 1st Pioneers (1860) on 19th January 1916 and sailed for Britain on HMAT *Ceramic* from Sydney on 14th April. He returned to Australia on 12th June 1919 and was discharged on 11th September. Frederick married Florence May Dobbs (1883–1965) in 1921 and they lived at Delwood, Arthur Street, Homebush, New South Wales. By 1936 they had moved to 20 Arthur Street, Homebush and to 11 Bayview Street, Concord by 1965. They had a son, Neville Walden Howell, born and died in 1922.
- Valentine John Howell (1884–1918) was a plumber. He enlisted in 18th Battalion (116) on 6th April 1915 and sailed for Egypt on HMAT *Ceramic* from Sydney on

Valentine Howell's grave in Ribemont Communal Cemetery Extension.

25th June. He was promoted lance corporal and was killed in action on 31st May 1918 (Ribemont Communal Cemetery Extension, France – IV K 6).

- Henry William Howell (1887–88).
- Clarice May Howell (1889–1940) married Robert Thomson (1893–1956), a plasterer, in 1922. They lived at Kerri Muir, Dunmore Street, Croydon Park, New South Wales and had three children. He enlisted on 24th January 1916 (2760), was posted to 30th Battalion and was awarded the MM for his actions at Ypres, Belgium on 4th–6th October 1917. He was wounded by a gunshot to the right elbow on 14th April 1918 and returned to Australia on 11th June 1919 for discharge.
- Frank Hall Howell (1891–1975) was a carpenter. He married Christina Elizabeth Maders (1891–1974) in 1915. They lived at Melnotte, 56 Janet Street, Drummoyne. They had five children including:
  - Valerie Anne Howell (1918–70) married Dudley Michael Rush Hellmrich (1919–83) in 1943 and they had two children. He served in 19th Line of Communication Signals during the Second World War, reaching the rank of sergeant and was discharged on 20th August 1945.
  - Robert Wilfred Howell (1920–2001) enlisted in the Royal Australian Air Force on 26th May 1942 (65212) and was posted to No.3 Operational Training Unit as a leading aircraftman before being discharged on 10th May 1945. He married in 1942 and had five children.
- Robert Hugh Howell (1896–1945) married Dulcie Louise Fletcher (1893–1977) in 1927. They lived at Lurnea, Clement Street, Enfield and had a daughter, Doreen Betty Howell in 1930.
- Walter Roy Howell (1903–79) was a carpenter. He married Johanna Elizabeth Olsen (1903–85) in 1926. They were living at 42 Boyle Street, Enfield in 1928, at 54 Boyle Street, Enfield in 1932, 53 William Street, Hornsby in 1943, 95 Taylor Street, Lakemba in 1949 and 335 Stacey Street, Bankstown in 1954. They had four children.

Snowy's paternal grandfather, John Reform Howell (c.1830–81), a carpenter and upholsterer, was born at Brighton, Sussex. He married Catherine née Prigg (born 1827) in 1854 at St Mary, Lambeth, London. Catherine was born at St John's, Newfoundland, daughter of Sergeant John Prigg. They were living at Croydon Road, Streatham, London in 1861 and in a cottage on Tooting Common, Streatham in 1871. They emigrated to Australia on the *Tyburnia*, arriving on 5th October 1874. In addition to John they had five other children, all born

SV *Tyburnia* was built by Alexander Stephen & Sons in Glasgow in 1857.

Albany Barracks, originally Parkhurst Barracks, was completed in 1798. The barracks were decommissioned in the early 1960s and the site is now Albany Prison. Snowy's grandfather, Samuel Aird Sweeny, was born at the barracks in 1819.

Snowy's grandfather, Samuel Aird Sweeny, married Mary Ann Hall at Manchester Cathedral in 1844.

Burwood Public School, Sydney was attended by Snowy Howell.

in London – Sarah Elizabeth Howell 1855, Louisa Mary Ann A Howell 1859, Eliza Lilian Howell 1862, Rose Howell 1864 and Edith Ellen Howell 1869.

His maternal grandfather, Samuel Aird Sweeny (also seen as Sweeney) (1819–65), was born at Albany Barracks, Isle of Wight, Hampshire. He was a railway clerk in 1841 living at Sowerby Bridge, Yorkshire before moving to 9 Spring Gardens, Doncaster, Yorkshire by 1851. He married Mary Ann née Hall (c.1824–1914) in 1844 at Manchester Cathedral, Lancashire. She was born at Sidmouth, Devon. They emigrated to Australia, leaving Liverpool on 21st April 1855 on the *Exodus*, arriving at Sydney on 26th July. Samuel became a police constable in the New South Wales Police Force. He was promoted acting inspector on 2nd December 1855 and retired on 2nd September 1858. They moved to Darlinghurst, New South Wales where he worked as a collector. In 1871 Mary was living at 58 Great Barcom Street, Darlinghurst. By 1873 she was at 62 Great Barcom Street, Darlinghurst, by 1879 at Selwyn Street, Paddington and at Elveslea, Dunmore Street, Croydon at the time of her death in 1914. In addition to Martha they had six other children – Samuel George Valentine Sweeny 1845, Julianna Sweeny 1848, Aird Sweeny 1850 (served in the Surry Hills Volunteer Rifles), Frederick Sweeny 1853, William Sweeny 1855 and Mary Ann Sweeny 1861.

Snowy was educated at Croydon Park Public School, Sydney and Burwood Public School, Sydney. He became a bricklayer and builder after completing an apprenticeship at Campsie, near Enfield, where he played rugby for Enfield Federals Club.

Snowy enlisted in Sydney on 3rd June 1915. He was described as 5′ 7″ tall, weighing

The camp at Tel El Kebir.

SS *Huntsgreen* (9060 tons) was originally a German ship, the *Derflinger*, built in Danzig in 1907 for North German Lloyd, Bremen. In 1914 she was captured at Port Said, renamed *Huntsgreen* and operated as a troopship. She returned to North German Lloyd in 1923 and resumed the Bremen–New York route. She returned to the Far East service in 1928 and in 1932 was scrapped at Bremerhaven.

147 lbs, with sandy hair, blue eyes and his religious denomination was Church of England. He was posted to Liverpool, near Sydney and embarked there for the Middle East with 7th Reinforcement Group for 1st Battalion on HMAT A67 *Orsova* on 14th July. He disembarked at Alexandria, Egypt and went on to Heliopolis. He served with 1st Battalion at Gallipoli from 1st November until returning to Alexandria aboard SS *Huntsgreen* and on to Tel El Kebir on 28th December. He was charged with being absent without leave 8th–12th January 1916 and was awarded seven days Field Punishment No.2 and forfeited five days pay.

SS *Ivernia* was built by Swan Hunter on the Tyne in 1899 for Cunard. In August 1914 she was hired as a troop ship. In 1916, William Thomas Turner, former captain of RMS *Lusitania*, took command. On 1st January 1917, while carrying 2,400 troops from Marseilles to Alexandria, she was torpedoed by UB-47 in the Kythira Strait off Greece with the loss of 120 lives. (Municipal Archives of Trondheim)

He embarked at Alexandria for Marseilles, France on HMT *Invernia* on 22nd March 1916 and attended a course at the Trench Mortar School, Wallon-Cappel near Hazebrouck 5th–11th April. Snowy was again absent without leave on 18th May and was wounded by a gunshot to the back at Pozières on 22nd July. Having been evacuated to No.44 Casualty Clearing Station on 23rd July, he was transferred to 27th Ambulance Train next day for No.23 General Hospital, Étaples. He was evacuated to England via Le Havre for 3rd Northern General Hospital, Sheffield, Yorkshire on 2nd August and returned to France on 11th November. He was promoted lance corporal on 10th December and was posted to the

3rd Northern General Hospital had its headquarters at Collegiate Hall, Ecclesall Road in Sheffield and took over numerous buildings across the city. At full capacity it had over 1,400 beds.

Australian soldiers on the beach at Weymouth. An ANZAC Depot was set up there in May 1915 based around Monte Video House in Chickerell, two miles from the town. The New Zealand Depot moved to Hornchurch, Essex in April 1916 and Weymouth became No.2 AIF Command Depot. Recovering wounded were sent there when not expected to be fit for six months. Most soldiers repatriated to Australia as a result of their wounds passed through Weymouth, including Snowy Howell. The Depot expanded to three camps – Monte Video, Westham and Littlemoor. The former still exists as Wyke Regis Training Camp.

Snowy Howell receives his VC and MM from the King in the Forecourt of Buckingham Palace on 21st July 1917.

Divisional School of Instruction 29th December–28th January 1917. Promoted corporal 6th February.

Awarded the MM for his actions at Demicourt on 9th April when he led his rifle bombing section in an attack. His section was held up on several occasions by machine gun fire, and on each occasion he adopted sound offensive tactics and good use of his weapons and continued to advance, LG 26th May 1917. Awarded the VC for his actions at Bullecourt on 6th May 1917, LG 27th June 1917. The VC and MM were presented by the King at Buckingham Palace on 21st July 1917. Snowy's father was granted leave to attend the investiture, but was refused admittance to the buffet lunch. Snowy was granted leave 21st September– 5th October at Weymouth, Dorset and embarked for Australia on HMAT A35 *Berrima* on 31st October. He disembarked at

St Stephen's Presbyterian Church, Philip Street, Sydney where Snowy Howell married Sarah 'Sadie' Lillian Yates in 1919. The church was demolished in the 1930s.

Melbourne, Victoria on 30th December and was discharged on 5th June 1918 in Sydney.

Snowy Howell married Sarah 'Sadie' Lillian Yates (23rd August 1892–22nd September 1953), a nurse who had served in Fiji, at St Stephen's Presbyterian Church, Philip Street, Sydney on 1st March 1919. They lived at various addresses in New South Wales:

   1930 – 9 Dans Avenue, Coogee, Amiens Flats.
   1933 – 14 Boambillee Avenue, Vaucluse.
   1936 – Bella Vista, Moira Crescent, Coogee.
   1937 – 436 Park Road, Paddington.
   1939 – 106 Brook Street, Coogee.
   7 Alfreda Street, Coogee.

They had a daughter, Norma Lillian Howell (died 2001), who married Robert George Baker in 1946 at Perth, Western Australia. They had two sons – Ronald Robert Baker and Norman George Baker. Robert died in 1965 and Norma married Peter Tanner.

Sadie's father, Joseph George Yates (1869–1900), was born at Tambaroora, New South Wales. He married Hanna Maria née Gibbons (1865–1910), born at Darlinghurst, New South Wales, in 1887. In addition to Sadie they had four children – Joseph George Yates 1888, Francis Halliday Yates 1890, Charles Bertram Yates 1895 and Harry Neville Yates 1900.

Post war Snowy became a journalist, working on the advertising staff at Smith's Newspapers and later at the Bulletin Newspaper Pty Ltd. By 1933 he was the New South Wales representative for the Brisbane Daily Standard and The Worker.

An Anzac Dinner on 23rd April 1927, hosted by Lieutenant General Sir John Monash GCMG KCB VD, was attended by twenty-three VCs, but for an unknown reason the Duke of York was not invited. When Snowy Howell responded to the toast to the VCs proposed by Monash, he remarked, *If I were Prime Minister of Australia, there is one thing I would do. When any Royal personage was here, I would say to him, 'Monash and the Diggers are having a little dinner tonight. Come along old chap'*. Two days later Snowy took part in the Anzac commemoration service at the Exhibition Building, Melbourne, Victoria in the presence of the Duke of York. In the march past the VCs conceded pride of place to blinded soldiers who insisted on marching.

He attended the first AIF Re-Union Dinner at Sydney Town Hall on 8th August 1928 to celebrate the tenth anniversary of the commencement of 'The Big Push' together with seven other VCs. In November 1929 he was entertained at a luncheon at Government House by the Governor of Australia, Sir Dudley de Chair, and his wife, together with thirteen other VCs. On 7th November 1929, he was Initiated into Freemasonry, in Coogee Lodge No.322. He was affiliated with Literature Lodge No.500 and was Junior Warden 1934–35. Snowy attended the wedding of Walter Ernest Brown VC DCM at Christ Church, Bexley, New South Wales on 4th June 1932 together with seven other VCs.

Snowy re-enlisted at Paddington, New South Wales on 14th October 1939 (N69450) and was appointed orderly room sergeant of 2nd Garrison Battalion on 23rd October. He reported sick with an old bayonet wound at Randwick Hospital, Sydney on 11th December and was discharged as a sole supporter of dependants on 17th December. It was not long before he was in uniform again. He re-enlisted on 25th June 1940 at Paddington (N75435), understating his age by three years. He was posted to Headquarters Eastern Command, Victoria Barracks, Paddington and promoted corporal on 16th October. He was later promoted staff sergeant and was discharged on 12th February 1941. During this period Snowy published a book, *ANZAC DAY, 1940 – ANZACS & ARABS*. He joined the United States Army Services of Supply, South West Pacific Area, Transportation Corps as a deckhand on 5th September 1944 and served aboard tug ST*131*. She travelled from Hollandia to San Pedro Bay, Philippines towing two barges of high-octane fuel in October–November 1944, arriving three days after the initial landings on Leyte at the beginning of the campaign to liberate the islands from Japanese occupation. During the journey she survived an attack by suicide bombers and a monsoon.

Snowy Howell in 1956 (State Library of Western Australia).

Snowy attended the funerals of William Currey VC at St Stephen's Church, Macquarie Street, Sydney on 3rd May 1948 and Thomas Bede Kenny VC at Mary Immaculate Church, Waverley, New South Wales on 17th April 1953. After his wife died in 1953, Snowy lived with his daughter at Applecross, Perth, Western Australia, but about 1960 went to Gunyidi, Western Australia, a rail siding with a very small population. He assisted in the woolsheds by cooking, sweeping and general odd jobs. The isolation was not to his liking and he often travelled to Perth before moving back there about 1962. He attended the VC Centenary Celebrations at Hyde Park, London on 26th June 1956, travelling on SS *Orcades* with other Australian VCs.

Snowy Howell died at the Repatriation Hospital, Hollywood, Perth, Western Australia on 23rd December 1964 and was cremated at Karrakatta Crematorium, Perth on 29th December. A commemorative plaque was placed on the Western Australian Garden of Remembrance Memorial Wall 1 Row I. He is commemorated in a number of other places:

- Howell Place, Gowrie, Canberra, Australian Capital Territory.
- Howell Club, Randwick Barracks, Avoca Street, Randwick, New South Wales.
- Howell Avenue, Matraville, Randwick Shire, New South Wales.
- Howell Street, Crib Point, Melbourne, Victoria.
- Howell Street, Lalor, Melbourne.
- Victoria Cross Memorial, Campbell, Canberra dedicated on 24th July 2000.
- Victoria Cross Memorial, Queen Victoria Building, George Street, Sydney.

- Portrait photographs of George Howell VC and Bede Kenny VC are displayed at the Coogee – Randwick Returned Services League Club.
- Named on one of eleven plaques honouring 175 men from overseas awarded the VC for the Great War. The plaques were unveiled by the Senior Minister of State at the Foreign & Commonwealth Office and Minister for Faith and Communities, Baroness Warsi, at a reception at Lancaster House, London on 26th June 2014 attended by the Duke of Kent and relatives of the VC recipients. The Australian plaque is at the Australian War Memorial.
- The Secretary of State for Communities and Local Government, Eric Pickles MP, announced that Victoria Cross recipients from the Great War would have commemorative paving stones laid in their birthplace as a lasting legacy of local heroes within communities. The stones would be laid on or close to the 100th anniversary of their VC actions. For the 145 VCs born in Australia, Belgium, Canada, China, Denmark, Egypt, France, Germany, India, Iraq, Japan, Nepal, Netherlands, New Zealand, Pakistan, South Africa, Sri Lanka, Ukraine and United States of America, individual commemorative stones were unveiled at the National Memorial Arboretum, Alrewas, Staffordshire by Prime Minister David Cameron MP and Sergeant Johnson Beharry VC on 5th March 2015.

The Pacific Star.

In addition to the VC and MM he was awarded the 1914–15 Star, British War Medal 1914–20, Victory Medal 1914–19, War Medal 1939–45, Pacific Star, Australia Service Medal 1939–45, George VI Coronation Medal 1937, Elizabeth II Coronation Medal 1953, US Merchant Marine Pacific War Zone Medal, US Merchant Marine World War II Victory Medal 1941–45. In addition he was awarded the US Army Sea Duty Ribbon, US Merchant Marine Combat Bar, Philippines Defense Ribbon and Philippines Liberation Ribbon; the latter two were established in 1944 by the Philippines Commonwealth Government. The Philippines Defense Ribbon was awarded for service in the defence of the Philippines 8th November 1941–15th June 1945 and the Philippines Liberation Ribbon was for participation in the liberation of the Philippines 17th October 1944–3rd September 1945. Both were originally issued as ribbon bars, but in 1945 they were established as medals. Howell was entitled to both, but it is assumed that they were not claimed. The Pacific Star was not claimed by the family until 2012.

The US Merchant Marine Pacific War Zone Medal.

His daughter, Norma, sold the VC group (less the War Medal 1939–45 and Australia Service Medal 1939–45, which were retained by a family member) in 1982 through Spinks' Australian representative Edward Joslin for A$14,000. The group was purchased by John Meyers, owner of the Maryborough Military and Colonial Museum. He sold the group for A$600,000 in the Noble Numismatics auction on 8th April 2011 at Hotel InterContinental, Macquarie Street, Sydney. The buyer was media mogul Kerry Stokes, who presented it to the Australian War Memorial, Anzac Parade, Canberra, Australian Capital Territory, Australia.

GS/55295 CORPORAL GEORGE JARRATT
8th Battalion, The Royal Fusiliers (City of London Regiment)

George Jarratt was born at Kennington, Surrey on 22nd July 1891. His surname is also seen as Jarrett. His father, Leviticus 'Levi' Jarratt (1852–1923), served as a sapper in the Royal Engineers at South Camp, Aldershot, Hampshire and was discharged on 19th April 1883. In 1891 he was a packer, in 1901 an electrical engineer and by 1911 a general shop keeper. He married Frances née Cole (1855–1929) on 24th October 1880 at Aldershot. She was a servant at Acton, Middlesex in 1871 and a stay machinist in 1881, lodging at 56 Downing Street, Farnham. The family was living at 53 Farmer's Road, Newington St Mary, London in 1891, at 23 Smith Street, Lambeth, London in 1901 and by 1911 at 28 White Hart Street, Lambeth. George had six siblings:

- Frances Helena Jarratt (1882–1968) married Charles Ernest Orford (1880–1939) in 1907 at St Andrew, Farnham. Charles was a painter when he enlisted in the Royal Navy (300995) on 1st July 1902 for twelve years as a stoker. He was described as 5′ 5¾″ tall, with light brown hair, grey eyes and fresh complexion and gave his date of birth as 24th September 1882. He served on HMS *Duke of Wellington*, *Calliope*, *Warrior*, *Erebus*, *Firequeen*, *Sutley*, *Victory II*, *Heclar*, *Diadem*, *Hawke*, *King Alfred*, *Fisgard*, *Neptune*, *Pembroke*, *Drake*, *Prince of Wales*, *Cardiff*, *Champion* and

Kennington about the time George Jarratt was born there.

Conquest. Appointed stoker 1st class 1st July 1906, acting leading stoker 20th August 1909, acting stoker petty officer 17th November 1910, stoker petty officer

17th November 1911, acting mechanic 1st January 1915, mechanic 1st January 1916 and retired on 30th June 1924. They were living at 97 Prince Albert Road, Eastney, Hampshire in 1911 and at Roseberry House, 8 Chestnut Road, Kingston on Thames in 1918. They had four children – Eileen May Orford 1908, Violet Elizabeth Orford 1911, Edward AE Orford 1913 and Frances E Orford 1924.

• Elsie May Jarratt (1883–1964) was a tailoress in 1901 and a military tailoress in 1911. She married Charles E Barnes in 1911 at Lambeth and they had three children – Grace W Barnes 1912, Frances HJ Barnes 1920 and Dudley A Barnes 1925.

• Randolph William A Jarratt (1885–1912) was a clerk in a merchant's office in 1901. He married Elizabeth Marie Kates (born 1884) in 1909 at Rochford, Kent. He was a commercial traveller by 1911 and the family was living at Not Hill View, Hammer, near Shottermill, Hampshire. Randolph and Elizabeth had a son, Leslie R Jarratt 1910. Elizabeth married Henry Wheeler in 1915 at Camberwell.

• Edith Annie Jarratt (1888–1948) was a numberer (cheque) in 1911. She died unmarried.

• Sidney James Jarratt (1893–1946) was a junior clerk in a distillery in 1911. He married Lucy Payne in 1918 at Southwark and they had four children – George M Jarratt 1920, Lucy F Jarratt 1922, Gerald S Jarratt 1928 and John Jarratt 1930. Sidney enlisted in the Royal Naval Volunteer Reserve on 18th January 1912 in London (5/2584). He was described as 5′ 8¼″ tall with light brown hair, blue eyes and medium complexion. He served on HMS *Hercules*, *Vanguard*, *Pembroke I* and *Lion* and was promoted ordinary seaman on 20th August 1912 and able seaman on 1st January 1913. He was commissioned as a temporary sub-lieutenant on 11th May 1918 and served aboard HMS *Vivacious*. He served in the Royal Naval Volunteer Reserve during the Second World War as a temporary lieutenant 29th May 1940. He was promoted lieutenant commander and was on the staff of HMS *Vernon* when he died on 4th September 1946. He is buried at Troqueer Cemetery, Dumfriesshire (H 2 19).

• Percy Clarence Jarratt (1896–1955) was an office boy in a wholesale chemists in 1911.

George's paternal grandfather, Henry Jarratt (1827–75), was an agricultural labourer and hop grower in 1861. He married Ellen née Raggett (1829–87) in 1849 at Elstead, Surrey and they lived at Wordhills, Farnham. She was living at Birchen Reeds, Farnham, Surrey in 1881 as an annuitant. In addition to Levi they had twelve other children – William Jarratt 1850, James Jarratt 1853, Martha Jarratt 1855, Peter Jarratt 1857, Anne Jarratt 1859, George William Jarratt 1862, Henry Jarratt 1864, Harry Jarratt 1865, twins Edwin and Ellen Jarratt 1867, Elizabeth Jarratt 1870 and Mary Jarratt 1872.

George's maternal grandfather, Henry Cole (c.1816–72), was a porter in 1861. He married Jane née Martin (c.1824–62) in 1842 at Alton, Hampshire. They lived at West Street, Farnham. By 1871 Henry was a labourer, living with his daughter Emma and son John at Factory Yard, Farnham. In addition to Frances, George and Jane had seven other children – Thomas Cole 1845, Mary Ann Cole 1846, Catharine Cole 1848, Henry Cole 1849, Clara Cole 1852, Emma Cole 1857 and John Cole 1860.

The Rise, Sunningdale, Berkshire where Gertrude's family was living in 1911.

George was employed as a clerk at the Beefeater Gin distillery in Kennington and was also a scoutmaster. He enlisted in the Royal West Kent Regiment in 1914 (12991) and served in 12th (Reserve) Battalion until transferring to the Royal Fusiliers. There is no mention of his service in the Royal West Kent Regiment on his medal index card.

He married Gertrude M née Elkins (born 1892) in the 2nd quarter of 1915. She was born at Slough, Buckinghamshire (now Berkshire) and was a draper's assistant in

George Jarratt's name on the Arras Memorial.

St Mark's Church, Kennington. George Jarratt is named on the war memorial, the cross in front of the second column from the left.

Gertrude carrying Joyce receives her husband's VC from the King outside Buckingham Palace on 21st July 1917.

1911 at Southwark. Gertrude's father, Albert Edward Elkins (1863–1922), was born at Much Wenlock, Shropshire. He married Margaret Garland née Roots (1867–1942) in 1891 at Greenwich. She was born at Deptford, London. Albert was a cycle salesman in 1901 when the family was living at 10 Cottage Grove, Newington, London. By 1911 they had moved to Osborne Cottage, The Rise, Sunningdale, Berkshire. In addition to Gertrude they had six other children including – Edwin Albert Elkins 1894, Ethel Maria Elkins 1900, Winifred Hilda Elkins 1907 and Vera Maggie Elkins 1908.

George and Gertrude had a daughter, Joyce EM Jarratt, born in the 4th quarter of 1916, registered at Wandsworth, London. Joyce married Albert E Harwood in 1941 and they had three sons – Geoffrey R Harwood 1945, Terence P Harwood 1947 and Robert G Harwood 1955. Joyce died in 1960 and Albert married Rosa E Taylor in 1963.

George went to France on 21st March 1917. **Awarded the VC for his actions near Pelves, France on 3rd May 1917, LG 8th June 1917.** He was killed during his VC action on 3rd May 1917 and is commemorated on the Arras Memorial. The VC was presented to his widow and daughter by the King outside Buckingham Palace on 21st July 1917. George is named on the war memorial at St Mark's Church, Kennington, South London.

In addition to the VC he was awarded the British War Medal 1914–20 and Victory Medal 1914–19. The medals were reportedly sold to the trustees of the Royal Fusiliers Museum by Gertrude in 1963 and are held by the Royal Fusiliers Museum, Tower of London.

Gertrude was living at 28 Stanley Road, Southgate, Middlesex at the time of her husband's death. She married Ernest W Pearce (1890–1964) in the 4th quarter of 1921 at Paddington, London. They lived at 67 North Street, Southgate and in 1964 were living at Southminster, Essex.

2389 PRIVATE JOERGEN CHRISTIAN JENSEN
50th Australian Infantry Battalion AIF

Joergen Jensen was born on 15th January 1891 at Løgstør, Aalborg, Denmark. His father, also Joergen Christian Jensen, was a farmer and wool merchant. His mother was Christiane or Christiana née Sorensen of Løgstørmark, Denmark. In addition to Joergen, they had three other children.

Joergen junior became a sailor and moved to England in 1908, but emigrated to Australia, disembarking in Melbourne, Victoria in March 1909. He worked as a labourer at Morgan, South Australia, also at Port Pirie

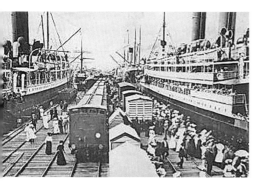

Melbourne Pier around the time that Joergen arrived there in March 1909.

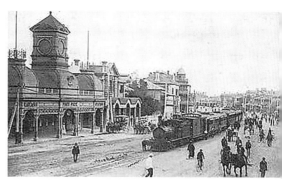

Ellen Street in Port Pirie.

and at one time worked on a River Murray steamer. He was naturalised British on 7th September 1914 in Adelaide, South Australia, because there was no Australian Citizenship Act until 1948.

Joergen enlisted at Keswick Barracks, Adelaide on 23rd March 1915. He was described as 5′ 8¾″ tall, weighing 161 lbs, with fair complexion, brown hair, brown eyes, a tattoo on his right forearm and he gave his religion as Church of England. He embarked at Adelaide aboard HMAT A30 *Borda* with 6th Reinforcement Group for 10th Battalion, 3rd Australian Brigade, 1st Australian Division on 23rd June and disembarked at Alexandria, Egypt before moving to Heliopolis. He embarked at Alexandria for Gallipoli on 19th September and was involved in operations at Gallipoli from 28th September with 10th Battalion. He was admitted sick to 2nd Australian Light Horse Field Ambulance 30th September–5th October. Following the evacuation of Anzac at Gallipoli, he returned to Egypt and disembarked at Alexandria from HMAT A48 *Seang Bee* on 29th December.

Joergen had a number of disciplinary problems, starting on 19th April 1916 when he was absent from tattoo. He was apprehended the following day and awarded two days Field Punishment No.2 and forfeited two days pay. On 5th June he embarked at Alexandria for Marseilles, France arriving on 12th June. On 14th August he was wounded

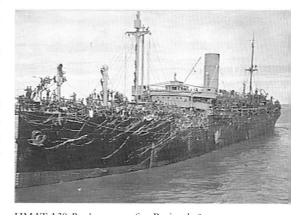

HMAT A30 *Borda* was one five Peninsula & Oriental Steam Navigation Company liners for the single-class emigrant service to Australia. *Borda* was the last to be completed and was launched in December 1913, making her maiden voyage in April 1914. She was requisitioned by the Australian Government and after the war returned to the London–Australia route. Her final voyage was in 1929 and in 1930 she was broken up at Kobe, Japan.

by a gunshot to the left shoulder near Pozières and was admitted to 3rd Canadian General Hospital, Dammes-Camiers near Étaples later that day. He was evacuated to Britain aboard HMHS *Stad Antwerpen* on 16th August and treated at Graylingwell War Hospital, Chichester, Sussex. While he was recovering his disciplinary record worsened. He was absent without leave 21st–22nd September, resulting in him being confined to camp for two days and forfeiting two days pay. He transferred to 1st Convalescent Depot, Perham Down, Hampshire on 23rd September and No.4 Command Depot, Wareham, Dorset on 27th October. He was absent again on 27th November, resulting in him being detained for twelve days and forfeiting twenty-four days pay. For avoiding embarkation on 11th January 1917, he received twenty-eight days Field Punishment No.2.

Dammes-Camiers, near Etaples.

Joergen eventually embarked at Folkestone, Kent for Étaples aboard SS *Princess Clementine* on 16th January 1917. He transferred to 50th Battalion, 13th Australian Brigade, 4th Australian Division on 28th January. **Awarded the VC for his actions at Noreuil on 2nd April 1917, LG 8th June 1917.** Promoted lance corporal on 4th April and corporal on 4th July. The VC was presented by the King in the Forecourt of Buckingham Palace on 21st July.

A large ward at Graylingwell War Hospital, Chichester. It was completed as an asylum in 1897 and was almost entirely self-sufficient, with market gardens and two farms worked by able-bodied patients. At the outbreak of war the asylum was requisitioned as a military hospital and the inmates were relocated to other asylums. The first casualties arrived on 24th March 1915 and the hospital was returned to civilian use in 1919. During the Second World War the Summersdale block was used to treat acute battle neurosis casualties. Graylingwell Hospital closed for inpatients in 2001 and for outpatients in 2009.

On 12th July, he transferred to 13th Training Battalion at Codford, Wiltshire, arriving on 17th July, and was at the School of Musketry, Hayling Island, Hampshire 6th–13th August. He was absent again 17th–21st September and was severely reprimanded and forfeited five days pay. He embarked at Folkestone for Le Havre on 2nd October and rejoined 50th Battalion on 6th October. Appointed temporary sergeant on 5th November. Joergen was seriously wounded by a gunshot to the head on patrol near Villers-Bretonneux on 5th May 1918 and reverted to corporal. He was evacuated to 12th Australian Field Ambulance before being transferred to 26th

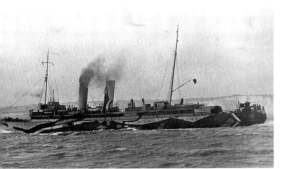

SS *Ville de Liège* about to enter Dover harbour.

During the First World War, Codford became a huge base for ANZAC forces. 13th Training Battalion was responsible for carving a huge (53m x 45m) AIF badge into the chalk of 'Misery Hill', which can still be seen. In the cemetery there are sixty-six New Zealander and thirty-one Australian burials. The association with the Anzacs is perpetuated each year with an Anzac Day remembrance ceremony.

General Hospital at Étaples on 7th May. He was evacuated to Britain aboard SS *Ville de Liege* on 18th May and treated at Richmond Military Hospital, Surrey until transferred to No.1 Australian Auxiliary Hospital, Harefield, Middlesex on 29th May.

Following sick leave, 31st May–14th June, he moved to No.1 Australian Command Depot, Sutton Veny, Wiltshire on 18th June. Joergen was one of ten Australian VCs who returned to Australia aboard HMAT D21 *Medic* to support recruiting, embarking on 24th August and arriving at Melbourne on 15th October. On 29th November, he and Private Hausler DCM were welcomed back to Renmark, South Australia during the interval of a performance by Eroni Brothers Circus. The performance was followed by refreshments at Hisgrove's Café provided by the Patriotic Committee.

Joergen was discharged in Adelaide on 12th December 1918, medically unfit for further service. He worked at the Truro Hotel, Truro, South Australia then in Adelaide as a marine store dealer and later as a 'bottle-oh' (Australian slang for a liquor shop attendant). On 13th

No.1 Australian Auxiliary Hospital, Harefield Park, Middlesex. In November 1914, Charles Billyard-Leake, an Australian resident in the UK, offered his home, Harefield Park House and grounds, to the Minister of Defence in Melbourne for use as a convalescent home for wounded AIF soldiers. It became the only solely Australian hospital in England. As the house could only accommodate a quarter of the number expected, hutted wards were built in the grounds. The first patients arrived on 2nd June 1915 and by August there were 362. The King and Queen visited, speaking to every patient confined to bed. By October 1916, the Hospital had 960 patients and later that year it became a general hospital as well as a convalescent home. The hospital closed in January 1919. The site is now Harefield Hospital.

The Truro Hotel at Truro, South Australia was established in 1863.

HMAT D21 *Medic* (11,985 tons) was built in 1899 by Harland & Wolff in Belfast for the Oceanic Steam Navigation Co Ltd. She carried passengers and refrigerated cargo. In 1928 she was renamed *Hektoria* by new owners and converted to a whale factory. On 11th September 1942 she was sunk by U-*211* and U-*608* en route from Liverpool to New York.

July 1921, he married Katy Herman (née Arthur) (1888–1953) at Adelaide Registry Office, South Australia. Katy was a divorcee, having married Joseph Louis Herman in 1910 at Norwood and had two daughters – Lois Kathleen Herman 1911 and Elsa Audrey Herman 1912. Joergen and Katy lived at St Peters, Adelaide, South Australia. In 1923, Katy married Harold George Sweet and lived at 52 O'Connell Street, North Adelaide.

Joergen never fully recovered from his war wounds and was admitted to Royal Adelaide Hospital in alcoholic mania and died shortly afterwards on 31st May

Royal Adelaide Hospital.

1922. He was buried with full military honours in the Light Oval Section, Adelaide (West Terrace) Cemetery (4 West, Grave 3). He is commemorated in a number of other places:

- Victoria Cross Memorial, Campbell, Canberra dedicated on 24th July 2000.
- Jensen Lane, Wodonga, Victoria on White Box Estate built on the former Bandiana Army Camp.
- Jensen Street, Crib Point, Melbourne.
- A statue in his former hometown of Løgstør, Aalborg, Denmark.
- A display at the Port Pirie sub-branch of the Returned & Services League, South Australia.
- Victoria Cross Memorial, Queen Victoria Building, George Street, Sydney, New South Wales.

Joergen Jensen's grave in Adelaide (West Terrace) Cemetery.

- VC Honour Roll in the Memorial Hall of Adelaide B1 Torrens Training Depot, King William Street, Adelaide, the former HQs for 10th Battalion, Royal South Australia Regiment and the Adelaide University Regiment of the Citizens Military Forces/Army Reserve.
- Bronze paving blocks in North Terrace, Adelaide commemorate the South Australian 150th Jubilee, one of which is dedicated to Joergen Jensen.
- Named on one of eleven plaques honouring 175 men from overseas awarded the VC for the Great War. The plaques were unveiled by the Senior Minister of State at the Foreign & Commonwealth Office and Minister for Faith and Communities, Baroness Warsi, at a reception at Lancaster House, London on 26th June 2014 attended by the Duke of Kent and relatives of the VC recipients. The Australian plaque is at the Australian War Memorial and the Danish plaque is at Churchillparken in Copenhagen, Denmark.
- The Secretary of State for Communities and Local Government, Eric Pickles MP, announced that Victoria Cross recipients from the Great War would have commemorative paving stones laid in their birthplace as a lasting legacy of local heroes within communities. The stones would be laid on or close to the 100th anniversary of their VC actions. For the 145 VCs born in Australia, Belgium, Canada, China, Denmark, Egypt, France, Germany, India, Iraq, Japan, Nepal, Netherlands, New Zealand, Pakistan, South Africa, Sri Lanka, Ukraine and United States of America, individual commemorative stones were unveiled at the National Memorial Arboretum, Alrewas, Staffordshire by Prime Minister David Cameron MP and Sergeant Johnson Beharry VC on 5th March 2015.

In addition to the VC, he was awarded the 1914–15 Star, British War Medal 1914–20 and Victory Medal 1914–19. His VC was donated to the Australian War Memorial by his stepdaughter, Mrs Lois Winger of Largs Bay, Adelaide at a ceremony attended by Queen Margrethe II of Denmark in February 1987. It is displayed in the Australian War Memorial's Hall of Valour, Anzac Parade, Canberra, Australian Capital Territory, Australia.

4195 PRIVATE THOMAS JAMES BEDE KENNY
2nd Australian Infantry Battalion AIF

Bede Kenny, as he preferred to be called, was born at Paddington, Sydney, New South Wales, Australia on 29th September 1896. His father was Austin James Kenny, a butcher from Auckland, New Zealand. His mother was Mary Christina née Connolly, whose father, Thomas Connolly of Drinane, Ballygar, Co Galway, Ireland, emigrated to Australia in 1860. Mary was living at Park Parade, Bondi, New South Wales in 1915 and was working as a nurse at Drynane Private Hospital there in 1917. She later moved to 35 Gibb Street, Waverley, New South Wales. Bede had two siblings, a younger brother Edward Kenny and a sister Berenice Kenny. Bede was educated at Waverley College run by the Christian Brothers' at Waverley, New South Wales and became a pharmaceutical student.

On 14th September 1915, Bede enlisted in the Australian Imperial Force at Warwick Farm, Sydney, New South Wales and was posted to Liverpool, New South Wales. He was described as 6 tall, weighing 154 lbs, with brown complexion, brown eyes, black hair and his religious denomination was Roman Catholic. On his enlistment papers he gave his occupation as chemist's assistant. He embarked on HMAT A60 *Aeneas* at Sydney with the 13th Reinforcement Group on 20th December 1915 and disembarked at Alexandria, Egypt in January 1916. He moved to Tel el Kebir before joining 54th Battalion at Zeitoun on 16th February and transferring to 2nd Battalion on 27th February. Bede was posted to 1st Training Battalion at Tel el Kebir on 17th April and later to France, reporting to 1st Division Base Depot at Étaples on 1st August. He rejoined 2nd Battalion in the bombing platoon on 11th August and was involved in the fighting at Pozières on the Somme.

Awarded the VC for his actions at Hermies, France on 9th April 1917, LG 8th June 1917. He was promoted lance corporal the same day. Bede's dark complexion and cheery disposition caused him to be compared to 'Chunder Loo', who featured in boot polish advertisements of the time. The nickname stuck and

Chunder Loo.

An Australian Base Depot and Hospital were located at Sutton Veny in Wiltshire during the First World War. No.1 Australian Command Depot was a holding unit for men proceeding to the Western Front, many of them reinforcements who had trained on nearby Salisbury Plain. The Australian YMCA operated a rest house at Greenhill House (now Sutton Veny House). After the Armistice, 1st Australian General Hospital moved to Sutton Veny and remained until late 1919. Of the 143 Australians buried in the cemetery at St John the Evangelist Church, 101 died from Spanish Flu after the Armistice, including two nurses. Every year, the community holds an Anzac Day service and children decorate every grave with flowers. There is an Anzac Chapel inside the church and close by the AIF badge, cut into the chalk downland by troops during the war, is still maintained. One of Sutton Veny's own war dead was Private Arthur Pond, 11th Battalion AIF. He enlisted at Perth, Western Australia and was killed in action at Lihons on 10th August 1918 (Villers-Bretonneux Memorial, France).

many members of the Battalion did not initially connect him with the award of the VC.

Bede reported sick with trench foot on 21st April 1917 and was evacuated to England via Rouen on 2nd May. He was admitted to Richmond Military Hospital on 4th May until sent to No.2 Australian Command Depot at Chickerell, Weymouth, Dorset for convalescence on 2nd June. While there he reported sick again from 22nd June to 20th July. On 21st July he was presented with the VC by the King in the forecourt of Buckingham Palace. Bede was charged with being absent without leave 22nd July–9th August and on the day he returned he was sick again until 18th August.

He recovered sufficiently to attend physical and bayonet courses at Devonport, Devon and Aldershot, Hampshire 15th October–21st December and was posted to No.1 Australian Command Depot at Sutton Veny, Wiltshire on 10th January 1918. He embarked at Folkestone, Kent for Étaples, France on 6th May and rejoined 2nd Battalion on 9th May. On 26th June, he was wounded in the Merris sector, but remained at duty. Promoted corporal 1st August and returned to England on 4th August for duty at AIF HQ in London. On 24th August, he embarked on HMAT D21 *Medic* with fellow VCs John Carroll, John James Dwyer, Reginald Inwood,

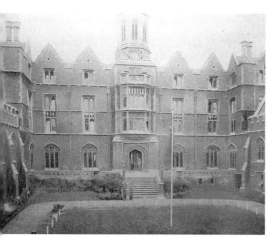

The Australian Imperial Force Headquarters in London was located in Horseferry Road, Westminster.

Australian VCs invited home by Australian PM, Billy Hughes to assist in a recruiting campaign aboard HMAT D21 *Medic* shortly before she berthed at Port Melbourne. Bede Kenny is in the back row second from the left (AWM).

Joergen Jensen, Leonard Keysor, Stanley McDougall, Walter Peeler, William Ruthven and John Whittle. They returned to Australia to support recruiting and disembarked at Sydney on 9th October, where they were welcomed by Major General Lee, Commandant of New South Wales. Bede rejected an offer to join the military police, who he disliked intensely, and was assigned to recruiting duties until being discharged in Sydney on 12th December 1918.

After the war, he worked for Clifford Love & Co Ltd, manufacturers, importers and merchants, as the northern New South Wales traveller. Later, he joined the Sunday Times in Sydney and finally worked as a traveller for Penfolds Wines, trading with hotels around Sydney from Surry Hills to Woolloomooloo. He was also an executive of the Waverley College Old Boy's Union for over thirty years.

Bede attended a number of commemorative events. He was at the Anzac commemoration service on 25th April 1927 at the Exhibition Building, Melbourne, Victoria in the presence of the Duke of York (later King George VI) and took part in the march past with twenty-five other VCs. An Anzac Dinner was held two nights before, hosted by Lieutenant General Sir John Monash GCMG KCB VD, and attended by twenty-three VCs,

The twenty-six VC winners lining up prior to the Anzac commemoration service on 25th April 1927 at the Exhibition Building, Melbourne, Victoria. Bede Kenny is the tallest man in the front row, eleventh from the left, next to a man in a light coloured suit.

Lieutenant General Sir John Monash (1865–1931) is probably the most famous Australian military commander. Although born in Melbourne, his parents were German Jews and he spoke German fluently. He graduated as a Master of Engineering in 1893, Bachelor of Law in 1895 and Doctor of Engineering in 1921. As an engineer, he played a major role in introducing reinforced concrete to Australia and with his law degree was also able to act in contract arbitrations. His military career began with the university militia company in 1884 and by 1912 he was commanding 13th Infantry Brigade. He took up soldiering full time on the outbreak of war and overcame much anti-German and Jewish prejudice to command 4th Australian Brigade in Egypt and Gallipoli, 3rd Australian Division in France and the Australian Corps. With the latter, he spearheaded the Allied advance on 8th August 1918 at the Battle of Amiens, which started the 'Hundred Days Advance to Victory'. When he died, his state funeral was attended by 300,000 mourners.

Bede attended the wedding of Walter Ernest Brown VC DCM (1885–1942) in 1932. Brown was born in Tasmania and was a grocer before enlisting in 1915. He was awarded the VC for his actions at Villers-Bretonneux with 20th Battalion AIF in July 1918. He lied about his age in the Second World War and served in the Royal Australian Artillery. He is believed to have been killed in action on 15th/16th February 1942 at Singapore. His remains were never recovered.

including Bede Kenny. For an unknown reason the Duke of York was not invited. On 8th August 1928, he was one of eight VCs who attended the 1st AIF Reunion Dinner at Sydney Town Hall to celebrate the 10th Anniversary of the commencement of 'The Big Push'. In November 1929, he attended a luncheon at Government House with the Governor of Australia, Sir Dudley de Chair, together with thirteen other VCs. On 4 June 1932, he was one of eight VCs attending the wedding of Walter Ernest Brown VC DCM at Christ Church, Bexley, New South Wales.

Bede Kenny married Kathleen Dorothy Buckley (c.1899–1970), a florist, on 29th September 1927 at St Mary's Cathedral, Sydney. Kathleen's father, John J Buckley (1859–1942), born at Spital, Tipperary, Ireland, emigrated to Australia aboard the *Montmorency*, arriving at Sydney from Liverpool on 27th August 1864. He married

St Mary's Cathedral, Sydney was still under construction in the 1920s. Bede Kenny married Kathleen Buckley there on 29th September 1927.

Montmorency (812 tons), owned by the Black Ball Line, was built at Quebec, Canada in 1854. She had made a previous voyage to Sydney and Melbourne with immigrants. Her first voyage to Moreton Bay, Queensland finished on 16th October 1860, bringing 310 people. *Montmorency* made four other voyages, including the one in 1864 bringing Bede Kenny's father-in-law, John Buckley. Early in 1866, she again set off for Australia. The voyage was difficult and Captain James Cooper and the other officers had to carry loaded revolvers to avoid a mutiny. After landing her passengers, *Montmorency* loaded with wool for London and arrived at Napier, New Zealand on 24th March 1867. The following day, a fire broke out and the ship was burned out.

Catharine née Kelly (c.1863–1931) c.1887 at Temora, New South Wales and in addition to Kathleen they had nine other children. Bede and Kathleen had three children:

- Judith Kenny, born on 27th June 1930, died of rheumatic fever on 4th December 1943.
- Bede Kenny, born on 18th August 1931, also died of rheumatic fever on 6th February 1946.
- Hilary J Kenny married Paddy Sparks and they lived at Portland, New South Wales.

Bede suffered from the effects of trench foot and was also partially deaf due to his war service. He died from a combination

Concord Repatriation Hospital, New South Wales where Bede Kenny died, was built 1939–42 as a general hospital for the Australian Army (113th Australian General Hospital) with 2,000 beds. In 1974, it began providing care for the community and in 1993 transferred to the Central Sydney Area Health Service as Concord Repatriation General Hospital (Frank Hurley).

of illnesses at Concord Repatriation Hospital, New South Wales on 15th April 1953. Following a requiem mass at Mary Immaculate Church, Waverley, he was buried in the Roman Catholic section of Botany Cemetery, Matraville, New South Wales (Section 3, Row 12, Grave 441) with his daughter Judith and son Bede. His wife attended the 1956 Victoria Cross Centenary celebrations in London, England. She was buried with them in 1970. Bede is commemorated in a number of places:

- Bede Kenny VC Club opened at East Hills Barracks in March 1988, during which a plaque was unveiled by Commander 1st Division, Major General Mike Jeffery (later Governor-General of Australia). Bede's daughter, Mrs Paddy Sparks, was guest of honour.
- Kenny Street, Crib Point, Melbourne, Victoria.
- Kenny Avenue, Chifley, Sydney, New South Wales.
- Kenny Place, Fairfield West, Sydney, New South Wales.
- Kenny Road, Pagewood, Sydney, New South Wales.
- Kenny Road, Gallipoli Barracks, Enoggera, Brisbane, Queensland.
- Kenny Street, Balwyn North, Melbourne, Victoria.
- Waverley College, Birrell Street, Waverley, New South Wales:
  - Sgt Bede Kenny VC Memorial Award, comprising a plaque and gold medallion, presented each September by Waverley College Cadet Unit at the annual parade to the most efficient NCO.
  - Kenny Building used by the middle school was named in 1996. In 2006, it was rededicated to commemorate the centenary of his entry into Waverley College and members of his family attended.
  - VC Guard in the Waverley College Cadet Unit, founded in 2009 in memory of Bede Kenny VC. Members wear a badge in the colour of the VC ribbon.
- Named in the Australian War Graves Garden of Remembrance, Rookwood, New South Wales.
- Victoria Cross Memorial, Campbell, Canberra, dedicated on 24th July 2000.
- Victoria Cross Memorial, Queen Victoria Building, George Street, Sydney, New South Wales.
- His photograph (and that of George Howell VC MM) is displayed at Coogee-Randwick-Clovelly Returned Services League Club, St Pauls, New South Wales.
- Named on one of eleven plaques honouring 175 men from overseas awarded the VC for the Great War. The plaques were unveiled by the Senior Minister of State at the Foreign & Commonwealth Office and Minister for Faith and Communities, Baroness Warsi, at a reception at Lancaster House, London on 26th June 2014 attended by the Duke of Kent and relatives of the VC recipients. The Australian plaque is at the Australian War Memorial.
- The Secretary of State for Communities and Local Government, Eric Pickles MP, announced that Victoria Cross recipients from the Great War would have commemorative paving stones laid in their birthplace as a lasting legacy of local

heroes within communities. The stones would be laid on or close to the 100th anniversary of their VC actions. For the 145 VCs born in Australia, Belgium, Canada, China, Denmark, Egypt, France, Germany, India, Iraq, Japan, Nepal, Netherlands, New Zealand, Pakistan, South Africa, Sri Lanka, Ukraine and United States of America, individual commemorative stones were unveiled at the National Memorial Arboretum, Alrewas, Staffordshire by Prime Minister David Cameron MP and Sergeant Johnson Beharry VC on 5th March 2015.

In addition to the VC, he was awarded the British War Medal 1914–20, Victory Medal 1914–19 and George VI Coronation Medal 1937. His family sold the medals for A$46,000 at auction at Spinks in Australia on 24th November 1985. On 15th February 1986 they were handed over to the Director of the Australian War Memorial, Air Vice Marshal JH Fleming, by the National President of the Returned Services League, Sir William Keys. They are held in the Hall of Valour, Australian War Memorial, Treloar Crescent, Campbell, Australian Capital Territory.

MAJOR FREDERICK WILLIAM LUMSDEN
Royal Marine Artillery attached Headquarters 32nd Division

Frederick Lumsden was born at Fyzabad, India on 14th December 1872. His father was John James Foote Lumsden MA (1837–1902), born at Old Machar, Aberdeen. He joined the Indian Civil Service on 6th August 1856 and was attached to North-Western Provinces on 12th October 1857 as an Assistant in the Benares Division from 3rd November. Numerous appointments followed – Assistant Magistrate and Collector at Mirzapur November 1857; Joint Magistrate and Deputy Collector at Gorakhpur 14th July 1858; Assistant Settlement Officer 2nd Grade 26th May 1862; Assistant Settlement Officer 1st Grade December 1864; Officiating Magistrate, Collector and Assistant Settlement Officer at Gorakhpur 4th September 1866; Assistant Settlement Officer at Azamgarh 5th

November 1866, 18th November 1867 and 8th March 1868 and in-between was Officiating Magistrate and Collector 25th July 1867 and 26th February 1868; leave to Europe 29th April 1868–26th January 1871; Joint Magistrate and Deputy Collector at Banda 20th February 1871; in charge of sub-division of Karwi March 1871; Officiating Magistrate and Collector at Farukhabad 24th July 1871; Officiating Magistrate and Collector at Benares 12th October 1871; Officiating Magistrate and Collector at Gorakhpur 8th March 1873, confirmed on 31st July 1874; special duty

Benares (now Varanasi), where Frederick's father started his career in the Indian Civil Service.

Gorakhpur station. All four of Frederick's brothers were born in the city.

to Naini Tal 20th July–29th September 1875, then resumed at Gorakhpur 6th October 1875; Magistrate and Collector at Mirzapur 27th February 1877; Officiating Commissioner Rae Bareli Division 3rd April 1878; transferred to Fyzabad Division 8th November 1878 and confirmed as Commissioner 2nd December 1879. His final appointment was Commissioner of Benares and Member of the Board of Revenue for the North West Provinces. Frederick senior married Margaret 'Marguerite' Lowther (late Coxon, née Whyte/White) (1836–1918) on 9th May 1863 at Agra, India. She was born at Meerut, India. He retired in 1891 and was living at Skene House, Aberdeenshire in 1894 and at 393 Great Western Road, Aberdeen when he died in 1902. In 1914, Marguerite was living at Strawberry Bank, Eskbank, Midlothian and her death in 1918 was registered at Croydon, Surrey. Frederick junior had five siblings; the four brothers were all born at Gorakhpur, India:

- Philip James Lumsden MB MCh (1864–1937) was educated at Edinburgh Royal High School and Edinburgh University before being commissioned as a captain in the Indian Medical Service on 29th September 1888. Promoted major 29th December 1900, lieutenant colonel 29th December 1908 and colonel 1st December 1918. He served with 7th Hariana Lancers as medical officer. Philip married Beatrix Katie Wilson (c.1878–1965) in 1899 at Hanworth, Middlesex. They had a son, Douglas Rupert Shepherd Lumsden (1903–89), who married twice – Beryl Mary Brander in 1927 and Hannah M Downey in 1943.
- John Stuart Shepherd Lumsden (1867–1906) was also educated at Edinburgh Royal High School and Edinburgh University (MB MCh). He was commissioned in the Indian Medical Service on 28th July 1891 and served with 40th Bengal Infantry. Promoted major on 28th July 1903. He married Lilian Jacob (1874–1928) in 1896 at Fort Sandeman, Baluchistan, India. She was born at Maharashtra, India, daughter of Henry Priestley Jacob, Educational Inspector at Sind.
- Maud Laura Lumsden (1870–1951) was born at Byth House, King Edward, Aberdeenshire. She married Thomas Henry Holloway in 1905 at Harrow,

Middlesex. He was a retired wine merchant (born c.1833) of Lincoln House, High Street, Harrow. Maud was living at 10 Victoria Villas, Kilburn, London at the time. Thomas had been married twice previously. First to Elizabeth Stratton (c.1836–80) in 1863 and they had a son, Wilfrid Stratton Holloway, in 1873. His second wife was Emma Harriet Jordan (1853–95) in 1881 and they also had a son, Baliol Blount Holloway (1883–1967).

- Claude Stanley Lumsden (twin with Douglas) (born 1874) was a rubber planter in India. He married Constance Louise Lamb Daniel (1891–1973) in 1918 at Wandsworth, London. They had a daughter, Sheila Lumsden.
- Douglas Gordon Lumsden (twin with Claude) (born 1874) was a planter in India.

Frederick's paternal grandfather, John Lumsden of Keir, Belhelvie, Aberdeenshire married Helen née Shepherd, daughter of the Reverend Robert Shepherd in 1812 at Old Machar, Aberdeen. He was a merchant in 1841, living with his family at South College Street, Old Machar, Aberdeen. In addition to Frederick they had eleven other children. Frederick's maternal grandfather, Samuel White, a schoolmaster sergeant in the Bengal Horse Artillery, married Margaret née Lowther in India. In addition to Margaret they had four other children, all born in India.

Frederick was educated at The Gym (old Chanonry House Gymnasium School), Old Aberdeen and Bristol Grammar School 1886–88. In 1881, he was living at 11 Leven Terrace, St Cuthberts, Edinburgh, Scotland with his aunt, Helen Lumsden and his brother John and sister Maria.

Frederick was trained at the Royal Military College Sandhurst 1888–90 and was commissioned on 1st September 1890. Promoted lieutenant 1st September 1891. He acquired a number of qualifications in gunnery, torpedo, musketry, signalling, equitation and military law at the Royal Naval College, Greenwich, HMS *Excellent* and in Army schools. On 17th December 1894 he embarked on the battleship HMS *Nile* and served in the Mediterranean and Malta. He joined the Ascension Island garrison on 20th January 1896 on the strength of HMS *Penelope*, a guardship at Simon's Bay, Cape of Good Hope. Promoted captain 16th June 1897. He embarked on the battleship HMS *Resolution* in the Channel Squadron June 1900, but on 10th October 1901 went back to the Mediterranean aboard HMS *Formidable*.

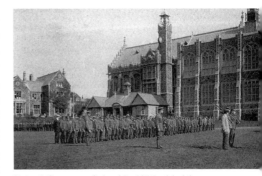

Bristol Grammar School in 1914 with 4th Gloucestershire drilling in the grounds. The school was founded in 1532 and was also attended by Brigadier General Manley Angell James VC DSO MBE MC (1896–1975), Sir Allen Lane (1902–70) founder of Penguin Books, cricketer Tom Graveney (born 1927), actor Timothy West (born 1934) and Michelle Goodman (born 1976), the first female RAF officer to be awarded the DFC.

HMS *Nile*, was a Trafalgar Class battleship and only sister ship to HMS *Trafalgar*. She was the last British battleship with a single citadel and the first to mount secondary armament of quick-firing guns. She was commissioned on 30th June 1891 and joined the Mediterranean Fleet until 1898 when she became port guardship at Devonport. In 1903 she went onto the Reserve and was sold for scrap in July 1912.

HMS *Formidable* the lead ship of her class of pre-dreadnoughts, commissioned in 1904 and served with the Mediterranean Fleet until transferring to the Channel Fleet in 1908. In 1912 she joined the 5th Battle Squadron. On 1st January 1915 she was sunk by two torpedoes from U-*24* off Start Point, Devon with the loss of 547 of her crew of 780. A storm blew up after *Formidable* sank and a raft of bodies was blown along the coast to Lyme Regis, where the Pilot Boat pub cellar was used as a temporary mortuary. The landlord's dog, a half collie crossbreed named 'Lassie', licked the face of one victim, Able Seaman John Cowan, and stayed beside him, keeping him warm. To everyone's surprise, Cowan awoke and made a full recovery. The 1938 novel, *Lassie come home* by Eric Knight may have been inspired by this story, which was eventually picked up by Hollywood and a number of films and television series followed.

Frederick was a student at the Staff College, Camberley in 1908 and spent six months in Germany in 1909–10, gaining a 1st Class Interpreter Certificate. From 4th June 1910 he was GSO2 Straits Settlement Command in Singapore until 30th April 1914. During this tour of duty he was appointed brevet major 1st September 1911 and promoted major 10th June 1913. In Singapore he received exceptional reports, being judged thoughtful, capable, reliable, hardworking and displaying tact and judgment. In 1913, he was recommended for accelerated promotion.

On 16th December 1894, Frederick Lumsden married Mary Ellen Augusta Harward (17th August 1873–25th January 1933) at Portsea, Hampshire. She was born at Attock, India, daughter of Lieutenant General Thomas Netherton Harward (1829–1908). Thomas was commissioned from the Royal Military Academy, Woolwich into the Bengal Artillery on 8th December 1848. He saw action during the Indian Mutiny with Havelock's Force from Allahabad to Lucknow and was Mentioned in Despatches. His final appointment in 1884 was GOC Royal Artillery

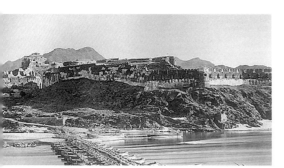

Attock, on the banks of the Indus, about eighty kilometres from Rawalpindi in Pakistan, is where Frederick's wife, Mary Harward, was born in 1873. In 1849 Attock Fort was seized by the British and renamed Campbellpur after Sir Colin Campbell. Its name reverted to Attock in 1978. The city was begun in 1903 near the Fort and in 1915 the first oil well was drilled, resulting in the population soaring from a few thousands to more than 100,000 today.

The Army Staff College at Camberley originated from Colonel Le Marchant's staff college, founded in 1799. In 1802 it became the Senior Department of the new Royal Military College, then at High Wycombe and later at Sandhurst. In 1858 the Senior Department became the Staff College and in 1870 separated from the Royal Military College. The purpose-built accommodation seen here was constructed 1859–63. From 1903 Colonial forces officers were admitted and in 1905 a few Royal Navy and Royal Marines officers were also introduced each year. Except for during the world wars, it operated until 1997, when it merged into the new Joint Services Command and Staff College, together with its Royal Navy and Royal Air Force equivalents. Its Commandant in 1936–37 was a fellow VC, then Major General Viscount Gort.

Lahore Division before he retired in March 1885. He wrote, *Hereward The Saxon Patriot: a history of his life and character with a record of his ancestors and descendants, AD 455–AD 1896*, which traces the Harward family. Thomas married Ellen Halemann née Atkinson (1836–1907) in 1853 at St Andrew's Church, Singapore. After moving back to England, they lived at Hampton Court Palace, Middlesex. In addition to Mary they had eight other children in India including:

- Frederick Thomas Lane Harward (born 1856) who went to Canada.
- Auberon George Netherton Harward (born 1860) served in the Cape Mounted Police and afterwards in the Government Education Department, South Africa.
- Arthur John Netherton Harward (1867–1938) was commissioned into 21st Hussars on 5th October 1887 and transferred to the Indian Staff Corps to serve with 48th Pioneers as a lieutenant on 1st September 1888. Promoted captain 5th October 1898, major 5th October 1905, lieutenant colonel 5th October 1913 and brevet colonel and colonel 3rd June 1915. Awarded the CB, LG 23rd October 1919. He married Grace Isabella Swifte (1870–1957) in 1904 at Bombay, India. She was the daughter of Colonel Joshua Waddington Swifte (1839–1904). Arthur and Grace had two sons.

Frederick's and Mary's only child, May Sunbeam Violet Lumsden (1895–1948), married Major Albert 'Bertie' Kemblis North (1876–1935), 4th Oxfordshire and Buckinghamshire Light Infantry, in 1917 at Portsmouth. Albert was commissioned on 9th April 1898 and was promoted captain on 4th June 1902. He served as a major during the First World War and was partially blinded on the Somme in 1916 while leading an attack; he killed six Germans before being wounded and left for dead. His body was recovered a few days later and he was about to be buried when his voice was heard shouting, *My bloody head hurts*. Albert worked at St Dunstan's Hostel for Blinded Soldiers until his death. He was the youngest of six sons of North North, all of whom served in the Army:

St Dunstan's was founded by Arthur Pearson in 1915, because of the increasing numbers of blind soldiers returning from the front. The first hostel was in Bayswater Hill, London before moving to St Dunstan's Lodge in Regent's Park, from which it took its name. In 1938 a purpose built training, convalescent, care and holiday centre opened at Ovingdean, Brighton. The charity moved to Harcourt Street, London in 1984 and in 2012 changed its name to Blind Veterans UK.

* Brigadier General Bordrigge North North CB MVO, King's Own Royal Lancaster Regiment (c.1863–1936).
* Captain Louis Aylmer North, Royal Scots Fusiliers (1866–1901), was commissioned on 14th December 1887 from the Militia. He served with the Manchester Regiment from 2nd June 1901 and died of wounds in South Africa on 3rd December 1901.
* Lieutenant Colonel Edward Bunbury North CMG DSO (born 1869), was commissioned in the Royal Lancaster Regiment in 1892 and transferred to the Royal Fusiliers later that year. He was employed with the Egyptian Army and took part in the Nile Expeditions of 1898 and 1899. MID, LG 30th September 1898 and Turkish Order of the Medjidie 4th Class. Took part in the South African War 1899–1900: Relief of Ladysmith, Colenso, Tugela Heights, Pieters Hill, Transvaal and Cape Colony. ADC to GOC North East District 1901–02. Attached to the General Staff War Office 1904–05. Brigade Major, 2nd West Riding Infantry Brigade, Northern Command and later 147th Brigade 1912–15. Served on the Staff in France & Belgium from April 1915. Brigade Major, 124th Brigade October 1915–September 1916. CO 4th Royal Fusiliers September 1916–September 1917 and then CO 10th Royal West Surrey until January 1918. Served on the Staff thereafter for the rest of the war. MID, LG 4th January 1917 and 8th July 1919. Half Pay from 18th May 1921.
* Lieutenant Colonel Piers William North DSO MVO, Royal Berkshire (1871–1959), was commissioned in 1891. Took part in the South African War 1899–1901:

Orange Free State, Transvaal and Orange River Colony. Served with Mounted Infantry. MID, LG 10th September 1901. Recalled during the First World War. Served with the Royal Marines March–August 1915 and the Machine Gun Corps December 1915–May 1916. CO 20th Durham Light Infantry October 1916–July 1917. Served in France March–May 1915 and December 1915–May 1917 and at Gallipoli June–August 1915. Wounded twice. MID, LG 25th May and 21st December 1917.

• Lieutenant Colonel Oliver Henry North DSO (1874–1980), was commissioned in the Lancashire Fusiliers in 1900 having had commissioned service with Bethune's Mounted Infantry January–May 1900. Assistant Superintendent Gymnasia Eastern Command 1907–11. Staff Captain in France August 1914–July 1915 and Assistant Provost Marshal July–October 1915. Served with 8th King's (Liverpool) from September 1916 and was CO November 1916–March 1918. Served with the Machine Gun Corps from March 1918. MID LG, 7th April & 22nd June 1915, 18th December 1917 and 8th July 1919. Brevet lieutenant colonel 3rd June 1919.

May and Albert had two children:

• Violet Iris L North (born 1919) married Lieutenant Anthony Edgar Tausig, Intelligence Corps, in 1942, son of Herman Tausig of Prague, Czechoslovakia. He was a sergeant in the RAOC before being commissioned on 18th April 1941 (183070). Promoted war substantive lieutenant 1st October 1942, temporary captain 14th January 1944 and captain 1st May 1947. They had a son, John Alan Tausig, in 1946.

• Frederick Lumsden North (1921–2009) was a proficient rugby player and also an accomplished race rider. He was commissioned in The Queen's Own Royal Regiment (West Surrey) on 29th March 1941 (180043) and was promoted war substantive lieutenant 29th September 1942 and temporary captain 1st October 1943. He relinquished his commission on 27th October 1946 and was granted the rank of honorary major. He married three times. Firstly to Elisabeth Marker in 1955 and after she died to Patricia Albuquerque, who also predeceased him, and finally to Margaret. There were no children. Freddie was one of the first bridge professionals of post war England, opening The Sussex School of Bridge in 1950 and working for P&O, running bridge on cruise ships. He wrote over twenty books and contributed regularly to various bridge magazines. He also excelled at duplicate bridge, becoming one of the English Bridge Union's first Grand Masters, winning his first national title in 1948, the Sydney Woorward Cup, with Peter Heywood. He won numerous other competitions – Daily Telegraph Cup 1950, 1955–56, 1963 & 1967, National Pairs 1952 with Chris Hunt, Field Cup 1958 opposite Maurice Harrison-Gray, Pachabo Cup with John Pugh 1959 and 1962 representing Sussex CBA (he was its President for nearly thirty years from 1972). They also won the Gold Cup in 1962 with Harrison-Gray, Rockfelt and the

Sharples brothers and Crockfords 1967 with Louis Tarlo and Claude Rodrigue. Freddie represented Great Britain in the World Pairs Olympiads of 1962 and 1966 and played with Dimmie Fleming in the 1962 World Pairs. He also represented England in several Camrose Trophy matches in the late 1950s and 1960s.

May married, secondly, Captain Charles Arthur Freer Fowke MBE MC (1893–1969) in August 1942. Charles was commissioned into 3rd Oxford & Buckinghamshire Light Infantry on 1st March 1912. He was mobilised on 5th August 1914 and embarked at Southampton on 16th October, disembarking at St Nazaire. Having sprained or broken a tendon in his left foot, he was evacuated on the HMHS *Carisbrook Castle* on 20th October for treatment at Osborne House, Isle of Wight. Promoted lieutenant 10th December 1914 and rejoined for duty on 15th January 1915. Promoted captain 6th November 1915. Awarded the MC, LG 11th January 1916. He received a gunshot wound to the chest on 10th March 1916 at Arras and it was not until 13th December 1918 that a Medical Board found him fit for General Service again. He embarked at Cork on 6th September 1919 and disembarked at Constantinople on 1st October. He embarked at Constantinople on 15th November and was demobilised on 29th November 1919. Charles was mobilised again during the emergency 9 April–4 June 1921. He had to relinquish his commission due to ill health on 29th April 1926. Charles was the Poultry Area Organiser for the Ministry of Agriculture and Fisheries when he was awarded the MBE (LG 12th June 1947).

Frederick returned to Britain on 3rd June 1914 and served on HMS *Illustrious* 2nd–18th August 1914. He then commanded No.1 Howitzer (15″) in the Howitzer Brigade RMA and took it to France on 15th February 1915. It fired its first round from Locre on 6th March. On 19th April, he took command of the four guns of the Howitzer Brigade RMA. Appointed GSO3 HQ First Army 27th July, Brigade Major 21st November and Staff Officer with Canadian Corps Troops on 27th November. On 27th January 1916 he was appointed GSO2 HQ V Corps and on 17th January 1917 GSO2 with HQ 32nd Division. Brevet lieutenant colonel 1st January 1917. **Awarded the DSO for outstanding service and devotion to duty, LG 1st January 1917. Awarded the VC for his actions at Francilly, France on 3rd/4th April 1917, LG 8th June 1917.**

Frederick was appointed to command 17th Highland Light Infantry 7th–12th April 1917, in order to qualify for command of a brigade. **Awarded a Bar to the DSO for his actions near Fayet, France probably on 9th April 1917; he made a reconnaissance of an enemy position, moving over open ground under heavy fire, bringing back valuable information and rendering invaluable services throughout the operations, LG 11th May 1917. Awarded a 2nd Bar to the DSO for his actions near Fayet, France probably on 10th April 1917: in charge of a large reconnaissance party, he carried out the task allotted with conspicuous success, skilfully withdrawing the party at a critical time** and saving many casualties, LG 11th May 1917.

Appointed temporary brigadier general to command 14th Brigade on 12th April 1917. He was on leave in Britain 6th–16th July. The VC, DSO & two Bars were presented by the King outside Buckingham Palace on 21st July 1917. Frederick was wounded on 2nd August, but returned to duty on 5th August. He was wounded again on 30th August, but remained at duty. Promoted lieutenant colonel 25th October 1917 under the provisions of Order in Council of 15th January 1878 for specially meritorious services in the field during which he was awarded the VC and DSO plus two bars and for good service in command of a unit on active service, LG 6th November 1917.

He was awarded a 3rd Bar to the DSO for actions on 2nd December 1917 around Volt Farm, Mallet Copse and Double Copse near Ypres during a large raid in which part of his Brigade formed the left flank in support of 97th Brigade; at the first objective there was a slight hesitation due to heavy small arms fire and exhaustion, but he led the assault on a group of seven pillboxes and then conducted a valuable reconnaissance of the enemy position before supervising the withdrawal, remaining with the covering party and was the last to leave the enemy position, LG 22nd April 1918. Awarded the CB, LG 3rd June 1918. Mentioned in General/ Field Marshal Sir Douglas Haig's Despatches dated 30th April 1916, 13th November 1916, 11th November 1917 and 7th April 1918, LG 15th June 1916, 4th January 1917, 11th December 1917 and 20th May 1918 respectively. Awarded the Belgian Croix de Guerre, 14th September 1918.

In October 1914, the RMA formed two artillery brigades for the Western Front, one was anti-aircraft, the other was equipped with twelve 15″ Howitzers. It had about 1,000 all ranks, but the guns were deployed singly, not in batteries. The first Howitzer landed in France on 15th February 1915. The 15″ Howitzer was designed by Coventry Ordnance Works, based on its design for the successful 9.2″ Howitzer used by RGA siege batteries. The 635 kgs shell could only be fired to a maximum range of 9,700m. The howitzer alone weighed 10.75 tons (ninety-four tons total per installation) and each required three Foster-Daimler steam tractors to move it. Only twelve were ever deployed and they were turned over to a less than enthusiastic Army in 1916. Although the shell was devastating, the gun was difficult to move, had a very slow rate of fire and because of its poor range had to be mounted close to the front, where it was vulnerable to counter-battery fire. During the war 25,332 rounds were fired and dud 15″ shells are still found periodically. One was recovered during the construction of the Thiepval Visitor Centre on the Somme. The howitzers were scrapped in 1920.

Frederick was temporary GOC of 32nd Division, 6th–7th May 1918. On 4th June 1918 he was in the Brigade's trenches at Blairville, near Arras when an enemy attack was imminent. Having moved into an exposed position to evaluate the situation, he was shot in the head by a sniper and died instantly. He is buried in Berles New Military Cemetery (111 D 1). The Brigade was taken over by another VC winner, Lewis Pugh Evans.

Frederick left £1,290/8/6 and probate was granted to Geoffrey Holt Stilwell, a banker. Mary was living at 28 Ashworth Mansions, Elgin Avenue, London in June 1918 and at Hampton Court Palace in 1928. Frederick is commemorated in a number of places:

Frederick Lumsden's grave in Berles New Military Cemetery.

• Lumsden Road, Eastney, Southsea, Hampshire.
• Lumsden Block, Stanley Barracks, Bovington, Dorset.
• Lumsden Memorial unveiled on 25th July 1920 outside the Royal Marines Museum at Eastney. It has since been moved to the Museum's memorial garden.
• Plaque at St Andrew's Garrison Church, Eastney, Hampshire was transferred to the chapel of Stonehouse Barracks, Plymouth, Devon on the closure of St Andrew's.
• Aberdeen War Memorial.
• His portrait hangs in Bristol Grammar School.
• The Secretary of State for Communities and Local Government, Eric Pickles MP, announced that Victoria Cross recipients from the Great War would have commemorative paving stones laid in their birthplace as a lasting legacy

A memorial plaque in Berles New Military Cemetery. Unfortunately his surname is spelled incorrectly.

Aberdeen War Memorial forming one side of Cowdary Hall was dedicated on 29th September 1925, the same day that George V opened Cowdary Hall and Art Museum. The granite lion statue was designed by Aberdeen sculptor, William MacMillan, who also designed the World War I Victory Medal.

of local heroes within communities. The stones would be laid on or close to the 100th anniversary of their VC actions. For the 145 VCs born in Australia, Belgium, Canada, China, Denmark, Egypt, France, Germany, India, Iraq, Japan, Nepal, Netherlands, New Zealand, Pakistan, South Africa, Sri Lanka, Ukraine and United States of America, individual commemorative stones were unveiled at the National Memorial Arboretum, Alrewas, Staffordshire by Prime Minister David Cameron MP and Sergeant Johnson Beharry VC on 5th March 2015.

The Lumsden Memorial at the Royal Marines Museum, Eastney (Jonathan Saunders).

Frederick was a Freemason, Initiated into the Navy Lodge (No.2612) on 17th May 1907, Passed to the Second Degree on 18th June and Raised to the Sublime Degree of a Master Mason on 14th October.

In addition to the VC and DSO with three Bars, he was awarded the Companion of the Order of the Bath, 1914–15 Star, British War Medal 1914–20, Victory Medal 1914–19 with Mentioned-in-Despatches Oakleaf and Belgian Croix de Guerre. The VC group was purchased by the Royal Marines Museum in April 1973, where it is held.

CAPTAIN THAIN WENDELL MACDOWELL
38th Battalion (Ottawa), Canadian Expeditionary Force

Thain MacDowell was born on 16th September 1890 at his grandparent's home, The Parsonage, Lachute, Quebec, Canada. His father, the Reverend John Vincent MacDowell (c.1853–94), a Methodist inister, married Eleanor Eliza née Ireland (born c.1864). The family was living at Carp, Ontario in 1890 and later moved to Lyn. Eleanor married JF Richardson, a cheese maker, in 1897. They lived at Maitland, Ontario and later at Lyle Close, Brockville, Ontario. Thain had four siblings:

- Cuyler Melanethon MacDowell (born 1884) was a clerk when he enlisted in the Royal Marine Artillery on 20th October 1901 at Liverpool (9772). He was described as 5′ 7½″ tall with fresh complexion, dark brown hair, hazel eyes and his religious denomination was Wesleyan. He served on HMS *Implacable* January 1904–July 1906 and was discharged in January 1910. He enlisted in the CEF on 24th February 1915 at Halifax, Nova Scotia. He had served previously for eight and a half years in the

The railway station at Lachute c.1900.

Royal Marine Artillery. He was described as 5′ 8½″ tall, with dark complexion, grey eyes, black hair and his religious denomination was Methodist. He served in England with 2nd Heavy Battery, Ammunition Column, Reserve Brigade CFA, 11th Siege Battery and 3rd Brigade CGA. He was promoted to sergeant (228) and on 26th May 1917 was commissioned as a lieutenant. In France, where he was wounded, he served with 2nd Heavy Battery and 3rd Brigade CGA. His service was recognized by being Mentioned in Despatches and awarded the French Croix de Guerre (LG 7th June 1919). Cuyler married Margaret Ogle.
- Newell Lansing MacDowell (1888–1966) moved to Portland, Maine, USA in 1905. By 1915 he was a clerk with the Canadian Briscoe Motor Co Ltd at Brockville, Ontario. Newell married Agnes Edna Dowsley (c.1888–1982) in 1917 and they lived at 155 King's Street, Brockville. Agnes was the daughter of Judge JK Dowsley. Newell enlisted in the CEF on 17th April 1917. He was described as 5′ 6″ tall, with medium complexion, blue eyes, black hair and his religious denomination was Methodist. He was commissioned as a lieutenant and was taken on strength at Rockville Camp, Ottawa on 24th August 1917, but did not go overseas. Newell and Agnes had at least three children including – Catherine D MacDowell and Wendell D MacDowell.
- Merrill Whedon MacDowell (1891–1978) was a manufacturer. He joined the Militia, 41st Regiment (Brockville Rifles), and served for three months in 156th Battalion CEF (formed from Brockville Rifles) before being commissioned as a lieutenant in 59th Battalion CEF on 25th February 1916. He later served in 4th Canadian Mounted Rifles and was awarded the MC for leading his platoon to within fifty metres of his objective, maintaining his position and inflicting heavy losses on the enemy in a counterattack (LG 18th July 1917). Merrill married Mary Rebecca Fraser (born 1893) in 1918 and they had a daughter, Janice Elizabeth MacDowell, in 1922.
- Eula Grace MacDowell (1894–1988) served as a nurse at Brockville Hospital during the war. She married Clifford Frank Dumbrille (1892–1969), a merchant, in 1919. They had at least one son, Richard MacDowell Dumbrille, who was

Postmaster of Augusta Township, Maitland, Ontario, where he also helped preserve the architectural heritage by purchasing and restoring old buildings. He was awarded the Order of Canada (Canada Gazette 26th June 1976) and Commander of the Order of St John (27th October 2004). He married Sara Jane and they had three children.

Thain's paternal grandparents, James MacDowell and Eleanor née Blair, were born in Ireland. His maternal grandfather, Francis Charles Ireland, married Sophia née Fish. In addition to Eleanor they had at least one son, James Ireland, who became a clergyman. He officiated at the wedding of his nephew, Merrill MacDowell, in 1918.

  Thain was educated at:

- Maitland Public School, Ontario.
- Brockville Collegiate Institute on Pearl Street East, Brockville, Ontario. He was inducted into the Institute's Hall of Excellence in 2003.
- Victoria College, University of Toronto (BA 1915). He was a letterman in football and hockey and captained the Jennings Cup champion ice hockey team in 1911–12. The Jennings Cup, instituted in 1898, has been contested every year since and is the longest consecutively awarded ice hockey trophy in the world. He held the 'Athletic Stick', awarded to the Victoria College athlete in his graduating year who most satisfactorily meets the conditions of holding four colours for various sports and exhibits leadership

The original Brockville Collegiate Institute seen here was built in 1889. The school expanded and in 1908 a north wing was added. The building was destroyed by fire in 1929 and the new Institute opened two year later.

and sportsmanship. He was also rink manager and Athletic Union President. He was granted an Honorary MA on Armistice Day 1918 as the graduate who achieved the highest military honour, representing … *thousands of graduates and undergraduates who have done their duty, fought, even died, having performed countless deeds of valour which in their sum constitutes Canada's glory*.

While at university he joined the Canadian Officer Training Corps and also served in The Queen's Own Rifles of Canada. On 19th November 1914, he joined the Militia as a provisional lieutenant in 41st Regiment (Brockville Rifles). Thain was commissioned as a lieutenant in 38th (Ottawa) Battalion CEF on 9th January 1915 and was assigned to B Company. He was described as 5′ 9″ tall, with ruddy/dark

Founded as the Upper Canada Academy by the Wesleyan Methodist Church in 1831, the College opened under a royal charter from King William IV in 1836. Although the school taught liberal arts subjects, it was unofficially a Methodist seminary. In 1841 it was incorporated as Victoria College and received a charter from the Upper Canadian Legislature. In 1884 Victoria University was formed when the College federated with Albert University. Six years later Victoria University federated with the University of Toronto and in 1892 moved to its current location on Queen's Park Crescent, Toronto. The College has the Royal Standard that covered Queen Victoria's coffin in 1901. In 1928 Union College federated with the theology department of Victoria College to became Emmanuel College.

38th Battalion's colours were presented on 31st July 1915, just before it sailed for Bermuda.

complexion, blue/grey eyes, dark brown hair and his religious denomination was Wesleyan. He attested in the CEF on 1st February and carried out training at London, Ontario.

Thain was promoted captain on 19th July and sailed for Bermuda on 8th August, where he suffered from dengue fever. He sailed for England on 29th May 1916, arriving at Plymouth on 9th June. Further training followed before going to France, landing at Le Havre on 13th August. **Awarded the DSO for his actions on 18th November in an attack on Desire Trench and Desire Support Trench at Petit Miraumont on the Somme. He led B Company in bombing three machine guns that had been holding up the advance. After severe hand-to-hand fighting he captured three officers and fifty men. Although wounded in the left hand by a grenade and suffering concussion, he initially remained at his post, LG 10th January 1917.** He was admitted to No.7 Stationary Hospital at

Patients and staff of No.7 Stationary Hospital at Boulogne.

Boulogne on 21st November and was then evacuated to Britain on HMHS *St Denis*, where he was treated at 2nd Western General Hospital, Manchester 24th–30th November. A medical board at 86 Strand, London on 1st December found him unfit for General Service for three weeks.

Another medical board at 76 Strand, London on 27th December found him fit for General Service and he returned to France on 14th January 1917, rejoining 38th Battalion on 17th January. Appointed acting major while commanding a company 1st March 1917. **Awarded the VC for his actions on Vimy Ridge, France on 9th–13th April 1917, LG 8th June 1917. Mentioned in Sir Douglas Haig's Despatch of 9th April 1917, LG 1st June 1917.** He was presented with the VC and DSO by the King at Buckingham Palace on 21st July.

Thain was wounded during his VC action and suffered from tonsillitis a week later, resulting in him being treated at No.7 Stationary Hospital, Boulogne 24th April–1st May. He was granted ten days leave from 8th June, but contracted trench fever on 28th June. He was admitted to 12th Field Ambulance on 3rd July and then 22nd Casualty Clearing Station for a week before transferring to 24th General Hospital, Étaples on 10th July. He had a mental breakdown (war neurasthenia) and was evacuated to Britain. As a result he relinquished his rank as acting major and was taken on strength of the Eastern Ontario Regimental Depot on 15th July. The

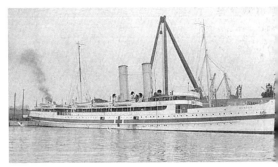

HMHS *St Denis* (2,570 tons) was built at Clydebank in 1908 for the Great Eastern Railway's Harwich–Hook of Holland service and was originally named SS *Munich*. She was requisitioned during the First World War as a hospital ship and renamed *St Denis*. She was acquired by the London & North Eastern Railway in 1923 and continued on the Hook of Holland route. In 1940, while involved in the evacuation of Amsterdam, she became trapped and was scuttled. The Germans salvaged her and she was eventually scrapped in 1950.

Thain MacDowell receives the VC and DSO from the King at Buckingham Palace on 21st July 1917.

same day he was admitted to Mrs Mitchison's Hospital, Clock House, Chelsea until 24th July when a medical board at 12 Bowers Street, London found him unfit for service and he was granted two months sick leave in Canada, travelling on SS *Metagama* on 3rd August. He spent the next three months at Brockville Hospital, Ontario where he was nursed by his sister Eula. A medical board at the Discharge Depot, Quebec found him unfit for General Service for two months on 13th August. His leave in Canada was extended and a medical board at Kingston, Ontario found him fit for General Service on 29th January 1918. He sailed for Britain on 5th February and on 1st March was posted to Headquarters Overseas Military Forces of Canada and to the Canadian Training Centre at Bexhill 4th July–25th November. During this period he may have attended a staff course at Clare College, Cambridge.

Mrs Mitchison's Hospital at the Clock House, Chelsea Embankment, London is now private flats. Mrs Mary E Mitchison (1897–1999) opened it in her home in 1916 as an auxiliary military hospital for officers. It had thirty beds and was affiliated to Queen Alexandra's Military Hospital a short distance away at Millbank. By the time it closed in April 1918, the hospital had treated 366 patients.

A medical board at 12 Bowers Street, London on 29th August found that, although he was of a nervous disposition, he was fit for General Service. Appointed temporary major 10th October. He returned to Canada on 7th December and was involved in demobilisation work. A medical board at Kingston, Ontario on 18th December found he was nervous, tired easily and had difficulty sleeping; he was fit for Home Service in Canada only. Thain was attached to Fleming Court Hospital, Ottawa as an outpatient from 3rd March 1919. He was admitted to Ste Anne de Bellevue Military Hospital suffering from neurasthenia 16th August–15th October. His case was reviewed on 13th October and it was concluded he would not be fit for General Service.

SS *Metagama* was built in Glasgow in 1914 for the Canadian Pacific's North Atlantic service. Her maiden voyage on 26th March 1915 was from Liverpool to St John, New Brunswick. Although she often carried troops, she remained in service with Canadian Pacific throughout the war. By 1930 reduced demand for transatlantic travel caused her to be laid up and she was broken up in 1934.

He was demobilised on 14th October 1919. However, he continued with the military and was appointed brevet major in the Ottawa Regiment (Duke of Cornwall's Own) on 1st May 1920. In 1927 he transferred to the Reserve of Officers and in 1933 was appointed Honorary Lieutenant Colonel of The Frontenac Regiment at Napanee, Ontario.

In civilian life Thain was appointed Private Secretary to the Minister of National Defence at Ottawa 1923–28. He was subsequently director of several mining companies as well as President of the Chemical Research Foundation. He remained very active and was proficient at golf, hockey and baseball. He travelled to London for the VC Garden Party at Buckingham Palace on 26th June 1920, the VC Dinner at the Royal Gallery of the House of Lords on 9th November 1929 and the VC Centenary Celebrations at Hyde Park on 26th June 1956. A man claiming to be Thain MacDowell paraded wearing a miniature VC in Sydney, New South Wales, Australia in 1937 and 1938. He was identified as Donald McDonald and claimed to have served in the Black Watch. He also paraded under the name of Evans VC. He was one of several known VC impostors in Australia at that time. During the Second World War Thain gave lectures to the Canadian Army.

On 1st July 1929, Thain MacDowell married Norah Jean Hodgson (1898–1983) and they lived at 354 Côte Saint Antoine Road, Westmount, Quebec. They had two sons:

- Thain H MacDowell.
- Angus J MacDowell (born 1937), composed the march, *The 48th Highlanders of Canada Pipes and Drums.*

One of Norah's brothers, Jonathan Archibald Hodgson (1896–1974), married Anne Churchill Hyde (1909–2006). Her father, Charles Edward Hyde (1880–1918), served as a lieutenant in 13th Battalion CEF and was killed in action on 7th August 1918 (Hangard Wood British Cemetery, France – I A 4).

Thain MacDowell died following a heart attack at Nassau, Bahamas on 27th March 1960. He is buried in Anglican Section 3, Oakland Cemetery, Brockville, Ontario (Lot 112). He is also commemorated in a number of other places:

- Lieutenant Colonel Thain Wendell MacDowell Auditorium of the Royal Canadian Legion Branch 96, Park Street, Brockville, Ontario was

Thain MacDowell's grave in Oakland Cemetery, Brockville (Wikipedia).

dedicated on 29th October 2009. His son, Angus, and nephew, Richard MacDowell Dumbrille, spoke on behalf of the family, of whom more than twenty were present. A bronze plaque outlining Thain's service was unveiled.

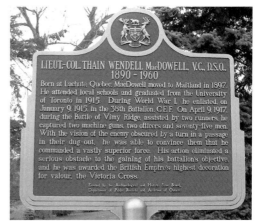

The memorial plaque to Thain MacDowell in Maitland, Ontario (Alan L Brown of ontarioplaques.com).

- In Kenora District, Ontario the seventy kilometres long MacDowell River, named on 12th December 1939, flows into MacDowell Lake, named on 25th March 1938, where there is a First Nation Indian reservation, MacDowell Township.
- Memorial plaque unveiled by his widow on 2nd September 1970 at the intersection of County Road 2 and Church Street at Maitland, Ontario. It was one of a series erected by the Ontario Department of Public Records and Archives.
- His portrait in the Canadian War Museum, General Motors Court, 330 Sussex Drive, Ottawa, Ontario.
- A wreath is taken each Remembrance Day from the cenotaph at Brockville and placed on his grave for one week.
- A wooden plaque bearing fifty-six maple leaves each inscribed with the name of a Canadian-born VC holder was dedicated at the Canadian Forces College, Toronto on Remembrance Day 1999.
- Named on a Victoria Cross obelisk to all Canadian VCs at Military Heritage Park, Barrie, Ontario dedicated by The Princess Royal on 22nd October 2013.
- Named on one of eleven plaques honouring 175 men from overseas awarded the VC for the Great War. The plaques were unveiled by the Senior Minister of State at the Foreign & Commonwealth Office and Minister for Faith and Communities, Baroness Warsi, at a reception at Lancaster House, London on 26th June 2014 attended by the Duke of Kent and relatives of the VC recipients. The Canadian plaque was unveiled outside the British High Commission in Elgin Street, Ottawa on 10th November 2014 by The Princess Royal in the presence of British High Commissioner Howard Drake, Canadian Minister of Veterans Affairs Julian Fantino and Canadian Chief of the Defence Staff General Thomas J Lawson.
- The Secretary of State for Communities and Local Government, Eric Pickles MP, announced that Victoria Cross recipients from the Great War would have commemorative paving stones laid in their birthplace as a lasting legacy of local heroes within communities. The stones would be laid on or close to the 100th anniversary of their VC actions. For the 145 VCs born in Australia, Belgium,

Canada, China, Denmark, Egypt, France, Germany, India, Iraq, Japan, Nepal, Netherlands, New Zealand, Pakistan, South Africa, Sri Lanka, Ukraine and United States of America, individual commemorative stones were unveiled at the National Memorial Arboretum, Alrewas, Staffordshire by Prime Minister David Cameron MP and Sergeant Johnson Beharry VC on 5th March 2015.

• Two 49 cents postage stamps in honour of the ninety-four Canadian VC winners were issued by Canada Post on 21st October 2004 on the 150th Anniversary of the first Canadian VC's action, Alexander Roberts Dunn VC.

In addition to the VC and DSO he was awarded the British War Medal 1914–20, Victory Medal 1914–19, George VI Coronation Medal 1937 and Elizabeth II Coronation Medal 1953. The VC is held by the University of Toronto Memorial Trust.

LIEUTENANT DONALD MACKINTOSH
3rd attached 2nd Battalion, Seaforth Highlanders (Ross-shire Buffs, The Duke of Albany's)

Donald Mackintosh was born at the Superintendent's House, Western Infirmary, Partick, Glasgow on 7th February 1896. His father was Colonel Donald James Mackintosh CB MVO MB CM LL.D FRS Edin (1862–1947). He was a medical student in 1881, lodging at 142 St Georges Road, Barony, Lanarkshire and by 1891 he was living at Queen's Park, Langside, Cathcart, Renfrewshire. In 1899 he was appointed Member of Council of the St Andrew's Ambulance Association. On 12th October 1901 he was commissioned as a surgeon lieutenant in The Glasgow Companies, Volunteer Medical Staff Corps and served as  Chairman of the Medical and Executive Committee of the Scottish National Red Cross Hospitals during the South African War. Mentioned in Field Marshal Earl Roberts' Despatch dated 1st March 1902 (Edinburgh Gazette 17th June 1902) and awarded the MVO 4th Class (LG 9th November 1902). Donald was promoted lieutenant colonel on 1st April 1908 to command 3rd Scottish General Hospital and was Assistant Director of Medical Services, 65th (2nd Lowland) Division from 1st April 1912, supervising the administration and organisation of all Military, War and Territorial General Hospitals in the Glasgow area. As a civilian, Donald was appointed Infirmary Superintendent of Western Infirmary, Glasgow and was appointed Chairman of Council of the St Andrew's Ambulance Association in 1911. Knight of Grace, Order of St John of Jerusalem, LG 23rd June 1914. He suffered

The Western Infirmary in Glasgow, where Donald Mackintosh senior was the Superintendent. The hospital was built in 1874 and expanded in 1911.

Stobhill Hospital opened in 1904. In September 1914 it was requisitioned as 3rd and 4th Scottish General Hospitals and returned to civilian use in 1920.

The Station Hotel, Perth where Donald's parents married in December 1894.

from cardiac dilation as a result of influenza debility, together with vertigo and shakes. A series of medical boards from 1st March 1916 onwards found him unfit until 16th June, when he was cleared for light duties. On 22nd June he was employed as Administrator of Hospitals and cleared for Home Service on 15th July, but was permanently unfit for General Service and was transferred to the Territorial Force Reserve on 26th July. Awarded CB (LG 24th January 1917) and Mentioned in Despatches (LG 25th January 1917). In 1917 he inspected Military and War Hospitals in Eastern Command for the Economics Committee of the War Office. He retired from the Territorial Army Reserve on reaching the age limit in November 1924 and was appointed DL Glasgow on 1st November 1929. Donald senior married Margaret 'Maggie' née Fullarton (1862–1956) at Station Hotel, Perth on 19th December 1894.

Donald junior had a sister, Anna Fullarton Mackintosh (1904–92), who was living at 108a University Avenue, Glasgow at the time of her marriage to John Blair (born c.1905) in 1933 at Wellington Church, Glasgow. John was a chartered accountant of 111 Douglas Street, Glasgow. They were living at 14 West Corennie Gardens, Glasgow in 1956.

Donald's paternal grandfather, also Donald Mackintosh (born c.1832), was a schoolmaster at Dykehead, Shotts, Lanarkshire. He married Agnes née Dawson (c.1835–68) in 1854 in Glasgow. When she died, he married Marion Dickie Cowan (born 1843). They were living at School House, Shotts in 1881. Donald's maternal grandfather, Thomas Taylor Fullarton (c.1816–75), was a farmer of Redstone, Cargill. He married Janet 'Jessie' née MacFarlane (c.1825–1906) at Cargill in 1850. In addition to Maggie they had five other children:

St Ninian's Preparatory School was founded in 1879 by Arthur John Caswall Dowding, father of Air Chief Marshal Hugh Dowding (1882–1970), who was born and educated at the school. The school was attended by two other VCs – David Younger and George Findlay. In 1987 the RAF Association and RAF Benevolent Fund bought the school, which was renamed Dowding House. It provides sheltered housing for former RAF personnel and dependants.

- James Fullarton (1852–1926) was a farmer of 220 acres at Redstone, Cargill. He died unmarried at Royal Infirmary, Perth.
- Janie Fullarton, born c.1855.
- Agnes Fullarton (c.1856–1907) died unmarried.
- Jessie Fullarton (1857–64). On 26th February 1864, she was asked to collect an item from a cupboard at home that was also used by her father to store gunpowder. She placed a candle too close and it exploded, resulting in severe burns to her and serious damage to the house. Jessie died a few hours later.
- Isabella Fullarton, born c.1859.

Donald was educated at Glasgow Academy, St Ninian's School at Moffat and Fettes College (Moredun House) from 1911 until December 1913 (OTC). He enlisted into 3rd Scottish General Hospital RAMC on 14th August 1914 (6A) as a sergeant. He was described as 5′ 8″ tall and weighed 157 lbs. Having been discharged to the Reserve on 13th February, he was commissioned into the Special Reserve of Officers, Seaforth Highlanders on 20th February 1915 and posted to 9th Battalion. He went to France on 29th September 1915 and was promoted lieutenant on 2nd February 1916. He received a gun shot wound to the left arm and shoulder on 21st March 1916 and was treated at No.1 British Red Cross Hospital, Le Touquet from the 23rd until being evacuated to England on 2nd April. He was treated at Yorkhill War Hospital,

Sir William Fettes (1750–1836) founded the school in memory of his only son, William, but it was not built until 1870. It was a boys school until 1970 and became fully co-educational in 1983. Ian Fleming's character, James Bond, attended Fettes College. Coincidentally a real James Bond did attend Fettes and was a frogman with the Special Boat Service. In addition to Donald Mackintosh, three other members of the school have been awarded the VC – William Herbert Anderson, Hector Lachlan Stewart MacLean and Matthew Fontaine Maury Meiklejohn. Another old boy is Tony Blair, PM of the United Kingdom 1997–2007.

Glasgow and joined 3rd (Reserve) Battalion for light duties on 15th August. Having been declared fit for General Service on 21st November, he joined 2nd Battalion on 13th January 1917. Donald attended the XV Corps Lewis Gun School 20th January–5th February.

Awarded the VC for his actions north of Fampoux, France on 11th April 1917, LG 8th June 1917. He was killed during his VC action and is buried in Brown's Copse Cemetery, Roeux (II C 49). He is also commemorated in a number of other places:

- Glasgow Academy War Memorial, Colebrooke Road, Glasgow.
- Glasgow University War Memorial, University Avenue, Glasgow.
- Memorial plaque and window in Elder Memorial Chapel, Western Infirmary, Dumbarton Road, Glasgow unveiled by the matron, Miss Gregory Smith, on 12th December 1925. The memorial is also to the VC's father, Colonel DJ

No.1 British Red Cross Hospital in the Casino at Le Touquet was also known as the Duchess of Westminster's Hospital.

Donald Mackintosh's grave in Brown's Copse Cemetery, Roeux.

Donald's parents receive his Victoria Cross from the King on 21st July 1917.

The memorial in the Chapel at the Western Infirmary, Glasgow to Donald and his father.

Mackintosh CB MVO. A tablet was also unveiled in memory of two nurses, Sister Ella Maud Bond and Staff Nurse Margaret S Dewar, who lost their lives during the war.

- Fettes College War Memorial, East Fettes Avenue, Edinburgh.
- Named on his parents' grave in Dalnottar Cemetery, Great Western Road, Old Kirkpatrick, Glasgow.

As Donald never married, the VC was presented to his parents by the King outside Buckingham Palace on 21st July 1917. In addition to the VC, he was awarded the 1914–15 Star, British War Medal 1914–20 and Victory Medal 1914–19. His VC is held by The Highlanders' Museum, Fort George, Ardersier, Inverness.

SECOND LIEUTENANT THOMAS HAROLD BROADBENT MAUFE
124th Siege Battery, Royal Garrison Artillery

Thomas Maufe was born at Warlbeck, King's Road, Ilkley, Yorkshire on 6th May 1898. He was known within the family as Squash. His father, Frederic Broadbent Muff (1857–1938), a master linen draper, was later chairman of Bradford's leading departmental store, Brown Muff & Co Ltd, known locally as the Harrods of the North. He married Helen Mann née Statham (1861–1923) in 1885 in Islington, London. By 1900 the family was living at Warlbeck, King's Road, Ilkley. On 30th July 1909 he changed the surname Muff to Maufe by Deed Poll inspiring the local ditty:

In Bradford 'tis good enoof
To be known as Mrs Muff
But in Ilkley by the river Wharfe
'Tis better to be known as Mrs Maufe!

In 1814 Elizabeth Brown opened a drapery at 11 Market Street, Bradford. In 1828 her son Henry joined the firm and in 1846 he went into partnership with his brother-in-law, Thomas Muff, to form Brown Muff & Co. They expanded the business and a new building was constructed in 1870. New stores were opened in Skipton, Bingley and Doncaster in the 1960s, but financial difficulties in the 1970s led to the company being sold to Rackhams, part of House of Fraser. The Bradford store closed in 1995.

At the time of the 1901 Census, Helen was one of twenty boarders at the South Cliffe Hotel, Bellevue Road, Southbourne, Hampshire, with sons Statham and Philip. Coincidentally Andrew and Margaret McRae Bruce were also staying at the hotel with their family, including son William, who was awarded the VC in the First World War. Frederic remained in Ilkley with daughter Frances and sons Frederick and Thomas. When he died in 1938, Frederic's estate was valued at £44,071/5/8. Thomas had four siblings:

- Statham Broadbent Maufe (1887–1916) married Constance Hilda Madeline Tennent (1887–1935) in 1914. On 16th December 1906, Statham was commissioned in 2nd Volunteer Battalion, The Prince of Wales's Own (West Yorkshire Regiment), which was absorbed into the Territorial Force on 1st April 1908. Promoted lieutenant and transferred to 6th Battalion as a university candidate 1908. Regular commission 24th August 1910, backdated to 18th September 1909, and remained in 2nd Battalion. Promoted lieutenant 10th November 1910. Served abroad 10th January 1910–5th April 1913 and was attached to 3rd Battalion from 30th March 1913. Joined 11th (Service) Battalion on 19th October 1914 as temporary captain and adjutant. Promoted captain 13th November 1914 and appointed temporary major 16th January 1915. Went with the Battalion to France on 25th August 1915. Appointed second-in-command 21st February 1916. **MID, LG**

The sun setting on Statham Maufe's grave in Heilly Station Cemetery, Méricourt-L'Abbé, France.

15th June 1916. Statham died of wounds at 36th Casualty Clearing Station at Heilly on 5th July 1916 and is buried at Heilly Station Cemetery, Méricourt-L'Abbé, France (I A 7). He is also commemorated on Ilkley War Memorial on Grove Road, which was unveiled by his brother, Thomas Maufe VC, on 23rd July 1922. Constance married Jonathan Richard Greenbank (c.1898–1966), sub-manager of a bank, in 1920 at Scarborough, Yorkshire.
- Philip Broadbent Maufe (1888–1975) married Marguerite Humphris Carter (1892–1968) in 1914. He became a director of the family business, Brown Muff & Co Ltd. They had three sons:
  - Michael Humphris Maufe (1916–2004) read aeronautical engineering at Christ's College, Cambridge and became an apprentice with the Bristol Aircraft Company. Emergency Commission in the Royal Air Force Volunteer Reserve as pilot officer on probation (79636) in the Administrative & Special Duties Branch 25th May 1940, having failed the eye test to become a pilot. Transferred to the Technical Branch on 24th November 1940 and and promoted war substantive flying

officer 25th May 1941 and temporary flight lieutenant 1st January 1943. Served at the Airborne Forces Experimental Establishment. Promoted flight lieutenant 1st March 1951 with seniority from 25th November 1948. Relinquished his commission on 12th November 1953. Michael married Lucy Holmes in 1941 and they had two children – Penelope S Maufe 1943 and Anthony M Maufe 1946. He joined the family business of Brown Muff & Co Ltd and eventually became managing director. His passion for flying vintage gliders was sparked when his favourite uncle, Thomas Maufe VC, treated him to a joy ride in a powered aircraft. He was eighty years old when he last flew solo.

◦ David H Maufe (1919–2011) was a farmer. He married Ann B Hastings-Turner (1919–66) in 1940 at Fakenham, Norfolk. They had four children – Miranda Maufe 1942, Georgina Maufe 1945, Tessa Maufe 1948 and Tarquin D Maufe 1951. David married Edith G Holbert in 1970 and Jane Rawnsley in 1973. He died in Maryland, USA.

◦ Garry Humphris Maufe (1922–2009) enlisted in the Royal Norfolk Regiment on 22nd May 1940. While on guard duty one night a fellow soldier shot himself in the shoulder to avoid being sent overseas, but the bullet ricocheted into his heart and killed him. Garry commenced training as an artillery officer cadet, but received an Emergency Commission in 1st King's Royal Rifle Corps (232567) on 18th April 1942 and was promoted war substantive lieutenant on 18th October 1942. He served in North Africa and Italy 1943–45. In Italy he crossed the Marano River under fire and was hit in the back by a bullet that inflicted only a severe bruise. On another occasion a shell landed near his feet, but sank deep into the mud before exploding ineffectually. **Awarded the MC for his actions on 4th January 1945 at Mezzano; he was woken at 4.30 a.m. by activity near his farmhouse headquarters. A sergeant in a forward position had lost two men and needed ammunition urgently. He set off in a carrier at dawn with a driver and 6215394 Rifleman Thomas Vickery Walker. They killed several enemy in ditches as the carrier drove about 550 metres along a narrow track to reach the sergeant and his men. He then joined a Canadian unit and flushed out about seventy Germans who fled back to their lines, (LG 21st June1945).** Rifleman Walker was awarded the MM. Garry entered Austria on 2nd May and came upon a German Mark III tank that had run out of petrol. He climbed onto the turret and discovered an SS officer inside with the 75 mm gun trained on his carriers. He persuaded the German to surrender and drove his prisoner to headquarters. Having been released to the Unemployed List in 1946, he took up farming on 500 acres of Lord Leicester's Holkham estate at Burnham Thorpe, Norfolk and started a successful commercial plum orchard. He married Marit S Børstad, a Norwegian au pair, in 1949 and they had four daughters – Marguerite N Maufe 1950, Zoe B Maufe 1953, Inger-Lise C Maufe 1956 and Kaja S Maufe 1962.

• Gwendolen Broadbent Maufe (1890–1957) married Richard Graham Lane (1888–1944) in 1910. He was a coal merchant, leaving an estate valued at

£121,545/13/11d when he died. Gwendolen was living at 6 Oakhill Avenue, Hampstead, London at the time of her death, leaving £33,472/14/7 in her will. They had four children – Rosemary G Lane 1921, Jean Lane 1922, John Frederick Graham Lane 1926 and Graham S Lane 1926.

- Frederick William Broadbent Maufe (1895–1980) was a twin with sister Frances. He was a cadet colour-sergeant in the Junior Division of the Uppingham School Officer Training Corps. He was commissioned in 4th West Riding (Howitzer) Brigade RFA (TF) on 25th May 1914 and allocated to 11th West Riding (Howitzer) Battery. Appointed temporary lieutenant 7th January 1915. Transferred to A Battery (10th West Riding) and went to France on 15th April 1915. Appointed acting captain while second-in-command of a battery 28th October 1917–14th August 1918. **MID, LG 18th May 1917. Awarded the MC when brigade forward observation officer, keeping up communication and sending back important information under heavy fire during an attack. Before going up he personally led the ammunition wagons singly to the battery position while the track was being heavily shelled. By his coolness he undoubtedly saved many casualties, LG 18th January 1918 and 25th April 1918. Awarded a Bar to the MC for twice attending to wounded under shell fire and carrying them clear of danger. Later, when the battery again came under shell fire, he cleared the detachments to a flank and led them back at the double to the guns, the fire of which was urgently needed. He filled a vacancy caused by a casualty in the most exposed gun emplacement and worked the gun until cease fire with the remaining men of the detachment. He had the most inspiring effect on the men and his fine example kept all the guns in action, LG 18th January 1918 and 25th April 1918.** Seconded as temporary captain 15th August 1918. Promoted captain 8th January 1919 backdated to 13th April 1918. Restored to RH & RFA (TF) establishment 22nd January 1919. He was a captain in 1st West Riding Brigade RFA (TF) on 31st July 1920. Frederick was commissioned as a temporary captain in the West Riding Brigade RFA (Defence Force) on 11th April 1921 and relinquished it on 6th July 1921. Promoted major in 69th (West Riding) Field Brigade (TA) on 21st October 1926 and lieutenant colonel on the Unemployed List on 10th June 1936. **Awarded the Territorial Decoration, LG 20th February 1931.** He was the Military Member, York (West Riding) Territorial Army and Auxiliary Forces Association in 1946. He transferred to the Territorial Army Reserve of Officers (20099) until he exceeded the age limit of liability to recall on 21st February 1951. Frederick married Frances Armitage in 1925 and they had three daughters – Rachel A Maufe 1926, Jane A Maufe 1929 and Susan A Maufe 1931.
- Helen Frances Broadbent Maufe (born 1895) was a twin with brother Frederick. She married Francis Anson Arnold-Forster (born 1890) in 1921. He was commissioned in 6th Duke of Wellington's (West Riding Regiment) on 1st April 1908. He transferred to 11th West Riding (Howitzer) Battery, 4th West Riding (Howitzer) Brigade RFA (TF) and was promoted lieutenant on 31st July 1909.

Transferred to 4th West Riding (Howitzer) Ammunition Column in 1913. Promoted captain 1st July 1913. He was serving in France prior to 31st December 1915. Appointed temporary major 20th March 1916 and promoted major 1st June 1916. **Awarded DSO, LG 1st January 1918, corrected 8th March and 11th April 1918.** Francis was commissioned in the Defence Force as a major in 2nd West Riding Brigade RFA on 10th July 1920 and relinquished his commission in the Defence Force on 22nd July 1921. He was a major in 70th (2nd West Riding) Brigade RFA (TA) in 1921 and transferred to the Territorial Army Reserve of Officers on 11th July 1925. **Awarded the Territorial Decoration, LG 3rd July 1923.** He was recalled as a major (20069) on 1st June 1939 and retired, having exceeded the age limit, on 1st September 1948.

Thomas' paternal grandfather, Thomas Parkinson Muff (c.1822–1901), was a draper. He married Eliza née Ingham (c.1819–89) in 1844. They were living at 4 Bellevue, Manningham, Bradford in 1861 and at Woodbank, Ilkley by 1881. In 1845 Thomas entered into partnership with Henry Brown, husband of his sister Betsy, in a linen and woolen draper's and tailor's shop in Market Street, Bradford. The shop was established by Henry's mother, Elizabeth Brown, in 1814 and was taken over by Henry in 1834. Thomas was employing twenty-four people in 1861. The partnership was dissolved by mutual consent on 29th September 1871 and a new business, Brown Muff & Co Ltd, opened in larger premises in Market Street. It became Bradford's leading departmental store (taken over as Rackhams in 1978). By 1881 Thomas was a master draper, employing forty-two people. When he died his estate was valued at £165,419/19/9. In addition to Frederic, Thomas and Eliza had five other children – Emily Muff c.1845, Rachel Alice Muff 1847, Henry Muff 1850, Charles James Muff (1851–1928) and Thomas William Muff 1855. Charles James Muff married Annie Maria McConnel (1862–1929) in 1884 and they had three children including:

• Ernest Gordon Muff (1885–1916) married Emily Cissie Harris (1888–1962) in 1910 and they had a daughter, Eileen Gordon Maufe in 1913. He served as G/18238 Private EG Maufe in 11th Queen's Own (Royal West Kent Regiment) and was killed on 6th October 1916 (Thiepval Memorial, France). Emily married Henry EJ Dalton (1878–1942) in 1920.
• Charles Gordon Muff (1889–1940) married Joyce Rankin (1895–1969) in 1916. He was commissioned in 6th West Yorkshire (TF) and served in 1/6th Battalion. Promoted lieutenant 7th November 1917 and attached to 1/5th Battalion in 1918. **MID twice, LG 23rd May 1918 and 8th July 1919.** He transferred to the Territorial Force Reserve on 29th September 1920 and the Territorial Army Reserve of Officers (49326) on 29th November 1921. Retired from the Reserve on 6th October 1939, having reached the age limit. Charles and Joyce had five children – Simone Maufe 1917, Gabriel Maufe 1919, Oliver G Maufe 1923, Elizabeth Maufe 1925 and Ambrose G Maufe 1927.

Augustus Wooldridge Godby founded a new school in Ilkley in 1889, 'to prepare the sons of gentlemen for entrance to the Royal Navy and to public schools'. After fourteen years the school moved to its current location at Greystone Manor, Ghyll Royd. At that time the boys attended hunts, trained with rifles and boxed.

Uppingham School, founded in 1584, remained small until expanding in the 19th century. By the 1960s it had 600 pupils. The first girl attended in 1973. Famous alumni include: Jonathan Agnew, the BBC's Chief Cricket Correspondent; Rowan Atkinson, actor and comedian; Vera Brittain's brother, Edward Brittain, whom she wrote about in *Testament of Youth*; Sir Malcolm Campbell and Donald Campbell, world land and water speed record holders; Stephen Fry, actor, comedian and writer; Lieutenant General Sir Brian Horrocks, commander of XXX Corps in the Second World War; CRW Nevinson, official war artist in both World Wars; William Henry Pratt, stage name Boris Karloff; John Schlesinger, film director; and Rick Stein, chef, restaurateur and television broadcaster.

His maternal grandfather, Reverend William Mann Statham (1830–1902), was an Independent minister of the Church. He married Mary Lamb née Pledge (1837–1918) in 1856. They were living at West Parade Terrace, Kingston upon Hull, Yorkshire in 1871. By 1891 he was Rector of Iver Heath, Buckinghamshire living at The Firs, Hillingdon, Middlesex. In addition to Helen they had three other children – Mary Morison Statham 1857, William Arnold Statham (1859–1935) and Emily Lamb Statham 1863. William Arnold Statham was a barrister who contested unsuccessfully the Bethnal Green constituency for the Conservatives in the 1895 General Election. He married Gwendoleyne Pearl SB Roberts-Cowley (1882–1968) in 1903 at Westminster.

Thomas was educated at Ghyll Royd School, Greystone Manor, Ilkley Road, Burley-in-Wharfedale January 1907–1912 and then at Uppingham School, Rutland until 1915, where he was in West Deyne House.

Thomas was trained at the Royal Military Academy Woolwich and commissioned on 10th May 1916. He went to France on 20th July 1916. **Awarded the VC for his actions at Feuchy, France on 4th June 1917, LG 2nd August 1917 and 31st March 1919.** The VC was presented by the King at Buckingham Palace on 29th August 1917. He was presented with a silver casket by the town of Ilkley in recognition of his bravery. Appointed acting captain 3rd July 1917–3rd March 1919, acting major 4th March 1919, reverting to acting captain 14th April–1st June 1919. Promoted lieutenant 10th November 1917 and captain 25th June 1919. He

Clare College was founded in 1326 as University Hall. In 1338 it was refounded as Clare Hall by an endowment from Elizabeth de Clare, granddaughter of Edward I. In 1856 it changed its name to Clare College and admitted women from 1972. Amongst its many famous alumni are: naturalist Sir David Attenborough; broadcaster, political analyst and former MP Matthew Parris; Richard Stilgoe, songwriter and musician; and war poet Siegfried Sassoon.

The Royal Military Academy Woolwich was founded in 1741 to train artillery and engineer officers. New buildings came into use in 1806. From 1920 the Academy also trained Royal Signals officers. It closed in 1939 and its last commandant was Major General Philip Neame VC. Thereafter all regular officers training was conducted at the Royal Military Academy Sandhurst, which had previously only trained infantry and cavalry officers. The Woolwich site was sold in 2006 and was converted and extended into 334 houses and apartments.

transferred to the Regular Army Reserve of Officers (Class I) on 25th June 1919 and resigned his commission on 31st July 1935.

After the war he studied civil engineering at Clare College Cambridge (BA & MA) 1919–22 and trained at the Royal School of Mines in Kensington. Thereafter he worked in tin smelting at Gravesend and tin mining in Cornwall. Later he was a director of Brown Muff & Co Ltd of Bradford. His address in November 1921 was Woodlands Rise, Ilkley.

Thomas Maufe married Mary Gwendolen née Carr (22nd September 1904– 20th January 1978) on 4th June 1932 at St Margaret's, Ilkley. It was the fifteenth anniversary of his VC action. The reception was held at Wells House and they honeymooned in Scotland. Gwen was a well known local tennis player. Prior to the marriage he was living at Stonedene, Ilkley. In 1942 they were living at Whitethorne, Rupert Road, Ilkley. They had two children:

• Adrianne Helen Maufe (born 16th April 1935) married James Farquhar Thomson (1929–90) at Westminster in 1957 and they had four children – Lyn Susan Thomson 1957, Tracy Fiona Thomson 1959, James Robert Farquhar Thomson 1960 and Timothy David Farquar Thomson 1963.
• Anthony Peter B Maufe (born 9th May 1941) married Carol N Searle in 1965 and they had two children – Simon NB Maufe 1965 and Clare Victoria Maufe 1969.

Gwen's father, George Carr (1865–1935), was a stuff merchant in 1901. He married Florence Marianne née Tee (1873–1954) in 1893. In 1901 they were living at Cragg Mount, Rawdon, Yorkshire. By November 1929 they were at Hillside, Wells Road, Ilkley and at other times lived at North Hill, Ilkley and Whitethorn, Myddelton, Ilkley. In addition to Mary they had four other children – Hugh Dixon Carr 1895, Helen Carr 1898, George Philip Carr 1900 and Christopher Glyn Carr (1907–63). Christopher enlisted in the Royal Army Service Corps and rose to acting lance sergeant until being granted an Emergency Commission (121028) on 21st February 1940. Promoted lieutenant 1941, war substantive captain 12th August 1942 and temporary major 12th August 1942–1949. He was appointed GSO2 Training Branch, HQ Combined Operations on 28th August 1946. He converted to a short service commission as a captain on 1st August 1949 with seniority from 12th August 1942. Promoted major on 21st February 1953 and transferred to the Regular Army Reserve of Officers on 1st April 1957 until relinquishing his commission on 1st April 1959. He lived at Lyncroft, Skipton Road, Ilkley and died unmarried on 14th May 1963.

Around 1936 Thomas was diagnosed with diabetes. At the outbreak of the Second World War he wanted to rejoin, but was refused on account of his medical condition. He served as a private in the Ilkley Company, 29th West Riding (Otley) Battalion Home Guard instead. On 28th March 1942 he was killed during a training exercise at Manor Farm, Blubberhouses Moor, near Ilkley when a mortar bomb exploded in the tube. Private Henry Galloway was also killed and Private John Ford was seriously injured. Thomas is buried in Ilkley Cemetery (A 768). He left £24,797/17/5 gross, £20,546 net. He is commemorated in a number of other places:

The Royal School of Mines was established in 1851 as the Government School of Mines and Science Applied to the Arts in Jermyn Street, London. It merged with the Royal College of Chemistry in 1853 and its name changed in 1863 to the Royal School of Mines. It moved to South Kensington in 1872 and in 1907 was incorporated into Imperial College of Science and Technology. The impressive building on Prince Consort Road opened in 1913.

Thomas and Gwen's grave in Ilkley Cemetery.

- Maufe Way, Ilkley was named after him in 1997.
- Memorial stone cairn at Blubberhouses, North Yorkshire erected on 27th May 1946 near where he and Henry Galloway were killed.
- Blue stone tablet in Uppingham School's Galilee Chapel dedicated to the five Old Uppinghamians who were awarded the VC. The others were Wilward Clarke, John Collings-Wells, Arthur Lascelles and George Maling.
- Memorial stone in the Garden of Remembrance behind Bradford Cenotaph unveiled on 26th July 1999 and dedicated to seven men associated with Bradford who were awarded the VC.
- Royal Military Academy Woolwich VC Honour Board, Woolwich, London now in the RMA Sandhurst Library.
- Royal Artillery VC Memorial in the ruins of St George's Chapel, the former Garrison Church at Woolwich, which was reduced to a roofless shell by a V1 in 1944.
- Brass plaque in St George's Memorial Church, Ypres, Belgium dedicated to the 447 boys of Uppingham School who gave their lives in the Great War and 250 in the Second World War.

The memorial to seven men associated with Bradford who were awarded the VC in the Garden of Remembrance behind Bradford Cenotaph.

Ilkley War Memorial.

- Bronze memorial plaque for 1939–45 on the gates of Nevill Holt Manor House, Nevill Holt, Medbourne, Leicestershire. A preparatory school associated with Uppingham was established there in 1919, well after Thomas' school days.
- Ilkley War Memorial.
- Clare College War Memorial, Cambridge.

In addition to the VC he was awarded the British War Medal 1914–20, Victory Medal 1914–19 and George VI Coronation Medal 1937. The VC is held privately.

427586 PRIVATE WILLIAM JOHNSTONE MILNE
16th Battalion (Canadian Scottish), Canadian Expeditionary Force

William Milne was born on 21st December 1891 at 8 Anderson Street, Cambusnethan, near Wishaw, Lanarkshire, Scotland. His father, David Milne (1860–1917), was a carting contractor living at 43 Hope Street, Newmains, Lanarkshire in 1885. David married Agnes née McCormick (1860–1948), a domestic servant, in October 1885. By 1901 the family was living at 10 Anderson Street, Cambusnethan, Lanarkshire. When David died, only nine days after his son's VC was gazetted, he was a road surface man. William had seven siblings:

- Alexander Milne born in 1887.
- Jane Milne born in 1889.
- David Milne (1894–1984) married Martha Snodgrass (c.1887–1936) in 1918 and they had three children – Sarah Anne Milne 1919, an unnamed child born and died 1919 and Martha Milne c.1921.
- Margaret Milne born in 1895.
- Agnes Milne born in 1897.
- Helen 'Nellie' Milne born in 1900.
- Elizabeth Milne born in 1903.

William's paternal grandfather, Alexander Milne (1830–89), was a ploughman. He married Jane née Baker (c.1832–1909) in 1853. They were living at Upper Thainston Cottages, Fettercairn, Kincardineshire in 1861 and at Auchcairnie Cottage, Fourdoun, Kincardineshire in 1871 and 1881, by when

Cambusnethan, near Wishaw, Lanarkshire where William Milne was born.

he was an agricultural labourer (overseer). When he died he was a farm grieve. Jane was living at Balbegno Cottages, Fettercairn in 1891. In addition to David they had six other children – Susan Milne 1853, Helen Stewart Milne 1855, Mary Ann Milne 1857, William Milne 1864, James Milne 1865 and Alexander Milne 1871.

William's maternal grandfather, Michael McCormick (c.1822–93), was a coal miner. By 1871 he was a mineral weigher in an ironworks. He married Jane née Johnston (c.1818–99) at Douglas, Lanarkshire in 1848. They were living at 3 Roadend Row,

Fettercairn, Kincardineshire where William's paternal grandparents lived.

Gasswater, Ayrshire in 1851. By 1871 they were at 44 Hope Street, Cambusnethan, Lanarkshire and by 1881 at 43 Hope Street. In addition to Agnes they had five other children – Margaret McCormick c.1847, William McCormick c.1852, Jane McCormick c.1854, John McCormick c.1856 and James McCormick c.1858.

William was educated at Newmains Public School, Cambusnethan and in 1901 he emigrated to Canada to work at Kirkland Farm, near Caron, Moose Jaw, Saskatchewan, owned by Walter Cumming. He enlisted at Moose Jaw on 11th September 1915 and was described as 5′ 5½″ tall, with fair complexion, blue eyes, dark brown hair and his religious denomination was Presbyterian. William sailed for Britain with 46th Battalion on SS *Lapland* from Halifax on 23rd October 1915, arriving at Devonport on 30th October. He undertook basic training at Bramshott and was treated at Connaught Military Hospital, North Camp, Aldershot 26th March–3rd April and 2nd–8th June 1916 for gonorrhoea, during which time his pay was stopped. He sailed for France on 16th June and transferred to 16th Battalion next day, reporting to the unit in the Ypres Salient on 20th June. He took part in the Battle of the Somme from August and was in action at Pozières and on the Ancre Heights on 8th October, during which Piper James Cleland Richardson of 16th Battalion won the VC for his part in the attack on Regina Trench. William was

Kirkland Farm, near Caron is about thirty kilometres from Moose Jaw, Saskatchewan. William worked there for Walter Cumming (the farm is still in the family) until September 1915. In 1995 the Government of Saskatchewan placed a memorial plaque at the farm. A ceremony was held there on 13th September 2015 to commemorate the centenary of William's walk to Moose Jaw. It was attended by Lieutenant Governor Vaughn Solomon Schofield, members of the armed forces, government and local residents (Moose Jaw Times-Herald).

Bramshott Camp.

SS *Lapland* was built for the Red Star Line in 1908. She operated across the North Atlantic and in April 1912 brought the surviving members of *Titanic*'s crew back to England. From October 1914, *Lapland* worked under the British flag on charter to Cunard. In 1917 she was mined, but reached Liverpool. Later that year she was requisitioned as a troopship and carried 1st Aero Squadron, the first American air unit to reach France. She returned to the Red Star Line in 1920 and in June that year carried Douglas Fairbanks and Mary Pickford on their honeymoon. Her last voyage was in 1932.

admitted to No.2 Canadian Field Ambulance on 28th November with influenza. He was transferred to the Divisional Rest Station and No.3 Canadian Field Ambulance on 3rd December until rejoining the Battalion on 19th December.

Awarded the VC for his actions near Thélus on Vimy Ridge on 9th April 1917, LG 8th June 1917. He was killed during his VC action and is commemorated on the Canadian National Vimy Memorial, France. William never married and the VC was posted to his family in Lanarkshire. He is also commemorated in a number of other places:

- On a memorial to fourteen Lanarkshire VCs dedicated at Hamilton, Lanarkshire on 19th April 2002.
- Two 49 Cent postage stamps in honour of the ninety-four Canadian VCs were issued by Canada Post on 21st October 2004 on the 150th Anniversary of the first Canadian VC's action, Alexander Roberts Dunn.

Connaught Military Hospital, North Camp, Aldershot (actually Farnborough) opened in 1898 and closed in 1948. Most of it has since been demolished but the entrance block was retained as part of the Normandy Barracks Officers Mess.

- Victoria Cross obelisk to all Canadian VCs at Military Heritage Park, Barrie, Ontario dedicated by The Princess Royal on 22nd October 2013.
- Named on one of eleven plaques honouring 175 men from overseas awarded the VC for the Great War. The plaques were unveiled by the Senior Minister of State

at the Foreign & Commonwealth Office and Minister for Faith and Communities, Baroness Warsi, at a reception at Lancaster House, London on 26th June 2014 attended by the Duke of Kent and relatives of the VC recipients. The Canadian plaque was unveiled outside the British High Commission in Elgin Street, Ottawa on 10th November 2014 by the Princess Royal in the presence of British High Commissioner, Howard Drake, Canadian Minister of Veterans Affairs Julian Fantino and Canadian Chief of the Defence Staff, General Thomas J Lawson.

William Milne's name is engraved with 11,284 other Canadians with no known grave on the Canadian National Vimy Memorial.

In addition to the VC he was awarded the British War Medal 1914–20 and Victory Medal 1914–19. His next-of-kin is eligible to receive the Canadian Memorial Cross. When William's mother died, the VC passed to his sister Nellie. It was later acquired by a Scottish collector and in 1979 by Jack Stenabaugh, from Huntsville, Ontario. He put the VC group up for sale through Christie, Mason & Woods Ltd in London. It was the

The Lanarkshire VC memorial in Hamilton (Scotland's War).

last Canadian Vimy Ridge VC in private ownership and the Canadian War Museum wanted it, but did not feel justified in spending most of its annual budget on a single item. Public subscriptions were called for and the VC group was bought on 25th July 1989 for £41,000. It is held by the Canadian War Museum in Ottawa, Ontario.

LIEUTENANT RUPERT THEODORE VANCE MOON
58th Australian Infantry Battalion, AIF

Rupert Moon was born on 14th August 1892 at Bacchus Marsh, Victoria, Australia. He was nicknamed Mick. His father, Arthur Moon (1856–c.1933), was born at Hurstbourne Priors, Hampshire. He was a clerk and land agent in 1871 and a clerk at Exeter Probate Court in 1881, living with his parents. Arthur joined the Devon Volunteers and lived at Crediton for some years. He married Ellen 'Nellie' née Dunning (1851–1934) on 5th February 1884 at St Olave's Church, Exeter, Devon. Her sister, Eliza Sutherland Dunning, was married in the same church the following month. Arthur and Ellen emigrated to Australia shortly afterwards, where he became an inspector at the Collins Street Branch of the National Bank of Australasia, Melbourne, Victoria. They were living at 22 Murphy Street, Fawkner, Victoria in 1914, at 4 Lambert Street, Toorak, Victoria in 1919 and at Hawksburn Road, South Yarra, Victoria in 1933. Nellie was living with her daughters, Constance and Dorothy, at 8 Darling Street, South Yarra, Victoria by 1924. Rupert had four siblings:

- John Dunning Moon (1885–99).
- Arthur Stapley Moon (1894–1960) was a bank clerk who also served in 49th Infantry, Citizen's Military Force. He was known as Phil. He enlisted in 8th Light Horse Regiment AIF on 17th August 1915 (2134) at Melbourne, Victoria, described as 5′ 6¾″ tall, weighing 158 lbs, with fresh complexion, blue eyes, fair hair and his religious denomination was Church of England. Posted to 24th (Depot) Battalion AIF, Royal Park, Victoria 12th November and transferred to Reinforcements Williamstown, Victoria on 13th January 1916. Promoted lance corporal 28th January and embarked on HMAT A43 *Barunga* at Melbourne on 7th April with the 15th Reinforcement bound for Egypt. He was taken on strength of 3rd Light Horse Training Regiment, Tel el Kebir, on 10th May and transferred to 4th Light Horse Regiment on 30th May at Abou Hammad (2134A) to be with his brother Rupert. He was admitted to No.3 Australian General Hospital, Abbassia with constipation 4th–7th June and pyrexia 7th–9th June, before rejoining his unit at Tel el Fara. Arthur was charged with taking a mule from barracks without permission at Belah on 11th March 1918, for which he forfeited two days' pay and reverted to trooper. He suffered a gunshot wound to the left leg on 14th July and was admitted to 36th Stationary Hospital, Gaza on 16th July, transferring to 24th Stationary Hospital, Kantara next day and 14th Australian General Hospital, Port Said on 19th July. After sixteen days' leave in Cairo, stationed

Bacchus Marsh, Victoria where Rupert Moon was born.

Rupert Moon's parents married at St Olave's Church, Exeter in 1884.

at Moascar Garrison 12th–29th October, he rejoined his unit at Tripoli on 18th November. Promoted lance corporal 23rd March 1919 and returned to Australia on SS *Essex* departing Kantara on 15th June 1919. Arthur was discharged at 3rd Military District, Victoria Barracks, Melbourne on 8th September 1919 and resumed his duties as a bank clerk. He was Mentioned in Despatches. He was living at the Farmer's Arms Hotel, Nhill, Victoria in 1924. Arthur married Annie Bruerton Claridge Ford (1905–64), a nurse at Ballarat Hospital, Victoria, in 1930. They had two children, Campbell Moon and Shannon Moon, and were living at 286 Williams Road, Fawkner, Victoria in 1931. He was the manager of various banks – Goroke National Bank, Wannon, Victoria in 1936, Hume National Bank, New South Wales in 1943 and 60 Main Street, Mornington, Victoria in 1949.

- Constance Josephine Moon (born 1890) was a bank clerk. She married Geoffrey Ashburton Thompson (1894–1961) c.1924. Geoffrey was a student living at 85 Rose Street, Armadale, Victoria in 1921. He qualified as a medical practitioner and they moved to 114 Albany Road, Victoria Park, Swan, Western Australia in 1925 before moving to 23 Mount Street, Perth by 1943. By 1980 Constance was living at 78 Minora Road, Nedlands, Western Australia.
- Dorothy Nell Moon (1888–1962) died unmarried.

Rupert's paternal grandfather, John Moon (1818–91), born at Lapford, Devon, was a noted cattle and game fowl breeder on his estate at Kelland Barton. John married Elizabeth Jane née Gay (1822–77) at Torrington, Devon in 1843. He was land agent and steward for the Earl of Portsmouth's estate at Hurstbourne Priors, Hampshire and later was an agent to Sir Massey Lopes. In July 1867 he was a land agent and surveyor when he was declared bankrupt. They were living at Maristow Cottage, Tamerton Foliot, Devon in 1861, 8 Longfield Place, Plymouth, Devon in 1867, while he conducted his business from 30 Westwell Street and 2 Moor View Terrace, Charles, Plymouth in 1871. In addition to Arthur they had five other children:

- Edmund Gay Moon (1843–84).
- Sarah Anne Moon (1845–1922) married John Partridge (1839–99) in 1866 at Tamerton Foliot, Devon. John was a farmer and they were living at North Hilldown, Bow, Devon in 1881. Sarah was living with her stepmother, Mary Anne Moon, at Searle Street, Crediton in 1891 and at 81 Ballater Road, Brixton, London at the time of her death in 1922. They had six children – John Moon Partridge 1867, Annie Madeline Partridge 1871, Jessie Maud Partridge 1872, Mary Kathleen Partridge 1877, Arthur St George Partridge 1879 and Walter Gay Partridge 1886.
- Frank Moon 1847.
- Harry Moon (1853–1923) was a law clerk for a pharmaceutical society. He married Donna Holmes (1864–1952) in 1895 at Camberwell, London. They were living at 1 St Margaret's Road, Brockley, Kent in 1911.

- Walter Moon (1863–1949) married Marion Richards (born 1868) in 1895 at Holy Trinity Church, Barnstaple, Devon. Walter was a bank clerk in 1891 and manager of Lloyds Bank, Salisbury by 1911, when the family was living at 16 Bourne Avenue, Salisbury. They had three children – Vera Ethel Moon c.1900, Ivy Frances Moon 1901 and Harold Curtis Moon c.1908. When he died his estate was valued at £27,014/5/8. Harold was commissioned in the Royal Artillery (194575) on 5th July 1941.

John married Mary Ann Bromfield (born 1854) in 1880 at Bedwelty, Monmouthshire and was living with her at Roseville, Searle Street, Crediton, Devon in 1881. Mary was born at Worcester. He was Surveyor to the Urban Sanitary Authority at Crediton and Sanitary Inspector and Collector of Rates to the Crediton Improvement Commissioners. He was also Honorary Secretary of the Cottage Garden and Horticultural Society, Crediton and North Devon Race Meetings and the Crediton Fat Stock, Root and Poultry Show, frequently judging at agricultural shows in Devon and Wales and also at Smithfield. His estate was valued at £10,140/13/5 when he died. Mary was living as a caretaker with her widowed sister, Frances Jane Murrell, at 38 Ebury Street, St George, Hanover Square, London in 1911.

His maternal grandfather, Jonathan 'John' Dunning (c.1816–75), was born at North Tawton, Devon. He married Mary Cock née Stevens (c.1818–82) at Penzance, Cornwall in 1843, where she was born. John was a commercial traveller in drapery goods. The family was living at 3 Park Place, Exeter, Devon in 1851, at 1 Belle Air Place, Exeter in 1861 and later at Mount Radford, Exeter. In addition to Ellen they had five other children:

- Mary 'Minnie' Stevens Dunning (born 1845) married Caleb Thomas, a civil engineer, in 1875.
- Eliza Sutherland Dunning (1849–1924) was a schoolmistress, living as head of household with her mother and sister Helen at 15 David's Hill, Exeter in 1881. When she married Frank Stapley (1858–1944) at St Olave's Church, Exeter in 1884, she was a school principal. Frank was an architect and town planner who went to South Africa in 1880, where he practised in Cape Town and on the Kimberley diamond fields. After contracting fever in 1883 he returned to England. Eliza and Frank migrated to Victoria, Australia. He worked for William Salway, a leading Melbourne architect, and also with Melbourne City Council's surveyors department 1887–93 before venturing out on his own. He designed domestic, commercial and industrial buildings, including the West Melbourne Stadium. Frank held a number of prominent appointments – Melbourne's Chief Advocate of Town Planning, member of Melbourne City Council 1901, Lord Mayor of Melbourne 1917–18, President of the Royal Victorian Institute of Architects 1920–21, Alderman of Melbourne 1921–39, Foundation Chairman of the Metropolitan Town Planning Commission 1922, Chairman of Melbourne

Council Parks and Gardens Committee and he was also a member of the Melbourne and Metropolitan Board of Works, the Health Commission and the National War Memorial Committee. He was living at 18 Park Street, South Yarra when he married Edith Ellen Simms (1888–1978) in September 1924 at St James's Anglican Church, West Melbourne. Edith was a barmaid living at 22 Drummond Street, Carlton, Victoria 1912–14. They were living at 44 Gardiner Parade, Kooyong, Victoria in 1943.

Frank Stapley as Lord Mayor of Melbourne 1917–18.

- Kate Dunning (born 1850) was a schoolmistress of Blenheim House, Exeter. She married Henry Martyn in 1876 at Exeter. He was an accountant. They emigrated to Victoria, Australia aboard the *MacDuff*, arriving in August 1877.
- John Ashburton Dunning (born 1854).
- William Stoneman Dunning (1856–76). He was staying with his uncle, William Stoneman Dunning, at Tudor Road, Penge, Surrey in 1871. William was a seaman when he died of smallpox aboard the *Blenheim* at Rangoon, Burma on 16th March 1876. He is buried in Rangoon Town Cemetery.

Rupert spent his childhood years at Maffra, Gippsland, Victoria. He was educated at Kyneton Grammar School, Victoria and worked as a bank clerk at the National Bank of Australasia, Melbourne and at branches at Kyneton, Casterton, South Melbourne, Bairnsdale, Maffra and Geelong.

He had served in the Militia and enlisted in the AIF on 21st August 1914 and was posted to Broadmeadows Camp, Melbourne, Victoria (153). He was described as 5′ 5¾″ tall, weighing 139 lbs, with fair complexion, blueish eyes, brown hair and his religious denomination was Church of England. He embarked at Melbourne with A Squadron, 4th Light Horse Regiment, as a trumpeter on HMAT A18 *Wiltshire* on 20th October. *Wiltshire* assembled with the first convoy on 1st November at King George's Sound, Albany, Western Australia to transport the first detachment of the Australian and New Zealand Imperial Expeditionary Forces to the Middle East. Rupert disembarked at Alexandria, Egypt on 10th December and moved to Mena. He was admitted to Mena Hospital in April 1915 and discharged on the 25th. He embarked at Alexandria for Gallipoli on 15th May. On 29th September he was admitted to hospital, but rejoined his unit next day. Promoted lance corporal 23rd November and returned to Egypt aboard HMT *Caledonia*, arriving at Alexandria on 27th December. He transferred to Regimental Headquarters and was appointed provisional acting sergeant trumpeter at Heliopolis on 20th January 1916 and provisional sergeant trumpeter on 9th February. Promoted sergeant 6th March and embarked at Alexandria for France on 10th June, arriving at Marseilles on 17th June with II ANZAC Mounted Regiment (two squadrons of 4th Light Horse and a squadron of Otago Mounted Rifles).

On 9th September Rupert was commissioned and transferred to 58th Battalion. He went on leave to England on 7th January 1917 and joined 5th Australian Division School of Instruction on 18th February, returning to his unit on 28th March. Promoted lieutenant 6th April. **Awarded the VC for his actions at Bullecourt, France on 12th May 1917, LG 14th June 1917.** The VC was presented by the King at Buckingham Palace on 3rd August 1917.

Rupert was admitted to 8th Australian Field Ambulance and was transferred to No.29 Casualty Clearing Station at Grevillers and 20th General Hospital at Camiers on 14th May. He was evacuated to Reading War Hospital, Berkshire aboard HMHS *Pieter de Coninck* from Calais on 26th May and transferred to 1st Southern General Hospital, Birmingham, Warwickshire on 28th May. He was placed on the Supernumerary List on 11th August and returned to Australia on 10th January 1918 on SS *Corinthic*. He re-embarked at Sydney, New South Wales on HMAT A14 *Euripides* on

No.2 Australian General Hospital at Mena Camp, in the shadow of the Great Pyramid at Giza.

The *Caledonia* (9,223 tons), an Anchor Line ship built in Glasgow in 1904, was requisitioned as a troopship in 1914. She was torpedoed and sunk by U-65 on 4th December 1916, 125 miles southeast of Malta. Only one life was lost. The master, Captain James Blaikie (1861–1930), aimed his crippled ship at the submarine and damaged it so severely that it had to limp to port on the surface and was not in service again until April 1917. The Germans took Blaikie prisoner and he was in danger of being shot for his attack on U-65, but the British made it clear through neutral American channels that such an action would result in retaliation against a German prisoner. Blaikie spent the rest of the war in a prison camp and on his return he was awarded the DSC, LG 24th May 1919.

1st May, transferred to the armed merchant cruiser HMS *Teutonic* at New York on 14th June and disembarked at Liverpool, Lancashire on 2nd July.

He was posted to the School of Musketry, Tidworth, Hampshire on 17th July and embarked at Southampton on 14th August, landing at Le Havre, France two days later. He rejoined his unit on 19th August, but was detached to 60th Battalion 23rd–26th August and was posted to Fourth Army School of Instruction in France on 3rd October. He rejoined 58th Battalion on 3rd November. Appointed

Pieter de Coninck (1,767 tons) was one of four Belgian Government mail steamers used as ambulance transports from 16th March 1917 to 28th March 1919. She was built in 1910 and could carry 377 casualties.

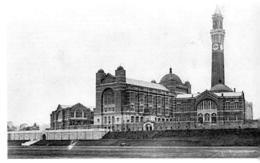

From 1909 the new buildings of the University of Birmingham were earmarked as a war hospital of 520 beds. Plans were put into action in August 1914 and the first casualties arrived on 1st September. More university and other suitable buildings were taken over and at its peak 1st Southern General Hospital had space for 130 officers and 2,357 other ranks. In May 1917 the former Poor Law Infirmary on Dudley Road was separated from it and became 2/1st Southern General Hospital.

temporary captain 5th February–17th April 1919 and was on leave in England 4th–29th March. Granted the honorary rank of captain 17th April. Rupert left France on 23rd April, arriving at Southampton next day. He embarked on SS *Port Lyttleton* on 10th June and disembarked at Melbourne, Victoria on 3rd August. His appointment in the AIF was terminated on 4th October 1919 and he transferred to the Reserve of Officers.

Rupert resigned from the National Bank of Australasia on 1st December 1919 and worked in Malaya as an assistant manager of a rubber plantation. He returned to Australia and worked as a bookkeeper and jackeroo on a property near Corowa, New South Wales, before returning to the National Bank of Australasia. After holding posts at various branches, including North Melbourne and Foster, he became an accountant with the Geelong firm of Dennys Lascelles Ltd, wool brokers. He becoming its managing director in 1948 and retired in 1960. He was a member of a number of clubs in Victoria – Naval

SS *Teutonic* was launched in 1889 for the White Star Line under the British Auxiliary Armed Cruiser Agreement. Indeed she was Britain's first armed merchant cruiser, although her eight 4.7″ guns were removed in peacetime. She gained the Blue Riband in 1891, but lost it the following year to the *City of Paris* and was the last White Star ship to hold it. During the Boer War she served as a troop transport and in 1901 survived a tsunami. In 1911 she was transferred to the Dominion Line for the Canadian service. At the start of the First World War she became a merchant cruiser in 10th Cruiser Squadron. In 1916 she was refitted with 6″ guns and was used as a convoy escort ship as well as a troopship. She was scrapped at Emden in 1921 (Detroit Publishing Company).

and Military, Victorian Racing, Moonee Valley Racing, Geelong Racing, Victoria Amateur Turf and Barwon Heads Golf.

Rupert Moon married Susan Alison May 'Sammy' Vincent (1st May 1906–3rd March 1998) on 17th December 1931 at St George's Presbyterian Church, Geelong. They lived at Calder Park, Mount Duneed, Victoria and 13 Bostock Avenue, Barwon Heads, Victoria. Rupert and Sammy had two children – Moira Moon and Michael Moon.

Sammy's father, Robert Vincent (died 1935), married Leslie née Robertson (died 1940). They lived at Prospect House, Western Beach, Geelong, Victoria. In addition to Sammy they had a son, Robert Trevor Vincent (1898–1938). He volunteered for service with the Light Horse and enlisted on 29th July 1918 at Melbourne (V79375). He was described as 5′ 8¾″ tall, weighing 145 lbs, with fair complexion, hazel eyes, dark brown hair and his religious denomination was Presbyterian. Having carried out basic training at Recruit Depot Battalion, Broadmeadows Camp, Victoria he was due to go to Egypt with 8th General Service Reinforcements, but with the armistice on 11th November further reinforcements were not needed and he was demobilised on 24th December 1918. He married Ella Mary 'Weenie' Napthine (born 1900) in 1925. Robert was a keen aviator and used an aeroplane for business purposes. He won the handicap section in the Adelaide Centenary Air Race in 1936 with Mr CD Pratt. Robert was commissioned in the Royal Australian Air Force on 16th October 1939 at Broadford, Victoria and was posted to the Flying Training School. He and Pilot Officer JR Whitford, champion pilot of the Royal Aero Club of New South Wales in 1938, were killed when their aircraft crashed on 29th November 1939. Weenie married Captain Klaas Hemke-Henkes (1891–1945). She was awarded the OBE for charity on fund raising activities, LG 30th December 1975.

Rupert served in the Volunteer Defence Corps during the Second World War and was appointed captain in 6th Victorian Battalion on 9th September 1942. He was Assistant Staff Captain of South West Group January 1943–September 1944.

An Anzac Dinner on 23rd April 1927, hosted by Lieutenant General Sir John Monash GCMG KCB VD, was attended by twenty-three VCs including Rupert Moon, but for an unknown reason The Duke of York was not invited. Two days later Rupert took part in the Anzac commemoration service at the Exhibition Building, Melbourne, Victoria in the presence of the Duke of York. In the march past the VCs conceded pride of place to blinded soldiers who insisted on marching.

Rupert was one of ten VCs presented to Queen Elizabeth II and HRH The Duke of Edinburgh at Melbourne Cricket Ground on 25th February 1954. He attended the VC Centenary Celebrations at Hyde Park, London on 26th June 1956, travelling on SS *Orcades* with other Australian VCs. He was one of seven VCs who attended the funeral of William Dunstan VC in March 1957. Rupert was one of seventeen Australian VCs at the opening of the VC Corner at the Australian War Memorial in 1964 by the Governor General, Viscount De l'Isle VC.

Rupert Moon died at Bellarine Private Hospital, Whittington, Victoria on 28th February 1986. He was the last but one surviving Australian VC from the Great War; William Joynt outlived him by nine weeks. He was given a funeral with full military honours on 4th March at All Saint's Anglican Church, Hitchcock Avenue, Barwon Heads, Victoria. He is buried in the Church of England Section, Mount Duneed Cemetery, Victoria and is commemorated in a number of other places:

- RV Moon Handicap over 2,050 metres, run each September as part of the Moonee Valley Stakes day meeting in Melbourne, Victoria.
- A memorial garden at Mount Duneed Cemetery dedicated in his honour on 12th May 2008.
- 'The Captain R.V. Moon VC Army Reserve Trust' started with a donation from Rupert Moon to the Naval and Military Club, Melbourne in the 1980s. The trust fund exists to encourage the traditions of the Army Reserve and the welfare of its members.
- Moon Lane, Wodonga, Victoria on the White Box Rise estate, built on land formerly part of Bandiana Army Camp.
- Named on Victoria Cross Memorial, Campbell, Canberra, dedicated on 24th July 2000.
- Named on Victoria Cross Memorial, Queen Victoria Building, George Street, Sydney, New South Wales.

The memorial garden at Mount Duneed Cemetery (Mount Duneed Progress Association).

- Named on one of eleven plaques honouring 175 men from overseas awarded the VC for the Great War. The plaques were unveiled by the Senior Minister of State at the Foreign & Commonwealth Office and Minister for Faith and Communities, Baroness Warsi, at a reception at Lancaster House, London on 26th June 2014 attended by the Duke of Kent and relatives of the VC recipients. The Australian plaque is at the Australian War Memorial.
- The Secretary of State for Communities and Local Government, Eric Pickles MP, announced that Victoria Cross recipients from the Great War would have commemorative paving stones laid in their birthplace as a lasting legacy of local heroes within communities. The stones would be laid on or close to the 100th anniversary of their VC actions. For the 145 VCs born in Australia, Belgium, Canada, China, Denmark, Egypt, France, Germany, India, Iraq, Japan, Nepal, Netherlands, New Zealand, Pakistan, South Africa, Sri Lanka, Ukraine and United States of America, individual commemorative stones were unveiled at the National Memorial Arboretum, Alrewas, Staffordshire by Prime Minister David Cameron MP and Sergeant Johnson Beharry VC on 5th March 2015.

In addition to the VC he was awarded the 1914–15 Star, British War Medal 1914–20, Victory Medal 1914–19, George VI Coronation Medal 1937, Elizabeth II Coronation Medal 1953 and Elizabeth II Silver Jubilee Medal 1977. His VC is held in the Hall of Valour, Australian War Memorial, Treloar Crescent, Campbell, Australian Capital Territory, Australia.

9887 SERGEANT EDWARD JOHN MOTT
1st Battalion, The Border Regiment

Edward Mott was born at Drayton, Abingdon, Berkshire on 4th July 1893. His father was John Mott (1847–1928), an agricultural labourer. He married Jane Sophia Harris (1847–91) in 1867 and they were living at Abingdon Road Cottage, Drayton in 1881 and at 21 Church Street, Drayton in 1891. Edward's mother was Lydia née Bradfield (1853–1901), a tailoress. She married John William Woodley (1852–83), a railway porter, in 1874 and they were living at Grey's Lane, Rotherfield Greys, Oxfordshire in 1881. John Mott and Lydia Woodley were married on 23rd September  1892 at Abingdon. The family was living at Ladygrove, Sutton Courtney, Abingdon in 1901. By 1911 John was living at Spring Terrace, Shippon, Berkshire. Edward had seventeen siblings from his parents' three marriages:

396 Victoria Crosses on the Western Front January–July 1917

- Charles Mott (1868–1925) was a ploughboy in 1881. He enlisted in the Militia, 3rd Royal Berkshire (1937) at 49th Regimental District, Reading on 22nd November 1886. He was described as a labourer, 5′ 3¾″ tall with fresh complexion, hazel eyes, dark brown hair and his religious denomination was Church of England. He was discharged by purchase on 20 February 1877. Charles married Mary Palmer (1869–1949) in 1895. By 1901 he was the publican of 'The Wheatsheaf', 26 West Helen Street, Abingdon. The family was living at Ivy House, East Helen Street, Abingdon in 1911. Charles and Mary had a daughter, Winifred Annie Mott, in 1897. She was a drapery apprentice in 1911, married William S Lee in 1921 and had a daughter, Dorothy M Lee, in 1922.
- Joseph Mott (1869–1927) was a ploughboy in 1881 and later a cowman. He enlisted in 4th Queen's Own Hussars at 49th Regimental District, Reading on 20th February 1891 and was discharged next day unfit for service due to skin disease. He was described as 5′ 6¾″ tall with fresh complexion, blue eyes, dark brown hair and his religious denomination was Church of England. Joseph married Charlotte Anne Weston (1869–1935) in 1893. Charlotte had a daughter, Dorothy Josephine J Weston, born in 1891. The family was living at Lower Range, Drayton Challow Marsh, Wantage, Berkshire in 1911. Joseph and Charlotte had ten children – Frederick Charles Mott 1893, Nora Kathleen M Mott 1896, Lilian Edith J Mott 1898, Thomas Cedric Henry Pretoria Mott 1900, Gladys Agnes A Mott 1902, Cyril John Mott 1904, Arthur William Mott (born and died 1906), Cecil Ronald 'Bill' Mott 1907, Ethel Irene M Mott 1910 and Ivy Winifred E Mott 1912. The eldest, Frederick Charles Mott, died of wounds whilst serving with 2nd Royal Berkshire (9390) on 28th October 1916 and is buried at Bancourt British Cemetery, France (III M 14). 'Bill' Mott served as a lance corporal in the Corps of Military Police during the Second World War.
- Rosanna Mott born and died 1872.
- William John Mott (1873–1945) was a carman at a corn store in 1911. He married Alice Minns (born 1877) in 1915. She had previously married Joseph Vasey (1875–1912), a coal merchant, in 1901 and had three children – Ernest Vasey 1903, William Joseph Vasey 1904 and Gwendoline May Vasey 1905.
- Archibald Bradfield Woodley (1875–1930), a cloth cutter, married Gertrude Laura Broughton (1874–1951) in 1897. They were living at 22 Abingdon Road, Drayton in 1901. They had a son, Archie Ellis B Woodley in 1898, who married Alice Chivers in 1921 and had a daughter, Shirley A Woodley in 1929.
- Henry John Mott (1875–1963) married his step-sister, Edith Mary Woodley (1879–1940) in 1897 (see below). Henry was a general labourer on the Great Western Railway in 1911, living with his family at Scutts Lane, Wroughton, Wiltshire. They had five children – Millicent Edith Mott 1897, Lydia Maud Mott 1901, Raymond Woodley Mott 1906, Reginald John Mott 1908 and Grace Evelyn Mott 1910.
- Sidney John Woodley (1877–1967) was a stonemason.

- Esther Rose Mott (1878–1914) married Charles Henry Nutt (1875–1942) in 1900. He was a Corporation labourer in 1911, living with his family at 9 Church Lane, Hinksey, Oxford. They had six children – Charles Henry Nutt 1901, Leonard Arthur Nutt 1903, Stanley Nutt 1904, William John Nutt 1907, Elsie Maria Nutt 1910 and Gladys Kate Nutt 1913.
- Edith Mary Woodley (1879–1940) was a general domestic servant in 1891. She married her step brother, Henry John Mott (1875–1963) in 1897 (see above).
- Susan May Mott (1880–1967) married Frederick Arthur Harris (1881–1967) in 1901. He was a fishmonger's assistant in 1911 and the family was living at 12 Marshalls Road, Sutton, Surrey. They had two children – Reginald Stanley Harris 1902 and Leslie Albert Harris 1907.
- Lydia May Woodley (1881–1923) was a general kitchen maid in 1901. She married Frank Channon (1862–1948) in 1910. He was a grocer's assistant in 1891, living with his previous family at 69 Rosebury Road, Fulham, London. By 1911, Frank was a store manager and they were living at 119 Eleanor Cross Road, Waltham Cross, Middlesex. Frank had nine children from his previous marriage to Emma Jessie Evans (1864–1907) in 1883 – Frank Channon 1884, Henrietta Channon 1887, Gilbert Channon 1889, Edward Channon 1890, Bessie Channon 1893, Sidney John Channon 1894, Leonard Channon 1896, Walter Channon 1900 and Herbert Channon 1901. Lydia and Frank had a daughter, Vera M Channon, in 1914.
- John Edgar Mott born and died 1882.
- Florence Jessie Woodley (born 1883) was a general domestic servant in 1901. She married Frederic George Hill (born 1888), an electrician, in 1912 and they had a daughter, Phyllis K Hill, in 1914.
- George Heber Mott (1884–1974), a chauffeur, enlisted in the Canadian Overseas Expeditionary Force at Valcartier on 23rd September 1914 (37139), declaring he was born in 1886. He was described as 5′ 3″ tall with fair hair, blue eyes, dark brown hair and his religious denomination was Methodist. His given date of birth was 23rd September 1886, but he probably lost a couple of years to ensure he was accepted. He served for a year and five months on MT duties. George was deemed to have enlisted in the British Army (25984 later M/337537) on 2nd March 1916 and was called up on 5th August 1917 for service in the Army Service Corps. He gave his employment as motor mechanic. His height was just under 5′ 2″ and he had a glass left eye and flat feet. His religious denomination had changed to Church of England and his address was 38 The Leys, Chipping Norton. He was discharged at his own request on 18th August 1917.
- Annie Mott (1887–1961) never married.
- Albert James Mott (1895–1952) married Elsie May Mazey (1901–82) in 1925.
- Francis 'Frank' Vincent Mott (1897–1970) married Clara Hilda Jones (1901–87) in 1927 and had three children – Sydney A Mott 1927, Dennis C Mott 1928–29 and June M Mott 1931.

Edward was educated at Abingdon Council School. He enlisted on 31st December 1910 and took part in the Gallipoli landings on 25th April 1915. **Awarded the DCM for his actions on 28th April 1915 at Krithia, leading his company to successive fire positions and also for bravery and good service in attacking over difficult country, LG 3rd July 1915. He was Mentioned in General Sir Ian Hamilton's Despatch of 12th June 1915, LG 5th August 1915.** When the Helles sector was evacuated in January 1916 he accompanied his unit to Egypt and moved to France in March. Edward was wounded and shell shocked on 30th June 1916 and evacuated to England, but returned to France later.

Awarded the VC for his actions south of Le Transloy, France on 27th January 1917, LG 10th March 1917. The VC was presented by the King at Buckingham Palace on 4th April 1917. Edward was discharged as no longer physically fit for service on 16th March 1919 and was awarded the Silver War Badge (B207316) on 12th June.

Edward Mott married Evelyn Maud née Hopgood (17th April 1899–17th March 1979) on 2nd September 1918 at Alverstoke, Hampshire. They lived at 38 New Yatt Road, Witney, Oxfordshire and had eight children:

- Kenneth J Mott, registered in the 1st quarter of 1920 at Edmonton, Middlesex. He married Nora J Orgill (born 1922) in 1944 at Amersham, Buckinghamshire and they had a son, Andrew J Mott, in 1956.
- Rona A Mott, registered in the 2nd quarter of 1922 at Edmonton. She married Kenneth R Stone in 1942 at Abingdon, Berkshire and they had three children – Jennifer Y Stone 1947, Robert J Stone 1948 and Raymond HN Stone 1958.
- George H Mott, registered in the 2nd quarter of 1923 at Edmonton.
- Nora E Mott, registered in the 3rd quarter of 1925 at Edmonton. She married Horace C Cook in 1949 at Abingdon and they had four children – Anthony C Cook 1950, Ann E Cook 1951, David G Cook 1954 and Edith Cook 1957.
- Norman E Mott, registered in the 3rd quarter of 1927 at Abingdon. He married Olive Morris in 1951 at Oxford and they had two children – Jaqueline Mott 1952 and Lesley S Mott 1954.
- Ena D Mott, registered in the 1st quarter of 1931 at Abingdon. She married Royston PV Snellock (born 1927) in 1950 at Abingdon and they had three children – Paul EG Snellock 1952, Vega L Snellock 1955 and Dawn A Snellock 1958.
- Bernard R Mott, registered in the 3rd quarter of 1933 at Abingdon. He married Margaret A Everett (born 1932) in 1956 and they had two children – Sally J Mott 1957 and Wendy J Mott 1961.
- Edna J Mott, registered in the 4th quarter of 1942 at Abingdon. She married Bernard J Coggins in 1962 and they had two children – Lynda Fiona A Coggins 1967 and Helen Coggins 1968.

Edward's father-in-law, George Hopgood (1873–1942) joined the Royal Navy (No.147389) on 14th August 1891 for twelve years and was described as 5′ 9″ tall

HMY *Victoria and Albert* (4,700 tons) was launched in 1899 and entered service in 1901, seven months before Queen Victoria died. She was the third yacht to carry the name and was used by four sovereigns before being decommissioned in 1939. During the Second World War she was an accommodation ship to HMS *Excellent* at Portsmouth and was broken up in 1954, when she was replaced by HMY *Britannia*.

Selfridge's on Oxford Street, London opened in 1909.

with brown hair, light blue eyes and fresh complexion. He served on HMS *St Vincent*, *Garnet*, *Victory* and *Excellent* as an Able Seaman before joining the Royal Yacht *Victoria & Albert* on 16th January 1896. He married Agnes née Bundey (1880–1939) in 1898 and in 1901 was living with his family at 38 Richmond Road, Alverstoke, Hampshire. The family had moved to 98 Queens Road, Gosport, Hampshire by 1911. George transferred to the Reserve on 4th October 1913 and was recalled on 2nd August 1914, serving on HMS *Dolphin*, *Victory*, *Virginian* and *President* until 18th July 1919. In addition to Evelyn, George and Agnes had five other children – Annie Vera Hopgood 1904, Hughbert Charles Hopgood 1908, Ena Agnes Hopgood 1909, George F Hopgood 1911 and Lilian M Hopgood 1913.

Edward Mott on the right with Bernard Freyberg VC at a reunion on Horse Guards Parade probably in the late 1950s. Bernard Freyberg was the last Western Front VC of 1916 and Edward Mott was the first of 1917.

After leaving the Army, Edward became a commissionaire at Selfridge's on Oxford Street, London. He was a member of the VC Guard at the Interment of the Unknown Warrior on 11th November 1920. From 1926 until October 1940 he worked at an RAF depot and then ran a family building firm with his son Bernard.

Edward Mott died at his home at 38 New Yatt Road, Witney, Oxfordshire on 20th October 1967. He was cremated at Oxford Crematorium, where his ashes were scattered.

The Department for Communities and Local Government decided to provide a commemorative paving stone at the birthplace of every Great War Victoria Cross recipient in the United Kingdom. Edward's stone is scheduled to be dedicated at Vale of White Horse District Council, Banbury, Oxfordshire on 29th January 2017 to mark the centenary of his award.

In addition to the VC and DCM, he was awarded the 1914–15 Star, British War Medal 1914–20, Victory Medal 1914–19 with Mentioned-in-Despatches Oakleaf, George VI Coronation Medal 1937 and Elizabeth II Coronation Medal 1953. The VC was reported stolen in the 1930s, but probably went missing in the 1920s. A replacement, issued on 9th September 1937, was purchased by the Regiment at a Glendinings auction on 3rd March 1967 for £1,950. It is held by the King's Own Royal Border Regiment Museum, Carlisle Castle. Lester Watson (1889–1959), an investment banker from Boston, Massachusetts, amassed an impressive collection of 411 British gallantry and campaign medals during his life. His son, Hoyt, donated the collection to Cambridge, Massachusetts, USA and it is on loan to the Fitzwilliam Museum, Cambridge, England, including the original VC, DCM and 1914–15 Star awarded to Edward Mott. It is not known what became of the original British War Medal 1914–20 and Victory Medal 1914–19.

51507 LANCE CORPORAL HAROLD SANFORD MUGFORD
8th Cavalry Brigade Machine Gun Squadron, Machine Gun Corps

Harold Mugford was born at 149 Keetons Road, St James', Bermondsey, London on 31st August 1894. His father, Richard John Sanford Mugford (1873–1949), was a solicitor's clerk. He married Rose Lilian née Parsons (1874–1956) on 5th September 1892 at St Olave, London. The family was living at 56 Camilla Road, Bermondsey in 1892, at 149 Keetons Road, Bermondsey by 1901 and at 2 Gillett Avenue, East Ham, London by 1911. Richard and Rose later moved to Ambleside, Walnut Road, Chelston, Torquay, Devon. Rose lived at 27 Upton Road, Torquay after her husband's death. Harold had two brothers:

• Richard Henry Mugford (1892–1934) was educated at East Ham Technical College and was a provision merchant's clerk in 1911. He served in the Essex Yeomanry 1911–13 as a trooper until he went to Shanghai, China to work as a Customs Official. He returned to enlist in 1st King Edward's Horse (The King's Overseas Dominions Regiment) Special Reserve (855) on 15th December 1914; he was 5′ 11″ tall and weighed 153 lbs. Richard embarked at Southampton with A Squadron on 1st June 1915 and landed at Le Havre next day. He was charged with neglect of duty in the field on 1st January 1916, but was admonished. He was granted leave in Britain

29th April–7th May and was appointed unpaid lance corporal on 5th November. Promoted lance corporal on 7th January 1917 and acting corporal on 4th February. He was granted leave in Britain 29th May–8th June and was promoted corporal and acting sergeant on 4th June. He reverted to lance sergeant on 8th July but was appointed acting sergeant on 21st July and sergeant on 8th December. He served in Italy with his unit December 1917–March 1918 and was awarded the MM on 29th December 1917, LG 13th March 1918. When he applied for a commission in early 1918, he was 6′ tall and weighed 175 lbs. He commenced training at No.3 Officer Cadet Battalion, Parkhurst on

Keeton's Road, Bermondsey, an area that was bombed heavily on 7th September 1940 with many casualties (Southwark Local History Library and Archive).

23rd May 1918 and completed the course, but was demobilised on 6th January 1919. He was gazetted to a commission in the Devonshire Regiment on 5th February 1919, which he relinquished on 1st September 1921. Richard married Dora Kate George (née Beeston) (1883–1968) in 1926. Dora had been married previously to Frederick W George in 1915 and had a son, Anthony F George, in 1916. Richard and Dora lived at 51 West Street, Bognor Regis, Sussex. He was a supervising agent when he became unemployed and gassed himself in an apartment at Denbeigh Street, Pimlico, London on 8th November 1934. His suicide note stated, *Only young men in their early twenties are wanted nowadays. What am I to do? I can live on the charity of my relatives or make away with myself, and I choose the latter.* A verdict of 'suicide while of unsound mind' was recorded at an inquest at Westminster the following day. Richard left £240/15/7 to his widow. Dora was living at 57 West Street, Bognor Regis at the time of her death in 1968. She left £6,425 in her will.

• Percy Cecil Mugford (1898–1917) enlisted in the Essex Regiment at Brentwood, Essex (2893 later 200769) and served with 1/4th Battalion in Palestine. He was killed in action in the First Battle of Gaza on 26th March 1917 and is commemorated on the Jerusalem Memorial.

Harold's paternal grandfather, Richard Mugford (1838–1919), was born at Newton Abbot, Devon. He married Mary Ann Sarah née Sanford (1843–1904) at St Giles, London in 1865. By 1881, Richard was an HM Customs Examining Officer in Bermondsey, London living with his family at 32 Galley Wall Road. In addition to Harold's father, Richard and Mary had a daughter, Isabella Rose Mugford (1869–1958), a feather mounter in 1891, who died unmarried at Torquay, Devon.

Harold's maternal grandmother, Jane Parsons (born 1850), was the daughter of Edward and Sarah Parsons. Jane was a machinist skirt maker, living with her daughter Rose at 26 Abbeyfield Road, Rotherhithe, Surrey in 1881. In the Census of that year she was recorded as a widow. By the 1891 Census, she had moved to 58 Camilla Road, Bermondsey, London with Rose and was recorded as married. Rose's father is unknown.

Harold was educated at Shrewsbury Road School, Forest Gate and was then employed as a clerk by the shipping group Messrs Furness Withy. He enlisted in the Essex Yeomanry (852 later 51507) on 18th December 1912 and was mobilised in August 1914. He went to France on 29th November 1914 and saw action around Ypres and at Loos in 1915. On three occasions he was buried by shells exploding close to his dugout. On 29th February 1916 he transferred with the Essex Yeomanry Machine Gun Detachment to 8th Cavalry Brigade Machine Gun Squadron on the formation of brigade machine gun squadrons and companies.

Awarded the VC for his actions at Monchy-le-Preux, France on 11th April 1917, LG 26th November 1917. As a result of the injuries he sustained during his VC action, he was evacuated to England and underwent six operations. Both legs were amputated above the knee and shrapnel was removed from his hip, tongue and jaw. Harold was confined to a wheelchair for much of the rest of his life. The VC was presented by the King outside Buckingham Palace on 3rd July 1918. Harold was discharged on 12th July and was awarded the Silver War Badge (No.379066) on 20th July. The following month he was presented with a cheque for £300 by the Mayor of East Ham.

Harold worked for an oil company in London and on 23rd April 1919 he married Amy Mary née Key (1894–1978) at All Saints' Church, Forest Gate, London. She was a shorthand typist in a solicitor's office in 1911. There were no children. They lived at Mill House, Little Waltham, Essex before moving to Ashburton, 20 Chignall Road, Chelmsford, Essex. Amy's parents were William John Key (1856–1947), born in Lincolnshire, and Amy Maria Atkins née Hale (1860–1940), born at Warminster, Wiltshire. They married in 1888 at Stepney, London. William was an Inspector of Works with the Borough Council, living with his family at 17 St John's Road, East Ham, London in 1901 and at 22 Lathom Road, East Ham by 1911. Amy senior was a dressmaker. In addition to Amy junior, they had two other children, including William Robert Key (born 1892), who was a bank clerk in 1911.

Harold's former employers paid him a pension until he died and then to his wife until her death. Despite his disability, Harold remained very active and was vice-president of the Chelmsford Amateur Operatic and Dramatic Society. He died at Chelmsford and Essex Hospital, Essex

Little Waltham in Essex, where Harold and Amy lived for some time.

Chelmsford and Essex Hospital.

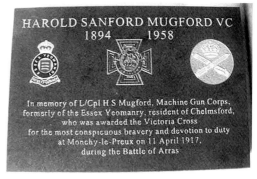

The memorial in St Peter's Chapel, Chelmsford
Cathedral (Essex Branch, Western Front Association).

on 16th June 1958 and was cremated at Southend-on-Sea
Crematorium, where his ashes were scattered in the June
area. Harold left £12,594/10/7 and when Amy died in
1978 she left £59,184. He is commemorated on a memorial
plaque in St Peter's Chapel, Chelmsford Cathedral,
unveiled by Lord Petre, Lord Lieutenant of Essex, in June
2006.

In addition to the VC, he was awarded the 1914–15
Star, British War Medal 1914–20, Victory Medal 1914–
19, George VI Coronation Medal 1937 and Elizabeth II
Coronation Medal 1953. As they had no children, Harold
bequeathed his medals to Messrs Furness Withy after
the death of his wife. The company donated them to the
Imperial War Museum on permanent loan.

Harold Mugford later in life.

CAPTAIN HENRY WILLIAM MURRAY
13th Australian Infantry Battalion AIF

Henry Murray was born on 1st December 1880 at Clairville,
Evandale, near Launceston, Tasmania; now the site of
Launceston airport. He was probably the most highly
decorated Commonwealth soldier of the First World War.
He was known as Harry and in the Army as Mad Harry. His
father, Edward Kennedy Murray (1840–1904), was born at
South Esk, Tasmania. He had a farm at Woodstock, near
Evandale, before moving to Northcote, near St Leonard's.

Harry's mother, Clarissa née Littler (1841–1933), was born at Launceston. Edward and Clarissa were married on 27th June 1867 at her father's house in John Street, Launceston. She was living at 33 Erina Street, Launceston in 1919. Harry had a poor relationship with his father, which stemmed partly from being taken out of school to work on the farm while his older brothers received a better education. Harry had eight siblings:

- Albert Edward Murray (1868–1919) was educated at Launceston Church Grammar School. He moved to Western Australia with his brother Charles in the late 1880s. By 1893 he was known as Albert Edward Beresford Murray when he married Edith 'Ada' Henrietta Johnstone (c.1875–1956) (also seen as Johnson or Johnston) at Broken Hill, New South Wales. Albert and Edith had nine children – Edith Elizabeth Clarissa Murray 1894, Thelma Olga Beresford Murray 1896, Alba Louisa Murray 1898, Margurite Alice Linden Murray 1902, John Albert Desmond Arthur Murray 1902, Iris Alexandra Beresford Murray c.1903, Edward Murray 1906, Henry William Murray 1910 and Agnes Joan Patricia Murray 1912. Albert was the keeper of the Australia Hotel, Kanowna, Kalgoorlie, Western Australia in 1910. He had known Miss Eva Downey for about one month when they and some friends visited various hotels on the night of 30th April 1919 in a taxi driven by William Gustave Weylandt. At ten minutes past midnight Murray shot Miss Downey in the head with a revolver at Rokeby Road, Subiaco, Perth before turning the gun on himself. He left several suicide notes, one to his daughter 'Tot', one to a lady friend and a third unsigned in an unaddressed envelope.
- Charles Francis Murray (1870–1943) was also educated at Launceston Church Grammar School. He married Kathleen Ada Stewart (1887–1954) in 1909 and they had ten children – Charles Stewart Murray 1909, Edward Kennedy Murray 1911, Ian Murray 1914, Joan Francis Murray, Kathleen Joyce Murray c.1917, Vera Amie Murray 1919, Gordon Russell Murray 1921, Ronald Murray 1922 and Madge Murray 1924. They were living at Menzies, Kalgoorlie, Western Australia in 1916 and were at Williams, Forrest by 1925. Kathleen Joyce Murray married William Bowe Stubbs (c.1917–42), who died serving as a Pilot Officer in the Royal Australian Air Force (415284) on 25th June 1942 and is buried in the Church of England Plot at Parkes General Cemetery, New South Wales (Section 24, Grave 4).
- Amie Clarissa Littler Murray (1872–1966) married Frank Herbert Adams (1870–1951) in 1895 and they had five children – Mary Walmsbury Adams 1896, Keith Murray Adams 1899 who served in the Royal Navy, Kathleen Amy Adams 1903, Margery Francis Adams 1908 and Annie Clarissa Littler Adams 1911.
- Marion Annie Murray (1873–1963) married David Gray and had three daughters – Dulcie Gray 1897, Philomena Gray 1898 and Nell Gray 1900.
- Helen 'Nellie' Frances Murray (1875–1959).

- Jennie Gertrude Murray (1877–1966).
- Hannah Goodall Murray (1879–1962), married Joshua Reynolds Cocker (1867–1958) in 1907 and they had three children – Clarissa Jocelyn Cocker 1909, Benjamin Murray Cocker (born and died 1910) and Benjamin Murray Cocker 1911.
- Annie 'Dot' Summers Murray (1882–1963) married David Cocker (1870–1941) in 1910. He was a solicitor. They had seven children – David Cocker (born and died 1911), David Cocker 1912, Henry William Cocker 1913, Joshua North Cocker 1915, Margaret Grey Marks Cocker 1917, Leslie Henley Cocker 1919 and Joseph Murray Cocker 1922. Margaret Grey Marks Cocker was the first Launceston woman to become a qualified legal practitioner and was called to the Bar in the Supreme Court at Hobart, Tasmania on 5th May 1941.

Harry's great grandfather, Kennedy Murray (1764–1853), was born in Glasgow, Lanarkshire, Scotland. He was convicted of stealing a box of six small knives, a pair of striped garters and some 'knittings' from the house of a widow, Agnes Dunlop, in 1786 and was sentenced to fourteen years penal servitude. He arrived in Port Jackson, Sydney, New South Wales on 14th February 1792 on the transport ship *Pitt* and was sent to Norfolk Island, New South Wales on 1st October 1796. He married Ann White (1771–1820), who was sentenced to five years penal servitude for stealing a roll of cloth and had arrived in New South Wales in 1790 aboard the transport ship *Neptune*. Kennedy and Ann had a son, Harry's grandfather, who was also Kennedy Murray (1799–1860). Kennedy junior left for Tasmania with his mother on 20th January 1813. He married Sarah MacQueen (1805–39) in 1819 and they had eight children – Sarah Murray 1819, Anne Murray 1821, Thomas John Murray 1825, William Kennedy Murray 1827, Elizabeth Mary Murray 1829, James Francis Murray 1832, George Richard Murray 1835 and Catherine MacQueen Murray 1837.

Kennedy did well and built his home, Prosperous House, together with a schoolhouse, stable, granary, storehouse and outhouses. He was employing five convict servants by April 1831 when he was granted a further 320 acres of land by George Arthur, Lieutenant-Governor of Van Diemen's Land. On 1st May 1839 he married Harry's grandmother, Hannah née Goodall (1815–1904), at St John's

The *Pitt* was the largest transport of the time used to move convicts. She was chartered to the East India Company 1786–98 and her officers were entitled to carry their own trade goods as well as convicts, resulting in the ship being overcrowded. Her voyage to Sydney as a convict transport in 1792 took 212 days. Harry's great grandfather was one of the 402 convicts aboard, of whom twenty men and nine women died en route and a further 120 men were sick on arrival, resulting in further deaths (JW Edy).

Norfolk Island's beauty is in stark contrast to the brutal convict colony that was established there. It is now a holiday resort with World Heritage historical sites. James Cook sighted the island on his second voyage on HMS *Resolution* in 1774 and named it after the Duchess of Norfolk. In 1786 it became an auxiliary settlement in the colonisation plan for New South Wales. The first convicts arrived in March 1788 and the last left in May 1855. In June 1856, 194 descendants of Tahitians and HMS *Bounty* mutineers arrived, resettled from the Pitcairn Islands.

Church, Launceston. She was born at Newcastle, Co Meath, Ireland. In addition to Harry's father, Edward, they had seven other children:

- Francis Goodwin Murray (1842–1919) married Jessie Lucy Wadham (1855–1901) in 1875 and they had a daughter, Florence Stewart Murray, in 1884.
- William Usher Murray (born c.1843) married Elizabeth Marianna Wilson and had seven children.

Conditions aboard the transport *Neptune* were even worse than on *Pitt*. She was one of the Second Fleet ships, along with *Surprize* and *Scarborough*, sailing with 421 male and seventy-eight female convicts on 19th January 1790. She spent sixteen days at the Cape of Good Hope in April, taking on provisions and twelve more male convicts. *Neptune* arrived at Port Jackson on 28th June after 160 days. The treatment of the convicts aboard was the most horrific in the history of transportation. Most were chained below decks for the duration, disease was endemic, rations totally inadequate and the disciplinary regime was brutal; convicts suspected of petty theft were flogged to death. As a result, during the voyage 158 convicts died and 269 were sick when landed. One of those lucky to survive was Harry's great grandmother, Ann White.

- Henry Murray (1844–1927).
- Hannah Sarah Murray (1846–1937) married Augustus East Littler (1843–80) in 1867 and they had seven children. Hannah later married Francis Seymour Stevens.
- Albert Goodall Murray (1848–1925) married Catherine Jane Revell (died 1936) in 1880 and they had nine children.
- Jane Maria Murray (1850–1903) married Henry Samuel Fookes and they had eight children.
- Mary Anne (also seen as Maryanne and Marianne) Goodwin Murray (1853–1910) married Arthur Alfred Littler (1851–1921), the VC's maternal uncle, in 1877 and they had eight children.

Harry's maternal grandfather was Charles Littler (1806–69), born at Waltham Abbey, Essex, England. The Littlers owned silk mills and there were a number of naval and military officers in the family. He married Annie née Summers (1817–89) in 1838 at St Martin-in-the-Fields, London. The family suffered financial difficulties, so Charles decided to try his luck in Australia and emigrated to Tasmania via Adelaide in 1838. He had been an accountant, but worked his way as a free settler aboard the *Henry Porcher* as a hospital attendant to the ship's surgeon. He became gatekeeper at the Female House of Correction, Launceston, working for £40 a year plus rations and Annie became a sub-matron at the same institution for £20 a year plus rations. They were referred to later in a document relating to an inquiry into female prison discipline as Charles Littlehouse (Littler) and Mrs Littlehouse (Littler). In addition to Harry's mother, Clarissa, they had seven other children:

- Augustus East Littler (1843–80) married Hannah Sarah Murray (born 1846) in 1867 and they had seven children, one of whom, Charles Augustus Murray Littler, served as a captain in 52nd Battalion AIF and was awarded the DCM and DSO before being killed in action on 3rd September 1916 (Villers-Bretonneux Memorial, France).
- Walter Lemonde Littler (1845–1902) married Millicent Jane Richards (1848–95) in 1868 and they had seven children.
- William Thomas Littler (1847–1922) was a master mariner who emigrated to England, where he married Helen Sophia Smith (c.1835–1914) in 1871. They were living at 20 Bruce Grove Road, Tottenham in 1911, having had one child who did not survive infancy.
- Henry Charles Littler (1849–1924) married Annie Rosina Horne and they had a son.
- Arthur Alfred Littler (1851–1921) married Mary Anne Goodwin Murray (1853–1910), the VC's paternal aunt, in 1877, and they had eight children.
- Annie Francis Littler (born 1856) married Robert William Harrison.
- Frank Edwin Littler (1858–92) married Helen Brand Flett (1862–1932) in 1883 and they had three children.

Blackboy Hill Camp, Bellevue, Western Australia in 1914 (Australian War Memorial).

Troops marching through Melbourne.

Harry was educated at Evandale State School, near Launceston until 1894, when his father removed him to work on the farm. His education was continued by his mother. He moved to Western Australia about 1909/10 to work on his brother Charles' farm, Comet Vale. Harry was given food and lodgings, but no pay. He then

HMAT A40 *Ceramic* loading in 1915. SS *Ceramic* was built in Belfast for the White Star Line 1912–13 and worked the Liverpool–Australia route. In 1914 she was requisitioned as HMAT A40 *Ceramic* and survived a number of U-boat attacks. She returned to the White Star Line to resume civilian service in November 1920. When White Star merged with Cunard in 1934, *Ceramic* was sold to Shaw, Savill & Albion, but carried on working the same route. In February 1940 she was again requisitioned as a troopship. In the South Atlantic on 11th August, she collided at speed with the cargo ship *Testbank*. Both ships were damaged, but remained afloat. *Testbank* made Cape Town under her own power. *Ceramic*'s passengers were transferred to RMS *Viceroy of India* and she was assisted to Walvis Bay in South West Africa by a tug. After emergency repairs she went to Cape Town for renovation before resuming service. On 3rd November 1942, *Ceramic* left Liverpool for Australia carrying 641 passengers and crew and 12,362 tons of cargo as part of Convoy ON 149. When it dispersed, she continued unescorted and at midnight on 6th/7th December she was hit by a torpedo from U-*515* in mid-Atlantic. A few minutes later two more torpedoes hit the engine room. However, she remained afloat and was abandoned in good order. Three hours later, U-*515* fired two more torpedoes, which sank her immediately. It was a stormy night and the heavy sea capsized some lifeboats. U-*515* returned to look for *Ceramic*'s Master, Herbert Elford, to ascertain the ship's destination. One lifeboat was sighted around noon but, with the storm raging, the U-boat crew seized the first available survivor, Sapper Eric Munday RE. Despite searches by neutral craft, no other survivors were picked up. Munday spent the rest of the war at Stalag VIII-B in Silesia (Australian War Memorial).

worked as a courier for a mining company at Kookynie, north of Kalgoorlie, carrying gold and mail by bicycle or on horseback on a trip of 210 miles every two weeks. Later he became a bushman, employing a gang of sleeper cutters near Manjimup, near the Karri forests of the southwest.

Harry served in the Launceston Volunteer Artillery Corps (Militia) 1902–08. He enlisted in the Australian Imperial Force at Perth on 30th September 1914 and was posted to Blackboy Hill Camp, Bellevue, Western Australia, where he joined the machine gun section of 16th Australian Infantry Battalion (315). He was described as 5′ 8½″ tall, weighing 152 lbs, with fair complexion, grey–green eyes, dark-brown hair and his religious denomination was Congregationalist. He would have enlisted earlier, but had to dispose of his business first.

Harry was offered a commission but at that time preferred to remain as a soldier. The Battalion entrained for Fremantle on 21st November and sailed for Melbourne, Victoria aboard the troopships *Indarra* and *Dimboola*. At Broadmeadows the Battalion joined 4th Australian Infantry Brigade under Brigadier General John Monash. On 17th December, the Brigade marched through Melbourne, the salute being taken by the Governor General, Sir Ronald Craufurd Munro Ferguson. Harry's Battalion embarked at Melbourne on 22nd December on HMAT A40 *Ceramic* and arrived at Alexandria, Egypt on 1st February 1915. It then travelled by train to Zeitoun, near Cairo and marched to camp at Heliopolis.

On 12th April the Battalion embarked for Mudros on the Transport *Haida Pascha*, where it carried out some training before re-embarking and landing at Ari Burnu, Gallipoli, on 25th April. Harry was promoted lance corporal on 13th May 1915. He was slightly wounded on Pope's Hill as No.2 on a machine gun with his mate, Lance Corporal Percy Charles Herbert Black, as No.1. Black was also wounded, but they both refused to leave their posts. Harry was wounded by a bullet in the right

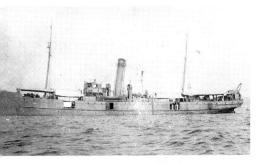

The Auxiliary Minesweeper HMS *Clacton* (820 tons) owned by the Great Eastern Railway Company, Harwich. On 3rd August 1916 she was sunk by U-*73* in Kavalla Bay, Aegean Sea.

RMS *Franconia*, operated by Cunard, made her maiden voyage in February 1911 between Liverpool and Boston, USA. She was requisitioned as a troopship in early 1915. On 4th October 1916 she was sunk by UB-*47*, 200 miles east of Malta. There were no troops aboard, but twelve of her crew of 314 were lost.

knee on 30th May and was evacuated by the Auxiliary Minesweeper *Clacton* and then the Transport *Franconia* next day. **Awarded the DCM for his actions in the period 9th–31st May 1915, during which he exhibited exceptional courage, energy and skill, inflicting severe losses on the enemy, while being twice wounded, LG 5th August 1915.**

The Convalescent Depot at Mustapha, Egypt.

He was treated at 15th General Hospital, Alexandria from 15th June and discharged to the Convalescent Depot, Mustapha on 25th June. His knee was permanently stiff and he was classified 'permanently unfit for further military service'. He was to embark on a hospital ship for return to Australia on 3rd July, but persuaded an ambulance driver to take him to the wharf at Alexandria, where he boarded HMT *Scotian* and got back to his unit on Gallipoli. He was wounded again on 8th August, but remained at duty.

On 13th August Harry transferred to 13th Battalion as a sergeant and was commissioned the same day. He contracted dysentery and enteritis on 26th September and was evacuated to Mudros and Alexandria on 29th September on HMHS *Valdivia*. In Egypt he was admitted to 2nd Australian General Hospital at Ghezireh with colitis. Having recovered, he embarked on HMT *Tunisian* at Alexandria for Gallipoli on 14th November and rejoined his unit on 7th December.

Following the evacuation of the Anzac sector at Gallipoli, he went to Alexandria via Mudros, arriving on 3rd January 1916. Promoted lieutenant at Moascar on 20th January and captain at Ismailia on 1st March. The unit embarked on the *Transylvania* at Alexandria for Marseilles, France on 1st June. Harry was appointed Landing Officer at the dock gates. As some Australian reinforcements disembarked from their ship, they broke ranks and headed for the city. Harry ordered them back and, when they refused, he stood in front of them with revolver drawn; they returned to their ship.

Awarded the DSO for his actions in an attack on Mouquet Farm on the Somme on 14th–15th August 1916, during which he was twice wounded, but assumed command of the Company following the death of the commander. The objective was secured following a bayonet charge and Harry beat off four counterattacks, but he was eventually forced to order his force of one hundred to retire, bringing with them a number of prisoners. During this action an enemy bullet started a man's equipment exploding and Harry tore it off him at great personal risk, LG 14th November 1916.

While leading a patrol of two other men they were attacked by a German bombing party of five. One of Harry's men lost his foot and the other was hit in the eye. Harry jumped into the German pit and was struck on the helmet and revolver with

Pre war HMHS *Asturias* was operated on the Southampton–
Buenos Aires route by The Royal Mail Steam Packet
Company. On 1st February 1915 she was hit by a torpedo,
but it failed to detonate. The author JRR Tolkien returned
to Britain aboard her, having gone down with trench fever
on the Somme in October 1916. On 20th March 1917, en-
route from Avonmouth to Southampton, she was torpedoed
by UC-*66*, but managed to beach near Bolt Head, Devon.
She was salvaged and used as a floating ammunition hulk at
Plymouth. In 1920, she was purchased by the Royal Mail
Line, repaired as a cruise liner, renamed *Arcadian* and sailed
the Mediterranean and Caribbean until scrapped in 1933.

While in Britain this photograph of
Harry was taken with his uncle, former
Captain William Littler, and his cousin,
Keith Adams, then serving in the Royal
Navy.

knobkerries, but shot two of his attackers. The three remaining enemy fled and
Harry threw a Mills bomb after them. He then carried the man who had lost his foot
back to his own lines, assisted by the man with the injured eye.

On 30th August he was wounded by shrapnel to the leg and back and evacuated
to 49th Casualty Clearing Station. On 9th September, he was evacuated from Le
Havre to England aboard HMHS *Asturias* and admitted to 4th London General
Hospital at Denmark Hill, where he shared a ward with Albert Jacka VC and his
mate from 16th Battalion, Percy Black. He was discharged on 5th October and
returned to France on the 19th. **Mentioned in Sir Douglas Haig's Despatch of
13th November 1916, LG 4th January 1917.**

Harry contracted influenza on 3rd February 1917 and had a temperature of
103 degrees, but refused to be hospitalised. **Awarded the VC for his actions at
Stormy Trench, northeast of Gueudecourt on 4th February 1917, LG 10th
March 1917.** He was appointed temporary major on 18th April. **Awarded a Bar
to the DSO for his actions in an attack near Bullecourt on 12th April 1917.
The tanks failed to cut the wire, but he led his company over 1,100m of fire-
swept ground and breached the Hindenburg Line. The newly won trenches
were soon isolated, but he went along the whole frontage, organising the
defence and encouraging the men of all units by his cheerfulness, bravery
and skill. He ordered artillery support but conflicting messages meant it
was not provided andn when ammunition ran low, the troops were forced
out of the Hindenburg Line with heavy losses, LG 18th June 1917.** Amongst
the dead was Harry's mate, Percy Black, by then a major in 16th Battalion with

the DSO, DCM and Croix de Guerre (Villers-Bretonneux Memorial). Harry's VC and DSO & Bar were presented by the King in Hyde Park London on 2nd June 1917.

Harry was promoted major on 12th July and assumed command of 13th Battalion on 4th November, during the absence of the CO, Lieutenant Colonel JMA Durrant DSO. **Mentioned in Sir Douglas Haig's Despatch of 7th November 1917, LG 28th December 1917.** He was granted leave to Paris 13th January–1st February 1918 and was posted to 4th Australian Machine Gun Battalion on 8th March, assuming command as temporary lieutenant colonel on 15th March. Orders to proceed to England to undertake a machine gun course were cancelled. Promoted lieutenant colonel on 24th May. Harry was attached to II American Corps 24th September–2nd October 1918 in an advisory role. **Awarded the Order of St Michael and St George for his actions during the period 18th September–11th November**

Percy Charles Herbert Black DSO DCM (1877–1917), Harry's great mate in the machine gun team at Gallipoli. Having been awarded the DCM with Harry, Percy was commissioned in August 1915. In 1916 he was a major on the Western Front, where he was awarded the DSO and French Croix de Guerre. At Mouquet Farm he was shot in the neck and evacuated to London, but later returned to the front. He was killed in the First Battle of Bullecourt on 11th April 1917. His body was never found despite a determined search by Harry Murray. Percy is commemorated on the Villers-Bretonneux Memorial.

1918 while commanding the machine guns of the Division and those of an attached Machine Gun Battalion during the capture of the Hindenburg Outpost Line. As Liaison Machine Gun Officer with II American Corps, he contributed to the success of that Corps in breaching the main Hindenburg Line near Bellenglise, 3rd June 1919.

He returned to Britain on special leave 4th November–6th December. **Mentioned in Sir Douglas Haig's Despatches of 8th November 1918 and 16th March 1919, LG 31st December 1918 and 11th July 1919. Awarded the French Croix de Guerre, LG 7th January 1919.** He was posted to Australian Imperial Force Headquarters in London on 8th June 1919. While awaiting repatriation, he and fellow VC, William Joynt, were put in charge of parties of farmers and aspirant farmers to tour farming districts in Britain from 27th June to 27th September. They also went to Denmark to study agricultural methods.

Harry left England on 19th November aboard the Orient Line transport, *Ormonde*, along with generals Birdwood and Monash. A large crowd assembled to welcome them at Victoria Quay in Fremantle, but Harry managed to slip away and travelled to his sister's home in Launceston, Tasmania. His appointment was terminated on 9th March 1920 in Tasmania and he joined the Reserve of Officers. He took a property of 3,230 hectares at Blairmach, Muckadilla, eighty kilometres from Richmond in northern Queensland. On 13th October 1921 he married Constance Sophia Cameron (4th August 1877–12th September 1930) at Camlet, Bollon, Queensland. Constance was an estate agent and part owner of Cameron and Company, a stock and station agency at St George. They lived at Blairmach until 1925, when Harry went to New Zealand. The marriage was dissolved on 11th November 1927 and there were no children. Constance died in Glasgow, Lanarkshire, Scotland in 1930.

Harry married Ellen 'Nell' Purdon Cameron (24th August 1904–2nd September 2000) on 20th November 1927 (also seen as 30th November) at the Registrar's Office, Auckland. Nell was the niece of his first wife, Constance. They returned to Queensland, where Harry purchased Glenlyon Station at Richmond, a 74,000 acre grazing property, in April 1928. He lived there for the rest of his life. Nell and Harry had two children:

- Douglas Edward Neill Murray, born on 6th October 1930, was named after Lieutenant Colonel Douglas Grey Marks, CO of 13th Battalion 1917–18. He married Heather Ballantyne Kelman and they had four children – Christopher Henry Murray, Donald Ian Murray, Julie Frances Murray and Megan Lisa Murray. Douglas retired to Townsville, Queensland, where he owned a six acre property, growing mangoes, lychees and avocados.
- Clementine 'Clem' Helen Macarthur Murray, born on 2nd January 1934, married Ian Niveson Kelman and they had two daughters – Neta Ellen Kelman and Sally Helen Kelman.

Harry wrote several articles for the 'Reveille' magazine of the New South Wales Returned Services League of Australia. In December 1935 he wrote on the subject of discipline in the AIF:

Throughout history, great generals have always recognised the supreme value of discipline. It has been alleged that although Australian troops made good soldiers they lacked discipline. This I could never agree with, because I maintain that it was the discipline, traditions, and code of the A.I.F. that enabled Australia to play a creditable part in the Great War. Without discipline, one can never have an army – nothing but a rabble. . . . For my own part, without discipline and training I could never have done my day's work, and it is to the system of discipline enforced by the A.I.F. that I lift my hat, because it transformed thousands of men – nervy and highly-strung like myself – enabling them to do work which, without discipline, they would have been quite incapable of performing.

As the outbreak of the Second World War appeared imminent, he was appointed to command 26th Battalion (The Logan and Albert Regiment), 11th Brigade at Townsville on 21st July 1939 (Q30751). He was granted leave without pay 1st–13th October 1941. On 21st October he was mobilised for full-time service with the Australian Military Forces at Sellheim, Queensland. At that time his second-in-command in 26th Battalion was Major Edgar Towner VC. He attended No.1 Motor Transport Course at Mount Annerley 13th–25th November. 26th Battalion became an Australian Imperial Force unit in 1942. Harry was sick 7th April–6th August 1942 and, due to his age, he was posted to the Supernumerary List on 11th August. He assumed command of 23rd Battalion, Volunteer Defence Corps, on 19th August, serving with York Force in northern Queensland (QX48850). Harry was treated for an infected left arm at 116th Australian General Hospital 20th February–4th March 1943. He was granted leave without pay 1st September–1st October 1943 and his appointment was terminated on 8th February 1944.

In 1954 Harry was presented to Queen Elizabeth and the Duke of Edinburgh at Brisbane during their Royal Visit of Australia. When asked what he did, he replied, *Between wars I grow wool*. Harry travelled on SS *Orcades* with other Australian VCs who were part of the 301 Victoria Cross recipients from across the Commonwealth to attend the VC Centenary Celebrations at Hyde Park, London on 26th June 1956.

On 6th January 1966 Harry was a passenger in a car driven by his wife when it had a puncture and overturned on the Leichhardt Highway near Condamine. He was admitted to Miles Hospital on the Darling Downs, Queensland, where he suffered a heart attack and died next day. His funeral with full military honours took place at St Andrew's Presbyterian Church, Ann Street, Brisbane on 14th January 1966. It was followed by cremation at Mount Thompson Crematorium, Brisbane, where a memorial stone commemorates him and his wife Nell, who subsequently remarried as Waugh. Harry is commemorated in a number of other places:

• Murray Crescent, Canberra, Australian Capital Territory.
• Murray Street, Wodonga, Victoria on White Box Rise estate built on part of the former Bandiana Army Camp.
• Murray Street, Crib Point, Melbourne, Victoria.
• The nineteen wards at Hollywood Private Hospital, Perth, Western Australia are named after VCs and GCs, including Henry Murray.
• The 'Henry Murray Australia's Most Decorated Soldier Class 1 Handicap' horse race is held by the Tasmanian Turf Club over 1,400m annually on Anzac Day at Launceston Racecourse. It is one of four Anzac Day races at Launceston named after Tasmanian born VCs.
• 'Lieutenant Colonel Harry Murray VC Honours Scholarships' established in 2010 by the Tasmanian Minister for Veterans' Affairs are awarded by the University of Tasmania Foundation and funded by the Tasmanian State Government. Two one year scholarships are available annually for students in their final year who intend

undertaking an honours year of study with the focus of their thesis examining Tasmanians' involvement in war.

- The Victoria Cross Memorial, Campbell, Canberra dedicated on 24th July 2000. A portrait of him hangs in the Hall of Valour at the Australian War Memorial.
- A memorial plaque in the Garden Of Remembrance, Pinaroo Cemetery, Albany Creek, Queensland.
- The Victoria Cross Memorial, Hobart Cenotaph, Tasmania, dedicated on 11th May 2003.
- A bronze statue of Harry was unveiled at Evandale, Northern Tasmania by the Governor General of Australia, General Michael Jeffrey, on 24th February 2006. The statue cost A$85,000, the money being raised by volunteers over two years. Those present included Harry's son Doug, his daughter Clem Sutherland, Veteran Affairs Minister Bruce Billson and Tasmanian Premier Paul Lennon. A ceremony was held at the statue on 5th February 2007 to mark the 90th Anniversary of his VC action.

The bronze statue of Harry Murray at Evandale, Northern Tasmania (Diana Kupke).

- 'The Murray Memorial Room' at Evandale Community Centre commemorates his life and deeds.
- The Victoria Cross Memorial, Queen Victoria Building, George Street, Sydney, New South Wales.
- A bronze bust at Jack Brown Lions Park Richmond, Queensland.
- Named on one of eleven plaques honouring 175 men from overseas awarded the VC for the Great War. The plaques were unveiled by the Senior Minister of State at the Foreign & Commonwealth Office and Minister for Faith and Communities, Baroness Warsi, at a reception at Lancaster House, London on 26th June 2014 attended by the Duke of Kent and relatives of the VC recipients. The Australian plaque is at the Australian War Memorial.
- The Secretary of State for Communities and Local Government, Eric Pickles MP, announced that Victoria Cross recipients from the Great War would have commemorative paving stones laid in their birthplace as a lasting legacy of local heroes within communities. The stones would be laid on or close to the 100th anniversary of their VC actions. For the 145 VCs born in Australia, Belgium, Canada, China, Denmark, Egypt, France, Germany, India, Iraq, Japan, Nepal, Netherlands, New Zealand, Pakistan, South Africa, Sri Lanka, Ukraine and United States of America, individual commemorative stones were unveiled at the National Memorial Arboretum, Alrewas, Staffordshire by Prime Minister David Cameron MP and Sergeant Johnson Beharry VC on 5th March 2015.
- His VC action featured in Issues No. 789 and 1326 of the Victor Comic on 3rd April 1976 and 19th July 1986.

In addition to the VC, CMG, DSO & Bar and DCM, he was also awarded the 1914–15 Star, British War Medal 1914–20, Victory Medal 1914–19 with Mentioned-in-Despatches Oakleaf, War Medal 1939–45, Australia Service Medal 1939–45, George VI Coronation Medal 1937, Elizabeth II Coronation Medal 1953 and the French Croix de Guerre with Bronze Palm. In September 2015 his daughter, Clem Sutherland, put her father's medals into the care of the Australian War Memorial for permanent display in the Hall of Valour.

CAPTAIN JAMES ERNEST NEWLAND
12th Australian Infantry Battalion AIF

James Newland was born on 22nd August 1881 at Highton, Geelong, Victoria, Australia. His father, William Anthony Newland (1859–1921), was a labourer and later a railway employee. His mother, Louisa Jane née Wall (1857–1947), married William in 1879 at Geelong, Victoria. James had ten siblings:

• William Andrew Newland (1880–1949) enlisted as a trooper in 2nd Scottish Horse on 15th February 1901 (31696) and served during the Second Boer War in South Africa until being discharged on completion of service on 14th September 1901. He enlisted in 4th Light Horse on 11th February 1902 (2221) and served again in the Second Boer War in 4th and 10th Australian Light Horse rising to sergeant. He received a gunshot wound to the right calf. On 19th August 1914 he enlisted in 4th Light Horse Regiment as a corporal (483) at Broadmeadows Camp, Victoria and was assigned to the Machine gun section. He was described as a mechanical engineer, 5′ 6″ tall with fair complexion, greyish eyes, reddish hair and his religious denomination was Methodist. He transferred to 8th Light Horse at Broadmeadows as a private on 17th October and was promoted sergeant on 28th October. William sailed for Gallipoli via Alexandria, Egypt on HMT *Menominee* on 10th May 1915 and received a gunshot wound to the chest at Walkers Ridge on 26th May. Having been evacuated on HMHS *Dunluce Castle* to Egypt on 30th May, he was admitted to No.2 Australian General Hospital, Ghezireh Palace, Cairo the following day. Having recovered partially he was invalided to Australia on HMAT *Ballarat* on 3rd September and was discharged medically unfit at 3rd Military District, Victoria on 22nd December 1915. on 22nd August 1914 and served in 1st Company, Army Service Corps AIF (210), returning to Australia on 20th October 1918. He married Elizabeth Grace Allin (1894–1966) in 1914 and they had four children – Blanche Elizabeth Newland 1915, William Allin Newland 1916, Irene Jean Newland 1919 and Nancy Newland 1923.

- Stella Louise Newland (1883–1937).
- George Benjamin Newland (1884–1968) served in 58th Battalion AIF (2754) from 15th July 1915 and returned to Australia on 8th April 1919. He married Mary Flora O'Donnell (1890–1916) and they had five children – George Richard Newland 1910, Ronald Herbert Newland 1911, Ann Veronica Newland 1912, Gordon Lindsay Newland 1913 and Blanche May Newland 1915. George married Eva Moore and had nine more children – Joyce Newland 1922, Elva Newland 1924, Golding Newland 1926, Alison Newland 1928, Phyllis Newland 1928, Noel Newland 1930, Dorothy Newland 1932, Mervyn Newland 1934 and Lorna Newland 1938.
- Edith Blanche Newland (1886–1957).
- Ethel Winifred Newland (1888–1974) married Joseph William George and they had a daughter, Mary Josephine George.
- Herbert Leslie Newland (1890–1964) was a Police Constable and also served for three years in the Royal Australian Artillery until being discharged at own request. He enlisted in 2nd Field Artillery Brigade Ammunition Column (1537) on 1st September 1914 at Broadmeadows Camp, described as 5′ 11″ tall and weighing 180 lbs. He sailed from Australia on 24th September and was promoted corporal on 22nd July 1915. He was hospitalised at Gallipoli on 21st August and evacuated to New End Section Hospital, Heath Street, Hampstead, London on 10th September with tonsillitis. Herbert returned to duty on 9th February 1916 and arrived in Cairo, Egypt on 14th February. Appointed acting sergeant at Tel el Kebir on 8th March and joined 23rd Battery there the following day. He arrived at Marseilles, France on 28th March, was promoted sergeant on 12th March and transferred to 21st Field Artillery Brigade on 15th May. He was appointed temporary battery sergeant major on 1st November. Herbert was commissioned on 30th November and transferred to 1st Division Artillery Column and was detached to the Artillery School of Instruction the same day. He returned to 21st Field Artillery Brigade on 6th January 1917 and transferred to the Divisional Ammunition Column on 21st January and 1st Medium Trench Mortar Brigade on 2nd February. He was promoted lieutenant on 27th February. Having been granted leave on 17th July, he was admitted to No.7 Stationary Hospital, Boulogne with gonorrhoea and transferred to No.39 General Hospital, Boulogne the following day. He was discharged to Base Details on 22nd August and rejoined his unit on 25th August. He transferred from V1A Heavy Trench Mortar Battery to X1A Medium Trench Mortar Battery on 30th October and was granted leave to Britain 4th–19th February 1918. He transferred to the Australian Corps Heavy Trench Mortar Battery on 15th February. Herbert embarked at Le Havre on RMS *Durham Castle* on 13th October, arrived at Melbourne on 23rd October and was granted special leave. He was discharged medically unfit for active service on 2nd April 1919. He rejoined the Victorian Police and served as Sergeant-in-Charge of police stations at Queenscliff, Geelong and St Kilda. At St Kilda he was appointed Sergeant-in-Charge of the first guard section at the new Melbourne

Shrine of Remembrance. He married Catherine Milne Scott (1896–1951) and had at least one son, Leslie Alexander Newland in 1924.

• Irene Victoria Newland (1892–1925) married Albert Victor Hyde (born 1893–) in 1920 and they had a daughter, Winifred Irene Hyde the same year. He served as a senior naval cadet July 1908–January 1911 and enlisted in the Australian Imperial Force on 2nd July 1915 (2739). He was assigned to 9th Reinforcements, 21st Battalion and went to Gallipoli with 14th Battalion. He later served in France. Before he left Australia, Irene gave him a gold locket, which probably saved his life when a shell exploded in front of him, severely damaging the locket. His right leg was fractured and his body was riddled with shrapnel. He begged a doctor not to amputate his leg, but was unfit to continue serving and was evacuated to Australia on 5th February 1918 in the rank of sergeant. He was a public servant when he enlisted in the Australian Militia Forces on 19th May 1932 at Ripponlea, Victoria for three years with 46th Battalion (B4747). He was promoted corporal on 16th November 1932, sergeant the following day and was discharged on 21st October 1933.

• Alfred Lindsay Newland (1894–1916) was a labourer. He enlisted at Broadmeadows Camp on 19th February 1915 (656), described as 6′ ¼″ tall, weighing 175 lbs, with fresh complexion, light blue eyes, brown hair and his religious denomination was Methodist. He was assigned to 22nd Infantry Battalion AIF as a private on 1st May and sailed for Gallipoli on 30th August. He sailed to Alexandria, Egypt on 7th January 1916 and was taken on strength at Moascar Garrison on 1st March. He was promoted corporal on 10th March, but this was cancelled and he was promoted sergeant on 12th March instead. He returned to duty from the School of Instruction at Zeitoun the following day and disembarked at Marseille, France on 19th March. Alfred was served as a 2nd lieutenant commissioned and assigned to in 6th Company, Australian Machine Gun Corps on 18th October. AIF and He was killed in action on 9th November 1916 (AIF Burial Ground, Flers – X L 1). His conduct was brought to the notice of the Secretary of State for War on 13th August 1918 for valuable services in action.

• Elsie Mildred Newland (1896–1962) married Charles Hutchinson and they had six children – Joy Hutchinson, Geoffrey Hutchinson, Clifford Hutchinson, Shirley Rae Hutchinson, Olive Hutchinson and Jean Hutchinson.

• Redvers Cecil Newland (1900–72) was a police constable in Geelong. He married Bella Fairweather (1904–84) from Rutherglen, Lanarkshire, Scotland in 1928 and they had a son, Maxwell James Newland in 1937. Redvers was appointed Licensing Inspector in the Chief Secretary's Department, Victoria in July 1954. Redvers and Bella were visiting Scotland when he died at Perth on 29th July 1972.

James' paternal grandfather, James Newland (1824–77) at Norton, Hertfordshire. He was a railway labourer, living at Norton in 1851. He married Elizabeth née Currell (born c.1823) in 1849 at Hitchin and they emigrated to Victoria, Australia in 1852. In addition to William they had seven other children:

- Charlotte Ann Newland (born 1843).
- Alfred Currell Newland (born 1845) married Elizabeth Osborne in 1871 in Victoria and they had seven children – Annie Elizabeth Newland 1872, Alfred George Newland 1874, John Newland 1875, Florence Lucy Newland 1877, Edith Victoria Newland 1881, Bessie Newland 1884 and Charles Osborne Newland 1887.
- Kate Elizabeth Newland (1851–52), died at sea in the Indian Ocean during the voyage to Australia.
- George James Newland (born and died 1854).
- Martha Jane Newland (1855–91) married John Kemp (died 1918) in 1872 and they had eight children – Suzanna Jane Kemp 1873, Francis Kemp 1875, Charlotte Elizabeth Kemp, Martha Harriot Kemp 1880, John William Kemp 1882, Arthur Edward Kemp 1884, Flora Alice Kemp 1887, Clarice Phebe Kemp and a male Kemp 1891.

James' brother, 2nd Lieutenant Alfred Lindsay Newland, is buried in AIF Burial Ground, Flers.

- Samuel George Newland (1857–1939) married Eliza Loveday (1860–1906) in 1881 at Belmont, Victoria and they had six children – George Edward Newland 1882, Horace William Newland 1884, Horace Loveday Newland 1886, Beatrice Elizabeth Newland 1887, Leopold Thomas Newland 1889, Claude Stanley Bolden Newland 1892, Lionel Claude Newland 1895 and Oliver Marcus Bolden Newland 1897.
- James Edward Newland (born 1862) married Fanny Elizabeth Tozer (born 1868) in 1888 and they had three children – Richard William Newland 1889, James Henry Herbert Newland 1890 and Frank Alfred George Newland 1893.

His maternal grandfather, William Wall (1819–1907), married Louisa Jane née Thomas (1816–86) in December 1844 at Bodmin. They emigrated to Australia, arriving at Geelong, Victoria on 5th January 1853. William was living with his family at Belmont, Corio, Victoria in 1903. In addition to Louisa they had five other children:

- James Robert Wall (1847–1926) married Jessie Maria Wells (1857–1935) in 1882 in Victoria. They had eight children – James Robert William Wall 1883, Louisa Wall 1884, Jessie Maria Wall 1885, Mary Ann Wyatt Wall 1887, Albert Ernest Wall 1888, Arthur Henry Wall 1889, Alexander Wall 1890 and Lucy Wyatt Wall 1891.
- Mary Ann Wall (1849–1908) married Thomas Henry Hall (1856–1940) in 1876 in Victoria. They had six children – Rhoda Ellen Hall 1878, Eva Jane Hall 1882, Alice Lavinia Hall 1885, Minnie Blanche Hall 1887, Albert Henry Hall 1888 and Ruby Maud Hall 1890.

- John Thomas Wall (1850–1907) married Mary Ann Wright (1853–1930) in 1875 at Geelong. They had twelve children – Grace Adelaide Wall 1875, Louisa Emily Annie Wall 1877, Mabel Trefina Ethal Wall 1879, John Thomas Wall 1881, Percival Ernest Wall 1883, Blanch Adelaide Wall c.1884, Blanche Edith Wall 1885, Edith May Wall 1887, Ernest Charles Herbert Wall 1890, Annie Lilian Myrtle Wall 1892, Claude Cleveland Wall 1895 and Rosaline Muriel Wall 1898.
- Benjamin Wall (1852–1917) was born at sea aboard the barque *Time & Truth*. He married Susannah Mary Ann Tregonning (1861–1917) in 1880 at Geelong and they had a daughter, Alice Louisa Wall 1881.
- Andrew Wall (1859–1932) married Annie Parker (1862–1954) in 1886 at Camperdown, Victoria. They had eight children – Alfred Henry Wall 1887, Charles Norman Wall 1888, Annie Lillian Wall 1889, Arthur Stanley Wall 1892, Herbert Benjamin Wall 1893, Harold Victor Wall 1895, Roy Cameron Wall 1903 and Nellie Louisa/e 1904.

James enlisted in Melbourne on 11th February 1902 (2354) and served with 4th Battalion, Australian Commonwealth Horse in the South African War. He embarked on SS *Templestowe* on 26th March 1902, disembarked at Durban and took part in operations in the Transvaal. The peace treaty was signed shortly afterwards and he embarked at Durban aboard SS *Manchester Merchant* on 28th June 1902 for Australia. He then served as a gunner (1439) in the Royal Australian Artillery in Victoria 27th July 1903–14th September 1907. Promoted to acting bombardier 1st November 1904, bombardier 3rd December 1904 and corporal 1st December 1905. James was a policeman in Tasmania, March 1909–August 1910. He married Florence May née Mitchell (1885–1924) at Sheffield, Tasmania on 27th December 1913 and they lived at 'Hazeldene'.

James rejoined the Army in Hobart, Tasmania and served in the Australian Instructional Corps from 11th August 1910. He attended a qualifying course as a staff sergeant major at the School of Musketry, Randwick, New South Wales, passing out on 3rd September 1912. He also attended a machine gun course at the School of Musketry, passing out on 20th December 1913. When war broke out, he enlisted in the AIF on 17th August 1914 as regimental quartermaster sergeant with 12th Battalion (No.2) at Pontville, Tasmania. He was described a 5′ 9″ tall, weighing 175 lbs, with fair hair, blue eyes and fair complexion. He was known as 'Skipper'. James embarked for Egypt from Hobart aboard HMAT *A2 Geelong* on 20th October, disembarking at Alexandria before moving to Heliopolis. He was appointed temporary warrant officer class two in the Permanent Military Forces on 29th January 1915.

James landed at Gallipoli on 25th April 1915 and received a gunshot wound to the arm between then and 28th April when he was evacuated. He was commissioned on returning to 12th Battalion on 22nd May and was appointed Battalion Transport Officer in Egypt on 9th June. Promoted lieutenant 15th October and posted to the

Manchester Liners, founded in 1898 as a result of the construction of the Manchester Ship Canal, operated across the Atlantic and in the Mediterranean. Two new ships joined the fleet in 1899–1900, *Manchester Port* and *Manchester Merchant*. During the Second Boer War, four of the Company's ships, including *Manchester Merchant*, were requisitioned to transport troops, horses and supplies. Returning to Manchester from New Orleans on her first voyage after her war service in January 1903, a fire started in her cargo. She was scuttled on the west coast of Ireland and broke up in bad weather. A new *Manchester Merchant* was launched in 1904. The Company continued until 1985, when its ships, restricted in size by the Manchester Ship Canal, could no longer compete with larger container ships.

A mailship arriving at Durban harbour about the time of the Second Boer War.

Transport Section at Maadi, Egypt on 3rd November. He reported sick with dengue fever on 12th November and was in hospital at Ghezireh until 23rd November.

Appointed honorary captain 1st March 1916 and Adjutant of 12th Battalion on 15th March. He embarked at Alexandria on 29th March and landed at Marseilles, France on 5th April. **Mentioned in General Sir Douglas Haig's Despatch of 13th November 1916 (2nd Supplement to LG of 2nd January 1917, published on 4th January 1917), as a result of his actions at Pozières on the Somme on 21st August, when he led his company in a successful attack on trenches northeast of Mouquet Farm. He was recommended for the MC and later the French Croix de Guerre for this incident, but received the MID instead.**

On 4th December, he reported sick with pyrexia of undetermined origin and was admitted to No.2 General Hospital at Le Havre until 12th December. He joined 1st Australian Division Base Depot at Étaples on 14th December and was attached to HQ 2nd Australian Brigade from 18th December until 21st January 1917. After some leave in England, he was wounded by shrapnel in the face near Bapaume on 26th February. He was discharged to Base Details, Boulogne on 5th March and rejoined the Battalion on 25th March.

Awarded the VC for his actions at Boursies and northeast of Lagnicourt, France 8th–9th April and 15th April 1917, LG 8th June 1917. The VC was presented by the King in the forecourt at Buckingham Palace on 21st July.

Troops being trained by the Australian
Instructional Corps at the School of Musketry
(later Small Arms School), Randwick, New South
Wales.

HMAT *A2 Geelong* departing Hobart on 20th
October 1914 with James Newland aboard (AWM).

During the Second Battle of Bullecourt on 5th May, he received a gunshot to
the left arm and was evacuated to England. He departed England on 21st July and
disembarked at Melbourne, Victoria on 18th September. He was promoted warrant
officer class two in the Permanent Military Forces on 14th November 1917 and
his appointment with the AIF was terminated in Victoria on 2nd March 1918 as
medically unfit. He was on the Reserve of Officers, 6th Military District, Tasmania
on 1st October 1920 and carried out full time duty as a captain in the Reserve until
31st December 1921, but this was not recognised as continuous employment in a
permanent capacity until 1927. Meanwhile he was promoted warrant officer class
one in the Permanent Military Forces on 31st December 1921. He was appointed
honorary captain in the Australian Instructional Corps on 1st January 1922 and
was posted as Quartermaster of 8th Battalion, transferring to 49th Battalion on 8th
September and 38th Battalion on 17th April 1923.

Florence died of tuberculosis in 1924 at Bendigo, Victoria and James married
Vivienne Heather née Broughton (1900–77) on 30th April 1925 at St Paul's Anglican

The first parade of 12th Battalion AIF at Pontville, Tasmania (AWM).

All that remained of Mouquet Farm after the intense fighting there in 1916 (AWM).

Casino Lechin was one of six buildings taken over by No.2 General Hospital in Le Havre.

Church, Bendigo. They lived at 54 Brigg Street, Caulfield, Melbourne, Victoria and had a daughter, Heather Dawn Newland (born 1926), who married as Hartley George Robinson (1925–2006) and they had three children. Hartley enlisted in the Royal Australian Naval Reserve on 20th January 1943 (PM.5653) as a probationary Sick Berth Attendant (SBA), described as 5′ 5³/₈″ tall, with fresh complexion, blue eyes and brown hair. He trained at HMAS *Cerberus*, Victoria and qualified as a SBA on 14th May. He was based at various establishments – the shore-based HMAS *Penguin*, Sydney 4th October 1944; mobile repair ship HMAS *Whang Pu* at Madang Harbour, New Guinea and Morotai, Dutch East Indies 1st November; HMAS *Penguin* 23rd April 1945; shore-based HMAS *Lonsdale*, Port Melbourne 24th April; HMAS *Penguin* 18th May; HMAS *Whang Pu* 20th June; repair vessel HMAS *Platypus* in New Guinean waters 1st September; HMAS *Whang Pu* 15th October; corvette HMAS *Ballarat* 23rd November; HMAS *Lonsdale* 13th December; HMAS *Cerberus* 17th December; and HMAS *Lonsdale* 28th June 1946. He was awarded a Good Conduct Badge on 20th January 1946 and demobilised on 15th July 1946.

On 16th June 1926, James was a founder member of Bendigo Legacy, which still cares for the families of deceased or incapacitated service veterans. He was at the Anzac commemoration service on 25th April 1927 at the Exhibition Building, Melbourne, Victoria in the presence of The Duke of York (later King George VI) and took part in the march past with twenty-five other VCs. In November 1929, he attended a luncheon at Government House with the Governor of Australia, Sir Dudley de Chair, together with thirteen other VCs.

James completed a Rifle and Bayonet Course at the Small Arms School, Randwick on 16th December 1929 and was appointed honorary major on 1st May 1930. He was posted to A Branch, Army Headquarters, Melbourne on 10th May 1940 until

The Exhibition Building, Melbourne where James Newland took part in the Anzac commemoration service on 25th April 1927 in the presence of the future King George VI.

St Paul's Anglican Church, Bendigo where James married his second wife, Vivienne Broughton, on 30th April 1925.

being retired on 22nd August 1941 as honorary lieutenant colonel. He was appointed Deputy Commissioner of the Northern Territory Division of the Australian Red Cross Society April–September 1941 and became a Senior Examiner at No.2 Small Arms Ammunition Factory, Footscray, Melbourne on 2nd January 1942.

James Newland died of heart failure at his home at 54 Brigg Street, Caulfield on 19th March 1949. His funeral with full military honours on 21st March was at Bathurst's Chapel, Glenhuntly Road, Elsternwick, Victoria and he is buried in the Methodist Section at East Brighton Cemetery, Melbourne, Victoria (G 174a). He is commemorated in a number of other places:

- Newland Street, Canberra, Australian Capital Territory.
- Newlands (sic) Street, Crib Point, Melbourne, Victoria.
- Newland Street, Wodonga, Victoria on White Box Estate on the former Bandiana Army Camp.
- Newland Avenue, Milperra, Sydney, New South Wales.
- Newland Place, Yarrawarrah, Sydney.

Army Headquarters in Victoria Barracks, Melbourne. The barracks also housed the Australian War Cabinet during the Second World War (AWM).

The Queen's South Africa Medal was awarded to military personnel, civilian officials and war correspondents who served in South Africa during the Second Boer War from 11th October 1899 to 31st May 1902. There were twenty-six clasps for individual actions and campaigns. James received the clasps for 'Transvaal' and 'South Africa 1902'.

The Victoria Cross Memorial at Hobart commemorates the thirteen VC recipients from Tasmania. In the left background is the Hobart Cenotaph (Hobart War Memorial).

- Newland Street, Fig Tree Pocket, Brisbane, Queensland.
- Newland Reserve, Sadlier Avenue, Milperra, Sydney.
- Newland Barracks (formerly Geelong Barracks), Myers Street, Geelong, Victoria was opened by Brigadier Steve Aird, Commander 4th Brigade on 9th December 2006 – it is currently occupied by HQ A Company, 8th/7th Battalion, Royal Victoria Regiment and the Geelong Unit of the Australian Army Cadets.
- His tunic and a replica set of medals are displayed at Fort Queenscliff, King Street, Queenscliff, Victoria.
- Victoria Cross Memorial, Campbell, Canberra, dedicated on 24th July 2000.
- Victoria Cross Memorial, Hobart Cenotaph, Tasmania, dedicated on 11th May 2003.
- Victoria Cross Memorial, Queen Victoria Building, George Street, Sydney, New South Wales.
- Memorial plaque at Battery Point, Anglesea Barracks Memorial Garden, Hobart, Tasmania.
- Lieutenant Colonel James Ernest Newland Room, Geelong Returned and Services League.

- Named on the Honour Board of Old Laverton School, Melbourne, Victoria with his brothers William, Herbert and Lindsay.
- Named on one of eleven plaques honouring 175 men from overseas awarded the VC for the Great War. The plaques were unveiled by the Senior Minister of State at the Foreign & Commonwealth Office and Minister for Faith and Communities, Baroness Warsi, at a reception at Lancaster House, London on 26th June 2014 attended by The Duke of Kent and relatives of the VC recipients. The Australian plaque is at the Australian War Memorial.
- The Secretary of State for Communities and Local Government, Eric Pickles MP announced that Victoria Cross recipients from the Great War would have commemorative paving stones laid in their birthplace as a lasting legacy of local heroes within communities. The stones would be laid on or close to the 100th anniversary of their VC actions. For the 145 VCs born in Australia, Belgium, Canada, China, Denmark, Egypt, France, Germany, India, Iraq, Japan, Nepal, Netherlands, New Zealand, Pakistan, South Africa, Sri Lanka, Ukraine and United States of America, individual commemorative stones were unveiled at the National Memorial Arboretum, Alrewas, Staffordshire by Prime Minister David Cameron MP and Sergeant Johnson Beharry VC on 5th March 2015.

In addition to the VC, he was awarded the Queen's South Africa Medal 1899–1901 (clasps 'Transvaal' & 'South Africa 1902'), 1914–15 Star, British War Medal 1914–20, Victory Medal 1914–19 with Mentioned-in-Despatches Oakleaf, George VI Coronation Medal 1937, Permanent Forces of the Empire Beyond the Seas Long Service & Good Conduct Medal, Meritorious Service Medal (Commonwealth of Australia), War Medal 1939–45 and Australia Service Medal 1939–45. His medals were donated to the Australian War Memorial, Treloar Crescent, Campbell, Australian Capital Territory by his daughter in 1984, where they are held in the Hall of Valour.

3/1836 SERGEANT JOHN WILLIAM ORMSBY
2nd Battalion, The King's Own (Yorkshire Light Infantry)

John Ormsby was born at 14 Tunnacliffe Yard, Old Westgate, Dewsbury, Yorkshire on 11th January 1881. His father, William Ormsby (1838–97), a peddler or licensed hawker and later a night watchman for Dewsbury Corporation, was born in Ireland. His mother was Caroline née Brook. Her age given in various official documents varies wildly. In the 1881 Census she was thirty-seven (born c.1844), but in the 1911 Census she was sixty-two (born c.1849). When she died in 1912, her age was recorded as fifty-eight (born c.1854). After William died, Caroline was living at 8 Belgrave Street, Flatts, Dewsbury. By 1911, she was living with her daughter, Mary

Horan, at 48 Hodgsons Yard, Vulcan Road, Dewsbury. John had sixteen siblings, of whom only two survived to adulthood. Those known are:

- Anthony Ormsby born and died 1875.
- Patrick James Ormsby (1876–1943) married Martha Jane Hall (1878–1944) in 1897. He was a paver in 1911, living with his family at 17 Swallow Road, Dewsbury. They had twelve children – John William Ormsby 1898, Mary Ormsby 1899, Harriet Ann Ormsby 1901, James Ormsby 1903, Edward Ormsby 1905, Joseph Ormsby 1908, William Ormsby 1909, Martha Jane Ormsby 1912, Patrick J Ormsby 1914, Michael Ormsby 1916, Teresa Ormsby 1921 and Agnes Ormsby 1923. The eldest, J/40616 Ordinary Seaman John William Ormsby, was also the VC's godson. He was a mill hand when he enlisted in the Royal Navy on 1st June 1915, giving his date of birth as 7th April 1897 and name as John Willie Ormsby. He was only 5′ 1¼″ tall with dark brown hair, blue eyes and fresh complexion. He was on the strength of HMS *Victory I* until joining HMS *Colleen*, the depot ship for the Auxiliary Patrol Service at Queenstown, Ireland on 2nd February 1917. He transferred to HMS *Begonia*, a Q-ship renamed Q-10, operating as SS *Dolsis Jessop* and was lost when HMS *Begonia* was involved in a collision with a U-boat on 6th October 1917 and sank off Casablanca. He is commemorated on the Portsmouth Naval Memorial.
- Mary Ann Ormsby (1877–85).
- Emma Ormsby (1882–85).
- Anthony Ormsby born and died 1884.
- Edward Ormsby (1886–89).
- Mary Emma Ormsby (1888–1931) married John William Horan (1882–1966) in 1908. He was a wood sawyer and she was a cloth rag sorter in 1911. They were living at 48 Hodgson's Yard, Vulcan Road, Dewsbury. They had five children – Mary Horan (1911–12), twins Mary E Horan and Rodger Horan 1920, Winifred Horan 1922 and Teresa/Theresa Horan born and died 1931. Mary E Horan married Harry Winder in 1939. Harry served in the Royal Navy as an Able Seaman (P/JX 196158). He died on 14th February 1942 on the strength of HMS *President III*, the training establishment in Bristol for those serving on Defensively Equipped Merchant Ships, and is commemorated on the Portsmouth Naval Memorial. He was aboard the Panamanian ship *Ramapo* as a DEMS gunner when she was torpedoed by *U-108* about 180 miles north of Bermuda with the loss of all forty aboard. His date of death is recorded as 14th February by the CWGC, but *U-108*'s log states the attack took place on 16th February. Mary married Fred Davies in 1946 and they had two children – Peter F Davies 1946 and Pauline A Davies 1954.

John was educated at St Paulinus Catholic Primary School, Dewsbury, but when he enlisted he was almost illiterate. He was employed as a labourer until enlisting in the Northumberland Fusiliers on 16th October 1899 (6083) as John Willie Ormsby. He gave his age as nineteen years and nine months. He was posted to 2nd Battalion on 22nd December 1899 and 3rd Battalion on 12th February 1900. On 25th April 1900, he was sentenced to eight days detention with hard labour for absence 13–20th April. Appointed unpaid lance corporal 26th February 1902, but it was short-lived as on 12th April a Regimental Court Martial sentenced him to fourteen days detention with hard labour for conduct to the prejudice of good order and military discipline. John served in the West Indies from 30th April 1902 and South Africa from 23rd July. He was posted to 1st Battalion in Mauritius on 12th December 1903 and served there until 8th February 1906 and then in India until 8th November 1907. He was awarded Good Conduct Badges on 22nd April 1904 and 22nd April 1906. John was posted to the Depot on 17th October 1907 and arrived in England on 9th November for transfer to the Reserve on 14th November 1907. He was discharged from the Reserve on 15th October 1911.

John Ormsby married Catherine 'Kate' née Burns (4th February 1881–1938) on 26th October 1908. She was a rag sorter for Mr Thomas H Graham, rag and mungo merchant, at Hoyle Head Mill, Dewsbury. Her parents, John Burns (c.1849–1911) and Mary 'Maria' née McGee (c.1856–1925) were born in Dublin, Ireland. Catherine was a rag sorter in 1901 and 1911. They lived at various addresses in Dewsbury – 10 Back Belgrave Street in 1911; 5 Firth Street, Boothroyd Lane in 1917; later in Victoria Road, Springfield, Batley Carr; and after Kate died he was at Park Avenue, Westtown. Kate and William had four children:

Port Louis, Mauritius.

- William John Ormsby (1909–61) married
  Martha J Moorhouse (1917–2004) in 1937. They had five children – David P Ormsby 1939, John W Ormsby 1941, Margaret P Ormsby 1941, Jean C Ormsby 1943 and Patricia S Ormsby 1944.
- Helen 'Lena' Ormsby (1910–37) married Lionel Bennett Richardson (1907–70) as Helena Ormsby in 1930 and they had a son, Francis A Richardson later that year.
- Henry 'Harry' Ormsby (1912–13).
- Mary Victoria Ormsby, born and died 1917.

One of Kate's sisters, Anne Elizabeth (born 1879) married David Rochford (1882–1917) in 1916. David enlisted in 1/4th King's Own Yorkshire Light Infantry on

15th November 1914 (201419) and went to France on 15th June 1915. He was hit in the back with shrapnel and suffered gas poisoning and was admitted to hospital at Le Tréport. Anne was notified by telegram and travelled to be by his side, but arrived an hour after he had been buried. He died on 27th July 1917 and is buried in Mount Huon Military Cemetery, Le Tréport (II H 1).

On 18th August 1909 John was sentenced to seven days hard labour for assault. He re-enlisted when war broke out and went to France on 11th November 1914. **Awarded the MM, almost certainly for actions during the Battles of the Somme, LG 11th November 1916. Awarded the VC for his actions at Fayet, France on 14th April 1917, LG 8th June 1917.** The VC ribbon was presented to him by Major General AR Montagu-Stuart-Wortley, GOC 32nd Division, on 11th June 1917. The VC was presented by the King at Buckingham Palace on 30th June 1917.

When he returned to Dewsbury a large crowd gathered in the Market Place before the Town Hall. William was taken there in procession, with his wife and family, from the railway station, surrounded by wildly cheering crowds. The procession included A (Batley) and B and C (Dewsbury) Companies of the West Riding Volunteers, together with members of various local groups and organisations including St Paulinus' Church Lads' Brigade and officials of Dewsbury Irish National League Club. At the Town Hall, he was welcomed by the Mayor, Alderman W France, and other dignitaries, including Father Frederick Mitchell, the Parish Priest of Our Lady and St. Paulinus' Church. The crowd in the Market Place was estimated at over 20,000 with 5,000 more in Boothroyd Lane to welcome him to the family home. Unfortunately, Jessie Woods, a neighbour of the Ormsby family, died after falling from the roof of her cottage, where she had climbed to get a better view.

John was discharged on 16th April 1919 and was presented with a horse and cart and £500 to start a green-grocery business, but he used it as a general carrier and marine stores dealer. The business was not a success and he was later employed by Dewsbury Corporation Highways Department for thirty years. John formed the 'Ormsby Boxing Troupe', training young boys to box and play rugby. One of his boxers, Paddy Lyons, a middleweight, was active from 1939 until 1945 and had thirty-three professional bouts, winning a number of championships. William was a life member of the Irish National Club in Dewsbury and the Horbury and Keighley British Legion, as well as being active with the King's Own Yorkshire Light Infantry Regimental Association.

St Paulinus Church was designed by Edward Welby Pugin, son of Augustus Pugin, architect of the interior of the Houses of Parliament. It opened in June 1871 (Taking Stock).

John served in the Home Guard or civil defence in the Second World War, as he was awarded the Defence Medal. He was presented to the future Queen, Princess Elizabeth, on 31st October 1951 at Queen Elizabeth Barracks, Strensall, York in her capacity as Colonel-in-Chief of the King's Own Yorkshire Light Infantry. John always wore his medals during ex-servicemen's parades and functions, …. *for those who never came home – the real heroes.*

John Ormsby died at the home of his son at 28 Low Road, Dewsbury on 29th July 1952. A full military funeral with requiem mass at St Paulinus Church on 1st August was followed by burial in Dewsbury Cemetery (R 718). A firing party from the King's Own Yorkshire Light Infantry fired three volleys over the grave and the Last Post and Reveille were played. A headstone was erected in the 1980s organized by local resident Albert Mercer and paid for by the Regiment. The year of birth was shown incorrectly as 1889 and this was corrected in 2008. He is also commemorated at John Ormsby VC Way, Shawcross Business Park, Dewsbury opened by the Mayor of Dewsbury, Councillor J Brooke, on 16th May 1992.

In addition to the VC and MM, he was awarded the 1914 Star with 'Mons' clasp, British War Medal 1914–20, Victory Medal 1914–19, Defence Medal, George V Jubilee Medal 1935 and George VI Coronation Medal 1937. The VC was presented to the Regiment by his son, John William Ormsby, but the other medals remain with the family. The VC is held by the King's Own Yorkshire Light Infantry Museum, Doncaster Museum & Art Gallery, Chequer Road, Doncaster.

John William Ormsby's grave in Dewsbury Cemetery (Peter Bennett).

731 LANCE SERGEANT FREDERICK WILLIAM PALMER
22nd Battalion, The Royal Fusiliers (City of London Regiment)

Frederick Palmer was born at Hammersmith, London on 11th November 1891. His father, Thomas Palmer (1865–1921), was born at Martley, Worcester. He was an omnibus driver in 1891 and a taxi cab driver in 1901. His mother was Rhoda née Smith, born at Stanton Lacy, Shropshire in 1861. Thomas' and Rhoda's marriage was registered in the 1st quarter of 1887 at Brentford, Middlesex. The family was living at 213 King Street, Hammersmith, London in 1891 and 9 Russell Gardens, Kensington, London in 1901. By 1911, Thomas was living without Rhoda at 36

King Street, Hammersmith, London.

A humorous wartime publication by Cecil Palmer & Haywood.

Godolphin Road, Hammersmith. It is understood that Rhoda married Arthur W Allport in 1925. Frederick had six siblings, but only three were living in 1911:

• Harry Cecil Palmer (born 1889) was a publishing manager in 1911 and later set up the publishers, Cecil Palmer & Haywood. He enlisted in the Royal Air Force as a Private Class 2 on 29th July 1918 (181201) at the Cadet Distribution Depot, Hampstead, London for training as a Cadet (Flying). He was described as 5′ 8½″ tall, with fair hair, blue eyes, fresh complexion and his religious denomination was Church of England. He was posted to No.1 School of Aeronautics at Wantage Hall, Reading, Berkshire on 24th August and to No.9 School of Aeronautics on 26th October. He transferred to the Class G Reserve on 22nd February 1919 (49231) and was deemed to have been discharged on 30th April 1920.

• George Ernest Palmer (1893–1963) was a horse dealer's assistant in 1911. He is believed to have married Kathleen Shipton in 1917 and had four children – Kathleen R Palmer 1919–21, Eileen E Palmer 1922, Joyce A Palmer 1924 and George R Palmer 1928.

• Eva Emily F Palmer (1894–1911).

Frederick with his first wife Daisy (Palmer family).

Frederick was educated at King William Street School, Hammersmith. He was employed by Messrs Simpkin, Marshall, Hamilton, Kent & Co Ltd and later by the publishers Erskine MacDonald. When war broke out he was the business manager of the magazine 'Poetry Review'. Frederick Palmer married Daisy Lily née Dightam

(1893–1923) in the 3rd quarter of 1914 at St Olave, London. She was a waitress at the Aerated Bread Company, Ludgate Hill, London in 1911.

Daisy's brother, Frederick Percy Charles Dightam (1896–1920), was a clerk in 1911. He enlisted in 9th Rifle Brigade (S3903) on 10th September 1914, but was discharged on 21st October with heart trouble. He enlisted again at Camberwell on 22nd June 1917 in 22nd (Reserve) London Regiment (684002) and transferred to the Machine Gun Corps (115089) as a rangetaker. He was described as 5′ 11½″ tall with pale complexion, grey eyes, light brown hair and his religious denomination was Church of England. He was posted to various MGC battalions at Grantham from 17th August. Appointed acting lance corporal on 1st December. He went to France with 267th Company MGC on 12th January 1918 and was promoted lance corporal the same day. Appointed acting corporal on 22nd April, but was admitted to hospital on 6th May with an anal abscess and reverted to lance corporal. He was transferred to 10th Canadian Stationary Hospital at Calais before being evacuated to Britain on 11th May. He was treated at Leith War Hospital, Seafield near Edinburgh until 28th July, then Edinburgh War Hospital, Bangour until 12th September and Lewisham Military Hospital London 14th September–4th December. He was also treated at Arnothill Auxiliary Hospital, Falkirk. Frederick was awarded the MM, LG 2nd August 1918.

14 Platoon at Roffey Camp, Horsham, Sussex. Frederick is second from the right (Palmer family).

He was demobilised to the Class Z Reserve on 8th February 1919, despite suffering from tuberculosis, possibly brought on by being gassed on 21st March 1918 and by constant exposure on active service, He was assessed as 100% disabled and granted a pension of £1/10/- per week, rising to £2/3/4 from 3rd September 1919. Frederick Dightam died on 2nd January 1920.

Frederick Palmer enlisted on 22nd September 1914 and served in 14 Platoon, D Company. He went to France on 16th November 1915 and was promoted corporal on 21st September 1916. **Awarded the MM for his actions on Redan Ridge on the Somme**

Bombers involved in a raid in June 1916 on Vimy Ridge. From left to right – front row, Johnny Bone, T Moore, A Jennings – rear row, S Roberts, Syd Rogers, Sergeant Rowlands and Frederick Palmer (Palmer family).

between **13th and 15th November 1916, LG 19th February 1917.** The specific circumstances leading to the award are not known.

Awarded the VC for his actions north of Courcelette, France on 16th/17th February 1917, LG 3rd April 1917. Promoted sergeant 18th February 1917. Frederick was commissioned in the Battalion on 14th March. On 3rd May he was commanding a composite group of survivors north of Oppy Wood and spent sixteen hours stuck in the German wire with every man in his platoon a casualty. He was wounded in the head in this action and evacuated to England for treatment. The VC and MM were presented by the King in Hyde Park on 2nd June 1917.

Frederick later served in the RFC and transferred to the RAF. On 1st July 1918, he was appointed temporary second lieutenant RAF Kite Balloon and joined No.2 Balloon Training Wing at Richmond. He went to France on 7th July. Promoted lieutenant RAF Kite Balloon Officer on 14th September and served in 16th Balloon Company. On his first operational trip his balloon was shot down by German fighters and he had to bale out. He transferred to the Unemployed List on 18th May 1919.

Frederick may have been the model for the Royal Fusiliers War Memorial at Holborn, but this is not certain. Early in the 1920s he moved to Malaya and became a director of several companies at Penang, Ipoh, Kuala Lumpur and Singapore, including Kyle, Palmer & Co, an import and export business, and Kenneison Bros Ltd.

Frederick and Daisy had a son, Victor Cecil Frederick Palmer (18th August 1919–February 1991) at Battle, Sussex. He was commissioned as a probationary second lieutenant Royal Marines on 18th January 1938. Acting lieutenant 17th December 1939, confirmed as lieutenant 1st February 1940, acting captain 7th February 1942, acting major 1st December 1942 and 8th January 1945 with 27th Battalion. Acting captain 13th May 1947 with seniority backdated to 14th September 1944. He relinquished his commission on 1st November 1947 and joined his father in business in Malaya. He married Joan H Webster (born 1923) in 1944 at Gloucester and they had three children, including Jennifer Palmer born in 1945. Daisy died in childbirth together with the baby, registered in the 1st quarter of 1923 at St Columb, Cornwall.

Frederick represented Malaya at the biennial conference of the British Empire Service League in London on 17th July 1923 and met the King. During the financial crisis in 1929, his company went broke. The insurance companies let him down and he never took out insurance again thereafter.

While in hospital in Singapore in 1929, suffering from stomach problems resulting from his war wounds, Frederick met a nurse, Doris Kimsinn née Seah (19th May 1908–2nd October 2004). She was the daughter of Quee Boon Seah, a Chinese Magistrate in Singapore, and En Tet née Hyu. Frederick and Doris were married on 24th December 1937 and lived at 2 Walton Road, Singapore. They had three children:

- Donald William Miraumont Palmer (15th August 1938–16th September 2008) married Margaret Lambert in 1964 and they had a daughter, Andrea Jane M Palmer in 1966. Donald was Marketing Director of Allhallows College Ltd 1995, Marketing Consultant, Swallow International Consultants Ltd 1998 and Education Consultant, JDR Composite Solutions Ltd 2000–07. He died in France.
- Dorothy 'Dot' Veronica Gwendolene Palmer (2nd May 1940–10th June 1995) married John Donald Crowle (born 1941) in 1964 and they had two children – Fiona Elizabeth C Crowle 1965 and Alistair John W Crowle 1967. John was commissioned as a pilot officer (General List) with the Equipment Branch RAF (4254655) on 6th October 1960, rising to wing commander on 1st July 1978 and retired on 15th August 1996.
- Brian Vivian Walton Palmer (born 28th January 1949) married Susan Hall in 1970.

Frederick with his second wife Doris and their three children about 1950 (Palmer family).

When war broke out Frederick went back into the RAF. He was commissioned as a probationary pilot officer (87556) with the Administrative and Special Duties Branch on 7th November 1940 and was employed on station/airfield defence duties. He served with:

- No.10 Operational Training Unit 7th November 1940–19th June 1941, including attending a course at No.1 Ground Defence Gunners School 22nd February–14th March 1941.
- No.21 Operational Training Unit from 20th June 1941.
- No.22. Operational Training Unit, Bomber Command from 6th November 1941.

Appointed acting flight lieutenant on 20th July 1941. He was confirmed in the rank of pilot officer, promoted war substantive flying officer and appointed acting squadron leader on 6th November 1941. He transferred to the RAF Regiment on its formation on 1st February 1942.

Doris and her two children had remained in Singapore and the family home was destroyed when the Japanese invaded. When Singapore fell to the Japanese in February 1942, Doris and the children were marched north and spent the rest of the war in a refugee camp. Frederick had no news of them until they were reunited in 1946.

Later in the war, Frederick third from left seated, with a group of RAF Regiment NCOs (Palmer family).

Frederick meets the Princess Royal at Torquay, summer 1940 (Palmer family).

Frederick commanded No.2742 Field Squadron, RAF Regiment at the RAF Regiment Depot from 10th June 1942. Promoted war substantive flight lieutenant on 6th November and was appointed to command No.2826 Light Anti-Aircraft Squadron, RAF Regiment at Hawkinge the day before. Between 7th and 11th June 1943 he attended the Senior Anti-Gas Course at Rollestone Camp on Salisbury Plain. Appointed acting wing commander on 10th May 1944 and moved to Kenley with two detachments to RAF Friston (27th June–22nd August and 1st–27th September 1944). Frederick was mainly employed on ground defence duties within Britain, but may have spent some time in West Africa. He relinquished his commission on account of medical unfitness on 13th March 1945 and retained the rank of wing commander. **Mentioned in Air Ministry Despatch dated 14th June 1945, Supplement to LG of 8th June 1945 published on 14th June 1945**.

Frederick returned to Singapore after the war, but retired in 1949 due to ill health. The family moved to England and settled at Hordle, Hampshire. He died at Lymington Hospital, Hampshire on 10th September 1955 and was cremated at Bournemouth Crematorium. His ashes were interred in the family grave at All Saints Parish Churchyard, Hordle, Lymington. He left £8,107/4/3 in his will.

In addition to the VC and MM, he was awarded the 1914–15 Star, British War Medal 1914–20, Victory Medal 1914–19, Defence Medal, War Medal 1939–45 with Mentioned-in-Despatches Oakleaf, George VI Coronation Medal 1937 and Elizabeth II Coronation Medal 1953. The medals were held by the family until 1st June 2006, when they were handed over to the Royal Fusiliers Museum at the Tower of London on permanent loan.

808887 PRIVATE JOHN GEORGE PATTISON
50th Battalion (Calgary), Canadian Expeditionary Force

John Pattison was born on 8th September 1874 at Woolwich, London, England. His birth was registered as John George Wicking. His natural father is not known. His mother, Mary Ann Wicking (1856–1928), was a domestic servant at 39 Manor Road, Deptford in 1871 and by 1881 was a domestic cook at the Refreshment and Lodging House of Henry Miller at 1 Broadway, Deptford, Kent. Also working there, as a waiter, was Henry 'Harry' Alfred Pattison (1854–1919). He was born Henry Alfred Sancto and changed his surname to his grandmother's maiden name before 1881. Henry and Mary were married in Woolwich in 1881. By 1891 Henry was a railway stoker and the family was living at 52 Milton Court Road, New Cross, Deptford. By 1901 he was a railway engine driver and the family had moved to 86 Milton Court Road and by 1911 to 92 Milton Court Road. Henry died at the footplate of his engine at Brighton, Sussex in April 1919. John had two siblings, both of whom died very young – Harry Pattison (1888–92) and Ethel May Pattison (1890–92).

John's paternal grandfather, Robert Pattison Sancto (1828–97) was a painter and glazier. He married Caroline née Beacon (c.1830–84), a dressmaker, in 1852. The family lived at Ospringe Road, Faversham, Kent. In addition to Henry they had two other children – Henrietta Augusta Sancto 1853 and Caroline Pattison Sancto 1860.

John's maternal grandfather, John Wicking (born c.1816), was a labourer at the Royal Arsenal, Woolwich. He married Sarah née Hands (c.1818–82), a charwoman, in 1837. In 1861 the family was living at 2 Friths Buildings, Eltham, Kent and by

Broadway, Deptford where John's parents worked at the Refreshment and Lodging House of Henry Miller.

Beresford Square in Woolwich with the Arsenal gates on the left. John's maternal grandfather was a labourer there.

Ospringe Road, Faversham, Kent where John's paternal grandparents lived.

St James' Church, Hatcham where John was a member of the Church Lads' Brigade.

1871 had moved to 13 Fenwick Street, Woolwich. In addition to Mary Ann they had five other children – John Perry Wicking 1845, Sarah Wicking 1849, Esther Elizabeth Wicking 1851, Samuel Wicking 1853 and Emma Wicking 1859.

John was educated at Clifton Hill School, Clifton Road, Deptford, London and was a member of St James' Company, Church Lads' Brigade, Hatcham, London. He then worked as a boilermaker's mate in a shipyard. On 29th September 1895 he married Sophia Louisa Ann Allen (1875–1947) at St Saviours, London. They were living at 53 Milton Court Road, Deptford in 1901. John and Sophia had four children:

- Ethel May Pattison, born 1896 at Greenwich, London.
- Henry John Pattison, born 1898 at Deptford, London. He enlisted in 82nd Battalion CEF in 1916 and transferred to 137th Battalion to be with his father. They sailed for England and carried out basic training together, but Henry was too young for active service and remained in England. He received a letter from his father, written on 2nd June 1917, the day before he died, giving details of the award of the VC. In August 1917 Henry joined his late father's unit in France and was presented with a miniature VC medal and ribbon, which he was permitted to wear on his right breast in honour of his father.
- Helena Margaret Pattison, born 1900 at Deptford. Her name has also been seen as Eleanor Margaret Pattison.
- George Alfred Pattison, born 1905 at Greenwich.

The family emigrated to Canada in June 1906 and settled initially in Rapid City, Manitoba. By 1916 they were living at 1622 First Avenue, Westmount, Calgary, Alberta, but a year later Sophia had moved to Suite 12, Curtis Block, Calgary. John was working as an engineer in 1912 in the Operation and Construction Department, Canadian Western Natural Gas Company at Calgary. However, his enlistment documents state that he was a labourer.

On 6th March 1916, John enlisted at Calgary and requested assignment to 82nd Battalion CEF to be with his son, Henry. The request was denied and he went to 137th Battalion CEF, which was raised in Calgary. John was described as 5′ 2½″ tall, with medium complexion, brown eyes, dark brown hair, three tattoos on each forearm or wrist and his religious denomination was Church of England. He sailed for England on RMS *Olympic* on 22nd August 1916, arriving at Liverpool on 29th August. After basic training he was transferred to 21st Reserve Battalion on 10th January 1917 and drafted to 50th Battalion in France on 1st February.

Awarded the VC for his actions on 10th April 1917 on Vimy Ridge, LG 2nd August 1917. He was involved in the successful attack on The Pimple on 12th April and was in action again on 7th May, receiving multiple wounds, including one to his foot. He was admitted to No.1 Canadian Field Ambulance until 11th May, then rejoined the Battalion, but was retained with the base details while his foot recovered. 50th Battalion was in action at the generating station at Liévin, near Lens, France on 3rd June when it came under heavy fire. All available men were recalled from the base, including John Pattison. He was not involved in the attack, but was in a post in Callons Trench when a direct hit by an enemy shell wiped out all the men in it. The post was taken by the Germans and Pattison was reported missing, presumed dead. He was buried by the Germans and a wooden cross was placed over his grave. The grave was located three months later and his body was exhumed and buried in La Chaudière Military Cemetery, near Arras, France (VI C 14). John is commemorated in a number of other places:

- Pattison Mountain in the Victoria Cross Range of Jasper National Park, Alberta, Canada was named after him by the Geographical Society of Alberta in 1951.
- Pattison Bridge, Calgary, Alberta opened in 1967.
- Roll of Honour at Deptford Town Hall, South East London.
- A plaque at Lewisham Civic Centre bears the names of eight local men awarded the VC – Harold Auten, George Evans, Philip Gardner, Sidney Godley, Alan Jerrard, George Knowland, Noel Mellish and John Pattison. It was unveiled in May 1995 by the only survivor, Captain Philip Gardner VC.
- Twenty-two Berberis shrubs represent the twenty-two members of the Church Lads' Brigade who were awarded the VC at the Church Lads & Church Girls Brigade Memorial Plot at the National Memorial Arboretum, Alrewas, Staffordshire.

John Pattison's grave in La Chaudière Military Cemetery, near Arras.

- Victoria Cross obelisk to all Canadian VCs at Military Heritage Park, Barrie, Ontario dedicated by the Princess Royal on 22nd October 2013.

- Named on one of eleven plaques honouring 175 men from overseas awarded the VC for the Great War. The plaques were unveiled by the Senior Minister of State at the Foreign & Commonwealth Office and Minister for Faith and Communities, Baroness Warsi, at a reception at Lancaster House, London on 26th June 2014 attended by the Duke of Kent and relatives of the VC recipients. The Canadian plaque was unveiled outside the British High Commission in Elgin Street, Ottawa on 10th November 2014 by The Princess Royal in the presence of British High Commissioner Howard Drake, Canadian Minister of Veterans Affairs Julian Fantino and Canadian Chief of the Defence Staff General Thomas J Lawson.
- Two 49 Cent postage stamps in honour of the ninety-four Canadian VCs were issued by Canada Post on 21st October 2004 on the 150th Anniversary of the first Canadian VC's action, Alexander Roberts Dunn.
- His portrait by Ethel Wright hangs in the boardroom of the Canadian Western Natural Gas Company in Calgary, Alberta.
- Named on the Clifton Hill County School War Memorial.

It was intended to hold the VC investiture at Buckingham Palace and his son Henry was notified to receive it, but this was cancelled. Instead the VC was presented to his widow by the Lieutenant-Governor of Alberta, HE Robert George Brett, at Victory Park, Calgary on 10th April 1918. Deptford Borough Council presented an illuminated scroll to John's son, Henry, at a ceremony at New Cross Town Hall on 9th November 1918. John's father, Henry Alfred Pattison, also attended and signed the Borough Roll of Honour. Sophia was offered employment by the Calgary Gas Company Ltd and retired from the company on 2nd May 1940. She was introduced to King George VI during his visit to Canada on 3rd June 1939. John's son Henry attended the VC Centenary celebrations in London in 1956.

In addition to the VC he was awarded the British War Medal 1914–20 and Victory Medal 1914–19. As he died on operational duty, his next-of-kin is eligible to receive the Canadian Memorial Cross. The VC is held by Glenbow Museum, 9th Avenue SE, Calgary, Alberta, Canada, which also has the colours of 137th Battalion CEF.

2ND LIEUTENANT ALFRED OLIVER POLLARD
1/1st Battalion, The Honourable Artillery Company Infantry

Alfred Pollard was born at Rycroft, Melbourne Road, Wallington, Surrey on 4th May 1893. His father, James Alfred Pollard FCII (1859–1933), was born at Heckmondwike, near Dewsbury, Yorkshire. He was an insurance broker and was eventually appointed Director of Alliance Assurance Company, St James Street, London. James married Ada Jane née Payne (1861–1953) in 1883. She was born at Ryde, Isle of Wight. They lived at three addresses within Wallington, Surrey over forty-five years and by 1911 were at 'Tidbury', 2 Belmont Road, Wallington. Alfred had four siblings:

- James Frank Pollard (1889–1916) was an insurance clerk with the Alliance Assurance Company at Croydon and enlisted in the Honourable Artillery Company (404) on 1st March 1909. He attended annual camps 1909–1913 and re-engaged on 1st March 1913 and 1st March 1914. When war broke out he was mobilised on 5th August 1914 and was desperate to get to the front. There seemed little prospect of doing so with the HAC and he deserted on 15th August and immediately enlisted in 1st Grenadier Guards (17341) as Frank Thompson. He went to France on 4th January 1915 and was formally discharged from the HAC on 20th January 1916 to re-enlist in the Brigade of Guards. Frank was killed at Ginchy, France on 10th September 1916, days before his commission was gazetted. He is commemorated on the Thiepval Memorial.

The Alliance Assurance Company building in St James Street, London. Alfred worked there for a while before the war and his father eventually became a director.

- Lily Ada Pollard (1885–1974) married Dr Arthur MacGregor Warwick (1888–1967) in 1913 at St Paul's Cathedral in Calcutta, India. Arthur worked for the Bengal United Tea Company as a medical practitioner. During the First World War, Lily served in France from May 1915 onwards and was Matron of a French Red Cross hospital in Boulogne. She qualified for the Great War medal trio. Arthur was commissioned in the Royal Army Medical Corps on 19th April 1915 and was attached to 1st Royal Warwickshire. He was awarded the MC for his actions on 30th August 1918 in an attack on St Servin's Farm during which he cleared his aid post of all casualties, organised stretcher-bearers and brought in a large number of wounded lying in the open, LG 1st February 1919. They

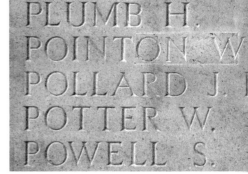

James Frank Pollard's name on the Thiepval Memorial.

had a daughter, Ada VM Warwick (1920–69), who married Peter I Wright in 1950. Lily and Arthur divorced in 1923. He married Jeanne Kuhne (1898–1986) in 1925 and they had a son, Frederick Warwick, in 1934. Jeanne was born in Tunxi District, Xiuning County, Anhui, China.

- Eva Kate Pollard (1887–1917) was an elementary school teacher in 1911.
- Amy Grace Pollard (1891–1965) was a student of cooking and domestic economy in 1911. She married Harold Herbert Pugh (1891–1933) in 1925 and they had three children – Frank Pugh 1926, Elizabeth Jean Pugh 1927 and Katherine I Pugh 1928.

Alfred's paternal grandfather, James A Pollard (c.1834–88), was a master at Upper School, Heckmondwike, near Dewsbury, Yorkshire. By 1871 he was an insurance clerk. He married Catherine née Ledward (c.1833–99) in 1857. In 1871 they were living at 12 Fairlight Terrace, Camberwell, Surrey, by 1881 at 4 Clifton Terrace, Camberwell and later at 69 Ivanhoe Road, Denmark Park, Surrey. She was living at 184 Brighton Road, Croydon, Surrey at the time of her death in 1899. In addition to James they had three other children – Elizabeth Ann Pollard 1858, George Arthur Pollard (1863–1939) and Beatrice Adelaide Pollard 1874. George joined the Salvation Army in 1881 and was commissioned as a lieutenant. He worked at Peckham in London and Portadown in Ireland before returning to Marylebone in London and later at New Basford, Nottinghamshire. He came to the attention of General William Booth, the founder, and was promoted captain and posted to New Zealand in January 1883. In New Zealand, George married Alice Pearcey (c.1864–1942) in October 1883, a Captain in the Salvation Army, whom he first met in Peckham. In April 1885 he was promoted colonel and posted to Sydney, New South Wales, opening thirty-three Corps headquarters in two and a half years. He returned to London in 1891 and was promoted commissioner around 1895. He accompanied General Booth on tours to Australasia 1895 and 1899 and USA 1902. After organising the International Congress in London in 1904, his health broke down and he resigned the following year. He took an executive position with J Lyons & Co and became a director in 1919. George and Alice had seven children – Christopher Pollard 1885, Arthur Howard Pollard 1886, Beatrice Emma Pollard 1888, Elizabeth Ledward Pollard 1890, James Bramwell Pollard 1893, Herbert Edward Pollard 1895 and Leslie Innes George Pollard 1901.

Alfred's uncle, George Arthur Pollard, pictured with his wife Alice, was a pioneer of the Salvation Army movement in New Zealand and Australia.

His maternal grandfather, Oliver Payne (c.1835–1910), was a carpenter and joiner in 1861. He was born at Cowes, Isle of Wight. He married Sophia née Rayner (c.1829–1915), a dressmaker, in 1859. The family was living at Castle Street, Ryde, Isle of Wight in 1861. By 1871 they had moved to 4 Peacock Street, St Mary Newington, London and by 1881 to 177 Newington Butts, St Mary Newington. In addition to Ada they also had Eva Rose Payne (1867–1936).

Founded in 1551, the Merchant Taylors' School was in London until 1933, when it moved to a new site at Sandy Lodge, Northwood. Amongst its numerous famous alumni are Clive of India (Baron Clive of Plassey), Titus Oates and the actor Boris Karloff.

Alfred was educated at Merchant Taylor's School 1906–08 and was then employed as an insurance clerk by Alliance Assurance Company, St James' Street, the same company as his father. When war broke out, he asked the branch secretary if he could enlist, but was rejected. As he left the office at the end of that day he told the secretary, *You'll always remember I asked you, sir!* Next morning he went to enlist and did not return to the office.

He enlisted in the Honourable Artillery Company on 8th August 1914 (1023) and commenced training at its headquarters at Armoury House on 11th August. At the end of August he volunteered for active service and was allotted to No.8 Section, 10 Platoon, C Company. The Battalion was inspected by its Captain-General and

SS *Westmeath* was built in 1903 in West Hartlepool as *Everton Grange* for the Houlder Line. In November 1911 she was sold to the New Zealand Shipping Co and renamed *Westmeath*. In 1915 she transferred to the Union Steam Ship Company of New Zealand, which was taken over by Peninsular & Oriental Steam Navigation Co in 1917. In July 1917 she was torpedoed by UC48 in the English Channel inbound from South America, but survived. In 1925 she was sold to Soc Ligure de Navigazione a Vap, Genoa, Italy and renamed *Nordico* Two years later she was sold to D&E Fratelli Bozzo, Genoa, laid up in 1930 and went for scrap in 1932.

Colonel, the King, and moved into camp at Aveley, Essex, expecting to have six months training. Some introductory marksmanship training was carried out at Pirbright ranges, Surrey. The unit moved by train to Southampton, Hampshire on 18th September and embarked on SS *Westmeath* for St Nazaire, France. The Battalion was in camp there for further training and also undertook various duties, including guarding prisoners in the hospital. His Company moved to BEF Headquarters at St Omer and on 5th November travelled by bus to Bailleul for attachment to the Lahore Division, but they were not required as it was assumed from the unit title that they were artillery. The Battalion was then attached to 7th Brigade, 3rd Division and went into the trenches in front of Kemmel in early December.

Alfred collapsed with suspected jaundice after coming out of the line on 25th December and was evacuated through the medical chain to a base hospital on 31st December. He was concerned at being regarded a shirker in the Battalion and begged the doctors not to repatriate him. He was released on 4th January 1915, having actually had a chill on his liver. At Rouen he was billeted in a transit camp with the first group of reinforcements for the Battalion and fell out with the camp sergeant major for not attending morning parade, drill, fatigues and duties for eight days. Alfred did not believe they applied to him as he had front-line experience and managed to avoid punishment before returning to the Battalion. He was then appointed batman to Second Lieutenant Douglas Stalman Davis, a newly commissioned former sergeant and also volunteered as a cook in the company officers' mess. Promoted acting lance corporal 4th May and acting corporal 17th June.

Alfred took part in the attack on Bellewaarde on 16th June, during which he was a company runner. Promoted corporal in the same month and was also involved in a night attack in support of 1st Wiltshire, during which he first encountered the art of bombing. He went home to Wallington for a few days leave on 31st July and on return submitted an application for a commission. While that was being processed, he attended a bombing course at the Second Army Grenade School at Terdeghem and returned to the Battalion to take charge of the bombing platoon on 23rd September. Promoted sergeant 26th September and later that day was acknowledged by the commander of 3rd Division for his work in preparing fourteen bomb storage shelters.

Awarded the DCM for his actions at Sanctuary Wood, Hooge, near Ypres (Second Battle of Bellewaarde) on 30th September 1915, LG 16th November 1915. The Germans blew a mine under 4th Middlesex's position and Alfred's bombing platoon was ordered to retake it. The platoon commander worked along the lip in one direction with half of the platoon, while Alfred led the rest in the opposite direction. He was joined by five Royal Scots bombers, making a party of twenty-one men. During the attack a German bomb hurled him back against a barricade, knocking him

unconscious and spraying him with numerous splinters. He came round and shook himself back into action, continuing to throw bombs and issue orders to encourage his men. His example renewed their confidence when they were shaken due to superior enemy numbers. Although there were only seven men unwounded and they were under accurate sniper fire from trees less than forty metres away, Alfred was determined to take the crater. He jumped over the barricade to collect a bag of bombs and was handing them to another man when the latter pitched forward on his face dead.

Pollard was shot through the right shoulder by the same bullet, but initially felt nothing. With one arm useless, he believed he could still direct operations, but his legs gave way and the attack had to be abandoned. Second Lieutenant Rupert Price Hallowes, 4th Middlesex, was posthumously awarded the VC for the same action. Alfred's CO, Lieutenant Colonel Harold T Hanson, recommended him for the VC and was disappointed when he received the DCM instead.

Rupert Price Hallowes, 4th Middlesex, was posthumously awarded the VC for the same action at Sanctuary Wood in which Alfred Pollard was awarded the DCM.

Alfred was evacuated to a casualty clearing station and to a base hospital the following day. He was transferred to England for treatment at Crumpsall Infirmary, Manchester on 6th October, where he underwent two operations to remove the bullet. He was discharged for two weeks convalescence leave and joined 3/1st Reserve Battalion at Richmond, Surrey, where the CO, Colonel William Evans, offered him a commission. Alfred spent two more weeks on convalescence leave over Christmas to allow his wounds to heal properly and was commissioned on 19th January 1916. He was allocated to the bombing school before attended a three weeks' officers training course at Chelsea Barracks, London. Rejoining the Reserve Battalion, by then at Blackheath, he undertook further grenade training.

Alfred embarked for France on 24th May and rejoined 1st Battalion at Hesdin on 30th May. He was appointed to B Company on 5th June and was also Battalion Bombing Officer, earning the nickname 'Bombo'. During a series of

Chelsea Barracks was built in the 1860s and rebuilt a century later, mainly for public duties Guards battalions. It was sold by the MOD in 2007. At the time of writing the site had been cleared and work had commenced on building 448 homes plus gardens, shops, a playground and sports centre.

night reconnaissance patrols in preparation for an attack on the Somme, he injured his knee on rusty barbed wire and it became badly infected. He was evacuated to a casualty clearing station and then to a base hospital at Wimereux in mid October. Having had two weeks special leave in England from 1st November, he returned to a base hospital at Le Havre, France on 14th November before rejoining the Battalion at Nouvion. On 21st December he was posted to the newly formed 63rd Division School of Instruction as a bombing instructor, but resigned after only six days and returned to the Battalion in the first week of January 1917. He took command of 7 Platoon in B Company and was back in the front line on 13th January.

Awarded the MC for his actions at Grandcourt on the Somme on 7th–8th February 1917, LG 26th March 1917. He led a patrol on a difficult reconnaissance into the village to establish the enemy's dispositions, but took a wrong turn on his return and the patrol stumbled in behind the German line before getting away. The next night he led his company after the OC was wounded in an attack north of the Ancre at Baillescourt Farm, during which he was hit three times, twice on the helmet and once below the shoulder blade. He took his objective in a sunken road and Miraumont Alley and beat off two counterattacks under very heavy shellfire. He and two others repelled the advance of a German squad along the captured trench with grenades and assisted in repulsing a stronger counterattack. He held the position for eight more days and seven nights until relieved. Only thirty-five men remained from the original strength of 150.

Appointed acting captain while a company commander 23rd February. He sprained his ankle falling into a trench in the dark on 19th March 1917 and was evacuated through a casualty clearing station to a base hospital, relinquishing the rank of acting captain the same day. He returned to the Battalion on 12th or 13th April.

Awarded a Bar to the MC for his actions near Gavrelle on 16th April 1917, LG 18th June 1917. He carried out a dangerous reconnaissance of the enemy front line under very heavy fire and obtained most valuable information, setting a splendid example of courage and determination. Having cut the enemy wire, he entered the German trench to find it full of enemy. Beating a hasty retreat he lost a man, went back to find him and had to run along the enemy parapet for almost a hundred metres to find a gap through which to escape. All the time he was in full view of the enemy in the light of numerous star shells.

Awarded the VC for his actions at Gavrelle, France on 29th April 1917, LG 8th June 1917. Major General Lawrie, commanding 63rd Division, came to congratulate him and Haine the next day. Pollard was in bed completely naked when the General came into his tent, but he graciously understood the situation. Appointed acting captain 15th May–29th October and promoted lieutenant 19th July. The VC, MC & Bar and DCM were presented by the King outside Buckingham Palace on

21st July 1917. He and Bill Haine VC were invited to a celebratory lunch at Armoury House with the Honourable Artillery Company following their investiture. Alfred had scarcely made a speech in his life and when asked to do so he stood up and said, *Thank you very much everybody* and sat down again. The audience did not think a lot of his effort so they asked Reginald to elaborate. He stood up and said, *I think Alf's said all there is to say*, and promptly sat down too.

Alfred attended a Lewis gun course at Le Touquet on 26th December. From March 1918 he trained Americans at Étaples and was then attached to a US Division to advise on training. He was later appointed Adjutant of No.2 Reinforcement Camp at Quiberville, but returned to England on 11th July possibly due to previous wounds. He returned to the Battalion in mid October 1918, but contracted influenza. After the Armistice he served in Germany in the Occupation Forces with Second Army's Deputy Provost Marshal at Spa and Köln from 2nd December until demobilised on 23rd February 1919. He remained in the Honourable Artillery Company until transferring to the Territorial Army Reserve as a captain on 8th December 1921. Alfred was a member of the VC Guard at the Interment of the Unknown Warrior on 11th November 1920. He ceased to belong to the Territorial Army Reserve of Officers (43297) having exceeded the age liability to recall, on 26th October 1949.

From the age of eighteen Alfred was infatuated with Mary Ainsley (1891–1976) and they married on 4th June 1918, at Christ Church, Purley, Surrey. The marriage ended, childless, in divorce in 1923. The experience had a profound effect on Alfred and for a few years he became somewhat reckless. Mary's father, Matthew William Ainsley (1856–1934), was a licensed victualler. He married Mary Louisa née Davies (1864–1938) in 1888. The family was living at 2 Eastern Villas, Edmonton, Middlesex in 1891 and Rhine House, Fore Street, Edmonton in 1901. By 1911 they had moved to 421 Fore Street, Edmonton and later to 'Trefilan', 88 Foxley Lane, Purley, Surrey. In addition to Mary they had four other children:

• Mary Ainsley, born and died 1889.
• Dylis Charlotte Ainsley (1889–1985).
• Conyers Ainsley (1892–1937) was an agricultural student in 1911, boarding at 1 The Gable, Wye, Kent. He died in Christchurch, New Zealand.
• Olive Ainsley (1896–1980) married Edward Phillips Holder (1895–1978) in 1925. Edward was the brother-in-law of Bill Haine, who was awarded the VC with Alfred Pollard. Edward joined the Honourable Artillery Company (1028) and was promoted to sergeant. He went to France on 29th December 1914, was commissioned on 7th December 1916 and continued to serve until 4th October 1923. In the Second World War, Edward enlisted in the Royal Artillery TA (125069) and was promoted lance bombardier before being commissioned in the Royal Army Service Corps on 27th March 1940.

Alfred found it difficult to find work following demobilisation, partly due to his outlook resulting from his war service. In a newspaper article in November 1932, he wrote that the award of the Victoria Cross was the greatest thing that had happened in his life, but *war decorations have no practical value in peacetime … Their possession, instead of being an asset, frequently act as a definite hindrance in the fight for existence.* He was offered his old job with Alliance Assurance and had remained on the payroll throughout his service. However, after four and a half years of active outdoor life, the prospect did not appeal. He declined the offer and resigned from the Company, but the Board of Directors voted him the generous gift of a year's salary. He took a variety of jobs, including training salesmen for an American firm, director of Low Engineering Company, a small aero-engineering firm, and broadcasting for the BBC.

In 1923, while working as a commercial traveler, he was fined £5 and costs and had his license endorsed at Biggleswade for driving a motorcar to the public danger at Sandy on the night of 22nd September. He knocked down and severely injured Herbert Dent, an agricultural labourer, who was walking with a bicycle in the road.

On 15th July 1924, Alfred was granted a Short Service Commission in the General Duties Branch of the Royal Air Force as a probationary pilot officer and was posted to No.2 Flying Training School, RAF Digby. He transferred to No.5 Flying Training School, RAF Sealand, Chester on 29th January 1925. He qualified as a pilot in May 1925 and became a member of the Royal Aero Club on 13th May. Having qualified, he served with No.13 (Army Co-operation) Squadron at RAF Andover (now Army Headquarters) from 17th August 1925 flying Bristol fighters. Promoted flying officer 15th February 1926. He resigned his commission on 15th December 1926. Although his service was short, he gained a reputation for humorous pranks, frequently risking the displeasure of senior officers. At a guest night in the Officers' Mess he let loose a small pig in the dining room, causing utter chaos as the mess waiters tried to catch the animal. On another occasion, with

Alfred Pollard while serving in the RAF.

The Bristol Fighter first flew in September 1916 and entered service on the Western Front in April 1917. It remained in service with the RAF and other nations in the army cooperation and light bombing roles until withdrawn in 1932.

fellow officers, he put two cars in the mess anteroom at RAF Digby, necessitating the removal of the doors to get the vehicles out again. For this he was confined to his quarters by the station commander, Wing Commander Arthur Tedder.

After leaving the Royal Air Force, Alfred decided to write a book. He struggled at first and earned only £65 in the first year, but by 1929 he was writing full time, including as a columnist on a number of London and provincial newspapers. He also compiled a fortune telling game named Zodiac. His published works include:

Factual – The Royal Air Force, 1934; Boy's Romance of Aviation, 1935; Romantic Stories of Air Heroes, 1937; Epic Deeds of the RAF, 1940; Leaders of the Royal Air Force, 1940; Bombers Over the Reich, 1941; The Army of Today, 1942.

Thriller and adventure novels, including – Pirdale Island; Rum Alley; Murder HideandSeek, 1931; The Death Flight, 1932; The Riddle of Loch Lemman, 1933; The Phantom Plane, 1934; Murder in the Air; The Secret of Castle Voxzel, 1935; Unofficial Spy; The Death Game; Hidden Cipher, 1936; The Murder Germ; Flanders Spy, 1937; Black Out; Air Reprisal, 1938; The Secret Formula; Murder of a Diplomat, 1939; The Secret Pact; ARP Spy; Secret Weapon, 1941; Wanted by the Gestapo; Invitation to Death, 1942; The Death Squadron, 1943; Gestapo Fugitive; The Fifth Freedom, 1944; Blood Hunt, 1945; Double Cross, 1946; A Deal in Death; The Iron Curtain, 1947; The Death Curse; David Wilshaw Investigates; The Secret Vendetta; Dead Man's Secret; Red Hazard; The Poisoned Pilot, 1950; The Death Parade; The Golden Buddha; Death Intervened, 1951; Counterfeit Spy; The Dead Forger, 1952; Criminal Airman; The Buckled Wing, 1953; Homicidal Spy, 1954; The Missing Diamond; Sinister Secret, 1955; Smugglers' Buoy, 1958; Wrong Verdict, 1960.

His autobiography – Fire Eater; The Memoirs of a VC, 1932.

Marshal of the Royal Air Force Arthur William Tedder, 1st Baron Tedder, GCB (1890–1967). He joined the Colonial Service and went to Fiji in February 1914, but returned when war was declared. He held a reserve commission in the Dorsetshire Regiment, but a knee injury ruled out infantry service and he transferred to the RFC as a pilot and later squadron commander. He was promoted wing commander in 1924 and commanded RAF Digby and No.2 Flying Training School, where Alfred Pollard incurred his displeasure. In the Second World War, Tedder was Air Officer Commanding RAF Middle East Command, involved in operations in the Mediterranean and North Africa and commanded Mediterranean Air Command during the invasions of Sicily and Italy. In 1944 he was Eisenhower's Deputy as Supreme Commander for Operation Overlord. Post war, Tedder was Chief of the Air Staff and retired in 1951 (Walter Stoneman).

Alfred was a prolific author. *Epic Deeds of the RAF* was published in 1940, one of six factual books he wrote on the RAF and flying.

Black Out was one of fifty thrillers and adventure novels he wrote between 1931 and 1960.

Alfred wrote his autobiography, *Fire Eater: The Memoirs of a VC*, in 1932.

Alfred's second marriage was to Violet Irene Swarbrick (1900–61) on 5th September 1925, registered at Brentford. There were no children. She took a job selling stationery and office equipment for Kalamazoo to supplement her husband's income as an author. They moved to Flat 2, 'Linkwood', 18 Queen's Park Gardens, Bournemouth, Hampshire (Dorset from 1974) in 1949. Violet's father, Robert Alfred Swarbrick (1871–1949), was a civil engineer. He married Lilian née McKeand (1863–1940) in 1892. In addition to Violet, they also had Lilian Daphne G Swarbrick (born 1893), who married Clement Richard Chown (1891–1970) in 1915 and had three children – Richard Robert William Chown 1917, Charles Stanley Malcolm Chown 1919 and Clement M Chown 1921.

Alfred was a committee member of the Victoria Cross and George Cross Association and became very close friends with Bill Haine, with whom he won the VC. On 4th December 1960 he went outside his home at Queen's Park Gardens, Bournemouth to fix a dislodged panel in a strong wind. Back inside he sat in the kitchen to read the Sunday paper when he suddenly gasped and fell to the floor He could not be resuscitated and a post mortem on 6th December revealed he had died of a coronary thrombosis. He was cremated at Bournemouth Crematorium, where his ashes were scattered.

In addition to the VC, MC & Bar and DCM he was awarded the 1914 Star with 'Mons' clasp, British War Medal 1914–20, Victory Medal 1914–19 with Mentioned-in-Despatches oakleaf, George VI Coronation Medal 1937 and Elizabeth II Coronation Medal 1953. His medals and sword were presented to the Honourable Artillery Company by his nephew, Richard Robert William Chown, son of his sister-in-law, Lillian, in 1961. The VC is held by the Honourable Artillery Company Museum, Armoury House, City Road, London.

LIEUTENANT CHARLES POPE
11th Australian Infantry Battalion AIF

Charles Pope was born on 5th March 1883 at 21 Morrison Buildings, Mile End Old Town, East London, England. His father was William Pope, born at Stapleford Abbotts, Essex in 1853. His mother, Jane née Clark (c.1859–88), married William in 1878 at Poplar, London. William was a constable in the Metropolitan Police Force in 1881, living with his family at 21 Morrison's Buildings. By 1885 they had moved to 10 Cuthbert Street, London. In 1891 William was a traveller, living with his children at Back Lane Cottage, Billericay, Essex. He married Sarah Ann Barkwith née Swaine (born 1848) in 1897 at Billericay, Essex. She had previously been married to Charles George Barkwith (1845–96) and had three children by him – Sarah Ann Elizabeth Barkwith 1868, Emily Barkwith 1873 and Charles Barkwith 1875. By 1901, William was a bar retailer living at 47 Marcus Street, West Ham and had moved to 176 Clyde Road, South Tottenham by 1911, where he was an off licence beer retailer. Charles had four siblings:

• Mary Maud Pope (1879–1955) was living with her paternal aunt and uncle, Charles and Mary Pigrome, at James Street, Barking in 1881, but was back with her father by 1891. She married George Gregory (born 1864) in 1897 at Marylebone, London. He was born at Colebrook, Devon and was a horse keeper and stable groom in 1901, living with his family at 4 Abley Gardens Mews, St Marylebone. By 1911 he was a coachman, living with his family at Burton Cottage, Ballards Lane, Finchley, Middlesex. They had three children – William Henry Gregory 1897, Kathleen Gregory 1899 and Robert George Gregory 1901.

The Improved Industrial Dwellings Co Ltd erected two blocks of flats on opposite sides of Commercial Road in Mile End Old Town in 1874. The Morrison Buildings were named after the Chairman, Walter Morrison MP. In 1899 there was a resident carpenter, George Plumby. The building on the north (No.35a) is still there, but the one on the south (1–54 a, b, c & d), seen here in 1972, has been demolished (www.stgite.org.uk).

• William Pope (born 1881) was an electrical engineer, living at 4 High Road, Kilburn, London in 1902. By 1911 he was running his own electrical engineering business, living with his father and step-mother at 176 Clyde Road, South Tottenham. A William Pope of the correct age died in Islington in 1958.

- Annie May Pope (1885–96).
- John Pope (1886–1918) enlisted in the Militia at Stratford, East London on 23rd January 1902. He was described as a labourer, 5′ 4¼″ tall, weighing 105 lbs, with fresh complexion, brown eyes, brown hair and his religious denomination was Church of England. He emigrated to Australia c.1909 and served in 51st Battalion AIF (3163). He was killed in action on 25th April 1918 in France and is commemorated on the Villers-Bretonneux Memorial.

Charles' paternal grandfather, also William Pope (c.1813–84), was a coachman, publican and shopkeeper living with his family at the Plough, Navestock, Essex in 1861. He married Sarah née Surridge (c.1821–96) in 1846 at Greenwich, London. She was living at 27 Sabine Green, Ongar, Essex in 1891. In addition to William they had five other children:

- Ann Elizabeth Pope (born 1844).
- Mary Pope (1847–1912) married Charles Pigrome (1847–1919) in 1872 at Poplar, London. He was a carpenter and joiner. They were living at 37 Cambridge Avenue, Willesden, London in 1911.
- Emma Pope (1852–1923) married George Whitney Lagden (1844–1926), a domestic gardener, in 1873 at Poplar, London. They were living at Hannington School House, Northamptonshire in 1891, Weston Favell, Northamptonshire in 1901 and 4 Stenson Street, Northampton in 1911. They had seven children including – William Lagden 1876, Alfred Lagden 1878, Albert Oliver Lagden 1880, Elsie Lagden 1882, Lucy Lagden 1884 and Mary Lagden 1887.
- James Pope (1856–1937) was a police constable. He married Edith Tavener (1855–1930), registered as Taverner, in 1879 at Shoreditch, London. They were living at 29 John Street North, Marylebone, London in 1881, at 20 Little Grove Street, St Marylebone in 1891 and at 29 Hethpool Street, Paddington in 1911. They had nine children including – James William Pope 1881, Albert Edward Pope 1882, Archibald Pope 1884, Ernest Pope 1890, Gertrude Pope 1892, Frederick Pope 1894 and Jenny Pope 1899.
- Thomas Pope (born 1859) was a plumber and painter in 1881, living with his sister and family at James Street, Barking, Essex.

Charles was only five when his mother died and his father had to seek help from family members to look after his children. Charles was sent to live with his paternal grandmother in 1891 at Sabine Green, Navestock, Essex. He was educated there and on 24th April 1899 he enlisted in the Royal Marine Artillery (8103), adding a year to his age. He was described as a general labourer, 5′ 7½″ tall, with fresh complexion, blue eyes and light brown hair. He served aboard HMS *Renown* 30th October 1900–13th April 1904 and was discharged on 3rd June. He emigrated to Canada soon after leaving the Royal Marines and was employed by the Canadian Pacific Railways.

452   Victoria Crosses on the Western Front January–July 1917

HMS *Renown* (12,865 tons) was a second–class battleship launched at Pembroke Dockyard in May 1895 and completed in January 1897. She was well armed with 4 x 10″ guns, 10 x 6″ QF guns, 12 x 12 Pdr QF, 8 x 3 Pdr Hotchkiss guns and 5 x 18″ torpedo tubes. She was also heavily armoured. She served as flagship for the Commander in Chief, Vice-Admiral Sir Nowell Salmon VC at the 26th June 1897 Diamond Jubilee Fleet Review at Spithead. Later that year she became flagship of the North America and West Indies Station until May 1899. After a refit, she transferred to the Mediterranean Fleet as flagship to Vice Admiral Jackie Fisher. In 1902, she carried the Duke and Duchess of Connaught on a royal tour of India and rejoined the Mediterranean Fleet in April 1903, resuming as flagship later that year. In 1905 she was converted into a royal yacht and in October carried the Prince and Princess of Wales on a royal tour of India. In 1907 she carried King Alfonso XIII and Queen Victoria Eugenia of Spain on a visit to and from the United Kingdom. *Renown* was converted to a stoker's training ship in 1909. On 2nd April 1914 she was sold for scrap and broken up at Blyth.

He returned to London in 1906 and joined the Chelsea Division of the Metropolitan Police Force.

On 13th December 1906 Charles Pope married Edith Mary née Smith (born c.1883) at St Luke's Anglican Church, Chelsea, London. After emigrating to Australia they lived at various addresses in Perth, Western Australia – 117 Glendower Street, 14 Dangan Street, 1093 Ham Street, 630 Murray Street and 248 Fitzgerald Street. Charles and Edith had two children:

- Edith Maude Pope (15th September 1907–15th August 1996) was born at Belgrave, London. She worked for Dalgety & Co Ltd, William Street, Perth, Western Australia and married Francis Errol Nicolson (c.1904–60). He was born at Durban, South Africa and they settled there, having two children.
- Charles William Pope (14th October 1909–25th May 1996) was

The parish church of St Luke was built in the 1820s at the time when Chelsea was expanding from a village into a district of London. The idea for the new church came from the Rector of Chelsea, Reverend Gerald Wellesley, brother of the 1st Duke of Wellington. Charles Dickens married Catherine Hogarth there on 2nd April 1836, just two days after the publication of his first success, the first part of *Pickwick Papers*. Robert Baden-Powell's parents married there on 10th March 1846.

born in London. He worked for Mason James Truscott & Co, Chaff Merchants, Northam, Western Australia. He married Daisy Sophia White (1915–2000) in 1935 and they had two children.

A Metropolitan policeman of the period when Charles Pope served in the Force.

Charles resigned from the Police in 1910 and emigrated to Australia, where he was employed as a furniture salesman by Blain & Co, Beaufort Street, Perth, Western Australia. He then worked for the Temperance & General Insurance Co, Perth. He enlisted in the Australian Imperial Force in Perth on 25th August 1915 and was posted to Blackboy Hill, Greenmount, Perth. He was described as 5′ 11″ tall, weighing 142 lbs, with fresh complexion, blue eyes, light brown hair and his religious denomination was Church of England. Charles was promoted through the ranks to sergeant and was commissioned on 10th February 1916.

On 15 July 1916 he embarked on HMAT A31 *Ajana* at Fremantle, Western Australia with 18th Reinforcement Group for 11th Battalion. He disembarked at Plymouth, Devon on 1st September and joined 3rd Training Battalion at Perham Down on Salisbury Plain, Wiltshire. Charles embarked at Southampton, Hampshire for Le Havre, France on 7th December and was posted to A Company, 11th Battalion on 10th December. Promoted lieutenant on 26th December.

Awarded the VC for his actions near Louverval, France on 15th April 1917, LG 8th June 1917. He was killed during his VC action and was originally buried

11th Battalion recruits having a hurried meal during training at Blackboy Hill Camp.

where he fell. His body was exhumed after the war and interred in Moeuvres Communal Cemetery Extension, France (V D 22). Charles is commemorated in a number of other places:

- Pope Place, Fairfield West, Sydney, New South Wales.
- The nineteen wards at Hollywood Private Hospital, Perth, Western Australia are named after VCs and GCs, including Charles Pope.
- Pope Terrace, Wodonga, Victoria on White Box Rise Estate built on the former Bandiana Army Camp.
- Victoria Cross Memorial, Campbell, Canberra dedicated on 24th July 2000.
- Victoria Cross Memorial, Queen Victoria Building, George Street, Sydney, New South Wales.
- Memorial plaque at the State War Memorial, King's Park, Perth dedicated on 26th January 1996.
- Named on one of eleven plaques honouring 175 men from overseas awarded the VC for the Great War. The plaques were unveiled by the Senior Minister of State at the Foreign & Commonwealth Office and Minister for Faith and Communities, Baroness Warsi, at a reception at Lancaster House, London on 26th June 2014 attended by the Duke of Kent and relatives of the VC recipients. The Australian plaque is at the Australian War Memorial.

In addition to the VC, he was awarded the British War Medal 1914–20 and Victory Medal 1914–19. The VC was presented to his widow by Sir Ronald Craufurd Munro-Ferguson GCMG, Governor General of Australia, at a parade at Karrakatta Camp,

SS *Ajana* (7759 tons) was built by Russell & Co at Port Glasgow and launched on 22nd February 1912 as a passenger/refrigerated cargo vessel for Australind Steam Shipping Co Ltd of London. In November and December 1914 she was converted at Cockatoo Island Drydock, Sydney to transport 427 troops and 304 horses. Her first trip commenced on 19th December 1914 from Sydney, carrying 7th Light Horse Regiment. She joined the Second Convoy on 2nd January 1915 after embarking troops at Fremantle and disembarked in Egypt on 1st February 1915. On 14th April 1917 she was attacked by a U-boat in the English Channel, but escaped. On 29th July she was chased by a U-boat off the northwest coast of Ireland and escaped again. In November 1919 she was sold to New Zealand Shipping Co and renamed *Otarama*. She was sold again in February 1928 to D & E Fratelli Bozzo of Genoa and renamed *Amaranto*. She was broken up at Genoa in November 1932.

Charles Pope's grave in Moeuvres Communal Cemetery Extension, France.

Sir Ronald Craufurd Munro-Ferguson (1860–1934) started with a military career in the Grenadier Guards. In 1884 he was elected to Parliament, but was defeated in the general election in November 1885. In a by-election in August 1886 he was elected MP for Leith Burghs and became private secretary to Lord Rosebery, a leading Liberal. His support for the imperial policies of the Conservative government during the Boer War meant he was not called upon to join the Cabinet in the Liberal governments of Cambell-Bannerman or Asquith. In February 1914 he accepted the post of Governor General of Australia, having refused South Australia in 1895 and Victoria in 1910. He remained in post until October 1920 and is acknowledged to have been the most successful Governor General to date. Back in Britain he was raised to the peerage as Viscount Novar and was appointed by Liberal PM, David Lloyd George, to be Vice President of the Committee of the Council of Education. In the government of Andrew Bonar Law, he was Secretary of State for Scotland and was later Chairman of the Political Honours Committee. He died childless and the title with him.

Perth, Western Australia on 23rd November 1917. His medals are held in the Hall of Valour, Australian War Memorial, Treloar Crescent, Campbell, Australian Capital Territory. Charles Pope was the only Metropolitan Police Officer to be awarded the VC in the First World War and the Commissioner, Sir John Stevens, laid a wreath at Charles' grave on 14th May 2001.

Edith was living at 258 Newcastle Street, Perth in 1921. She found it hard to make ends meet as a widow and a letter from her was published in the *West Australian* on 21st November 1921. She complained about the unfair administration of pensions, whereby men suffering some incapacity were able to work and also received a pension, but widows had to struggle with scarcely enough to keep their families. She married William Hamilton Burnett Woods in 1922 and they moved to 62 Dickens Street, Elwood, Victoria. However, the marriage did not last and she took out a court order for maintenance against him in 1929. It was not fully complied with and Woods was last heard of in Darwin in November 1940. Edith fell on hard times again and in 1942, while living at 161 Central Avenue, Maylands, Perth, sought restoration of her widow's pension.

2251 PRIVATE WILLIAM RATCLIFFE
2nd Battalion, The Prince of Wales's Volunteers (South Lancashire Regiment)

William Ratcliffe was born at 38 Newhall Street, St Thomas', Liverpool on 18th February 1884 according to his birth certificate. However, the baptismal register records his birth on 18th January and baptism on 21st January. William always celebrated his birthday in January. His father, also William Ratcliffe (1854–1917), was a general porter in 1881, a corn porter at East Waterloo Dock in 1891 and a dock labourer by 1901. He married Mary Ann née Kelly (1851–92) on 5th February 1876 at St Vincent de Paul Catholic Church, St James Street, Liverpool. To help support the family she collected scraps of wood and chopped them for kindling, which she sold on street corners. The family lived at a number of addresses in Liverpool:

1876 – 59 Jordan Street.
1881 – 7 Court, House 5, Blundell Street.
1888 – 7 Court, Newhall Street.
1891 – 8 House, 12 Court, Fisher Street.
1896 – 1 Court, 1 House, Pilgrim Street.
1901 – 13 Parliament Street.
1892 – Crump Street.
1904 – 19 Caryl Street.

William junior had six siblings:

• Sarah Ratcliffe (1876–1955) had three children (father unknown) – Mary Ann Ratcliffe 1904, William Ratcliffe 1907 and John Joseph Ratcliffe 1908. Sarah married John Humes (registered as Hulme) (c.1875–1948) in 1909. It is believed that her three children changed their name to Humes. John was a ship's scaler in 1911. They were living at 1 Court House B, Chester Street, Liverpool in 1911 and by the late 1940s were at 30 Head Street, Liverpool. John and Sarah had a daughter, Margaret Humes (1911–90), who married Cornelius Walsh in 1938 and they had a daughter, Noreen Walsh also in 1938. Cornelius served as a private in 1st South Lancashire (3650251) and was killed in action at Dunkirk on 20th May 1940. He is buried at Outtersteene Communal Cemetery Extension, Bailleul, France (5 A 52). After John's death Sarah moved to 29A St Oswald Gardens, Old Swan, Liverpool.

St Vincent de Paul Catholic Church, St James Street, Liverpool where William's parents married in 1876. It was designed by Edward Pugin, son of Augustus, who designed the Houses of Parliament. Edward was responsible for designing over a hundred catholic churches in Britain and Ireland.

East Waterloo Dock Liverpool, where William's father was a porter.

- Peter Ratcliffe (1878–1915) enlisted in 2nd King's (Liverpool) Regiment on 18th September 1896 at Liverpool (5412). He gave his age as eighteen years and eleven months and was described as 5′ 8¾″ tall, with fresh complexion, brown eyes, black hair and his religious denomination was Roman Catholic. He went to South Africa with the 1st Battalion on 25th November 1897 and qualified as mounted infantry on 30th June 1898. On 27th December 1898 he was sentenced to ten days hard labour in prison by the civil authorities for failing to pay a fine of £1 for riotous behaviour. He served in the Second Boer War, but returned to England on 21st March 1900 and was posted to Ireland. Peter was discharged on 12th June 1901 from Curragh Camp, Ireland having been found medically unfit for further service. He became a dock labourer. Peter married Margaret Melia (born 1881 and possibly died 1920) in 1902 and they were living at 1 Worthington Street, Liverpool in 1911 and at 1 Court House, Back Grafton Street, Liverpool in 1915. Peter enlisted in 13th King's on 22nd September 1914 (12237), but while training at Bournemouth, Dorset was declared *unlikely to become an efficient soldier* and was granted a medical discharge in December. He joined the Merchant Navy as a fireman and was serving aboard RMS *Lusitania* when she was torpedoed by U-*20* off the Old Head of Kinsale, Ireland on 7th May 1915. His body was not recovered and he is commemorated on the Tower Hill Memorial, London. Margaret and Peter had five children – Mary Jane Ratcliffe 1902, Peter Ratcliffe 1904, William Ratcliffe 1908, David Ratcliffe 1911 and Sarah Ratcliffe 1914.
- Mary Jane Ratcliffe (1880–1956) was living at 14 Court, 6 House, Rathbone Street, Liverpool when she married Peter Joseph Rowan (1874–1940) in 1897 (also seen as Rowen). He was a boiler cleaner in 1911. They had eleven children – Mary Ann Rowan 1900, Sarah Rowan 1902, John Marco Rowan 1904, Josephine Rowan 1905, Rose Alice Rowan 1907, Peter Frederick Rowan 1910, William Rowan 1912, Mary Jane Rowan 1914, Winifred Rowan 1916, Veronica Rowan 1921 and Joseph F Rowan 1923. Sarah emigrated to the USA, Peter to Rhodesia and Veronica to Newfoundland.
- Thomas Ratcliffe (1886–88).
- Alice Ratcliffe (born 1889) was living at 14 Brindley Street, Toxteth Park, Liverpool when she married Thomas H Hughes in 1915 and they had a child.
- John Ratcliffe (born and died 1892).

William's paternal grandfather, John Ratcliffe (c.1795–1879), married Jane née Tolbut (c.1814–85). They were living at 7 Gore Street, Toxteth Park, Lancashire in 1851 and by 1871 had moved to 131 Chatsworth Street, Liverpool. In addition

RMS *Lusitania* arriving in New York at the end of her maiden voyage in September 1907. William's brother, Peter, went down with her when she was torpedoed by U-20 in May 1915.

to William they had four other children – Thomas Ratcliffe c.1836, Ann Ratcliffe 1839, Alice Ratcliffe 1846 and Sarah Ratcliffe 1851.

His maternal grandfather, Peter Kelly, a labourer, was born c.1820 in Ireland. He married Mary née Rutledge, also born c.1820 in Ireland. They were living at No.11 Court, Brick Street, Liverpool in 1861. In addition to Mary they had two other children – James Kelly c.1840 and Margaret Kelly c.1853.

William was educated at St Vincent de Paul's Roman Catholic School, Norfolk Street, Liverpool. He left school c.1895 and was employed as a messenger boy and luggage handler at Liverpool Docks.

St Vincent de Paul's Roman Catholic School, Norfolk Street, Liverpool where William was educated to the age of eleven. It has since been demolished and replaced with a new school.

By 1900 he was working for Edmund Ranson, a cow keeper, at 3 Raffles Street, Liverpool. He enlisted in 3rd South Lancashire at Liverpool on 19th September 1900 as William Radcliffe (7412). He was described as 5′ 5⅜″ tall, weighing 115 lbs, with fresh complexion, brown eyes and brown hair. He gave his age falsely as eighteen years and eight months. After forty-nine days he enlisted in the Durham Light Infantry on 14th November, but his service record ends there. He is believed to have served in India and was discharged in 1911.

He returned to the docks in Liverpool and in 1911 was living at 84 St James Street. William was recalled in early August 1914 and posted to 16 Platoon, D Company, 2nd South Lancashire at Tidworth, Hampshire. He went to France on 6th December. **Awarded the MM for his actions in the Wulverghem area on 14th April 1917**

The barracks at Tidworth were built from 1904 onwards and were state of the art at the time. William Ratcliffe was there briefly in 1914. It had its own branch railway line and station.

– the Battalion was out of the line, but his company was involved in working parties when it suffered casualties from snipers. He went out and accounted for seven enemy marksmen, LG 28th July 1917.

Awarded the VC for his actions near Messines, Belgium on 14th June 1917, LG 2nd August 1917. William was wounded and evacuated to England, where he was treated at the Fentham Institute, Hampton-in-Arden, Warwickshire, an auxiliary military hospital, where he remained until the end of August. He visited his old school at the beginning of September and was posted to 3rd (Reserve) Battalion at Barrow-in-Furness, Lancashire, where the MM was presented by Lieutenant Colonel Herbert DSO on 24th September. The VC was presented by the King outside Buckingham Palace on 26th September 1917. On 13th October he kicked off a football match between South Liverpool and Tranmere Rovers at Aigburth; South Liverpool won 4–2. That evening he attended a dinner in his honour hosted by the National Union of Dock Labourers in Liverpool. Lord Derby was present and in his speech indicated that a sum of money would be presented to Ratcliffe when the war was over, "… as it was against military regulations to reward a man with money for doing his duty".

William receives his VC from the King on 26th September 1917.

William may have returned to France, but that is not certain. He was discharged to the Class Z Reserve on 11th February 1919. The medal roll for the Victory and British War Medals indicate he served with 2nd, 11th, 7th and 2nd Battalions in that order and also in the Manchester Regiment (61444) before his second period with the 2nd Battalion. There is no mention of the Manchester Regiment on his medal index card.

William Ratcliffe during a visit to his old school.

He returned to the docks for the rest of his working life, but fell on hard times in the 1920s, when he was lucky to get two days' work a week. He lodged briefly with his sister Mary Jane and her husband Peter Rowan in Brindley Street, Liverpool before moving into lodgings. When he was invited to the VC Dinner at the House of Lords, London on 9th November 1929, he stated, *I have hopes of getting the fare and I hope no one will mind my going in this old suit*. A new one was donated anonymously and he was able to attend.

In 1946, while working on the quayside of Queen's Dock, he was struck by heavy bags of castor oil seed that had fallen from a sling while being offloaded from a vessel. He sustained injuries to his neck, spine and pelvis and was completely deaf in one ear, with limited hearing in the other. He was unfit for further employment and retired with a pension of £2 per week from the Dock Board. He moved in with his sister Sarah at 30 Head Street following the death of her husband in 1948. They both moved to 29A St Oswald's Gardens, Old Swan, Brindley Street until Sarah died in 1955. Thereafter his niece, Margaret Walsh, and her daughter Noreen, who lived nearby, supported him. They accompanied him to

St Oswald's Gardens in the Old Swan area of Liverpool has been redeveloped since this picture was taken.

the 1956 VC Centenary Celebrations, for which he received a new suit, black trilby, gloves and shoes from a Liverpool tailoring firm.

William began showing signs of dementia in 1962. In March 1963, he slipped on ice and fell on his way home. At Broadgreen Hospital he was unable to remember his address. His niece, Margaret, rang the police to report he was missing from home and he was eventually found in the hospital. He needed regular supervision and was transferred to residential care at Kirkdale House, 241 Westminster Road, Kirkdale. He developed bronchopneumonia and died there on 26th March 1963. He is buried in the grave of his sister and brother-in-law, Sarah and John Humes, in the Roman Catholic Section of Allerton Cemetery, Liverpool (19–274). He is commemorated in a number of other places:

William Ratcliffe VC MM later in life.

- A memorial to Captain Noel Chavasse VC & Bar MC was unveiled in Abercromby Square, Liverpool in July 2008, opposite No.19, where the Chavasse family lived and close to No.13, where Ernest Alexander's VC father lived. The names of fifteen other VCs associated with Liverpool are also inscribed on the memorial, including William Ratcliffe.
- Victoria Cross Memorial, Liverpool Town Hall.
- A memorial plaque was commissioned by the National Union of Dock Labourers and Riverside Workers in their branch office in St James Place, off Upper Parliament Street, Liverpool. It was rescued when the building was demolished c.1976 and cared for by the Kettle family who eventually contacted Liverpool historian Bill Sergeant, who approached Liverpool Council. It is displayed in Liverpool Town Hall

William Ratcliffe's grave in Allerton Cemetery (Dave Blyth).

following a ceremony conducted by the Lord Mayor, Councillor Hazel Williams, on 21st September 2010. Many family members attended.

• The Department for Communities and Local Government decided to provide a commemorative paving stone at the birthplace of every Great War Victoria Cross recipient in the United Kingdom. William's stone is scheduled to be dedicated at West Derby, Liverpool, Merseyside on 14th June 2017 to mark the centenary of his award.

In addition to the VC and MM he was awarded the 1914–15 Star, British War Medal 1914–20, Victory Medal 1914–19, George VI Coronation Medal 1937 and Elizabeth II Coronation Medal 1953. They are owned privately, but since November 2007 have been on loan to the Imperial War Museum, where they are displayed in The Lord Ashcroft VC Gallery.

53730 LANCE SERGEANT ELLIS WELLWOOD SIFTON
18th Battalion (Western Ontario), Canadian Expeditionary Force

Ellis Sifton was born on 12th October 1891 at Wallacetown, Ontario, Canada. His father, John James Sifton (1863–1949), was a farmer of Irish extraction. He married Amelia née Bobier (1853–1912) and they were living at Dunwich, Elgin, Ontario in 1901. Ellis had two sisters:

• Ella Sifton born 1886.
• Lila 'Millie' Amelia Sifton born 1888.

Ellis's paternal grandfather, Robert H Sifton (c.1810–77), was born at Clonmel, Co Tipperary, Ireland. His parents went to Canada in 1818, where Robert became a stonecutter, contractor, builder and railroad contractor. He married Mary Jane née Ellis (1827–1916) in 1845 in Ontario. She was also born in Ireland. They were living at Dunwich, Elgin West, Ontario in 1891. In addition to John they had seven other children – Rebecca Sifton 1849, William Charles Sifton 1851, Joseph Sifton c.1854, Bamlet Ellis Sifton 1856, Edwin S Sifton 1862, Harry L Sifton 1865 and Frank Sifton.

Ellis's maternal grandfather, John Bobier (1800–80) was born at Ennisconthy, Co Wexford, Ireland. He married Jane Mill née Wellwood (1811–85) in 1829 at Trinity Parish, St Thomas, Ontario. She was born at Carlow, Ireland. In addition to Amelia they had twelve other children – Joshua Bobier 1830, William Bobier 1832, Mary Ann Bobier 1834, Thomas Bobier 1836, Sarah Jane Bobier 1838, Harriet Bobier 1840, John Bobier 1842, Joseph Bobier 1844, Richard Bobier 1847, Louisa Bobier 1849, David Bobier 1850 and Alfred F Bobier 1857.

Halifax, Nova Scotia was the start and finish point for many trans-Atlantic convoys. On 6th December 1917 the city was devastated when a French cargo ship collided with a Norwegian ship in the harbour. Almost 3,000 tons of explosives detonated and about 2,000 people died and over 9,000 were injured.

Ellis Sifton before leaving Canada (Elgin County Archives).

Little is known of Ellis's early life other than he became a farmer and was a member of the Wallacetown Rifle Association for five years prior to enlistment. He enlisted at St Thomas's, Ontario on 23rd October 1914 and was described as 5′ 7¾″ tall, with fair complexion, grey eyes, fair hair and his religious denomination was Church of England. During basic training he was allocated to 18th Battalion CEF and was promoted lance corporal. He sailed from Halifax, Nova Scotia on 21st April 1915 on SS *Grampian*, arriving at Bristol,

SS *Grampian* in Prince's Dock, Glasgow, the city where she was built in 1907 for the Allan Line. From September 1914 she became a troop transport carrying elements of the CEF to Britain, but between these voyages she undertook commercial work. In 1917 the Allan Line was taken over by Canadian Pacific. *Grampian* was burned out in March 1921 while under refit at Antwerp and was scrapped in 1925.

The Wesleyan Soldier's Home at Shorncliffe Camp. The camp was first established in 1794 and during the First World War it was used for troops transiting to France. In 1915 a Canadian Training Division formed there.

Soldiers tending Ellis Sifton's grave
(Department of National Defence).

Ellis Sifton's name commemorated at Lichfield
Crater Cemetery.

Lichfield Crater Cemetery at Thélus is rather
unusual as it is one of two mine craters (the other
being Zivy) used by the Canadians in 1917 for
burials on the Vimy battlefield. The crater is a mass
grave for fifty-seven men, fifteen of whom are
unknown, killed on 9th and 10th April 1917. There
is one exception, a South Lancashire Regiment
soldier who died in April 1916, whose grave was
found on the crater lip and is the only one with
a headstone. The names of the remainder are on
three panels beneath the Cross of Sacrifice.

Gloucestershire on 29th April. Further
training was carried out at Shorncliffe
Camp, Kent and he was promoted
corporal on 10th September. He sailed
to France from Folkestone, Kent on
14th September, landing at Boulogne
the following day. Ellis was a transport
driver with 2nd Divisional Train from
1st February 1917, but was keen to rejoin
his unit. Promoted lance sergeant on
14th March 1917.

The memorial plaque to Ellis Sifton at St Peter's
Church, Tyrconnel, Wallacetown, Ontario (Alan L
Brown of ontarioplaques.com).

**Awarded the VC for his actions
at Neuville St Vaast, France on 9th
April 1917, LG 8th June 1917.** Ellis
was killed during his VC action and was
buried in Lichfield Crater Cemetery, Thélus, France where he is commemorated
on Panel 3. As he never married the VC was presented to his father by the Duke
of Devonshire, Governor General of Canada at the Canadian National Exhibition
in Toronto on 1st September 1917. Ellis is commemorated in a number of other
places:

- A memorial plaque commissioned by the Ontario Department of Travel and Publicity with the assistance of the Archaeological and Historic Sites Board of Ontario, was dedicated at St Peter's Church, Tyrconnel, Wallacetown, Ontario on 21st May 1961. The ceremony, which was attended by his sisters Ella and Lila, was sponsored by the London Branch of the 18th Battalion Association, presided over by Captain Edward Shuttleworth, who served with Ellis.
- Canadian Book of Remembrance.
- A wooden plaque bearing fifty-six maple leaves each inscribed with the name of a Canadian born VC holder was dedicated at the Canadian Forces College, Toronto on Remembrance Day 1999.
- Named on a Victoria Cross obelisk to all Canadian VCs at Military Heritage Park, Barrie, Ontario dedicated by the Princess Royal on 22nd October 2013.
- Named on one of eleven plaques honouring 175 men from overseas awarded the VC for the Great War. The plaques were unveiled by the Senior Minister of State at the Foreign & Commonwealth Office and Minister for Faith and Communities, Baroness Warsi, at a reception at Lancaster House, London on 26th June 2014 attended by the Duke of Kent and relatives of the VC recipients. The Canadian plaque was unveiled outside the British High Commission in Elgin Street, Ottawa on 10th November 2014 by The Princess Royal in the presence of British High Commissioner Howard Drake, Canadian Minister of Veterans Affairs Julian Fantino and Canadian Chief of the Defence Staff General Thomas J Lawson.
- The Secretary of State for Communities and Local Government, Eric Pickles MP, announced that Victoria Cross recipients from the Great War would have commemorative paving stones laid in their birthplace as a lasting legacy of local heroes within communities. The stones would be laid on or close to the 100th anniversary of their VC actions. For the 145 VCs born in Australia, Belgium, Canada, China, Denmark, Egypt, France, Germany, India, Iraq, Japan, Nepal, Netherlands, New Zealand, Pakistan, South Africa, Sri Lanka, Ukraine and United States of America, individual commemorative stones were unveiled at the National Memorial Arboretum, Alrewas, Staffordshire by Prime Minister David Cameron MP and Sergeant Johnson Beharry VC on 5th March 2015.
- Two 49 cents postage stamps in honour of the ninety-four Canadian VC winners were issued by Canada Post on 21st October 2004 on the 150th Anniversary of the first Canadian VC's action, Alexander Roberts Dunn VC.

In addition to the VC he was awarded the 1914–15 Star, British War Medal 1914–20 and Victory Medal 1914–19. His next-of-kin is eligible to receive the Canadian Memorial Cross. His VC was donated to the St Thomas YMCA following the death of his last surviving sister. It was later donated to the Elgin County Pioneer Museum at St Thomas, Ontario, but his other three medals were reported lost. On 4th October 1974 replacements were issued to the Museum after pre payment.

40989 PRIVATE ERNEST SYKES
27th Battalion (4th Tyneside Irish), The Northumberland Fusiliers

Ernest Sykes was born at Quick View, Mossley, Lancashire on 14th April 1885. His father is not recorded on his birth certificate. When Ernest married in 1905, his father was recorded as Robert Sykes (deceased), a selfactor minder. However, when he married in 1938 his father was recorded as John Sykes, a cotton spinner (operative). Ernest's mother was Ruth Sykes (1848–99), born at Honley, Yorkshire. She was a cotton frame tenter, living with her mother at Carr Hill Road, Saddleworth in 1881, and a cotton card room hand in 1885. She was living at 27 Lees Road, Mossley in 1891 with her three children and sisters, Ada and Hannah. Ernest had two sisters:

* Helena 'Lena' Sykes (1887–1965) married Robert Clayton (1886–1964) in 1906 and they had eight children – Hannah Clayton 1907, Joseph Clayton 1912, John Clayton 1915, Lena Clayton 1918, Samuel Ernest Clayton 1920, Ronald Clayton 1923, Gilbert Clayton 1928 and Dorothy Clayton 1930.
* Mary Sykes (1889–1938) married James Edward Lees (1884–1934) in 1911 and they had four children – Leonard Lees 1911, John Lees 1914, Ben Lees 1920 and Mary Lees 1923.

Ernest's maternal grandfather was Benjamin Sykes (1821–72), a woollen spinner in 1841 and a handloom weaver by 1851. He married Mary (also seen as Ann) Brierly/Brierley (born c.1821 and died before 1890) in 1843. She had a son, Isaac Brierley, in December 1840. By 1861 the family was living at Uppermill, Saddleworth. Ann was living at Carr Hill Road, Saddleworth, Yorkshire in 1881. In addition to Ruth they had eight other children – Allen Sykes 1844, Grace Sykes 1849, Hannah Sykes c.1851, Emma Sykes c.1853, Inkerman Sykes 1856, Ned Sykes 1858, Ada Sykes c.1865 and Hannah Sykes 1869. Hannah married Harry Taylor (c.1865–1903), who served in 105th Regiment (2500) from 31st December 1880. On enlistment he was almost 5′ 7½″ tall, weighed 120 lbs, with fair complexion, brown hair, brown eyes and his religious denomination was Church of England. He transferred to the King's Own Light Infantry (South Yorkshire Regiment) when 105th and 51st Regiments amalgamated on 1st July 1881. He served in India 7th February 1883–14 December 1890 and took part in the Burma campaign 1886–87 (India Medal 1849–95 with Burma 1885–7 clasp). Good Conduct Badges were awarded on 14th July 1885 and 31st December 1886 and one was forfeited on 19th July 1890. Posted to 2nd Battalion on 29th August 1887 and transferred to the West Yorkshire Regiment on 19th November 1887 (2100).

Stalybridge with St George's Church on the right on Cocker Hill.

Mossley Station, where Ernest worked as a platelayer from 1911 until he enlisted (Ed Pollock).

Promoted lance corporal on 26th September 1889, but reverted to private on 6th June 1890 and returned to Britain on HMS *Euphrates* 20th November–12th December 1890. He had a colourful medical history including dyspepsia, gonorrhoea, ague, syphilis and other complaints. Discharged 30th December 1892.

Ernest was educated at St George's School, Stalybridge. Thereafter he was employed as a woollen feeder in 1901, but was a foundry labourer at the time of his marriage in January 1905. By the birth of his first son, in December 1906, he was a woollen mill hand and by May 1910 was a woolen teaser. From 1911 he was a platelayer working for the London & North Western Railway at Mossley.

Ernest Sykes married Alice Bredbury (also seen as Bradbury) (1883–1920), a cotton weaver, on 16th January 1905 at Saddleworth Register Office. Both gave their address as 4 Buckley's Place, Springhead. They were living at 4 Croft Place, Milnsbridge, Huddersfield, Yorkshire in 1911 and later at 3 Bank Street, Mossley. Alice's death was registered in the 1st quarter of 1920 at Ashton-under-Lyne, almost certainly due to complications in childbirth. Ernest and Alice had three children:

• Percy Sykes (1906–79) was born at 237 Klondike Place, Outlane, Longwood, Huddersfield, Yorkshire. He was a bleacher in a cotton works. He married Sarah Hannah Hall (born 1907) in 1926 and they had four children – Annie Sykes 1927, Margaret Sykes 1928, Doris Sykes 1931 and Joan Mary Sykes 1933. The marriage failed and Sarah went to live in London and may have changed her name to Grantham. Doris was raised by her grandfather, Ernest, until he remarried in 1938, when Sarah took Doris to London, where she worked for Mr and Mrs Saper, confectioners. Doris married Fred Whatmough in1971 and they had a daughter, Victoria Elizabeth Whatmough. Doris was the matron and Fred the warden of Castleshaw Residential Centre, Waterworks Road, Delph, Lancashire. It was founded in 1895 to give delicate and poverty-stricken children from Oldham a holiday in rural surroundings. In 1958 it became a camp school run on youth hostel lines.

- Harold Sykes (1910–91) born at 4 Croft Place, Milnsbridge, Huddersfield, worked on the railways at Mossley as a porter. He married Norah Howarth in 1935 and they had six children – Joan Sykes 1936, David H Sykes 1937, Martyn R Sykes 1943, Jeffrey H Sykes 1945 and twins Howard P Sykes and Stephen E Sykes 1947.
- Ivy Sykes (1920–90), born at Ashton-under-Lyne, Lancashire. She married William Nightingale Woffenden (1920–96) in 1942. They had two children – Katina C Woffenden 1944 and David E Woffenden 1949.

Ernest enlisted in 7th West Riding at Halifax, Yorkshire on 31st August 1914 (13425). His Medal Index Card shows he entered the Balkans Theatre (Gallipoli & Aegean Islands) on 18th July 1915. However, 7th West Riding went to France in April 1915 and the only West Riding Regiment battalion to serve at Gallipoli was the 8th. It left Liverpool in July 1915 and was at Mudros prior to landing at Suvla, Gallipoli on 6th August 1915. It is therefore concluded that Ernest transferred to the 8th Battalion between August 1914 and July 1915. He was seriously wounded in the foot but refused to have it amputated in Egypt and was sent home, where he underwent several operations to save it.

When he was passed fit for active service in 1916, he transferred to 25th and later 27th Northumberland Fusiliers (40989). **Awarded the VC for his actions at Roclincourt, near Arras on 9th April 1917, LG 8th June 1917.** On 12th July 1917 he arrived home on leave to an enthusiastic reception on the station platform. He was met by his wife and two sons, the Mayor and members of the Town Council and Corporation. After the civic reception, he was carried shoulder high to his home through cheering crowds.

The VC was presented by the King outside Buckingham Palace on 21st July 1917. On 27th July he and Lance Corporal Thomas Bryan received a civic reception at the Empire Theatre, Newcastle. The Lord Mayor presented them with war loans, a clock and a wallet of Treasury notes. Ernest was presented with a silver tea service by the officers of his Battalion. A week after his investiture, the people of Mossley turned out to greet him at a presentation in Market Square, where the Mayor gave him an illuminated address, a gold watch and other gifts, including £100 of War Bonds. Ernest was discharged on 26th May 1918, no longer fit for active service.

Ernest Sykes with the King during his investiture on 21st July 1917.

He returned to work with the London & North Western Railway in the Engineering Department and later became a ticket collector at Stalybridge, before becoming a guard. He remained with the railways for the rest of his working life. He attended the unveiling

Morley Lane, Milnsbridge, Huddersfield in the background beyond the Huddersfield Narrow Canal.

Stalybridge Station, where Ernest was a ticket collector (JW Sutherland).

of the LNWR War Memorial at Euston Station by Earl Haig in October 1921.

On 4th April 1938, Ernest Sykes married Gladys née Clough (23rd May 1893–1971), a domestic cook, at Huddersfield Register Office. Both gave their address as 8 Morley Lane, Milnsbridge, Huddersfield. During the Second World War, Ernest served in 25th West Riding (Huddersfield) Battalion, Home Guard.

Ernest died at his home at 17 Thornfield Avenue, Lockwood, Yorkshire on 3rd August 1949 and is buried in Lockwood Cemetery, Meltham, near Huddersfield (F 227). He is also commemorated in a number of other places:

Ernest Sykes later in life in railway guard's uniform.

- Memorial at Mossley Station unveiled on 11th August 2014.
- A London & North Western Railway Claughton Class locomotive (No.2035), built in 1920, was named *Private E. Sykes V.C.* in February 1922. Two other Claughtons were also dedicated to LNWR employees who had been awarded the VC – JA Christie and W Wood. LNWR was absorbed into London, Midland & Scottish Railway in 1923 and No.2035 was renumbered No.5976. When it

The London & North Western Railway War Memorial at Euston Station was dedicated by the Archbishop of Canterbury and unveiled by Earl Haig on 21st October 1921. It commemorates the 3,719 LNWR employees who died in the First World War and was designed by the company architect, R Wynn Owen. It also commemorates the men and women of the London, Midland & Scottish Railway who died in the Second World War.

was moved from the Manchester area, the nameplate transferred to No.158 in April 1926, to continue the association with the city. It was renumbered No.6015 in May 1926 and was withdrawn from service in March 1933 for rebuilding as a Patriot Class. On completion it was renumbered No.5537 on 25th June 1934. When the railways were nationalised in 1948, British Railways renumbered it No.45537. It was withdrawn from service in June 1962 and scrapped, but the nameplate was presented to the Royal Northumberland Fusiliers Museum at Alnwick Castle in 1967 and is displayed there.

The Patriot Class locomotive No.45537, *Private E. Sykes V.C.*, awaiting scrapping after being withdrawn from service in 1962. The nameplate was saved and can be seen at the Royal Northumberland Fusiliers Museum at Alnwick Castle.

• Blue Plaque at George Lawton Hall, Stamford Street, Mossley, Ashton-under-Lyne, Manchester unveiled by his granddaughter, Miss Joan Sykes, in September 1996. The Hall also has an Ernest Sykes Room.
• Named on a Blue Plaque to all Tameside VCs at the entrance to Ashton Town Hall unveiled on 20th April 1995. The other named VCs are John Buckley, William Thomas Forshaw, Albert Hill, James Kirk, Andrew Moynihan, Arthur Herbert Procter and Harry Norton Schofield.
• Joint memorial plaque to him and Charles Coverdale VC at Huddersfield Town Hall.

In addition to the VC, he was awarded the 1914–15 Star, British War Medal 1914–20, Victory Medal 1914–19, Defence Medal and George VI Coronation Medal 1937. The Defence Medal does not form part of the group and may not have been claimed. It is believed that Ernest donated his VC to the Regiment just before he died and it was handed over by his eldest son, Percy. His other medals and a copy VC were sold at Sotheby's in 1981 and were believed to be in Canada until the campaign medals were sold to a private buyer for £6,000 at a Dix Noonan Webb auction on 12th May 2015. The VC is held by the Royal Northumberland Fusiliers Museum, Alnwick Castle.

30144 PRIVATE HORACE WALLER
10th Battalion, The King's Own (Yorkshire Light Infantry)

Horace Waller was born at 11 Woodhill Terrace, Batley Carr, Dewsbury, Yorkshire on 23rd September 1896. His father was John Edward Waller (1868–1936), known as Edward. He ran a family plumbing business, Strickland Waller & Sons, started by his father. Horace's mother, Esther née Myers (1871–99), married Edward in 1891 at Pateley Bridge and they lived at 11 Warwick Road, Dewsbury. After Esther died, Edward moved in with his widowed mother at 82 Upper Road, Dewsbury. He married Sarah Elizabeth Prescott (1864–1953) in 1903 at Holy Trinity Church, Batley Carr. They were living at 'Laurel Bank', Heald's Road, Dewsbury, Yorkshire in the 1920s.

Horace had one brother from his father's first marriage, John Strickland Waller (1891–1937). He was also a plumber and married Agnes Hannah Watson (1887–1971) in 1919 at Mansfield, Nottinghamshire. They had two children – Horace Waller 1920 and Dorothy Waller 1924.

His paternal grandfather, Strickland Waller (1840–98), a plumber and glazier, married Sarah née Shaw (1845–1916) at the Parish Church, Dewsbury in 1865. He started the family plumbing business in Batley Carr, which was run by his wife

Holy Trinity Church, Batley Carr where Horace's father married for the second time in 1903 and where Horace is commemorated on two memorials inside the church. The gateway on the right forms the Second World War memorial (Betty Longbottom).

after his death. The family lived at various times at Beckett Road, Rushworth Street, Earls Heaton and Upper Road all in Dewsbury. In addition to John they had four other children:

- Susannah Waller (1866–1952), a binder of rugs in 1891, married William James Stubley (1866–1950), a commercial clerk, in 1895. They were living at 29 Warwick Road, Batley in 1901 and at 109 Mill Road, Batley Carr in 1911.
- Mary Ellen Waller (1871–1957) (registered as Mary Alice) married Herbert Edwin Spink (1871–1952) in 1894. They had a son, Harold Spink, in 1903.
- Annie Waller (1877–1956) married Willie Halmshaw (1868–1914), a butcher, in 1904. They had a daughter, Elsie Halmshaw, in 1905.

- Arthur Waller (1879–1956) married Lilian Emsley (1884–1950) in 1906 and they lived at Healds Road, Dewsbury. They had two children – Eric Waller 1904 and Irene Waller 1908.

His maternal grandfather, John Myers (c.1839–1901), was a spindle maker. He married Eliza née Trigg (1839–1916) in 1863. The family lived at various times at Addison Street, Bowling Road Lane, and Sunny Bank Road all in Bowling. By 1881 John was employing five men and seven boys. In 1911 Eliza was living at 7 Round Street, West Bowling. In addition to Esther, John and Eliza had two other children:

- Thomas Myers (born 1866) was a spindle maker. He married Margaret Rowling (1864–1926) in 1887. They were living at 7 Leatham Street, Bradford in 1891, at 18 Rosslyn Place, Bradford in 1901 and at 2 Waverley Place, Bradford in 1911. They had two children – Marion Myers 1888 and Nellie Myers 1889.
- John Arthur Myers (1876–1940) married Florence Ashley (1878–1955) in 1900. John was an assistant in a sport's outfitters in 1911. The family lived at 399 Bowling Old Lane, Bradford. They had two children – Vera Myers 1900 and Mona Myers 1910.

Horace was educated at:

Batley Grammar School, attended by Horace Waller from 1909, was founded in 1612 by the Reverend William Lee. When the comprehensive system of education was introduced, the school became independent and fee paying. It became fully co-educational in 1996 and later returned to the maintained sector as one of the first free schools. Former pupils include Joseph Priestley (1733–1804), the discoverer of oxygen and Sir Owen Willans Richardson (1879–1959), Professor of Physics at Princeton University and King's College, London, who was awarded the Nobel Prize for Physics in 1928.

Batley was the centre of the shoddy trade, recycling old woollen rags and clothing into blankets, carpets etc (Kirklees Image Archive).

- Miss Whitworth's Seminary, Albert Terrace, Halifax Road, Dewsbury 1902–05.
- Purlwell Council School, Batley Carr 1905–09.
- Batley Grammar School from 1909, where he won a County Minor Scholarship in 1910.
- Dewsbury Technical College in 1913, while also working for the family plumbing business of Strickland Waller & Sons.

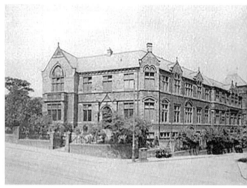

The dedication of Dewsbury War Memorial in September 1924.

Dewsbury Municipal Technical College and School of Art (Albert Lyles).

Horace enlisted on 30th May 1916 after twice being rejected for medical reasons. He went to France in December 1916. **Awarded the VC for his actions south of Héninel, France on 10th April 1917, LG 8th June 1917.** He was killed during his VC action and is buried in Cojeul British Cemetery (I C 55). His will was administered by his father; he left £184/7/2. Horace is commemorated in a number of other places:

• Horace Waller VC Parade, Shawcross Business Park, Dewsbury.
• The family grave in Dewsbury Cemetery.

Batley Grammar School's First World War Memorial. Other bronze panels have been added for the Second World War and subsequent conflicts (Philip Wheeler).

Horace Waller's grave in Cojeul British Cemetery, a short distance from where he won his VC on 10th April 1917. Captain Arthur Henderson VC MC, who was killed on 24th April 1917, is also buried in the Cemetery. The 64th Brigade memorial is in the background.

Batley War Memorial. The names of the dead are inscribed on the surrounding fence pillars (Kirlees Council).

Horace Waller's name on the family grave in Dewsbury Cemetery.

- Batley Carr Holy Trinity Church War Memorial and on a separate memorial.
- Batley Grammar School Memorial.
- Dewsbury War Memorial.
- Batley Carr War Memorial.
- Joint memorial plaque at Dewsbury Town Hall with John William Ormsby VC MM.

As Horace never married, the VC was presented to his parents by the King outside Buckingham Palace on 21st July 1917. In addition to the VC, he was awarded the British War Medal 1914–20 and Victory Medal 1914–19. The VC was purchased for £8,800 by Spink & Son from Christie's on behalf of a private client on 25th February 1980. Its current whereabouts are not known.

The memorial to Horace Waller in Holy Trinity Church, Batley Carr. His name is also on the First World War Memorial in the church.

SECOND LIEUTENANT FRANK BERNARD WEARNE
3rd attached 11th Battalion, The Essex Regiment

Frank Wearne, known as Bernard, was born at 45 Matheson Road, Fulham, London on 1st March 1894. His father, also Frank Wearne (1856–1924), was a wine merchant, co-founder of Feuerheerd Wearne, which was taken over by Gonzales Byass, producers of Tio Pepe sherry. He married Ada née Morris (1860–1947) in

1888 at Steyning, West Sussex. The family was living at 49 (later 45) Matheson Road, Fulham in 1891, at 89 Greencroft Gardens, Hampstead by 1901 and later at The Manor Lodge, Royal Avenue, Worcester Park, Surrey. When Frank died on 16th January 1924 he left £18,490/16/4 to his widow; and when she died on 17th March 1947 she left £37,217/3/4. Bernard had five siblings:

• Edith Ann Wearne (1889–1956) married Thomas Clinton Pears (1882–1912) in 1910, great great grandson of Andrew Pears, founder of the soap manufacturers, A & F Pears Ltd. They lived at Mevagissey, St Johns Road, Isleworth. Thomas joined the Pears company in 1903 and was appointed manager of the Lanadron Works, a subsidiary firm, on the corner of London Road and Linkfield Road, Isleworth. He was also responsible for Lanadron Rubber Estates Ltd in Malaya. On 10th April 1912 they boarded RMS *Titanic* at Southampton. He died when the liner went down five

Greencroft Gardens, Hampstead, where the Wearne family was living in 1901.

Bernard's sister, Edith, survived the sinking of RMS *Titanic* in April 1912.

Edith's husband, Thomas Pears, went down with the *Titanic* and his body was not recovered.

RMS *Titanic*, the second of the White Star Line's three *Olympic* class liners, at Southampton. She was the largest ship afloat at the time and was said to be unsinkable. However, on her maiden voyage she collided with an iceberg and sank early on 15th April 1912 with the loss of 1,514 passengers and crew out of the 2,224 aboard.

days later, but Edith survived. Thomas left £16,763/10/7. His body was not recovered and he is commemorated on the family grave in Isleworth Cemetery. Edith served as a nurse in the British Red Cross and drove an ambulance. She later served in the Women's Royal Naval Service as a chauffeur. After the war she shared a London flat with Norah Frances Crowe (born 1880) and married Norah's brother, Douglas Valentine Crowe (1887–1969), in 1919. Douglas was a tea planter on the Periaburrar Estate, Munmaar PO, near Periyakulam (previously Travancore), southern India. They had two children – Sheila Marian Crowe 1920 and Frank Wyndham Crowe 1924. Frank was commissioned in the Royal Artillery on 24th April 1943 (271527).

- Frank Morris Wearne (1891–92).
- Keith Morris Wearne (1892–1917) entered the Royal Military College, Sandhurst in 1910 and was commissioned in 1st Essex Regiment on 14th February 1912. He served in India and South Africa and was promoted lieutenant on 6th September 1914. Keith received a severe gunshot wound to his left leg on 2nd May 1915 at Gallipoli and was admitted to Deaconess Hospital, Alexandria, Egypt on 8th May. He was evacuated to England aboard HMHS *Delta* embarking at Alexandria on 6th July and arriving at Southampton on 13th July. He was admitted to Lady Evelyn Mason's Hospital, 16 Bruton Street, London. Medical boards on 28th July, 28th September, 13th December 1915 and 12th February 1916 found him unfit for various periods and he was sent on leave 28th July–27th September, extended to 27th November then to 12th February 1916. Promoted captain 17th October 1915. He was posted to 3rd Reserve Battalion for light duties. Medical boards at Felixstowe on 29th March, 10th May and 10th June found him unfit for General Service, but fit for Home Service. Finally a medical board at Felixstowe on 10th July found him fit for General Service. He returned to France in April 1917 as a captain and was killed by shellfire on 21st May 1917. Keith is buried in Orange Trench Cemetery, Monchy-le-Preux, France (Special Memorial 3).
- Geoffrey Alleyne Wearne (1896–1971) enlisted in the Canadian Expeditionary Force (55951) at Toronto on 12th November 1914. He was described as a twenty-three years old student, 5′ 9″ tall, with fair complexion, grey eyes, fair hair and his religious denomination was Church of England. He was in a trench when the Germans blew a mine beneath it and was severely shell-shocked, resulting in him becoming very aggressive after demobilisation in 1919. He was engaged to May Joyce Carey (1898–1970) in 1920, but before they married he was certified insane and spent the rest of his life in a mental hospital.
- William Roy Wearne (born 1899) was commissioned in the Grenadier Guards on 30th January 1918 and was promoted lieutenant on 30th July 1919. He married Vera Manville-Hales in 1924 and during the Second World War was commissioned as acting pilot officer, Administrative and Special Duties Branch RAF (118530) on 7th January 1942. Promoted flying officer 1st October 1942 and last appears

in the Air Force List in July 1945. It is understood they subsequently moved to South Africa.

Bernard's paternal grandfather, Henry Wearne (c.1811–85), was a woolen draper. He married Louisa née Hammon (c.1826–1906) in 1851 at Sellindge, Kent. They were living at 9 Eldon Road, Kensington in 1861. At 5 Phillimore Terrace, Chelsea in 1871 and at 59 Warwick Gardens, Chelsea by 1881. In addition to Frank they also had seven other children:

• Harry Wearne (born 1852) was a manufacturer's clerk in 1871 and an agent by 1881.
• Hammon Wearne (1854–1921) was a stockbroker. He married Caroline Morris (born c.1871) in 1889 and they lived at 13 Fourth Avenue, Hove and later at Arundel House, 22 The Drive, Hove, Sussex. They had four children – Phyllis Margaret Wearne 1891, Mary Beryl Wearne 1893, John Herbert Wearne 1895 and Kenneth Martin Wearne (1896–1917). Kenneth enlisted in the Inns of Court OTC (5671) on 16th August 1915. He was 5′ 5½″ tall and weighed 119 lbs. He applied for commission on 3rd April 1916, by when he was 5′ 7″ tall and weighed 128 lbs. He was admitted to No.1 Company, Inns of Court OTC on 25th April and was commissioned on 7th July 1916 in 10th, attached 5th, Queen's (Royal West Surrey). He was killed on 20th September 1917 and is commemorated on the Tyne Cot Memorial, Belgium.
• Mary Louisa 'Daisy' Wearne (1857–1910) married Martin Southwell Skeffington (1842–1924) in 1875, a partner in the publishing firm of Skeffington & Son. They had five children – Winfred Marian Skeffington 1876, Harold Ernest Skeffington 1877, Kate Beryl Skeffington 1880, Henry John Skeffington 1881 and Herbert Neville Southwell Skeffington 1884. Harold was commissioned in the Army Printing and Stationery Service on 15th December 1917. He married three times – Constance Evelyn Jones in 1911, Ada V Dixon in 1931 and Elizabeth Lillian Day in 1939. Herbert enlisted in the AIF on 18th August 14 (No.4). He was a photographer, described as 5′ 11″ tall, weighing 152 lbs, with dark complexion, brown eyes, brown hair and his religious denomination was Church of England. He joined 3rd Field Company Australian Engineers and departed Australia on HMAT A2 *Geelong* on 22nd September. Promoted lance corporal 13th March 1915 and departed Alexandria on 5th April. He embarked on HMAT A50 *Itonus* on 2nd June and joined his unit at Gallipoli on 8th June. Appointed company quartermaster sergeant 27th July. He reported sick on 30th August and was admitted to 1st Australian General Hospital at Heliopolis with dysentery on 2nd September, transferred to 3rd Auxiliary Hospital on 5th September and to Ras-el-Tin Convalescent Hospital 8th October–15th November. He rejoined his unit on 9th December and was attached to HQ 1st Australian Division Engineers on 29th December at Tel-el-Kebir. Herbert transferred to 1st Pioneer Battalion on 10th

March 1916 as regimental quartermaster sergeant. He embarked at Alexandria on 26th March, disembarked at Marseilles on 2nd April and was on leave in France 27th April–5th May. Herbert was commissioned on 10th June, promoted lieutenant 10th September and was struck off strength of the AIF on 23rd October on transferring to the Royal Flying Corps Special Reserve and joining No.2 Royal Flying Corps School of Instruction at Oxford. He was appointed flying officer 22nd June 1917 and posted to 57th Squadron on 14th July. On 28th July 1917 he was shot down flying BE No.A7448 over Wielsbeke, fifteen kilometres northeast of Courtrai. His observer, Lieutenant AC Malloch, a Canadian, was wounded and taken prisoner, but Herbert was killed. The Germans dropped a message to this effect over the British lines soon afterwards and reported his death in the *Norddeutche Allgemeine Zeitung* on 18th August. He is buried in Wielsbeke Communal Cemetery, Belgium (Grave 3).

- Herbert Wearne (born 1859).
- Perry Wearne (1861–1946) married Helen Myrtle Dow (1871–1948) in 1902 at St Marylebone. Helen was born at Madison, Wisconsin, USA. They had a daughter, Margaret Louisa Wearne in 1905.
- Kate Dora Wearne (1863–1954) never married.
- Edith Jane Wearne (1865–86).
- Emile Collin Wearne (1868–1951), a member of the Stock Exchange, married Adela Maude Whitlock (1877–1963) in 1909. They were living at Boxmoor, Hertfordshire in 1911 and at Matale, 21 Lodge Hill Road, Lower Bourne, Farnham, Surrey in 1955 . They had two children – Adrian Collin Wearne 1910 and Hammon Oliver Collin Wearne 1912.

His maternal grandfather, William Morris, was a watchmaker. He married Caroline née Buckland in 1854 at St Mary's Church, Lewisham, London. They were living at Tranquil Vale, Blackheath, London in 1860. In addition to Ada they had two other daughters – Jane Morris 1858 and Caroline Morris 1862.

Bernard's grandparents, William and Caroline Morris, lived at Tranquil Vale, Blackheath.

Bernard was educated initially by Reverend DH Marshall of Ovingdean. He won a scholarship in 1908 to Bromsgrove School, Worcestershire, where he became Head Monitor before leaving in 1912. He was a member of the 1st XV and a corporal in the Officer Training Corps. Bernard went to Corpus Christi College, Oxford in 1913,where he was a member of the UOTC, but because of the war he never finished the course.

He enlisted on 3rd September 1914 at Westminster and joined B Company,

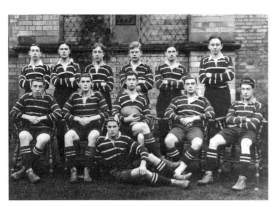

The Bromsgrove School rugby team outside the chapel in 1911. Bernard Wearne is standing on the far right. At least two of the other boys in the photograph were killed in the war.

Corpus Christi College, Oxford, founded in 1517, has a reputation for Classics. Amongst its former students are the Miliband brothers, David, former Foreign Secretary, and Ed, former leader of the Labour Party.

18th (1st Public Schools) Battalion, Royal Fusiliers on 15th September (2214). He was described as 5′ 11″ tall, weighing 154 lbs with dark complexion, brown eyes, brown hair and his religious denomination was Church of England. He was medically fit, but short sighted in both eyes. He was promoted lance corporal 23rd November, but reverted to private on 30th December. Bernard applied for a commission on 29th April 1915 and was commissioned in 3rd (Reserve) Battalion, Essex Regiment on 16th May 1915. He was attached to 10th Battalion on 5th June. He went to France on 13th December. On 5th June 1916 near Carnoy he and three scouts managed to capture a member of the German 62nd Regiment. **Mentioned in Sir Douglas Haig's Despatch of 30th April 1916, LG 15th June 1916.** Bernard received a serious gunshot wound to the right arm on a reconnaissance on 3rd July. He was evacuated from Le Havre on HMHS *Egypt* on 4th July arriving at Southampton on 6th July, and was treated at 1st London General Hospital, where a medical board on 21st August found him unfit for six months. He

In August 1914 1st London General Hospital took over St Gabriel's College in Camberwell. In December 1915 huts were erected in Myatt's Fields to accommodate 520 more patients and by 1917 the Hospital had expanded to 231 beds for officers and 1,038 for enlisted men. Vera Brittain, author of *Testament of Youth*, worked there as a VAD Nurse.

was sent on leave until 20th February 1917. A medical board at Kingston-on-Thames on 24th February found him unfit for General Service for two months, but fit for Home Service and he joined 3rd Battalion on 4th March. A medical board on 6th April passed him fit for General Service and he joined 11th Battalion on returning to France in May 1917.

Bernard Wearne's name on the Loos Memorial.

Awarded the VC for his actions east of Loos, France on 28th June 1917, LG 2nd August 1917. As Bernard never married, the VC was presented to his father by the King at Buckingham Palace on 20th October 1917. It was the only VC awarded to the Essex Regiment during the First World War. Bernard was killed during his VC action on 28th June 1917 and is commemorated on the Loos Memorial.

In addition to the VC he was awarded the 1914–15 Star, British War Medal 1914–20 and Victory Medal 1914–19. His father bequeathed Bernard's and Keith's medals to his son William. Bernard's medals were auctioned at Sotheby's in 1977 for £7,000 and by Spink's on 17th December 1997 for £54,000, when they were purchased by Lord Ashcroft. They are displayed in the Imperial War Museum's Lord Ashcroft Gallery.

8763 LANCE CORPORAL JAMES WELCH
1st Battalion, The Royal Berkshire Regiment

James Welch was born at Stratfield Saye, near Silchester, Hampshire on 7th July 1889. His father, Daniel Welch (c.1860–1911), was an agricultural labourer. His mother, Martha Ellen née Hiscock (1865–1944), was a general servant in 1881. Daniel and Martha married in 1886 and the family lived at Fair Oak, Stratfield Saye. James had eleven siblings:

• George Welch (born 1886) was an agricultural labourer in 1911.
• Agnes Mary Welch (born 1887) married George Wonderfull Marjoram (1887–1958) in 1909. He was a chimney sweep and they were living at Chapel Street, Diss, Norfolk in 1911. George had enlisted in the Army Service Corps on 12th January 1904 at Diss, Norfolk (T/21646). He

was described as 5′ 2½″ tall, weighing 109 lbs, with fresh complexion, blue eyes, brown hair and his religious denomination was Church of England. He had previously been rejected for military service due to his height. On 28th October 1904 he was imprisoned for three days for disobedience to orders. George transferred to the Reserve on 11th January 1906 and was mobilised on 6th August 1914 at Woolwich, London. He went to France with 8th Divisional Train as a driver on 26th August. Numerous promotions followed – acting

Fair Oak Green, Stratfield Saye. The village is best known for being the country seat of the Duke of Wellington.

lance corporal 16th January 1915, acting corporal 8th February, acting sergeant 15th February, paid lance corporal 12th May 1916, acting company sergeant major 31st November 1916 and corporal 5th March 1919. He transferred to the Class Z Reserve on 25th July 1919 and was discharged on 31st March 1920. Agnes and George had three children – twins Hilda Ellen Marjoram and Mary Hope Marjoram 1909 and George James Marjoram 1911.

• Daniel Welch (born 1891) was an agricultural labourer in 1911.
• Minnie Welch (1892–1965) married William Hiscock in 1917.
• Eleanor Welch (born 1894) was a kitchen maid domestic in 1911.
• Frances May Welch (1896–1969) was a housemaid in 1911.
• Gertrude Welch (born 1898) is believed to have married George W Richards in 1918, registered at Hartley Wintney.
• Dorothy Matilda Welch (1900–57) married Joseph W Wheatley in 1928 and they had three children – Francis JW Wheatley 1929, Alice M Wheatley 1931 and Dorothy E Wheatley 1935.
• Christopher Welch (1901–68) married Teresa M Brake (c.1906–41) in 1924 and they had six children – Teresa PH Welch 1925, Christopher W Welch 1928, James Alfred Welch 1931, Robert Edward Welch 1933, Arthur P Welch 1937 and Walter F Welch 1939.
• Edward Charles Welch (born 1902).
• Hilda Ann Welch (born 1906) married Robert J Evans in 1939.

James' paternal grandfather, George Welch (c.1829–1901), was an agricultural labourer. He married Mary Anne née Lucas (c.1827–82) in 1853. She had married Charles Woolford in 1845 and had two children – Charles Woolford 1847 and Eliza Ann Woolford 1850. Charles and Mary were living at Bridge Street, South Lynn, Norfolk in 1851 and he died later that year. George and Mary were living at Bramley, Hampshire in 1871 and Western Green, Stratfield Saye in 1881. In addition to Daniel they had three other children – Laura Ann Welch 1854, James Welch 1856 and Harry Welch 1861.

James' maternal grandfather, Peter Hiscock (1836–1917), was also an agricultural labourer. He married Elizabeth née Hunt (1838–1906) in 1858. They were living at Southend Road, Stratfield Saye, Hampshire in 1881, at Ash Street, Ash, Surrey in 1901 and Greaves Cottages, Ash, in 1901. In addition to Martha they had nine other children – Ann Elizabeth Hiscock 1859, George Hiscock 1861, James Alfred Hiscock 1863, Charles Hiscock 1868, Agnes Charlotte (also seen as Margaret Agnes) Hiscock 1870, Albert Edward Hiscock 1873, William Henry Hiscock 1874, Nelly Ann Hiscock 1877 and Edward John Hiscock 1881. In 1911 Peter Hiscock was living with his sister Ann Elliott, a widow, at Hartley Wespall, near Basingstoke.

James' aunt, Agnes Charlotte Hiscock (1870–1946), married George Gates (c.1870–98) in 1889 as Margaret Agnes Hiscock. George was a general labourer and they were living at 282 High Street, Aldershot in 1891. They had five children – Agnes Mary Gates 1890, George Charles Gates 1891, Charles William Gates 1893, Elizabeth Ann Gates 1896 and Beatrice Florence Gates 1898. Elizabeth and Beatrice were living with their grandparents, Peter and Elizabeth Hiscock in 1901, Beatrice being recorded as Rebecca. Agnes married Henry 'Harry' Gardener (1880–1949) in 1901 and they lived at 5 White Cottages, Gravel Road, Farnborough. Harry was a Royal Artillery soldier and appeared in the 1901 Census, aged twenty-one, born at Weymouth, Dorset. By the 1911 Census he was a Royal Field Artillery ammunition column foreman at Deepcut, Surrey aged forty-two and his place of birth was Bath, Somerset. Agnes and Harry had three children – Harry Gardener 1901, Agnes Gardener 1903 and Dorothy 'Dolly' Gardener 1904.

James Welch while recovering from wounds.

James was educated at Stratfield Saye School and was then employed as a farm labourer. He enlisted on 25th January 1908 and served with 2nd Battalion in India. He went to France on 6th November 1914 and was wounded at Neuve Chapelle and on the Somme. During one of these occasions he was evacuated to the Woofindin Convalescent Home, Sheffield where he met his wife, Daisy née Barnes (1886–28th June 1968). They were married in the 4th quarter of 1915 and she was living at 24 Stothard Road, Crookes, Sheffield in 1917. They had five children:

• Daisy Victoria Welch (1918–85) married Edmund Straw (1918–66) in 1940 and they had two children – Edmund D Straw 1941 and Ronald J Straw 1944.
• James Oppy Welch (1920–59) served in the York & Lancaster Regiment during the Second World War. He married Hilda M Asher (born 1919) in 1942 at Horsham,

Sussex and they had four children – Susan H Welch 1944, Philip J Welch 1947, Sheila D Welch 1951 and John P Welch 1955.
- William CV Welch born and died 1921.
- Margaret Ellen Welch (1922–2012) married George L Holt (1921–) in 1946. She married Benjamin 'Benny' H Blunden (born 1913) in 1973. Benny had married Doris H Morris in 1933 and had two children – John M Blunden 1934 and Michael LG Blunden 1935.
- Francis D Welch (born 1923) married Margery Slater in 1950.

Daisy's father, William Barnes (born 1855), was a farmer at Stacey Farm, Storrs, Bradfield, Wortley, Yorkshire. By 1901 he was a stone carter. He married Sarah

188 Western Road, Crookes, Sheffield, where the Welch family lived.

WAAF members of 939 (West Riding) Balloon Squadron RAAF hauling in.

James Welch being sent off by fellow workers of CH Lea Ltd as he departed for the VC Dinner at the House of Lords in November 1929 (Sheffield City Council).

James' and Daisy's grave in North Cemetery, Bournemouth (Memorials to Valour).

Ann née Wood (1855–96) in 1878. By 1901 William was living with his children at 24 Shepherd Road, Nether Hallam, Sheffield. In addition to Daisy they had six other children – Lucy Barnes 1879, Edith Barnes 1880, Frank Barnes 1883, Helen 'Ellen/Nellie' Barnes 1885, William Barnes 1888, May Barnes 1889 and Thomas Barnes 1896.

James was promoted corporal on 21st April 1917, but all accounts of his VC action, including the citation, refer to him as a lance corporal, so perhaps it was a backdated promotion. **Awarded the VC for his actions near Oppy, France on 29th April 1917, LG 27th June 1917.** He was evacuated to Queen Mary's Military Hospital, Whalley, Blackburn, Lancashire for treatment. The VC was presented by the King outside Buckingham Palace on 21st July 1917. Promoted sergeant August 1918 and was discharged unfit for further service on 11th April 1919. He was awarded Silver War Badge No. B268911 on 18th April.

He settled in Sheffield and worked as a property repairer and later for CH Lea's (Sheffield Cardboard Box Company). The family lived at 188 Western Road, Crookes. During the Second World War he served as a sergeant in B Flight, 939 (West Riding) Balloon Squadron RAAF in Sheffield and at one time led a small team travelling the city to pinpoint unexploded bombs for bomb disposal teams. He worked as a foreman at Joseph Pickering & Sons Ltd, cardboard box manufacturers, in the late 1940s and early 1950s.

James and Daisy moved to Bournemouth, Hampshire in 1960. He died at his home, 80 Pinehurst Park, West Moors, Bournemouth (transferred to Dorset 1974) on 28th June 1978 and was cremated at Bournemouth Crematorium. His ashes were interred in his wife's grave in North Cemetery, Bournemouth (Section F9–18). Coincidentally his wife also died on 28th June, but in 1968.

In addition to the VC he was awarded the 1914 Star with 'Mons' clasp, British War Medal 1914–20, Victory Medal 1914–19, Defence Medal, War Medal 1939–45, George VI Coronation Medal 1937, Elizabeth II Coronation Medal 1953 and Elizabeth II Jubilee Medal 1977. The VC was purchased for £9,000 by the Duke of Edinburgh's Regiment in 1979. It is held by The Rifles (Berkshire & Wiltshire) Museum, The Wardrobe, The Close, Salisbury. The Elizabeth II Jubilee Medal 1977 was not with the medal group when presented to the Museum.

24866 SERGEANT ALBERT WHITE
2nd Battalion, The South Wales Borderers

Albert White was born on 1st December 1892 at 62 Teulon Street, Kirkdale, Liverpool, Lancashire. His father, Thomas White (c.1862–1922) was born in Dundee, Forfarshire. He moved to Liverpool c.1881 and lived in lodgings at 14 Lockhart Street. By 1891 he was a railway porter and may also have worked for the Leyland Line shipping company.

He married Elizabeth 'Eliza' Ann née Falls (1861–1909) on 26th March 1883 at St Nicholas Church, Liverpool. She was a domestic servant at the home of Thomas Dodd, 25 Upper Pitt Street, Liverpool in 1881. In 1891 the family was living at 23 Tillard Street, Kirkdale and by 1901 had moved to 124 Arlington Street, Kirkdale. Albert had six siblings:

St Nicholas Church, Liverpool where Albert White's parents married on 26th March 1883.

• Thomas Henry White (born 1887) was a biscuit maker in 1901 and later a stable lad domestic. He enlisted in the Royal Navy as a boy on 6th August 1904 and was assigned to HMS *Pembroke*. He was described as 5′ 2″ tall with fresh complexion, grey eyes and brown hair. He served on a number of ships and shore establishments – HMS *Northampton* 7th October, HMS *Calliope* 17th November, HMS *Hawke* 12th January 1905, HMS *Victory* 1st May. He signed on as a man on 24th May 1905 for twelve years, by when he had grown to 5′ 3½″. Other ships followed – HMS *Revenge* 1st September 1905, HMS *Victory* 17th February 1906, HMS *Barmouth* 21st April, HMS *Victory* 1st June 1909, HMS *Fisgard* 6th July, HMS *St Vincent* 3rd May 1910 (he spent seven days in the cells on four occasions), HMS *Victory* 28th May 1912, HMS *Duke of Wellington* 7th August, HMS *Victory* 20th November 1914, HMS *Dido* 26th January 1915, HMS *Victory* 30th May, HMS *Alert* 4th September, HMS *Dalhousie* 22nd May 1916, HMS *Victory* 29th May, HMS *Victorious* 2nd December, HMS *Colleen* 1st February 1917, HMS *Gibraltar* 25th April 1918 and HMS *Haslar* 1st December. He was demobilised to the Reserve as a leading stoker on 28th March 1919, but served on HMS *Victory* again 9th April–4th June 1921. Thomas married Agnes Reid (registered as Reade) in 1913 and they had at least one child – Thomas Henry White in 1914.

- Robert James White (born 1887) enlisted as a boy in the Royal Navy on 25th September 1905 (229688). He was described as 5' 1¾" tall, with brown hair, grey eyes and fresh complexion. He served on HMS *Emerald, Impregnable, St George, Vivid* and *Europa*. By the time he transferred to man service he had grown to 5' 5". He served on HMS *Implacable, Vivid, Majestic, Hawke, Snipe, Astraea, Charybdis, Blake, Defiance, Belerophon* and *Lion*. He transferred to the Royal Naval Reserve on 10th June 1921.
- Elias White (born 1889) married Agnes Jones in 1911.
- Jessie Ellen M White (1898– c.1965) was living at 58 Lamb Street, Liverpool in 1918. She married Edward McArdle in 1922 and they had four children – Edward A McArdle 1923, Patricia McArdle 1925, Anthony McArdle 1928 and Joan McArdle 1934.
- Florence White (born 1902).
- Edward White (1903–40) served as 3763878 Corporal E White in 1/9th Manchester and was killed in action on 27th May 1940 near Poperinge, Belgium. He is buried in Dozinghem Military Cemetery (XVII B 5).

HMS *Northampton*, launched in December 1876, was flagship of the North America and West Indies Station until put into reserve in 1886. She became a boys' training ship in 1894 and was broken up in 1905. Albert's brother, Thomas, was a boy trainee on her in 1904.

HMS *Implacable*, a Formidable Class battleship, was commissioned in September 1901 and served with the Mediterranean Fleet until 1908, then the Channel and Atlantic Fleets. In 1912 she joined the Home Fleet and on the outbreak of war returned to the Channel Fleet. She supported the landings at Cape Helles, Gallipoli on 25th April 1915 and served mainly in the Mediterranean until June 1917, when she returned to Britain. She was sold for scrap in 1921. Albert's brother, Robert, was serving on her in 1910.

Albert's paternal grandfather, John White a shipwright, died before 1894. His maternal grandfather, Elias/Eleas Falls (died 1879), was a ship's steward. He married Ellen née Hewitt (born c.1842) in 1858 at Liverpool. She was born in Ireland and was living with her parents at Stockport, Cheshire in 1851. She was living with her mother at 95 Frederick Street, Liverpool in 1861 and by 1881 had moved to 9 Bailey Street, Liverpool. In addition to Eliza they had four other children – Mary Ellen

Falls 1859, Elias Falls c.1871, Robert Falls c.1875 and Emily Falls 1875.

Albert was educated at Everton Terrace Industrial School, Liverpool, which catered for troublesome pupils. Albert was a high-spirited lad and one of the tough nuts on his street. He was employed as a merchant seaman, working as a trimmer aboard the White Star liner SS *Laurentic* in 1910. He was living in Haddock Street, Liverpool in 1914.

Albert enlisted in 3rd South Lancashire on 25th July 1910 (1099), giving his date of birth as 25th July 1892 and occupation as ship scaler. He was described as 5′ 2½″ tall, weighing 124 lbs, with hazel eyes, fresh complexion, brown hair and his religious denomination was Church of England. His service was short lived as he deserted from the Depot at Warrington, Lancashire on 6th October. He enlisted in the RAMC (43785) on 23rd October 1914 and transferred to 2nd South Wales Borderers on 1st June 1915. He served with the Mediterranean Expeditionary Force from 30th June and was at Gallipoli from 21st July, including Suvla in August. He returned to Egypt on 11th January and moved to France on 17th March. Promoted sergeant 2nd July 1916. He was offered a commission and returned to Britain on 10th January 1917 for training, but withdrew because he could not afford the expense due to supporting his younger siblings Jessie, Edward and Florence from his military wage. He returned to France on 17th April 1917.

Awarded the VC for his actions at Monchy-le-Preux, France on 19th May 1917, LG 27th June 1917. He was killed during his VC action

SS *Laurentic* (14,900 tons) started life with the Dominion Line in 1908 as SS *Alberta*, but changed name when taken over by the White Star Line in 1909. Her first voyage was between Liverpool and Quebec, commencing on 29th April 1909. When the murderer Dr Hawley Harvey Crippen escaped from Britain on SS *Montrose* he was recognised by the Captain, who radioed back his suspicions. Chief Inspector Walter Dew of the Metropolitan Police boarded the faster SS *Laurentic* and reached Canada ahead of Crippen to effect his arrest on 31st July 1910 and brought him back to Britain for trial and subsequent hanging. She was in Montréal when war broke out and was immediately commissioned as a troop ship for the CEF and in 1915 was converted into an armed merchant cruiser. *Laurentic* was sunk by two U-boat laid mines off Ireland on 25th January 1917; 354 passengers and crew were lost. The ship was carrying 43 tons of gold (valued in 2014 at £380M). All but 1% of this was recovered by RN divers between 1917 and 1924.

The wide expanse of Suvla Bay from Walker's Ridge at ANZAC.

and is commemorated on the Arras Memorial. As he never married the VC was presented to his father by the King outside Buckingham Palace on 21st July 1917. He is commemorated in a number of other places:

Albert White's name on the Arras Memorial.

- Memorial panel to South Wales Borderers VCs in Harvard Chapel, Brecon Cathedral, Powys.
- A memorial to Captain Noel Chavasse VC & Bar MC was unveiled in Abercromby Square, Liverpool in July 2008, opposite No.19, where the Chavasse family lived and close to No.13, where Ernest Alexander VC's father lived. The names of fifteen other VCs associated with Liverpool are also inscribed on the memorial, including Albert White.
- Memorial Roll of Honour in the Hall of Remembrance at Liverpool Town Hall.
- Victoria Cross Memorial, Liverpool Town Hall.
- Victoria Cross Honours Board, South Wales Borderers Museum, Brecon, Powys.

The memorial to Captain Noel Chavasse VC & Bar MC in Abercromby Square, Liverpool, which also commemorates fifteen other VCs associated with Liverpool, including Albert White.

In addition to the VC he was awarded the 1914–15 Star, British War Medal 1914–20 and Victory Medal 1914–19. The VC is held privately.

2902 SERGEANT JOHN WOODS WHITTLE
12th Australian Infantry Battalion AIF

John, or Jack as he was generally known, Whittle was born on 3rd August 1882 at Huon Island, Port Cygnet District, near Gordon, Tasmania. His father, Henry William Whittle (c.1850–1902), was a labourer. His mother, Catherine Theresa née Sullivan (1857–1918), married Henry on 4th February 1878 at Brighton, Tasmania.

She was living at 103 Harrington Street, Hobart at the time of her death on 23rd November 1918. Jack had nine siblings:

- Albert William Whittle (1879–1915) married Alice Maud Scott (1881–1977) in 1912.
- Mary Violet Whittle (born 1880) married Ronald Campbell Swinton (born 1885) in 1907 and they had a daughter, Doris Kathleen Swinton in 1910.
- Arthur Ernest Whittle (born 1881).
- Esther May Whittle (born 1884).
- Herbert Willisy/Willessie Whittle (1885–86).
- Michael Joseph Whittle (1890–1957) married Olive Irene Mary Harrison (1892–1958) and they had a child.
- George Henry Whittle (born 1891) was a wharf labourer before enlisting in 12th Battalion AIF on 17th August 1914 at Brighton, Tasmania (900439). He was promoted corporal and returned to Australia on 31st March 1919.
- Francis Leslie Whittle (1893–c.2002).
- Thomas Clyde Whittle (1897–c.1976) served as a gunner in 36th Battery, Royal Australian Garrison Artillery AIF from 14th July 1915 (2735) and returned

Davey Street, Hobart, with Harrington Street running off to the left (Henry Hall Baily).

to Australia on 23rd July 1919. He married Olga 'Irene' Esta Maggie Franklin (née Parker) (1910–54). Olga was previously married to Stanley Eyiens Frederick Franklin, with whom she had three children – Lucy May Franklin 1927, Claude Eyiens Franklin 1929 and Charles Thomas Franklin c.1930. The marriage ended in divorce. Thomas and Olga had four children including Yvonne Olga Whittle (1934–2005), who married as Gilbert.

Jack served for three and a half years with the Senior Cadets. He enlisted for service in South Africa and embarked with 4th (2nd Tasmanian Imperial Bushmen) Contingent from Hobart aboard SS *Chicago* on 27th March 1901 (347). He disembarked at Port Elizabeth, South Africa on 24th April and took part in operations in Cape Colony. He embarked at Durban aboard SS *Manila* on 22nd May 1902, disembarked at Hobart, Tasmania on 25th June and was discharged on 30th June. Soon afterwards he enlisted in the Royal Navy as a stoker for five years on the Australia Station, serving aboard HMS *Challenger* and HMS *Pioneer*. He then served in the Australian Permanent Military Forces in the Australian Army Service Corps, 31st Battery Royal Australian Artillery and the Tasmanian Rifle Regiment.

HMS *Challenger*, a second-class protected cruiser, built at Chatham and launched in May 1902. She was commissioned in May 1904 and served on the Australia Station until going into reserve in October 1912. During the First World War, she was in the Ninth Cruiser Squadron off West Africa before moving to East Africa. She was scrapped in 1920.

HMS *Pioneer* (2,200 tons) was a third-class protected Pelorus Class cruiser with a top speed of 19.5 knots. She was armed with 8 x 4″ guns, 8 x 3 Pdr guns, two field guns, three Maxims and 2 x 14″ torpedo tubes. *Pioneer* was laid down at Chatham in 1897, launched in June 1899 and commissioned in July 1900. She was on the Mediterranean Station until 1904. In September 1905, she became a drill ship with the Australian Squadron and joined the Royal Australian Navy on 1st March 1913. On 16th August 1914 she captured the German merchant ship *Neumunster* and ten days later captured the liner *Thuringen*. In December, she was assigned to the blockade of German East Africa and helped contain the German cruiser *Königsberg* in the Rufiji River. On 30th July 1916 she fired 100 x 4″ shells during the bombardment of Dar-es-Salaam, but in August returned to Australia and was paid off. Despite being obsolete, she probably saw more action than any other Australian ship in the First World War. She was used as an accommodation vessel until 1922. The hulk was sold in 1926 and *Pioneer* was scuttled off Sydney Heads in February 1931. She is seen here during a refit at Simonstown, South Africa.

Jack Whittle married Emily Margaret Roland on 23rd July 1909 at the Archbishop's House, Hobart, Tasmania. They lived at 255 Macquarie Street, Hobart before moving to 29 Forsyth Street, Glebe, Sydney, New South Wales c.1929. Jack and Emily had two sons and three daughters, including Ivan Ernest Whittle (30th April 1923–7th September 1943). Ivan was a process worker when he enlisted in 2/33rd Battalion (NX97110). He was killed with many others when a Liberator aircraft crashed into the Battalion marshalling area near Port Moresby, New Guinea (Port Moresby (Bomana) War Cemetery – B2 A 26).

Jack enlisted in the Australian Imperial Force at Claremont, Tasmania on 6th August 1915 (2902) from 13th Remount Depot. He was described as 5′ 8½″ tall, weighing 182 lbs, with dark complexion, brown eyes, black hair and his religious denomination was Roman Catholic. He was posted to Claremont as acting corporal and embarked with 26th Battalion, 6th Reinforcement Group at Brisbane, Queensland on 21st October aboard HMAT A48 *Seang Bee*. He transferred to HMAT A38 *Ulysees* departing Melbourne, Victoria on 27th October. Having disembarked at Alexandria, Egypt he moved to Heliopolis and was admitted to 1st

Troops training at Claremont.

Macquarie Street, Hobart where Jack and Emily Whittle lived.

Australian General Hospital there 14th–17th January 1916. He was posted to 12th Battalion on 1st March, initially reverting to the ranks, but was promoted corporal on 14th March and lance sergeant on 13th April. While he was abroad, Emily's address was c/o A Roland, Rosebank, Middleton Channel, Tasmania.

The Battalion embarked at Alexandria on 29th March and disembarked at Marseilles on 5th April. He received a gunshot wound to his right arm on 21st June and was admitted to 3rd Australian Field Ambulance, then transferred immediately to 1st Australian Casualty Clearing Station and then to a General Hospital at Camiers on 22nd June. He was evacuated to England from Calais aboard HMHS *Stad Antwerpen* on 23rd June for treatment at 1st Eastern General Hospital, Cambridge. On 30th June, he was transferred to 1st Australian Auxiliary Hospital, Harefield Park, Middlesex and was discharged to No.1 Command Depot, Perham Down, Wiltshire on 4th August. Jack embarked at Southampton for France on 21st August. Having returned to 12th Battalion on 16th September, he was

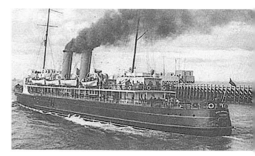

Stad Antwerpen, a 1,384 tons passenger ship built in 1913 by Societe Cockerill, Hoboken, Belgium, was owned by the Belgium government. She was used to transport wounded across the Channel during the war and returned to normal service afterwards until being broken up in 1934. In the picture she is leaving Ostende.

No.1 General Hospital occupied most of the large buildings in Étretat, including La Villa Orphée, the former summer home of the composer Jacques Offenbach.

promoted sergeant on 14th October. Jack reported sick with laryngitis on 30th November and was treated successively at 3rd Australian Field Ambulance, New Zealand Stationary Hospital at Amiens, then by Ambulance Train No.24 on 1st December to No.1 General Hospital at Étretat until discharged to duty on 10th December.

Awarded the DCM for his actions on 27th February 1917, during the German withdrawal to the Hindenburg Line when A Company attacked Le Barque and Ligny-Thilloy at dawn – on the left flank Whittle bombed an enemy machine gun post, forcing the Germans to flee, LG 26th April 1917. Awarded the VC for his actions at Boursies on 8th–9th April 1917 and Lagnicourt on 15th April 1917, LG 8th June 1917.

Jack reported sick with psoriasis on 20th April and was admitted to 3rd Australian Field Ambulance, transferring to 56th Casualty Clearing Station next day until discharged to duty on 23rd April. However, the problem persisted and he was evacuated to 3rd Training Battalion in England on 6th May and admitted to Fargo Military Hospital, Larkhill, Wiltshire on 18th May. He was discharged to duty on 24th May, but was re admitted to Fargo Military Hospital with the same complaint on 3rd August until discharged to duty on 18th August. During this period he was released so the VC and DCM could be presented by the King at Buckingham Palace on 21st July.

Jack returned to France on 26th August. He was tried by Field General Court Martial at Le Havre on 1st October for drunkenness and conduct to the prejudice of good order and military discipline on 27th September; while the CO was addressing a parade, he called out in a loud voice, *but we are good soldiers though*. He was reduced to corporal, spent four days in detention and rejoined his unit in Belgium on 8th October. The sentence was remitted by GOC Lines of Communication Area on 15th October.

Jack received a shrapnel wound to a finger on 19th March 1918 and was admitted to 1st Australian Field Ambulance and then 2nd Australian Casualty Clearing Station the following day. He was moved to 53rd General Hospital at Wimereux and discharged to No.1 Convalescent Depot on 27th March, rejoining his unit on 11th April. The same day, he mutilated his pay book, for which he was reprimanded on 30th April. On 9th June, he was posted to Second Army Central School until 13th July. He was wounded again on 25th July with shrapnel to the right elbow and was admitted to 3rd Australian Field Ambulance next day and transferred to 1st Australian Casualty Clearing Station before moving almost immediately to a general hospital. He was evacuated to England on 31st July and, according to his service record, was admitted to the Central Military Hospital, Eastbourne, Sussex. However, no trace of a military hospital within Eastbourne can be found, although Summerdown Camp Military Convalescent Hospital was nearby. He transferred to 3rd Australian Auxiliary Hospital, Dartford, Kent on 14th August.

On 24th August Jack embarked aboard HMAT D21 *Medic* with eight other Australian VCs and disembarked at Melbourne, Victoria on 11th October to assist with recruiting. Jack was discharged in Tasmania on 15th December 1918. It is understood that he re-enlisted for a short period in 1930 in 4th Battalion (Australian Rifles).

Tooth's Brewery in Sydney, where Jack was employed for a period.

Jack struggled to find work and in 1932 made a desperate plea, *I have been trying to struggle on for some time, but the children are badly in need of boots and clothing for the winter, and I cannot get any work*. Within a month, he was employed as an inspector by the Western Assurance Company and was later given other jobs, including at Tooth's Brewery in Sydney.

As with other VCs, Jack was in demand to attend key events. He was at the Anzac commemoration service on 25th April 1927 at the Exhibition Building, Melbourne, Victoria in the presence of The Duke of York (later King George VI) and took part in the march past with twenty-five other VCs. An Anzac Dinner was held two nights before, hosted by Lieutenant General Sir John Monash GCMG KCB VD, and attended by twenty-three VCs, including Jack Whittle. For an unknown reason the Duke of York was not invited. On 8th August 1928 he was one of eight VCs who attended the 1st AIF Reunion Dinner at Sydney Town Hall to celebrate the 10th Anniversary of the commencement of 'The Big Push'. In November 1929 he attended a luncheon at Government House with the Governor General of Australia, Sir Dudley de Chair, together with thirteen other VCs.

On 7th February 1934 Jack was walking across University Park, Sydney when a small boy yelled that his three-year old brother had fallen into the lake. Jack dived in, found the boy in the weeds, brought him to the bank and applied artificial respiration for half an hour. The boy was revived and taken to hospital. Jack went home in a taxi without leaving his name, but was traced by the Royal Life Saving Society and was awarded its Certificate of Merit. He was ill for a fortnight from the effects of swallowing the foul water in the lake. A few weeks later, on 13th March, he became a Freemason, being Initiated into Saint Andrew Lodge, Sydney (No.7). On 26th January 1945, he was examining a service rifle on the verandah of his home, when it went off, shattering his left index finger. He was found unconscious and taken to the Royal Prince Alfred Hospital.

Jack Whittle died of a cerebral haemorrhage at his home at 27 Avenue Road, Glebe, Sydney on 2nd March 1946 and is buried in the Roman Catholic Section, Rookwood Cemetery, Sydney (Grave 63). He is also commemorated in a number of other places:

- Whittle Street, Canberra, Australian Capital Territory.
- Whittle Lane, Wodonga, Victoria on White Box Rise Estate built on the former Bandiana Army Camp.
- Whittle Street, Crib Point, Melbourne, Victoria.
- Victoria Cross Memorial, Campbell, Canberra, dedicated on 24th July 2000.
- Victoria Cross Memorial, Hobart Cenotaph, Tasmania, dedicated on 11th May 2003.
- Victoria Cross Memorial, Queen Victoria Building, George Street, Sydney, New South Wales.
- Named on one of eleven plaques honouring 175 men from overseas awarded the VC for the Great War. The plaques were unveiled by the Senior Minister of State at the Foreign & Commonwealth Office and Minister for Faith and Communities, Baroness Warsi, at a reception at Lancaster House, London on 26th June 2014 attended by the Duke of Kent and relatives of the VC recipients. The Australian plaque is at the Australian War Memorial.
- The Secretary of State for Communities and Local Government, Eric Pickles MP, announced that Victoria Cross recipients from the Great War would have commemorative paving stones laid in their birthplace as a lasting legacy of local heroes within communities. The stones would be laid on or close to the 100th anniversary of their VC actions. For the 145 VCs born in Australia, Belgium, Canada, China, Denmark, Egypt, France, Germany, India, Iraq, Japan, Nepal, Netherlands, New Zealand, Pakistan, South Africa, Sri Lanka, Ukraine and United States of America, individual commemorative stones were unveiled at the National Memorial Arboretum, Alrewas, Staffordshire by Prime Minister David Cameron MP and Sergeant Johnson Beharry VC on 5th March 2015.
- Plaque on Wall 7, Panel E at New South Wales Garden of Remembrance, Lidcombe.

In addition to the VC and DCM, he was awarded the Queen's South Africa Medal 1899–1902 (clasps 'Cape Colony', 'Orange Free State', 'South Africa 1901' & 'South Africa 1902'), 1914–15 Star, British War Medal 1914–20, Victory Medal 1914–19, George V Jubilee Medal 1935 and George VI Coronation Medal 1937. The medals were owned by John Edwards of Port Macquarie, New South Wales until he died in June 2006. On 20th November 2014, they were sold at auction (Lot 107) to a private bidder at a Noble Numismatics

The King George V Silver Jubilee Medal commemorated the 25th anniversary of the King's coronation. 85,235 medals were issued, a proportion to each Commonwealth country, including 6,500 to Australia. The medals were awarded at the discretion of the local government, but in general went to members of the Royal Family and household, ministers, government and local government officials and members of the armed forces.

sale at Dixson Room, State Library of New South Wales, Macquarie Street, Sydney for the hammer price of A$500,000 (£274,240). They are held in the Hall of Valour, Australian War Memorial, Treloar Crescent, Campbell, Australian Capital Territory.

SECOND LIEUTENANT FREDERICK YOUENS
13th Battalion, The Durham Light Infantry

Frederick Youens was born at The Marsh, High Wycombe, Buckinghamshire on 14th August 1892. His father, Vincent Youens (1868–1952), was a basket maker and later a hotel porter, living at Belgrave, 64 Desborough Park Road, High Wycombe. His mother, Lizzie née Russell (1868–1958), had a son, Vincent John V Russell (1887–1966), who later changed his surname to Youens. Vincent Youens and Lizzie Russell married on 23rd September 1888 at High Wycombe parish church and they lived initially on London Road, Chepping Wycombe. By 1901 they were living at 17 Ship Street, High Wycombe and at 11 Gordon Road, High Wycombe by 1911. Vincent enlisted in A Company, 1/4th Royal West Kent Regiment on 18th October 1914 at Tunbridge Wells, Kent (200928). He was described as 5′ 7″ tall, with brown eyes, brown hair and claimed his age was thirty-seven years and seven months. He was posted to Jubbulpore, India where a congenital deformity of the right foot (overlapping and hammer toes) was discovered and he also developed dermatitis. He was admitted to hospital on 1st December 1915 for ten days but refused an operation. A medical board on 26th December found that due to his age he was liable to break down during the summer and recommended he return to Britain. A medical board at Tunbridge Wells on 1st August 1917 recommended his discharge which occurred on 5th September, no longer physically fit for war service. His place of residence was the Angel Inn, Pauls Row, High Wycombe, but Lizzie was living at 59 Salisbury Road, Chatham, Kent and later at 42 Luton Road, Chatham. When Frederick enlisted in September 1914 he was unable to give an address for his father. After Frederick's death in July 1917, his mother did not include his father or either brother on a list of near relatives. Frederick had six siblings:

Wycombe Marsh where Frederick Youens was born.

- William John Youens (1888–1971).
- Albert Youens (1890–1958) was a basket maker in 1911. It is understood he married Mabel Merritt (1907–31) in 1929 and had a son, Glynn A Youens later that year.
- Dorothy Youens (born 1895). It is understood she married Harry Hosking in 1918.
- Edith May Youens (born 1897) married Henry W Stone in 1914.
- Ethel Eva Youens (born 1899) married Harold R Green in 1920 and they had a daughter, Peggy J Green in 1921.
- Florence Annie Youens (born 1901) married Herbert B Moyes (born Herbert Frederick B Moyes in 1901) in 1928. They had two children – Jose B Moyes 1928 and Betty E Moyes 1933. Herbert died in 1958.

High Wycombe parish church (All Saints) where Frederick's parents, Vincent and Lizzie, were married on 23rd September 1888.

Frederick's paternal grandfather, John Youens (1837–1912), was a basket manufacturer. He married Dinah née Taylor (1838–1911) at High Wycombe, Buckinghamshire in 1854. They were living at 7 Laura Place, High Wycombe in 1871 and at 3 Church Square, High Wycombe by 1881. In addition to Vincent they had ten other children:

- William Youens (1855–1924) married Eliza Amelia Sitch (1858–1947) in 1876 at Pembroke. They were living at 55 Lamcote Road, Nottingham in 1881 and at 3 Stretton Road, Nottingham in 1891. They had nine children – Bertie Youens 1880, John George Youens 1882, Frances Katherine Youens 1884, Leah Youens 1887, Frederick Thomas Youens 1889, William Youens 1890, Clara Youens 1893, Christina Youens 1896 and Winifred Youens 1901.
- Emma Youens (born 1858) married William Johnson (born 1858) in 1876. They were living at St Stephen's Villas, Clewer, Berkshire in 1881, at 91 West End Road, High Wycombe by 1891 and at Desborough Road, High Wycombe by 1901. They had two children – William Alexander Johnson 1878 and Florence Clara Johnson 1881.

Pauls Row, High Wycombe with the Angel Inn on the left. This was Vincent's place of residence when he was discharged from the Army on 5th September 1917.

- Michael Youens (born 1860) was a basket maker. He married Alice Ugler (1861–1925) in 1879. They were living at 10 Georges Terrace, High Wycombe in 1881, at Totteridge Road, High Wycombe by 1891 and at Penington Road, High Wycombe by 1901. They had seven children – Morna Youens 1880, Olivette Youens 1882, John Youens 1883, Michael Youens 1886, Vincent Youens 1888, Bertram Youens 1890 and Gertrude Youens 1892.
- Clara Youens (1863–1939) married John Hart Grimsdale (1861–1949), a carpenter, in 1884. They were living at 9 Prospect Cottages in 1891, at 21 Putney Bridge Road in 1901 and at 3 Southfield Terrace, Merton Road in 1911, all addresses in Wandsworth. They had six children – Ethel Elizabeth Grimsdale 1884, Clara Hart Grimsdale 1886, John Grimsdale 1888, Arthur Grimsdale 1890, Gertrude May Grimsdale 1895 and Sidney Hart Grimsdale 1902.
- Florence Mary Youens (born 1865) married Henry Richards (born 1868), a coachbuilder, in 1890. She was a boarding house keeper at Margate, Kent in 1911, living with her father and sister Christine. They had two children including, Florence Eleanor Richards 1893.
- Fanny Youens (born 1870) married Thomas Edward Gill (born 1869), a boat-builder, in 1893. They were living at 14 The Groves, Chester, Cheshire in 1901 and at Aikmans Gardens, Chester in 1911. By 1911 Thomas was the manager of a boat company and Fanny was the manageress. They had two sons – Edward Stanchell Gill 1894 and Harry Youens Gill 1905.
- Adelina Youens (1872–1936) married Charles Challis (1869–1945), a coachman, in 1898. They were living at 43 Linver Road, Fulham, London in 1901. They had a daughter – Muriel Frances K Challis in 1900.
- Frederick Youens (1874–1946), a basket maker, married Annie Luttman/Lutman (1874–1965) in 1896. They were living at 23 Bridge Street, High Wycombe in 1901. They had a son, Frederick Gilbert Youens in 1897.
- Christine Youens (1875–1964) was living with her father and sister Florence in 1911. She married Sidney Robert Probets (1883–1950) in 1913. They had a son, Dennis S Probets in 1916.
- Leah Youens (1878–85).

His maternal grandfather, John Russell (1842–1936) worked in a paper mill and lived at The Marsh, Chepping Wycombe. He married Elizabeth née Jones (c.1841–1935) in 1861. In addition to Lizzie they had another eight children:

- Susanna Russell (born 1862) was a rag porter and had a daughter, Rosetta Green Russell in 1879. She married Joseph Green (born 1863), a band sawyer, in 1883, who may have been Rosetta's natural father. They were living at Chepping Wycombe in 1891. They had two daughters – Edith May Green 1886 and Elizabeth Ada Green 1888.
- Sarah Russell (1863–73).

- Annie Russell (born 1866).
- William Russell (born 1870) was a cutter man in a paper mill in 1891. He married Susan Elizabeth Main (1872–1959) in 1892. By 1911 he was a works foreman and they were living at Basildon, near Higham, Kent. They had five children – Gilbert Main Russell 1893, William Haddon Russell 1895, Vera Joyce Queenie Russell 1900, Enid Doris Russell 1904 and Raymond Hector Russell 1905.
- John Russell (born 1873) was a chair polisher in 1891.
- Charles Albert Russell (born 1877), known as Albert, was an errand boy in a paper mill in 1891. He married Amelia Fordham (born 1879) in 1899. By 1901 he was a wheelwright and they were living at Victoria Street, High Wycombe. They had a daughter, Amelia Elizabeth C Russell in 1899.
- Flora Russell (1879–1959) married William Grace (1878–1963) in 1903. He was a foreman machinist in a chair factory in 1911. They were living at Walmer, West Wycombe Road, High Wycombe in 1911. They had three children – Frederick William Grace 1905, John H Grace 1913 and Norman R Grace 1919.
- Sarah Russell (born 1874). It is understood she married George Brown (born 1876) in 1899. George was a labourer for a chair manufacturer and they were living at 1 Croom Cottages, Upper Marsh, High Wycombe in 1911. This couple had five children – Leslie George Brown 1900, Ronald Brown 1901, Stanley Brown 1906, Ruby Ethel Brown 1908 and Marjorie E Brown 1916. A Sarah Brown of the correct age died in 1960.

Frederick was educated at the National and Royal Grammar Schools in High Wycombe. He was at the Grammar School 1906–11 after winning a scholarship. There he was a prominent member of the school debating society, the Officer Training Corps and took part in amateur dramatics. He was noted for his performance as Mrs Malaprop in Richard Brinsley Sheridan's play, *The Rivals*, in 1910. Frederick was also a member of the Medway Swimming Club. He passed the Junior and Senior Oxford Locals with honours and the London Matriculation in the first division in 1910. In 1912 he was an assistant schoolmaster at St Peter's School, Rochester and before enlisting he was a teacher at Chalvey Junior School, Slough, Berkshire. He gained a scholarship to go to Oxford.

   He enlisted as a private in the Royal Army Medical Corps (34900) at Chatham on 5th September 1914 and joined E Company, RAMC School of Instruction at Aldershot next day. He was described as 5′ 5½″ tall, weighing 114 lbs with fresh complexion, brown eyes, brown hair and his religious denomination was Church of England. He transferred to 7th East Surrey on 12th May 1915 (G7/9019). He went to France on 1st June and received a gunshot wound to the right arm whilst attending to the wounded at Loos on 13th October. He was treated at 23rd General Hospital, Étaples and was evacuated to England on HMHS *Dieppe* on 22nd/23rd October. It took him a year to recover, during which he applied for a commission in the East Surrey Regiment on 30th May 1916. At that time he was 5′ 7″ tall and weighed 139 lbs. He served with 3rd (Reserve) Battalion, East Surrey from 28th July 1916, based at Kingston-on-Thames, Dover and Hertford. Promoted lance corporal 1st August and acting corporal 4th October. He joined No.9 Officer Cadet Battalion at Gailes on 5th October, was commissioned in 13th Durham Light Infantry on 24th January 1917 and went directly to France.

Awarded the VC for his actions near Hill 60, near Ypres, Belgium on 7th July 1917, LG 2nd August 1917. As a result of the wounds he sustained during his VC action, he died at 70th Field Ambulance on 7th July 1917, and is buried in Railway Dugouts Burial Ground (Transport Farm), Zillebeke, Belgium (I O 3). He is commemorated in a number of other places:

• Plaque and portrait at Royal Grammar School, High Wycombe.
• Fraser Youens House, Royal Grammar School, High Wycombe, named after the school's two VCs, Ian Edward Fraser and Frederick Youens, opened as a boarding house on 10th October 1999.
• Youens Road, High Wycombe.
• Memorial plaque at All Saints Church High Wycombe dedicated by the Bishop of Buckingham, Dr Robert Hay, on 13 December 1947.
• Named on the war memorial in St Andrew's Church, High Wycombe. The memorial was moved to a new St Andrew's Church on Hatters Lane when the Gordon Road church was demolished about 1960.
• Named on the war memorial outside High Wycombe Hospital.
• Named on the war memorial in St Peter's Churchyard, Chalvey, Slough, Berkshire. The memorial was unveiled by Major General Carteret Carey, Acting Governor of

Frederick's grave in Railway Dugouts Burial Ground (Transport Farm) as it appears today and with the original wooden grave marker.

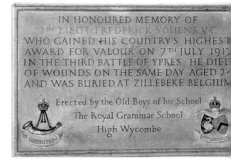

Frederick's memorial plaque in All Saints Chu... High Wycombe (Peter Underwood).

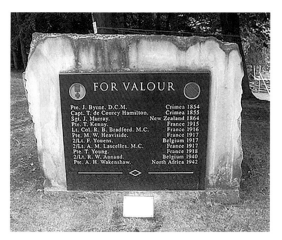

The commemorative stone honouring the eleven Durham Light Infantry soldiers awarded the VC in the grounds of the Durham Light Infantry Museum.

The war memorial in St Peter's Churchyard, Chalvey, Slough, close to where Frederick taught at the Junior School (Postcards from Slough).

Windsor Castle, and blessed by the Bishop of Buckingham, Dr Philip Eliot, on 28th June 1921.

• A commemorative stone honouring the eleven Durham Light Infantry soldiers awarded the VC was unveiled in the grounds of the Durham Light Infantry Museum on 8th September 2001 by Brigadier Robin MacGregor-Oakford MC. The stone was funded by the Durham Light Infantry veterans' group, 'The Faithful Inkerman Dinner Club'. The ceremony was attended by the Regiment's sole surviving VC holder, Captain Richard Annand.

In addition to the VC he was awarded the 1914–15 Star, British War Medal 1914–20 and Victory Medal 1914–19. As he never married, the VC was presented to his mother by the King at Buckingham Palace on 29th August 1917. The medals were sold at auction twice and were purchased for £4,900 by the Regiment. The VC is held by the Durham Light Infantry Museum, Aykley Heads, Framwell Gate, Durham.

Sources

The following institutions, individuals and publications were consulted:

Regimental Museums

Royal Marines Museum, Southsea; Light Infantry Office (Yorkshire), Pontefract; RHQ The Argyll and Sutherland Highlanders, Stirling; The Royal Gloucestershire, Berkshire and Wiltshire Regiment Museum, Salisbury; Lancashire County and Regimental Museum, Preston; Household Cavalry Museum, Windsor; Royal Green Jackets Museum, Winchester; Honourable Artillery Company Archives, London; South Wales Borderers and Monmouthshire Regimental Museum, Brecon; Green Howards Museum, Richmond, Yorkshire; RHQ Queen's Lancashire Regiment, Preston; RHQ Prince of Wales's Own Regiment of Yorkshire, York; Border Regiment and Kings Own Royal Border Regiment Museum, Carlisle; Canadian War Museum, Ottawa; Royal Artillery Historical Trust.

Individuals

Doug and Richard Arman, Daphne Barker, Margaret Blunden, Major (Ret'd) R Booth, David Broadhead, PR Brooks, Nancy Brunt, Alick Burge, Elizabeth Chapman, Norah Cook, Alistair Crowle, John Crowle, Tom Dresser, John Fanning, Dennis Foster, Mike Gomersall, David Harvey, Derek Hunt, Alan Jordan, Sue Knight, Alasdair Macintyre, Robert Mansell, Peter Maufe, Tony and Pat Mills, Richard Milward, Andrew Mott, Robert Mott, Brian Palmer, Doris Palmer, Donald Palmer, Joan Palmer, Nora Pearce, Brandon Smith, David Snoxell, Wendy Sutherland, Vic Tambling, Alister Williams, Lt Col Les Wilson MBE.

Record Offices, Libraries and Local Museums

Buckinghamshire County Records and Local Studies Service; High Wycombe Reference Library.

Newspapers

Buckinghamshire Advertiser; High Wycombe Leader.

Schools and Universities

Bromsgrove School; Fettes College; Uppingham School.

Divisional Histories

The History of the Second Division 1914–18. E Wyrell. Nelson 1921. Two volumes.

A Short History of the 6th Division August 1914–March 1919. Editor Maj Gen TO Marden. Rees 1920.

The Eighth Division in War 1914–18. Lt Col J H Boraston and Capt CEO Bax. Medici Society 1926.

History of the 12th (Eastern) Division in the Great War 1914–18. Editor Maj Gen Sir AB Scott. Compiler PM Brumwell. Nisbet 1927.

The 18th Division in the Great War. Capt GHF Nichols. Blackwood 1922.

The 23rd Division 1914–19. Lt Col HR Sandilands. Blackwood 1925.

The 25th Division in France and Flanders. Lt Col M Kincaid-Smith. Harrison 1919.

The Story of the 29th Division – A Record of Gallant Deeds. Capt S Gillon. Nelson 1925.

The 33rd Division in France and Flanders 1915–19. Lt Col GS Hutchinson. Waterlow 1921.

The Thirty-Fourth Division 1915–19 – The Story of its Career from Ripon to the Rhine. Lt Col J Shakespear. Witherby 1921.

The History of the 40th Division. Lt Col FE Whitton. Gale & Polden 1926.

The History of the Fiftieth Division 1914–19. E Wyrell. Percy, Lund, Humphries 1939.

The Royal Naval Division. D Jerrold. Hutchinson 1923 (63rd Division).

Brigade Histories

History of the 50th Infantry Brigade 1914–19. Anon. Oxford University Press 1919.

The 54th Infantry Brigade 1914–18 – Some Records of Battle and Laughter in France. E R. Gale & Polden 1919.

Regimental/Unit Histories – in seniority order:

The Royal Marine Artillery 1804–1923, Volume II. E Fraser & LG Carr-Laughton. Royal United Services Institute 1930.

Britain's Sea Soldiers, A Record of the Royal Marines During the War 1914–19. Compiler Gen Sir HE Blumberg. Swiss 1927.

Short History of the Royal Dragoons. Anon. Gale & Polden 1954.

History of the Royal Dragoons 1661–1934. CT Atkinson. University Press.

The Royal Artillery War Commemoration Book. Anon. G Bell 1970.

History of the Royal Regiment of Artillery, Western Front, 1914–18. Gen Sir M Farndale. Dorset Press 1986.

ARTYVICS – The Victoria Cross and The Royal Regiment of Artillery. Marc J Sherriff. Witherbys, Aylesbury St, London.

Irish Heroes in the War, The Tyneside Irish Brigade. J Keating. Everett 1917.

The Royal Fusiliers in the Great War. HC O'Neill. Heinemann 1922.

A History of the 22nd Service Battalion Royal Fusiliers (Kensington). Editor Maj C Stone. Privately published 1923.

From Vimy Ridge to the Rhine, Letters of Christopher Stone. Edited by GD Sheffield and GIS Inglis. Crownwood Press 1989.

The East Yorkshire Regiment in the Great War 1914–19. E Wyrell. Harrison 1928.

This Righteous War. BS Barnes. Richard Netherwood 1990.

A Short Diary of the 11th (Service) Battalion of the East Yorkshire Regiment 1914–19. Some of Them. Goddard, Walker and Brown 1921.

The 16th Foot, A History of the Bedfordshire and Hertfordshire Regiment. Maj Gen Sir F Maurice. Constable 1931.

The Story of the Bedfordshire and Hertfordshire Regiment Volume II – 1914–58. Compiled by Lt Col TJ Barrow DSO, Maj VA French and J Seabrook Esq. Published privately 1986.

The Green Howards in the Great War 1914–19. Col H C Wylly. Butler & Tanner 1926.

The Green Howards – For Valour 1914–18. Anon. Published 1964.

The History of the Green Howards – 300 Years of Service. G Powell. Arms and Armour 1992.

The History of the South Wales Borderers 1914–18. CT Atkinson. Medici Society 1931.

History of the East Surrey Regiment, Volume II 1914–17 and Volume III 1917–19. Col HW Pearse & Brig Gen HS Sloman. Medici Society 1924.

The Border Regiment in the Great War. Col HC Wylly. Gale & Polden 1924.

Tried and Valiant, The History of the Border Regiment 1702–1959. D Sutherland. Leo Cooper 1972.

A History of the South Staffordshire Regiment 1705–1923. JP Jones. Whitehead Bros 1923.

History of the South Staffordshire Regiment. Col WL Vale. Gale & Polden 1969.

The History of the Seventh South Staffordshire Regiment. Editor Maj AH Ashcroft DSO. Boyle, Son & Watchurst 1919.

The South Lancashire Regiment. Col BR Mullaly. White Swan Press.

Ich Dien, The Prince of Wales's Volunteers (South Lancashire) 1914–34. Capt H Whalley-Kelly. Gale & Polden 1935.

Regimental War Tales 1741–1919, Told for the Soldiers of the Oxfordshire and Buckinghamshire Light Infantry. Lt Col AF Modder-Ferryman & Lt Col RB Crosse. Slatter & Rose 1942.

Oxfordshire and Buckinghamshire Light Infantry Chronicle 1916–17, Volume 26, 1st July 1916–30th June 1917. Compiler Lt Col AF Modder-Ferryman. Eyre & Spottiswoode.

The Story of the 2/4th Oxfordshire and Buckinghamshire Light Infantry. Capt GK Rose. Blackwell 1920.

Essex Units in the Great War 1914–19, Volume I, 1st Battalion The Essex Regiment and Volume VI Service Battalions The Essex Regiment. JW Burrows. John H Burrows 1923 and 1935.

The Royal Berkshire Regiment, Volume II 1914–18. FL Petre. Reading The Barracks 1935.

History of the King's Own Yorkshire Light Infantry in the Great War, Volume III 1914–18. Lt Col RC Bond. Percy Lund, Humphries 1930.

The King's Own Yorkshire Light Infantry, Register of Officers 1755–1945. CP Deedes.

Faithful, The Story of the Durham Light Infantry. SGP Ward. Nelson 1962.

The Durham Forces in the Field 1914–18, Volume II, The Service Battalions of the Durham Light Infantry. Capt W Miles. Cassell 1920.

Officers of the Durham Light Infantry 1758–1968 (Volume 1 – Regulars). M McGregor. Published privately 1989.

Seaforth Highlanders. Editor Col J Sym. Gale & Polden 1962.

Argyllshire Highlanders 1860–1960. Lt Col GI Malcolm. Halberd Press.

An Reisimeid Chataich, The 93rd Sutherland, Now 2nd Battalion The Argyll and Sutherland Highlanders (Princess Louise's) 1799–1927. Brig Gen AEJ Cavendish. Butler & Tanner 1928.

Fighting Highlanders – The History of the Argyll and Sutherland Highlanders. PJR Mileham. Arms and Armour Press 1993.

The History of the Prince of Wales's Leinster Regiment (Royal Canadians), Part II The Great War and the Disbandment of the Regiment. Editor Lt Col FE Whitton. Gale & Polden 1924.

Stand To – A Diary of the Trenches 1915–18. Capt FC Hitchcock. Hurst & Blackett 1937.

The History of the Rifle Brigade in the War 1914–18. Volume I, August 1914–December 1916. R Berkley. Rifle Brigade Club 1927.

As above. Volume II, January 1917–June 1919. WW Seymour. Rifle Brigade Club 1936.

As above. Appendix – List of Officers and Other Ranks of the Rifle Brigade awarded Decorations or MID for services during the Great War. Compiled by Lt Col TR Eastwood and Maj HG Parkyn. Rifle Brigade Club 1936.

Rifle Brigade Chronicles 1915–1920. Editor Col W Verner. John Bale 1916–1921.

A Rifle Brigade Register 1905–63, Part 1 – A Roll of Officers who have served in the Regiment. Compiled by Col WPS Curtis. Culverlands Press 1964.

Machine Guns, Their History and Tactical Employment (Being also a History of the Machine Gun Corps 1916–22). Lt Col GS Hutchinson. MacMillan 1938.

The Honourable Artillery Company in the Great War 1914–19. Editor Maj G Goold Walker. Seeley Service 1930.

In Adversity: Exploits of gallantry and awards to the RAF Regiment and its associated forces 1921–95. Sqn Ldr Nicholas G Tucker. Jade Publishing 1997.

They Dared Mightily. Lionel Wigmore, Jeff Williams & Anthony Staunton 1986.

Tales of Valour from The Royal New South Wales Regiment. Maj Gen GL Maitland 1992.

The Story of the Fifth Australian Division. Capt AD Ellis MC. Hodder & Stoughton 1920.

Canada in Flanders. Sir Max Aitken 1916.

The History of The 16th Battalion (The Canadian Scottish) Canadian Expeditionary Force in the Great War, 1914–1919. Lt Col HM Urquhart DSO MC ADC. Trustees & Regimental Committee of The 16th Battalion.

The New Zealand Division 1916–1919. A Popular History Based on Official Records. Col H Stewart CMG DSO MC. Whitcombe & Tombs Ltd, Auckland 1921.

General Works

A Bibliography of Regimental Histories of the British Army. Compiler AS White. Society for Army Historical Research 1965.
A Military Atlas of the First World War. A Banks & A Palmer. Purnell 1975.
The Times History of the Great War.
Topography of Armageddon, A British Trench Map Atlas of the Western Front 1914–18. P Chasseaud. Mapbooks 1991.
Before Endeavours Fade. REB Coombs. Battle of Britain Prints 1976.
British Regiments 1914–18. Brig EA James. Samson 1978.
Orange, Green and Khaki, The Story of the Irish Regiments in the Great War 1914–18. T Johnstone. 1992.
The Ypres Salient, A Guide to the Cemeteries and Memorials of the Salient. M Scott. Gliddon Books 1992.
Norfolk and Suffolk in the Great War. G Gliddon. Gliddon Books 1988.
Boom Ravine. Trevor Pidgeon. Leo Cooper 1998.

Biographical/Autobiographical

The Dictionary of National Biography 1901–85. Various Volumes. Oxford University Press.
The Cross of Sacrifice, Officers Who Died in the Service of the British, Indian and East African Regiments and Corps 1914–19. SD and DB Jarvis. Roberts Medals 1993.
Australian Dictionary of Biography.
Whitaker's Peerage, Baronetage, Knightage & Companionage 1915.
Our Heroes – Containing Photographs with Biographical Notes of Officers of Irish Regiments and of Irish Officers of British Regiments who have fallen or who have been mentioned for distinguished conduct from August 1914 to July 1916. Printed as supplements to Irish Life from 1914 to 1916.
The Bond of Sacrifice, A Biographical Record of all British Officers Who Fell in the Great War. Volume I Aug–Dec 1915, Volume II, Jan–Jun 1915. Editor Col LA Clutterbuck. Pulman 1916 and 1919.
The Roll of Honour Parts 1–5, A Biographical Record of Members of His Majesty's Naval and Military Forces who fell in the Great War 1914–18. Marquis de Ruvigny. Standard Art Book Co 1917–19.
Bloody Red Tabs: General Officer Casualties of the Great War 1914–1918. Frank Davies and Graham Maddocks. Leo Cooper 1995.
The Dictionary of Edwardian Biography – various volumes. Printed 1904–08, reprinted 1985–87 Peter Bell Edinburgh.
Mad Harry – Australia's Most Decorated Soldier. George Franki & Clyde Slatyer.
A Slice of Parish Life – A History of the Church of Our Lady and St Paulinus, Dewsbury, 1841–1971 (William Ormsby VC MM). Fr Nicholas Hird 2014.

Fire-Eater: the Memoirs of a VC. Alfred Pollard. 1932.
Lumsden, Frederick William (1871–1918), *Royal Marines Officer.* Donald F Bittner.
  Oxford University Press 2004–05.

Specific Works on the Victoria Cross

The Register of the Victoria Cross. This England 1981 and 1988.
The Story of the Victoria Cross 1856–1963. Brig Sir J Smyth. Frederick Muller 1963.
The Evolution of the Victoria Cross, A study in Administrative History. MJ Crook.
  Midas 1975.
The Victoria Cross and the George Cross. IWM 1970.
The Victoria Cross, The Empire's Roll of Valour. Lt Col R Stewart. Hutchinson 1928.
The Victoria Cross 1856–1920. Sir O'Moore Creagh and EM Humphris. Standard Art
  Book Company, London 1920.
Heart of a Dragon, VC's of Wales and the Welsh Regiments. W Alister Williams. Bridge
  Books 2006.
VC Locator. D Pillinger and A Staunton. Highland Press, Queanbeyan, New South
  Wales, Australia 1991.
Black Country VCs. B Harry. Black Country Society 1985.
The VC Roll of Honour. JW Bancroft. Aim High 1989.
A Bibliography of the Victoria Cross. W James McDonald. WJ Mcdonald, Nova Scotia
  1994.
Canon Lummis VC Files held in the National Army Museum, Chelsea.
Recipients of the Victoria Cross in the Care of the Commonwealth War Graves
  Commission. CWGC 1997.
Victoria Cross Heroes. Michael Ashcroft. Headline Review 2006.
Monuments to Courage. David Harvey. 1999.
Beyond the Five Points – Masonic Winners of The Victoria Cross and The George Cross.
  Phillip May GC, edited by Richard Cowley. Twin Pillars Books, Northamptonshire
  2001.
Our Bravest and Our Best: The Stories of Canada's Victoria Cross Winners. Arthur
  Bishop 1995.
A Breed Apart. Richard Leake. Great Northern Publishing 2008.
Beyond Their Duty – Heroes of the Green Howards. Roger Chapman. Green Howards
  Museum 2001.
VCs of the First World War: Arras & Messines 1917. Gerald Gliddon 1998.

Works on Other Honours and Awards

Distinguished Conduct Medal 1914–18, Citations of Recipients. London Stamp
  Exchange 1983.
Recipients of the Distinguished Conduct Medal 1914–1920. RW Walker.
The Distinguished Service Order 1886–1923 (in 2 volumes). Sir O'Moore Creagh and
  EM Humphris. JB Hayward 1978 (originally published 1924).

Official Publications and Sources

History of the Great War, Order of Battle of Divisions. Compiler Maj AF Becke. HMSO.

History of the Great War, Military Operations, France and Belgium. Compiler Brig Gen Sir JE Edmonds. Published by HMSO in 14 volumes, with 7 map volumes and 2 separate Appendices 1923–48.

Location of Hospitals and Casualty Clearing Stations, BEF 1914–19. Ministry of Pensions 1923.

List of British Officers taken Prisoner in the Various Theatres of War between August 1914 and November 1918. Compiled from Official Records by Messrs Cox & Co, Charing Cross, London 1919.

London Gazettes.

Census returns 1841–1911.

Officers and Soldiers Died in the Great War.

Service records from the Australian War Memorial.

Service records from the Library and Archives of Canada.

Service records from the New Zealand Government Archives.

Official History of Australia in the War of 1914–1918, Volume IV – The Australian Imperial Force in France, 1917. 11th Edition 1941.

Official History of the Canadian Army in the First World War – Canadian Expeditionary Force 1914–19. Col GWL Nicholson 1962.

National Archives

Unit War Diaries under WO 95.

Imperial Yeomanry Attestation Papers under WO 128/13.

Military maps under WO 297.

Medal Cards and Medal Rolls under WO 329, 372 and ADM 171.

Royal Navy service records in the Public Record Office under ADM 157, 159, 188 and 337.

Soldier's Service Records under WO 97, 363 and 364.

Army Officer's Records under WO 25, 76, 339 and 374.

RAF Officer's Records under Air 76.

Births, Marriages and Deaths records formerly held at the Family Records Centre, Islington, London.

Official Lists

Navy List.

Army List – including Graduation Lists and Record of War Service.

Air Force List.

Home Guard List 1942–44.

Indian Army List 1897–1940.

India List 1923–40.

Reference Publications

Who's Who and Who Was Who.
The Times 1914 onwards.
The Daily Telegraph 1914 onwards.
Kelly's Handbook to the Titled, Landed and Official Classes.

Internet Websites

I hesitate to include websites because they change frequently, but the following deserve
a mention:
History of the Victoria Cross – www2.prestel.co.uk/stewart – Iain Stewart.
Commonwealth War Graves Commission – www.yard.ccta.gov.uk/cwgc.
Scottish General Registry Office – www.origins.net/GRO.
Free Births, Marriages and Deaths – www.freebmd.com
Memorials to Valour – http://www.memorialstovalour.co.uk – Steve Lee.

Periodicals – various editions of:

This England.
Coin and Medal News.
Journal of The Victoria Cross Society.
Orders and Medals Society Journal.

Useful Information

Accommodation – there is a wide variety of accommodation available in France. Search on-line for your requirements. There are also numerous campsites, but many close for the winter from late September.

Clothing and Kit – consider taking:

Waterproofs.
Headwear and gloves.
Walking shoes/boots.
Shades and sunscreen.
Binoculars and camera.
Snacks and drinks.

Customs/Behaviour – local people are generally tolerant of battlefield visitors but please respect their property and address them respectfully. The French are less inclined to switch to English than other Europeans. If you try some basic French it will be appreciated.

Driving – rules of the road are similar to UK, apart from having to drive on the right. If in doubt about priorities, give way to the right, particularly in France. Obey laws and road signs – police impose harsh on-the-spot fines. Penalties for drinking and driving are heavy and the legal limit is lower than UK (50mg rather than 80mg). Most autoroutes in France are toll roads.

Fuel – petrol stations are only open 24 hours on major routes. Some accept credit cards in automatic tellers. The cheapest fuel is at hypermarkets.

Mandatory Requirements – if taking your own car you need:
Full driving licence.
Vehicle registration document.
Comprehensive motor insurance valid in Europe (Green Card).
European breakdown and recovery cover.
Letter of authorisation from the owner if the vehicle is not yours.
Spare set of bulbs, headlight beam adjusters, warning triangle, GB sticker, high visibility vest and breathalyzer.

Emergency – keep details required in an emergency separate from wallet or handbag:
Photocopy passport, insurance documents and EHIC (see Health below).
Mobile phone details.
Credit/debit card numbers and cancellation telephone contacts.
Travel insurance company contact number.

Ferries – the closest ports are Boulogne, Calais and Dunkirk. The Shuttle is quicker, but usually more expensive.

Health

European Health Insurance Card – entitles the holder to medical treatment at local rates. Apply online at www.ehic.org.uk/Internet/startApplication.do. Issued free and valid for five years. You are only covered if you have the EHIC with you when you go for treatment.

Travel Insurance – you are also strongly advised to have travel insurance. If you receive treatment get a statement by the doctor (*feuille de soins*) and a receipt to make a claim on return.

Personal Medical Kit – treating minor ailments saves time and money. Pack sufficient prescription medicine for the trip.

Chemist (*Pharmacie*) – look for the green cross. They provide some treatment and if unable to help will direct you to a doctor. Most open 0900–1900 except Sunday. Out of hours services (*pharmacie de garde*) are advertised in Pharmacie windows.

Doctor and Dentist – hotel receptions have details of local practices. Beware private doctors/hospitals, as extra charges cannot be reclaimed – the French national health service is known as *conventionné*.

Rabies – contact with infected animals is very rare, but if bitten by any animal, get the wound examined professionally immediately.

Money

ATMs – at most banks and post offices with instructions in English. Check your card can be used in France and what charges apply. Some banks limit how much can be withdrawn. Let your bank know you will be away, as some block cards if transactions take place unexpectedly.

Credit/Debit Cards – major cards are usually accepted, but some have different names – Visa is Carte Bleue and Mastercard is Eurocard.

Exchange – beware 0% commission, as the rate may be poor. The Post Office takes back unused currency at the same rate, which may or may not be advantageous. Since the Euro, currency exchange facilities are scarce.

Local Taxes – if you buy high value items you can reclaim tax. Get the forms completed by the shop, have them stamped by Customs, post them to the shop and they will refund about 12%.

Passport – a valid passport is required.

Post – postcard stamps are available from vendors, newsagents and tabacs.

Public Holidays – just about everything closes and banks can close early the day before. Transport may be affected, but tourist attractions in high season are unlikely to be. The following dates/days are public holidays:

1 January
Easter Monday
1 May
8 May
Ascension Day
Whit Monday
14 July
15 August
1 & 11 November
25 December

In France many businesses and restaurants close for the majority of August.

Radio – if you want to pick up the news from home try BBC Radio 4 on 198 kHz long wave. BBC Five Live on 909 kHz medium wave can sometimes be received. There are numerous internet options for keeping up with the news.

Shops – in large towns and tourist areas they tend to open all day. In more remote places they may close for lunch. Some bakers open Sunday a.m. and during the week take later lunch breaks. In general shops do not open on Sundays.

Telephone

To UK – 0044, delete initial 0 then dial the rest of the number.

Local Calls – dial the full number even if within the same zone.

Mobiles – check yours will work in France and the charges. Beware roamer charges and/or disable them before getting on the ferry.

Emergencies – dial 112 for medical, fire and police anywhere in Europe from any landline, pay phone or mobile. Calls are free

British Embassy (Paris) – 01 44 51 31 00.

Time Zone – one hour ahead of UK.

Tipping – a small tip is expected by cloakroom and lavatory attendants and porters. Not required in restaurants, when a service charge is included.

Toilets – the best are in museums and the main tourist attractions. Towns usually have public toilets where markets are held; some are coin operated.

Index